POWER AND RESISTANCE

POWER AND RESISTANCE

SIXTH EDITION

CRITICAL THINKING ABOUT CANADIAN SOCIAL ISSUES

— EDITED BY —

WAYNE ANTONY
JESSICA ANTONY
and
LES SAMUELSON

Fernwood Publishing
Halifax • Winnipeg

Editing: Curran Faris
Cover design: John van der Woude
Printed and bound in Canada

Published by Fernwood Publishing
32 Oceanvista Lane, Black Point, Nova Scotia, B0J 1B0
and 748 Broadway Avenue, Winnipeg, Manitoba, R3G 0X3

www.fernwoodpublishing.ca

Fernwood Publishing Company Limited gratefully acknowledges the financial support of the
Government of Canada through the Canada Book Fund, the Manitoba Department of Culture, Heritage
and Tourism under the Manitoba Publishers Marketing Assistance Program, the Province of Manitoba,
through the Book Publishing Tax Credit, the support of the Province of Nova Scotia through the
Department of Communities, Culture and Heritage and the support of the Canada Council for the Arts.

Canada   Canada Council   Conseil des arts   NOVA SCOTIA Manitoba
          for the Arts   du Canada

Library and Archives Canada Cataloguing in Publication

Power and resistance: critical thinking about Canadian social issues
/ Wayne Antony, Jessica Antony & Les Samuelson, editors. -- Sixth edition.

Includes bibliographical references and index.
ISBN 978-1-55266-853-5 (softcover)

1. Social problems—Canada. 2. Canada—Social conditions. I. Antony, Wayne Andrew,
1950-, editor II. Antony, Jessica, editor III. Samuelson, Leslie, 1953-, editor

HN103.5.P68 2017   305.0971   C2016-908074-9

Contents

Acknowledgements

Thanks to everyone who has been involved in this, the sixth edition of *Power and Resistance*. To all the authors, those who are new to *Power and Resistance* and those who revised chapters for this edition, our thanks: your insights and hard work are sincerely appreciated and contribute to what we think is a great book. To the Fernwood team involved with making this book — Beverley Rach for overseeing production, Curran Faris for copy editing, John van der Woude for the cover design, Brenda Conroy for designing the book and Debbie Mathers for pre-production — thank you. From Wayne and Les, thanks to Jessica for joining the editorship of *Power and Resistance*; we hope you can help keep its politics going for years to come. Finally, to all the people who struggle for social justice in Canada: it is your dedication and selflessness that inspired the book that we hope plays some small part in creating a society in which everyone is valued and respected.

Wayne Antony
Les Samuelson
Jessica Antony

About the Authors

JESSICA ANTONY is a managing editor at Fernwood Publishing. She is a member of the Department of Rhetoric, Writing and Communications at the University of Winnipeg, where she has taught academic writing since 2009. Jessica also works as a freelancer, providing editing, writing and consulting services for both fiction and non-fiction works.

WAYNE ANTONY is a co-publisher at Fernwood Publishing. He is also a founding member of the Canadian Centre for Policy Alternatives-Manitoba (CCPA-MB) and has been on the board of directors since its inception. Prior to becoming involved with the CCPA-MB, he worked with the Winnipeg political activist organizations, the Socialist Education Centre and Thin Ice. Wayne also taught sociology at the University of Winnipeg for eighteen years. He is co-author of three reports on the state of public services in Manitoba (for CCPA-MB) and is co-editor (with Les Samuelson) of five editions of *Power and Resistance*, co-editor (with Dave Broad) of *Citizens or Consumers? Social Policy in a Market Society* and *Capitalism Rebooted? Work and Welfare in the New Economy* and co-editor (with Julie Guard) of *Bankruptcies and Bailouts*.

SUSAN BOYD is a distinguished professor in the Faculty of Human and Social Development, University of Victoria. She is the author of seven books, including *More Harm than Good: Drug Policy in Canada* (co-authored with Connie Carter and Donald MacPerson) and numerous articles on drug policy. She is on the Steering Committee of Canadian Drug Policy Coalition and works with community organizations that advocate for drug policy reform and harm reduction initiatives.

JAMIE BROWNLEE currently teaches at Carleton University and conducts research in the Canadian and international political economy, higher education, environmental politics and climate change, corporate crime and access to information law. He is the author of *Ruling Canada: Corporate Cohesion and Democracy* and *Academia, Inc.: How Corporatization is Transforming Canadian Universities*. He is also the co-editor of *Access to Information and Social Justice: Critical Research Strategies for Journalists, Scholars, and Activists*.

CONNIE CARTER is currently a senior research officer at the B.C. Representative for Children and Youth and was former senior policy analyst at the Canadian Drug Policy Coalition. She has held a number of scholarships including the Joseph Armand Bombardier Ph.D. Fellowship (2006–09) from the Social Sciences and Humanities Research Council. With Susan Boyd and Donald MacPherson, she is co-author of *More Harm than Good: Drug Policy in Canada*.

WENDY CHAN is a professor of sociology at Simon Fraser University. Her work examines the criminalization of marginalized groups in the context of immigration, criminal justice, mass media and welfare system. Her most recent book is the co-authored (with Dorothy Chunn) *Racialization, Crime and Criminal Justice in Canada*.

MARK HUDSON is an associate professor of sociology and coordinator of the Global Political Economy Program at the University of Manitoba. He writes and researches about the entanglement of environments and political economy. He is the author of *Fire Management in the American West: Forest Politics and the Rise of Megafires* and co-author (with Ian Hudson and Mara Fridell) of *Fair Trade, Sustainability, and Social Change*.

MURRAY KNUTTILA is a professor of sociology at Brock University and an adjunct member of the Department of Sociology and Social Studies at the University of Regina. He is co-author (with Wendee Kubik) of three editions of *State Theories* and the author of *Paying for Masculinity: Boys, Men and the Patriarchal Dividend*.

NORMAND LANDRY is Canada Research Chair in Media Education and Human Rights and a professor at TÉLUQ, Université du Québec. Normand's work focuses on communication rights, media education, social movement theory, law and democratic communications.

DONALD MACPHERSON is currently the director of the Canadian Drug Policy Coalition and has an adjunct faculty appointment in the Faculty of Health Sciences at Simon Fraser University. Formerly he was North America's first drug policy coordinator at the City of Vancouver, where he worked for twenty-two years. He is the author of *Four Pillars Drug Strategy*. In 2007 he received the Kaiser Foundation National Award of Excellence in Public Policy in Canada. With Susan Boyd and Connie Carter, he is co-author of *More Harm than Good: Drug Policy in Canada*.

ELIZABETH MCGIBBON is a professor in the Faculty of Science at St. Francis Xavier University. Her publications and research focus on critical health studies, emphasizing the structural determinants of health, ecological health, social justice and human rights. She is a co-investigator in a Canadian Institutes for Health Research study, "Indigenous Heart Health in Manitoba From a Two-Eyed Seeing Perspective." Elizabeth is author of *Oppression: A Social Determinant of Health* and *Anti-Racist Health Care Practice*.

SALLY MILLER has worked in sustainable food and agriculture for almost twenty years in Canada and in the U.S. She has extensive experience as a consultant and manager in a variety of organic and natural food and agriculture co-operatives and enterprises. Her publications include *Edible Action: Food Activism and Alternative Economics*, *Belongings: The Fight for Food and Land* as well as various research reports and articles on food, farming and land.

PAMELA D. PALMATER is a member of Eel River Bar First Nation, one of the First Nations belonging to the Mi'kmaw Nation in New Brunswick. She is a lawyer, author and social justice activist and currently serves as an associate professor and chair in Indigenous Governance at Ryerson University. Her recent publications include *Beyond Blood: Rethinking Indigenous Identity* and *Indigenous Nationhood*.

TRACEY PETER is an associate professor of sociology at the University of Manitoba. Her general research and publication interests include: mental health and well-being, issues of homophobia and transphobia, LGBTQ-inclusive education, trauma and violence, suicide prevention, social inequality and marginalization, youth and research methods/statistics.

DENNIS PILON is an associate professor of political science at York University. His research and publications focus on elections, electoral reform and democratization, as well as class analysis and the question of identity in politics, particularly working class identity. He is the author of *The Politics of Voting: Reforming Canada's Electoral System* and *Wrestling with Democracy: Voting Systems as Politics in the Twentieth Century West.*

JAMES POPHAM is an assistant professor of criminology at Wilfrid Laurier University. His research focuses on two areas: cyber deviance and social justice. He is currently working on projects that unite these two interests.

LES SAMUELSON is an associate professor of sociology at the University of Saskatchewan. He has an active interest in social justice initiatives, especially at the community level. His research interests include justice reform, especially as it pertains to Indigenous people, and international crime, justice and human rights. He is co-editor (with Wayne Antony) of five editions of *Power and Resistance.*

LESLIE REGAN SHADE is a professor in the Faculty of Information at the University of Toronto. Her research focus since the mid-1990s has been on the social and policy aspects of information and communication technologies, with particular concerns towards issues of gender, youth and political economy.

JIM SILVER is a professor in and chair of the Department of Urban and Inner-City Studies at the University of Winnipeg. He is a founding member of CCPA-Manitoba and is a member of the Manitoba Research Alliance. Jim's research interests are in inner-city, poverty-related, and community development issues. His most recent books are *Solving Poverty: Innovative Strategies from Winnipeg's Inner City* (2016) and *Poor Housing: A Silent Crisis* (co-edited with Josh Brandon; 2015).

ELIZABETH SHEEHY the is vice dean research, and held the Shirley Greenberg Chair for Women and the Legal Profession Faculty of Law 2002–05 and 2013–16, at the University of Ottawa. She was co-counsel for the Women's Legal Education and Action Fund (LEAF) and has participated in the legal work for many ground-breaking cases. Elizabeth sat on the University's Task Force on Respect and Equality ("Rape Culture") and is on the advisory board for Informed Opinions and the board for the Ottawa Rape Crisis Centre. Her most recent books are an edited collection, *Sexual Assault in Canada: Law, Legal Practice and Women's Activism,* and *Defending Battered Women on Trial: Lessons from the Transcripts.*

CATHERINE TAYLOR is a professor in the Faculty of Education and the Department of Rhetoric, Writing, and Communications at the University of Winnipeg. Her recent work on research ethics, LGBTQ well-being, LGBTQ-inclusive education and confrontations between LGBTQ and heteronormative discourses has been published widely in scholarly books and journals.

RHON TERUELLE is a postdoctoral research scholar at the Department of Communication, Media and Film, University of Calgary. His research focuses on social movements and collective action in relation to digital media and civic mobilization. In particular, he investigates various communication tactics employed by grassroots organizations with particular concerns about meaningful social change, racial equality and the environment.

1

Social Problems and Social Power

Individual Dysfunction or Social Injustice?

Wayne Antony, Les Samuelson and Jessica Antony

YOU SHOULD KNOW THIS

- Of the 338 members of the federal parliament, nearly 90 (26.6 percent) self-identified as businessman or woman, while just under 50 (14.9 percent) self-identified as lawyer. There are over 30 consultants, about 30 executives, managers and senior administrators, 30 teachers and over 20 journalists. Less than 10 (3 percent) self-identified as something akin to trades and skilled labour, with about the same number indicating "farmer" as their affiliation.
- Two-thirds of First Nations in Canada have had at least one drinking water advisory in the last decade. Between 2004 and 2014, 400 out of 618 First Nations had a water problem — 93 percent of Saskatchewan and New Brunswick First Nations and 87 percent of First Nations in Alberta had drinking water advisories. On any given day, there are more than 150 boil water advisories in effect in First Nations. The longest water advisory is twenty years at Neskantaga First Nation, Ontario.
- The average member of Canada's 100 most highly-paid CEOs earned as much by 12:18 p.m. on the second working day of 2016 as was earned by the average Canadian full-time employee in the entire year.
- Among patients fifty years or older, women are less likely than men to be admitted to an ICU and to receive selected life-supporting treatments, and they are more likely than men to die after critical illness.
- In 2014, 58,000 girls and women and 28,000 boys and men were injured or killed by a family member; one woman was killed by a family member every four days, while every six days a woman was killed by an intimate partner, and every twenty-three days a man was killed by an intimate partner. It is estimated that at least 70 percent of violence within families is not reported.
- Total media revenue in Canada in 2014 was $75.4 billion, up from $19 billion in 1984. Of the revenue in TV, Bell accounts for over 33 percent (with 70 TV channels); Bell and Shaw account for over 50 percent, and the "Big Five" (Bell, Shaw, Rogers, CBC and Quebecor) account for 90 percent. The Big Four (the Five excluding CBC) account for 57 percent of all telecom, Internet and media revenue, twice as much as ten years ago. Canada tops the list of media concentration in thirty industrial countries.
- Canadian governments support oil, gas and coal industries with $2.9 billion in subsidies and $2.9 billion in public financing per year. For the G20 countries, the total government support is $444 billion per year.
- In 2015, the tar sands production of 2 million barrels per day uses 11,000–44,000 litres of water per second; planned expansion to 3 billion barrels per year will use an estimated 7 million litres of water per second, more water than there is in the Athabasca River.

Sources: CCPA 2016; Public Health Agency of Canada 2016; Winseck 2016; CBC News 2015; Fowler et al. 2007; Parliament of Canada n.d.; Oil Change International Institute 2015; Pannozzo 2016.

WHAT ARE WE TO MAKE OF THESE "THINGS YOU SHOULD KNOW"? Pollution of our air, water and soil; poverty that is increasingly widespread and persistent; the epidemic of sexual violence on campuses; the difficulties faced by immigrants and refugees; the consequences of colonialism and more. This book is about trying to figure out the who, what, when, where, how and why of the conflicts, troubles and dilemmas that confront us in Canada.

In a simple but absolutely crucial sense, how we think about social issues depends on how we approach thinking about social life in general. At the risk of oversimplification, we can say that there are two basic approaches to getting below the surface of our social lives. There is what we will call the neoliberal approach — some might see this as a "traditional" way of looking at social problems — and there is what we will call the "critical" approach. Many other books on social issues tend to describe three approaches based on traditional divisions in sociology: function-alist, interactionist and conflict theories. (In Chapter 2 Murray Knuttila describes some of the social and political theories that make up these two approaches in detail: the traditional includes pluralism, rational choice and institutionalism, and the critical includes Marxism, neo-Marxism and feminism.)

> How we think about social issues depends on how we approach thinking about social life in general.

One way of describing these different ways of understanding social life is to go back to a classic statement on the nature and value of the "sociological imagination" made almost sixty years ago. In 1959, U.S. sociologist C. Wright Mills distinguished between "private troubles" and "public issues." Using the gendered language that was typical in his day, Mills wrote:

> [Private] troubles occur within the character of the individual and within the range of his immediate relations with others; they have to do with his self and with those limited areas of social life of which he is directly and personally aware. [Public] issues have to do with matters that transcend these local environments of the individual and the range of his inner life. They have to do with the organization of many such milieux into the institutions of [a] historical society as a whole, with the ways in which various milieux overlap and interpenetrate to form the larger structure of social and historical life. (Mills 1959: 8)

For some analysts, again at the risk of a little oversimplification, social problems are mainly about private troubles; for others, social problems involve public issues.

The Neoliberal Approach: Individuals and Freedom

For the neoliberal approach, society is essentially a bundle of private troubles. In his distinc-tion between troubles and issues, Mills was pointing to a profound bias in North American (actually, specifically U.S. or maybe Anglo-American) thinking: the tendency to see society in individual terms. In this neoliberal way of thinking, the understanding or explanation of how society works really comes down to the choices that individual people make. As human beings, we decide what we will eat, where we will live, what work we will do, how we will treat others, whether we will go to university or community college, what music we will listen to, who or if we will marry and so on. Almost always, it is assumed, we choose to do what is best for us as individuals. If we need to, we may decide to co-operate with others to achieve some of our goals, but fundamentally and ultimately we act for ourselves. Even so, these choices are and should be constrained, but only within very wide boundaries. We cannot act in ways that threaten others — their lives, their freedom or their rights. For instance, we cannot take our neighbour's new car just because driving around in it will make us feel good or because we need a car.

> In this neoliberal way of thinking, the understanding or explanation of how society works really comes down to the choices that individual people make.

These constraints on individual choice, the traditional approach argues, tend to have two bases: obvious and natural boundaries and those on which everyone (or at least a majority) agrees. We know, even without there being laws against it, that we cannot take someone else's car just because it may be good for us. We also agree with laws that protect our property and our lives. But, according to the neoliberals, the legal constraints on freedom must be kept to a minimum.

This is a perspective that is also preoccupied with social order and social stability, that is, the social imperative for individuals and the parts of a social system to be working together. Achieving this ability to effectively work together, what many neoliberals call social "equilibrium," comes from a set of beliefs, values and morals that are widely shared and accepted and that hold the system together. In other words, there is an assumption that a consensus exists among the members of society that freedom is paramount, individual merit and responsibility are important and family values, hard work and respecting others' property are what society and life are all about. More than that, neoliberals contend that the social system does generally fit together and function effectively and that it is generally, and must be, in a long-term state of equilibrium. For some (probably most) traditional social analysts, the democratic capitalism that currently dominates and characterizes the societies of the developed industrial world epitomizes just such a free, prosperous and stable social world (see Klein 2007).

Social theorists who call themselves pluralists share this emphasis on freedom (see Chapter 2 for details about pluralism). Pluralists argue that capitalist, liberal democracies are free because there are no groups that dominate society, at least not for long periods of time or over many sectors of a society. These societies have a free press, and most people have access to the information that they need in order to know what is going on. Everyone is free to vote and to try to influence social and political processes — for pluralists, elections are the great political equalizer, as one person/one vote makes us all the same. Everyone is free to pursue any form of education and work, and the accompanying lifestyle, they desire. Without these kinds of individual freedoms such a society would break down.

Pluralists note that there are powerful people and groups in a society, but that power is always restricted and tempered by the power held by other individuals and groups. As Murray Knuttila (Chapter 2) says, "complex industrial societies are typically divided into different kinds of groups, classes and factions based on a multitude of religious, class, occupational, regional, ethnic and sexual differences, for example, corporations, unions, cultural groups, professional associations, special interests and community groups." So many different groups make it at least difficult for one kind of group to exercise power and authority over all of society for long periods of time — for example, the power of corporations is limited by the rights of unions and consumer groups.

In its most radical form, this traditional, individualistic approach can lead to the claim — made by Margaret Thatcher, prime minister of Britain from 1979 to 1990 — that there is no society, only individuals. This sense of radical individualism underlies the neoliberal revolution, of which Thatcher was the political architect in England (in the U.S. it was Ronald Reagan, who was president from 1980 to 1989). Neoliberalism developed out of classic liberalism of the late seventeenth and eighteenth centuries when the ideas of freedom — life, liberty and property — took hold. Developing into a political movement, liberalism was meant to undo the grasp that aristocracy, hereditary privilege and the divine right of kings had over societies, particularly in the governing of societies, especially in Western Europe and the U.S. For the emerging powerful class of entrepreneurs and business people, hereditary aristocracy (and conservatism) kept them from having much political influence in their society (see Chapter 6 for more on the emergence of liberal democracy).

Neoliberalism has taken up the essential core of liberalism in its focus on individual freedom, liberty and personal responsibility. The term is used mostly in a political economy sense, proclaiming that the competitive, free market is "an ethic unto itself, capable of acting as a guide to all human action, and substituting for all previously held ethical beliefs ... hold[ing] that the social good will be maximized by maximizing the reach ... of [the] market ... seek[ing] to bring all human action into the domain of the market" (Harvey 2005: 3). In a broad political sense, neoliberalism rests on a holy trinity: eliminating the public sector, liberating corporations from government regulation and bare-bones social spending (Klein 2007: 17). The public sector is seen with much suspicion in that it is inherently inefficient, costly and a waste of taxpayers' money (Knuttila, Chapter 2). Thus, where markets for the things we need to exist are not in place, such as health care, social security, water, education and so on, they must be created (Harvey 2005: 3–5). In strictly economic terms, this means that it is the state's responsibility to ensure the conditions of profitability for private corporations, the economic equivalent of individuals.

In more general social terms, neoliberals see society as made up of freely interacting individuals — the basic unit of society — who are responsible and held accountable for the choices they make (Harvey 2005: 65). If there is even such a thing as the common good, it is produced when these freely interacting individuals are not restricted in the pursuit of their own best interests. For neoliberals, most restrictions on individual freedom, especially in the form of government regulation, are counterproductive to a prosperous and harmonious society.

The Critical Approach: Social Structure, Power and Social Justice

In this book we approach social issues in a different way. We look at society through a critical lens. Keeping in mind Mills's distinction between public issues and private troubles, this approach begins with the observation that to understand our lives we need to examine the institutions — the social structure — of our community and society. As Mills (1959: 10–11) argues, what we experience in our lives is both caused and constrained by the various and specific social settings — or social structures — that we are part of. As such, "to understand the changes of many personal milieux we are required to look beyond them.... To be aware of the idea of social structure and to use it with sensibility is to be capable of tracing [the] linkages among a great variety of milieux. To be able to do that is to possess the sociological imagination." In other words, to fully understand our lives and the society in which we live involves utilizing a structural or institutional — not an individualistic — framework.

> If we think about how our choices play out in everyday life, one of the first things we recognize is that some people have a wider range of choices than others.

One way of getting at what this means is to return to the idea of the individual choices that we can and do make. If we think, even for just a minute, about how our choices — clothes, food, jobs, partners, education — play out in everyday life, one of the first things we recognize is that the choices we are presented with are not unlimited. Our choices, for example, are largely influenced by where and when we live, who we are — women, men, transgendered, Indigenous, white — or if we have children, go to school, work part-time or full-time, and so forth.

As soon as we give this reality some thought, we will also notice that some people have a wider range of choices than others. For instance, some people have the privilege to choose whether or not they go to university. Others can choose which university they will go to (regardless of whether it is close to home or far away). But many others do not have these choices available to them; the option of attending university is not even on their radar. Instead, they have to work to support themselves and others close to them. Or, as Jamie Brownlee shows so clearly in Chapter 9, many people cannot take on the large debt that university education requires (unless, of course, they live in one of the Scandinavian countries where such education is fully paid for by the state). Elizabeth McGibbon (in Chapter 7) demonstrates that whether or not we will be sick with certain kinds of diseases, like diabetes, is strongly related to our income and whether or not we are Indigenous. That is, not everyone is free to make any choice — there are barriers; there are inequalities between individuals.

For critical thinkers, a key feature of our social structure, and the second main component of a critical approach, is social inequality. Inequalities are not just about individual lifestyle choices. It is true that some people may want bigger cars, the latest clothing fashions, to dine at the most expensive restaurants or to live in luxurious houses while others may not want any of these things. And social structure and inequality do not mean that we do not make choices about our behaviour — we do have what sociologists call "agency" (see Knuttila 2016). The point, however, is that the existence of social inequality means a narrowing of life choices for many people, not just in what they may want but also in what they can do and become. That is, inequality is actually about power differences, not merely lifestyle differences.

Power resides in social relationships, and it can take many forms. Power can be exercised by virtually anyone, almost anywhere. A CEO tells the executive committee that they must devise plans to increase profits by 20 percent over the next four fiscal quarters. The Commissioner of the WNBA fines players for wearing Black Lives Matter t-shirts on the court. The big kid in grade 6 forces a smaller kid to give up a place in the cafeteria queue. In other words, there are many possible bases of power, especially when it comes to one individual pitted against another.

> Power involves the ways in which people in particular social groups can force people in other social groups to act in certain ways.

But even in these examples the people acting are not just individuals. That is, power is not randomly distributed; it has a social basis and social patterns. Power, in the social sense, involves the ways in which people in particular social groups can influence, force, coerce and direct people in other social groups to act in certain ways, narrowing their choices in life. These powerful social groups tend to coalesce around race, gender, class and sexuality:

- white people expropriating land from Indigenous people, labelled "Indian" people by Canadian legislation, who then find that their social and economic activities cannot conform to their own views of who they want to be and what kind of direction they want to pursue as individuals and as nations (see Pamela Palmater, Chapter 3);
- men using their physical strength and capacity for violence to control women, while the surrounding culture encourages such behaviour and society as a whole turns a blind eye, providing many women with little choice but to cope with the fallout (see Elizabeth Sheehy, Chapter 11);
- rising tuition and debt levels blocking access to higher education for underprivileged families (see Jamie Brownlee, Chapter 9).
- heterosexual people deciding that their sexual choices are "normal," thus complicating and denigrating the lives of and experiences of LGBTQ people (see Tracey Peter and Catherine Taylor, Chapter 13).

Power can also be enacted through the state or government. For example, James Popham and Les Samuelson (Chapter 5) show that what the state legislates as criminal offences in Canada are not always the most harmful or dangerous behaviours. For example, most of us, at one time or another, will have money unwillingly taken from us by corporations, through everything from misleading advertising to predatory pricing to violations of labour standards regulations. The great financial meltdown of 2008 was, as Popham and Samuelson describe, actually the pilfering of hundreds of millions of dollars from citizens by various financial corporations through devious, irresponsible actions that were not defined as criminal. It is estimated that $11 trillion was drained from households during the crisis. But most of these harmful business activities are not defined and treated as criminal theft, while taking money unwillingly from a convenience store owner certainly is. Big business has enough power to ensure that the state will protect its need to maximize profits.

Relations of power also occur in other contexts. Sally Miller (Chapter 15) tells us about how the ways in which we think about food reflect the desire of agri-business to control food production and distribution. As she points out, we tend to see food mainly in terms of supply and demand, as commodities to be bought and sold — agri-business spends much time and resources making sure we see it this way. But taking the culture and compassion out of food — that is, turning food into nothing more than commodities — and denying that adequate, safe, nutritious food is a human right not only ensures that large numbers of people will go hungry because they are "unwilling to pay" the going prices, but also increases the profits and control of food by multinational corporations.

Knowing that our society is characterized by inequality and the relations of power does not mean that we can be certain of how power will operate. For example, Murray Knuttila (Chapter 2) sets out a critical theory of how the state acts on behalf of the interests of powerful groups (power that relates to class, gender and race). But as Knuttila argues, while we know that such powerful interests dominate society, we cannot specify ahead of time the actual mechanisms through which power is exercised. We can do this theoretically or abstractly — Knuttila discusses in general the direct and indirect ways in which the powerful influence the state to do what they want it to do. But, an understanding of how power actually operates can come only through careful historical research, by uncovering the ways in which the powerful try to protect their interests, sometimes through the state and sometimes elsewhere, and the ways in which they are successful, and unsuccessful.

So, as you can see, there are some basic disagreements about the nature of society and how it is organized and how it operates. These disagreements find their way into thinking about social issues and their causes. In general, thinking about social issues involves trying to understand not only what comes to be seen as a social problem but also how to resolve those problems, both of which are connected to what we think causes social problems and how society is organized and structured.

Defining Our Changing Problems

In thinking about social issues, we have to first consider what behaviours and conditions are social problems. Without getting into a long discussion of how to "define social problems" (which many social problems textbooks do), it is sufficient to say that social problems are behaviours and conditions that both (objectively) harm a significant group of people and behaviours and conditions that are (subjectively) defined as harmful to a significant group of people. Both elements are part of identifying what is a social problem. Augie Fleras tells us that defini-tions of social problems are generally divided between conditionalists and constructionists (Fleras 2005; see also Nelson and Fleras 1995: 1–9). Conditionalists define social problems as conditions that are seen as threatening and harmful by a significant segment of the population. Constructionists, on the other hand, define social problems in terms of people's reactions

> Social problems are behaviours and conditions that both (objectively) harm a significant group of people and behaviours and conditions that are (subjectively) defined as harmful to a significant group of people.

to conditions that are or are perceived as harmful — such circumstances become social problems because people act together to change them. Donileen Loseke (1999: 5–13) says that social problems involve both the actual harm caused by behaviours and conditions and what people worry about. In other words, there are both objective (the conditions) and subjective (how things are seen) elements to social problems.

These definitions, which are representative, are useful and accurate (see Eitzen, Zinn and Smith 2011 for a recent but similar discussion). But beyond agreement at a very general level that social problems have an objective and a subjective element and people want to do something about them, what we think of as a social problem is not so simple. Our definitions and conceptions of social problems are tied up with how we see society being organized.

The Things that Hurt Us: Objective Element of Social Problems

- In 2013, Canada ranked fifteen out of seventeen industrialized countries for child poverty, and in March 2015, 852,137 Canadians used food banks, more than double the number for 1989. Between 1976 and 2011, average housing prices have increased by 613 percent while average household income has increased by 17.5 percent (Chapter 6).
- In 2015, the Office of the Correctional Investigator of Canada reported that almost 25 percent of federal prisoners are Indigenous; in the Prairie Provinces it is 48 percent, and more than 36 percent of females in federal jails are Indigenous. Yet, Indigenous people are 4.3 percent of the population in Canada (Chapter 3).
- Women students reported 179 sexual assaults to their campus authorities in Canada in 2013, a rate that is 21 percent higher than assaults reported in 2012 and 66 percent higher than 2009. Despite this rise in reports of campus sexual assault, only twenty-four of one hundred post-secondary institutions in Canada had, by 2016, adopted a stand-alone policy for sexual violence on campus (Chapter 11).
- The oil and gas sector is the largest contributor to Canada's greenhouse gas emissions at 25 percent, and oil and gas emissions are projected to increase by 45 percent between 2005 and 2020. The oil sands accounts for most of the emissions growth, and they are projected to be 67 percent of emissions between 2005 and 2020 (Chapter 10).
- In a national survey, over half of LGBTQ high school students report hearing homophobic comments, and over 60 percent were verbally harassed about their sexual orientation every day. As a result, many live with high levels of emotional stress leading to their isolation and disengagement at school, feeling schools are unsafe places and contemplating suicide (Chapter 13).

These facts all indicate serious circumstances that negatively impact the lives of many people. There is no doubt that particular social conditions and behaviours that cause suffering to a significant set of people are problems, both for those people and for society. Equally, there is no doubt that such conditions are objectively real. We can observe and articulate those conditions, even though it may be difficult to define just when a social condition becomes a social problem — what level of harm needs to be done and to how many people before we define it this way? Yet, in many ways, all that this part of the definition tells us is that we can and must articulate who is being harmed in order to call something a social problem.

It is important to note that the conditions that can become a social problem are actually the behaviours of some groups of people. They are not some kind of abstracted circumstances that exist outside of people's behaviours and relationships to one another. This is often obvious: the violence suffered by women is obviously about the behaviour of, mainly, men. Poverty is about how income and economic resources are distributed through the labour market, which is really businesses and employers deciding who will get paid what for which kind of work. Greenhouse gas emissions are about politicians and big business deciding that the tar sands' economic value is more important than keeping the temperature of the earth from rising.

All too often, though, neoliberal social analyses accept as self-evident the problematic nature of some set of social conditions. In this view, there are behaviours that clearly, objectively and obviously disrupt the functioning of society as it exists. For example, we are so often told that violence is a serious problem in our society. From many sources we are relentlessly warned about the dangerousness of certain parts of the cities we live in. There can be no doubt that violence is harmful and disruptive to anyone who encounters it. Yet, as James Popham and Les Samuelson (Chapter 5), and Elizabeth Sheehy (Chapter 11), show us, we are much more likely to encounter violence at work or at the hands of people we know intimately (mainly males) than in those "certain parts of the city." This is not to make light of or dismiss so-called "stranger violence," for it does occur. In these terms, the nature of the problem of violence is not self-evident, even though violence is harmful.

> Neoliberal social analyses accept as self-evident the problematic nature of behaviours that disrupt the functioning of society as-it-exists.

To take another example: Like many revolutionary technologies before it, the Internet is often self-evidently taken to be a sign of social progress (in fact, there tends to be a generalized sense that all technological change is progress). There is no doubt that the Internet has made life more interesting, easier and richer for many people; indeed, the instant communication it facilitates about other parts of the world is a positive feature. Yet, as Normand Landry and Rhon Teruelle (Chapter 16) point out in their examination of the new social media, technological design can hide vested interests: corporations who own the social media sell private information to marketers and governments use Internet devices to keep close watch on all citizens. In a related example, the so-called "sharing economy" of AirBnB, Uber, Lyft and the like have found new ways to utilize the Internet to develop ways for people to get some of things they need, designed at least initially to contribute to the ideals of community sharing (rather than corporate exploitation). However, those non-corporate enterprises have become just what they proclaimed they would avoid. Very quickly the sharing economy has become a "playground of billionaires and exploited workers" and is really just a typical capitalist marketing scheme (Slee 2015: 163). In these and other ways, the new social media can actually be a social problem.

Thus, we do have to ask about and determine the objective contours of the conditions we define as social problems. But when we talk about social conditions we are actually talking about people's needs. So — to think this through critically and as the above examples illustrate — we also have to ask about whose needs are being met by the existing social set-up. And, on the other side of that coin, we have to ask about whose needs might be better met by disrupting the functioning of society as it exists. That is, taking some social condition as self-evidently problematic ignores who is raising the question. Some social actors — academics, bureaucrats, politicians, business people — are positioned so that society functions well for them. As such, they often characterize social conditions from their standpoint and in their interests. This difference of standpoint at times manifests itself in disputes about the facts. For example, there is a long-standing dispute over how many people are poor in Canada. For many years there has been a dispute about how to measure poverty in Canada and elsewhere (Jim Silver, Chapter 6). Many poverty analysts say that a definition that takes into account the general level of income in a society makes sense. But another definition is championed by the Fraser Institute, a Canadian think-tank that draws its support from corporations and wealthy people. According to their way of defining and measuring it, there is very little real poverty in Canada. From their point of view, most of the people who are defined as poor in Canada have food, shelter and access to education and health care. They say that truly poor Canadians should be like the poor in the so-called undeveloped world, who are destitute, unable to afford the bare physical necessities of life. In this view, "poverty ... has been virtually eliminated. It is simply not a major problem in Canada" (Sarlo, cited in Chapter 6). Such a characterization is clearly in the interests of the groups who support the Fraser Institute and those the Fraser Institute supports.

> We have to ask whose needs are being met by the existing social set-up. And, whose needs might be better met by disrupting the functioning of society as-it-exists.

In a related context, there is a world food crisis, given the large numbers of starving and hungry people around the world, the magnitude of which is not disputed. Yet this hunger becomes a particular kind of problem depending on how it is framed and from whose standpoint it is viewed. Sally Miller (Chapter 15) tells us that the Food and Agriculture Organization of the United Nations knows, and tells the world through its reports, that there is actually about one-and-a-half times the food needed to feed everyone in the world. Yet, the food crisis is mostly presented as one in which more food production is necessary. The real problem, according to Miller's analysis, is the dysfunctional ways food is distributed by a system largely controlled by multinational agri-business and governments in developed countries. Framing hunger as a worldwide lack of food serves the needs of these powerful interests rather than the needs of the starving people in the world. Miller gives the example of Haiti, which went from providing almost all its staple food, rice, to becoming an importer of rice, mainly from the U.S. Thus, how we think and talk about a particular social condition is important to defining it as a social problem.

The Stories That Are Told: The Subjective Element of Social Problems

Many traditional analysts, like almost all critical analysts, take the step beyond seeing a social situation as self-evidently, or objectively, a problem. They go on to argue that social conditions become problems or issues when "some value cherished by publics is felt to be threatened" (Mills 1959: 8). That is, it is not "just the facts" and social harm that lead a social condition to be defined as a social problem. A condition or behaviour can become a social problem if it threatens an important social value or if it is perceived by the public or by a critical mass of people as being such a threat (see Nelson and Fleras 1995: 8; Loseke 1999: 5, 8–9; Fleras 2005: 7). Values are certainly not irrelevant in building an understanding of why some behaviours or conditions are deemed to be social problems. In this regard, both neoliberal and critical social scholars would agree that values (and perceptions) are an important part of the social problem process. There is, however, a tendency among neoliberal scholars to define problems as arising from a violation of an assumed value consensus within society. When we conceptualize and study social issues, we must ask and be clear about the cherished values that are being threatened. It is on this issue — what values and whose values — that neoliberal and critical scholars part company.

The case of immigration into Canada is very much about values. Wendy Chan (Chapter 4) tells us that it is the feelings of insecurity that makes immigration a problem for many Canadians. It is true that there has been a significant increase in the level of immigration to Canada since the 1980s, accounting for half the population growth in 1980–2000. Yet, the people who see immigration as a problem tend to call for strict regulations and law enforcement to deal with the maladaptation of immigrants (in terms of their work skills and our economic needs, and their cultural norms) and with the criminals and terrorists who enter Canada as refugees. For them, it is not just too many immigrants, but not enough "good" immigrants that do not threaten the safety, prosperity and harmony of Canada. A 2016 Angus Reed Institute poll showed that 68 percent of people surveyed feel that immigrants do not do enough to fit into Canada, such as shedding their culture and language, and 79 percent say immigration should be for Canada's economic needs not crises elsewhere in the world (Proctor 2016). But, as Chan demonstrates, it is difficult to establish that there is lax enforcement of immigration law or that immigrants are actually an economic drain. Lurking behind the transformation of Canadian immigration law and enforcement and the idea that immigration is a problem is racism. When we drill down into the actual practices of immigration policy and enforcement, the matter of "good" immigrants is not really about skills and adaptation. The new immigrants — who in recent decades have come mainly from Asia and Africa — actually threaten to upset a decades-old policy aimed at "keeping Canada white." Thus, in analyzing social problems we need not only to clearly identify the values that are at risk, but also, more importantly, to ask about whose values are at risk.

We also cannot assume that public perceptions are freely formed. Some scholars within the traditional neoliberal framework do suggest that "a problem exists when an influential group defines a social condition as threatening to its values" (Sullivan and Thompson 1988: 3) or when there is a "critical mass" of the general public who see a behaviour/condition as problematic (Fleras 2005: 7). Janet Mosher (2014) refers to the ability of "claims makers" to convince the rest of us that some condition or group is a problem and to define the problem in ways that suit their interests. She investigates how so-called welfare fraud is treated in legislation, enforcement and public discourse as a crime, while tax evasion (which robs society of much more money) is not treated as a crime and is controlled by much less stringent civil regulation. As Mark Hudson argues in Chapter 10 regarding the government's failure to allow for public participation in the development of the Alberta Tar Sands, "What we see … is a systematic closure of public participation in energy resource management in Alberta. This … suggests that the state may no longer see democratic participation as an integral part of its legitimacy — a major issue in relations of power and resistance." In general, these powerful elites tend to define environmental issues as in conflict with economic needs and believe that acting aggressively to alter environmental degradation will cause economic harm. Neighbourhood, environmental and other groups, with access to fewer resources, face difficult struggles in challenging how environmental concerns are defined by governments, corporations and their expert scientists.

> The people who have access to the means of public discourse can dominate the public agenda not only by defining what will be seen as social problems but also by framing how certain issues or conditions will be seen as problems.

The people who have access to the means of public debate and discourse can dominate the public agenda not only by defining what will be seen as social problems but also by framing how certain issues or conditions will be seen as problems. Powerful and socially privileged groups tend to have more access to the means of public discourse. Corporations and the wealthy people who own and control the mass media do not force all of us to think in particular ways, but they have more influence than others regarding what social issues will get into the public domain, and they are more likely than not to frame these issues in ways that support the status quo. A good example of this is how illness is understood. As Elizabeth McGibbon (Chapter 7) shows us, the main causes of illness are the "social determinants of health" — income, housing, racism, access to good food — rather than lifestyle choices or "genes and germs." As she says: "When individuals and families live in a chronic state of stress due to the relentlessness of racism, or a chronic state of crisis about where money for the rent cheque or the next family meal is coming from, then the adrenal system becomes fatigued. Results include immunosuppression, diabetes, heart disease and depression. In other words, the body's stress handling system becomes chronically overburdened." So Indigenous people in Canada, for example, are much more prone to diabetes, respiratory illness, heart disease, suicide and depression than non-Indigenous Canadians. But the dominance of the "biomedical gaze" championed by the media, the medical establishment and health care corporations frames illness almost exclusively in terms of genetics and lifestyle rather than on an unhealthy, for some, social structure of privilege and power, in this case, racism and colonialism

Corporations and the wealthy also have privileged access to think-tanks and policy networks. Organizations such as the Canadian Council of Chief Executives and policy research institutes such as the Fraser Institute and Conference Board of Canada were organized precisely to produce statistics and analyses that shape the social-issues and public-policy agendas in Canada. These organizations have multi-million-dollar budgets financed by donations from corporations and wealthy Canadians (most of whom are also male and white) (Brownlee 2005).

Closer to home, Jamie Brownlee (Chapter 9) shows that through the shift to a more corporate model of organization with more and more private funding, universities are becoming businesses more than institutions of research and free thinking. Administrators are more concerned about marketing and branding than academic research, which "has led to a significant growth in the share of institutional resources devoted to advertising and promotional campaigns." This has also led to a censoring of academic research and writing. Brownlee writes, "Preoccupation with brand image means that 'controversial' research by professors, criticism of universities by faculty and students, as well as public displays of dissent or resistance on campuses are increasingly viewed as a threat to the university's brand name. On some campuses, new student conduct and use-of-space policies are denying students the opportunity to assemble and speak freely."

For critical analysts, then, the focus is on social power and not merely social values and perceptions. C.W. Mills, so many years ago, highlighted the tendencies in sociology that led to what he terms the "cultural and political abdication" of classical (or neoliberal) social analysis. He castigates value-oriented theories and analyses (like those of his influential contemporary, Talcott Parsons) that are obsessed with the concept of the normative order — that norms and values are the most important element of social analysis. Such an approach, says Mills, absolves the analyst from any concern with power and political relations, thereby legitimating the existing structures and social arrangements that produce major inequalities in our society. Without putting norms and values into the context of social inequality, such a view turns the values, views and experiences of society's dominant groups into society's values, views and experiences. To update and modify an old phrase: "What is good for Apple, is good for society."

Resolving Our Problems: Changing Individuals?

The other key aspect in thinking about social issues is trying to figure out how to resolve them. Proposing solutions to social problems is really extrapolating from what causes them. Even more obvious than the link between our understanding of society and what gets defined as a social problem is the connection between that understanding and the kinds of solutions proposed to resolve social problems.

Given its general social outlook, not surprisingly, the traditional approach tends to see the problems of a community or society in individual, pathological terms. If you see the current society as fundamentally good and sound, then its problems have to be the results of some "bad apples." In other words, these analyses usually see social problems as emanating from the personal inadequacies of individuals, from their "private troubles." These personal inadequacies are,

> If you see the current society as fundamentally good, then its problems have to be emanating from the personal inadequacies of individuals.

in turn, often seen as deriving from inappropriate socialization and dysfunctional behaviour choices. For example, the predominant view of violence between men and women is just such an individualistic approach. In this view, women, it is argued, are just as violent as the men with whom they have intimate relationships. The power dynamics present in, for example, cases of domestic violence or rape, are left out of the equation, effectively silencing women who are the victims of rape and sexual assault. If rape and sexual assault are individual problems, then authorities often turn to women to ask what they did wrong or what they failed to do to protect themselves. In fact, the "unfounding rate" — that is, the rate at which police disbelieve complainants — for sexual assault is higher than that of any other crime in Canada (Elizabeth Sheehy, Chapter 11). Given this individualistic frame, it is not really surprising, says Elizabeth Sheehy, that "men who rape count on the silencing effect of this crime." Furthermore, the ways in which our knowledge about violence against women at the hands of men is constructed socially aids this silencing effect. Sheehy argues, "Police data has been recognized as incomplete both because so few women choose to report to police but also because police recording practices for this category of crime are deeply problematic given the documented biases that infect them." In addition to the inadequacies of police data, crime victimization surveys are also often inaccurate "because they are not specifically tailored to identify for women the range of behaviours that constitute 'sexual assault' in legal terms, nor are the interviewers trained to spend time gaining the confidence of interviewees and responding with empathy."

The neoliberal focus on individual change can and does take on a broader, more community-oriented approach. It is argued by neoliberals that whole groups of people need to adjust and change their behaviour to solve their problems. For example, from the time of Confederation the assimilation of Indigenous people has been and has been seen as the dominant "solution" to the problems within and of their communities. At the time of the *Indian Act*, the goal of assimilation was blatantly overt. Former deputy superintendent of Indian Affairs Duncan Campbell Scott made this goal and its ultimate objective absolutely clear in arguing for the *Indian Act*: "I want to get rid of the Indian problem. ... *Our objective is to continue until there is not a single Indian in Canada* that has not been absorbed into the body politic and there is no Indian question, and no Indian Department, that is the whole object of this Bill" (cited in Chapter 3). The 1969 federal government White Paper in Indian Policy advocated for the end to special recognition for Indians, of the Department of Indian Affairs and the *Indian Act*. One specific element of this approach, for example, is to give Indigenous people individual, rather than band, title to treaty and reserves lands so they can be bought and sold just like any other plot of land. This is a plan touted often by political scientist Tom Flanagan to end Indigenous poverty. He explains the overall objective of the land proposal, like the Indian Act and the White Paper before it: "Call it assimilation, call it integration, call it adaptation, call it whatever you want: it has to happen" (Flanagan 2000: 196, cited in Chapter 3). In other words, if Indigenous people became and acted more like non-Indigenous people (in this context by not holding on to outdated, economically counterproductive views of land ownership), their problems (of poverty) would come to an end.

In recent years, the traditional focus on individualism has taken a new twist: neoliberalism.

Many within the neoliberal model call for using the competitive market as a model in all our social undertakings. In this view, the market or business way of doing things, as opposed to a collective approach, is seen as the solution for our economic woes and for a host of other social and political problems — neoliberalism calls for not only deregulating our economy but also applying business principles to schooling, cultural production, assistance to the destitute, prisons, environmental protection and so on. In a nutshell, the market is seen as being based on and promoting the individual freedom that will pave the way to a prosperous and harmonious society. In health care and education, for example, this push has taken the form of privatization, the various ways of shifting authority, ownership, ideology, production and/or delivery of public services from state-controlled to private, market-oriented organizations and frameworks (see Antony et al. 2007; Harvey 2005: 64). Privatization can involve selling public resources to for-profit corporations, but it also occurs when management of public social programs is turned over to corporations and when public institutions, whose goals are far broader than profit making, are managed through corporate models as if they are profit-making businesses.

Jamie Brownlee (Chapter 9) gives us a detailed examination of the privatization of university education in Canada. With the switch to a corporate structure, universities are more and more at the whim of their private funders, and this occurs at the cost of academic freedom. In addition, the focus on private funders and their interests has led to a change in curriculums and academic programs, and "universities are devoting more resources to vocational and applied fields, while arts and basic science programs are downgraded." Despite the fact that humanities, liberal arts and basic science programs have produced graduates who have succeeded in the Canadian job market, the need to satisfy corporate and private funders has led to this major change in the academic focus of many universities.

What the education example, and the reserve land solution outlined above, show is that privatization — far from resolving problems of health care and education — has all kinds of negative consequences. Put simply, these examples of tindividual, market solutions do not solve our education (and other) problems because they do not address the abiding inequalities that are at their root.

Resolving Our Problems: Resistance and Social Justice

The contributors in this book use a different approach, one that sees social inequality as underlying the problems we face. Social harm, and thus social problems, arise from excesses of private power and are exacerbated when public resources are shifted to the control of elites such that benefits go to the privileged (Barlow 2005: 142). For example, the critical perspective shifts our view and understanding of poverty from looking at what poor people do to problematizing wealth, or to paraphrase Linda McQuaig and Neil Brooks, "the trouble [is] with billionaires" (cf. McQuaig and Brooks 2010). Seen in this way, the search for solutions takes a different tack. "Critical perspectives ask not only whether individual people have maintained their responsibility to the community, but also whether the community has maintained its responsibility to individuals. The approach does not focus on individual flaws; rather, it questions societal structures ... inequality and disenfranchisement, abuse

> For critical observers, social problems are partly the result of choices — the choices of powerful groups in society.

and victimization, classism, racism, and sexism" (Brooks 2002: 47). The neoliberal approach all too often blames the victim of social problems.

In a sense, for critical observers, social problems are partly the result of choices — the choices of powerful groups in society. As Pamela Palmater (Chapter 3) shows, in the case of Indigenous peoples, it is not their failure to assimilate into Canadian society that explains their various dire circumstances, but rather Canada neglecting to live up to its treaty obligations. As she says, almost from the very beginning, through various subtle and not so subtle means, "getting rid of Indians has been the corner-stone of Indian policy." Colonialism, the actions and choices of non-Indigenous settlers, is not historical but ongoing. It includes funding Indigenous education at a third (or more) less than non-Indigenous education, an *Indian Act* that attempted to "thin blood lines" by denying status to Indigenous women who married non-Indigenous men and taking Indigenous children from their communities through residential schools, the Sixties Scoop and, more recently, the child welfare system (where Indigenous children, less than 4 percent of the population, make up over 40 percent of the children and youth in a system that the Canadian Human Rights Tribunal ruled has been systematically underfunded). For Palmater, the issue is not a lack of assimilation into the dominant society (the choices and actions of Indigenous peoples) but coercive attempted assimilation (the choices and actions of powerful non-Indigenous peoples).

Thus, for a critical approach to social problems, solutions lie in resistance and social justice action — in working to overturn the basic social inequalities of our unjust social structure.

> For a critical approach, solutions lie in resistance and social justice action — in working to overturn the basic social inequalities of our unjust social structure.

One aspect of being human is "an instinct for freedom ... to control [our] own affairs ... [not] to be pushed around, ordered, oppressed, etc., and ... a chance to do things that make sense" (Chomsky 1988: 756). What we also see when we look carefully is that Canadians do act to resist inequality, and we do this in a variety of ways. We do it as individuals and as collectivities; we do it through the state and in non-state organizations. We do not always do it intentionally, and some resistance may be more symbolic than material. But the logic of inequality and oppression forces us to reject and try to change fundamental elements of our society.

Individually, we engage in numerous day-to-day, small activities that are part of the long-term process of changing society. For instance, we buy what we need (as opposed to what we are told we want) from local producers and worker co-operatives; we refuse to be silent around racial slurs and we show our children that men must be involved in caring for them and cleaning our houses. In this vein, Jessica Antony (Chapter 12) shows us in the context of tattooing that women, as individuals, do not necessarily consume the commodification agenda of capitalism. It has been profitable for a burgeoning tattooing industry to distance itself from the "deviants" associated with tattoos in the past, thereby stripping permanent body art of any meaning other than as a new form of fashion. What she found in talking to tattooed women is that while many do not see their tattoos as "political," neither do they see them as being akin to wearing fashionable clothing. Tattoos have meaning — from spiritual to familial to feminist — because people want and need meaning in what they do. They do resist the tendency in capitalism to make consumption the only meaningful activity and to promote the idea that everything should be about consumption.

We also join with others in resisting inequality and pursuing social justice. The most obvious of these collective actions are the social movements that have already changed our world — the movements we are familiar with, including feminist organizations, labour unions, anti-racist groups, gay and lesbian rights organizations and environmentalists. The democracy that we probably take for granted did not arrive full blown but rather because of the collective action of non-elite Canadians. As Dennis Pilon (Chapter 8) demonstrates from the very start, the "founding fathers" were not concerned to develop a political system that included the voices of all citizens. In fact, as he says, "The founders of Canada were not democrats," they were more concerned with creating a governing system to protect and enhance their capitalist enterprises. Wresting control of government from aristocracies but putting in place a system that gave voice only to "propertied men" gave rise to the popular and working class, unions and "occupy-like events and movements" demanding a voice for all people rather the fully intended stunted democracy. Over the years, similar movements — the One Big Union, the Winnipeg General Strike, the huge strikes of post-World War II to the Occupy movements of the 2000s — continually pressed for moving "democracy" towards "self governance" for all people and not to be just about elections.

Sometimes the distinction between individual and collective resistance can be blurred. Leslie Shade, Normand Landry and Rhon Teruelle (Chapter 16) show us that "botnets" and "swarming" are, in an important sense, individual actions; they are not the typical kind of collective action of street protests and demonstrations that are organized and carried out in a face-to-face manner. Nonetheless, they do bring people together in a co-operative action. The success of "Operation Payback, meant to launch a global 'cyberwar' against censorship ... was unique because it relied on ... the keen co-operation of those who are usually the unwilling accomplices of hackers and pirates." As is the case with much resistance, activist use of social media subverts the purposes and prescribed uses of technology that is owned by economically and politically powerful groups.

Despite the demands and desires of some neoliberals that government disappear from the social scene, it is clear that we cannot live in a society without some form of state. It is through the state, albeit a more participatory and fully democratic one, that we can make the kinds of collective decisions we must make if we are to live together and realize our collective responsibility to each other. Government is a key part of our social lives. Thus it is no surprise that collective resistance can and does also take place through the state. Tracey Peter and Catherine Taylor (Chapter 13) discuss some of the ways that homophobia can be overturned in schools and in society generally. While they recognize the limits of a declaration like the *Charter of Rights and Freedoms* in producing a discrimination-free society, for example, and do see the important place of Gay Student Alliances for creating safe spaces for LGBTQ students, they are optimistic that lobbying governments can have positive social change results. They tell us that schools have become safer for LGBTQ students where school divisions have mandated a "whole-system approach" to include gender and sexual minority content in policies, programs and curriculum.

Still, collective action against inequality does not necessarily take place through the state, nor does it have to. At the very least, given the scale of state activities, these institutions can be insensitive to the needs of some people and, in some cases, oppressive. Jim Silver (Chapter 6) shows that poverty in Canada has become seemingly intractable, in large part because almost every approach that has tackled economic conditions in recent years has been market-oriented and too often state-centred. He shows us that along with some necessary changes in government social- and labour-market policies and state support, a key strategy for anti-poverty action is within poor communities themselves. In particular, he says, community-based economic development can and will plug the many holes through which wealth produced in poor communities "leaks out" to corporations and other groups. Just as importantly, social enterprises that are developed and run locally can provide the skills development and self-confidence necessary for dispossessed people to eliminate poverty, a change that will benefit everyone in society, not just the poor.

Power and Resistance

At their core, social problems are about inequality — they are about power and resistance. The chapters in this book emphasize that — depending on class, race, gender and sexual orientation — people face inequalities of treatment and life chances. Emphasizing power means first of all recognizing that some groups have privileged access to the resources that make life viable in our society. More importantly, a critical emphasis means revealing how those groups act to maintain and enhance their privilege, thereby creating problems for other groups of people. These inequalities — inherent in an unjust social structure — are the social problems in and of Canadian society. Our focus is not just on documenting existing conditions but also on ways of generating emancipatory resistance and social justice change.

Glossary of Key Terms

Inequality: The more or less narrow life choices and life chances for individuals and groups of people. Inequality refers not just to what people have; it is not only differences in lifestyle, but also what they can do and what they can become.

Neoliberal(ism): A theory and ideology about political economy that claims human well-being is maximized by liberating individual entrepreneurs within social and political institutions that enhance property rights and the free market. Public goods and community should be replaced with private property and individual responsibility. Where there are not markets, such as in education, health care and social security, they must be created.

Objective element of social problems (conditionalism): The basis in reality for whether a social condition or behaviour pattern is a problem or not. This basis involves identifying who is harmed and who benefits, and in what ways, from a social condition or behaviour pattern.

Power: The ability to set limits on the behavioural choices for ourselves and for others. Power is clearly in play when individuals and groups act in ways that achieve their desires, needs and interests against those of others. Power has many bases and faces, from the schoolyard bully to influence over public discourse.

Private troubles: Occur within the character of the individual and within the range of immediate relations with others; they have to do with the self and with those limited areas of social life of which we are directly and personally aware.

Public issues: Matters that transcend the local environments of the individual and the range of inner life. They have to do with the organization of many such milieux into the institutions of a historical society, with the ways in which various milieux overlap and interpenetrate to form the larger structure of social and historical life.

Resistance: Acting to change the basic social inequalities of society. Resistance can be an individual act and can occur in collectivities; it happens through the state and in non-state organizations. It is not always intentional, and some resistance is more symbolic than material. But the logic of inequality forces us to reject and try to change fundamental elements of our society.

Social justice: An ideology and activist goal focused on realizing equality in society. Rather than an "equality of sameness" (treating un-alikes as if they were alike) the focus is on achieving an "equality of difference" to ensure that all social groups have access to social, political and economic resources in society and that there are no constraints on life choices based on social group differences.

Structure: Social and political structures are the patterns of behavioural relationships between groups of people in society. They include how men and women, racialized people, young and old, wealthy and poor, governments and citizens relate to one another.

Subjective element of social problems (constructionism): In regard to social issues, this is often called public perception. What people perceive as real will guide their actions and their understanding of society. This aspect of social problems refers to what people think are the consequences — who is harmed and who benefits — of a social condition or pattern of behaviour.

Questions for Discussion

1. Take an issue in the neighbourhood or city you live in, or the university you go to. What are the "facts" about it? Where do you get information about those facts? Who provides that information? Is there a debate about the facts? What individuals, groups and organizations represent the various elements of the issue and its debate? What resources do they have to make their case known to other people and groups and/or to government?

2. Does a focus on structure and inequality mean that individuals bear no responsibility for social problems and their solutions?

3. How are the following issues "private troubles"? How are they public issues? Youth gangs, online bullying and equal pay for equal work.

4. For the issue you thought about in question 1, think about possible solutions. What government policies are involved? What changes might help? What community organizations and resources are there to help resolve the issue? What new community resources could be developed?

Resources for Activists

Briarpatch: briarpatchmagazine.com
Canadian Centre for Policy Alternatives: policyalternatives.ca
Canadian Dimension: canadiandimension.com
Council of Canadians: canadians.org
Democracy Now!: democracynow.org
Herizons: herizons.ca
New Internationalist: newint.org
Rabble: rabble.ca
This Magazine: this.org

References

Antony, W., E. Black, S. Frankel, D. Henley, P. Hudson, W. Land, D. Lewycky, E. Ternette, and R. Tychonick. 2007. *The State of Public Services in Manitoba*. Winnipeg: Canadian Centre for Policy Alternatives–Manitoba.

Barlow, M. 2005. *Too Close for Comfort: Canada's Future Within Fortress North America*. Toronto: McClelland and Stewart.

Brooks, C. 2002. "New Directions in Critical Criminology." In Bernard Schissel and Carolyn Brooks (eds.), *Marginality and Condemnation: An Introduction to Critical Criminology*. Winnipeg and Black Point, NS: Fernwood Publishing.

Brownlee, J. 2005. *Ruling Canada: Corporate Cohesion and Democracy*. Winnipeg and Black Point, NS: Fernwood Publishing.

CBCNews. 2015. "Bad Water: 'Third World' Conditions on First Nations in Canada." October 15 <cbc.ca/news/canada/manitoba/bad-water-third-world-conditions-on-first-nations-in-canada-1.3269500>.

CCPA (Canadian Centre for Policy Alternatives). 2016. "Power Lunch." *CCPA Monitor* March/April.

Chomsky, N. 1988. *Language and Politics*. Montreal: Black Rose Books.

Eitzen, D.S., M. Zinn, and K. Smith. 2011. *Social Problems, 12th edition*. New York: Pearson.

Fleras, A. 2005. *Social Problems in Canada: Conditions, Contstructions and Challenges*. Toronto: Pearson Education.

Fowler, R.A., N.S. Sabur, P. Li, D.N. Jurrlink, R. Pinto, M.A. Hladunew, and N. Adhikari. 2007. "Sex- and Age-Based Differences in the Delivery and Outcomes of Critical Care." *Canadian Medical Association Journal* 177, 12.

Harvey, D. 2005. *A Brief History of Neoliberalism*. Oxford: Oxford University Press.

Klein, N. 2007. *The Shock Doctrine: The Rise of Disaster Capitalism*. Toronto: Knopf Canada

Knuttila, M. 2016. *Paying for Masculinity: Men, Boys and the Patriarchal Dividend*. Winnipeg/Halifax: Fernwood Publishing.

Loseke, D. 1999. *Thinking About Social Problems*. New York: Aldine de Gruyter.

McQuaig, L., and N. Brooks. 2011. *The Trouble with Billionnaires: How the Super-Rich Hijacked the World and How We Can Take it Back*. Toronto: Penguin Canada

Mills, C. Wright. 1959. *The Sociological Imagination*. New York: Oxford University Press.

Mosher, J. 2014. "Welfare Fraudsters and Tax Evaders: The State's Selective Invocation of Criminality." In C. Brooks and B. Schissel (eds.), *Marginality and Condemnation, 3rd edition*. Winnipeg and Black Point, NS: Fernwood Publishing.

Nelson, E., and A. Fleras. 1995. *Canadian Social Problems*. Englewood Cliffs, NJ: Prentice Hall.

Oil Change International Institute. 2015. "Empty Promises: G20 Subsidies to Oil, Gas and Coal Production." <priceofoil.org/2015/11/11/empty-promises-g20-subsidies-to-oil-gas-and-coal-production/>.

Pannozzo, L. 2016. *About Canada: The Environment*. Halifax and Winnipeg: Fernwood Publishing.

Parliament of Canada. n.d. "Occupations of Members of the House of Commons." <op.parl.gc.ca/parlinfo/Lists/Occupation.aspx?Menu=HOC-Bio&Section=03d93c58-f843-49b3-9653-84275c23f3fb&Parliament=b67c82bf-0106-42e5-9be1-46ecb5feaf60&Name=&Party=&Province=&Gender=&CurrentParliamentarian=False&Occupation=&OccupationType=>

Polaris Institute. 2008. "Boiling Point." <polarisinstitute.org/boiling_point_0>.

Proctor, J. 2016. "CBC-Angus Reid Institute poll: Canadians want minorities to do more to 'fit in': Majority polled also said immigration policies should put Canada's economic needs first." <cbc.ca/news/canada/british-columbia/poll-canadians-multiculturalism-immigrants-1.3784194>.

Public Health Agency of Canada. 2016. *The Chief Public Health Officer's Report on the State of Public Health in Canada 2016. A Focus on Family Violence in Canada*. Ottawa. <healthycanadians.gc.ca/publications/department-ministere/state-public-health-family-violence-2016-etat-sante-publique-violence-familiale/alt/pdf-eng.pdf>.

Raphael, D. 2009. "Poverty, Human Development, and Health in Canada: Research, Practice and Advocacy." *Canadian Journal of Nursing Research* 41, 2.

Slee, T. 2015. *What's Yours Is Mine: Against the Sharing Economy*. Toronto: Between the Lines.

Sullivan, T., and K. Thompson. 1988. *Introduction to Social Problems*. New York: Macmillan.

Winseck, D. 2016. "Modular Media." CCPA *Monitor* July.

2

Matters of the State Still Matter

Political Power and Social Problems

Murray Knuttila

YOU SHOULD KNOW THIS

- Canada is a federation, meaning political power is divided among and between a federal, or national, legislature located in Ottawa and provincial or territorial legislatures located in provincial and territorial capitals. In addition, there are smaller local or regional city, town and other municipal councils and assemblies.
- While the distribution of political powers was originally specified in the *British North America Act* of 1867 and the 1982 *Constitution Act*, there are constant debates and shifts involving different political ideologies and positions with regard to the precise distribution of powers between the various levels.
- Democracy did not come easily to all Canadians. In 1916, Saskatchewan, Manitoba and Alberta granted women the right to vote, but it was not until 1920 that women could vote in federal elections. Aboriginal persons could not vote until 1960. People in jail could not vote until after the Supreme Court ruled in 2002 that preventing them from voting was unconstitutional.
- According to opensecrets.org, pharmaceutical and health product companies in the United States spent $3,320,985,764 (USD) on lobbying the U.S. governments between 1998 and 2016.
- In 2015, individuals paid significantly more income tax than did the corporate sector. Personal income tax totaled nearly $135.7 billion while the corporate sector paid $39.4 billion, only 29.0 percent of what individuals pay. In 2000, personal tax amounted to $82.3 billion while the corporate share was $28.2, only 34 percent of what individuals pay.

Sources: Centre for Responsive Politics 2106; Department of Finance 2015; Department of Finance 2002.

THE TITLE OF THIS BOOK, *POWER AND RESISTANCE*, SAYS MUCH about the complex and changing world of the early decades of the twenty-first century because we often associate the word "power" with making things happen or implementing change, while "resistance" implies disagreement with the direction of such change. Power is a commonly used word in everyday life and in the social sciences; however, it is also among the most contested and misunderstood words. While the editors of this collection define social power as "the ways in which people in particular social groups can force people in other social groups to act in certain ways," in this chapter we will take a somewhat broader view since this chapter deals with political power. In the various chapters that follow, we will see many different social actors, classes, interests and collectivities working to change various aspects of our society in order to make it more egalitarian, just, fair and sustainable, or sometimes resisting changes that would make it even less egalitarian, just, fair and sustainable. The chapters describe various arenas in which power is exercised and resisted, and while the outcomes vary in terms of the consequences for individuals, groups and society as a whole, most, if not all, are impacted by the actions, policies and programs of the state and government; hence our focus is on the state and its relationship to social issues. If we are to understand the state, the dynamics of political power, specific state policies and actions and the overall social role of the state, we must delve into the field of state theory and consider some of the theoretical frameworks that have been used to analyze and explain the role of the state in capitalist society.

The emphasis here tends to be on a macro or a structural approach, which means that social problems are examined and explained in terms of structural and social relations and processes. Because the state (also referred to as the polity) in Western capitalist societies is generally understood as the institution that is primarily concerned with the organization of political and social power and the exercise of authority in the interests of social stability and order, an adequate understanding of social problems requires an analysis of the role of the state. First off, the state (or polity) and the government are often confused and conflated. The state is generally understood as referring to the overall institutional and organizational apparatus through which social power is exercised and decisions impacting society generally are made, ostensibly on behalf the population of a defined territory. In Western liberal democracies, there are a variety of different institutional state forms typically composed of legislatures and assemblies, cabinets, executive branches, bureaucratic and regulatory structures, plus modes and means of law and regulatory enforcement. The nature and operation of the formal decision-making apparatus of states are typically articulated in a constitution. Government on the other hand, represents a particular assemblage of people who are formally in control of the apparatus of the state for a limited period of time and, in liberal-democratic states, are subject to renewal or replacement through periodic elections. While government will be mentioned, what follows will focus on the state.

The state in capitalist society has been the subject of debate and controversy since it emerged as part and parcel of the emergence of capitalism about 500 years ago. During the fifteenth and sixteenth centuries, formally organized states claiming sovereignty over various territories emerged in various parts of Western Europe and England. While early political philosophers such as Thomas Hobbes may have worried about the "problem of order" and argued for a strong state to prevent citizens from mutual destruction, it was Karl Polanyi in the *Great Transformation* who explained that a state was necessary in order to establish the preconditions for capitalism. A strong state was necessary to establish the rudimentary requisites for capitalist enterprise such as uniform currencies, standardized weights and measures, legal codes, enforceable contracts and the like, without which capitalist commerce and industry would not have been possible. As the nature of the classes with dominant economic power changed and evolved, so did the structures and dynamics of the state. It is important to understand how popular-based social and political movements changed and democratized many Western states; however, we will jump ahead and consider some of the ways that twentieth and twenty-first century capitalist states have acted and been explained. We will begin with a perspective on the nature of the state that held sway for much of the last century.

Pluralism

If you studied political science or political sociology at most Western universities throughout much of the twentieth century, you would likely have learned that complex industrial societies (although they were capitalist, these societies tended to be identified as just "industrial") faced an age-old problem relating to political or social decision-making: How does the state in a society composed of different individuals, groups and interests develop goals, priorities and social policies that broadly represent the public and enjoy widespread support? You would have been taught that the state in Western society has evolved in a manner that allows it to recognize the rights of individuals, the potential dangers of discord in an excessively individualistic society and the need for a functioning political system that makes important social decisions on behalf of all citizens. Indeed, you may have been taught that such a state structure is one of the major accomplishments of Western liberal-democratic society.

Charles Merriam (1964) was among the first to systematically argue that the United States represents a social system that has successfully addressed the key issue of how a society divided into many classes, groups and factions might establish a system of political decision-making that is open and democratic, and capable of representing the common or public good. However, it was the work of Robert Dahl (1967, 1972) that established the dominance of what has come to be called the pluralist approach. According to Dahl, complex industrial societies are typically divided into different kinds of groups, classes and factions based on a multitude of religious, class, occupational, regional, ethnic and sexual differences. Corporations, unions, cultural groups, professional associations, and special interest and community groups are some examples of these factions. When understood in this context, the function of government and the political decision-making process mainly involves mediation and arbitration among and between the interests, desires and motivations of these factions.

Pluralists argue that Western democracies — with the U.S. system being typical — are sets of structures and processes that fulfill the best possibilities for democratic political activity in an advanced industrial society. For pluralists, the electoral system, with its "one-person one-vote," is a great equalizer or "leveller." Regardless of an individual's income, social status or background, on election day every person is deemed to be equal. The fact that everyone is entitled to one vote means all citizens potentially have the same power and opportunity to make an impact on the political process.

> For pluralists, the electoral system with its "one-person one-vote" is a great equalizer or "leveller." Regardless of an individual's income, social status or background, on election day every person is deemed to be equal.

The political process is not, however, just about elections. Individuals, groups, associations and classes have other opportunities to influence government policies and actions. Pluralism holds that liberal-democratic systems are open societies with multiple modes of communication available to citizens to ensure that most people have access to information about what the government is doing and the activities of the state. When the government is about to decide on an issue, the individuals and groups interested in that issue will know about it and have the opportunity to present their case to the government. Lobbying is available to all, even if the participants did not support the particular party or individual who was victorious in the electoral process.

Based on this sort of analysis of Western democracies, pluralists argue that political power is dispersed across a multitude of individuals, classes, associations and interests that compete through the electoral and lobbying processes to influence government. The existence of a plurality of centres of power means that in the long term no one of those centres is able to dominate. The government must be willing to accommodate all of the various interests, or else it runs the risk of becoming viewed as being corrupt and tied to one centre of power, incapable of acting as a neutral mediator or arbitrator of possible disputes of conflicts. If this happens, the government will face certain electoral defeat once it becomes apparent to all the various interests that they have become excluded from the political process. Assuming that the various excluded interests comprise the majority, they will be in a position to develop a coalition and remove the offending government from power.

In summary, pluralists claim that the liberal-democratic polity facilitates social decision-making in a complex and divided society. The polity is the site of mediation and "trade-offs," as the government seeks to establish policies and priorities that it sees as representing the interests of the majority (Dahl 1967: 24). No centre of power is dominant or able to consistently get its way, at least over the long term. "You win some, you lose some" truly characterizes how different interest groups fare in the political process. An example might be the necessity of granting workers the basic right to organize unions while maintain a labour relations regime that also empowers the corporate sector with the power to make major economic decisions.

Some pluralists suggest that the political process may not be quite this smooth. Charles Lindblom (1977), for example, notes that the concentration of economic power in capitalist society has significant implications for political processes. Social and political stability within capitalist systems requires a smooth, functioning economy; therefore, it is important that the state does everything in its power to see that certain economic conditions prevail. On this basis, Lindblom and many others show that businesses occupy a "privileged position." The enormous resources controlled by the corporate sector can give it overwhelming advantages in the competition to influence the government — a situation contrary to pluralist analysis. To return to the example of the right of workers to form unions, should that right fundamentally threaten the economic power of a corporation, the company might simply close the operation, throwing all its employees out of work.

The critical questions raised by the privileged political position of corporations was clearly a problem for pluralists and pluralism; however, there were other pressing issues across the West that resulted in the emergence of alternate approaches. Even as most of the Western world enjoyed the prosperity of the post-WWII boom, economic, social and political conditions provided the context for a renewed interest in the work of Karl Marx. In North America, a number of key developments rocked the stability of the post-WWII social order, including the emergence of the civil rights movement, second-wave feminism, the counter culture, student movements, various anti-war movements directed at ending the West's involvement in wars in Indo-China and demands for gay and lesbian rights. Internationally, social movements aimed at decolonialism in the so-called Third World, the emergence of organized terrorism, instability in the Middle East and the growing power of multinational corporations and transnational trade and financial agreements pointed to the incapacity of pluralism to explain the real world of power and domination. Meanwhile, more of Marx's original writings were available to the English-reading public, including scholars whose re-examination of Marx led them to argue that many of his ideas were in fact incompatible with the ideas and practices of regimes such as that in the Soviet Union. What emerged were alternate theoretical perspectives that became variously referred to as critical theory, neo-Marxism or simply conflict theory.

The State in Capitalist Society

Although there is no systematic and well-developed conception of the state in Marx's original works, he was interested in political power on both a practical and a theoretical level. In *The German Ideology* (1970: 80), Marx and Engels argued that the state must be understood within the context of capitalist economic structures that are predicated on a society divided into two main classes, the working class and the capitalist class: "The State is the form in which the individuals of a ruling [capitalist] class assert their common interests." Marx and Engels made other statements on the nature of the state in capitalist society, sometimes in quite simplistic terms, as in their claim that "the executive of the modern state is but a com-mittee for managing the common affairs of the whole [capitalist class]" (1952: 44). In other works they present more complex pictures of the state (Marx 1972a, 1972b, 1972a, 1972b), but the constant theme was that the state is a central part of the process of capitalist-class domination of the economy and of society.

Following Marx's death, some of his ideas were reinterpreted and restated by Engels, Lenin and others. The Russian Revolution of 1917 became an important worldwide development and resulted in the emergence of what Russell Jacoby (1971: 121) calls a "bolshevized" Marx. Some critics argue that Marxism was turned into a rigid and simplistic caricature of Marx's thinking in the form of "Soviet-style Marxism" (Marcuse 1961). However, during the 1960s, interest in Marx re-emerged among political activists and scholars loosely referred to as neo-Marxists, resulting in a number of efforts to further examine the role of the state in capitalist society.

Early Neo-Marxist Perspectives

Instrumental Marxism

Among the first systematic neo-Marxist treatments of the state was Ralph Miliband's *The State in Capitalist Society*. One of Miliband's explicit purposes was to demonstrate the inadequa-cies of the pluralist model (1973: 6). He points out that a key feature of capitalist society is its class structure, with the dominant economic class — those who own and control the means of producing goods and services in society, capitalists — overwhelmingly holding and controlling economic power. To put it briefly, Miliband argues that the state tends to act in the interests of the capitalist class, with most of its actions geared towards trying to ensure that the capitalist system continues to operate as it does (that is, in ways that benefit the capitalist class). Furthermore, the development of large-scale corporations that continually concentrate and centralize economic power have made the capitalist class even more powerful — indeed, so powerful that the capitalist class controls political power and should thus be understood as forming a "ruling elite."

To illustrate capitalist class control of the operation of the state, Miliband breaks the state down into its various components: the elected government, the bureaucracy and administrative apparatus, and the military. He shows that either representatives of the capitalist class or people sympathetic to the interests of the capitalist class tend to control the primary decision-making positions in all the major branches of the state. Miliband argues that the upper levels of the "officialdom" of the state apparatus (uppermost leadership), including the administrative and bureaucratic arms, are overwhelming populated by individuals with business connections or who are pro-business (50–58). By "sympathetic" he is referring to how those in command positions in the state generally share lifestyles, networks and value systems with the capitalist class. He points out that most of those in these positions come from a similar class position and were educated and trained in a select group of education institutions that serve the sons (and sometimes the daughters) of the wealthy. Miliband rejects arguments about the state being a neutral mediator seeking to establish social policies and priorities for "the nation" in "the national interests." He says that arguments that appeal to ideas such as the "national interests" must be approached with a critical and wary eye because what is claimed to be the national interest is often just the interests of a dominant class. As we shall see, the power of a dominant class postulating its interests and worldviews as representing the interests and worldview of the entire society is an important form of social power. The jargon that is applied to this process might be stated as representing the ideological manipulations of public opinion designed to provide a façade of legitimation for class domination.

Structural Marxism

In *Political Power and Social Classes*, French neo-Marxist Nicos Poulantzas sought to provide a different type of theoretical approach based on the insights of Marx. For Poulantzas, the main task for neo-Marxists was not merely to criticize pluralism, but rather to provide an alternative theoretical approach.

Poulantzas argued that it is a mistake to simply examine the personnel of and personal connections between the capitalist class and the state. What really matters is the role and function of the state in the capitalist mode of production, not the particular individuals who staff the state. Since the central characteristic of the capitalist mode of production is its division into classes with fundamentally conflicting interests, concerns and unequal structural positions, some means of stabilizing the system and alleviating class conflict must be developed if this system is to survive. According to Poulantzas, because capitalism is inherently a class-based system based on relations of exploitation, domination and inequalities of power and wealth, it is prone to instability, conflict and crisis, thus requiring an institution such as the state to stabilize the whole system.

What followed was a lively debate and exchange between Miliband and Poulantzas. Yet for both, the state functions in the long-term interests of the capitalist class because the capitalist class has the most to gain from the smooth, conflict-free operation of the system.

Thus, two broadly neo-Marxist streams developed. Poulantzas understood the state largely in terms of the functions it performed for the capitalist class. This structuralist approach directs our attention to an understanding of the structures, roles and functions of the state by examining the overall structures, dynamic and logic of capitalism. We refer to the position as structuralist because it locates the need for the state in the class structures of capitalism and the inevitable necessity of class conflict that may threaten the very existence of the system. In short, were it not for the presence and functioning of the state, capitalist society may well not be possible, certainly not in a stable and ongoing form. Miliband examined more direct connections between the capitalist class and the state by looking at state personnel: the personal, lifestyle, interactive and ideological similarities between the capitalist class and those in charge of the state. However, both Miliband and Poulantzas understood that in acting to preserve the total capitalist system the state is also acting in the interests of the class that benefits most from the maintenance of the status quo.

Alternative Directions in Neo-Marxist Theory

Neither of these approaches was without problems and critics. Within the structuralist tradition, the state is simply assumed to operate in the interests of the capitalist class, with this assumption becoming the explanation of the state's role and actions. The instrumentalist approach has difficulty explaining those instances when there are no immediate or direct connections between the state and the capitalist class; yet it maintains that the state tends to operate so as to serve the long-term interests of capital. Several others (see Block 1977; Skocpol 1980; Szymanski 1978) argue for an alternate, non-pluralist approach that moves our understanding of the state beyond the Miliband-Poulantzas debate. Albert Szymanski's work is illustrative of such an approach.

In *The Capitalist State and the Politics of Class* (1978), Szymanski offers a critique of the existing approaches while recognizing some of their strengths. He maintains that it is necessary to recognize that in liberal-democratic society the capitalist class does not necessarily directly control the state since many elected politicians and state bureaucrats come from classes other than the capitalist class. However, the state does tend to act in the interests of the dominant class. Szymanski argues that the state is not purely controlled by the economic power of the capitalist class as some simple interpretations of Marx might have suggested — as one example, the state does occasionally enact policies that are economically important to the working class, such as social programs, environmental regulations and other components the social safety net. To explain these types of situations, Szymanski offers an analysis based on the idea that in liberal-democratic society the various classes, groups, associations and individuals can influence the operation, policies, actions and decisions of the state through direct and indirect linkages or mechanisms of power.

There are, Szymanski argues, three essential, direct mechanisms of power. The first mechanism is having members of the capitalist class in the operational and command positions of the state. The second is lobbying, which can influence the state. The third is the policy-formation process. Because governments and state agencies often rely on advice to make decisions, establishing organizations to offer that advice can be a mode of influencing the state. As we shall see, Szymanski argues that by virtue of the resources the dominant class controls and commands, it is better posed to engage or utilize these mechanisms of power.

In addition, he argues there are several indirect linkages through which the capitalist class can control or impact the actions of the state (Szymanski 1978: 24–25). These include the use of ideological power, economic power and funding electoral processes. Given that the state and governments operate within a larger ideological environment, it is possible to influence the state by influencing that environment, particularly through the process of public opinion. If a class or group can convince the majority of the people that everyone shares the same interests, then the public as a whole will resist any state actions that run counter to the interests of that group or class. As a result, the state's ability to act will be limited or constrained. Ruling classes always attempt to present their interests as the "national interest" or as the "public good" in order to constrain the actions of the state. For example, while free trade agreements may overwhelmingly operate in the interests of multinational corporate interests, they are typically presented as operating in the interests of everyone, as being for the so-called "public good." Since the capitalist class tends to own and control the major mechanisms of public information and debate — such as mass media and think-tanks — they have the means to develop an ideological consensus.

> Ruling classes always attempt to present their interests as the "national interest" or as the "public good."

In terms of economic power, the state and governments in capitalist society are dependent on the existence of a healthy and stable economy. The class that controls economic decision-making and planning is in a position to exert major influence on the state because, in the event that the state acts against their interests, they can decide not to invest or to withdraw investment or transfer investments elsewhere. Any of those actions will have a negative impact on employment, prosperity and indeed the entire social and political system. The actions and policies of the state are often constrained by the need to maintain "business confidence."

Lastly, there is the matter of how political processes are funded. In its simplest terms, the adage "he who is pays the piper, calls the tune" explains a lot about the dynamics of political power. At the political level, groups or individuals who are able to fund political parties and candidates can influence the policies and actions of governments when those parties are in power.

Szymanski thus offers an approach to the state in capitalist society that provides a way of explaining why and how, in specific instances, the state acts in the manner that it does, while avoiding the pitfalls of simple instrumentalist or abstract structuralist explanations. He argues that the overwhelming economic power of the capitalist class means that it is most capable of using the various mechanisms of power. In a liberal democracy, those mechanisms of power are available to everyone, but because the class structure means that economic resources are unequally allocated, in reality it is the capitalist class that has the overwhelming advantage in influencing the state. There is no doubt in Szymanski's mind that the state in a capitalist society operates in the interests of the capitalist class, but the process is complex and contradictory and is affected deeply by some historical developments in the role of the state in Western society over the past few decades.

Neoliberalism and the State

The state that Miliband, Poulantzas and Szymanski were attempting to explain was operating at a time characterized by a particular form of capitalist development. The era from the end of the Second World War to the early 1970s was one of general prosperity based on mass production and mass consumption of consumer goods under the international leadership of the United States. Although the twentieth century was punctuated by the horrors of two world wars, the Great Depression and revolutions in Russia and China, it also saw the emergence of the welfare state as part of a post-WWII political and class compromise in much of the Western world. A central element of post-Depression Western capitalism was an active state. The near total collapse of the capitalist system wrought by the Great Depression provided the context for the widespread acceptance of what we know as Keynesian economics and a new understanding of the role of the state. Keynes and his followers prepared to accept state intervention in the form of regulation and spending to increase the demand for goods and services thereby stimulating lagging economies. The Keynesian state became a key element in the post-WWII compromise and involved a set of social and political structures through which businesses, corporations, the labour movement and the state regulated economic, social and political affairs based on widespread sharing of the benefits that prosperity brought. This post–WWII social contract was based on the idea that unions would bargain (vigorously) on matters of pay and working conditions, but would not question the overall legitimacy of the capitalist system, including the right of business to run the economy. The state provided a social safety net — that is, social programs such as health insurance, Medicare, child protection legislation and even some minimal form of social assistance — and used its resources to direct investment and economic activity (especially economic development aid for selected regions and industries) for the benefit

> The Keynesian state became a key element in the post-WWII compromise through which corporations, the labour movement and the state regulated economic, social, and political affairs based on widespread sharing of the benefits of prosperity.

of both capitalists and the working class. Business was free to make most of the nation's economic decisions within these broad constraints. In particular, in key industrial sectors (autos, rubber, steel, for example), owners and managers were given a free hand to introduce technological change and other labour-saving innovations; workers, through their unions, would get wage increases in line with productivity gains plus inflation. This overall system came to be called "Fordism." However, Fordism ultimately contained the seeds of its own destruction.

According to David Harvey (2010), contradictions arise from the fact that capitalism, as a class-based system, is based on the necessity of continual economic growth. As a result, Fordism began to face a number of interrelated crises. The largely U.S.-led reconstruction of the core Western capitalist economies after WWII was designed to ensure that they remained in the capitalist world system, but an unintended result was the eventual emergence of growing rivalries within and between capitalist nations as Japan and Western Europe were rebuilt with new and more efficient technologies. In addition, capitalists, especially big business, found themselves with large amounts of cash and increasingly fewer profitable investment opportunities, even as the Western world enjoyed a period of prosperity. Ongoing investment in profitable ventures is a necessary precondition for sustained economic activity in the capitalist system (Harvey 2010: 45). Added to these problems were the advancing globalization of business and growing state fiscal deficits resulting from the expenditures associated with the welfare state and the expansion of public services.

The 1970s thus marked the emergence of a series of crises for the welfare state system. These crises included growing government deficits, international competition among capitalist economies, increasing regional disparities and growing internationalization of capital. In response to these upheavals, many governments began to implement a series of public policies that violated the existing informal social contract (Harvey 2005) by making widespread and deep cuts to a range of social programs, including Medicare, school support, daycare programs and international aid. All of these cuts were designed to reduce government spending and regulation, making the market more dominant in every aspect of our lives. Meanwhile, the corporate sector across the West abandoned its loyal working class, which was essential to its earlier prosperity, in search of low-wage production on a global scale.

> Neoliberalism was actually a return to classical liberalism, with its emphasis on the individual as the basic unit of society, as illustrated by then prime minister of Britain, Margaret Thatcher, who mused that there was really no such thing as society, only individuals.

Neoliberalism is conventionally used to describe the shift away from the post-WWII welfare state after the 1970s. To a large extent, neoliberalism was actually a return to elements of classical liberalism, which emphasized the individual as the basic unit of society, a point illustrated by then Prime Minister of Britain Margaret Thatcher, who mused that there was really no such thing as society, only individuals (Keay 1987). The welfare state was indicted as the root of all social and economic evils, with claims that it sapped individuals of their work ethic, cost hard-working taxpayers too much and empowered the state and its bloated bureaucratic apparatus with excessive power, resulting in intolerable and counterproductive state regulation. The market (that is, corporations) was deemed to be the supreme and ultimate decision-maker for economic matters, although the so-called market rationality was increasingly used to direct the operations of many social institutions, including education, social services and health care. Neoliberals argued that the state was to provide a minimal degree of economic oversight, acting essentially as a referee, to make sure that all sides played fair in terms of honouring contracts. The private sector, competition and the rule of the market were exalted to the status of common sense and a kind of natural order of things, while government, public service and the public sphere were denigrated and ridiculed as inherently inefficient, costly and a waste of taxpayers hard-earned money. David Harvey argues that there was more going on than might meet the eye: "My view is that it refers to a class project that coalesced in the crisis of the mid 1970s. Masked by a lot of rhetoric about individual freedom, liberty, personal responsibility and the virtues of privatisation, the free market and free trade, it legitimised draconian policies designed to restore and consolidate capitalist class power" (2010: 10). The key feature of this new political system is a nation-state that loses its central position; many state functions are taken over by non-government or private organizations, and corporations becomes fully internationalized.

As it turned out, the unregulated and unfettered corporation was not viable. A housing crisis and the stock market collapse in 2008–09 threatened the entire economic order; Western states rushed in with gargantuan bailout packages for a variety of sectors of the economy, such as banks, insurance companies and automotive companies. In the United States, for example, the state provided an initial bailout worth more that $700 billion, although some, such as Mike Collins (2015), argue that the final amount was actually in the trillions of dollars. Although the full impact of these measures is still a matter of debate, they did result in significant increases to debts and deficits that then again became a matter of concern for neoliberals. In Canada, the government of Steven Harper was forced to provide stimulus spending for some infrastructure projects and bailouts to major international corporations even while it continued to cut funding to many social programs that benefited marginalized people. In 2016, voters dramatically rejected the Harper Conservative government's neoliberalism and its obsession with debt reduction and its continued hacking away at Canada's social programs with the election of a Liberal government.

Over this period, the state changed from Fordist to neoliberal. It is important to note, however, that virtually all Western states cut social service programs and services, decreased funding to education (resulting in university students paying higher and higher tuition), and weakened many environmental regulatory regimes while spending more on the military. Still, the question remains, how do we understand the nature of the state in the twenty-first century and the manner by which that government will govern? These historical events show that the state, at times, did things that were good for people other than the wealthy and corporations as it sought to fix social and economic problems. But does that mean the state was a neutral umpire, or was it trying to keep capitalism alive?

Recent Development in State Theory

What this short diversion reminds us is the fact that the world is inherently a process, constantly changing, shifting and unfolding. As a socio-economic and political system, capitalism is likewise a dynamic system in which institutions, social dynamics and class structures change and unfold. When changes occur, such as the rise and decline of the welfare state, theoretical explanations and perspectives need to be revised or even be replaced. The real-world changes that occurred across most Western liberal-democratic regimes beginning in the 1970s necessitated and generated a series of new efforts to understand the nature, role and structure of the neoliberal state.

Rational Choice Theory

It should not come as a surprise that theorizing about the state was typically not a priority for neoliberal intellectuals because even the reduced state was viewed as somewhat of a necessary evil, just as the referee in a sports game is viewed with a measure of suspicion. The new reality was, after all, all about individualism, self-reliance, competition and winner-takes-all. In his overview, Martin Smith (2009) discusses rational choice theory as a relatively new stream of political thought. While Smith does not directly associate rational choice with neoliberalism, his identification of some core premises of rational choice thinking seem to align with some of the assumptions of neoliberals. Rational choice advocates assume that all individuals operate on the basis of maximizing those "utilities" (goods or services we desire or seek to satisfy a need or a want) that are in their self-interest and that align with their preferences (21). Stated more bluntly, within this worldview, humans tend to be self-interested, seeking those things that satisfy our wants and make us happy. Smith notes, "Rational choice theory exists within the liberal paradigm and hence is highly suspicious of state power" (56). The state's role and the use of political power is seen as largely the enforcement of contracts or the maintenance of order, including, when necessary, the legitimate use of force. Since rational choice theory holds that all actors, including those in the state apparatus and politicians, act largely out of self-interest, the approach would justify spending more money on the surveillance and monitoring of social service recipients and less on actual social services, since those who access social services are viewed with suspicion and are believed to be prone to ripping off the system. Lacking in rational choice theory, however, is a systematic approach to the actual dynamics of how the state works, both its structures and functions. As Smith puts it, "rational choice theory consequently develops a theory of the state and state power almost without reference to history, politics or power. States develop teleologically on the basis of self-interest" (57).

Given that rational choice theory focuses on self-interested individuals, one might assume that the approach also makes much of conflict or potential conflict. However, as Terry Moe argues, one of the weaknesses of the approach is its silence on power: "Political institutions are more than just structures of cooperation. They are also structures of power, and the theory does not tell us much about this. As a result, we get a one-sided and overly benign view of what political institutions are and what they do" (2005: 228). The lack of an adequate conception of or attention to state, government and political institutions among many rational choice advocates and the inability of an individual-focused approach to explain collective decisions led Peter Hall and Rosemary Taylor (1996) to argue for an approach to the state they called institutionalism.

Institutionalism

James March and Johan Olsen summarize the core position of this approach: "Institutionalism emphasizes the relative autonomy of political institutions from other institutions, classes and social interests, possibilities for inefficiency in history, and the importance of symbolic action to an understanding of politics" (1984: 734; see also 1989). Although institutionalism could be seen as a reaction to the emphasis on individual behaviour and the lack of any analytical explanatory capacity in rational choice theory, it also emerged at a time when the issue of the relative role of individual action ("agency") and social structure in understanding society was emerging.

Edwin Amenta and Kelly Ramsey note that political institutionalism placed political and other actors within the context of the institutions within which they operated: "The main theoretical framework is that macro level political institutions shape politics and political actors, who act under constraints that may influence their impact on states and policies, refashioning political institutions in the process, and so on." (2010: 27; see also Ishiyama 2015)

Institutionalism directs our attention away from a highly structural and functionalist view in which the state performed certain functions simply because that was its function within a particular social system, a criticism that had been directed at the structuralism of Poulantzas. Conversely, institutionalism also avoided the pitfall of postulating individual actors acting willy-nilly to see that their preferences and self-interests were enacted. Institutions, such as state bureaucracies, are deemed to have their own cultures and histories that enable individuals with interests, agendas and opinions to advance those agendas and priorities or to stifle and resist those with which they disagree. Institutionalism pays attention, for example, to the role of state agencies and the bureaucratic apparatus when there is a change in government because the established institutional priorities, culture and membership may have their own way of thinking and doing things. This is one of the reasons that after an election and a change of government there are significant changes to personnel within state bureaucracies and agencies. Additionally, as Andre Magan's study of the history of the Canadian Wheat Board illustrates, the personnel of state agencies can coalesce into a cohort of social actors that have their own ideas about how the organization should operate and its long-term agenda and interests.

Regulation Theory

The latter part of the twentieth century saw the emergence of an approach to the state that was also structural in focus and is referred to as regulation theory. A central assumption of regulation theory, rooted as it is in a broadly Marxian approach or viewpoint, is that the social and economic structures of capitalist society are unstable, prone to crisis and incapable of maintaining themselves in the long term without significant state intervention. Regulation theorists look at both the economic and non-economic processes and structural conditions — modes of regulation — that allow various manifestations of capitalism to exist and function despite inherent contradictions and class conflicts. They further assume that the modes of regulation that characterize a particular society or nation are the outcome of historically specific social, economic and political conditions (Jessop 1990: 309). While both Canada and the United State had what we would call, broadly speaking, Keynesian welfare states during the 1950s, 1960s and into the 1970s, the actual configuration of state services, policies and programs was significantly different, with, for example, Canada having a much more robust public health service regime.

The overall approach that emerges out of the regulationist perspective offers a useful antidote to approaches that exaggerate the separateness of the state from the economic processes;

however, all of the approaches we have been considering share a common weakness: they ignore the important fact that politics and control of the state in most Western societies have been controlled and dominated by men. Like most Western social science, the importance of sex and gender relations tends to be ignored, a fact that, as one would expect, gave rise to a new direction of state theory that sought to develop a feminist theory of the state.

Moving Beyond Class Politics: Feminism and the State

Thus far we have examined major analytical approaches to the study of the state that are quite different. In the case of pluralism, the polity is seen as part of a social decision-making process in which there are no dominant forces, interests or players who consistently get their way, at least in the long run. According to the various Marxist positions, the state in capitalist society is connected to the capitalist class instrumentally, structurally or through mechanisms of power, and as a result the state tends to function in the interests of that class. As a result of its ability to influence the state, the capitalist class is truly a ruling class, having both economic and political power. While these approaches are radically different, they share a common shortcoming — they are all blind to the possibility that sex and gender play an important role in the actions, policies and practices of the polity.

Not surprisingly, the most important and systematic critique of this lacuna has come from the various schools of feminist thought. Feminists have posed new questions concerning the nature and role of the state, especially as it relates to sex and gender relations, and base their arguments on two interrelated aspects. First, convincing arguments and evidence show that the state plays a central role in the subordination of women and the domination of men, also known as patriarchy. The second is the need for a radical rethinking of the existing theoretical frameworks in order to account for the role of the state in maintaining the patriarchal and heterosexual relations that characterize Western society.

> For feminists, the state plays a central role in the subordination of women and the domination of men and in maintaining the patriarchal and heterosexual relations that characterize Western society.

Mary McIntosh (1978) was among those associated with what is called second-wave feminism, and she argues that the state is involved in the oppression of women through its support of the household system, which in capitalist society is intimately linked to the creation of the conditions necessary for the continuing accumulation of wealth and power for the capitalist class. The household is the site of the production and reproduction of the essential commodity in capitalism: labour power. Further, the state plays a central role in the maintenance of the specific household form, the patriarchal family. Thus, in performing one of its main functions of maintaining the conditions necessary for the continuation of capitalism, the state oppresses women through various measures that serve to maintain the patriarchal family. Examples of this oppression are the early legislation in various countries that limited the work of children, the restriction of women's employment in many industries and the creation of female dependency through social support provisions that gave more resources and power to men.

Numerous feminist writers have elaborated on these themes. Michèle Barrett (1980) cautions against explaining the persistence of male dominance and the patriarchal family solely in terms of economic factors; she argues that we need to consider the role of ideology as well. She notes that the economic dependence of many women is accentuated by powerful and systematic patriarchal ideologies that reinforce notions of male dominance and superiority as natural and inevitable. Varda Burstyn (1985) questions the value of a Marxian concept of class for addressing sex and gender oppression. Indeed, she argues that the state has played a central role in both economic-class domination and gender-class domination because men have dominated state structures.

Jane Ursel (1986) develops a somewhat different argument. She advocates the importance of both material production and biological reproduction in determining the shape of human society. Ursel argues that the concept of capitalism, understood in Marxian analysis, is useful for understanding the nature of material production, while the concept of patriarchy is most appropriate for an analysis of reproduction. She notes that the state has played a central role in material production and biological reproduction, which serves the interests of those who benefit from the class-based relations of production in capitalist society and the male-based sexual oppression of patriarchal society.

The relationship between the state and sex and gender relations is complex. Norene Pupo examines the rise and role of what we might term "family-related" legislation in Canada, noting its contradictory nature:

> Through its vast system of laws, regulations, and the institutional structure of the welfare state, the state shapes both personal and social lives. Historically, women have both welcomed and resisted the encroachment of the state in the family home. The state at once is regarded as a source of protection and justice and as the basis of inequality. Such contradictions are inherent in a state under capitalism. (1988: 229)

She further notes that while the actions and policies of the state may appear to be liberating, in the long run they work to reproduce patriarchal relations. An example is the unintended consequences of some forms of state support that are paid to women and reinforce the notion that women are essentially consumers who look after the immediate needs of their families, as is the case when so-called family allowance or child support payments are provided to women.

Jenson and Stroick (1992) provide a similar analysis. Drawing on the experiences of women in France and England, they conclude that it is not possible to make generalized theoretical statements; however, they point out that within the system there is also "space for resistance" (229). The notion that people who are oppressed have opportunities to resist is of central importance. Similarly, Pat and Hugh Armstrong (1990) develop the argument that there are opportunities to use the contradictions in the system in a positive way.

Catharine MacKinnon (1989: 169) focuses on the negative impact that many state actions have for women: "The state ... institutionalizes male power over women through institutionalizing the male point of view in law. Its first state act is to see women from the standpoint of male dominance; its next act is to treat them that way." A theme of much feminist thought is the omnipresence of patriarchal ideologies that simply take for granted male dominance, control, strength and power, along with converse views of women and girls. MacKinnon concludes: "However autonomous of class the liberal state may appear, it is not autonomous of sex. Male power is systemic. Coercive, legitimized and epistemic, it is the regime" (170).

As noted above, since the 1980s many welfare state policies and the infrastructure to support them have been under incessant attack from the neoliberal right. As a result, even the minimal levels of support for vital public services, including health and education, have been steadily eroded. As North America moves more and more to hyper-neoliberalism, the position of women and many others who suffer the most egregious forms of oppression in a class-based patriarchal system deteriorates even further. Others (see Brodie 1996) explore the negative impact of the transformation of the welfare state into a neoliberal, market-oriented state, which has as its main concern global competition and not the welfare or rights of its citizens.

Carole Pateman (1989) provides a key critique of the inherent logic of most political theorizing. Pateman argues that the basic concepts of all Western political discourse and theory are founded on a set of assumptions and arguments that are patriarchal and thus exclusionary for women. The core language, concepts and discourse assume political actors are men. The sexist notion that men are somehow more rational and thus capable of engaging in political debate has deep roots in Western philosophy, but it took on a new form with the relegation of many women to the private sphere of the family and domestic work that characterized the industrial revolution.

While Pateman agrees that much of Western political theory and thinking about the state are predicated on patriarchal thought, Chantal Mouffe (1997) argues that it is an error to assume there is something essentially different about women that provides them with an alternate and presumably more democratic and humane conception of citizenship. Mouffe explains:

> The limitations of the modern conception of citizenship should be remedied, not by making sexual difference politically relevant to its definition, but by constructing a new conception of citizenship where sexual difference would become effectively irrelevant. (82)

Mouffe's comment means that we need to understand women as complex beings with their sex being only one of many possible markers of their various and complex social positions and statuses. Rather than allocating priority to an individual's sex, as is often the case with women, we should be prepared to indicate that an individual is, say, a union president, a teacher, a social worker, a mechanic and so on, and that this individual is from Manitoba and, oh yes, she is a woman. This would be different from the conventional discourse in which we tend to say "a woman president" or "a woman mechanic," for example.

In recent years, feminist theory, like every other stream of social theory, has been criticized for adopting overly simplistic approaches to complex social phenomena. Both postmodernists and third-wave feminists have been critical of feminist theory. In their work, *Third Wave*

Agenda (1997), Leslie Heywood and Jennifer Drake acknowledge that they are building on the foundation of earlier feminisms, but their intellectual and political project has a distinctly different focus. The new agenda demands a recognition and an incorporation of multiple social, economic and political voices of women. Patricia Madoo Lengermann and Jill Niebrugge-Brantley explain:

> Third-wave feminism's focal concern is with differences among women.... Third-wave feminism looks critically at the tendency of work done in the 1960s and 1970s to use a generalized, monolithic concept of "woman" ... and focuses instead on the factual and theoretical implications of differences among women ... [such as] class, race, ethnicity, age, and affectional preference. (1988: 332–33)

Third-wave feminists call for an explicit acknowledgement of women's varied lived experiences. Nelson and Robinson (2002: 96) note that "inclusive feminism" is critical of the apparent search by earlier feminists "for the essential experience of generic 'woman.'" Patricia Elliot and Nancy Mandell (1995: 24) refer to the new approach as "postmodern feminism," emphasizing the need to include the voices and perspectives of "women of color and women from developing countries" as well as "lesbian, disabled and working-class women." Nelson and Robinson (2002: 98) note that postmodern feminists maintain that there is not "a single or even a limited plurality of causes for women's oppression." Indeed Lengermann and Niebrugge-Brantley identify an additional characteristic of third-wave feminism: its tendency to maintain that not all suffering is equal. They quote Lourdes Arguelles's argument that there is a "calculus of pain" that is "determined by the intersection of one's individual life of global location, class, race, ethnicity, age, affectional preference, and other dimensions of stratification" (Lengermann and Niebrugge-Brantley 1998: 334). Put simply, the feminism of the 1960s emerged out of the experiences of mainly white, middle/professional-class women and reflected their critique of patriarchal capitalism and their needs. Various feminists and streams of feminism have since argued that the social analysis needed to be, ironically, more inclusive and diverse so as to be able to address the multiple forms of oppression confronted, for example, daily by working-class women of colour living in substandard housing in an urban ghetto.

Third-wave feminism is only beginning to develop an approach to the study of the polity. Yet, all feminists remind us that political power in patriarchal society will remain contested and complicated by multiple voices; however, like most social institutions, the actions, policies and regulations generated by the state will be tainted by the underlying power dynamics of patriarchy. For the student of social problems, perhaps the important thing is to engage with third-wave feminism's insistence that we pay attention to the nuances and subtleties of the everyday oppression of all women in patriarchy.

What Does the State Actually Do and Why Does It Matter?

In 1978, Göran Therborn published a book with the intriguing title, *What Does the Ruling Class Do When It Rules?* Based on the summaries presented above, it is not yet clear that we can answer this question in a concrete and historical manner. We are faced with a seemingly endless variety of theoretical options or perspectives (there are many more than those discussed above) and must employ what Roy Bhaskar called "judgemental rationality," the act of using both rational judgemental thought and evidence to decided which approach best helps us understand the nature of political power and actual state actions, decisions and policies. Some have argued that the democratic state in capitalist society is the site of competition by more-or-less balanced forces and interests all equally capable of influencing its direction, priorities and policies (pluralism). Others see the state as an institution or site of interaction between self-seeking, utility-maximizing individuals, although actual conception of the state and the nature of power among these thinkers is less than clear (rational choice approach). Marx tended to see the state in capitalist society as a capitalist state, tending to serve the long-term interests of the capitalist class, although he was not clear on the mechanisms by which capitalists actually managed to make the state theirs. Subsequent generations of scholars generally sympathetic to this notion suggested relatively straightforward linkages (instrumentalism), while others looked to the structural dynamics of a capitalist mode of production (structuralism). Scholars working from an approach called institutionalism argue that the state is a complex set of institutions each potentially with its own interests, agendas and priorities and capable of impacting and directing state actions and policies. Poulantzas argues that capitalism, as an economic order, requires a state to ensure the conditions for profit making (regulation school). Finally, there were those who pointed out that this entire debate about the state in capitalist society bears the hallmark of the society within which it occurred — capitalist patriarchy — and thus like most discourse it either ignores issues of sex and gender or applies sexist "logic."

Bob Jessop, over the past three decades or more, has been among the most prolific scholars in terms of studying, theorizing and writing about the state in capitalist society. Two aspects of his work stand out in terms of how we might answer the question posed by Therborn. Jessop's commitment to critical realism, with its focus on the mechanisms that actually cause events to occur, as opposed to merely describing events, is important. The second notable element of Jessop's work relates to his ongoing efforts to seeking clarity in terms of the need for a systematic theory of the state in capitalist society. Jessop employs what he calls a "strategic-relational approach":

> The state is an ensemble of power centres and capacities that offer unequal chances to different forces within and outside the state and that cannot, *qua* institutional ensemble, exercise power. This implies that it is not the state, as such, that exercises power. Instead, its powers (plural) are activated by changing sets of politicians and state officials located in specific parts of the state in specific conjunctures. The exercise of these powers generally takes account of the prevailing and, perhaps, future balance of forces within and beyond a given state. How far and in what ways

state powers (and any associated liabilities or weak points) are actualized depends on the action, reaction, and interaction of specific social forces located within and beyond this complex ensemble. (2010: 45)

More simply put, he is saying that the state is a set of power centres and decision-making capacities that can be engaged or employed by various social forces (classes, groups, organizations, individuals and associations) within and outside the state in order to influence the state's actions, decisions and policies. The precise nature, character and composition of the tactics and strategies that such social forces utilize and engage becomes a matter of investigation, research and analysis. With this Jessop makes it possible to place human decision-making and individuals back in the picture without losing sight of state/social structures, thereby making it possible to examine interests, actions, tactics and outcomes of struggles for power. Having said this, the answer to the questions about just how agents activate or exercise political power is not clear; however, there is a way of addressing this question that will allow us to understand the precise mechanisms that are in play in politics.

Mechanisms of Power: Connecting the Polity

If social analysis is to avoid the simplicity and descriptive tendencies that characterize various kinds of pluralist thought and the simple assumptions that inform some streams of Marxian thought, an approach is needed that provides for the possibility of empirical research into state actions and decisions and explains the events many just describe. It is not enough to merely resort to notions of functional importance, contribution to social stability, the facilitation of capital accumulation, or even perpetuating patriarchy.

It is useful to review what we know about liberal-democratic states. They are highly structured, complex, bureaucratic and formal institutions whose structures and operation are typically formally established and recognized in codified constitutions. The state structures are composed of the government, bureaucracies, agencies, the military and the judiciary. In liberal-democratic systems, the core of the decision-making and policy formation process resides within the government, that is, within the legislative and executive branches. Although there are instances in which state bureaucracies and agencies have altered the intended impact of government policies and actions, the legislature is the ultimate decision-making body. A central question is: How can we come to understand the political practices and processes that are central to the operation of the liberal-democratic state? More specifically: How do individuals, classes and groups in capitalist society influence the processes, operation, decision-making and activities of the liberal-democratic state? In attempting to answer these questions we need an approach that allows us to devote attention to the formal decision-making processes that centre on legislatures; however, since many important decisions that impact society occur outside the formal state apparatus, our approach needs to be broad enough to account for the larger context.

Szymanski suggests examining the linkages between classes, individuals and the state, or what he called the "mechanisms of power." These mechanisms of power are available not only to different classes and fractions of classes, but also to groups, organizations and associations and other social and economic actors. There are a number of distinct yet inter-related mechanisms of power for influencing the state, state decisions and policies.

Direct and Indirect Mechanisms of Power

The electoral process is one obvious direct mechanism of power. It involves a variety of pro-cesses from funding the election costs of a particular candidate and political parties to actually seeking office. These activities are geared to influencing the selection of those individuals involved in actual state decision-making. The precise options open will vary depending on the nature of the system, whether it is parliamentary or republican, and also on the voting procedures, whether they are preferential or "first past the post," and so on.

A second direct mechanism of power is lobbying government and state officials. Lobbying and pressure group tactics of various sorts can be directed at the president, the prime min-ister, the cabinet, the backbenches, agencies and bureaucracies. This sort of activity is often open to empirical investigation, making it possible to determine precisely if, when and how the mechanism is used.

A third direct mechanism of power available is the policy formation process. The develop-ment of public policy and legislation requires extensive information, and as a result, intricate networks of "experts" and think-tanks have emerged to provide information on complex issues. Though not of the calibre or importance of organizations such as the Trilateral Commission, organizations in Canada such as the Fraser Institute and the C.D. Howe Institute are active in advising governments and in publishing papers and reports, all purporting to offer sound ("scientific") advice to governments. The coverage that such reports and events receive in the mass media makes it difficult for governments and state personnel to simply ignore them. In addition, it is important to note that governments often solicit the "scientific" advice of such organizations when planning policy decisions.

In addition to these direct means of influencing state policy, there are more structural or indirect mechanisms related to the larger social and economic environment. One such indirect means is the use of the ideological mechanism of power. The use of ideological power represents an important but often subtle means of influence. This mechanism of power is the capacity to influence the ideology, or belief, and value system of society as a whole, and it can involve the dissemination of dominant ideologies through multiple institutional orders involving the educational order, religious institutions and the various elements of the mass media. This often means, for example, attempting to equate the interests of a particular class or group with the so-called national interest or the general will. When a group, individual or class is able to establish this equation, it becomes more difficult for the state to manoeuvre because certain actions can be perceived as being against the "national interest," "freedom," or the "public good."

Ideological power does not necessarily imply the intentional creation or manipulation of "public opinion," though that, of course, does sometimes occur. Much of what makes up a society's value and ideology system emerges and is articulated in an unintentional, unin-tended and even haphazard manner. Sexism, racism and even classism represent systems of belief that, once they become established as part of the value system of a society, emerge as powerful factors in the determination of state policy and actions. State policy-makers and decision-makers may very well act within the bounds of the accepted "logic" of "how things are." John Thompson (1984), Robert Connell (1983) and Jorge Larrain (1979) discuss these issues, as does Michèle Barrett (1980). Connell and Barrett stand out because they explicitly discuss both classism and the role of familial ideology.

Another indirect, but very important, mechanism of power is the relationship between the economy and the state. A number of writers operating from different perspectives have argued that capitalists and business possess a massive advantage over other classes (Miliband 1973; Lindblom 1977; Block 1977). It is important to understand that economic power is control over allocating resources and constitutes a mechanism of power in its own right.

The operations of the state are fundamentally influenced by activities and conditions within the economy (see, for example, Crouch 1979; Block 1977; Szymanski 1978). According to Crouch, social stability is dependent on a "healthy" economy, that is, on continuing investment, stable and increasing employment and general economic prosperity. The class that determines the pattern of investment and economic development therefore has substantial power to influence the larger environment within which the state operates. Block makes the same point, noting that a critical element in economic activity in capitalist society is "business confidence" and that those classes controlling the society's allocative resources have the capacity to influence the operations of the state through their control of "economic planning." The extent to which a class or group is capable of influencing the larger economic processes in a capitalist society will be a central determinant of its capacity to use this mechanism of power. Given that social stability tends to depend on economic stability, at least in capitalist societies, control over economic resources can thus be translated into political power.

Engaging Mechanisms of Power

The political and heuristic value of this approach to understanding the state can be made more forcefully by looking at some examples of how these various mechanisms of power can be and are actually employed. We will begin with one of the most simple and direct by asking the following question: Who runs the state?

Although it is but one mechanism, it is interesting to look at who controls the important decision-making and policy-setting processes of government. If we look at who runs for political office and who is elected, we see an interesting pattern. Prior to the 2015 election in Canada, Josh Dehaas (2015) undertook an analysis of the occupations of the various candidates by party affiliation. The sector of society from which the largest number of candidates came was the business community, representing 27 percent of all candidates. The second largest category was those already involved in government and politics (21.66 percent), some of whom may be from the business sector as well. This is also the case with the third largest group, lawyers, representing just over 18 percent of all candidates. Candidates from the trades, on the other hand, represented only 0.3 percent, while only 2.08 percent of all candidates were from agriculture. As to who was successful, here is a rough occupations summary of those who now sit in the Canadian House of Commons. Parliamentarians often offer more than one occupational identity, so these approximations are based on the first listed occupation when several occupations are noted. Of the 338 Members of the 42nd Parliament, nearly ninety (26.6 percent) self-identified as businessman or woman, business owner and entrepreneur. This was the largest group. The second largest group was lawyers, just under fifty (14.9 percent), with many noting a business connection. There are over thirty consultants and about the same number of executives, managers and senior administrators. There are also about thirty teachers and educators and over twenty journalists. Less than ten (3 percent) indicated something akin to trades and skilled labour, with about the same number indicating "farmer" as their first affiliation. It is clear who will be making important public policy decision in Canada between 2015 and 2019.

In Canada there are limits on the amount of money that individuals can contribute to candidates and parties; however, such limits do not mean that the political parties are equal in terms of the resources they have to run campaigns and conduct their political operations. A party whose ideologies, platforms, policies and proclivities are in the interests of those in the society with and in control of significant wealth will logically and empirically have more resources. While the individuals in various classes may face similar limits, individuals from some classes find it easier to meet that limit, and the proportion of members of that class making a donation that is subject to a tax benefit will be higher than members of lower classes or marginalized groups. The electoral spending laws and regulations vary from country to country. Canada has relatively strict rules, meaning there are not radical differences in terms of election spending; however, in the United States the stakes are much higher. In a provocatively titled article "How much does it cost to buy the Presidency?" Brian Hughes (2016) estimates that during the 2016 presidential campaign candidates will spend over $5 billion on TV ads alone.

One dimension of the operations and activities of government and the state that typically escapes much public attention are the activities of the various lobbyists. In Canada, lobbyists attempting to influence the federal government must be registered, so we have some data on their activities. According to the Office of the Commissioner of Lobbying, in December 2016 there were 881 consulting lobbyists, 1,664 corporate lobbyists and 2,854 organizational lobbyists, for a total of 5,399 (Office of the Commissioner of Lobbying 2016). The historical record indicates there is much activity going on. *Maclean's* (2012) compiled a list of top ten lobby groups in Canada in 2012.

This does not include the lobbying efforts directed at provincial and municipal governments; however, all this action in Canada pales when compared to the U.S. According to OpenSecrets.org (Center for Responsive Politics n.d.), in 2015 there were over 11,500 lobbyists in Washington, and they spent over $3.2 billion U.S.

The activities of lobbyists do not just involve the gentle art of persuasion, as Jeff Madrick points out. He argues that lobbyists working through and with think-tanks "write research papers and Op-Ed pieces and participate in countless open panel discussions" (2016: 51). Further, Madrick quotes Lee Drutman, who recently published a book on lobbying and lobbyists in the U.S., by explaining that the staff of lobbyists "develop talking points and explanations of why legislation makes sense, write speeches and letters of support of it, seek

Top Ten Canadian Lobby Groups, 2012

Organization or Corporation	Number of Communication Reports and Lobby Attempts, Jan–Sept 2012
Canadian Association of Petroleum Producers	178
Canadian Bankers Association	131
Canadian Cattlemen's Association	113
Mining Association of Canada	105
Canadian Federation of Independent Business	96
Alliance of Manufacturers & Exporters Canada	95
World Society for the Protection of Animals Canada	92
Chicken Farmers of Canada	92
General Motors of Canada Ltd.	92
Canadian National Railway	88

Source: *MacLean's* 2012.

out co-sponsors and supporters both within and outside government, and generally see a bill though from start to finish" (2016: 51).

In anticipation of the Alberta provincial election of 2015, with polls showing increasing support for the New Democratic Party, the *Edmonton Sun* ran a story titled "Corporate business leaders warn of risks to Alberta NDP government" (Lazzarino 2015). Under a picture of five dour faced business leaders, the story reported that these businessmen were concerned that an NDP government would be bad for business, jobs and the world in general, particularly at a time of falling oil prices. The story further noted that the five business leaders had contributed a total of $86,000 to the Progressive Conservative Party in Alberta. After the election, the *Financial Post* ran a headline referring to a remark by the CEO of Enbridge, a large energy company: "Enbridge Inc. CEO on NDP's sweeping Alberta victory: 'I'm really not that concerned'" (Hussain 2015). The not-so-subtle message is he is concerned, just not "that" concerned, while another headline in the same issue read "Alberta's oil patch faces new era of uncertainty after NDP's shock victory" (Cattaneo 2015). Even more dramatic and ominous was a *Financial Post* headline from Bloomberg, "How Alberta's NDP election victory could spark a stock selloff and stall investment in the oil patch," in which Rebecca Penty and colleagues quote an energy fund executive as saying, "It's completely devastating." Meanwhile, an analyst at Dundee Capital Markets said, "Capital is extremely mobile and can easily move out of Alberta at the first sign of uncertainty."

In a liberal-democratic system, all citizens, individuals, associations, groups and parties have the formal legal right to engage the types of mechanisms of power discussed above. All citizens can run for office, support parties financially and otherwise, lobby governments and officials, attempt to influence public opinion, make decisions regarding economic activities and so on. What emerges, however, when we undertake research into the actual capacity and ability of various interests and actors to engage these mechanisms of power are patterns of inequality. One only need ask the somewhat rhetorical question, what does it take to run for office, fund political activities, engage in lobbying, undertake public relations and ideological campaigns, and make important economic decisions? The answer is, of course, access to and control of resources. In a class-based society, those who control the major economic institutions make the major economic decisions. Having said this, it is important to remember that conceptualizing struggles over political power in a liberal-democratic society within the context of the mechanisms of power noted above does leave room for various social and economic interests to attempt to engage those mechanisms of power. This is why, as the title of this chapter indicates, matters of the state *do* matter! In the chapters that follow, you will learn more about the extent to which such access and control is equally or unequally distributed in contemporary Canada.

The Task for Critical Thinking

So much dramatic change has happened in the world of politics and state structures since the collapse of the Soviet Union: the short-lived booms of the 1990s and early twenty-first century, the terror of 9/11 and the wars that followed and the ongoing economic crisis of this decade. Amid these upheavals, some are left wondering if past theories of the state have any relevance in an era of market hegemony, global capitalism, U.S. international domination, a so-called war on terror and virtually countless regional, national and international conflicts. One response to this intense realignment of forces has been the argument that we have entered a new historical epoch or era characterized by fragmentation, instability, indeterminacy, conflicting and alternate definitions of reality and reconsiderations of the very notion of reality (Harvey 1989).

For those who see the current era as marking the transition from what has been called modernity to a fragmented postmodern era, the theories, arguments and narratives set forth above are not just irrelevant — they are also dangerous because they provide a false picture of reality as being subject to systematic and coherent analysis, understanding and, perhaps, improvement. We need not lapse into such political pessimism and paralysis because whether we understand it or not, and whether it is getting more complicated or not, our lives and the society in which we live still have a material and substantial reality that exhibits regularities and patterns of power and resistance. Further, it remains the task of critical thinkers not only to figure out what is happening in that reality but also to reflect on that reality by using a prism informed by a commitment to social justice. Neil Postman describes what happens when we lack an appropriate theoretical framework for understanding our world:

> It may be said here that when people do not have a satisfactory narrative to generate a sense of purpose or continuity, a kind of psychic disorientation takes hold followed by a frantic search for something to believe in or, probably worse, a resigned conclusion that there is nothing to find. The devil-believers reclaim a fragment of the great narrative of Genesis. The alien-believers ask for deliverance from green-grey

creatures whose physics has overcome the speed of light. The deconstructionists keep confusion at bay by writing books in which they tell us that there is nothing to write books about. (1999: 10)

Although there is no doubt that capitalism and the world it creates has been and is changing, the task of the critical thinker remains essentially the same — analyzing and understanding our social, economic and political world. The seemingly chaotic, fragmented and transitory dimensions of our lives today do not in themselves mean that we have passed into a new postmodern era because capitalism has always been dynamic and changing (Harvey 1989: 12). Harvey argues that what has changed is the nature of the social and political regulation of capitalism, not the fundamentals of capitalism (1989: 121–23). Likewise one could argue that, while significant improvements have been made in terms of the rights and the position of women in society, the continued existence of patriarchy remains a problem for those interested in more egalitarian sex and gender relations.

Politics and Power

How, you might ask, does this litany of theories, arguments and ideas prepare us to fully understand the various issues addressed throughout this book? What does any of this have to do with welfare systems, poverty, education, health, the media, crime, sexuality, violence against women and the complexities of racism? Although the various theories of the state and its role differ in many respects, they tend to agree that social issues are political in both the broad and narrow senses of the word. In the broad meaning of political, these issues have to do with power and human relations. In a narrow sense, they are political in that they are issues often debated, discussed and acted upon within political institutions of the state. How you analyze and understand the relationship between the activities of human social agents and the structures and dynamics of the institutions comprising the polity is therefore central to an understanding of these various issues. As you prepare to engage with the various issues taken up in this book, you can begin by asking yourself some fundamental questions about how you understand the workings of power at different levels of individuals, collectivities and major institutions of the state in capitalist society.

Glossary of Key Terms

Feminism: A diverse set of beliefs, political practices, social practices, social movements and sociological theories predicated on a set of underlying assumptions and principles that recognize the historical subordination and oppression of women. Feminists not only are committed to explaining this phenomenon, but also seek alternative non-oppressive modes of social organization.

Fordism: An economic and political system in which the state provides a social safety net and uses its resources to direct investment and economic activity. But business makes most of the economic decisions, especially in key industrial sectors where it is given a free hand to introduce technological change and other labour-saving innovations. Workers, through their unions, get wage increases in line with productivity gains plus inflation.

Instrumentalist Marxism: A neo-Marxist view, this approach places emphasis on personal and personnel connections between representatives of the capitalist class and the state. Instrumentalists maintain that the capitalist class is able to control and direct the activities of the state because the people operating the state either come directly from the capitalist class or share the values, ideologies and objectives of the capitalist class.

Mechanisms of power: An approach to the state stressing that there are a number of different means that can be employed to influence the state in capitalist society. This includes both direct (personnel and personal connections, lobbying and impacting policy formation) and indirect (using economic power, ideological power and political funding) mechanisms of power. All classes and individuals are able to use these mechanisms of power; however, the class and groups with overwhelming economic power are better able to exercise them.

Pluralism: Pluralists recognize that individuals will differ in terms of their income, social status or authority, but liberal-democratic systems prevent these from becoming entrenched social inequalities. Pluralists maintain that democratic electoral systems, an open process of decision-making and group lobbying ensure a democratic decision-making process because all groups and interests in society have a more or less equal opportunity to influence the government through electoral and lobbying activities.

State system/polity: All of the institutions, organizations and agencies connected with the political processes in societies including formally organized political institutions. In Western liberal democracies, the state system or polity includes the formally elected apparatus of government, the appointed officials, the state bureaucracy, the judiciary, police, military, and national and international agencies.

Structuralist Marxism: A version of neo-Marxist theory that sees the state's major role as attempting to prevent inherent conflicts and contradictions, related to fundamental class inequality, from destroying the capitalist system. It is the needs and logic of the system that determine the role and function of the state and not the connections of state personnel to the capitalist class.

Third-wave feminism: Emphasizes the necessity of recognizing the complexities of women's situations and experiences by rejecting any simple notion of women as a homogeneous category or group. Third-wave feminists draw attention to issues of class, race, ethnicity, age, geographic location, national identity and a host of other differences and divisions that combine to oppress women. Thus, there cannot be a singular, totalizing or universal feminist theory.

Questions for Discussion

1. Why might the polity or the state system be considered a "special institution"? What is unique about the decisions made in this institution?

2. What are the core tenets of the pluralist understanding of political power? Do these assumptions stand up to critical scrutiny given the inequality of incomes that typically characterize market society?

3. Is the state another dimension of domination in patriarchal domination? Explain your answer.

4. What are the essential differences between a power resource approach and an approach using the notion of mechanisms of power? Are the two compatible? Explain.

5. Can the state or the polity be understood without first understanding sex/gender power relations?

6. Compare and contrast how two different theories or approaches to understanding the state would explain the decline of the welfare state over the past three decades.

Resources for Activists

Bob Jessop: bobjessop.org/2014/05/08/interview-the-fessud-annual-conference-financialisation-and-the-financial-crisis/

David Held interviewing Noam Chomsky: globalpolicyjournal.com/videos/noam-chomsky-and-david-held

Feminism and State Theory: annualreviews.org/doi/abs/10.1146/annurev.soc.26.1.641?journalCode=soc

Naomi Klein on Neoliberalism: bigthink.com/videos/naomi-klein-on-global-neoliberalism

Pluralist Theory: youtube.com/watch?v=sIzpbffAp6s

References

Amenta, E., and K.M. Ramsey. 2010. "Institutional Theory." In K.T. Leicht and J.C. Jenkins (eds.), *The Handbook of Politics: State and Civil Society in Global Perspective*. New York: Springer.

Armstrong, P., and H. Armstrong. 1990. *Theorizing Women's Work*. Toronto: Garamond Press.

Barrett, M. 1980. *Women's Oppression Today: Problems in Marxist Feminist Analysis*. London: Verso.

Block, F. 1977. "The Ruling Class Does Not Rule." *Socialist Register* May–June.

Brodie, J. (ed.). 1996. *Women and Canadian Public Policy*. Toronto: Harcourt Brace.

Burstyn, V. 1985. "Masculine Domination and the State." In *Women, Class, Family and the State*. Toronto: Garamond.

Cattaneo, C. 2015. "Alberta's oil patch faces new era of uncertainty after NDP's shock victory." *Financial Post*. May 6. <business.financialpost.com/news/energyalbertas-oil-patch-faces-new-era-of-uncertainty-after-ndps-shock-victory?__lsa=c555-6932>.

Center for Responsive Politics (OpenSecrets.org). 2016. "Influence and lobbying: ranked sectors." <opensecrets.org/lobby/top.php?indexType=i>.

____. n.d. "Lobbying Database." <opensecrets.org/lobby/>.

Collins, M 2015. "The Big Bank Bailout." *Forbes* July 14. <forbes.com/sites/mikecollins/2015/07/14/the-big-bank-bailout/#6d5594483723>.

Connell, R.W. 1983. *Which Way Is Up: Essays on Sex, Class and Culture*. Sydney: Allen & Unwin.

Crouch, C. (ed.). 1979. *State and Economy in Contemporary Capitalism*. New York: St. Martin's Press.

Dahl, R. 1967. *Pluralist Democracy in the United States*. Chicago: Rand.

____. 1972. *Democracy in the United States*. Chicago: Rand.

Dehaas, Josh. 2015. "Election analysis: Most common occupations for candidates in each party." CTV News Oct. 9. <ctvnews.ca/politics/election/election-analysis-most-common-occupations-for-candidates-in-each-party-1.2602533>.

Department of Finance, Canada. 2002. "Annual Financial Report, 2000–2001." <fin.gc.ca/afr-rfa/2001/afr01_5-eng.asp>.

____. 2015. "Annual Financial Report of the Government of Canada, Fiscal Year 2014–2015." <fin.gc.ca/afr-rfa/2015/report-rapport-eng.asp>.

Elliot, P., and N. Mandell. 1995. "Feminist Theories." In Nancy Mandell (ed.), *Feminist Issues*. Scarborough, ON: Prentice-Hall.

Hall, P.A., and R. Taylor. 1996. "Political Science and the Three New Institutionalisms." *Political Studies* 44, 5

Harvey, D. 1989. *The Condition of Postmodernity*. Cambridge, MA: Blackwell.

____. 2010. *The Enigma of Capital and the Crisis of Capitalism*. New York: Oxford University Press.

Heywood, L., and J. Drake. 1997. *Third Wave Agenda: Being Feminist, Doing Feminism*. Minneapolis: University of Minnesota Press.

Hughes, B. 2016. "How much does it cost to buy the Presidency." *Huffington Post* Feb. 09. <huffingtonpost.com/brian-hughes/how-much-does-it-cost-to-_3_b_9189292.html>.

Hussain, Yadulla. 2015. "Enbridge Inc CEO on NDP's sweeping Alberta victory: 'I'm really not that concerned.'" *Financial Post* May 6. <business.financialpost.com/news/energy/enbridge-inc-ceo-on-ndps-sweeping-alberta-victory-im-really-not-that-concerned>.

Ishiyama, J.T. 2015. "Neoinstitutionalism." Encyclopedia Britannica. <britannica.com/topic/neoinstitutionalism>.

Jacoby, R. 1971. "Towards a Critique of Automatic Marxism: The Politics of Philosophy from Lukacs to the Frankfurt School." *Telos* 10 (Winter).

Jenson, J., and S.M. Stroick. 1992. "Gender and Reproduction, or Babies and the State." In M. Patricia Connelly and Pat Armstrong (eds.), *Feminism in Action*. Toronto: Canadian Scholars Press.

Jessop, B. 1990. *State Theory: Putting the Capitalist State in its Place*. University Park, PA: Pennsylvania State University Press.

____. 2009. "Redesigning the State, Reorienting State Power, and Rethinking State Theory." In C. Jenkins and K. Leicht (eds.), *Handbook of Politics: State and Society in Global Perspective*. New York: Springer.

Keay, D, 1987. "Interview with Margaret Thatcher." *Woman's Own*. <margaretthatcher.org/document/106689>. Also quoted in E. Knowles (ed.), 2003, *The Oxford Dictionary of Modern Quotations*, New York: Oxford University Press.

Larraín, J. 1979. *The Concept of Ideology*. Athens, GA: University of Georgia Press Lazzarino, D. 2015. "Corporate business leaders warn of risks to Alberta NDP government." *Edmonton Sun* May 1. <edmontonsun.com/2015/05/01/corporate-business-leaders-warn-of-risks-to-alberta-ndp-government>.

Lengermann, P.M. and J. Niebrugge-Brantley. 1988. "Contemporary Feminist Theory." In George Ritzer (ed.), *Sociological Theory*. New York: Alfred A. Knopf.

Lindblom, C.E. 1977. *Politics and Markets*. New York: Basic Books.

MacKinnon, C. 1989. *Toward a Feminist Theory of the State*. Cambridge, MA: Harvard University Press.

Maclean's Magazine. 2012. "The 10 lobby groups with the most contact with federal officials." November 27. <macleans.ca/news/canada/in-the-lobby/>.

Madrick, J. 2016. "How the Lobbyists Marxists Win in Washington." *New York Review of Books* April 7.

Magnan, A. 2016. *When Wheat Was King: The Rise and Fall of the Canada–UK Grain Trade*. Vancouver: UBC Press.

March, J.G., and J.P. Olsen. 1984. "The New Institutionalism: Organizational Factors in Political Life." *American Political Science Review* 78, 3.

____. 1989. *Rediscovering Institutions: The Organizational Basis of Politics*. New York: Free Press.

Marcuse, H. 1961. *Soviet Marxism*. New York: Vintage.

Marx, K. 1972a [1850]. *The Class Struggles in France*. Moscow: International.

____. 1972b [1852]. "The Eighteenth Brumaire of Louis Bonaparte." In Robert Tucker (ed.), *The Marx–Engels Reader*. New York: Norton.

Marx, K., and F. Engels. 1952 [1848]. *Manifesto of the Communist Party*. New York: International.

____. 1970 [1845]. *The German Ideology*. New York: International.

McIntosh, M. 1978. "The State and the Oppression of Women." In Annette Kuhn and Anne Marie Wolpe (eds.), *Feminism and Materialism: Women and Modes of Production*. London: Routledge and Kegan Paul.

Merriam, C.E. 1964. *Political Power*. New York: Free Press.

Miliband, R. 1973. *The State in Capitalist Society*. London: Quartet.

Moe, T.M. 2005. "Power and Political Institutions." *Perspectives on Politics* 3, 2.

Mouffe, C. 1997. *The Return of the Political*. London: Verso.

Nelson, A., and B. Robinson. 2002. *Gender in Canada, 2nd edition*. Toronto: Prentice-Hall.

Office of the Commissioner of Lobbying. n.d. The Registry of Lobbyists. <lobbycanada.gc.ca/eic/site/012.nsf/eng/h_00000.html>.

____. 2016. "Active Lobbyists and Registrations by Type." <lobbycanada.gc.ca/app/secure/ocl/lrs/do/lbsRegs>.

Pateman, C. 1989. *The Disorder of Women*. Stanford, CA: Stanford University Press.

Penty, R., R. Tuttle and E. Lam. 2015. "How Alberta's NDP election victory could spark a stock selloff and stall investment in the oil patch." *Financial Post* May 6. <business.financialpost.com/news/energy/how-albertas-ndp-election-victory-could-spark-a-stock-selloff-and-stall-investment-in-the-oil-patch?lsa=c555-6932>.

Polanyi, K. 1944. *The Great Transformation*. New York: Farrar and Rinehart.

Postman, N. 1999. *Building a Bridge to the 18th Century*. New York: Alfred Knopf.

Poulantzas, N. 1978. *Political Power and Social Classes*. New York: New Left Books.

Pupo, N. 1988. "Preserving Patriarchy: Women, the Family and the State." In Nancy Mandell and Ann Duffy (eds.), *Reconstructing the Canadian Family: Feminist Perspectives*. Toronto: Butterworths.

Skocpol, T. 1980. "Political Responses to the Capitalist Crisis: Neo-Marxist Theories of the State and the New Deal." *Politics and Society* 10, 2.

Smith, M. 2009. *Power and the State*. London: Palgrave Macmillan

Szymanski, A. 1978. *The Capitalist State and the Politics of Class*. Cambridge: Winthrop.

Therborn, G. 1978. *What Does the Ruling Class Do When It Rules?* New York: Schocken Books.

Thompson, J.B. 1984. Studies in the Theory of Ideology. Berkley: University of California Press.

Ursel. J. 1986. "The State and the Maintenance of Patriarchy: A Case Study of Family, Labour and Welfare Legislation in Canada." In J. Dickinson and B. Russell (eds.), Family, Economy and State. Toronto: Garamond Press.

3

Death by Poverty

The Lethal Impacts of Colonialism

Pamela D. Palmater

YOU SHOULD KNOW THIS

- More than 113 First Nations in Canada are without clean drinking water.
- Forty-eight percent of all children in foster care are First Nations.
- Sixty percent of First Nations children live in poverty.
- In the last decade, there has been a 90 percent increase in the rate of imprisonment of Indigenous women in Canada.
- If nothing changes in terms of schooling resources, it will take 28 years to close the education gap between First Nations and Canadians.
- If nothing changes, it will take 63 years to close the income gap between First Nations and Canadians.

Sources: Lorraine 2016; OAG 2004; Wilson and Macdonald 2010; FNCFCSC v. Canada 2016.

The themes that emerged from a review of the circumstances of the deaths and lives of the youth, was not a story of capitulation to death, but rather, a story of stamina, endurance, tolerance, and resiliency stretched beyond human limits until finally, they simply could take no more. (Office of the Chief Coroner for Ontario 2011: 99)[1]

FROM TIME IMMEMORIAL, THE SOVEREIGN INDIGENOUS NATIONS of what is now known as Canada have thrived in their rich, vibrant cultures with their own languages, customs and traditions, and have developed complex governments, laws and political structures. They prospered from their vast territories, careful management of the natural resources and strategic use of inter-tribal trading networks. While disputes did occur, their military strategies and treaty negotiating skills always served them well. Post-contact, these Nations fought to maintain their way of life despite the diseases and poverty that ravished their peoples. With the future of their peoples in the balance, Indigenous Nations in Canada risked all to assert, live and defend their sovereignty and control over their territories. Land was not only central to their identities, but they knew then, as they do now, that it is the gifts from the lands, waters, plants and animals that sustain their nations. The colonization of Indigenous peoples and territories by foreign countries targeted Indigenous lands and trading networks, literally stealing the lifeblood of Indigenous peoples. It should be no surprise, then, that First Nations, in what is now known as Canada, have gone from the richest peoples in the world to the most impoverished, as their lands, resources and ways of being were stolen from them through the violent process of colonization. Today, Canada may be full of political apologies,

> First Nations in what is now known as Canada, have gone from the richest peoples in the world to the most impoverished, as their lands, resources, and ways of being were stolen from them through the violent process of colonization.

but it is not a post-colonial country. In fact, federal, provincial and territorial laws and policies not only put First Nations in their current state of extreme poverty, but also keep them in this state. Federal laws assume jurisdiction over First Nations and every aspect of their lives, yet corresponding policies fail to live up to those constitutional responsibilities. Provincial and territorial laws don't fare much better as they run roughshod over Aboriginal and treaty rights, including Aboriginal title (constitutionally protected rights to their lands) (see, for example, *Haida Nation vs. B.C.* 2004: 513). The resulting dispossession and oppression of Indigenous peoples has left many of those who have survived sick, impoverished and suffering from inter-generational trauma.

While the focus here is on the ongoing colonization and dispossession of Indigenous peoples through government policies and funding mechanisms, it would be incomplete without an acknowledgement of the equally lethal damage done by corporate colonization and dispossession of Indigenous peoples. The violence and lethal nature of colonization hasn't changed much since contact — except for the colonizers themselves. Some argue that we have entered a second phase of colonization, or "re-colonization" of Indigenous peoples, which has the possibility of being just as lethal (Banerjee 1999: 7). Large domestic and multi-national corporations can be as politically powerful as governments, and their false promise of corporate social responsibility has wreaked havoc on Indigenous lands, waters and resources for decades (Frynas 2005: 581, 589–591). It only follows that so many uninformed commentators sought to blame First Nations for their current state of affairs when the previous Conservative government, led by former prime minister Stephen Harper, publically blamed the victims and portrayed them as threats to national security for trying to defend their lands and waters. Most Canadians would like to believe that they can move forward with reconciliation since the atrocities of the past are just that — in the past. Yet they fail to see that the second phase of colonization is equally as lethal — and it is delivered through corporations as well as governments. It is true that all Canadians benefit from the dispossession of Indigenous peoples — but corporations reap the biggest profits. The "new corporate colonialism" (Vidal 2013) — that is, the corporate quest for minerals, trees, oil and gas that amounts to blood money — has its origins in pre-confederation colonization, where large companies worked with colonial governments to help clear the lands for development and settlement (Hall 2010). The result then is the same as now: First Nations die premature deaths from the resulting extreme poverty and by violent extractive activities.

> The corporate quest for minerals, trees, oil and gas amounts to blood money and has its origins in the pre-confederation colonization, where large companies worked with colonial governments to help clear the lands for development and settlement.

Corporate colonization of Indigenous lands and resources, taken together with ongoing government colonization, creates significant barriers for Indigenous peoples and makes efforts at resistance and protection of lands and peoples very difficult. Governments have maintained their vise-like grip on First Nations through literally thousands of laws and regulations, in addition to tightly managed and chronically under-funded government programs. Just consider the plight of Pikangikum First Nation in Ontario. Despite all the natural wealth and beauty that surrounds the community, they have been living under a dark cloud for many years because their children are taking their own lives. This has attracted the attention of the Ontario Chief Coroner, who decided to look into what was happening in the community:

> Pikangikum is an impoverished, isolated First Nations community where basic necessities of life are absent. Running water and indoor plumbing do not exist for most residents. Poverty, crowded substandard housing, gainful employment, food and water security are daily challenges. A lack of an integrated health care system, poor education by provincial standards and a largely absent community infrastructure are uniquely positioned against a backdrop of colonialism, racism, lack of implementation of self-determination and social exclusion. They all contribute to the troubled youth. (2011: 99)

The health care residents do receive is "fragmented, chaotic and uncoordinated" with "clear gaps in service. Pikangikum First Nation's school burnt down in 2007 and hadn't been replaced despite empty promises by Indian and Northern Affairs Canada (INAC) to do so. Only now is a new school under construction — ten years later. The chronic underfunding of Pikangikum students as compared to Canadian students means that the students who are the most disadvantaged and have the greatest needs receive the least assistance. While the education funding gap can range from 20–50 percent, on average, First Nations receive 30 percent less than their provincial counterparts (Porter 2016; Drummond and Rosenbluth 2013). A community of only 2,400 people had 200 child welfare files open and 80 children in care. Due to the lack of housing and the high levels of overcrowding, when children are apprehended from their parents, they are sent to foster homes far away from their First Nation. Should anyone be surprised by the fact that sixteen children between the ages of 10 and 19 took their own lives in Pikangikum between 2006 and 2008 living under these conditions. The suicide crisis did not abate with the submission of the Coroner's report. In 2011 alone, two 16-year-old girls committed suicide within twenty days of one another (Patriquin 2012). The following six weeks saw two men and two women commit suicide. In fact, Pikangikum has the highest suicide rate in the world and has held it for over twenty years. This is what it means to be a First Nation person living under federal jurisdiction in Canada today. Yet few realize the true extent of First Nation poverty, its root causes or why it is getting worse.

The Reality of First Nation Poverty

First Nation poverty is not a new phenomenon, nor is it so hidden as to be unknown to either the public or our policy-makers. Doctors, academics and other experts have tried to bring First Nation poverty and its devastating social effects to the forefront for many years.

In countless reports and studies, the extreme poverty in First Nations has been described by researchers as "pervasive," a "national disgrace," a "national shame," "unacceptable" and an "emergency" situation of "intolerable" conditions (National Council on Welfare 2007; OCI 2000–2010; Eggerton 2007; OAG 2000–2010; RCAP 1996). Political leaders, organizations and commentators have described the extreme poverty in First Nations as a "crisis," an "epidemic" and a matter of "life or death" (Mary Simon, President of Inuit Tapiriit Kanatami and former Ontario Lieutenant Governor James Bartleman quoted in Eggerton 2007: 1). Former Lieutenant Governor James Bartleman calls the situation a "national shame" (Aboriginal Peoples Television Network 2011). Even a former prime minister referred to the underfunding of First Nation education as "immoral discrimination" (Talaga 2011). While historical colonial laws and policies created the dependency relationship, current federal laws and policies maintain the national crisis of poverty in First Nations, which in turn results in the premature deaths of First Nations peoples.[2] Incredibly, politicians have turned a blind eye to the problem while conditions in First Nations have worsened. While Canada has publically denounced the attitudes of superiority upon which assimilatory laws and policies were previously based, the majority of these laws and policies remain unchanged (Harper 2008; Venne 1981; Wilson 1993; Indian Act 1985). How can Canada in one instance defend the assimilatory registration provisions of the Indian Act, while at the same time support self-government? How can Canada promote economic self-sufficiency yet criminalize or otherwise restrict the economic activities of Indigenous peoples? These underlying conflicts in policy objectives act as significant impediments to progress. Policymakers will not be able to move forward in addressing the crisis of poverty in First Nations until these conflicting policy objectives are finally resolved.

The large national and multinational corporations involved in extractive industries like mining, forestry, fracking and oil and gas have added another layer to the ongoing colonization of Indigenous peoples and lands (Alfred 2009: 46). These corporations have been authorized, subsidized and protected by federal and provincial governments to carry out their extractive activities over Indigenous lands. The free, informed and prior consent of Indigenous peoples is rarely obtained, nor is due consideration ever given to the actual costs of extraction such as environmental damage, water contamination, air pollution and the destruction of plant, fish and animal habitat. Governments and industry have worked together to literally blockade Indigenous peoples from accessing their own economies based on their lands, waters, trading routes and resources. Governments have also essentially created legal and economic blockades through laws and policies that have excluded Indigenous peoples, while at the same time creating, maintaining and defending a system of forced dependence on government programs and services (Palmater 2015: 232). In refusing to address chronic underfunding of essential social services like food, water, housing and health, governments have told Indigenous peoples to work with corporations to address their conditions of poverty (Lukas 2015; Penner 2014).

Except there is no relief to be found with corporations as they offer mere beads and trinkets in exchange for the mass exploitation of Indigenous lands. For those corporations that offer anything at all, the most typical form of compensation is a promise for a few jobs or minor business contracts. Often these jobs never appear, and any discussions about Indigenous ownership and control over the impacted lands or resources ends with Indigenous peoples being sent back to government or facing expensive litigation. Environmental racism results in Indigenous peoples bearing the disproportionate burden of environmental destruction left behind by these corporations and makes this crisis of poverty even worse (Jacobs 2010). U.N. rapporteur James Anaya noted the dramatic contradiction of Indigenous poverty in the face of so many corporations making profits from Indigenous lands with government backing:

> One of the most dramatic contradictions indigenous peoples in Canada face is that so many live in abysmal conditions on traditional territories that are full of valuable and plentiful natural resources. These resources are in many cases targeted for extraction and development by non-indigenous interests. While indigenous peoples potentially have much to gain from resource development within their territories, they also face the highest risks to their health, economy, and cultural identity from any associated environmental degradation. Perhaps more importantly, indigenous nations' efforts to protect their long-term interests in lands and resources often fit uneasily into the efforts by private non-indigenous companies, with the backing of the federal and provincial governments, to move forward with natural resource projects. (UNHRC 2014: par 69)

Startling Statistics

According to the 2006 Census, there are 1,172,790 Aboriginal people in Canada.[3] There are approximately 698,025 First Nations individuals, a number which breaks down into 564,870 registered (status) Indians and 133,155 non-registered (non-status) Indians (Statistics Canada 2006).[4] As of 2011, there are 615 First Nations that represent more than 50 Nations (INAC 2015). B.C. has the largest number of First Nations (198) while Ontario has the second highest (126). In the twenty-year period from 1981 to 2001, the gap in educational attainment (completion of high school) between the non-Aboriginal population and the status Indian population increased from twice as high (66 percent versus 30 percent) to three times as high (51 percent versus 15 percent) (Statistics Canada 2004a, 2004b). The gap also widened slightly for university education, which went from five times as high (15 percent versus 3 percent) to a little over five times as high (26 percent versus 5 percent). The employment rates between 1981 and 2001 also showed a widening gap between status Indians and the non-Aboriginal population, which went from 56 percent and 75 percent, respectively, to 58 percent and 80 percent. This means the gap increased from 19 percent to 22 percent over twenty years. In 2000, the median total income of status Indians on and off reserve was reported at $13,932 and $16,949, respectively, compared to $30,023 for the non-Aboriginal population. In 2005, the statistics show there was no substantial change, as the median income for First Nations on reserve was still under $14,000 while for the non-indigenous population it was over $30,000 (Statistics Canada 2011). The situation is worse for status Indian women, whose average total income is $1,700 lower compared with status Indian men and $9,191 lower compared with non-Aboriginal women. A more recent statistical report noted that even when compared to

> When compared to so-called ethnic minorities, the Aboriginal income disparity gap is very large — making Aboriginal people the most disadvantaged group in Canada.

so-called ethnic minorities, the Aboriginal income disparity gap is "very large," making Aboriginal peoples the most disadvantaged group in Canada. Income gaps for Aboriginal people range from 10–20 percent for women and 20–50 percent for men, whereas for ethnic minorities it is 0–10 percent for women and 20–50 percent for men. Even "a little 'Aboriginality' is associated with very poor labour market outcomes" (Statistics Canada 2004a: 17, 18, 19).

First Nation governments also face significant funding inequities on essential social services when compared to funding provided for provincial services:

> The reality behind the myths is that the money provided by the Federal Government to First Nations is insufficient rather than excessive, well-accounted for rather than misused, and almost all goes to pay debts and obligations to First Nations rather than the generous hand-out it is most often portrayed to be. Only $7,200 is spent on each First Nation individual in comparison to $14,900 per non-Aboriginal person who has the added benefit of provincial funding. (AFN n.d.: 3–5)

Less than two-thirds of the INAC budget makes it past Canada's large Indian Affairs bureaucracy down to First Nations (see Barnsley 2002; AFN n.d.). While the objective of federal policy was to use a funding formula that would provide "equity, predictability and flexibility" in the funding of services like First Nation child and family services, just the opposite has occurred (McDonald, Ladd et al. 2000: 10).[5] Even INAC's own internal documents have admitted that "the lack of in-home family support for children at risk and inequitable access to services have been identified ... by INAC, as important contributing factors to the over-representation of Aboriginal children in the Canadian child welfare system" (2004). More recently, the Canadian Human Rights Tribunal found Canada had knowingly discriminated against First Nation children in care by providing less funding to those children because they are First Nations (FNCFCSC v. Canada 2016).

An independent national assessment of First Nation water and sewer systems released in July 2011 was conducted with 571 of 587 First Nations and found that 73 percent of all water systems and 65 percent of all waste water systems in First Nations are characterized as medium to high risk.

> Nationally, based on the 10 year projected populations, the combined water and wastewater servicing needs are estimated to be $4.7 billion plus a projected operating and maintenance budget of $419 million per year. The projected future servicing cost per dwelling unit is estimated to average $29,600 per unit with an annual operating and maintenance cost of $2,700 per unit. (Neegan Burnside Ltd 2011: I, 34)

These statistics must be considered in light of the 2003 report of the Office of the Auditor General of Canada, which found that First Nations were also facing a "critical shortage of housing" and, more specifically, "a shortage of 8,500 houses, which is forecasted to increase by about 2,000 units per year over the next 10 years." The report also revealed "44 percent of the 89,000 existing houses require renovations" (Barrados 2003; OAG 2003: 12).[6] Assembly of First Nations' research shows that the housing need is far more than the 8,500 referred to by the Auditor General and is much closer to 85,000 homes for over 615 First Nations (AFN 2011). Thus, the funding inequities and state of crisis exists in all social program areas, and these poor living conditions have led to predictable health and social outcomes.

Predictable Outcomes

In January 2011, the *American Journal of Public Health* published an article highlighting the number of deaths in the United States attributable to social factors. For example, the authors of the article "demonstrated a link between mortality and social factors such as poverty and low education." They also found that "negative social interactions, including discrimination, have been linked to elevated mortality rates, potentially through adverse effects on mental and physical health as well as decreased access to resources." In 2000, at least of 874,000 deaths in the United States were attributable to social factors like low education and poverty (Galea et al. 2011: e7).[7] Indigenous populations in Canada, Australia and New Zealand all face higher mortality rates, higher rates of chronic and infectious diseases and poorer overall health, leading to decreased life expectancies ranging from eight to twenty years less than non-Indigenous populations (Daniel et al. 2000). Socioeconomic factors are now widely acknowledged to be determinants of both health and life expectancy, and this is especially true for vulnerable groups like Indigenous peoples (Raphael 2016). Canadian studies also show that thousands of preventable deaths occur in Canada every year, and First Nations are over-represented in those numbers.

A study conducted on the prevalence of type 2 diabetes in Aboriginal communities showed that Aboriginal children suffer higher rates of meningitis, otitis media (middle ear infections), respiratory illnesses and iron deficiency anemia. The largest gaps found between Aboriginal and non-Aboriginal children related to the prevalence of type 2 diabetes, which the study considered to be epidemic. The study further noted that diabetes was similar to psychosocial illnesses like suicide, depression and substance abuse. Suicide, depression and substance abuse are also over-represented in young Aboriginal people, have their roots in colonialism and are greatly exacerbated by poverty and social marginalization (Campbell 2002: 1–5). In fact, a 2005 Health Canada report noted that suicide was among the leading cause of death in First Nations peoples aged 10–44 and accounts for over 22 percent of all deaths on Aboriginal youth aged 10–19 (Health Canada 2010). To put this in context, the suicide rate in 2000 for First Nations amounted to 1,079.91 years of lost life (more than three times the national rate), representing more "premature mortality" than for all circulatory diseases and cancers combined. Clearly, Aboriginal status and poverty is linked to the overall poor health and premature deaths of

> In 2005 suicide was among the leading causes of death in First Nations aged 10–44 and accounted for over 22 percent of all deaths in Aboriginal youth aged 10–19.

First Nations in Canada (Lemstra et al. 2009; see also National Collaborating Centre for Aboriginal Health 2009).

The *Canadian Medical Association Journal* noted that "Nunavut has recorded the largest tuberculosis outbreak in the territory's 10-year history" and specifically pointed to social factors like poverty and overcrowded housing as the primary causes (MacDonald et al. 2011). Across the country, over 17 percent of First Nation homes reported overcrowding, and although occupant density has decreased in the non-Aboriginal population, it has actually increased in First Nations (National Aboriginal Health Organization 2006: 3). Water-borne diseases from contaminated drinking water are also widespread on reserve and can cause severe illness and even death (ibid.: 8).[8] Given the extremely high numbers of First Nations who have unsafe drinking water and are under boil water advisories, First Nations have an increased risk of death and disease from contaminated water — but these are all preventable situations (14; Neegan Burnside Ltd. 2011: cf 17). The city of Winnipeg, Manitoba, has some of the best drinking water in the world. Indigenous peoples were literally kicked off their traditional lands so that the city could access the lake to provide clean water to its residents (Puxley 2015). The Indigenous peoples were not just relocated away from the water source, but construction of an aquaduct to facilitate the transfer of water to the city created an island on which Shoal Lake Reserve 40 is now located. Ironically, Shoal Lake First Nation doesn't have clean drinking water and has been under a boil water advisory for over seventeen years. Their long-standing water crisis is a prime example of the social impacts of blatant racism, discrimination and colonialism in Canada (Lorraine 2016).

There can be no greater evidence of ongoing racism and colonialism in Canada than the gross overrepresentation of Indigenous peoples in Canada's jails. In the last decade, under former prime minister Stephen Harper, the number of racialized people in Canadian prisons increased by 75 percent, while the numbers of Caucasians reduced significantly (Brosnahan 2013). The Office of the Correctional Investigator found the path to jail for First Nation people is directly linked to federal policies and the current poverty crisis in First Nations (Mann 2009: 4). The problem of overrepresentation of Aboriginal people in federal jails is actually getting worse as the number of Aboriginal inmates increased in the period from 1998 to 2008 by 19 percent — the increase of Aboriginal women in prisons was an incredible 131 percent (6). However, in the last decade under Harper, the Aboriginal inmate population increased by 50 percent, and the number of Aboriginal women in prisons doubled (Sapers 2015: 2). It is also worthy to note that over 28 percent of federal Aboriginal inmates were raised in the child welfare system, and another 15 percent were raised in residential schools (OCI 2013). While Aboriginal people make up less than 4 percent of the total population, Aboriginal children represent over 40 percent of the 76,000 children and youth in care (Aboriginal Justice Inquiry of Manitoba n.d.: Chapter 14; Blackstock and Trocmé 2004: 2).[9] Sapers also emphasized the fact that the increase in prison populations is not crime driven, but instead due to government policies (see also Brosnahan 2013). The evidence

> Aboriginal people make up less than 4 percent of the total population, yet Aboriginal children represent over 40 percent of the 76,000 children and youth in care.

showing the direct causal link between Canada's history of colonization, its modern day discriminatory policies and poverty in First Nations is overwhelming, yet Canada continues to ignore a growing problem.

Ignoring the Problem

Canada controls the lives of First Nations peoples and provides inequitable funding that results in conditions of extreme poverty, and research has shown that poverty leads to their premature deaths. The ongoing funding inequities for basic social services have resulted in third-world living conditions, poor health, barriers to education and employment, social dysfunction, overrepresentation in jails and children in care, and premature death in First Nations. At this rate, it will take at least twenty-eight years to close the education gap (OAG 2004) and sixty-three years to close the income gap (Wilson and Macdonald 2010: 3). Surely reconciliation cannot mean that Indigenous peoples must wait many more generations before substantive change occurs.

Canada seems to put more energy into protecting its reputation than into fulfilling its mandate to Indigenous peoples. For example, governments frequently skew the public's perception of Indigenous people in the wording used around funds that flow to First Nations. Instead of acknowledging that these funds represent legal obligations through treaties and other agreements, the government often portrays the funds as handouts. Much of Canada's lands and resources are unceded and still legally belong to First Nations, yet most First Nations do not reap the benefits of the trillions of dollars that have been made on their lands. Canadians, governments and large corporations reap the majority of the benefits, leaving Indigenous peoples in poverty. Former Aboriginal affairs minister John Duncan said that poverty is a local issue and not one the government can fix with more government money. He explained that the government purposely keeps the funding low to act as an incentive for Indigenous people to get off welfare (Macleod 2015). These kinds of statements lead the general public to believe that it is their tax money going to First Nations, when in fact Canadians don't pay enough taxes to pay for their own social programs, let alone constitutionally protected First Nation programs. About one-third of Canadian workers don't pay taxes at all (including corporations) (Moretti 2011). In total, Canadians paid about $127 billion dollars in federal, provincial and territorial taxes in 2012 (CBC News 2014a), yet health care alone costs about $141 billion (Palacios, Barua and Ren 2015).

The debate over the nature of the funding aside, most experts agree that the federal government chronically underfunds all First Nation social programs, and if we believe former minister Duncan, it does so purposely. The crisis in poverty continues to get worse without corresponding action to address it. The federal government has been in a holding pattern on this issue, perhaps as a means of trying to determine the true extent of their legal obligations and potential liabilities. Many court cases have not gone in Canada's favour on key issues like Aboriginal and treaty rights, but the recent Canadian Human Rights Tribunal case brought by Cindy Blackstock on behalf of the First Nations Child and Family Caring Society highlights in great detail both the extent of underfunded social programs and the devastating impacts it has on First Nations. Even the United Nations has taken notice of the "abysmal poverty" created and maintained in First Nations by Canada. Former special rapporteur for Indigenous peoples, James Anaya, explained in his report on Canada: "The most jarring manifestation of these human rights problems is the distressing socio-economic conditions of indigenous peoples in a highly developed country" (UNHRC 2014: par 15). He went on to conclude: "One of the most dramatic contradictions indigenous peoples in Canada face is that so many live in abysmal conditions on traditional territories that are full of valuable and plentiful natural resources" (par 69). Perhaps Canada is holding out for a more favourable decision from the Supreme Court of Canada? Whatever the reason, Canada's blatant pattern of ignoring First Nation poverty has made a crisis situation even worse.

Defer, Deflect, Deny

The federal government has taken what appears to be a three-step approach to avoid dealing with what has become one of the most significant policy issues facing Canada today. First, the federal government has become extremely adept at deferring significant and even crisis issues by calling for additional studies or research to examine the problem. Take the crisis in First Nation education, for example. The Assembly of First Nation's (AFN) website contains over thirty major reports addressing issue of the education gap between First Nations and Canadians, and many contain substantial and achievable recommendations. Yet, when the issue gained attention under Harper's term, the Aboriginal Affairs Minister announced that the federal government would spend over $600,000 to create a National Expert Panel on First Nation education to once again study the issue. It is as if the minister had forgotten that in 2002 the federal government created a National Working Group on Education, which provided recommendations regarding "strategies and measures required to foster excellence in First Nation elementary and secondary education" and to "reduce the gap in academic results between First Nations and other Canadians." Referring to a "multitude of reports and studies" that have been consistent in their recommendations, the group concluded that "First Nations must have the resources and the means to design, develop and deliver life-long education, on- and off-reserve" (Minister's National Working Group on Education 2002: t51, 2). Some thought that a change in government from Conservative to Liberal would be the answer to the First Nation education underfunding issue — yet many forget that it was the Liberals who originally imposed the 2 percent funding cap. That being said, Justin Trudeau had campaigned in First Nations on a platform that included a promise to add an extra $2.6 billion to First Nation education as well as to lift the 2 percent funding cap. Since being elected, Trudeau has broken both promises (Parkin 2016; Smith 2016). The first federal budget only offered a little over $1 billion during his actual four-year mandate, and the recent release of government documents prove that Trudeau did not lift the 2 percent funding cap (Smith 2016). The recommendations to increase First Nation control over their lives and to provide them with equitable funding are consistent throughout other reports across every sector, yet INAC continues to defer the problem through new studies, perhaps in hopes of different results (Palmater 2015: 175).

    There are times when deferring a crisis issue does not satisfy the media, and INAC is forced to publically address the issue. When this happens, deflection seems to be Canada's back-up plan to detract attention from responsibility. INAC appears to strategically use the media by making announcements about unrelated projects it recently or previously funded, or by offering commentary that indirectly blames or vilifies First Nations in another part of the country about completely unrelated matters. For example, the Auditor General's report for spring 2011 contained damning findings in relation to INAC and its failure to address issues like the gap in education, over-crowded housing and unsafe drinking water in First Nations (OAG 2011). Within minutes, INAC made an announcement about the Joint Action Plan with the AFN that would deal with issues like education and economic development and spoke of the "long-term prosperity of First Nation people" (INAC 2011b). Upon a closer reading, it was obvious that nothing new was contained in the announcement, as it simply highlighted initiatives that were already ongoing. A promise to set up a joint engagement process on an education framework (legislation) was old news as were the promises to remove the residential school provisions from the *Indian Act* and to increase government transparency of First Nations. The Joint Action Plan was successful, however, in deflecting attention away from the Auditor General's scathing report and INAC's continued failure to address its legislative responsibilities with regards to First Nations.[10]

Canada also denies the problem of First Nation poverty directly via its litigation and political positions and indirectly by simply failing to act and/or consistently ignoring alarms raised by its own federal officials. For example, Canada's litigation position in many court cases deny any responsibility for a wide variety of problems it has created, like gender discrimination in the *Indian Act*, despite Parliamentary reports which clearly confirm otherwise (Palmater 2011). The Office of the Correctional Investigator for Canada (OCI) and the Office of the Auditor General (OAG) have consistently tried to raise the alarm about First Nation poverty and discrimination and demand that Canada take action, all to no avail. In 2002, the OCI was alarmed that the over-incarceration situation was worsening for Aboriginal people (OCI 2002: 9); in 2006, OCI explained that Canada's lack of an action plan meant that the situation was as bad as it was twenty years ago (OCI 2006: 11–12); and in 2010, OCI found that "inequitable and differential outcomes for Aboriginal offenders" are the direct result of "federal correctional policies and practices" (OCI 2010: 43; see also Sapers 2009).[11] The OCI recently confirmed that increasing prison rates is due to federal policy and not to increasing crime rates (Sapers 2105; Brosnahan 2013). Incredibly, the OAG reports document Canada's similar track record for ignoring the crisis of poverty that is created and maintained largely by Canada's discriminatory laws and policies. According to the OAG, continued denial of the problem (and failure to act) will have disastrous results:

> The Office of the Correctional Investigator for Canada found that in 2010, inequitable and differential outcomes for Aboriginal offenders are the direct result of federal correctional policies and practices.

> The education gap between First Nations living on reserves and the general Canadian population has widened, the shortage of adequate housing on reserves has increased, comparability of child and family services is not ensured, and the

reporting requirements on First Nations remain burdensome. … There is a risk that living conditions on many First Nations reserves will remain significantly below national averages, with little prospect of a brighter future, until these concerns are addressed. (OCI 2010: 8)

In 2008, the Auditor General concluded that "current funding practices do not lead to equitable funding among Aboriginal and First Nation communities," which results in an inability for First Nations to provide adequate service to their communities. In fact, the inequities are such that when INAC adjusts the funding formula in Alberta, they will have increased the funding by 74 percent just to keep up with the province (OAG 2008: 1, 2). While INAC has acted on a few of the OAG's recommendations over the years, the OAG found that overall INAC has consistently failed to implement those recommendations that "are most important to the lives and well-being of First Nations people" (1). These are clear policy choices being made by Canada with the full knowledge of the devastating impacts these choices will have on the lives of First Nations. The Canadian Human Rights Tribunal's (CHRT) decision related to the discriminatory under-funding of First Nations child and family services referred to the federal government's own internal documents that showed the government knew that chronic under-funding led to an increase in child apprehensions but did it anyway (*First Nations Child and Family Caring Society of Canada et al. v. Canada* 2016).

Canada has shown a tendency to avoid addressing crises by engaging in endless studies on the subject, but avoids the collection of critical data that would support different policy choices. An example of this is the replacement of the mandatory long-form census with a voluntary one, which resulted in the Chief Statistician Munir Sheikh resigning his post (*Globe and Mail* 2010a, 2010b).[12] Even the provinces publically denounced the move, explaining that it "will undermine the accuracy of budget decisions and erode the ability to direct social programs to the most vulnerable" (*Globe and Mail* 2010c). Aboriginal groups also took issue with the move, and an internal memo at Statistics Canada came to a similar conclusion:

> Indian and Northern Affairs Canada's objectives are to improve the social and economic outcomes and well-being of Aboriginal peoples. Absence of reliable long-form data will not allow them to effectively manage, evaluate and measure performance of their programs in areas of Aboriginal health, housing, education and economic development. (Kumagai 2011)

In 2008, the OCI concluded that there was no evidence of improved data collection or analysis and "therefore, parliamentarians and Canadians have no way of evaluating the Correctional Service's progress, or lack thereof, in this priority area of concern. The lack of openness and the refusal to engage in full reporting on this critical file remain a serious concern to this office" (34–35). In 2003, the OAG found that INAC "did not have a plan in place to ensure the fulfillment of their obligations under the agreements, and it had not monitored whether the departments had fulfilled their obligations" (30). As the OAG put it:

We found that INAC has little information on the outcomes of its funding on the safety, protection, or well-being of children living on reserves. As a result, it is unaware of whether or to what extent its program makes a positive difference in the lives of the children it funds. In our view, the information INAC collects falls far short of the child welfare program and policy requirements. (2008: 28)

By not sharing the data collected, it was impossible to monitor or analyze compliance. The OAG also found that INAC lacked data related to actual education costs, cost comparisons for different delivery methods or appropriate performance and results indicators (OAG 2002: 14–15). This refusal to collect or share relevant data presents one of the most significant challenges for policy-makers in moving forward to address First Nation poverty. In 2014, the OAG could only assess the food subsidy program for northern Indigenous communities based on comparable data from 2009. Canada had failed to conduct annual reviews or to verify that subsidies even reach these Indigenous populations. Even on that limited data, the Auditor General found that INAC did not identify communities based on need or established criteria for food subsidies that are "fair or accessible" (OAG 2014: ch 6). The problem of data collection seems to be across all sectors — even police forces — making the accurate and timely tracking and identification of other crisis issues like murdered and missing Indigenous women and girls and those who committed these offences difficult (Palmater 2015: 149).

Blaming the Victim

The public at large is relatively uneducated about First Nation poverty and its historical roots. As a result, they can be easily swayed by the media and other commentators who blame First Nations for the current situation. Explanations for poverty in society are often divided into two main categories: blaming the victims as the author of their own circumstances, or looking to societal factors that create, contribute to or exaggerate the disadvantages faced by the impoverished (Varcoe n.d.: 3; Centre for Research on Inner City Health 200; Steckley and Cummins 2008: 185–186). According to the Institute of Medicine, standardized data collection is critical to understanding and eliminating racial and ethnic disparities in health care. A critical barrier to eliminating disparities and improving the quality of patient care is the frequent lack of even the most basic data on race, ethnicity and primary language of patients within health care organizations (Hasnain-Wynia, Pierce and Pittman 2004: v; see also Percival 2011). While the focus here is on societal factors that have created the situation, one cannot ignore the real role that blaming the victim has on society's reactions to people living in poverty, their lack of empathy and their failure to demand that their governments address the situation. Some have argued that poor people are "genetically inferior," resulting in a lesser IQ, for example (Varcoe n.d: 5). These types of arguments were once very common among those who looked to race to explain poverty. Other explanations are that certain groups of people have a "culture of poverty," so their specific attitudes or cultural values keep them in poverty (Varcoe n.d.). While these explanations do not hold up against close and informed scrutiny, they have allowed Canada's relatively privileged society to justify their ongoing advantage:

Blaming the poor for their poverty remains a popular way of understanding poverty in part because this provides explanations which do not threaten those with privilege.… The most painless way to do this is to believe, if only vaguely, that the poor are somehow unworthy. While this is never fully convincing, especially because of the problem of children who cannot be seen as deserving to be poor, nevertheless it reduces the moral pressure on the middle class and the wealthy to take seriously the problem of changing institutions to eliminate poverty. (Varcoe 2009: 6)

This makes it far easier to blame First Nations' cultures, attitudes, values or perceived race for the crisis of poverty in which they currently live than it is to acknowledge the hard truth. While current generations did not personally steal the land or create the discriminatory laws and barriers, they do benefit from the cheap "rent" and social programs funded in part from the resources and wealth from Indigenous lands. One need only refer back to the Winnipeg water issue as an example. Settlers not only benefit from historical Indigenous dispossession, but also have a role in perpetuating the crisis of poverty by not demanding change.

> Settlers not only benefit from historical Indigenous dispossession, but have a modern-day role in perpetuating the crisis of poverty by not demanding change.

While the prevalent attitude of blaming the victim can be explained, in part, by governments' negative public statements about First Nations, one cannot overlook the epic failures of federal, provincial and territorial governments in educating Canadians and their own bureaucrats about the real histories, laws and rights of Indigenous peoples and Canada's role in creating the current crisis situation. "Canadians remain remarkably insulated from the misery of the world.… We know that we are privileged.… Yet there remains within Canada an almost unspeakable reality, which, like a cancer, slowly sickens the body politic. This is the reality of life for Aboriginal peoples … who live in Third World conditions" (Warry 2008: 13). While the media cannot shoulder all the blame for the current public attitude towards First Nations, the significant role that the media plays in helping to foster a societal attitude of blaming the victim simply can't be ignored:

> The mainstream media play a pre-eminent role in shaping the view Canadians and the world have of the history and contemporary circumstances of First Nations people.… The violence of Oka, the blocked logging roads of British Columbia, casinos and cigarettes in Ontario and Quebec, skid row everywhere, and substance abuse are the topics profiled and the images fed to a mainstream public which, with no knowledge of history or contemporary community life, responds with a mixture of pity, distaste, and a way of thinking that lays blame on the victims rather than the perpetrators. (Benyon 1994)

By way of example, in 2005, cbc News reported on the evacuation of Kashechewan due to contaminated drinking water, yet followed it up with a story about alleged corruption in Natuashish (Warry 2007: 69–70).[13] Even if the leaders in Natuashish in Newfoundland had been corrupt (and the resulting INAC report said they were not), what would that have to do with the members of Kashechewan in northern Ontario? These are two different First Nations from two different provinces. "In short, such editorial decisions blame the victim and create the impression that Aboriginal peoples are responsible for their ill health, rather than decades of government inaction and centuries of colonialism. Is it a surprise then, that many Canadians blame Aboriginal people for their problems?" (ibid.). The ways in which society seeks to blame First Nations for their impoverished situation does not reflect historical or present reality but acts as a justification for their failure to act.

Perhaps the most significant factor in the blame the victim attitude is one which governments have refused to confront head on: blatant, overt racism. Just as there is no excuse on the part of governments for failing to address racism against Indigenous peoples in Canada, there is no excuse on the part of settlers for failing to push their governments to address racism or for taking individual steps to end racism in their own settler communities. The Truth and Reconciliation Commission Report, which released details about the atrocities committed in residential schools and their long-lasting intergenerational impacts, made the point that everyone is responsible to make change and lists recommendations involving more than just governmental changes (TRC 2015a). While it is true that not all Canadians know all the legal, political and historical complexities around the crisis, the public cannot say they are not aware of the problem. There have been many commissions, inquiries and investigations into racism in Canada's justice system, all of which were not only made public, but also turned into books, movies and widely covered in the media — let alone university and college courses that cover racism and the justice system (Palmater 2016). The Royal Commission on Donald Marshall's wrongful prosecution, the Ipperwash Inquiry on the police shooting of unarmed land defender Dudley George, the Manitoba Aboriginal Justice Inquiry and many others have all pointed to overt and systemic racism in policing and the justice system (Palmater 2016). Racism is not just offensive; racism is literally killing Indigenous peoples (Palmater 2015: 55, 59]. This crisis of poverty is a matter of life and death.

A Matter of Life and Death

INAC's Community Well-Being Index (CWB) shows that there remains a significant gap between First Nations and Canadians, and there has been little to no improvement since the turn of the century. INAC found that over one-third of all First Nations and Inuit communities showed a marked decline in CWB scores between 2001 and 2006 (INAC 2010: 11, 24). By way of comparison, the United Nations also has data related to well-being known as the Human Development Index (HDI), where Canada in 2010 ranked as the fourth best country in the world (Make Poverty History 2010). However, if the data is adjusted to consider only the conditions on First Nations and Inuit communities, then Canada would rank seventy-eigth, below countries like Cuba and Paraguay (Borrows 2003: 1). According to former national chief of the AFN Shawn Atleo, this has created a "life or death" struggle that requires a critical mass of public support to turn the tide (Aboriginal Peoples Television Network 2011). There is no doubt that society at large plays a role in putting pressure on governments; however, the need to end the current poverty crisis in First Nations is not a matter of good will or charity by the public. As Nelson Mandela put it, "Overcoming poverty is not a task of charity, it is an act of justice. Like Slavery and Apartheid, poverty is not natural. It is man-made and it can be overcome and eradicated by the actions of human beings. Sometimes it falls on a generation to be great" (Make Poverty History, n.d.). U.N. rapporteur James Anaya urged Canada to take action:

> Indigenous peoples' concerns merit higher priority at all levels and within all branches of government, and across all departments. Concerted measures, based on mutual understanding and real partnership with aboriginal peoples, through their own representative institutions, are vital to establishing long-term solutions. (UNHRC 2014: 2)

The barrier for developing just policy is contained in the fundamental settler/federal government's conflicting policy objectives: the assimilation (and elimination) of First Nations versus the re-building (and returning the lands and resources) of First Nations.

Resolving the Policy Conflict

Indian policy in Canada changed quickly from one based on nation-to-nation treaty making and recognition of Indigenous sovereignty (Moss Gardner-O'Toole 1991) to one of domination and aggressive assimilation (Long et al. 1982: 190; CBC News 2008; see also RCAP 1996). For the most part, Indigenous peoples have had very little input, if any, into the policy-making process and even less input on the laws that pertain to them (Gibbons 1984; Long et al. 1982). The policies and laws created to deal with Indians and the reserve lands to which they were relocated were based on several problematic assumptions about Indigenous peoples that have led to ineffective and even harmful results. The first assumption was that Indigenous peoples were inferior to Europeans, and the second was that Indigenous peoples were slowly dying off. When diseases, like smallpox, starvation and scalping bounties did not kill Indigenous peoples fast enough, the former deputy superintendent of Indian Affairs, Duncan Campbell Scott, led an aggressive policy of assimilation. His characterization of the *Indian Act* said it all: "I want to get rid of the Indian problem.... *Our objective is to continue until there is not a single Indian in Canada* that has not been absorbed into the body politic and there is no Indian question, and no Indian Department, that is the whole object of this Bill" (emphasis added; cited in RCAP (vol. 1) 1996: 183). Getting rid of Indians has been the cornerstone of Canada's Indian policy ever since. Despite apologies to the contrary, various provisions in the *Indian Act*, originally intended to speed up assimilation, are still in effect and, in fact, are vigorously defended by Canada.

For Canada, it was thought that thinning the

> Former deputy superintendent of Indian Affairs Duncan Campbell Scott's characterization of the Indian Act: Our objective is to continue until there is not a single Indian in Canada that has not been absorbed into the body politic and there is no Indian question, and no Indian Department, that is the whole object of this Bill.

blood lines of Indians with inter-marriage amongst whites could help speed up assimilation and thus the land acquisition process. This was to be accomplished in two ways: "bleed off" Indian women and their children from their communities and "transfuse" the communities with the incorporation of non-Indian women and their children (Palmater 2011). Statistics show that this amounted to an almost complete blood transfusion as 16,800 Indian women lost their Indian status and 16,000 non-Indian women gained their status (Harper 2008; see also Access to Information and Privacy Request to Indian and Northern Affairs Canada dated April 1, 2011). In addition to excluding Indian women and children from membership in their communities, these assimilatory laws also impacted the ability of men to provide for their families as engaging in colonial occupations required a significant sacrifice: to give up one's Indian identity (RCAP 1996; Palmater 2011; Venne 1981). If an Indigenous man wanted to get a university degree or become a doctor or lawyer, he was required to give up his status as an Indian, which meant that his Indian wife and children were automatically disenfranchised as well. The loss of one's status as an Indian meant that they were no longer entitled to live in their community, have a voice in the affairs of their Nation or access rights under the various treaties signed with the Crown. Treaty rights, which often protected the traditional means of providing for the community and Nation, like the right to hunt, fish and gather, or the right to trade, would also be inaccessible to anyone who received an education.

Over the years, there has been some movement by the federal government to amend political positions, but the core objectives of Indian policy are firmly rooted in modern legislation. "Because of the intensity of genocidal policies that Indigenous people have faced and continue to face, a common error on the part of anti-racist and post-colonial theorists is to assume that genocide is virtually complete, that Indigenous peoples, however unfortunately, have been 'consigned to the dustbin of history' (Spivak 1994) and no longer need to be taken into account" (Lawrence and Dua 2005: 123).

Although assimilation as a formal policy objective became less palatable politically, it nevertheless resurfaced in 1969 when former prime minister Pierre Trudeau and former minister of Indian Affairs Jean Chretien presented the White Paper on Indian Policy that advocated the abolishment of all special recognition for Indians, the abolishment of INAC and the abolishment of the *Indian Act*, as well as the transfer of reserve lands to individual Indians (Indian Affairs and Northern Development 1969). The reaction to this policy by First Nation leaders was so swift and so fierce that the plan was eventually abandoned, but the goal of the White Paper was not. Tom Flanagan, an outspoken academic against First Nations rights, explains the overall policy objective: "Call it assimilation, call it integration, call it adaptation, call it whatever you want: it has to happen" (Flanagan 2000: 196; see also Flanagan et al. 2010; Cairns 1999; Widdowson and Howard 2008; Helin 2008; Gibson 2009). Flanagan agrees with this long-held view and suggests that the solution to finally rid Canada of the burden of First Nations and their impoverished communities is for them to be assimilated into the general population. He views this process as being "historically inevitable" and largely complete and says it will remain as the basis of Canadian society (Cairns and Flanagan 2001: 51). The government trend now is to promote individual initiatives that look beneficial on the surface but will result in the eventual assimilation of First Nations.

For example, getting rid of the *Indian Act* and giving Indians individual interests in reserve lands are ideas currently being sold as positive solutions to address the situation of poverty, but they are also the original keys to Canada's assimilation policy (Flanagan 2000; Flanagan, Alcantra and Le Dressey 2010; see also Palmater 2010). Getting rid of the *Indian Act* might clear the path for more formal recognition of First Nation jurisdiction or it could be used to do away with all special recognition and federal responsibility, as were the proposals in the White Paper. The government's view of treaties was that they contained "limited and minimal promises," and their significance "will continue to decline" until they are finally "ended" (Canada 1969: section 5). Despite the subsequent constitutional protection afforded treaties in section 35 of the constitution, Canadian governments still minimize their relevance.

In essence this "policy" blames the victim, but in a larger, nation-based, not individual, sense. It is the racist idea that First Nations sovereignty and independence is somehow "backwards" or "primitive" and that is the cause of their poverty and troubles, not colonialism. Critics like Flanagan suggest that if First Nations would just become like settler capitalist societies they would be just fine. The urge to assimilate Indigenous peoples has not lessened over time and remains a powerful force against which Indigenous peoples strenuously resist (Alfred 2005; Alfred and Corntassel 2005). In order to move forward, Canada will have to decide what the underlying policy objective is with regards to Indigenous peoples. Will reconciliation be centred on assimilation and integration or self-determination and reparation? This policy decision will determine whether future initiatives will rid Canada of the problem of poverty in First Nations, or rid Canada of the "problem" of First Nations.

The proposed solutions that fall into the other category of rebuilding and supporting First Nations tend to be more comprehensive in nature. This is why the Royal Commission on Aboriginal Peoples (RCAP) was such an important report. The commissioners not only envisioned healthy, prosperous, self-governing First Nations that would take them from poverty to prosperity, but actually had a detailed plan and budget on how to get there. The report called for "sweeping changes" to the current relationship with the federal government that would be founded on the recognition of Aboriginal peoples as self-governing nations.

Recommendations made in RCAP related to the recognition of First Nation jurisdiction, equitable funding for core programs like education, child welfare and housing, and the resolution of long-outstanding land claims and treaties. The Commission's implementation strategy proposed that governments increase spending to reach $1.5 billion by year five of the strategy and $2 billion in the subsequent fifteen years. This would include new legislation that would clearly outline treaty recognition and processes as well as specifically recognize Aboriginal Nations as a third order of government. Aboriginal lands and resources would be expanded to support their governments and a new Aboriginal parliament would be created. The central theme was First Nation jurisdiction over every aspect of their lives from education to health to governance.

The more recent Truth and Reconciliation Commission Report echoed many of the same sentiments and issued calls to action that focused on addressing the crisis in First Nations with proper funding, legal recognition of rights and Indigenous-led solutions (TRC 2105b). For example, the first call to action calls on governments to ensure proper funding so that

Indigenous governments can run child and family services. Calls to Action seven through ten call on governments to work with Indigenous peoples to address education and employment, which includes proper funding of First Nation education and First Nation consent to any legislation developed as a part of that strategy. Other recommendations include providing adequate funding for health,

> The Truth and Reconciliation Commission Report issued calls to action that focused on addressing the crisis in First Nations with proper funding, legal recognition of rights and Indigenous-led solutions.

the preservation of Indigenous languages, the elimination of the overrepresentation of Indigenous peoples in jail and taking action on murdered and missing Indigenous women and girls (TRC 2105b).

Part of the problem policy-makers have and will continue to face is that they require clear, consistent direction from politicians on how to move forward on First Nation issues., That is, what is required is a policy objective that transcends the inevitable changes in government every four years, changes in political parties and the ever-changing ideological slants of academics, the media and the public. If Canada cannot decide whether it wants to eliminate First Nations or empower them, then we will continue to see social programs and policies that do more harm than good. Although the law has advanced Aboriginal and treaty rights somewhat, it should not be seen as a replacement for sound policy-making. As James Anaya noted, all the legal protections in Canada have not abated the human rights violations and extreme poverty in First Nations: "It is difficult to reconcile Canada's well-developed legal framework and general prosperity with the human rights problems faced by indigenous peoples in Canada that have reached crisis proportions in many respects" (UNHRC 2014: par 14). While jurisprudence may help guide policy-makers on the higher-level core matters, it is simply not feasible to address issues of poverty in the courts on a case-by-case basis. Incremental legislative or policy changes are not enough to combat the crisis of poverty in First Nations. Canada must finally reconcile itself to the fact that Indigenous peoples in Canada are here to stay and act on that constitutional and political reality.

Signs of Hope

However, despite the very slow progress to date and the lack of attention that the crisis of First Nation poverty has been given, there are signs of hope that come from the most unexpected places. Take for example, the situation at Attawapiskat First Nation in Ontario. This Cree community has been fighting for a new elementary school for decades (Wawatay News online 2008). So, their youngest members travelled all the way to Ottawa to bring the issue to the attention of the minister, who, sitting in his lush office, told 13-year-old Shannen Koostachin, that he did not have the funds to build them a new school. INAC had promised them a new school four times previously because their current school was full of mould, mice, cracked walls and reeked of diesel fuel (Goyette 2010). After Shannen passed away unexpectedly, those she inspired created the Shannen's Dream campaign to end the discrimination in funding for First Nation education across the country. All of the subsequent pressure and publicity seemed to work in Attawapiskat's favour (NDP 2011). The United Nations Committee on the Rights of the Child decided to investigate Canada's failure to protect the rights of First Nations children (Provincial Advocate for Children and Youth 2011). The public pressure and international spotlight on Canada essentially shamed INAC into announcing funding for a new school to be built in 2013 (INAC 2011b). It was finally built and opened in late 2014 (CBC News 2014b). None of this would even have been possible but for the courage of Cree youth to exercise their voices and stand up for their community (Provincial Advocate for Children and Youth 2011: 8).

There are also signs of hope that come from the very act of nation-building and cultural revitalization in First Nation communities. Take for example the changes to educational programming in Nunavut noted by the Standing Committee on Aboriginal Affairs and Northern Development in 2007 (Canadian Council on Learning 2007: 9). Since 1985, the Nunavut Sivuniksavut Program has offered Nunavut high school graduates culturally appropriate transitional programming. This program not only had an 80 percent completion rate but also resulted in a very high employment record for its students. Similarly, cultural revitalization goes hand in hand with traditional governance practices and the assertion of jurisdiction over their own affairs. In fact, research has shown that acts of self-determination and cultural revitalization can even reduce the number of suicides in communities (Chandler and Lalonde 2008, 1998).[14] This is due to the presence of "cultural continuity factors," which include the achievement of at least some measure of self-government and control over key services like health, education and policing and community facilities to preserve culture (ibid: 6). There is still a long way to go before all First Nations enjoy this kind of success in all aspects of their lives, but the formula for success is backed up by research. Policy-makers need to focus on (1) the redistribution (return) of Indigenous lands and resources; (2) the recognition of First Nation jurisdictions, laws and governance systems; (3) the provision of needs-based funding to critical First Nation social programs to address long-standing inequities created by discriminatory laws and policies; and (4) the implementation of fully supported cultural revitalization policies to achieve healthy, sustainable and self-determining Indigenous Nations.

> Acts of self-determination and cultural revitalization can reduce the number of suicides due to the presence of "cultural continuity factors" — the achievement of at least some measure of self-government and control over key services like health, education and policing and community facilities to preserve culture.

Conversely, it is clear without doubt that the long-term costs of doing nothing far outweigh the immediate investment required to eliminate the gaps in health, education and income between First Nations and Canadians (Coffey 1997). For example, the cost of incarcerating one Aboriginal person for one year is $100,000, which far outweighs the $13,200 it costs to send one Aboriginal person to university for one year (AFN 2010). Yet, First Nation post-secondary education funds have been capped since 1996. If these funds were raised to the more equitable level of $20,000 per person per year, even a four-year degree would still be cheaper than one year of prison. Educating First Nations "would add $179 billion to Canada's GDP by 2026 through employment and by reducing government expenditures on income support, social services, health care, and security" (AFN 2011: 4). Even the initial costs of resolving treaties and land claims are far outweighed by the long-term financial and other benefits. One study found that the benefits of settling treaties earlier resulted in greater benefits being delivered sooner (Price Waterhouse Coopers 2009). Conversely, the longer it takes to settle treaties, the overall net benefit to Canadians and First Nations is reduced. Thus, the quicker we address poverty in First Nations, the more we will all benefit (9–10).

Sovereignty and Living a Good Life

The colonization and aggressive assimilation policies of the past have turned thriving Indigenous Nations into small communities of people who are barely surviving. Understanding the historical context and root causes of the current crisis of poverty in First Nations is absolutely essential to developing policy solutions that can turn this trend around. Past laws and policies were explicitly designed to impoverish First Nations — current laws and policies maintain their impoverishment today. Canada controls the lives of First Nations and provides them with inequitable funding that results in conditions of extreme poverty, leading them to their premature deaths. The startling statistics illustrate the true extent of the chronic underfunding of essential social services, the cap on education funding, the lack of basic infrastructure and maintenance support and the discrimination experienced in health and justice services. This has led to predictable results, namely, lower educational achievement rates, poor health outcomes and high unemployment and suicide rates. There is a direct causal link between premature deaths in First Nations and the chronic poverty originally created and now sustained by federal policy. Justice Murray Sinclair did not mince words in the TRC report when he said that Canada has engaged in all forms of genocide in its dealings with Indigenous people — cultural, biological and physical genocide (TRC 2015a: 1). It is long past the time when we confronted the lethal nature of racism.

However, instead of acting on the current medical, legal and social science research, Canada's tendency appears to be to ignore the problem. Canada's ability to defer, deflect and deny the problem is bolstered by the blame-the-victim mentality of many right-wing commentators, media outlets, policy-makers and politicians. Policies have waivered back and forth between assimilation and promotion of self-government. Yet, the two objectives cannot both underpin future policy. Canada has used the impoverished condition of First Nations in the last 250-plus years as a justification for both the assumption of jurisdiction over them and the paternalistic management of Indian affairs. This has led to the current crisis of poverty and premature deaths in First Nations. Yet, First Nations have had far more experience in governing themselves and creating strong, prosperous, thriving nations than Canada has had tearing them down. Despite all the challenges, there are signs of hope in First Nations that offer small glimpses into what is possible. Increased employment rates, reduced suicide rates and improved educational rates are all possible with access to equitable funding and First Nation jurisdiction over key areas like health, education, justice and child welfare. The resolution of land claims and treaties not only benefit First Nations, but all Canadians. First Nations can create success in their communities by addressing federal control, inequitable funding and discrimination prevalent in federal policies. The well-being of future generations can be assured through cultural revitalization in First Nations. First Nation youth need to know that there is nothing wrong with them — it is the system under which they are controlled that needs to be addressed. They have no less of a desire to live and experience the world than anyone else. The deprivation associated with extreme poverty stretches them "beyond all human limits" until they simply can't take it anymore. Decades ago, anthropologists, sociologists and other researchers used to study First Nations and write reports documenting their cultures; today, coroners study First Nations and write death reports. First Nations deserve the same rights as other peoples to enjoy their sovereignty and have a fair chance to live the lives they believe in. They deserve a chance to live the "good life" that everyone else gets to take for granted.

Glossary of Key Terms

Assimilation: The process by which Indigenous peoples were expected to, or forced to, conform to the ideas, values, cultures and beliefs of the settler populations.

Blaming the victim: A devaluing act through which the victims of a crime, accident, hardship or wrongful act are held to be entirely or partially responsible for the harm committed against them, and which is often associated with negative, stereotypical and/or racist and sexist views about them.

Colonialism: The state practice of taking full or partial control over another territory and its inhabitants with a view to exploiting the lands, waters, peoples and resources for economic profit.

First Nation: Replaces the term "Indian band," which refers to a specific Indigenous community that occupies land set aside under the *Indian Act* for their use and benefit. In some circumstances, First Nations are one of several smaller communities that form part of larger traditional Indigenous Nations such as the Mi'kmaq or Cree.

Poverty: Often defined as a lack of money or financial wealth relative to others. In an Indigenous context poverty specifically includes a lack of the basic necessities of life, including food, water, sanitation, shelter, heat and access to medical care.

Self-determination: An internationally recognized right of peoples to freely determine their own political status and economic, social and cultural development as well as control and benefit from their traditional lands, waters and natural resources.

Treaty: A sacred agreement between individual First Nations and/or larger Indigenous Nations and the Crown as represented by Her Majesty the Queen (in the case of historic treaties) or the Crown as represented by Canada and/or the provinces (in the case of modern treaties) and may protect hunting and fishing rights, set apart lands for First Nations and/ or implement First Nation governments and related powers that are now constitutionally protected.

Questions for Discussion

1. How much of a factor is racism in the decisions made by federal and provincial governments in relation to First Nations?

2. Do Canadians, individually or collectively, share in any of the responsibility for the socio-economic conditions of First Nations today?

3. How will we know when the colonization of Indigenous peoples has ended?

Resources for Activists

350: 350.org
Amnesty International-Canada: amnesty.ca
Council of Canadians: canadians.org
David Suzuki Foundation: davidsuzuki.org
Defenders of the Land: defendersoftheland.org
First Nations Child and Family Caring Society of Canada: fncaringsociety.com
Idle No More: idlenomore.ca
Indigenous Nationhood: indigenousnationhood.blogspot.com
Mining Watch Canada: miningwatch.ca
Pam Palmater website: pampalmater.com

Notes

1. This report included a special chapter related to the deaths by suicide in Pikangikum First Nation between the years of 2006 and 2008 where sixteen children between the ages of 10 and 19 years of age took their own lives.
2. *Constitution Act, 1867* (U.K.), 30 and 31 Vict., c.3 [*Constitution Act, 1867*]. I have focused my research on First Nations, which at times includes data related to the Inuit as well. Both groups are subject to federal jurisdiction as per section 91(24) of the *Constitution Act, 1867*. The Metis are a newer social phenomenon having only existed 250-plus years. As they are under provincial jurisdiction and have very different histories and social conditions, they were not included in this research except where specifically noted.
3. The Census includes North American Indians or First Nations (both registered and unregistered), Métis and Inuit in that definition. It is also important to note that this report focuses on the Aboriginal identity statistics. Statistics Canada makes a distinction between those with Aboriginal identity and those who report Aboriginal ancestry: "Aboriginal identity refers to those persons who reported identifying with at least one Aboriginal group, that is, North American Indian, Métis or Inuit, and/or those who reported being a Treaty Indian or a Registered Indian, as defined by the Indian Act of Canada, and/or those who reported they were members of an Indian band or First Nation." Aboriginal ancestry, on the other hand, is defined as referring to "the ethnic or cultural origin of a person's ancestors, an ancestor being usually more distant than a grandparent. In the census, if a person reports at least one Aboriginal ancestry response, the person is counted in the Aboriginal ancestry population."
4. The non-registered Indian population increased 53 percent, more than twice that of the registered population (24 percent). "This growth may be in part related to provisions of the

Indian Act governing the transmission of registered status to children."

5. There are no routine price adjustments incorporated in the operations formula. There appears to have been no price adjustments to the formula since the 1994–95 fiscal year. FNCFS agencies indicated that they all thought that an adjustment for remoteness was necessary. DIAND has been limited to 2 percent budgetary increases for the department while expenditures for FNCFS agencies have been rising annually at an average rate of 6.2 percent. The average per capita per child in care expenditure of the DIAND-funded system is 22 percent lower than the average of the selected provinces.

6. INAC and CMHC have not been able to demonstrate that all reserve homes meet the national building code, and "although mould contamination has been identified as a serious and g rowing health and safety problem for several years, a comprehensive strategy and action plan has not yet been developed." Further, on pages 21–22, the Auditor General also criticized INAC for failing to give Parliament a complete picture that instead of housing stock increasing, "the average number of homes constructed since the adoption of the policy in 1996 actually declined by 30 percent."

7. The breakdown was as follows: "245,000 deaths in the United States in 2000 were attributable to low education, 133,000 to poverty, 162,000 to low social support, 39,000 to area-level poverty, 119,000 to income inequality, and 176,000 to racial segregation." They also found: "These mortality estimates are comparable to deaths from the leading pathophysiological causes. For example, the number of deaths we calculated as attributable to low education is comparable to the number caused by acute myocardial infarction (192 898), a subset of heart disease, which was the leading cause of death in the United States in 2000. The number of deaths attributable to racial segregation is comparable to the number from cerebrovascular disease (167 661), the third leading cause of death in 2000, and the number attributable to low social support is comparable to deaths from lung cancer (155 521)."

8. Safe drinking water and sanitation are essential for good health. Microbial contamination can lead to outbreaks of waterborne diseases. Chemical contamination of drinking water occurs less frequently but may also have health impacts, generally chronic and long-term. "The major threats to drinking water quality in Canada are microbiological contaminants — bacteria, viruses, and protozoa — such as E. coli, Giardia, Crytosporidum, and Toxoplasmosis. These water-borne pathogens cause adverse effects ranging from mild gastroenteritis (upset stomach) to severe diarrhea and death" (National Aboriginal Health Organization 2006: 12–14).

9. "The residential school system was a conscious, deliberate and often brutal attempt to force Aboriginal people to assimilate into mainstream society, mostly by forcing the children away from their languages, cultures and societies." Further, "We believe many of the reasons why the numbers of Aboriginal people are so disproportionately high in the child welfare system are the same as the reasons why they are so over-represented in the criminal justice system. 'Clients' of one system frequently become 'clients' of the other system. It would be impossible to present a complete picture of the criminal justice system, and the youth justice system, without also analysing the field of child and family services." During this period, nearly 11,000 children were forcibly removed from their homes. Also, on page 6 they explain that "social workers deprived of the information, skills and resources to address the poverty, disempowerment, multi-generational grief and loss of parenting knowledge defaulted to a practice of mass removals known as the 60s scoop" (Blackstock and Trocmé 2004: 2).

10. My preliminary research uncovered many more examples that will be further developed in a future publication. See also Warry 2008.

11. "I would be the first to acknowledge that many of the factors contributing to the excessively high

rates of aboriginal incarceration — poverty, social exclusion, substance abuse, discrimination — go well beyond the capacity of the correctional service to address in isolation. I am well aware that the federal correctional authority does not have control over the number of federally sentenced offenders. Nevertheless, the report states that the Correctional Service of Canada has the jurisdiction and the obligation, statutory and constitutional, to manage sentences in a culturally responsive manner. On this point the federal correctional service has fallen short, with negative consequences for aboriginal offenders and their communities." See also page 2: "Over the years, my office has issued a series of reports and recommendations regarding the treatment of aboriginal offenders under federal sentence. In fact, the very first annual report released by the Office of the Correctional Investigator more than 35 years ago documented instances of systemic discrimination against federally sentenced aboriginal offenders. Unfortunately, many of our recommendations made since then have gone unheeded or only partially addressed, or the response to them has not yielded the intended result" (OCI 2010).

12. It was also reported by Statistics Canada employees that the Conservative government was moving away from social statistics to those which focus exclusively on economic issues.

13. "On 26 October 2005, the CBC National News reported on the evacuation of the Kashechewan Reserve in Northern Ontario due to the failure of its water treatment system, which led to the contamination of drinking water. This was an important story that potentially could have been used to educate viewers about the poor water quality and other environmental health problems on hundreds of reserves. But the CBC chose to follow the evacuation story immediately with a feature on mismanagement by, and potential corruption in, the Natuashish Band Council" (Warry 2007: 69–70).

14. See page 4: "If instead, one's culture is marginalized, or vandalized, or turned into a laughingstock; and if (because of colonization or decolonization or globalization) the familiar and trustworthy ways of one's community are criminalized, legislated out of existence, or otherwise assimilated beyond easy recognition, then woe be upon those transiting toward maturity, and for whom otherwise customary ways and means of warranting one's personal persistence often no longer suffice. The predictable consequence of such personal and cultural losses is often disillusionment, lassitude, substance abuse, self-injury and self-appointed death at an early age" (Chandler and Lalonde 1998).

References

Aboriginal Justice Inquiry of Manitoba. n.d. "Report of the Aboriginal Justice Inquiry of Manitoba: Chapter 14 — Child Welfare." <ajic.mb.ca/volumel/chapter14.html>.

Aboriginal Peoples Television Network. 2011. "First Nations face 'life or death' struggle: Atleo." Moncton, NB. 12 July. <aptn.ca/pages/news/2011/07/12/first-nations-face-life-or-death-struggle-atleo/>.

AFN (Assembly of First Nations). n.d. "Federal Government Funding to First Nations: The Facts, the Myths, and the Way Forward." Ottawa: AFN. <csfs.org/Files/Public/Index/Archive/Federal-Government-Funding-to-First-Nations.pdf>.

____. n.d. Education. <afn.ca/en/policy-areas/education>.

____. 2010. "Taking Action for First Nations Post-Secondary Education: Access, Opportunity, and Outcomes — Discussion Paper." Ottawa. <afn.ca/uploads/files/pse-dp.pdf>.

____. 2011. "It's Our Time: A Call to Action on Education." <afn.ca/uploads/files/11-06-11_a_call_to_action_year_in_review.pdf>.

____. 2011. "Fact Sheet: Quality of Life of First Nations." Ottawa: Assembly of First Nations <afn.ca/

uploads/files/factsheets/quality_of_life_final_fe.pdf>.

Alfred, T. 2005. *Indigenous Pathways of Action and Freedom*. Toronto: University of Toronto Press.

____. 2009. "Colonialism and State Dependency." *Journal of Aboriginal Health* 42.

Alfred, T., and J. Corntassel. 2005. "Being Indigenous: Resurgences Against Contemporary Colonialism." *Government and Opposition* 597.

Banerjee, S. 1999. "Whose Mine Is It Anyway? National Interest, Indigenous Stakeholders and Colonial Discourses: The Case of the Jabiluka Uranium Mine." Presented at the Critical Management Studies Conference (Postcolonial Stream), Manchester, UK, July 14–16. <mngt.waikato.ac.nz/ejrot/cmsconference/1999/documents/PostColonialism/postcolonial.pdf>.

Barnsley, P. 2002. "How much goes to Indians? Not as much as you think!" *Windspeaker* 19, 11 <ammsa.com/node/25042>.

Barrados, M. (Assistant Auditor General of Canada). 2003. "Opening Statement to the Standing Committee on Public Accounts — Federal Government Support to First Nations — Housing on Reserve." 5 May. <oag-bvg.gc.ca/internet/English/osh_20030505_e_23387.html>.

Benyon, J. 1994. "First Nations: The Circle Unbroken, Review." *Canadian Journal of Education* 19, 2.

Blackstock, C., and N. Trocmé. 2004. "Community Based Child Welfare for Aboriginal Children: Supporting Resilience through Structural Change." <dev.cecw-cepb.ca/files/file/en/communityBasedCWAboriginalChildren.pdf>.

Borrows, J. 2003. "Measuring a Work in Progress: Canada, Constitutionalism, Citizenship and Aboriginal Peoples." In Ardith Walkem and Halie Bruce (eds.), *Box of Treasures or Empty Box? Twenty Years of Section 35*. Vancouver: Theytus.

Brosnahan, Maureen. 2013. "Canada's prison population at all-time high." cbc News, November 25. <cbc.ca/news/canada-s-prison-population-at-all-time-high-1.2440039>.

Cairns, A. 1999. *Citizens Plus: Aboriginal Peoples and The Canadian State*. Vancouver: ubc Press.

Cairns, A., and T. Flanagan. 2001. "Flanagan and Cairns on Aboriginal Policy." *Policy Options* 43 (September).

Campbell, A. 2002. "Type 2 Diabetes and Children in Aboriginal Communities: The Array of Factors that Shape Health and Access to Health Care." *Health Law Journal* 10: 147.

Canada, Government of. 1969. Statement of the Government of Canada on Indian Policy. <aadnc-aandc.gc.ca/DAM/DAM-INTER-HQ/STAGING/texte-text/cp1969_1100100010190_eng.pdf>.

Canadian Council on Learning. 2007. "Redefining How Success Is Measured in First Nations, Inuit and Metis Learning: Report on Learning in Canada 2007." Ottawa.

cbc News. 2008. "Residential Schools: A history of residential schools in Canada." May 16. <cbc.ca/news/canada/story/2008/05/16/f-faqs-residential-schools.html?sms_ss=facebook&at_xt=4d8618622dc81306%2C0>.

____. 2014a. "Tax Season Facts and Figures." January 28 <cbc.ca/news/business/taxes/tax-season-facts-and-figures-1.2504140>.

____. 2014b. "New Attawapiskat School Opens Today." August 14.

Centre for Research on Inner City Health. 2009. "Measuring Equity of Care in Hospital Settings: From Concepts to Indicators: 2009." <tmichaelshospital.com/crich/reports/measuring-equity-of-care-in-hospital-settings/>.

Chandler, M., and C. Lalonde. 1998. "Cultural Continuity as a Hedge Against Suicide in Canada's First Nations." *Transcultural Psychiatry* 35, 2: 191. <web.uvic.ca/~lalonde/manuscripts/1998TransCultural.pdf>.

____. 2008. "Cultural Continuity as a Protective Factor Against Suicide in First Nations Youth." *Horizons — A Special Issue on Aboriginal Youth, Hope or Heartbreak: Aboriginal Youth and Canada's Future* 10,

1: 68. <www2.psych.ubc.ca/~chandlerlab/Chandler%20&%20Lalonde%20(2008).pdf>.

Coffey, C. 1997. "The Cost of Doing Nothing: A Call to Action." Royal Bank of Canada. <rbcroyalbank. com/aboriginal/r_speech.html>.

Constitution Act, 1867 (U.K.), 30 & 31 Vict., c.3.

CTVNews. 2010. "Atlantic native groups challenge census in court." <ctvnews.ca/atlantic-native-groups-challenge-census-in-court-1.585107>.

Daniel, M., et al. 2000. "Rating Health and Social Indicators for Use with Indigenous Communities: A Tool for Balancing Cultural and Scientific Utility." *Social Indicators Research* 94, 2: 241 at 242.

Drummond, D., and E. Rosenbluth. 2013. "The Debate on First Nations Education Funding: Mind the Gap." Working Paper 49. Queen's University, Kingston, ON.

Eggerton, L. 2007. "Physicians Challenge Canada to Make Children, Youth a Priority." *Canadian Medical Association Journal* 1693, 176, 12: 1.

First Nations Child and Family Caring Society of Canada et al. v. Canada. 2016. Canadian Human Rights Tribunal 11, File No.: T1340/7008.

Flanagan, T., C. Alcantra, and A. Le Dressey. 2000. *First Nations? Second Thoughts.* Montreal: McGill-Queen's University Press.

____. 2010. *Beyond the Indian Act: Restoring Aboriginal Property Rights.* Montreal: McGill-Queen's University Press.

Frynas. J. 2005. "The False Developmental Promise of Corporate Social Responsibility: Evidence from Multinational Oil Companies." *International Affairs* 81, 3.

Galea, S., et al. 2011. "Estimated Deaths Attributable to Social Factors in the United States." *American Journal of Public Health,* June 16.

Gibbons, R. 1984. "Canadian Indian Policy: The Constitutional Trap." *Canadian Journal of Native Studies* 1.

Gibson, G. 2009. *A New Look at Canadian Indian Policy: Respect the Collective — Promote the Individual.* Vancouver: Fraser Institute.

Globe and Mail. 2010a. "Canada's long-form census debate." <theglobeandmail.com/news/politics/canadas-long-form-census-debate/article1647591/>.

____. 2010b. "Statistics Canada chief falls on sword over census." <theglobeandmail.com/news/politics/statistics-canada-chief-falls-on-sword-over-census/article1647348/>.

____. 2010c. "Provinces rally against Ottawa as anger over census mounts." <theglobeandmail.com/news/politics/provinces-rally-against-ottawa-as-anger-over-census-mounts/article1646827/>.

Goyette, L. 2010. "Still Waiting in Attawapiskat." *Canadian Geographic.* <canadiangeographic.ca/magazine/dec10/attawapiskat.asp>.

Haida Nation v. BC (Minster of Forests). 2004. 3 S.C.R

Hall, A. 2010. *Earth into Property: Colonization, Decolonization, and Capitalism.* Montreal: McGill-Queen's University Press.

Harper, S. 2008. "Statement of Apology to Former Students of Indian Residential Schools." 11 June. Ottawa: Government of Canada. <ainc-inac.gc.ca/ai/rqpi/apo/index-eng.asp>.

Hasnain-Wynia, R., D. Pierce, and M.A. Pittman. 2004. "Who, When, and How: The Current State of Race, Ethnicity, and Primary Language Data Collection in Hospitals." Health Research and Educational Trust, American Hospital Association. <aapcho.dreamhosters.com/download/PDF/HasnianWynia_WhoWhenHow.pdf>.

Health Canada. 2010. "A Statistical Profile." <hc-sc.gc.ca/fniah-spnia/pubs/aborig-autoch/2010-stats-profil-determinants/index-eng.php>.

Helin, C. 2008. *Dances with Dependency: Out of Poverty Through Self-Reliance,* 2nd edition. California: Ravencrest Publishing.

Indian Act, R.S.C. 1985, c. I-5 [*Indian Act*].

Indian Affairs and Northern Development. 1969. "Statement of the Government of Canada on Indian Policy Presented to the First Session of the Twenty-Eighth Parliament by the Honourable Jean Chretien, Minister of Indian Affairs and Northern Development." Ottawa.

INAC (Indian and Northern Affairs Canada). 2004. "Speaking Points: Domestic Affairs Committee." 13 December. <fncfcs.com/sites/default/files/fnwitness/DomesticAffairsCommittee-SpeakingNotes-Dec2004.pdf>.

____. 2010. "First Nation and Inuit Community Well-Being: Describing Historical Trends (1981–2006)." Ottawa. <aadnc-aandc.gc.ca/DAM/DAM-INTER-HQ/STAGING/texte-text/cwbdck_1100100016601_eng.pdf>.

____. 2011a. "Minister Duncan announces funding for a new school at Attawapiskat First Nation." 19 May. <aadnc-aandc.gc.ca/eng/1100100016328/1100100016329>.

____. 2011b. "Minister Duncan and AFN National Chief Atleo Announce Joint Action Plan." 9 June. <ainc-inac.gc.ca/ai/mr/nr/m-a2011/23495-eng.asp>.

____. 2015. "First Nations." <ainc-inac.gc.ca/ap/fn/index-eng.asp>.

Jacobs, B. 2010. "Environmental Racism on Indigenous Lands and Territories." Canadian Political Science Association. <cpsa-acsp.ca/papers-2010/Jacobs.pdf>.

Kumagai, D. 2011. "Native Groups Fight Feds in Court." <longformcensus.kingsjournalism.com/2011/03/aboriginal-groups-challenge-census-in-court/>.

Lawrence, B., and E. Dua. 2005. "Decolonizing Antiracism." *Social Justice* 32, 4: 120 at 123.

Lemstra, M., et al. 2009. "Suicide Ideation: The Role of Economic and Aboriginal Cultural Status after Multivariate Adjustment." *Canadian Journal of Psychiatry* 54. 9: 589 at 590

Long, A., et al. 1982. "Federal Indian Policy and Indian Self-Government in Canada: An Analysis of a Current Proposal." *Canadian Public Policy* 8, 2: 189, 190.

Lorraine, B. 2016. "Shoal Lake 40 water crisis an ugly reminder of Canadian colonialism." *Ricochet* June 22. <ricochet.media/en/1239/shoal-lake-40-water-crisis-an-ugly-reminder-of-canadian-colonialism>.

Lukas, M. 2015. "Canadian government pushing First Nations to give up land rights for oil and gas profits." *The Guardian*, March 3. <theguardian.com/environment/true-north/2015/mar/03/documents-harper-pushing-first-nations-to-shelve-rights-buy-into-resource-rush>.

MacDonald, N., et al. 2011. "Tuberculosis in Nunavut: A century of failure." *Canadian Medical Journal Association* 183, 7: 741.

Macleod, A. 2015. "Aboriginal peoples responsible to raise selves out of poverty, Conservative say." *The Tyee*, September 29. <thetyee.ca/News/2015/09/29/John-Duncan-Aboriginal-Poverty-Debate/>.

Make Poverty History. 2010. "The Facts." <makepovertyhistory.ca/learn/issues/end-poverty-in-canada>.

____. n.d. "Mandela's Speech: Extracts." <makepovertyhistory.org/extras/mandela.shtml>.

Mann, M. 2009. "Good Intentions, Disappointing Results: A Progress Report on Federal Aboriginal Corrections." Ottawa: Office of the Correctional Investigator.

McDonald, R., P. Ladd, et al. 2000. "First Nations Child and Family Services: Joint National Policy Review: Final Report." Ottawa: AFN. <fncfcs.com/sites/default/files/docs/FNCFCS_JointPolicyReview_Final_2000.pdf>.

Minister's National Working Group on Education. 2002. "Our Children — Keeps of the Sacred Knowledge: Final Report of the Minister's National Working Group on Education." AFN. <afn.ca/uploads/files/education/23._2002_dec_jeffrey_and_jette_final_report_to_min_national_working_group_ourchildrenkeepersofthesacredknowledge.pdf> at t 51.

Moretti, S. 2011. "One-third of Canadian adults pay no income taxes." *Toronto Sun* April 30

<torontosun.com/2011/04/30/onethird-of-canadian-adults-pay-no-income-taxes>.

Moss, W., and E. Gardner-O'Toole. 1991. "Aboriginal People: History of Discriminatory Laws." Ottawa: Library of Parliament. <publications.gc.ca/Collection-R/LoPBdP/BP/bp175-e.htm>.

National Aboriginal Health Organization. 2006. "First Nations Regional Longitudinal Health Survey (RHS) 2002/2003: Report on First Nations' Housing." Ottawa: NAHO. <fnigc.ca/sites/default/files/ENpdf/RHS_2002/rhs2002-03-report_on_first_nations_housing.pdf>.

National Archives of Canada. Record Group 10, vol. 6810, file 470-2-2, col.7, pp. 55 (L-3) and 63 (N-3).

National Collaborating Centre for Aboriginal Health. 2009. "Poverty as a Social Determinant of First Nations, Inuit, and Metis Health." <nccah.ca>.

National Council on Welfare. 2007. "First Nations, Métis and Inuit Children and Youth: Time to Act." Ottawa: National Council of Welfare. <publications.gc.ca/collections/collection_2007/hrsdc-rhdsc/HS54-1-2007E.pdf>.

NDP. 2011. "Attawapiskat school a victory for northern kids: Fight continues for equal rights for First Nations students across Canada." <ndp.ca/news/attawapiskat-school-victory-northern-kids-ndp>.

Neegan Burnside Ltd. 2011. "National Assessment of First Nations Water and Wastewater Systems: National Roll-up Report — Final." Ottawa: INAC. <adnc-aandc.gc.ca/DAM/DAM-INTER-HQ/STAGING/texte-text/enr_wtr_nawws_rurnat_rurnat_1313761126676_eng.pdf>.

OAG (Office of the Auditor General of Canada). 2000–2010. "Status Report of the Auditor General of Canada to the House of Commons." <oci-bec.gc.ca/cnt/rpt/index-eng.aspx#AR>

____. 2003. "Federal Government Support to First Nations—Housing on Reserves." <oag-bvg.gc.ca/internet/docs/20030406ce.pdf>.

____. 2004. "Report of the Auditor General: Chapter 5 — Education Program and Post-Secondary Student Support." <oag-bvg.gc.ca/internet/English/parl_oag_200411_05_e_14909.html>.

____. 2011. "Interim Auditor General's Opening Statement." 9 June. <oag-bvg.gc.ca/internet/English/osm_20110609_e_35409.html>.

____. 2014. "2014 Fall Report of the Auditor General of Canada." <oag-bvg.gc.ca/internet/English/parl_oag_201411_e_39950.html>.

OCI (Office of the Correctional Investigator). 2000–2010. "Annual Report of the Office of the Correctional Investigator." <oci-bec.gc.ca/rpt/index-eng.aspx>.

____. 2013. "Backgrounder: Aboriginal Inmates." <oci-bec.gc.ca/cnt/rpt/oth-aut/oth-aut20121022info-eng.aspx>.

Office of the Chief Coroner for Ontario. 2011. "Report of the Paediatric Death Review Committee and Deaths Under Five Committee, Annual Report, 2011." Ontario. <mcscs.jus.gov.on.ca/sites/default/files/content/mcscs/docs/ec167691.pdf>.

Palacios, M., B. Barua, and F. Ren. 2015. "The Price of Public Health Care Insurance." Fraser Research Bulletin, August. Calgary: Fraser Institute. <fraserinstitute.org/sites/default/files/price-of-public-health-care-insurance-2015-rev.pdf>.

Palmater, P. 2010. "Opportunity or Temptation: Plans for private property on reserves could cost First Nations their independence." Literary Review of Canada April. <reviewcanada.ca/reviews/2010/04/01/opportunity-or-temptation/>.

____. 2011. Beyond Blood: Rethinking Indigenous Identity. Saskatoon: Purich Publishing.

____. 2015. Indigenous Nationhood: Empowering Grassroots Citizens. Winnipeg and Halifax: Fernwood Publishing.

____. 2016. "Shining Light on the Dark Places: Addressing Police Racism and Sexualized Violence Against Indigenous Women and Girls in the National Inquiry." Canadian Journal of Women and the Law 28, 2: 253.

Parkin, T. 2016. "Trudeau's confused reconciliation agenda." *Toronto Sun* August 14. <torontosun.com/2016/08/14/trudeaus-confused-reconciliation-agenda>.

Patriquin, M. 2012. "Canada, home to the suicide capital of the world." *Maclean's Magazine* March 30.

Penner, D. 2014. "'Unprecedented Opportunity' in resource development, Prime Minister tells First Nations." *Vancouver Sun*, June 1 <vancouversun.com/business/resources/unprecedented+opportunity+resource+development+prime/9356519/story.html>.

Percival, T. 2011. "Political Governance and Health." 6 July presentation at Samoa Conference II. New Zealand collects health data at hospitals by ethnicity. "Chapter 12 — Persistent Poverty and Rising Inequality." in Contemporary American Society. <ssc.wisc.edu/~wright/ContemporaryAmericanSociety/Chapter%2012%20--%20Persistent%20poverty%20--%20Norton%20August.pdf>.

Porter, J. 2016. "First Nations students get 30 per cent less funding than other children, economist says." CBC News, March 14. <cbc.ca/news/canada/thunder-bay/first-nations-education-funding-gap-1.3487822>.

Price Waterhouse Coopers. 2009. "Financial and Economic Impacts of Treaty Settlements in BC." Executive Summary. <www12.statcan.ca/census-recensement/2006/as-sa/97-558/p1-eng.cfm>.

Provincial Advocate for Children and Youth. 2011. "Our Dreams Matter Too: First Nations children's rights, lives and education: An alternate report from the Shannen's Dream Campaign to the United Nations Committee on the Rights of the Child on the occasion of Canada's 3rd and 4th periodic reviews." <uvic.ca/icwr/docs/research/OurDreams-LoRes.pdf>.

Puxley, C. 2015. "The price of Winnipeg's water: Man-made misery for a native community." *Globe and Mail*, March 12 <theglobeandmail.com/news/national/the-price-of-winnipegs-water-man-made-misery-for-a-native-community/article23417422/>.

Raphael, D. 2016. *About Canada: Health and Illness, 2nd edition.* Halifax and Winnipeg: Fernwood Publishing.

RCAP (Royal Commission on Aboriginal Peoples). 1996. "Report of the Royal Commission on Aboriginal Peoples, vols. 1–5." Ottawa: Minister of Supply and Services Canada.

Sapers, H. 2009. "Evidence to Standing Committee on Aboriginal Affairs and Northern Development." 26 November. <parl.gc.ca/content/hoc/Committee/402/AANO/Evidence/EV4268865/AANOEV40-E.PDF>.

____. 2015. "Annual Report of the Office of the Correctional Investigator: 2014–15." <oci-bec.gc.ca/cnt/rpt/pdf/annrpt/annrpt20142015-eng.pdf>.

Smith, J. 2016. "First Nations Funding Cap Is Still There Despite Trudeau's Promise." *Huffington Post* June 16 <huffingtonpost.ca/2016/06/16/political-will-to-lift-first-nations-funding-cap-is-there-needs-time-chief_n_10515960.html>.

Statistics Canada. 2004a. "A profile of Canada's North American Indian population with legal Indian status." Ottawa: Statistics Canada: 10.

____. 2004b. "A profile of Canada's North American Indian population without legal Indian status." Ottawa: Statistics Canada.

____. 2006. "2006 Census: Aboriginal Peoples in Canada in 2006: Inuit, Métis and First Nations, 2006 Census: Highlights." Ottawa <www12.statcan.ca/census-recensement/2006/as-sa/97-558/p1-eng.cfm>.

____. 2011. Aboriginal Peoples: Fact Sheet for Canada. Catalogue # 89-656-X <statcan.gc.ca/pub/89-656-x/89-656-x2015001-eng.htm#a8>.

Steckley, J., and B. Cummins. 2008. "The Story of Minnie Sutherland: Death by Stereotype?" In *Full Circle: Canada's First Nations, 2nd edition.* Toronto: Pearson Education Canada.

Talaga, T. 2011. "Lack of proper schools for natives is 'immoral discrimination,' Martin says." *Toronto Star* May 18. <thestar.com/news/canada/2011/05/18/lack_of_proper_schools_for_natives_is_immoral_discrimination_martin_says.html>.

TRC (Truth and Reconciliation Commission of Canada). 2015a. *Honouring the Truth, Reconciling the Future: Summary of the Final Report of the Truth and Reconciliation Commission of Canada.* <trc.ca/websites/trcinstitution/File/2015/Honouring_the_Truth_Reconciling_for_the_Future_July_23_2015.pdf>.

____. 2015b. *Calls to Action.* <trc.ca/websites/trcinstitution/File/2015/Findings/Calls_to_Action_English2.pdf>.

UNHRC (United Nations Human Rights Council). 2014. Report of the Special Rapporteur on the rights of indigenous peoples - The situation of indigenous peoples in Canada <ohchr.org/Documents/Issues/IPeoples/SR/A.HRC.27.52.Add.2-MissionCanada_AUV.pdf>.

Varcoe, C. n.d. "Harms and Benefits: Collecting Ethnicity Data in a Clinical Context." Prepared for the Michael Smith Foundation for Health Research. <ciqss.umontreal.ca/Docs/SSDE/pdf/Varcoe.pdf> at 3.

____. 2009. "Harms and Benefits: Collecting Ethnicity Data in a Clinical Context." <ciqss.umontreal.ca/Docs/SSDE/pdf/Varcoe.pdf>.

Venne, S. 1981. *Indian Acts and Amendments 1868–1975: An Indexed Collection.* Saskatoon: University of Saskatchewan Native Law Centre.

Vidal, J. 2013. "Indonesia is seeing a new corporate colonialism." *The Guardian,* May 25. <theguardian.com/world/2013/may/25/indonesia-new-corporate-colonialism>.

Warry, W. 2008. *Ending Denial: Understanding Aboriginal Issues.* Toronto: University of Toronto Press.

Wawatay News online. 2008. "No new school for Attawapiskat students." 7 February. <wawataynews.ca/archive/all/2008/2/11/No-new-school-for-Attawapiskat-students_12628>.

Widdowson, F., and A. Howard. 2008. *Disrobing the Aboriginal Industry: The Deception Behind Indigenous Cultural Preservation.* Montreal: McGill-Queen's University Press.

Wilson, Z. (ed.). 1993. *The Indian Acts and Amendments 1970–1993: An Indexed Collection.* Saskatoon: University of Saskatchewan Native Law Centre.

Wilson, D., and D. Macdonald. 2010. *The Income Gap Between Aboriginal Peoples and the Rest of Canada.* Ottawa: Canadian Centre for Policy Alternatives. <ywcacanada.ca/data/research_docs/00000121.pdf>.

4

Keeping Canada White

Immigration Enforcement in Canada

Wendy Chan

AFTER ALMOST TEN YEARS OF CONSERVATIVE GOVERNMENT policy-making on immigration in Canada, the immigration system today is barely recognizable when compared to 2006, when the Tories were elected to power. As the Conservative government acknowledge in their 2014 annual report to Parliament, the immigration system has been "transformed" into a system that is "faster, more flexible and responsive" (CIC 2014). During their time in power, the Conservatives prioritized preventing fraud and abuse of the immigration and refugee system. Their enforcement agenda was bolstered by the irregular arrival of Tamil asylum seekers in 2010 and allegations of widespread fraud in various immigration programs. They implemented a broad range of reforms and legislation within the immigration system, citing the need to enhance enforcement measures, improve administrative efficiency and boost Canada's economy (Alboim and Cohl 2012). Overall support from the general public for their reforms was quite strong, particularly for the enforcement measures that were implemented. This is evident in the reactions to the arrival on the west coast of Canada of close to 500 Tamil refugee claimants in 2010 (*Vancouver Province* 2010). Their arrival fueled a public surge of anger that so many people would be allowed, once again, to bypass the normal channels of refugee processing and "jump the queue" (*Toronto Star* 2010a). Many voices defended the need for Canada to be open-minded about refugees, to avoid making racist remarks about the Tamils, but in this debate, they were in the minority. In response to this event, the government tabled Bill C-49, and then C-4, *Preventing Human Smugglers from Abusing Canada's Immigration System Act*, in an effort to "crack down" on human smuggling into Canada, and in February 2012, the bill became law.

Increased public support for more restrictive immigration policies were possible because the Conservative government had capitalized on the public's heightened anxiety around immigrants and refugees. However, these concerns had to be balanced by the recognition that in order to keep Canada's economy competitive globally, there would be a continued need for more immigrants to come to Canada in order to address the shifting demographics and the global war for talent (*Globe and Mail* 2014). Critics argued that the economic consequences of failing to act would result in slower economic development and growth for Canada. Yet the process of determining how to select the "best" immigrants continues to fuel debate and controversy. Canada wants to attract "good" immigrants while also ensuring that "undesirable" immigrants are not allowed in.

What are we to think about Canada's approach to immigration enforcement? Is it too harsh and racist, as many immigrants argue? Or is it not harsh enough because it permits immigrants and refugees who arrive through irregular channels to enter into Canada?

Many immigration scholars agree that successive reforms to immigration policies in Canada have resulted in increasingly harsh and punitive measures, particularly with regards to the enforcement provisions of the *Immigration Act*. Both the language used and the substantive changes contained in various amendments to the Act construct negative images of immigrants as "abusers" of Canada's "generous" immigration system, as "bogus" refugee claimants and as "criminals" who "cheat" their way into Canada. The latest immigration act, the *Immigration and Refugee Protection Act* (IRPA), exemplifies the criminalizing and retributive tone that is now commonplace in immigration policy-making. The convergence of criminal justice strategies with concerns regarding immigration control found in the IRPA, the most comprehensive set of amendments since the introduction of the *Immigration Act* in 1975, marks an important direction in Canadian immigration policy-making.

Yet immigration critics continue to argue that not enough is being done to ensure that the best immigrants are allowed entry while potential immigrants who pose a threat are screened out. Critics also argue that the rules must be the same for everyone, and therefore undocumented immigrants should not be given "special" treatment. A letter to the editor published in the *Burnaby Now* is typical:

> There is something fundamentally wrong with a system that encourages queue-jumping and rewards human traffickers. When people enter our home by breaking in through the back door, why are they given preferential treatment over law-abiding

immigrants and legitimate refugees who respectfully ring the front doorbell and patiently wait to be admitted? (2010)

Ironically, after being elected in early 2006, Stephen Harper's minority Conservative government — many of whose members were once among Canada's harshest immigration critics — recognized that these issues are more complex and difficult than newspapers would suggest.

Untangling the myths and controversies around immigration enforcement requires a critical examination of enforcement provisions in the IRPA. Taking a critical approach involves asking how immigration laws and policies acknowledge issues of gender, race and class differences in the development, interpretation and application of the country's approaches. The allegations of an effort to keep Canada white by excluding immigrants of colour call for a close consideration of how well (or not) immigrants of colour fare under the current immigration Act. As we shall see, the trend towards criminalizing and demonizing immigrants is nothing new, and race and racism have played an important role in organizing racial identities and enforcing a specific racial reality in Canada. Then too, the enforcement provisions of the *Immigration and Refugee Protection Act* seek to address public concerns over "problem" immigrants, which means that it is important to consider the rationale for these provisions, as well as the responses and criticisms to them. Is there an adequate balance between enforcement and protection for immigrants? The IPRA appears to mark racialized immigrants as criminals and outsiders, with enforcement provisions driven by the need to scapegoat and punish immigrants for a range of fears and insecurities, an approach legitimized by racist ideologies and practices. Immigrants of colour pay the price for Canadians' need to be reassured that their established way of life will not be lost and that immigrants are not "taking over" their country. The result is that many immigrants will continue to be marginalized and excluded as full participants in Canadian society.

> The allegations of an effort to keep Canada "white" by excluding immigrants of colour call for a close consideration of how well (or not) immigrants of colour fare under the current immigration Act.

Canadian Immigration Policy: Recent Years

Canada, like many Western democratic countries, experienced a continued decline in births after the 1960s, combined with a relatively low level of immigration. The implications of this demographic trend raised concerns about whether there would be enough people to keep the country afloat. In the 1980s, Brian Mulroney's Progressive Conservative government sought to address these problems, and boost the economy, by increasing levels of immigration, targeting both young people, particularly those of child-bearing age, and skilled immigrant workers. The result was a significant increase in immigration levels during the late 1980s and early 1990s. Between 1980 and 2000, immigration accounted for almost half of the country's population growth, with over 3.7 million immigrants admitted (Li 2003: 32). In comparison, between 1955 and 1970 Canada had admitted just over 1.6 million immigrants, accounting for 30 percent of total population growth. From 2000 onwards, immigration continued to hold steady, with approximately 250,000 immigrants admitted annually. The key shifts during this period are a reduction in family (26.6 percent in 2001 to 21.5 percent in 2010) and refugee (11.1 percent in 2001 to 8.8 percent in 2010) class immigrants and an increase in economic class immigrants (from 62.1 percent in 2001 to 66.6 percent in 2010) (Alboim and Cohl 2012: 61).

The composition of immigrants was also shifting. Whereas in the post-World War II period immigrants came mainly from Britain and continental Europe (87 percent of immigrants from 1946 to 1955), by the 1980s and 1990s Asia and the Pacific region had become the key source continent for immigrants (53.8 percent from 1970 to 2000). By 1998–2000, the top four source countries were China, India, Pakistan and the Philippines (CIC 2001a: 8), and a decade and a half later, these four countries, along with Iran, continue to be the top five source countries between 2000–14 (CIC 2015: 28). Much of this shift can be attributed to alterations in immigration policies in the 1960s. The changes allowed Canada to abandon national origin as a selection criterion and admit immigrants from all over the world. The implementation of the point system in 1967[1] and, subsequently, the *Immigration Act* of 1976 removed the explicit racial and ethnic discrimination found in previous policies, with the effect that many more immigrants from non-European countries were now being admitted into Canada (Li 2003: 33).

Throughout the 1980s and 1990s, the public debate about immigration was also heating up. The increasing numbers of non-white immigrants had not gone unnoticed and had contributed to a backlash that promoted views that Canada could not absorb all this "diversity" (Li 2001) and that the "quality" of immigrants was threatening to destroy the nation (Thobani 2000). While immigration was on the increase, so too were unemployment rates. Public-opinion polls highlighted immigration as a hot-button issue — primarily, many pollsters believed, because the public associated high unemployment rates with too much immigration (Palmer 1996; Economic Council of Canada 1991). Opinion polls recorded between 1988 and 1993 found that 30–45 percent of the Canadian population believed the country had too many immigrants and indicated that hostility towards immigrants was on the rise (Palmer 1996). The polls expressed fears and anxieties about immigrants not assimilating sufficiently and creating social problems. Clearly, the issue of immigration had become highly charged, with pro-immigration and anti-immigration sentiments being strongly asserted in all types of public forums.

The issue, however, was not so black and white. While immigration was increasing, only certain types of immigrants were gaining access to Canada. The gender, class and race dynamics of the immigration system were not lost on many critics. Although the point system appeared to be neutral in terms of how it evaluated potential immigrants, the resources provided to immigration offices abroad were having an impact on who actually got their applications processed in a timely manner. The United States, Britain and Western Europe had reasonably adequate immigration services, but in non-traditional source areas, such as Africa and parts of South Asia, immigration services were few and far between, resulting in administrative delays and long waiting periods. As well, the professional qualifications of potential immigrants from countries in the northern hemisphere were given greater weight than the qualifications of immigrants trained in the south (CCR 2000: 12). Wealthier applicants were also given preferential treatment in that they were not assessed on all criteria of the points system if they met the criteria of the investors program.[2] These hidden biases resulted in continued racial and ethnic as well as class-based discrimination by favouring potential immigrants from countries more similar to Canada than not.

Gender biases also played a role, particularly in the types of categories that immigrants slotted themselves into when they applied for entry into Canada. Typically, men are the primary or main applicants, and women are in the category of dependent spouse. Although many women who come to Canada are skilled, they may not have had access to a traditional education, which is recognized through the point system and which in turn makes it difficult for them to succeed as the main applicant. Abu-Laban and Gabriel (2002: 49) also point out that how skills are constructed relies on a sexual division of labour. Women's work, both paid and unpaid — for example, cleaning, caring, cooking — is devalued in the point system because it is classified as unskilled or semi-skilled, and offers few if any points. Furthermore, patriarchal attitudes continue to cast women into the role of being dependent on men, and Canadian immigration policies and practices rely on these assumptions in the processing of applications. The net effect is that potential female immigrants have the best chances of entering into Canada by assuming the role of dependent spouse regardless of whether they fit that category or not. For women who do not have male applicants to support their immigration applications, the chances of successfully immigrating are greatly diminished. The only category in which women's applications have been largely successful is when they are able to enter Canada through the Live-In Caregivers Program (LCP). This program allows women to migrate to Canada and work as a live-in caregiver, after which they can apply for permanent residence status once they have completed two years or 3,900 hours of work within four years of their arrival.[3] Yet the relationship of these women to Canada is still precarious because upon entering Canada they are not given landed status, only a temporary permit. They have to satisfy the contractual agreement with their employers before they become eligible for landed status and possibly citizenship.[4]

The worry over illegal immigration to Canada and the high numbers of refugee applications further intensified the debate about the effectiveness of Canada's immigration system. Although the problem of "illegal" entry is an accepted problem in any immigration system, a number of high-profile cases of immigrants and refugees (for example, Tamil boat people) seeking entry led the public to conclude that Canada's immigration system was no longer effective and that more reform was necessary. What the public wasn't aware of, however, was that most "illegal" immigrants were not in fact cases of people seeking entry, but of people whose visas had expired and who had not yet left the country. Furthermore, governments have never, historically, regarded the problem of "illegal" entry into Canada to be a major immigration issue. Indeed, over the years a number of amnesty programs had been implemented to regularize immigrants who lacked proper documentation (Robinson 1983). If a "crisis" situation did exist, it was more likely the result of the media and political opportunists creating a crisis in the public imagination, allowing it to run unchecked, resulting in uninformed speculation about Canada's immigration system.

Controlling Immigration and Immigrants

A key element of many Western countries' immigration programs includes determining who is denied access. In Canada, the perceived need to control the flow of immigrants resulted in a marked resurgence of strictures in Canadian policy in the 1980s, a trend that peaked in the 1990s and coincided with the politicization of immigration. Beginning with the *Immigration Act* of 1975, numerous reforms and amendments led to stricter and exclusionary requirements. Search and seizure provisions were expanded, and refugee claimants were photographed and fingerprinted upon arrival. Fines and penalties were increased for transportation companies that brought in individuals who lacked appropriate documentation (Kelley and Trebilcock 1998).

Various explanations have been offered for why these changes occurred. Many authors cite the breakdown in Canada's refugee system combined with the rise in requests for asylum as a major contributing factor (Creese 1992; Matas 1989). The backlog of applications, the cumbersome administrative process and allegations that the refugee system was being abused challenged the legitimacy of the system. Other explanations included the lack of consensus amongst the political parties over what is an acceptable level of immigration, along with the belief that immigrants applying to Canada should be more self-reliant. These conditions paved the way for independent immigrants (typically male, business class) to be viewed as more desirable than dependent immigrants (typically women and children, family class). Racist beliefs — to the effect that different racial and ethnic backgrounds of immigrants were eroding Canadian values and traditions — shaped the contours of the debates around these issues (Frideres 1996).

In 1987, the federal government introduced two major policy reforms, Bill C-55 and Bill C-84, in response to unanticipated high levels of refugee claims, which were placing a major strain on the immigration system. The *Refugee Reform Act* (Bill C-55) created the Immigration and Refugee Board of Canada (previously the Immigration Appeal Board) and restructured the refugee determination process to respond to the problem of unfounded refugee claims. Refugees were now required to undergo a screening hearing to determine the credibility of their claims. The *Refugee Deterrents and Detention Act* (Bill C-84) gave immigration officers and agents more power to detain and remove refugee arrivals, particularly those considered criminals or a security threat (Kelley and Trebilcock 1998: 386). Both of these reforms led to heated debates, with many critics arguing that the changes proposed were not well-thought-out pieces of legislation but, rather, a reactionary and knee-jerk response to an alleged refugee "crisis" that had been created by the media (Creese 1992: 140–41). Due to these intense debates, the implementation of these bills did not occur until January 1989. Interestingly, the procedure of screening refugees at the beginning of the refugee determination process was eventually eliminated when it was discovered that 95 percent of refugee claims were legitimate (Garcia y Griego 1994: 128). In other words, the speculation that many refugees were "bogus" was unwarranted; the process of forcing refugees to undergo a screening was eventually removed in 1992.

Attempts to curtail and control immigration continued into the 1990s, when two more pieces of legislation were introduced to address security concerns and the growing belief that illegal immigrants rather than legitimate refugees were infiltrating Canada's borders. Introduced in June 1992, Bill C-86 proposed primarily restrictive revisions to the refugee determination system. The restrictions included fingerprinting refugee claimants, harsher detention provisions, making refugee hearings open to the public and requiring Convention refugees[5] applying for landing in Canada to have a passport, valid travel document or "other satisfactory identity document" (CCR 2000). In addition, individuals with criminal or terrorist links would no longer be admissible. In July 1995, the government introduced Bill C-44, better known as the "Just Desserts" bill, in response to the killing of a Toronto police officer by a landed immigrant with a long criminal record. Sergio Marchi, the immigration minister, reminded Canadians that immigration is a privilege and not a right, and he proposed changes that would "go a long way to stopping the tyranny of a minority criminal element" (Marchi 1995). Bill C-44 made it easier to remove from Canada permanent residents who were deemed by the minister to be a "danger to the public." This would be done by restricting their ability to appeal their deportation orders or submit a refugee claim. The bill included additional measures to address fraud and multiple refugee claims.

Like the earlier reforms, these two bills were equally divisive and resulted in intense public and political debates. The most controversial change implemented was the discretionary power given to the immigration minister to deport a permanent resident. Widespread academic and public discussions ensued, with legal scholars arguing that returning discretionary power to the minister was "a throwback to a less enlightened era" (Haigh and Smith 1998: 291), and advocates for a fairer immigration policy arguing that the new provisions were racist and would have the result of increasing the criminalization of non-European individuals in Canada (Hassan-Gordon 1996; Noorani and Wright 1995). Yet some critics believed that Bill C-44 had not gone far enough in tightening up the system against false claimants and criminals. The Reform Party argued that a "criminal is a criminal" and that it was not sufficient to define "serious criminality" as offences carrying a ten-year sentence or longer (Kelley and Trebilcock 1998: 434). That party's position highlights how, despite the lack of research demonstrating any links between immigrants and high crime rates, public fear about crime, based only on several high-profile cases, could be easily manipulated to argue for tighter immigration controls.

These debates highlight how immigration had, by the mid-1990s, become a hot-button issue for politicians and policy-makers as the Canadian public became more involved in shaping Canada's immigration system. Teitelbaum and Winter (1998: 188) attribute this change to the presence of the Reform Party and its call in the 1993 election for an abandonment of the policy of multiculturalism and significant reductions in Canada's annual immigration levels. The right-wing populist movement in Canada, as elsewhere, used immigration and immigrants as easy targets in placing blame for the economic troubles of the time:

> By the mid-1990s, immigration had become a hot-button issue for politicians and policy-makers as the Canadian public became more involved in shaping Canada's immigration system.

The Fraser Institute report says newcomers pay about half as much in income taxes as other Canadians but absorb nearly the same value of government services, costing taxpayers roughly $6,051 per immigrant and amounting to a total annual cost of somewhere between $16.3-billion and $23.6-billion.

"It's in the interest of Canada to examine what causes this and to fix it," said Herbert Grubel, co-author of the report Immigration and the Canadian Welfare State. "We need a better selection process ... We're not here, as a country, to do charity for the rest of the world." (*National Post* 2011)

Such views coincided neatly with the shift to neoliberal approaches in public-policy development — approaches that fostered a belief in how the more vulnerable sectors of society, such as single mothers and immigrants, were to blame for the lack of jobs or high crime rate (Abu-Laban 1998: 194). Good immigrants, it was understood, were those who could look after themselves and their families. With this came the "common-sense" view that strong immigration controls were a necessary component of any effective immigration system. The harsh government reforms of the 1980s and 1990s delivered the message that security and enforcement were now key priorities in immigration policy making.

The Immigration and Refugee Protection Act of 2002

Crepeau and Nakache (2006: 4) note that while immigration controls emerged years before 9/11, those attacks gave authorities more incentive to radically overhaul policies and make them harsher towards unwanted migrants. Canada, like many other states affected by aspects of globalization, transformed immigration from an economic and population policy issue into a security issue. The introduction of the *Immigration and Refugee Protection Act* (IRPA) in 2002 thus marks an important shift in Canadian immigration policy making. As the Standing Committee on Citizenship and Immigration (2001) affirmed, "The *Immigration and Refugee Protection Act* represents a significant step in addressing current security concerns. Even though it was drafted before September 11th, the legislation was clearly created with the threat of terrorism in mind." The Canadian government's response in deterring these activities and individuals was to impose tighter sanctions and increase levels of scrutiny and authority for immigration officers.

According to Citizenship and Immigration Canada (CIC), the IRPA is intended to serve a number of different immigration goals, such as attracting skilled workers, protecting refugees, allowing family reunification and deterring traffickers. The aim, according to the Liberal government of the time, was to accomplish these goals by simplifying the legislation and striking the necessary balance between efficiency, fairness and security. CIC asserts that there is a need to "simplify," "strengthen," "modernize" and "streamline" the immigration system. A key priority in this set of policy reforms was to close "the back door to criminals and others who would abuse Canada's openness and generosity." This would be achieved by including in the Act the necessary provisions to "better ensure serious criminals and individuals who are threats to public safety are kept out of Canada, and, if they have entered the country, that they are removed as quickly as possible" (CIC 2001b).

The IRPA did have a significant impact on controlling immigration to Canada. Immigrant supporting organizations pointed to growing concerns and trepidation about an Act that was overly reactive and too obsessed with security issues. As the Maytree Foundation[6] (2001: 3) stated, IRPA "is much more about who cannot come to Canada and how they will be removed, than it is about who we will welcome, who we will protect, and how we will do that." The addition of several legislative amendments to IRPA such as the *Protecting Canada's Immigration System Act* in 2012 and the *Faster Removal of Foreign Criminals Act* in 2013 highlight how strong enforcement measures would remain a central feature of controlling immigration. Many organizations expressed an uneasiness that racialized immigrants would suffer the consequences of immigration officers' concerns about the need to maintain border security. Moreover, women refugees and immigrants would be likely to shoulder the burden of the many changes that encompassed racist and sexist practices.

Targeting Traffickers and Smugglers

Within the IRPA, the crime of human smuggling and trafficking involves several types of activities. It is an offence to organize, induce, aid or abet immigrants to Canada who do not have the necessary travel documents (s. 117). The trafficking of persons through abduction, fraud, deception, the use or threat of force or coercion (s. 118) and leaving a person or persons at sea for the purposes of helping them come to Canada (s. 119) are also offences subject to criminal penalties. The difference between trafficking and human smuggling rests in the distinction between coerced and consensual irregular migrants. People who are trafficked (usually into forced labour or prostitution) are assumed not to have given their consent and are considered victims, whereas migrants who are smuggled are considered to have willingly engaged in the enterprise (Bhabha 2005).

The penalty for organizing the smuggling of less than ten people is a maximum of ten years imprisonment or a $500,000 fine, or both, for the first offence, or a maximum of four-teen years imprisonment or a $1 million fine, or both, for subsequent offences. When ten persons or more are involved, the penalty is a maximum of life imprisonment or a $1 million fine, or both. Trafficking persons or leaving them at sea carries a maximum penalty of life imprisonment, a fine of $1 million, or both (s. 120). Aggravating factors (s. 121) such as the occurrence of harm or death during the offence or the association of the offence with a criminal organization will be considered in determining the penalty imposed.

The Canadian Council for Refugees (CCR) (2001) argues that attempting to deter the activities of human smuggling and trafficking can have the unintended conse-quence of criminalizing family members who help refugees escape from their home countries (given that the law does not distinguish between smugglers for profit and others who are just trying to help). While the claimants can escape prosecution if they are found to be refugees (s. 133), their family members are not equally protected because they can be denied an asylum hearing or lose permanent residence without the possibility of an appeal (Crepeau and Jimenez 2004). Nor are individuals who apply for asylum in good faith, but are rejected, adequately protected. Given the lack of differentiation, both categories of individuals — those who engage in human smuggling for profit and those who are motivated by humanitarian concerns — will suffer the same penalties.

Moreover, while these provisions are intended to bring Canadian immigration policy in line with international protocols such as the U.N. Convention against Transnational Organized Crime, and thus have included strong enforcement measures to curtail and deter human smuggling and trafficking in persons, the bill has no provisions for the protection of those being smuggled or trafficked, even though Canada is a signatory to the U.N. Convention on the Status of Refugees. It would seem that while Canada has sought to meet some of its international obligations, in other agreements that Canada has undertaken it has yet to fully realize compliance. As the CCR points out, "The migrant protocol states that the criminalization measures are not to apply to people who are smuggled into a country, whereas Bill C-11 [now the IRPA] gives an exemption only to those recognized as refugees." As a result, protection from prosecution is limited only to those who can make a successful refugee claim.

With the passing of Bill C-4, *Preventing Human Smugglers from Abusing Canada's Immigration System Act*, refugee advocacy groups and immigration lawyers believe that making a refugee claim in Canada will now be more difficult than ever before. They argue that the measures contained in this Act will do little to target smugglers and that the Act is more likely to exacerbate the suffering of asylum-seekers. Some of the key concerns about the Bill include detaining refugees, including children, for a year without the possibility of an independent review; denying refugee claimants access to an appeal process; denying some refugees the right to apply for permanent residency in Canada for five years and thus delaying their reunification with family members and denying refugee claimants freedom of movement because they will not be able to travel outside of Canada until they are permanent residents (CCR 2010a). The CCR also point out that the immigration minister has sole discretion to determine whether or not the arrival of a group of persons into Canada is irregular or not (CCR 2010b). Those deemed irregular will be subjected to all kinds of special rules. The CCR argue this effectively creates two classes of refugees, with those designated irregular, based on model of arrival, treated worse than the other group (CCR 2010b).

Although the bill was passed, a concerted campaign by refugee organizations challenging this bill led to a softening of the detention provisions whereby children under 16 would be exempt from mandatory detention, and a detention review would be available after fourteen days and every six months thereafter (the original proposal was no detention review for the first twelve months) (CCR 2015). Despite these minor amendments, the Canadian Council for Refugees observe, "draconian laws are now on the books — laws which five years ago were considered inconceivable in Canada" (CCR 2015). Today, refugees and asylum seekers continue to be scapegoated and attacked for seeking safety from persecution. Most immigration experts do not believe that the government's efforts to curtail the arrival of refugees will have much of an impact. Morrison and Crosland (2001) argue that the deterrent effect of such grossly exaggerated penalties is doubtful, since entry into the "Western

> Most immigration experts do not believe that the government's efforts to curtail the arrival of refugees will have much of an impact.

fortress" necessitates that irregular migrants and refugees use some kind of help to enter Western countries for any reason.

Interdiction and Detention

Attempts to prevent and deter irregular migrants from entering Canada have resulted in a number of measures that were initiated or retooled in the IRPA either to stop migrants from setting foot in Canada or to swiftly remove them. Interdiction measures include the Smart Border Agreement between Canada and the United States. In that agreement Canada increased the number of countries for which it requires visas to be held by foreign nationals to enter the country (DFAIT 2004). Coupled with this are penalties (up to $3,200 per traveller) against airlines, railways and shipping companies that fail in advance to check their passengers for adequate documentation (IRPA s. 148[1][a] and s. 279[1]). Finally, immigration officers are also stationed at various countries of origin or of transit with the aim of stopping migrants before they reach Canada (DFAIT 2004).

With the IRPA, immigration detention and the power to detain have been fortified. Sections 55 and 56 of the new Act state that someone can be detained if there are reasonable grounds to believe that the person would be inadmissible to Canada, a danger to the public or unlikely to appear for future proceedings. Enhanced powers have also been given to immigration officers at ports of entry to detain people on the basis of administrative convenience, suspicion of inadmissibility on the grounds of security or human rights violations and failure to establish identity for any immigration procedure under the Act. Immigration officers also have wider discretion to arrest and detain a foreign national but not a protected person without a warrant, even in cases where they are not being removed (s. 55[2]). The length of detention is not specified for any of these grounds although periodic reviews are mandatory. Thus, someone who fails to provide adequate identification can be detained for the same length of time as can a person who is considered a danger to the public (s. 58[1]). Children can be detained, but only as a measure of last resort (s. 60).

A report by the Canadian Border Services Agency (CBSA) on the Detention and Removal Program in Canada notes that considerable variation exists across the country in detention practices within the first forty-eight-hour period (CBSA 2010). While detainees in the Atlantic, Prairie and Pacific regions are released early, those in Central Canada are detained for longer periods. Similarly, the practice of detaining children and individuals with mental health issues also varies across the country (CBSA 2010). The report recommends a number of changes to improve services as well as reduce the cost of detention by exploring alternatives for low-risk detainees (CBSA 2010).

Many concerns have been raised about the nature of the detention provisions and the manner in which they are or will be executed. The fear amongst most immigrant and refugee organizations is that conferring greater powers to individual immigration officers will result in racial profiling and that a high proportion of racialized migrants will end up being detained (CCR 2001; Getting Landed Project 2002). Other worries include the broad arbitrary use of power by immigration officers, the possibility of long-term detention of migrants who fail to establish their identities, the criminalization of trafficked or smuggled migrants who will be detained for the purpose of deterring human traffickers and the use of detention on the basis of group status rather than on the particular circumstances of the person involved. It has also been revealed that immigrant detainees are not adequately treated while in detention. In an investigation of detention conditions at Canadian facilities, the Red Cross found that detainees were housed in triple-bunked cells and that there was a lack of support for children and inadequate medical care available (*Toronto Star* 2014a).

The United Nations High Commission for Refugees (UNHCR) states that it opposes any detention policy that is fashioned to deter asylum seekers or to discourage them from pursuing their refugee claims. Moreover, it cautions against establishing a policy that detains migrants on the basis of being "unlikely to appear" at an immigration hearing because of their "mode of arrival" to Canada because many refugees are forced to use smugglers in order to reach safety (UNHCR 2001: 29). Finally, it argues that the act of detaining a person for failing to establish their identity, which includes making determinations about the person's level of co-operation with authorities, calls for a recognition of the difference between a wilful intention to deceive and the inability to provide documentation (UNHCR 2001: 30). The UNHCR joins the voices of others (CCR 2001; Maytree Foundation 2001) who also recommend that the government needs to establish clear guidelines and criteria as to what constitutes a refusal to co-operate.

The drift towards the use of preventative detention to deal with migrants perpetuates the mistaken and prejudiced perceptions that those being detained are a threat to public safety and are behaving illegally rather than being people who actually need safety from danger (CCR 2010b). Indeed, the culture of criminalization within the present immigration system points to disturbing trends. Unlike convicted offenders, migrants can face indefinite lengths of detention as they wait for the arrival of their identity documents, and they can be detained on the basis of suspicion or convenience. When asked about the expanding use of immigration detention for asylum seekers, the immigration minister at the time, Jason Kenney, side-stepped the question, focusing instead on the claim that detention facilities were akin to "hotel-like conditions" and not jails, even though they are "run as medium-security prisons with fences topped with razor wire, centrally controlled locked doors, security guards and surveillance cameras everywhere" (Dawson 2014: 829–830).

Loss of Appeal Rights

The elimination of immigration appeals in Canada, particularly in cases where "serious criminality" is involved, is a measure that many other countries have not implemented to the same extent. Section 64 of the IRPA states that individuals found to be inadmissible on considerations of security, violating human rights, serious criminality, organized criminality or individuals convicted of a crime and given a term of imprisonment of two years or more may not be allowed to appeal to the Immigration Appeal Division. Although judicial review remains available, applicants who lose their right to appeal can apply to the federal courts but only with leave from the court and only if there is a purely legal issue that needs to be dealt with. Therefore, if a factual mistake is made, or if all the evidence was not reasonably considered by the original decision-maker (even if that person reached the wrong conclusion), the federal court will not intervene. The effect of this change is to disallow any of the discretion formerly exercised in determining whether an individual should or should not be removed based on the circumstances of their case. While these changes may make the system more efficient, they do so at the cost of diminishing the rights of immigrants. As one commentator notes, such an approach illustrates a move towards a "mechanical application of the rules," which is the antithesis of the just administration of the law (Dent 2002: 762).

The introduction of the Act also included provisions for the establishment of a Refugee Appeal Division, where refugee determinations could be reviewed. However, the number of Immigration and Refugee Board members was reduced from a panel of two to one to balance the right to an appeal for refugees (Crepeau and Nakache 2006: 15). In 2010, the Refugee Appeal Division was finally established, almost eight years after the implementation of IRPA. The provisions for the Refugee Appeal Division were part of the reforms found in the *Balanced Refugee Reform Act*. However, also contained in this Act were less welcoming reforms such as the denial of appeal to refugee claimants arriving from "safe countries of origin" (CCR 2010c). The problem with this country of origin criterion is that it is unclear what constitutes a "safe" country, and activists argue that refugee determination should never be based on a blanket judgment such as country of origin. Instead, each case is unique and requires an individual assessment in order to achieve a fair outcome (CCR 2010c). Although the government argued that designating some claims as "safe" will help to streamline the refugee determination process, critics fear that many claimants may fall through the cracks if they do not have access to a full hearing. When refugees and immigrants do have the right to an appeal, their access to the process is made all the more difficult because of reduced funding in legal aid. Depending on which province the appeal takes place in, some appellants may never see the inside of a hearing room because some provinces do not have any funding available to migrants.

Protecting Immigrants' Rights

Many critics of the IRPA note the erosion of immigrant rights in the legislation. The emphasis on security and terrorism has clearly overshadowed migrants' rights and the need for a more balanced approach. Kent Roach (2005) observes that governments have taken advantage of concerns around security to reconfigure immigration law to bypass the human rights of migrants. He states, "Immigration law has been attractive to the authorities because it allows procedural shortcuts and a degree of secrecy that would not be tolerated under even an expanded criminal law" (Roach 2005: 2).

Critics argue that the IRPA and its subsequent amendments have had a detrimental effect on racialized individuals, groups and communities. For example, the attempts by government to combat human smuggling and trafficking should not occur at the expense of further victimization of the migrants smuggled or trafficked. The National Association of Women and the Law (NAWL) and the United Nations High Commission for Refugees (UNHCR) assert that by failing to include adequate protection for trafficked or smuggled migrants, the Canadian government is reneging on its responsibility to international protocols. The UNHCR notes that many reasons exist as to why migrants resort to smugglers and traffickers. While many migrants are people searching for better economic opportunities, many others are refugees whose only option for escape is with the smugglers or traffickers. NAWL believes that this new category of immigration enforcement will result in smugglers and traffickers charging migrants higher prices to escape. For women and children, who are less likely to have the financial resources to pay, the possibilities of fleeing persecution, conflict and human rights abuses will become even more remote unless they are willing to pay the costs in the form of enforced prostitution and sexual violations (NAWL 2001). It has been strongly recommended that the Canadian government provide protection to migrants by granting them immigration relief, access to permanent residency or the opportunity to submit applications to stay on humanitarian and compassionate grounds (see briefs by NAWL 2001; CCR 2001; and UNHCR 2001). Affording migrants the necessary protection would help to alleviate their vulnerability to the smugglers or traffickers.

Racialized women migrants in particular will experience the impact of the IRPA in harsh and uncompromising terms because they are typically more vulnerable to the effects of migration. For example, a third of all women who immigrate to Canada do so through the family class category, which means that they are sponsored by a Canadian citizen or permanent resident who agrees to ensure that their essential needs are met so that the sponsored person will not resort to social assistance (NAWL 2001). In its brief to the Standing Committee on Citizenship and Immigration, NAWL (2001) recommended that family reunification be recognized as a fundamental human right and, specifically, that people who are being reunited with their families in Canada be given the right to obtain permanent residence in Canada in order to avoid the development of exploitative or abusive relationships. In its review of the first several years of the IRPA, NAWL points out that neither this recommendation nor any of the others it submitted has been implemented, although cursory attention to the issue of gender in immigration has been paid. It notes, "Almost four years after the adoption of the new legislation, the only tangible result of any gender based analysis of the legislative commitment to gender based analysis of the Act is the sex-disaggregated data in the Annual Report 2005" (NAWL 2006).

> Racialized women migrants are typically more vulnerable to the effects of migration.

The decrepit state of detention centres in Canada and the now increased potential for long-term detention of migrants add to the growing list of concerns that detainees' civil liberties will be violated, particularly when the majority of the detainees are racialized migrants. Indeed, many organizations believe that the heightened powers of detention are a racist and reactionary response to the arrival of boatloads of Chinese and Tamil migrants to the shores of British Columbia, many of whom were primarily economic migrants seeking a new life in Canada.[7] That their arrival resulted in their immediate detention without much public outcry highlights how racism, through the practice of racial profiling, was used to gain legitimacy for the government's practices. The assumption was that if one boatload of migrants were "bogus" refugee claimants, then all migrants would be as well, which justified the government's "tough"[8] stance on "illegal" immigrants (CBC Online 1999a, 1999b; CCR 2010a). Not surprisingly, issues of due process and other human rights abuses surfaced in a United Nations Human Rights Commission report over the treatment of the Chinese (*Canadian Press*, April 12, 2001; CBC Online 1999c) and again with the Tamil migrants (Amnesty International 2010). The U.N. investigator said that Canada "needed to avoid criminalizing the victims." Her report pointed to the poor psychological state of some of the Chinese women who were detained and how mistreatment by penitentiary guards had led one woman to attempt suicide. In her report, the U.N. investigator reminded Canadian authorities that the migrants had been doubly victimized because they were also the victims of the traffickers. Similarly, Amnesty International has expressed concern that by detaining irregular arrivals, the rights of refugees and migrants are violated "solely on the basis of how they have travelled to Canada and how many others have travelled with them" (2010). Like others, they remind Canada that this is in direct contravention to various U.N. covenants binding on Canada.

For many activists and scholars involved in debating and discussing the IRPA, the government's recognition of the importance of human rights does indeed appear to be either non-existent or timid at best. Crepeau and Nakache (2006) argue that governments need to recognize that the principle of territorial sovereignty is not incompatible with protecting individual rights and freedoms. One way of recognizing this principle is to clearly identify and justify all security exceptions to the recognition of human rights that are normally conferred by the state to migrants (Crepeau and Nakache 2006: 25). The extent to which Canada and other Western nations will give priority to human rights while pursuing an immigration agenda focused on security and control remains to be seen. Catharine Davergne observes:

> The proliferation of human rights norms over the last half century has not markedly increased rights entitlements at the moment of border crossing, nor has it significantly increased access to human rights for those with no legal status, those "illegals" beyond the reach of the law but at the centre of present rhetoric. (2004: 613)

As a result, the approach taken continues to reinforce the unequal distribution of rights on the basis of birthplace, and it leaves those who are unprotected vulnerable and open to intimidation and exploitation.

Race and Nation: National Fears and Immigrant Scapegoating

As the successor to the 1975 *Immigration Act*, the IRPA represents a different era of immigration policy making. The 1975 Act was born out of a perceived need for "race-neutral" categories of eligibility and non-discriminatory treatment of immigrants and is considered to be liberal in its approach.[9] The IRPA emerged out of the continuing racialization[10] of immigration, whereby immigrants of colour have come to be viewed not only as threats to the social cultural, and linguistic order of the nation, but also as threats to the security of the nation. Martin Rudner (2002: 24), for example, blames Canada's immigration policy for the presence of "large, identifiable homeland communities from societies in conflict," communities that presumably became an attractive arena for fostering international terrorist networks. These anti-immigrant sentiments are not new and were present in various forms during previous immigration debates. However, in recent times they occupy a greater role in framing immigration debates as a result of the negative representation of immigrants of colour by the media in Canada and the realignment of immigration policy-making towards a conservative agenda (Abu-Laban 1998; Teitelbaum and Winter 1998).

It would seem that public concerns and anxiety about immigrants and national security are linked to "perceived immigrant desirability and legitimacy," as Buchignani and Indra (1999: 416) remark, rather than to any real threat to Canada's borders or sovereignty. Garcia y Griego (1994: 120) concurs, stating, "Canada has never lost control over its borders, but it has, on more than one occasion, lost control over its own admission process." This state of affairs has been made possible through the belief that it is the "outsider," the migrant or foreign national, that poses the greatest threat and that this threat can only be contained by retaining a tighter control over the criteria for determining who can immigrate to Canada. This view is evident in statements made by Public Safety and Emergency Preparedness Canada (2004), which notes that "many of the real and direct threats to Canada originate from far beyond our borders."

The implication is that problems are imported into the country via immigrants and that only through the adoption of a security-driven, regulatory agenda will those problems be contained. Indeed, the flurry of immigration reforms post-9/11 is perhaps more a reflection of the government of the time demonstrating that it had matters under control than it is a proportionate response to security issues. What this allows for, as Maggie Ibrahim (2005: 169) points out, is the legitimization of new racist fears. Instead of focusing on how to support immigrants who are at risk, a security-driven approach emphasizes the need to protect citizens because the incorporation of immigrants will result in an unstable host state (Ibrahim 2005: 169). Of significant concern is that these sentiments are no longer being echoed by conservative, right-wing political parties and organizations only. They are also being legitimized by more liberal, humanitarian-focused groups such as the U.N. and liberal-minded academics (Ibrahim 2005).

Immigrants who do not fit into the predefined mould of what constitutes a "good immigrant" will increasingly become the target of the new security-focused state. It is no surprise that hate crimes have risen dramatically since 9/11 (Statistics Canada 2004) and that many people of colour speak of experiencing racial profiling on a daily basis at the hands of various law enforcement agents (Bahdi 2003). The public acceptance of racist treatment towards people of colour is evident in the way in which the Canadian mainstream media described Muslims during the June 2006 arrest of seventeen Muslim men in Canada. The *Globe and Mail*'s (2006) front-page story noted, "Parked directly outside his ... office was a large, gray, cube-shaped truck and, on the ground nearby, he recognized one of the two brown-skinned young men who had taken possession of the next door rented unit." As Robert Fisk points out, "What is 'brown-skinned' supposed to mean — if it is not just a revolting attempt to isolate Muslims as the 'Other' in Canada's

> Immigrants who do not fit into the predefined mould of what constitutes a "good immigrant" will increasingly become the target of the new security-focused state.

highly multicultural society?" (Fisk 2006). Backed into a corner, Muslim groups and organizations have no choice but to join this process of "Othering" by distancing themselves from the men arrested and attempting to calm an increasingly hostile public through reinforcing the idea of peace as the centrepiece of their religion (*Globe and Mail* 2006). Good Muslims, they argue, are not violent and do not engage in terrorist activities. Within all these discussions, it is clear that in a climate of fear, suspicion and hostility produced by the association between Muslims and terrorist activities, homogeneity becomes the default security blanket, now made all the more possible by the IRPA.

A close look at the enforcement provisions of the IRPA shows that the process of blaming and punishing immigrants allows for a "suitable enemy" to blame for the problems of society (Christie 1986). Few strategies are as effective as processes of criminalization for reinforcing an ideology of "us" and "them," with the immigrant, usually understood as non-white, poor, and/or female, occupying the status of the outsider (Bannerji 2000). The racialized, gendered and class-based nature of this marking ensures that in the construction and definition of who is Canadian access to this identity is far from equal. Casting immigrants into the role of the "other" has been beneficial in suppressing public fears and insecurities about immigrants "terrorizing" Canadians, taking jobs away from Canadians and overtaxing the welfare system.

As immigration authorities seek to reclaim their ability to secure Canada's borders, and to argue that the integrity of the immigration system has not been compromised by "illegal" migrants, an increase in the degree of punishment to offenders allows governments to demonstrate their power through the use of force. Such has been the case in the European Union, where resolutions and legislation were brought in to counter a broad range of terrorist activities (these include not just terrorist organizations, but also anti-globalization protests, animal rights activism and youth subcultures), resulting in the use of deportation and detention without trial against foreign nationals suspected of posing a security risk (Fekete 2004: 6).

Keeping Canada White

Historically, immigration control linked the decline of the nation with the sexual excesses and mental and moral degeneration of Aboriginal peoples and people of colour (Valverde 1991: 105). Racist ideas determined which groups of people would be regarded as having more character and thus be considered more "civilized." People of British descent were viewed as morally superior for their ability to self-regulate and exercise self-control (Valverde 1991: 105). Importantly, this position was not contested, but rather taken for granted by moral reformers at the turn of the century in Canada (Valverde 1991: 106). The historical studies on immigration by Barbara Roberts (1988) and Donald Avery (1995) confirm the presence of these beliefs. The Canadian government sought to attract the most desirable immigrants, which it had identified — not surprisingly — as white, British, English-speaking and Protestant. As Strange and Loo (1997: 117) note, "Determining who could become or remain Canadian was one more way to shape the moral character of the nation." Immigrants identified as "low quality" or morally degenerate would find

> Gendered and racialized ideologies shape the circumstances that define immigrants as undesirable.

themselves subjected to various forms of regulation, with deportation being the most drastic measure imposed. Here, gendered and racialized ideologies shaped the circumstances that would be defined as undesirable. For men, unemployment or left-wing affiliation were sufficient to warrant deportation, while for women, having children out of wedlock, carrying a disease like VD or tuberculosis or appearing to court more than one man would bring them to the attention of immigration officials (Strange and Loo 1997: 119). In terms of racial exclusions, simply being non-white was sufficient to be classified as undesirable. The exclusion of Black and Chinese people from Canada was made on the belief that they posed a moral threat that could not be overcome by any means, and therefore special measures needed to be taken to ensure that they did not corrupt the moral integrity of the nation (Bashi 2004; Strange and Loo 1997). Examples of measures taken included the *Chinese Immigration Act* in 1923, which excluded anyone of Chinese descent from immigrating to Canada, prohibiting the employment of white women by Asian employers and preventing Chinese people from forming families in Canada (Strange and Loo 1997: 120–21).

An overarching feature of immigration policies in Canada, both historically and at present, is to build a nation of people who fulfill the highest moral standards. As Strange and Loo (1997: 145) observe, ideals of purity, industry, piety and self-discipline were regarded as essential features of Canadianness. Few would argue that these standards continue to characterize and shape present-day immigration policies, often to the detriment of non-white immigrants seeking to come to Canada. Vukov (2003) points out how contemporary public articulations about desirable and undesirable immigrants in both the news media and governmental policy with respect to sexuality and security issues reinforce the long-standing fears that sexually deviant immigrants and criminals continue to threaten the process of replenishing and sustaining a secure population base. Likewise, Angel-Ajani (2003: 435) argues that this climate of anti-immigrant rhetoric relies on the dual discourses of criminalization and cultural difference. Within this climate of insecurity, a wide range of screening practices have been enacted to ensure that people belonging to designated groups are properly filtered out. The construction of Middle Eastern, West Asian and Muslim peoples as security threats to the nation since September 11, and the introduction of new policy measures to secure our border, underscore the ways in which definitions of undesirable immigrants are highly racialized (Vukov 2003: 345).

The narrative that emerges from the IRPA supports this vision of Canada, with the good immigrant reaffirming Canada's essential goodness and "the bad immigrant forcing otherwise generous people into taking stern disciplinary measures" (Razack 1999: 174). A critical component of this ongoing story is that "good" is equated with whiteness and with being Canadian, while "bad" is associated with being an immigrant, an outsider to the nation. Thobani's (2000) study of the Immigration Policy Review in 1994 highlights this most clearly. She found that throughout the public consultation process, Canadians expressed concerns that their national values were being eroded and degraded by immigrants who did not share these values (Thobani 2000: 44). While Canadians saw themselves as respectful, honest and hard working, immigrants were consistently represented as criminal, disease-ridden and lazy. Thobani notes that by placing immigrant values in the context of social and cultural diversity, definitions of immigrants and Canadians are reproduced in racialized terms. Audrey Kobayashi sums up the situation in asserting that immigration law is a central site for articulating how Canada imagines itself:

> Immigration law is in Canada one of the most significant cultural arenas, a contested territory wherein people's relations with one another and with the places they designate as home are expressed. To aid them in that expression, people have faith in the law; it establishes a moral landscape and it codifies our myths about ourselves. It is our recourse to defining ourselves and others, as well as a means of systematically reproducing our imagined reality. (1995: 71)

These comments highlight why the harsh treatment of immigrants, particularly immigrants of colour, is so uncontroversial. For to question how immigration practices are carried out within Canada would not just be a challenge to the fairness of the system, it would also call into question how Canada envisions itself. Such a challenge would be neither lightly accepted nor welcomed.

Scapegoating Immigrants

As the boundaries between insider and outsider become more ambivalent and converge with nostalgia for a bygone period of immigration, immigrants of colour are the ones classified and defined as inauthentic, "illegal" or outsiders. Anti-racists allege that racial identity remains a key marker of those who are not perceived as belonging, as "legitimate" immigrants of the nation. Even though Canada moved away from blatant forms of discrimination in its immigration policies in the 1960s and 1970s, racism and patriarchy continued to define spatial and/or social margins in portrayals of the dominant vision of the nation (Simmons 1998; Kobayashi 1995).

The racialization of immigration, which focuses on the process of constructing racial identities and meanings, enables ideas about "race" to proliferate. Now, cultural differences, rather than racial inferiority, become the distinguishing markers between us and them. Avtar Brah (1996: 165) writes that this form of racism is "a racism that combined a disavowal of biological superiority or inferiority with a focus on 'a way of life,' of cultural difference as the 'natural' basis for feelings of antagonism towards outsiders." This tendency has made it possible, for example, for recurring themes to continue to characterize immigration debates — themes alleging that too much racial diversity will lead to conflict, that immigrants have large families that expect to be supported by the welfare state, that immigrants are criminals with no respect for the law or that immigrant workers take jobs away because they are willing to work for low wages (Hintjens 1992). In Canada and other Western nations, immigrants are now required to speak the official languages as proof of their adequate assimilation into mainstream culture (Fekete 2004: 22). As Thobani (2000: 293) observes, such demands elevate Europeanness/whiteness over other cultures and ethnicities and clearly redefine the national Canadian identity as being "white" while seemingly appearing to be race-neutral.

The lack of public outcry over the treatment of immigrants in the new legislation suggests that the public's imagination has been captured in such a way that immigration is understood as a sign of Canada's decline. While Canada cannot do without immigrants, those who are admitted are expected to adhere to Canadian values and adopt a "Canadian" way of life. Non-compliance is not an option because the failure to assimilate has become a sign of being someone who is a potential contributor to uprisings and terrorist activities. While Canada has always been distrustful of racialized immigrants, the IRPA highlights how we need to find a "suitable enemy" for whom we can blame all our failures and insecurities. Recent amendments to the IRPA suggest that the emphasis on security and enforcement shows

> While Canada has always been distrustful of racialized immigrants, IRPA highlights how we need to find a "suitable enemy" for whom we can blame all our failures and insecurities.

no signs of abating. Russo points out that Harper's Conservative government accelerated the evolution of laws and policies linking law and order and security issues with immigration reform (Russo 2008).

Racialized immigrants have been, and continue to be, the scapegoats for a variety of economic and cultural insecurities (Beisel 1994). One consequence of this is that any benefits that immigrants provide to host societies like Canada are drowned out by the discourse of exclusion (*Toronto Star* 2006a). Yet it would be a mistake to believe that immigrants and those working within the immigrant community are unwittingly accepting the recent immigration reforms that construct refugees and asylum seekers as illegitimate and fraudulent. Although the Conservative government capitalized on the hardened public attitudes to bring forward an immigration reform agenda that marks only the most resourceful immigrants as "desirable," there remains a substantial number of Canadians who refuse to accept this portrayal of immigrants and refugees. By the end of their reign in government, a noticeable number of news articles pointed to a backlash against the Conservatives. Claims that Harper's Conservatives had forgotten about Canada's cherished tradition towards refugees and had taken the wrong path in managing the problem were more commonplace, as were criticisms about changes to the *Citizenship Act*. An opinion piece in the *Globe and Mail* captures this growing sentiment with the headline "A crying need to rework Canada's immigration policies" (*Globe and Mail* 2015) while another article in the *Toronto Star* newspaper asks "Has Canada's immigration system lost its heart?" (*Toronto Star* 2015).

The raft of punitive amendments implemented by the Conservative government has led to immigration advocacy groups developing a strong grassroots movement to challenge these reforms. Although largely hidden from public view, two recent gains made by immigration activists suggest that resistance to the immigration enforcement agenda has not been in vain. First, activists worked tirelessly to defeat efforts to deny health care to failed refugee claimants still in Canada. The Federal Court ruled that lack of access to health coverage while awaiting court processes in Canada was "cruel and unusual" treatment (CBC News 2014). Second, a ban on wearing niqabs at citizenship ceremonies was struck down and upheld by the Federal Court of Appeal, who stated that the ban violates the *Citizenship Act* as the greatest possible religious freedom must be allowed when administering the citizenship oath

(CBC News 2015). These victories suggest that there is a diverse range of views of immigrants and refugees, and many immigration advocacy groups continue to campaign and educate Canadians about the realities of migration. In addition, with the increasing support of the international community such as Human Rights Watch[11] and Amnesty International, current immigration and refugee reforms will be even more carefully scrutinized to ensure that Canada does not violate it's obligations to the global community. Audrey Macklin and Sean Rehaag sum it up:

> About 30,000 asylum seekers arrive in Canada each year. In the fall, shortly after the arrival of around 500 Tamils on a boat in British Columbia, some 30,000 Burmese refugees fled into neighbouring Thailand — over a period of 48 hours. Let's get some perspective. (*Toronto Star* 2010b)

Although it is an uphill battle, the path towards an inclusive and anti-racist immigration system in Canada continues to be fought on many different levels with numerous campaigns calling on the current Liberal government to take a humanitarian approach to immigrants and refugees. A recent decision by the Immigration Minister, John McCallum, to reverse the deportation order of a Roma family who had been persecuted in Hungary, but whose refugee claim was denied because their Toronto lawyer failed to adequately represent their case (CBC News 2016), is one of the many small victories that will shape how Canada treats its newcomers in the twenty-first century.

Glossary of Key Terms

Criminalize: Turning an activity into a criminal offence by making it illegal.

Deportation: The act of expelling a non-citizen from a country, usually on the grounds of illegal status or for having committed a crime.

Discrimination: The unjust or prejudicial treatment of different categories of people or things.

Immigrant: a person who comes to live permanently in a foreign country.

Protected person: A person who has been granted refugee protection by the government of Canada.

Refugee: A person in flight who seeks to escape conditions or personal circumstances found to be intolerable.

Smuggling: Consensual transactions where the transporter and the transportee agree to circumvent immigration control for mutually advantageous reasons.

Trafficking: The recruitment, transportation, transfer, harbouring, or receipt of persons, by means of the threat or use of force or other forms of coercion.

Questions for Discussion

1. Do you think immigration control is possible without engaging in racist or discriminatory behaviour?

2. How can we balance issues of security and enforcement with a more humanitarian approach? Are the two approaches incompatible?

3. How can we create a more welcoming and inclusive society for immigrants and refugees?

4. Should refugees who arrive in Canada via irregular means (e.g., on a boat with others) be treated differently than refugees who arrive through regular channels (e.g., on a plane)?

Resources for Activists

Border Criminologies: law.ox.ac.uk/research-subject-groups/centre-criminology/centreborder-criminologies

Canadian Association of Refugee Lawyers: carl-acaadr.ca

Canadian Council for Refugees: ccrweb.ca/

End Immigration Detention Network: endimmigrationdetention.com/

International Human Rights Program, University of Toronto: law.utoronto.ca/programs-centres/programs/international-human-rights-program

Migrations Map: migrationsmap.net/#/CAN/arrivals

Mosaic: mosaicbc.com

No One Is Illegal Vancouver: noii-van.resist.ca/

Notes

This chapter is an updated version of Wendy Chan, "Illegal Immigrants and Bill C-11: The Criminalization of Race," *What Is a Crime?* Law Commission of Canada (ed.), Vancouver: UBC Press: 2002.

1. With the point system, immigrants would be assessed on the basis of age, education, language skills and economic characteristics and be assigned points for each of these categories. Applicants who had a sufficient number of points would be eligible for entry (Boyd and Vickers 2000).

2. For more details about the investor's program, see Citizenship and Immigration Canada website: <cic.gc.ca/english/immigrate/business/iivc/>.

3. The Live-In Caregivers program underwent significant changes in December 2014 (*Toronto Star* 2014b). See Citizenship and Immigration Canada (CIC) website for information about the program: <cic.gc.ca/ENGLISH/work/caregiver/index.asp>.

4. Critics of this program have pointed out how many women are exploited and ill-treated by their employers. See Oxman-Martinez 2004; and Langevin and Belleau 2000.

5. A Convention refugee is anyone who holds a well-founded fear of persecution based on one or more of five grounds as defined in the U.N. Convention Relating to the Status of Refugees: reasons of race, religion, nationality, membership in a particular social group, or political opinion. See Galloway 1997.

6. According to its website, maytree.com, "The Maytree Foundation is a Canadian charitable foundation established in 1982. Maytree believes that there are three fundamental issues that threaten political and social stability: wealth disparities between and within nations; mass migration of people because of war, oppression and environmental disasters, and the degradation of the environment."

7. The public reaction to the Chinese migrants was generally one of hostility; they tended to be regarded as "bogus" refugees. Many of them were detained and eventually deported back to China. See briefs by Coalition for a Just Immigration and Refugee Policy 2001; NAWL 2001; the Getting Landed Project 2002; African Canadian Legal Clinic 2001; UNHCR 2001.

8. Supporters of the migrants argued the government had overreacted in this situation, while critics contended that the government needed to take harsher measures.

9. This view of the 1975 *Immigration Act* has been challenged by critical immigration scholars who contend that, while the Act did not directly discriminate against particular racial and ethnic groups, the outcome of the point system nonetheless resulted in differential access to immigration. See Thobani 2000; Jakubowski 1997.

10. Racialization "refers to the historical emergence of the idea of 'race' and to its subsequent reproduction and application" (Miles 1989: 76). This suggests that the criminalization of certain racialized groups within the Canadian context can be understood, first, in light of the ways in which white, majority groups have been constructed as race-less, and, second, within the context of historical relations between First Nations peoples, early settlers and recent immigrants and migrants.

11. Human Rights Watch 2011, "Open Letter to Canada's Prime Minister Stephen Harper and Federal Party Leaders on Human Rights Priorities," May 9. <hrw.org/en/news/2011/05/09/open-letter-canada-s-prime-minister-stephen-harper-and-federal-party-leaders-human-r>.

References

Abu-Laban, Y. 1998. "Welcome/Stay Out: The Contradiction of Canadian Integration and Immigration Policies at the Millennium." *Canadian Ethnic Studies* 30.

Abu-Laban, Y., and C. Gabriel. 2002. *Selling Diversity*. Peterborough: Broadview Press.

African Canadian Legal Clinic. 2001. "Brief to the Legislative Review Secretariat." <aclc.ne>.

Alboim, N., and K. Cohl. 2012. "Shaping the future: Canada's rapidly changing immigration policies." The Maytree Foundation. October. <maytree.com/wp-content/uploads/2012/10/shaping-the-future.pdf>.

Amnesty International. 2010. "Refugee Rights Must Be Protected in Anti-Smuggling Legislation." <amnesty.ca/iwriteforjustice/take_action.php?actionid=540&type=Internal>.

Angel-Ajani, A. 2003. "A Question of Dangerous Races?" *Punishment and Society* 5.

Avery, D. 1995. *Reluctant Host: Canada's Response to Immigrant Workers 1896–1994*. Toronto: McClelland and Stewart.

Bahdi, R. 2003. "No Exit: Racial Profiling and Canada's War Against Terrorism." *Osgoode Hall Law Journal* 41.

Bannerji, H. 2000. "The Paradox of Diversity: The Construction of a Multicultural Canada and 'Women of Colour.'" *Women's Studies International Forum* 23.

Bashi, V. 2004. "Globalized Anti-Blackness: Transnationalizing Western Immigration Law, Policy and Practice." *Ethnic and Racial Studies* 27.

Beisel, D. 1994. "Looking for Enemies, 1990–1994." *Journal of Psychohistory* 22, 1.

Bhabha, J. 2005. "Trafficking, Smuggling and Human Rights." *Migration Information Source* March.

Boyd, M., and M. Vickers. 2000. "100 years of immigration to Canada." *Canadian Social Trends* 58.

Brah, A. 1996. *Cartographies of Diaspora: Contesting Identities*. New York: Routledge.

Buchignani, N., and D. Indra. 1999. "Vanishing Acts: Illegal Immigration in Canada as a Sometimes Social Issue." In D. Haines and K. Rosenblum (eds.), *Illegal Immigration in America*. Westport, CT: Greenwood Press.

Burnaby Now. 2010. "Send illegal migrants back." August 18.

Canadian Press. 2001. "U.N. Rights Report Criticizes Canada for Treating Migrants Like Criminals." April 12.

CBC Online. 1999a. "Officials Recommend Migrants Remain in Custody." September 2. <cbc.ca/story/canada/national/1999/09/02/migrants990902.html>.

____. 1999b. "Department Seeks More Teeth to Detain Migrants." September 23. <cbc.ca/news/canada/dept-seeks-more-teeth-to-detain-migrants-1.193774>.

____. 1999c. "Chinese Migrants Denied Due Process, Critics Charge." November 5. <refugees1.freeservers.com/nov6cbcradio.htm>.

____. 2014. "Refugee health-cuts ruling appealed by Ottawa." October 1. <cbc.ca/news/politics/refugee-health-cuts-ruling-appealed-by-ottawa-1.2783819>.

____. 2015. "Niqab ban at citizenship ceremonies unlawful, as Ottawa loses appeal." September 15. <cbc.ca/news/politics/niqab-ruling-federal-court-government-challenge-citizenship-ceremonies-1.3229206>.

____. 2016. "Deported Roma refugee family receives permission to return to Canada." February 8. <cbc.ca/news/canada/toronto/roma-refugee-canada-return-1.3437968>.

CBSA (Canadian Border Services Agency). 2010. "CBSA Detentions and Removals Programs: Evaluation Study." <cbsa-asfc.gc.ca/agency-agence/reports-rapports/ae-ve/2010/dr-rd-eng.html>.

____. 2014. Number of Detainees on Immigration Hold 2011-2013 and Average Detention Days Per Detainee. Documents obtained through Freedom of Information Act (A-2014-00687 QC LN).

CCR (Canadian Council for Refugees). 2000. "A Hundred Years of Immigration to Canada 1900–1999: A Chronology Focusing on Refugees and Discrimination." <ccrweb.ca/history.html>.

____. 2001. "Bill C-11 Brief." <ccrweb.ca/en/library?page=3>.

____. 2010a. "C-47-Key Concerns." <ccrweb.ca/en/c49-key-concerns>.

____. 2010b. "Some Comments on Bill C-49." <ccrweb.ca/en/comment-c49>.

____. 2010c. "Refugee Reform: Weighing the Proposals." <ccrweb.ca/en/refugee-reform>.

____. 2015. "Sun Sea: Five years later. July 2015." <ccrweb.ca/en/sun-sea-five-years-later>.

Christie, N. 1986. "Suitable Enemies." In H. Bianchi and R. van Swaaningen (eds.), *Abolitionism: Towards a Non-Repressive Approach to Crime*. Amsterdam: Free University Press.

CIC (Citizenship and Immigration Canada). 2001a. *Facts and Figures 2000: Immigration Overview*. Ottawa: Minister of Public Works and Government Services.

____. 2001b. "Bill C-11 — Immigration and Refugee Protection Act: Overview." <cic.gc.ca/english/irpa/c11-overview.html>.

____. 2014. *Canada Facts and Figures 2013: Immigrant Overview-Temporary Residents*. Ottawa: CIC Research and Evaluation Branch.

____. 2015. *Canada Facts and Figures 2014: Immigrant Overview-Permanent Residents*. Ottawa: CIC Research and Evaluation Branch.

Coalition for a Just Immigration and Refugee Policy. 2001 "Position Paper on Bill C-11." Toronto.

Creese, G. 1992. "The Politics of Refugees in Canada." In V. Satzewich (ed.), *Deconstructing A Nation*. Halifax: Fernwood Publishing.

Crepeau, F., and E. Jimenez. 2004. "Foreigners and the Right to Justice in the Aftermath of 9/11."

International Journal of Law and Psychiatry 27.

Crepeau, F., and D. Nakache. 2006. "Controlling Irregular Migration in Canada." *IRPP Choices* 12, 1.

Davergne, C. 2004. "Sovereignty, Migration and the Rule of Law in Global Times." *Modern Law Review* 67.

Dawson, C. 2014. "Refugee Hotels: The Discourse of Hospitality and the Rise of Immigration Detention in Canada." *University of Toronto Quarterly* 83.

Dent, J. 2002. "No Right of Appeal: Bill C-11, Criminality, and the Human Rights of Permanent Residents Facing Deportation." *Queen's Law Journal* 27.

DFAIT (Department of Foreign Affairs and International Trade). 2004. "Canada's Actions against Terrorism since September 11." <dfait-maeci.gc.ca/anti-terrorism/canadaactions-en.asp>.

Economic Council of Canada. 1991. *New Faces in the Crowd: Economic and Social Impacts of Immigration.* Ottawa: Economic Council of Canada, Study No. 22-171.

Fekete, L. 2004. "Anti-Muslim Racism and the European Security State." *Race and Class* 46.

Fisk, R. 2006. "Has Racism Invaded Canada?" <counterpunch.org/2006/06/12/has-racism-invaded-canada/>.

Frideres, J. 1996. "Canada's Changing Immigration Policy: Implications for Asian Immigrants." *Asian and Pacific Migration Journal* 5.

Galloway, D. 1997. *Immigration Law.* Concord, ON: Irwin.

Garcia y Griego, M. 1994. "Canada: Flexibility and Control in Immigration and Refugee Policy." In W. Cornelius, P. Martin, and J. Hollifield (eds.), *Controlling Immigration: A Global Perspective.* Stanford: Stanford University Press.

Getting Landed Project. 2002. "Protecting the Unprotected: Submission to the House of Commons Standing Committee on Citizenship and Immigration." <cpj.ca/story-getting-landed-project>.

Globe and Mail. 2006. "Terrorism Cases Strikingly Similar." June 10.

____. 2014. "Canada must see immigration as a competitive edge." May 12.

____. 2015. "A crying need to rework Canada's immigration policies." September 18.

Haigh, R., and J. Smith 1998. "Return of the Chancellor's Foot? Discretion in Permanent Resident Deportation Appeals under the Immigration Act." *Osgoode Hall Law Journal* 36.

Hassan-Gordon, T. 1996. "Canada's Immigration Policy — Detention and Deportation of Non-Europeans." <hartford-hwp.com/archives/44/032.html>.

Hintjens, H.M. 1992. "Immigration and Citizenship Debates: Reflections on Ten Common Themes." *International Migration* 30.

Ibrahim, M. 2005. "The Securitization of Migration: A Racial Discourse." *International Migration* 43.

Jakubowski, L. 1997. *Immigration and the Legalization of Racism.* Halifax: Fernwood Publishing.

Kelley, N., and M. Trebilcock. 1998. *The Making of the Mosaic: A History of Canadian Immigration Policy.* Toronto: University of Toronto Press.

Kobayashi, A. 1995. "Challenging the National Dream: Gender Persecution and Canadian Immigration Law." In P. Fitzpatrick (ed.), *Nationalism, Racism and the Rule of Law.* Aldershot: Dartmouth.

Langevin, L., and M. Belleau. 2000. "Trafficking in Women in Canada: A Critical Analysis of the Legal Framework Governing Immigrant Live-in Caregivers and Mail-Order Brides." Ottawa: Status of Women Canada. <publications.gc.ca/site/eng/238946/publication.html>.

Li, P. 2001. "The Racial Subtext in Canada's Immigration Discourse." *Journal of International Migration and Integration* 2, 1.

____. 2003. *Destination Canada.* Don Mills: Oxford University Press.

Marchi, S. 1995. "Speech: Tougher Tools For Deporting Criminals." *Canadian Speeches* 9 (August/September).

Matas, D. 1989. *Closing the Doors: The Failure of Refugee Protection*. Toronto: Summerhill.

Maytree Foundation. 2001. "Brief to the Senate Committee on Social Affairs, Science and Technology regarding Bill C-11, Immigration and Refugee Protection Act." Toronto, October. <maytree.com/Publications&Resources/Publications /SenateBriefBillC11.htm>.

Miles, Robert. 1989. *Racism*. London: Routledge.

Morrison, J., and B. Crosland. 2001. "The Trafficking and Smuggling of Refugees: The End Game of European Asylum Policy?" Independent Expert Report/UNHCR Working Paper 38. <unhcr.org/research/working/3af66c9b4/trafficking-smuggling-refugees-end-game-european-asylum-policy-john-morrison.html>.

National Post. 2011. "Immigrants Cost $23B a Year: Fraser Institute Report." May 17.

NAWL (National Association of Women and the Law). 2001. "Brief on the Proposed Immigration and Refugee Protection Act (Bill C-11)." <nawl.ca/en/issues/entry/brief-on-the-proposed-immigration-and-refugee-protection-act-bill-c-11-memo>.

____. 2006. "Update: Immigration and Refugee Protection Act and Women." <nawl.ca/ns/en/is-irl.html#update>.

Noorani, A., and C. Wright. 1995. "They Believed the Hype: The Liberals Were Elected as 'the Friend of the Immigrant': A Year Later, They're Fanning the Flames of Crime Hysteria with their New Pals, the Tabloids and Preston Manning." *This Magazine* 28 (December/January).

Oxman-Martinez, J.H., and L. Cheung. 2004. "Another Look at the Live-in Caregivers Program." Metropolis Research Report No. 24. <migrantworkersrights.net/en/resources/another-look-at-the-live-in-caregivers-program-an-a>.

Palmer, D. 1996. "Determinants of Canadian Attitudes Toward Immigration: More than Just Racism?" *Canadian Journal of Behavioural Science* 28.

Public Safety and Emergency Preparedness Canada. 2004. "Securing Canada: Laying the Groundwork for Canada's First National Security Policy." <circ.jmellon.com/agencies/psc/>.

Razack, S. 1999. "Law and the Policing of Bodies of Colour in the 1990s." *Canadian Journal of Law and Society* 14.

Roach, K. 2005. "Canada's Response to Terrorism." In V. Ramraj, M. Hor, and K. Roach (eds.), *Global Anti-terrorism Law and Policy*. Oxford: Cambridge University Press.

Roberts, B. 1988. *Whence They Came: Deportation From Canada, 1900–1935*. Ottawa: University of Ottawa.

Robinson, W.G. 1983. "Illegal Migrants in Canada: A Report to the Honourable Lloyd Axworthy, Minister of Employment and Immigration." Ottawa: Employment and Immigration Canada.

Rudner, M. 2002. "The Globalization of Terrorism: Canada's Intelligence Response to the Post-September 11 Threat Environment." *Canadian Issues* 24 (September).

Russo, Robert. 2008. "Security, Securitization and Human Capital: The New Wave of Canadian Immigration Laws." *World Academy of Science, Engineering and Technology* 44.

Simmons, A. 1998. "Globalization and Backlash Racism in the 1990s: The Case of Asian Immigration to Canada." In E. Lacquian, A. Lacquian, and T. McGee (eds.), *The Silent Debate: Asian Immigration and Racism in Canada*. Vancouver: Institute of Asian Research.

Standing Committee on Citizenship and Immigration. 2001. *Hands Across the Border: Working Together at Our Shared Border and Abroad to Ensure Safety, Security and Efficiency*. Ottawa: Public Works.

Statistics Canada. 2004. "Pilot Survey of Hate Crime." June 1. <statcan.gc.ca/daily-quotidien/040601/dq040601a-eng.htm>.

Strange, C., and T. Loo. 1997. *Making Good: Law and Moral Regulation in Canada, 1867–1939*. Toronto: University of Toronto Press.

Teitelbaum, M., and J. Winter. 1998. *A Question of Numbers: High Migration, Low Fertility and the Politics of National Identity*. New York: Hill and Wang.

Thobani, S. 2000. "Closing Ranks: Racism and Sexism in Canada's Immigration Policy." *Race and Class* 42, 35.

Toronto Star. 2006a. "Letter To Editor: 'Afraid Every Morning I Wake Up.'" May 28.

____. 2010a. "Anger Greets Asylum-Seekers." August 16.

____. 2010b. "Playing Politics with Refugees." December 3.

____. 2014a. "Red Cross uncovers problems facing Canadian immigration detainees." September 25.

____. 2014b. "Ottawa to cap number of foreign caregivers in Canada." October 31.

____. 2015. "Has Canada's immigration system lost its heart?" May 31.

UNHCR (United Nations High Commissioner for Refugees). 2001. "Comments on Bill C-11: Submission to the House of Commons Standing Committee on Citizenship and Immigration." Ottawa, March. <ccrweb.ca/c11hcr.PDF>.

____. 2015. *Asylum Trends 2014*. <unhcr.org/cgi-bin/texis/vtx/search?page=&comid=4146b6fc4&cid=49aea93aba&keywords=Trends>.

Valverde, Mariana. 1991. *The Age of Soap, Light and Water: Moral Reform in English Canada, 1885–1925*. Toronto: McClelland & Stewart.

Vancouver Province. 2010. "Migrants' Journey Treacherous." August 16.

Vukov, T. 2003. "Imagining Communities Through Immigration Policies." *International Journal of Cultural Studies* 6.

5

Crime as a Social Problem

Social Inequality and Justice

James Popham and Les Samuelson

> ## YOU SHOULD KNOW THIS
>
> - The richest 10 percent of Canadians control nearly 50 percent of the country's wealth
> - Approximately 30 percent of Indigenous persons in Canada, 16 percent of women and 20 percent of racialized persons live below the poverty line
> - Self-reported crime rates do not differ among socio-economic groups
> - Two-thirds of federally incarcerated inmates in Canada have a history of unemployment
> - In 2015 the average cost for a one-day criminal defense in Canada was $6,992
> - As of 2015, one in four incarcerated persons in Canada were Indigenous, compared to 4.3 percent of the population; Indigenous women account for 35 percent of the incarcerated female population, effectively doubling in number since 2004
> - Despite being directed by the 1992 *Corrections and Conditional Release Act* to better support incarcerated Indigenous persons, Correctional Service Canada established just sixty-eight healing lodge beds for federally sentenced men and none for federally sentenced women.
> - During the 2014–15 fiscal year, Canada Revenue Agency pursued 125 suspected cases of tax evasion, of which 95 were convicted. Thirty-four individuals were incarcerated with an average sentence of twenty months.
>
> Sources: Jackson 2015; Statistics Canada 2011; Antonaccio et al. 2010; Canada 2015; McKiernan 2015; Canada Revenue Agency 2016.

ON MARCH 2, 1995, THIRTY-THREE YEAR OLD Jerry Dewayne Williams of Compton, California was sentenced 25 years to life in prison. He had stolen a slice of pizza. A year earlier, the state of California had passed a "three-strikes" law designed to incapacitate offenders who had at least two prior convictions for serious or violent crimes and were before the courts again. Any new felony conviction would automatically trigger this sentence. Until being repealed in 2013, the three-strikes law added nine thousand new life sentences to the state's prison population, disproportionately affecting young, impoverished, black men like Williams (*New York Times* 1995; Zimring, Hawkins and Kamin 2003).

Two decades after Williams' conviction, 16-year-old Ethan Anthony Couch of Keller, Texas, was sentenced to ten years of probation. He killed four people when he drove his pickup truck into a stalled vehicle while intoxicated. Couch's defence attorney had successfully argued that he was afflicted with "affluenza," a condition in which his wealth had provided him with "a mental condition [that] prevented him from linking his behaviour with consequences" (Douds et al. 2016). Legal provisions in both state and federal law allow for the consideration of socio-economic status as a mitigating factor in criminal trials, particularly for youth. In Couch's case, his wealthy background was leveraged as a defence against his reckless behaviours.

How can such travesties occur in a system that is intended to be objective? Why is the justice system so unjust? Jeffrey Reiman and Paul Leighton (2013) answer these questions in their compelling book *The Rich Get Richer and the Poor Get Prison*. As the title says, Reiman and Leighton argue that the U.S. justice system is fractured along economic lines, providing shelter and immunity from justice to those of the middle and upper classes of society. This division is symptomatic of an American ideology of justice that labels the poorest members of society as "typical criminals," exaggerating their harm to society. In fact, Reiman and Leighton observe:

> *For the same criminal behaviour,* the poor are more likely to be arrested; if arrested, they are more likely to be charged; if charged, more likely to be convicted; if convicted, more likely to be sentenced to prison; and if sentenced, more likely to be given longer prison terms than members of the middle and upper classes. (119; emphasis in original)

The authors could therefore argue that Jerry Williams and Ethan Couch were treated differently because they fall on opposing sides of the American ideology, precipitated by their relative economic power: Williams lived in poverty as a member of California's black working class, while Couch lived an insulated lifestyle amongst Texas's elite.

While Reiman and Leighton's focus is on economic inequality and its role in maintaining the "evils of the social order" (179), the true contribution from their research is identifying the often subtle ways in which systems of belief ("common sense") shape the treatment of marginalized populations within the justice system. They identify the instrumental (implicit) and structural (tacit) ways that social, media and political forces collude to inform public opinions about criminality by creating and replicating biases that manifest as ideology. In other words, our perceptions about crime are manipulated, sometimes intentionally, to reproduce "common sense" knowledge about "good guys" and "bad guys." For instance, viewers of csi: *Las Vegas* are subjected to depictions of killers that subtly link "racialized and poor subjects to anti-social, spontaneous, explosive, or random violence, embodying senseless acts of low or no self-control" (Bonnycastle 2009: 161). Such imagery is just one of the many forms in which perspectives can be subtly re-defined; regardless of format, instrumental and structural influences on ideology should be understood as means to emphasize arbitrary and unfounded divides in the public psyche.

Unfortunately, ideological divides in the administration of justice are not unique to the United States — indeed, scholars across the globe have

> Our perceptions about crime are manipulated, sometimes intentionally, to reproduce "common sense" knowledge about "good guys" and "bad guys."

identified the role of economic power in justice matters at all levels. Moreover, critical criminologists have repeatedly emphasized that our society is also characterized by other inequalities of power based upon class, race and gender: these analyses focus on how socio-legal practices reinforce class-based inequalities, the patriarchal subjugation of women and injustice for Indigenous peoples. These inequalities generate differences of involvement and treatment within our criminal justice system, from what is defined as crime, to the responses of criminal justice personnel to offenders and victims. Therefore, this chapter discusses the gaps in the Canadian way of justice *beyond* economic disparity, focusing on class, race and gender. Although each of these inequalities intersect with poverty, we argue that differences of treatment in the Canadian criminal justice system are often based on arbitrarily defined characteristics. These characteristics can be attributed to both activities *and* individuals, and are reflective of dominant ideologies rather than the level of "harm." Thus, for critical criminologists, a central "justice" concern is with how underlying social inequalities and processes operate to bring marginalized/oppressed people into the criminal justice system, while privileged individuals — if dealt with at all — tend to be treated leniently.

Class and Crime

Reiman and Leighton (2013) explain that the class-biased nature of law has two basic dimensions; one is the structure of the law, which generally means the legal codes and regulations that define harmful behaviours, and the second is the application of justice, which refers to the criminal justice processes that are used to identify and punish wrongdoers. Both dimensions are strongly influenced by wealthy individuals and corporations who use their advantageous social positions to indemnify themselves from responsibility. Furthermore, critical theorists hold that a relatively small group of individuals control much of the wealth and political power in our society while also maintaining relatively low profiles within the criminal justice system. In Canada, we have witnessed a rapid expansion of the income gap over the past four decades:

> While Canada falls well short of U.S. levels of inequality, the OECD notes, [Canada has] become much a more unequal since the early 1980s. Today, the top 10% own almost half of all wealth. According to the latest rankings, for 2013, the top 100 Canadians now collectively have a net worth of $230 Billion. This elite group are all worth more than $728 Million, and will likely soon consist entirely of billionaires.... Looking at income, the top 1% of Canadians now receive 12% of all taxable income, up sharply from 7% in the early 1980s. Over one half of all taxable income from capital gains goes to taxpayers earning more than $250,000 per year. (5)

Combined, these factors show a concentrated and highly influential pool of economic power that can be leveraged to dramatically shape the Canadian criminal justice system. While not necessarily acting in unison, these powerful members of society are often able to influence political-legal processes so that both the structure of the law and also the administration of justice overlooks the social, economic and physical harms inflicted upon society by them and the corporations they control. Put bluntly:

Corporate actors regularly and repeatedly violate … standards of moral and legal behaviour, do much more physical and economic harm than any other violators of these standards, and continue to be treated as upright members of our society, giving meaning to Clarence Darrow's aphorism that most people classified as criminals are "persons with predatory instincts without sufficient capital to form a corporation." (Glasbeek 2002: 118)

The tragic events in Lac-Mégantic, Quebec, represent a culmination of these effects. In the early hours of July 16, 2013, a train of seventy-two oil tankers operated by the Montreal, Maine, and Atlantic Railway Ltd. (MMA) carrying 7.7 million litres of crude oil derailed in Lac-Magentic's central business district. Many of the tank cars ruptured, flooding the streets with a highly flammable type of oil that ignited and exploded almost immediately. The catastrophic chain of events killed forty-seven people and destroyed an entire community in Quebec's Eastern Townships. Yannick Gangé, proprietor of the local cafe where many of the victims perished, recounted his experiences from that evening to the press:

> The exclusive members of society are often able to influence political–legal processes so that both the structure of the law and the administration of justice overlook the social, economic, and physical harms inflicted upon society by corporations and their elite.

While I was looking towards downtown the ground shook, the electricity cut out and a fireball turned the sky orange. I thought a meteor had hit.… One of my employees was calling [on the phone]. She was screaming, telling me that she was running away, that everything was on fire, it was chaos, the restaurant was gone, everything was gone, and people were still inside. I told her to calm down, that I'd go see. I got into the car and turned towards the Musi-Café. I saw the wagons blocking the road. I couldn't pass. There was a wall of fire hundreds of feet high. My kids were screaming and crying. I turned the car around. Then I started crying like a child. (Giovannetti 2013: 2)

In its review of the Lac-Mégantic disaster, the Canadian Transportation and Safety Board identified eighteen causes and contributing factors to the derailment and explosion, as well as sixteen findings as to risk. Many of these issues — including "[a] weak safety culture," "not having emergency assistance plans" and "ineffective training and oversight on train securement" — resulted from intentional decisions and attributable actions at MMA's executive level (Transportation Safety Board of Canada 2014: 10); however, no criminal charges were laid against MMA or its executives (Snider 2015). When criminal charges were finally laid months after the tragic events at Lac-Mégantic, they were directed at junior employees of MMA and the sole crew member operating the doomed train (Snider 2015), leaving many observers frustrated with the justice processes. Snider (2015) explains that this scapegoating approach diverted attention away from corporate malfeasance and failures of regulation.

Sadly, Canada has endured a legacy of tragic events brought on by corporate misdeeds.

The list below provides a number of examples that are similar in circumstance to the Lac-Mégantic disaster. An important observation here is that for each of these incidents official inquiries applied at least *some* of the blame to negligence at the corporate/executive levels of involved businesses and to date no criminal charges have been laid at the corporate/executive level (although in some cases, non-criminal charges and fines have been applied).

- 1982: The *Ocean Ranger* offshore oil rig, operating in the North Atlantic Ocean near St. John's Newfoundland, claimed eighty-four lives when the rig sunk in rough seas. A royal commission on the tragedy identified ineffective safety procedures and equipment.
- 1992: The Westray coal mine explosion in Plymouth, Nova Scotia, occurred when excessive coal dust in the shafts ignited, killing twenty-seven miners. Investigations determined that ineffective abatement procedures and lax safety measures contributed to the tragedy.
- 1997: The St. Joseph bus accident killed forty-three tourists and the driver when the bus's brakes failed and it plunged over a cliff near Les Éboulements, Quebec. A public inquiry later revealed that the bus was in poor repair and that the driver had been over worked.
- 2000: The Walkerton, Ontario, E. coli outbreak killed one person and affected more than 2,500 when unqualified workers were tasked with maintaining the town's water quality.
- 2003: A pipeline explosion in Etobicoke, Ontario, killed seven people and destroyed several buildings. An investigation revealed cost-cutting measures as a major precipitating factor.
- 2008: A series of explosions at the Sunrise Propane facility in North York, Ontario, killed two people and caused thousands to be evacuated from nearby homes. Later investigations found that the company had instructed employees to undertake illegal gas-transfer procedures.
- 2012: A roof collapse at the Eastwood Mall in Elliot Lake, Ontario, killed two people and injured twenty more. Investigations identified thirty years of negligent actions by the corporations who had pressured engineers to approve shoddy workmanship.
- 2012: Explosions at the Lakeland Mills facility in Prince George, British Columbia, killed two workers and injured many more. Inquiries by the B.C. Safety Authority determined that the incident was due to a failure to effectively recognize and manage explosion hazards.
- 2014: A fire at the Résidence du Havre nursing home in L'Isle-Verte, Quebec, killed thirty-two seniors, many of whom were immobile. A *commission d'enquête* found a number of safety issues related to the tragedy, such as leaving one overnight employee responsible for the entire facility.

The 1992 Westray mine explosion, listed above, provides a telling example of the divided nature of justice in Canada. Prior to the disaster, fifty-two non-criminal breaches of health and safety standards had been recorded at the mine, yet none had resulted in substantial changes to the unsafe working conditions or management policies. This is due, in part, to the non-confrontational manner of provincial and federal workplace safety regulations: the patchwork of legislation designed to protect Canadian workers offers few immediately enforceable sanctions against workplaces in violations (MacEachen et al. 2016). Additionally, research has demonstrated that Canadians experiencing precarious employment often avoid complaining about compromises to safety for fear of losing their jobs (Tucker and Turner 2013). After the explosion at Westray, an investigative royal commission concluded: "Westray management, starting with the chief executive officer, was required by law, by good business practice, and by good conscience to design and operate the Westray mine safely. Westray management failed in this primary responsibility" (Richard 1997). Despite findings, all of the non-criminal charges against the corporation were withdrawn. Subsequent to a final Supreme Court of Canada decision in March 2007, prosecution against two mine managers charged with twenty-six accounts of manslaughter and criminal negligence causing death was abandoned. Importantly, on March 31, 2004, Bill C-45, also known as the "Westray Bill," amended the *Criminal Code* to establish new legal duties and imposed serious penalties for workplace injuries or death; however, the Canadian Centre for Occupational Health and Safety (ccohs) reports that to date there have only been eight charges laid under this law (ccohs 2016).

A defining feature in these incidents is the role of economic power in determining who will and who will not be held accountable for the damages and loss of life experienced. A systematic pattern of downloading responsibility is apparent: guilt is passed down the chain of command until reaching an individual or entity who is unable to leverage economic power in their defence. In a sense, this pattern mirrors the social theory of individualization raised by Beck-Gersheim (2009), which explains that one must be able to negotiate risks that were traditionally governed by the state in order to succeed at life, and the easiest way to do so is to pass them on to others. Thus we see a domino effect where "citizens are in effect being asked (actually, they are not being asked) to bear greater risks — risks of which they are largely unaware, and have little or no role in establishing — so that corporations can increase their profits" (Campbell 2013: 17).

The risks that are thrust upon citizens entail both physical and economic harms. Consider, for example, the sub-prime mortgage crisis of 2008 and the worldwide recession that it instigated. Through the decade leading up to the September 2008 market collapse, hundreds of major financial institutions and thousands of traders were complicit in illegal, avoidable actions that were undertaken to maximize profit over public safety (Financial Crisis Inquiry Commission 2011). As Roberts explains, the economically powerful were gambling with other people's money:

> In the current crisis, commercial banks, investment banks, and Fannie and Freddie generated large short-term profits using extreme leverage. These short-term profits alongside rapid growth justified enormous salaries until the collapse came. Who lost when this game collapsed? In almost all cases, the lenders who financed the

growth avoided the costs. The taxpayers got stuck with the bill.... Ultimately, the gamblers were playing with other people's money and not their own. (2010: 16)

While there were no immediate physical harms from the rapid devaluation of investments and savings, the 2008 financial meltdown catapulted millions of people into extreme emotional duress as they watched their retirement plans dissolve and the forfeiture of their homes. Deregulation of the U.S. financial sector allowed the executives at two major government-sponsored lending agencies — the Federal National Mortgage Association ("Fannie Mae") and the Federal Home Loan Mortgage Corporation ("Freddie Mac") — to use their investors' wealth irresponsibly, while private financial services and banking institutions like the Lehman Brothers, Merill Lynch, Morgan Stanley and Goldman Sachs leveraged similar loopholes to gamble billions of investment dollars (Financial Crisis Inquiry Commission 2011). As the financial crisis unravelled, many of these organizations declared bankruptcy and engaged in actions tantamount to theft from shareholders, or the public.

All told, the irresponsible actions of economically powerful members of society directly harmed millions of people in North America, and billions more worldwide. As of 2011, an estimated 26 million Americans were unemployed as a direct result of the financial crisis. Similarly, $11 trillion was drained from household savings. Major banks JPMorgan Chase and Citigroup closed their doors and jeopardized the financial security of millions (Financial Crisis Inquiry Commission 2011). The impact of the financial meltdown was felt in Canada too: The Caisse de dépôt et placement du Québec, Canada's largest pension fund, reported losses of $39.8 billion jeopardizing the savings of millions of workers; and major employers like Chrysler and General Motors faced bankruptcy, ultimately shedding thousands of manufacturing jobs in Southern Ontario (Mendleson 2012). As of 2016, the financial crisis continues to impact Canada — for example, the national youth unemployment rate in Canada peaked at just over 16 percent following the 2008 crisis and now hovers just below 14 percent, three points above its pre-2008 low of 11 percent (Trading Economics 2016). Despite such harms, the U.S. and Canadian governments have been reluctant to criminally sanction the leaders of the complicit financial institutions. To clarify, only one executive was imprisoned as a result of the 2008 financial crisis. While fines amounting to approximately $190 billion *have* been levied by various governments, Cohan (2015) points out that lion's share of these costs will be paid out *by the shareholders* rather than complicit executives. Indeed, many of the bankers and traders involved in financial crisis were incentivized with extreme bonuses to act in unethical manners; some were even rewarded for their actions *after* the crisis began (Crotty 2009).

> Only one executive was imprisoned as a result of the 2008 financial crisis.

Contrast the "justice" faced by unscrupulous bankers who pilfered millions of dollars to that of Kimberly Rogers, who was convicted of welfare fraud:

Kimberly Rogers had died alone and eight months pregnant, in her sweltering apartment in Sudbury, Ontario, while under house arrest for welfare fraud. What many do not realize is that the policies and conditions that set the stage for this tragedy are still in place and in some respects have actually worsened.

Kimberly Rogers was charged with welfare fraud after collecting both social assistance and students loans to help cover the costs of attending four years of community college. She was convicted in April 2001 and the penalty was six months under house arrest (with the right to be allowed out of her hot apartment three hours per week); a requirement to repay more than $13 thousand in benefits; eighteen months' probation and loss of the right to have part of her student loan forgiven.

At the time of Roger's conviction, Ontario Works regulations specified that anyone convicted of welfare fraud would be automatically suspended from receiving benefits for three months. This stipulation has since been made tougher. Anyone convicted of welfare fraud in the province of Ontario will be banned for life from ever being able to collect social assistance. (Keck 2002)

After her May 2001 launch of the first Ontario citizen *Charter of Rights and Freedoms* challenge to Ontario's Welfare (Ontario Works Benefits) laws,

> Rogers' benefits were reinstated for the interim, but this was not the end of her problems. Even with Ontario Works benefits, she was unable to support herself and her unborn child. After a deduction of 10 percent (towards repayment to Ontario Works) Rogers received $468 per month. With $450 going towards paying the rent. Rogers was left with $18 to cover all other necessities.... "I ran out of food this weekend. I am unable to sleep and I cry all the time (Kimberly Rogers, affidavit to court May 2001). Tragically, while still under house arrest, Kimberly Rogers died just weeks after the Ontario Superior Court of Justice released its exceptional decision. (Keck 2002)

Glasbeek, exasperated by Rogers' case, observed:

> A study of welfare fraud documented that 80% of all persons convicted of welfare fraud of this type were given jail sentences. In contrast, another study shows that "prison" is imposed in 4 percent of all tax evasion cases, even though the amount stolen vastly exceeds that stolen by welfare abusers. Unemployment benefit frauds reveal the same pattern: the rate of incarceration is twice that by tax evaders. (2002: 123)

Corporations, even government corporations, and the privileged can apparently kill, maim and rob with relative impunity while the poor get prison — or worse, in the case of Kimberly Rogers. This is yet another iteration of the class bias in criminal law.

Another form of bias lies in the fact that corporate harmfulness is often not even defined as criminal. Most often, costly and harmful corporate behaviour, when classified as illegal, falls within regulatory law rather than the *Criminal Code*, where most street crime is placed. This distinction is often made on the basis of legal notions of culpability, which were established to prosecute individual offenders for street crime but not corporations or corporate officials for industry-related misdoings. There is dispute and confusion over whether the *Canadian Charter of Rights and Freedoms* under sections 7 and 1(d) is meant to enforce the rigid legal standards of *mens rea* (literally meaning "the guilty mind," which is a standard used to determine whether or not a criminal act was intentionally committed) requirements for the prosecution of corporate offenders. In Canada, the Crown must prove "blameworthiness" to get a *Criminal Code* conviction. It refers to "the guilty mind, the wrongful intention" — a necessary element in establishing criminal conduct" (Verdun-Jones 2007: 66). In addition to the problem of *mens rea*, corporations have been almost exclusively prosecuted for regulatory violations — such as those governing health and safety — and not for the consequences of those violations (Reasons, Ross and Patterson 1986; McMullan 1992). For example, a company would be fined for not installing safety bolts in a construction crane, but not prosecuted for the death of several workers who were below the crane when it collapsed. Corporations have frequent and vociferous input into the regulations governing them, generally under the guise of being enlisted to co-operate in creating "workable laws." The result is a lax system of regulation.

When critically interpreted, the tragic events discussed above reveal a trend of *in*justice in the Canadian criminal justice system that places the interests of the economic elite above all others. This point is emphasized by the lack of action in response to numerous tragedies, despite clear linkages between corporate intentions and outcomes. Rather than taking decisive action, the collective patchwork of provincial and federal legislation designed to govern Canadian workplaces has been rendered toothless through revision, loopholes and inaction. The economically bifurcated nature of the justice system is further retrenched by drawing comparisons between legal responses to corporate wrongdoing and the wrongdoing of the individual. While individuals, particularly those of low economic means, face the wrath of the justice system for relatively small infractions, we see no reciprocal action against the financial elite. To restate Reiman and Leighton, the rich get richer and the poor get prison — even in Canada.

Race and Crime

In post-colonial societies, Indigenous peoples and people of colour are overrepresented in the criminal justice system. Canada, Australia and the United States all have similar experiences (Samuelson 1995). This is not some accident of history, or the result of pathologies of "lawlessness" among non-white people, but rather a legacy of the destruction and dislocation of Indigenous peoples that took place under European colonial practices of political and economic subjugation. Much like Reiman and Leighton's thesis, critical criminologists argue that the Canadian justice system is designed protect the interests of specific social groups while omitting, intentionally or otherwise, those of Indigenous and non-white people. These arbitrary social divisions generally also align with economic marginality, further subjecting certain social groups to additional hardships. Essentially, Indigenous peoples are still treated as a colonial population, and Canada has been no exception in this practice. After all, the Canadian government has segregated many of its "Indians" in concentration camps, known as reserves, for over 150 years and has regulated their behaviour in all aspects of their lives.

Getting this colonialist fact recognized and changed in our ostensibly post-colonialist era is apparently much harder to do in Canada than in the international arena. Mary Ellen Turpel (Aki-Kwe) (1992) notes that Canadians like to think of themselves as strong supporters of international rights, ready to contribute troops under the United Nations banner, if need be, to places like Bosnia, Kuwait, Afghanistan and Iraq; but not so when the subject of First Nations rights is raised in international political circles. For example, as director of the Canadian Institute for Human Rights and Democratic Development, Ed Broadbent remarked in the early 1990s that he would be in a particularly difficult position when he raised questions about human rights abuses in other countries because "These countries will be saying to me: what about Aboriginal rights in Canada?"

Changes to this legacy have been slow in the first two decades of the twenty-first century. For example, Canada, in 2007, under the Conservative government, elected to vote against the United Nations Declaration on the Rights of Indigenous Persons; again in 2014 Canada voted against a U.N. guiding document designed to re-affirm the 2007 declaration. While we had been joined by Australia, New Zealand and the United States on the 2007 vote, Canada stood alone in its vote against the 2014 document. The government rationalized this dissenting vote by raising concerns over some of the document's language, with government bureaucrats interpreting clauses about "free, prior and informed consent" from Indigenous groups on legislation that may affect them as constituting a veto (Lum 2014). Unsurprisingly, this statement raised the ire of many domestic and international Indigenous leaders, who equated this concern with an attempt to maintain colonial legacies of guardianship. Although the federal government, under the Trudeau Liberals, reversed its opinion and officially adopted the declaration in 2016, many Indigenous observers have stated that this is only the beginning of a long process.

> Overrepresentation of Aboriginal people in the justice system holds for nearly all categories of offenders, all types of institutions, and all regions of the country.

The overrepresentation of Indigenous people in the justice system holds for nearly all categories of offenders, all types of institutions and all regions of the country — this is a trend that has remained in place since such information became available (Hartnagel 2009). Parliament and the Supreme Court of Canada have repeatedly tried to address the problem, at least on paper. For example, in 1996 Parliament passed section 718.2(e) of the *Criminal Code*, giving special consideration to the circumstances of Indigenous offenders. The Supreme Court, in 1999, upheld those new provisions in *R. v. Gladue*, affirming its remedial purpose in attempting to reduce the high rate of Indigenous incarceration. Unfortunately, little progress has been made. The incarceration of Indigenous persons is overrepresented in every Canadian jurisdiction as of 2015 — for instance, a 2013 report to the House of Commons identified the chronic state of Indigenous overrepresentation in Canada's prisons, with 21.5 percent of incarcerated persons identifying an Indigenous heritage, compared to 4.3 percent of the general population (Canada 2013).

While women in general constitute a pronounced minority in the justice system,

Indigenous women are the most disproportionately represented group in both provincial and federal institutions. The latest *Annual Report of the Office of the Correctional Investigator* (2015) devotes an entire section to this issue, explaining that "as a group, Aboriginal women have become the fastest growing offender category under federal jurisdiction." Specifically, Indigenous women account for 35.5 percent of the female incarcerated population in Canada, nearly double the 2005 population. Additionally, Indigenous women are more likely to be classified as maximum security, more likely to be considered high risk and more likely to be incarcerated on a drug offence. This overrepresentation has been growing in the past decade, accelerated by the implementation of tough-on-crime initiatives.

To fully understand Indigenous women's over-involvement in the justice system, and their (discriminatory) high-risk classifications, we must consider the kinds of lives that they often experience. Consider the following "life profile" of a federally sentenced Indigenous woman:

> She may leave home because she experienced violence (whether she was abused or she witnessed abuse) and her home life has become unbearable. Or she may live under very rigid conditions that she leaves because she wants to become independent. Or she may be lured away by friends who have a life of drugs, alcohol and partying. She may work the streets because she needs money to live on and she does not have the education, skills and training to get a job. She may be subjected to racism, stereotyping and discrimination because of her race and colour. However, her experience on the streets becomes violent as she continues to experience sexual, emotional, and physical abuse. She is likely to become involved in an abusive relationship. There are usually children born from this relationship and the social, emotional and economic struggle continues. The cycle of an unhealthy family continues. (Griffiths 2004: 187–88)

To make matters worse, when they are incarcerated, Indigenous women face additional factors that impede healing. As Wotherspoon and Satzewich pointed out in the early 1990s, these factors include "severely inadequate prison facilities and programs, cultural and gender-biased assessment standards, failure to acknowledge and treat the realities of Aboriginal women's abusive life histories, and unsympathetic prison regimes" (1993: 198). Decades later, the Correctional Investigator of Canada explained that these issues persist and, in fact, the breadth and depth of services designed to address the needs of Indigenous women had declined due to budget cuts and the tough-on-crime stance of the Conservative government. In several studies of prison programming, incarcerated Indigenous women reported that they experienced overcrowded conditions and inadequate, one-size-fits-all programming (Findlay et al. 2013).

Why does this over-incarceration exist in the first place? The statistics indicate that there are underlying factors. In the new corrections language, it is argued that there are "risks" within Indigenous people themselves that propel them towards illegal and anti-social behaviour. Chronic poverty, poor employment, little education, disrupted family lives, homelessness, violence, drug and alcohol (mis)use and so on are defined as risks for Indigenous individuals to become involved in criminal behaviour. Whether borne of financial troubles, socially constructed differences or colonial legacies, these structural outcomes (the "risks") are systemically acknowledged as personal inadequacies and used to justify further marginalization through "corrections." A critical analysis, however, offers another explanation: these conditions are the result of prejudice and discrimination among Canadians generally and criminal justice personnel in particular.

The over-involvement of Indigenous peoples in crime and with the justice system, and the resistance of Indigenous peoples to that experience, takes place within the political, social and economic context of ongoing colonialism. An over-involvement in crime is but one of the social problems generated by the relatively passive genocide perpetrated against Indigenous peoples, largely under the rhetoric and guise of assimilation. The Royal Commission on Aboriginal Peoples (1996) argued that Indigenous over-involvement indicates the existence of "social" rather than "criminal" problems. The most central social problems are the ones that society creates for Indigenous peoples — not those created by any individual criminal pathology. Put simply, the problem is racism.

> The Royal Commission on Aboriginal Peoples argued that Aboriginal over-involvement indicates the existence of "social" rather than "criminal" problems.

The frequent public perception of Indigenous people as "drunks," "lazy" and "criminal" has long confused symptoms with the underlying causes (Hylton 1982: 125). Confusing symptom with cause is convenient, because it allows for a one-way street of criminal justice policies and programs that address crime as the problem without seriously challenging the status quo of the Canadian political economy. Like most systems of domination, this condition depends on the development, by powerful people, of strong ideologies and typifications that justify their control over subject populations. This was certainly true historically in Canada, and unfortunately it continues in modern form. A recent poll of Canadians confirmed a general backlash of attitudes towards "Indian," Inuit and Métis people (Neuman 2016). Approximately 35 percent of the respondents held generally negative views of Indigenous persons in Canada, and one in ten (13 percent) viewed Indigenous persons through a stereotypical lens (for example, that they are privileged or receive tax breaks, rely on welfare; are alcoholics, etcetera). While this is an improvement in attitude compared to similar research from the mid-1990s, it nonetheless depicts serious gaps in knowledge about the lives and experiences of First Nations, Inuit and Métis persons in Canada. Perhaps the most alarming finding was that most affluent respondents, those who typically have the most social power in Canadian society, frequently rejected "the idea that mainstream society continues to benefit from poor treatment of Aboriginal people" (Neuman 2016: 50). This provides some clarity about the continued over-policing of Indigenous communities as this affluent portion of the Canadian population take up many of our policy- and decision-making roles. This imbalance is further explored by Jim Silver (Chapter 6).

Geoffrey York (1990), in the *The Dispossessed*, provides a telling picture of the disparate treatment Indigenous peoples experience in justice. He reports on a study of capital murder cases from 1926 to 1957, which found that the risk of execution for an anglo-Canadian who killed a white person was 21 percent, whereas an "Indian" who killed a white person in the same circumstances had a 96 percent risk of execution. Research discovered memos from Indian Affairs bureaucrats recommending that "Indian" offenders be executed because Indigenous peoples needed "special deterrence" (York 1990: 157). Into the late 1980s, differential charging of Indigenous people by police for relatively minor public-order offences was widespread. Research done in Regina, for example, "found that 30 percent of the Indians arrested for drunkenness were charged and sent to court; by contrast, only 11 percent of non-Natives were charged and sent to court" (149). The Aboriginal Justice Inquiry of Manitoba (AJI) concurred, stating that over-policing must be blamed on persisting stereotypical racist attitudes and actions directed against Aboriginal people (AJI 1991: 595).

The problem of racism in policing has become an important dimension of the concern about the relatively high number of killings by police of Black and Indigenous people in questionable circumstances (Forcese 1992). Commissions have been struck to evaluate this problem, but the poor record of implementation of Indigenous justice initiatives does not bode well for eliminating racist views among police and putting curbs on police practice. For example, there was a huge outcry within the Indigenous community over the shooting by police of Dudley George, an Indigenous man, at the 1995 Ipperwash protest and the subsequent initial finding of no guilt for the police. The 2006 inquiry into the Ipperwash incident found the shooting of Dudley George, an unarmed peaceful protester, was unjustified. A concern of the inquiry, apart from racist police action, was the question of whether or not the police received a provincial "political directive" to direct them to "deal" with the incident.

Unfortunately, but notably, the city of Saskatoon had consistently appeared in Amnesty International's annual list of human rights abuses. The organization's 2001 report described in detail what have come to be known as starlight tours, among other allegations of "patterns of police abuse against First Nation men in Saskatoon" (*StarPhoenix* 2001). One such starlight tour was experienced by Darrel Night, an Indigenous man who had an encounter with the police while leaving a party in Saskatoon's west side one evening:

> Arresting Night for "causing a disturbance," they handcuffed him and put him in the back of their cruiser. Night assumed that he was being taken to the drunk tank. Instead, the officers drove him to the outskirts of the city, more than two kilometres from the Queen Elizabeth Power Plant. According to Night, they swore at him, "Get the fuck out of here, you fucking Indian" and removed the handcuffs. The cruiser then proceeded to drive away. When Night yelled, "I'm going to freeze out here," the officers stopped the car and yelled back, "That's your fucking problem." (Comack 2012: 118)

The Crown subsequently laid charges against two Saskatoon police officers, who were both fifteen-year veterans, in the Night case. They were charged with unlawful confinement and assault and were convicted and sentenced to eight months' jail time — but they did four months. The 1990 freezing death of Neil Stonechild resulted in yet another inquiry. After fourteen years of police-judicial inaction, the 2004 *Report of the Commission of Inquiry into*

Matters Relating to the Death of Neil Stonechild (Saskatchewan 2004) was released. A witness, Jason Roy, stated that he saw Stonechild in the back of a police car on the night in question. He was shouting, Roy testified, "They gonna kill me." While the two constables involved denied the charges, the inquiry concluded, based on the police's own records, that they did have Neil Stonechild in their custody the night he died. Both officers were fired by police chief Sabo two weeks after the report's release.

This section once again illustrates the structured divisions in Canada's justice system. In addition to economic divisions, our system also incorporates laws and regulations that reflect the European, colonial roots of Canada's history. Those members of society who do not meet the ideological prerequisites of "traditional" Canadians are encumbered with hardships in addition to financial limitations, such as increased surveillance, incarceration and prejudice. By appending racially derived differences onto specific groups, society can download risk and ultimately justify "corrective" actions designed to annex undesirable characteristics. This process is typified through Canada's historic mistreatment of Indigenous populations, be it the use of residential schools, over-incarceration or arbitrary punishments like the starlight tours.

Gender and Crime

Gender often plays a decisive role in the justice that individuals experience. While women are less likely to face criminal charges, those who do enter the criminal justice system frequently encounter gendered approaches to justice and rehabilitation that fail to consider differences in circumstance (Brooks 2015a). For instance, the Office of the Correctional Investigator reported in 2015 that when compared to men, women in custody are twice as likely to have a serious mental health diagnosis, twice as likely to be serving a sentence for drug-related offences and more likely to be supporting dependents on the outside (50). When that final point is paired with the fact that more than 70 percent of incarcerated women are mothers to children under the age of 18, we can see why such considerations are necessary.

> When compared to men, women in custody are twice as likely to have a serious mental health diagnosis, twice as likely to be serving a sentence for drug-related offences and more likely to be supporting dependents on the outside.

Neglect of these circumstances is symptomatic of a patriarchal system that often omits gender from consideration. For most of its history, the field of criminology has almost entirely ignored women. For example, Albert Cohen, champion of the subcultural theory, which has been influential in criminology theory and practice, argued for the masculinity of criminology:

> My skin has nothing of the quality of down or silk, there is nothing limpid or flue-like about my voice, I am a total loss with needle and thread, my posture and carriage are wholly lacking in grace. … My wife, on the other hand, is not greatly embarrassed by her inability to tinker with or talk about the internal organs of a car, by her modest attainment in arithmetic, or by her inability to lift heavy objects. (1955: 137–38)

Similarly, Taylor, Walton and Young's 1973 ground-breaking book, *The New Criminology*, did not contain one word about women (Gregory 1986). An analysis of Canadian criminal justice (Griffiths and Verdun-Jones 1994) devotes only about 7 out of 660 pages to discussing women and justice. Even Reiman and Leighton, whose perspective has heavily influenced this chapter, argue that "anti-discrimination legislation has sharpened the public's moral condemnation of racial and gender discrimination" (2013: 85), implying that these issues have been "solved" in modern societies.

Unfortunately, gender issues have not been resolved — if anything, they have been amplified. For instance, the process of feminizing poverty has continued apace. Originally coined by leading feminist researcher Diana Pearce in the 1970s, this perspective stems from the systemic economic barriers faced by women because of traditional gender roles:

> In spite of increased labor-force participation, the occupational ghettoization and discrimination has prevented any improvement in women's earnings relative to men. Child support, which rapidly increasing divorce and illegitimacy rates makes more important, is so minimal in reality that even the one- or two-child family runs a high risk of becoming poor if the father leaves. And welfare, although it supports more of the eligible population than ever before, does so at an even more penurious level than in the past. (Pearce 1978: 34)

Thus Pearce (1978) illustrates how each of these barriers fall into place one-by-one to shuffle women into economic disadvantage. These barriers persist in Canada. For instance, approximately one in five single-mother Canadian families live below the poverty line, contrasted against just one in twenty two-parent families experiencing poverty (Evans 2010). Furthermore Jim Silver (Chapter 6) notes that single females have the highest rate of poverty in Canada at 36 percent, and female-headed single-parent families have the highest rate of poverty at just over 21 percent. The feminization of poverty and the role of economic power work together to severely limit a woman's access to justice.

Indeed, the gendered nature of justice was illustrated by the liberation thesis, a concept used through the late 1970s and into the mid-1990s. Beginning in the late 1960s, crime analysts identified an upswing in female criminality — for example, between 1968 and 2000, the reported crime rate for women in all *Criminal Code* offences grew by 184 percent, compared to 43 percent for men (Hartnagel 2004). Policy-makers and theorists sought to explain this phenomenon, and by the 1970s, a populist "converging roles theory," championed by Freda Adler (1975), began to gain prominence. Generally, this perspective argued that the female crime rate mirrors advancements toward social and economic parity with men. Thus, as women were "liberated" from traditional gender roles, the convergence thesis held that they would begin acting more and more like men in all aspects of life, including criminality.

While this theory was beneficial in that it "stimulated a shift from thinking of criminalized women as monstrous, pathetic and/or pathological to thinking of women as independent agents" (Comack 2015: 301), it was exploited by the media and policy-makers to construct a mythos of dangerous, violent female offenders. But, even in the context of these large rate increases, 2005 statistics show that women made up only a little over 18 percent of all persons accused for violations against the person and just over 24 percent for total violations against property (Statistics Canada 2009). Seventy-seven percent of the increase from 1968 to 1996 in women charged with *Criminal Code* offences was for non-violent crime (Hartnagel 2000). From 1968 to 2000 the proportion of all women charged for violent crime increased from 10 percent to 26 percent (Hartnagel 2004: 130). Increases in female violent crime, and female gangs, are receiving considerable media and academic analysis, but, into the late 2000s, "the highest rates for women charged continue to be for less serious thefts of property" (Hartnagel 2009: 147).

But is this because of role convergence? Many years ago, Holly Johnson and Karen Rodgers noted that women's involvement in crime "is consistent with their traditional roles as consumers, and increasingly, as low income, semi-skilled, sole support providers for their families" (1993: 98). They add:

> In keeping with the rapid increase in female-headed households and the stresses associated with poverty, greater numbers of women are being charged with shoplifting, cheque forging and welfare fraud. (ibid.)

Comack reiterates this view:

> Women's theft rates did go up in the late 1970s, but the robberies were not committed by women who had been influenced by women's liberation, nor were these women serious crooks. They were primarily the work of young single mothers who were experiencing the *feminization of poverty*. They bore no resemblance to news reporters' fictionalized versions of wild, violent women running amok, as was propagated through the 1970s and again in the 1990s. At all periods of history, when women have organized for women's rights, they have met with fierce resistance from men and women who represent the status quo (2015: 301)

While role convergence and a less "chivalrous" or "paternalistic" judicial system cannot totally be ruled out as factors in women's involvement in crime, a more fruitful explanation would lie elsewhere. Continuing extensive female job ghettoization, the feminization of poverty and the development of a youth consumer market frequently directed at teenage females (Greenberg 1977; Comack 2015) are more basic to the understanding of female patterns and rates of involvement in crime.

Thus, it is not surprising that most women serving sentences in federal and provincial corrections are from marginalized backgrounds: "Their past and current situations are likely to include poverty, histories of abuse, long term drug and alcohol dependency, responsibilities for primary care of children, limited educational attainment, and few opportunities to obtain adequately paid work" (Griffiths 2004: 187). Sadly, virtually every critical observer concurs that prison still only teaches women at best to "do their time," medicated if necessary. More likely, prisons only add another bitter layer to their life experiences and do not deal with their underlying problems and issues (Boritch 2002). Re-incarceration is thus too often a reality, as is a push to move them up the "high-risk" carceral scale of inmate classification, usually with added debilitation not rehabilitation.

The justice system's treatment of women who have been the victims of crime has also been the object of considerable critical scrutiny in the past three decades. The main areas of concern have been the system's biases, injustices and ineffectiveness in dealing with women who have been the victims of domestic violence and sexual assault (Comack 2004). To this end we might consider institutionalized responses to sexual assault in Canada. Bill C-127, a 1983 reform to the *Criminal Code*, abolished the legal charge of rape as well as the separate charges of indecent assault on a male and indecent assault on a female. In place of the rape law, the federal government amended the definition of assault to include sexual assault and also defined three levels of sexual assault. The intent was to increase the reporting of rape by victims by reducing the stigma of rape and to emphasize, as many academics and feminists had strenuously contended, that rape was primarily a violent act of male domination in sexual form.

Still, much skepticism remained over the extent to which these changes would produce any significant increase in the reporting of sexual assault by females, or would alter the judicial stereotyping and traumatization of sexually assaulted women. Women's advocates argued that the legislation merely paid lip service to the advancement of equality and would fail to produce societal changes (Allison 1991). Many of these fears were realized when, in 1992, "rape shield" provisions designed to protect victims from having to recount their previous sexual history during trials were repealed by the Supreme Court of Canada, leaving lawmakers scrambling to define the meaning of "no means no" (Tang 1998). Moreover, the actual effectiveness of the law has long been questioned. For example, victimization surveys conducted in 2014 — thirty years after C-127's passage — showed that more than 90 percent of sexual assaults were not reported to police by their victims (Canadian Centre for Justice Statistics 2015). Past studies indicate that in many cases victims do not make these reports because they are reluctant to get the police involved, believe the police will not help them and/or because they fear retaliation (Gomme 2007).

> Victimization surveys conducted in 2014 — 30 years after C-127's passage — showed that more than 90 percent of sexual assaults were not reported to police by their victims.

Perhaps one of the most illustrative examples of the patriarchal divide in the administration of justice came from Justice Robert Dewar, one of the highest ranking trial judges in the province of Alberta. After hearing the case against Kenneth Rhodes, who was charged with sexually assaulting a woman while she was intoxicated, Justice Dewar issued a highly controversial judgement that suggested the victim was complicit in the assault through her actions and dress. *Globe and Mail* columnist Christie Blatchford observed:

> He called the rapist, one Kenneth Rhodes, a "clumsy Don Juan," described the case as one of "misunderstood signals and inconsiderate behaviour" and blamed the 26-year-old victim for creating "inviting circumstances." He noted that she and a

girlfriend on the night in question wore tube tops with no bras (to my faint recollec-
tion, that is a given with tube tops), high heels and lots of makeup, said they wanted
to party and left the impression that "sex was in the air." (2011: 1)

Victim-blaming of this magnitude is symptomatic of a justice system that maintains out-
moded views about women that are reliant on historical misconceptions about inferiority
and incapacity. Recent studies of this issue have illustrated that successful victim-blaming
(for example, reduced penalties or exoneration of the accused based on arguments about
the victim "wanting it") reinforces the historical structural limitations imposed on women.
Further, insinuating a victim's culpability based on a pre-existing relationship or manner
of dress fortifies a double-standard of victimization that narrowly defines rape as a forceful
occurrence between strangers and diminishes the power of "no," particularly for women
(Hayes, Lorenz and Bell 2013).

A double standard is also present in corrections for women. A review of the treatment
of incarcerated women shows how they have been contradictorily portrayed by corrections
officials as both "poor and unfortunate" women in need of protection and as "scheming
temptresses who are lazy and worthless" (Cooper 1993: 33). Many feminists challenge the
"well-meaning," "in need of protection" dimension; at most, it masks the social control and
subjugation of women (Currie 1986). Put succinctly and accurately, "prison, as a microcosm
of society, reflects all those inequalities which discriminate against women, be their source
historical, social or administrative convenience" (Ekstedt and Griffiths 1988: 337). This
inequality has manifested in the way that women have been dealt with in the system — specifically, prior to the 1990s, all federally sentenced women from across Canada were gathered
into a centralized institution, the federal Prison for Women (P4W) in Kingston, Ontario. P4W
opened its doors in 1934, just across the road from the Kingston Penitentiary for Men and
was modelled after it. While federal penitentiaries for men were spread across the country
and included three levels of security, P4W was the only federal facility for women and all
prisoners were classified as maximum security risk (Brooks 2015b). This meant that women
from all corners of the country were housed in southern Ontario, adding significant financial
burden to any visitors (as explored above, many incarcerated women are single mothers).

It is thus not surprising that virtually every major commission investigating Canada's penal
system, from the 1938 Archambault Report onward, severely criticized conditions at P4W
and generally recommended its closure. They tended to conclude that the relatively small
number of female prisoners should be housed in their home provinces. Indeed, between 1968
and the late 1980s, no fewer than thirteen government studies, investigations and private-
sector reports had reiterated this basic conclusion (Cooper 1987). The recalcitrance of the
Canadian justice system to change is indicated by the 1979 firing of Berzins and Cooper,
whose task was to improve services and programs at P4W. The two women produced a review
of the programs at P4W, noting major deficiencies compared to those available to federally
incarcerated men. Their report did not meet with the approval of the Commissioner of
Corrections, although it did become public by accident.

Questions over the lack of change in Canadian corrections for women were raised again.

This time the group Women for Justice, distressed by the lack of change in corrections policy, filed a complaint with the Canadian Human Rights Commission, which acknowledged that incarcerated women had been systemically discriminated against through a lack of training and rehabilitation programs, which were readily available for incarcerated men (Task Force on Federally Sentenced Women 1990). This finding broke ground for a new Task Force on Federally Sentenced Women, commonly known as the Creating Choices commission. Upon reviewing the mistreatment of federally incarcerated women, the Creating Choices report established five fundamental principles for women in prisons:

1. empowering women (programs to raise self-esteem);
2. providing more meaningful choices in programs and community facilities (wider range of options);
3. treating women with respect and dignity (to enhance self-respect);
4. providing a physically and emotionally supportive environment; and
5. sharing responsibility for the women's welfare (co-operation by government, correctional, and voluntary organizations and members). (Task Force on Federally Sentenced Women 1990)

The plan called for regional facilities, a healing lodge and a community release strategy. Moreover, each of these facilities was to differ from traditional male-oriented correctional facilities.

After the publication of the Task Force report, the announcement was finally made that p4w would be closed and that five new regional facilities and a "healing centre" for Indigenous women would be built at Maple Creek, Saskatchewan. But change would not come easily at p4w. In April 1994, the male Institutional Emergency Response Team (IERT) from Kingston Penitentiary was sent to p4w to "quell a violent incident." The public release of the horrific, brutal institutional response to an inmate-staff confrontation, which was videotaped, resulted in a 1996 Commission of Inquiry (the Arbour Inquiry). The final report was critical of the substantial abuse of these inmates and the violation of numerous CSC formal procedures (Canada 1996). For example: "Mace was used to subdue three of the inmates.... Although Correctional Service policy contains elaborate provisions with respect to decontamination following the use of mace, in this case, decontamination was limited to pouring some glasses of water over the inmates' eyes" (Canada 1996: 31). The report concluded: "Nearly every step that was taken in response to this incident was at odds with the intent of the new [*Creating Choices*] initiatives" (24). More specifically, the Arbour Inquiry

> documented the violations of the rule of law, policy, and institutional regulations in a number of areas, including the use of segregation, the use of force by the IERT, and the manner in which the women had been strip-searched and subjected to body cavity searches. Serious concerns were raised as to whether the CSC was capable of implementing the necessary reforms to ensure that the rules of law and justice were adhered to without outside intervention and monitoring. The Arbour report also contained 14 primary recommendations relating to cross-gender staffing in

correctional institutions for women, the use of force and of IERTS, the operation of segregation units, the needs of Aboriginal women in correctional institutions, ways of ensuring accountability and adherence to the rule of law among correctional personnel, and procedures of handling inmate complaints and grievances. (Griffiths 2004: 182)

The mistreatment of women in all aspects of the justice process is once again symptomatic of a divisive system that aims to preserve the power imbalances present in Canadian society. In this case, gendered divisions support the arbitrary imposition of characteristics onto women, particularly at the intersection of economics, race and gender. These processes result in arbitrary divides that put more than half of the Canadian population at a disadvantage and reinforce, through self-fulfilling prophecy, patriarchal assumptions of incapacity. These misconceptions have manifested as systems of control in the justice system and are particularly well represented by the historical discrimination of incarcerated women.

Changing Society, Not Fighting Crime

All of this is not to say that no efforts are being made by politicians, scholars and social activists to change the criminal justice system. While advancements come in fits and starts — usually in response to a tragic event emerging from disparity — they nonetheless introduce a modicum of social justice into the Canadian system.

For example, the past decade has born witness to greater and greater scrutiny over the unethical practices engaged in by corporations and wealthy members of society. This is largely in response to major scandals, events like the fraudulent practices from corporations like Enron; the major Ponzi and fraudulent practices of wealthy business-people like Bernie Madoff and Conrad Black; and the contrivances of thousands of stockbrokers and banking executives that precipitated the 2008 financial crisis. Greater social awareness of these activities, spurred on the social protest movements like Occupy Wall Street, has driven legislators to develop effective and meaningful laws in response. To this end, the Fortieth Parliament of Canada brought Bill C-21 into law, which amended the *Criminal Code* to include minimum mandatory sentences for persons convicted of fraud greater than $1 million, and also restitutions provisions for persons harmed by their actions (Parliament of Canada 2011).

Similarly, Indigenous persons are beginning to affect change on multiple political and social fronts after decades of advocacy. For instance, after seven years of hearings from thousands of witnesses, the Truth and Reconciliation Commission of Canada produced a substantive document detailing the injustices experienced by Canada's First Peoples in the residential school system and provided ninety-four recommendations ("Calls to Action") to redress this legacy, "[advancing] the process of Canadian *reconciliation*" (Truth and Reconciliation Commission of Canada 2015: 319). The report offers seventeen recommendations to improve the administration of justice for Indigenous persons in Canada with the goal of reducing overrepresentation, and the Forty-Second Parliament, led by the Liberal Party and Prime Minister Justin Trudeau, accepted the report's findings and committed to developing a strategy that will see each of the report's recommendations implemented. While there are still significant challenges to the equitable treatment of Indigenous persons in Canada (the tragic number of missing and murdered Indigenous women is testament to this point) there is a greater sense of hope that inroads can be made.

> The Truth and Reconciliation Commission of Canada produced a substantive document detailing the injustices experienced by Canada's First Peoples in the residential school system and provided ninety-four recommendations to redress this legacy.

Recent political changes have also shifted perspectives and action directed toward equality in justice for women. On November 4, 2015, Prime Minister Justin Trudeau introduced a cabinet that was, for the first time in Canadian history, gender balanced. Moreover, the Prime Minister instructed Patty Hajdu, Minister of Status of Women, to "work with experts and advocates to develop and implement a comprehensive federal gender violence strategy and action plan, aligned with existing provincial strategies" (Office of the Prime Minister of Canada 2015). Prime Minister Trudeau said Hajdu would "be supported by the Minister of Justice to make any necessary criminal code changes and by the President of the Treasury Board who will develop strategies to combat sexual harassment in federal public institution."

Again, these advancements must be considered within the shadow of recent tragedy. In 2013, a coroner's inquest into the death of Ashley Smith, a young woman who was asphyxiated while in custody at a federal institution, identified a series of failures in respect of the treatment of women by Correctional Service Canada (Correctional Service Canada 2013).

To move beyond piecemeal and partial socio-legal reforms in criminal and social justice, we need to develop more comprehensive theoretical, analytical and policy-based critiques of our society. Yet these kinds of initiatives will only partially confront the status quo in Canadian society. To reduce the prevailing inequities we need to focus on society's structural and cultural conditions and its distribution of power, the elements that are at the centre of the problem. At this level, basic changes are difficult to achieve because they confront the underlying, socially entrenched inequalities of life conditions and power relations. As Jeffrey Reiman (2007) states, in order for a real "society" to exist there must be two-way-street social justice.

Harry Glasbeek puts this very well at the end of his book *Wealth by Stealth*:

> As C. Douglas Lummis argued in *Radical Democracy*, to be a democrat is not an abstraction. It is a state of being: "Democracy is a world that joins *Demos* — the people with *Krakia* — power.... It describes an ideal, not a method for achieving it.... It is a historical project ... as people take it up as such and struggle for it." These proposals take up what we have learned in the previous pages about the enemy of this historical project, and they are intended to help fuel the spirit of would-be democrats as they engage in their struggles to bring together *people* and *power*, break down the corporate shield, and lay the groundwork for a humanizing transformation of our polity. (2002: 283)

Only if we recover, and enrich our political lives as democratic citizens, will we be able to be effective participants in local and worldwide movements to tackle the enormous human problems we face.

Glossary of Key Terms

Charter of Rights and Freedoms, sections 7 and 1(d): Prior to 1941, corporations were immune to any criminal liability because *mens rea*, "guilty mind," could not corporately exist. Section 7 and section 1(d) of the Charter have been used to argue against this rigid *mens rea* requirement in prosecution of corporate crime.

Commission: A group of individuals who have been tasked with investigating a specific issue related to the well-being of society. In Canada, commissions are generally chartered by the Crown.

Corporate crime/suite crime: Harmful economic, human and environmental acts committed by corporate officials in the pursuit of organizational goals, usually profit, and generally unpunished by the state.

Critical criminology: Grounded in the Marxist concepts of social class conflict and advocacy of significant social change, this theory sees crime and criminal justice as reflecting and reproducing the inequalities in society. As well, it is an advocacy perspective in that the point of critical analysis is not just to study society, but to eliminate unjust social acts and inequalities.

European colonialism: The takeover by white settlers of land belonging to Indigenous peoples, resulting in their nearly complete genocidal destruction, both physically and culturally.

Ideology: The starting point for justice in many societies is their collective understanding of right and wrong, which constitutes a guiding ideology. Ideologies are generally malleable and are often shaped by the most powerful members of society rather than through democratic processes.

Individualization: Similar to neoliberalism, adherents to this social theory believe that people in modern societies are left to their own devices when it comes to navigating rules, laws and moralities.

Overrepresentation of Indigenous peoples: In Western Canada, since the Second World War, Indigenous peoples have been incarcerated both provincially and federally far in excess of their percentage of the general population.

Political economy: A form of analysis that links political and economic power. An influential study of political economy contends that wealth and political power are concentrated in the hands of a few individuals and corporations, giving them substantial political, legal and economic control over our ostensibly democratic society.

Post-colonial justice: An alternative system of justice for Indigenous peoples that includes Indigenous self-determination and resolution of land claims in conjunction with traditional healing and harmony restoration.

Prison for Women (P4W): A federal prison that opened in 1934 to house federally sentenced women. Conditions were very harsh, paternalistic and far inferior to prisons for men. Inmate despair and suicide were thus a major problem. The prison was closed in July 2000.

Sexual assault: The intentional use of force or threat thereof to engage in sexual behaviours without consent. Recent data from Statistics Canada suggests that approximately one in four women have experienced sexual assault and that only one in ten sexual assaults are reported to police.

Questions for Discussion

1. Critically evaluate the truth of the statement that "criminal law and the justice system protect us from serious economic and physical harm."

2. To what extent does the Canadian justice system treat upper-class individuals more favourably than lower-class people? Is Canada a "haven" for corporate crime?

3. Was it fair to sentence Paul Coffin to lecture business students on ethics, for having committed a $1.5-million-dollar fraud? Should he be sentenced to jail time given that the Crown appealed the sentence?

4. Explain the nature of the over-involvement of Aboriginal peoples in the justice system, and outline any signs of positive change in this area.

5. Are women treated better by the justice system than men are? Explain.

6. How likely is it that inequalities of involvement and treatment in the justice system based upon class, ethnicity, and gender will disappear in the near future? Will "law and order" criminal justice policies be a help or a hindrance to this project?

Resources for Activists

The Arbour Inquiry: caefs.ca/wp-content/uploads/2013/05/Arbour_Report.pdf

Lac-Mégantic runaway train and derailment: tsb.gc.ca/eng/rapports-reports/rail/2013/r13d0054/r13d0054-r-es.asp

Truth and Reconciliation Commission of Canada: trc.ca/websites/trcinstitution/index.php?p=3

References

Aboriginal Justice Inquiry of Manitoba. 1991. *The Justice System and Aboriginal People.* Volume 1. Winnipeg: Queen's Printer.

Adler, F. 1975. *Sisters in Crime.* New York: McGraw.

Allison, M. 1991. "Judicious Judgements? Examining the Impact of Sexual Assault Legislation on

Judicial Definitions of Sexual Violence." In Les Samuelson and Bernard Schissel (eds.), *Criminal Justice Sentencing Issues and Reform*. Toronto: Garamond.

Antonaccio, O., C. Tittle, E. Botchkovar, and M. Kranidiotis. 2010. "The Correlates of Crime and Deviance: Additional Evidence." *Journal of Research in Crime and Delinquency* 47, 3

Beck, U., and E. Beck-Gernsheim. 2009. "Losing the Traditional: Individualization and 'Precarious Freedoms.'" In A. Elliott and P. du Gay (eds.), *Identity in Question*. Thousand Oaks, CA: Sage Publications.

Blatchford, C. 2011. "Manitoba Judge Is Dead Wrong in Rape Case." *Globe and Mail*, February 24.

Bonnycastle, K.D. 2009. "Not the Usual Suspects: The Obfuscation of Political Economy and Race in CSI." In M. Byers and V. Johnson (eds.), *The CSI Effect: Television, Crime, and Governance*. Lanham, MD: Rowman and Littlefield.

Boritch, H. 2002. "Women in Prison in Canada." In Bernard Schissel and Carolyn Brooks (eds.), *Marginality and Condemnation: An Introduction to Critical Criminology*. Black Point, NS: Fernwood Publishing.

Brooks, Carolyn. 2015a. "Critical Criminology." In B. Schissel and C. Brooks (eds.), *Marginality and Condemnation: An Introduction to Critical Criminology, 3rd edition*. Black Point, NS: Fernwood Publishing.

____. 2015b. "Reforming Prisons for Women?" In B. Schissel and C. Brooks (eds.), *Marginality and Condemnation: An Introduction to Critical Criminology, 3rd edition*. Black Point, NS: Fernwood Publishing.

Campbell, B. 2013. *The Lac-Mégantic Disaster: Where Does the Buck Stop?* Ottawa: Canadian Centre for Policy Alternatives.

Canada, Office of the Correctional Investigator. 2015. *Annual Report of the Office of the Correctional Investigator 2014-2015*. Ottawa: Queen's Printer (Catalogue no. PS100E-PDF).

____. 1996. "Office of the Correctional Investigator Backgrounder: Aboriginal Inmates: The Numbers Reveal a Critical Situation." Ottawa: The Correctional Investigator Canada.

Canada Revenue Agency. 2015. "Criminal Victimization in Canada, 2014." *Juristat* 85-002X. Ottawa: CCJS.

____. 2016. *The CRA's Criminal Investigations Program*. <cra-arc.gc.ca/investigations/>.

CCOHS (Canadian Centre for Occupational Health and Safety). 2016. "Bill C-45 — Overview." Ottawa: Canadian Centre for Occupational Health and Safety. <ccohs.ca/oshanswers/legisl/billc45.html>.

Clinard, M., and P. Yeager. 1980. *Corporate Crime*. New York: Free Press.

Cohan, W. 2015. "How Wall Street's Bankers Stayed Out of Jail: The Probes into Bank Fraud Leading up to the Financial Industry's Crash Have Been Quietly Closed. Is This Justice?" *The Atlantic*, September.

Cohen, A. 1955. *Delinquent Boys: The Culture of the Gang*. New York: Free Press

Comack. E. 2004. "Feminism and Criminology." In Rick Linden (ed.), *Criminology: A Canadian Perspective*. Toronto: Thomson-Nelson.

____. 2012. *Racialized Policing*. Winnipeg and Halifax: Fernwood Publishing.

____. 2015. "The Sex Question in Criminology." In B. Schissel and C. Brooks (eds.), *Marginality and Condemnation: An Introduction to Critical Criminology, 3rd edition*. Black Point, NS: Fernwood Publishing.

Cooper, Shelagh. 1987. "The Evolution of the Federal Women's Prison." In E. Adelberg and C. Currie (eds.), *In Conflict with the Law: Women and the Canadian Justice System*. Vancouver: Press Gang.

____. 1993. "The Evolution of the Federal Women's Prison." In Ellen Adelberg and Claudia Currie (eds.), *In Conflict with the Law: Women and the Canadian Justice System*. Vancouver: Press Gang.

Correctional Service Canada. 2013. "Cornoner's Inquest Touching the Death of Ashley Smith." <csc-scc.gc.ca/publications/005007-9009-eng.shtml>.

Crotty, J., 2009. "Structural causes of the global financial crisis: a critical assessment of the 'new financial architecture.'" *Cambridge Journal of Economics* 33, 4: 563–580.

Currie, D. 1986. "Female Criminality: A Crisis in Feminist Theory." In B. MacLean (ed.), *The Political Economy of Crime*. Scarborough, ON: Prentice-Hall.

Douds, A.S., D. Howard, D. Hummer, and S.L. Gabbidon. 2016. "Public Opinion on the Affluenza Defense, Race, and Sentencing Decisions: Results from a Statewide Poll." *Journal of Crime and Justice* 39, 1: 230–242.

Evans, P. 2010. "Women's Poverty in Canada: Cross-Currents in an Ebbing Tide." In G. Goldberg (ed.), *Poor Women in Rich Countries: The Feminization of Poverty over the Life Course*. New York: Oxford University Press.

Ekstedt, J., and C. Griffiths. 1988. *Corrections in Canada*. Toronto: Butterworths.

Forcese, D. 1992. *Policing Canadian Society*. Scarborough, ON: Prentice-Hall.

Financial Crisis Inquiry Commission, United States. 2011. *The Financial Crisis Inquiry Report: Final Report of the National Commission on the Causes of the Financial and Economic Crisis in the United States*. Washington, DC: US Government Printing Office.

Findlay, I., J. Popham, and P. Ince. 2014. *Through the Eyes of Women: What a Co-Operative Can Mean in Supporting Women During Confinement and Integration*. Saskatoon, SK: Community-University Institute for Social Research

Greenberg, D. 1977. "Delinquency and the Age-Structure of Society." *Contemporary Crises* l.

Giovannetti, J. 2013. "Last Moments of Lac Mégantic: Surviors Share their Stories." *Globe and Mail*, November 28.

Glasbeek, Harry. 2002. *Wealth by Stealth: Corporate Crime, Corporate Law and the Perversion of Democracy*. Toronto: Between the Lines.

Gomme, Ian. 2007. *The Shadow Line: Deviance and Crime in Canada*. Toronto: Thomson-Nelson.

Gregory, J. 1986. "Sex, Class and Crime: Towards a Non-Sexist Criminology." In B. MacLean (ed.), *The Political Economy of Crime*. Scarborough, ON: Prentice.

Griffiths, Curt. 2004. *Canadian Corrections*. Toronto: Thomson-Nelson.

Griffiths, C., and S. Verdun-Jones. 1994. *Canadian Criminal Justice*, 2nd edition. Toronto: Harcourt Brace.

____. 1992. "White Collar and Corporate Crime." In R. Linden (ed.), *Criminology: A Canadian Perspective*, 2nd edition. Toronto: Harcourt Brace.

Hagan, J., and R. Linden. 2009. "Corporate and White Collar Crime." In R. Linden (ed.), *Criminology: A Canadian Perspective*, 6th edition. Toronto: Nelson

Hartnagel, T. 2000. "Correlates of Criminal Behaviour." In R. Linden (ed.), *Criminology: A Canadian Perspective*, 4th edition. Toronto: Harcourt Brace Canada.

____. 2004. "Correlates of Criminal Behaviour." In Rick Linden (ed.), *Criminology: A Canadian Perspective*. Toronto: Thomson-Nelson.

____. 2009. "Correlates of Criminal Behaviour." In R. Linden (ed.) *Criminology: A Canadian Perspective*, 6th edition. Toronto: Nelson.

Hayes, R.M., K. Lorenz and K.A. Bell. 2013. "Victim Blaming Others: Rape Myth Acceptance and the Just World Belief." *Feminist Criminology* 8, 3.

Hylton, J. 1982. "The Native Offender in Saskatchewan: Some Implications for Crime Prevention Programming." *Canadian Journal of Criminology* 24.

Jackson, A. 2015. "The Return of the Gilded Age: Consequences, Causes and Solutions." Ottawa: The

Broadbent Institute. <d3n8a8pro7vhmx.cloudfront.net/broadbent/pages/3987/attachments/original/1431376127/The_Return_of_the_Gilded_Age.pdf?1431376127>.

Johnson, H., and K. Rodgers. 1993. "A Statistical Overview of Women and Crime in Canada." In E. Adelbery and C. Currie (eds.), *In Conflict with the Law*. Vancouver: Press Gang.

Keck, J. 2002 "Remembering Kimberly Roger." *Perception* 25, 3/4.

Lum, Z. 2014. "Canada is the Only UN Member to Reject Landmark Indigenous Rights Document." *Huffington Post*, October 2.

MacEachen, E., A. Kosney, C. Ståhl, F. OHagan, L. Redgrift, S. Sanford, C. Carrasco, T. Emile and Q. Mahood. 2016. "Systematic review of qualitative literature on occupational health and safety legislation and regulatory enforcement planning and implementation." *Scandinavian Journal of Work, Environment and Health* 41, 1: 3–16.

McMullan, J. 1992. *Beyond the Limits of the Law*. Winnipeg: Fernwood

McKiernan, M. 2015. "The Going Rate: The 2015 Canadian Lawyer Legal Fees Survey Shows Litigation Fees Have Returned to Pre-recession Rates." *Canadian Lawyer Magazine* June

Mendleson, R. 2012. "Canada Manufacturing Job Losses: Study Finds Laid-Off Auto Workers still Struggling Years Later." *Huffington Post*, July 12.

Neuman, K. 2016. *Canadian Public Opinion on Aboriginal Peoples: Final Report*. Toronto: Environics.

New York Times. 1995. *25 Years for a Slice of Pizza*. March 5.

Office of the Prime Minister of Canada. 2015. *Minister of Status of Women Mandate Letter*. <pm.gc.ca/eng/minister-status-women-mandate-letter>.

Parliament of Canada. 2011. *Legislative Summary of Bill C-21: An Act to Amend the Criminal Code (sentencing for fraud)*. Ottawa: Queen's Printer (Catalogue no. 40-3-C21-E).

Pearce, D. 1978. "The Feminization of Poverty: Women, Work, and Welfare." *The Urban and Social Change Review* 11, 1–2.

Reasons, C., L. Ross, and C. Patterson. 1986. "Your Money or Your Life: Workers' Health in Canada." In S. Brickey and E. Comack (eds.), *The Social Basis of Law*. Toronto: Garamond.

Reiman, Jeffrey. 2007. *The Rich Get Richer and the Poor Get Prison*, 8th edition. Boston: Pearson.

Reiman, J., and P. Leighton. 2013. *The Rich Get Richer and the Poor Get Poorer*. Boston: Allyn and Bacon.

Richard, K. 1997. *The Westray Story, A Preidctable Path to Disaster: Report of the Westray Mine Public Inquiry*. Halifax, NS: Lieutenant Governor in Council.

Roberts, R.D., 2010. *Gambling with Other People's Money: How Perverted Incentives Caused the Financial Crisis*. Fairfax, VA: Mercatus Center.

____. 1996. *Bridging the Cultural Divide*. Ottawa: Supply and Services.

Samuelson, L. 1995. "Canadian Aboriginal Justice Commissions and Australia's 'Anunga Rules: Barking Up the Wrong Tree.'" *Canadian Public Policy* 21, 2.

Saskatchewan. 2004. *Commission of Inquiry into Matters Relating to the Death of Neil Stonechild*. <qp.gov.sk.ca//Publications_Centre/Justice/Stonechild/Stonechild.pdf>.

Snider, Laureen. 1985. "Legal Reform and the Law: The Dangers of Abolishing Rape." *International Journal of the Sociology of Law* 4.

____. 2015. *About Canada: Corporate Crime*. Black Point, NS: Fernwood Publishing.

Statistics Canada. 2011. "2011 National Household Survey: Data tables" (Catalogue No. 99-014-X2011037). <www5.statcan.gc.ca/olc-cel/olc.action?objId=99-014-X2011037&objType=46>.

Tang, K.L., 1998. "Rape Law Reform in Canada: The Success and Limits of Legislation." *International Journal of Offender Therapy and Comparative Criminology* 42, 3: 258–270.

Task Force on Federally Sentenced Women. 1990. *Creating Choices*. Ottawa: Correctional Service of Canada.

Taylor, I., P. Walton, and J. Young. 1973. *The New Criminology: For a Social Theory of Deviance.* London: Routledge.

Trading Economics. 2016. *Canada Youth Unemploymnet Rate 1976–2016.* <tradingeconomics.com/canada/youth-unemployment-rate>.

Transportation Safety Board of Canada. 2014. *Lac-Mégantic Runaway Train and Derailment Investigation Summary.* Ottawa: Queen's Printer (Catalogue no. R13D0054).

Truth and Reconciliation Commission of Canada. 2015. *Honouring the Truth, Reconciling for the Future: Summary of the Final Report of the Truth and Reconciliation Commission of Canada.* Ottawa: Queen's printer.

Tucker, S., and N. Turner. 2013. "Waiting for Safety: Responses by Young Canadian Workers to Unsafe Work." *Journal of Safety Research* 45: 103–110.

Turpel, M. [Aki-Kwe]. 1992. "Further Travails of Canada's Human Rights Record: The Marshall Case." In J. Mannette (ed.), *Elusive Justice: Beyond the Marshall Inquiry.* Halifax, NS: Fernwood Publishing.

Verdun-Jones, S. 2007. *Criminal Law in Canada.* Toronto: Thomson-Nelson.

Wotherspoon, T., and V. Satzewich. 1993. *First Nations: Race, Class, and Gender Relations.* Scarborough, ON: Nelson.

York, G. 1990. *The Dispossessed: Life and Death in Native Canada.* Toronto: Little

Zimring, F., G. Hawkins, and S. Kamin. 2003. *Punishment and Democracy: Three Strikes and You're Out in California.* New York: Oxford University Press.

6

Persistent Poverty

A Matter of Political Will

Jim Silver

YOU SHOULD KNOW THIS

- In 2013 Canada ranked an abysmal fifteenth out of seventeen industrialized countries in the incidence of child poverty.
- By 2006, the poverty rate was approximately 40 percent for Indigenous children, more than double the rate for all children. For First Nations children the poverty rate was 50 percent; for First Nations children in Manitoba it was 62 percent, and in Saskatchewan 64 percent.
- In 1996, the incidence of poverty for members of racialized groups was double, and by 2006 was triple that for the Canadian population overall.
- The incidence of low income for Canadians over age 65 has risen from 7.6 percent in 2000 to 11.1 percent in 2013, and for single seniors, who are disproportionately women, the rate is 27.1 percent.
- In March 2015, 852,137 people in Canada used food banks, which is more than the population of large cities such as Winnipeg, Hamilton or Quebec City, and more than double the 378,000 who had used food banks in 1989.
- In 2010 there were 61 billionaires in Canada. They owned twice as much wealth as the approximately 17 million Canadians in the bottom half of the income distribution.
- The average member of Canada's one hundred most highly paid CEOs earned as much by 12:18 PM on the second working day of 2016 as was earned by the average Canadian full-time employee in the *entire year.*
- Canada now ranks twenty-fourth for government expenditures on social programs amongst the thirty-five Organization for Economic Cooperation and Development (OECD) countries.
- Using international poverty measurements, Canada ranks nineteenth out of thirty industrialized nations for poverty among adults, twenty-first for families with children and twentieth for children.

Sources: Conference Board of Canada 2013; Macdonald and Wilson 2013; Block and Galabuzi 2011; Jackson 2016; Food Banks Canada 2015; Stanford 2011; Mackenzie 2016; Mikkonen and Raphael 2010; Raphael 2009.

IN A COUNTRY AS WEALTHY AS CANADA we could largely eliminate poverty, if we chose to do so. It's a matter of political will. Rates of poverty in some industrialized countries — the Nordic countries in particular — are very low, while those in other industrialized countries — Canada and especially the U.S. — are very high. This suggests that different ways of doing things — different societal arrangements and public policies — produce different levels of poverty. The end of this chapter provides the broad outlines of a strategy that would dramatically reduce the incidence and severity of poverty in Canada.

What Is Poverty?

The concept of poverty is often misunderstood. We can think of two broad categories: the poverty related "only" to a shortage of income; and that which is more complex, including a multitude of factors that worsen poverty's impact. These are best seen as being on a continuum, with poverty as a shortage of income, often a temporary phenomenon that may not cause lasting damage to those who experience it, at one end of the continuum — a student whose income is relatively low during her years at university, for example — and poverty as a more complex, multi-faceted and often long-term and even inter-generational phenomenon (and includes a shortage of money, but also many other severe symptoms) that produces great and often long-term damage to those who experience it, at the other end of the continuum.

When we think of poverty as a shortage of income, it is useful to differentiate between absolute poverty and relative poverty. Absolute poverty occurs when people have so little money that they cannot acquire the bare necessities of life. This is not the most common form of poverty in Canada, although it certainly does exist — think of Canada's many homeless people, sleeping on the streets or in crowded shelters — and when it does occur it produces many of the negative consequences associated with what is referred to as complex poverty. Relative poverty, by contrast, occurs when people's incomes are such that they can acquire some or most of the bare necessities of life, but are excluded from anything resembling a "normal" life.

Poverty at the other end of the continuum, complex poverty, exists when people experience not only a shortage of income, but also a host of other causally connected problems that can erode their spirit and trap them in a cycle of poverty. These include a high incidence of poor housing, poor health, low educational outcomes, exposure to street gang activity and related violence, social exclusion, racism and the stigmatization and stereotyping of entire communities and their residents. The effects of complex poverty are often internalized by the poor, resulting in a loss of self-confidence, an erosion of self-esteem and, in some cases, even a sense of hopelessness. This process has been described using two metaphors:

> One is the notion of a complex web — a web of poverty, racism, drugs, gangs, and violence. The other is the notion of a cycle — people caught in a cycle of inter-related problems. Both suggest the idea of people who are caught, trapped, immobilized, unable to escape, destined to struggle with forces against which they cannot win, from which they cannot extricate themselves. The result is despair, resignation, anger, hopelessness, which then reinforce the cycle, and wrap them tighter in the web. (CCPA-Mb 2005: 24)

This complex poverty has grown in urban centres in North America and Europe, especially in the past forty years, and is partly the product of global economic changes and the "retreat of the state" that are associated with the rise of neoliberalism. Often this poverty is racialized and spatially concentrated.

> The effects of complex poverty are often internalized by the poor, resulting in a loss of self-confidence and an erosion of self-esteem, and in some cases even a sense of hopelessness.

Its complexity and deep-rootedness is such that although we could solve it, there are no quick or easy solutions.

Poverty by the Numbers

Poverty is typically depicted in quantitative terms, using one or more of several possible measurements of annual income.

The low-income measure (LIM) has typically been used for making international comparisons and is increasingly being used in Canada, in part because the method is fairly simple: those experiencing low income or poverty have incomes that are 50 percent or less of the median income, adjusted for family size.

The market basket measure (MBM) includes actual expenditures on shelter, food, clothing, transport and other basic household needs, so as to produce a "modest, basic standard of living" (Statistics Canada 2011). Adjustments are made for family size and for costs in varying geographic locations. A family of a particular size and in a particular community experiences low income or poverty if their income is not sufficient to purchase this basket of essentials. This measure depends, of course, on just what is and is not included in the basket.

The after-tax low-income cut off (A/T LICO) has in the past been the most frequently used measure of poverty, although Statistics Canada, which produces the data, does not call it a measure of poverty but of low income. With the A/T LICO, the low-income threshold is reached when a family spends 20 percent more of its after-tax income than does the average family on food, clothing and shelter. Adjustments are made to accommodate seven different family sizes and five different ranges of community population, resulting in thirty-five different LICOs. For example, a family of four living in a community of 30,000 people would have a different A/T LICOthan a family of three living in a city of 1.2 million people. The base year for this calculation is 1992, in which year the average family spent 43 percent of its after-tax income on food, clothing and shelter. Those households that spend 63 percent (20 percent more than the average family) or more of their income on these three essentials have low income, or are in poverty.

All measures are, at least in part, arbitrary. A strict reliance on any of these quantitative measures can obscure as much as it reveals because, as important as money is in a monetized society such as ours, complex poverty is about more than a shortage of money.

Nevertheless, a quantitative approach can be useful, yielding insight into the temporal and spatial incidence of poverty. That is, a quantitative approach can help us understand if poverty rates are going up or down over time, if they are higher in some countries than others, or in some regions of a country than others, and which categories of people are most likely to be poor.

As shown below, the total number of people living in poverty in 2011, as defined by the A/T LICO, is roughly the same as in 1976. The numbers grew until the mid-1990s and have declined since. When we measure the *proportion* of people living in poverty, the trends over time depend in part upon which measure we use. If we use the A/T LIM, the rate of poverty has remained high; if we use the A/T LICO, it has declined steadily since the mid-1990s.

Thousands of Persons in Low-Income, LICO After Tax

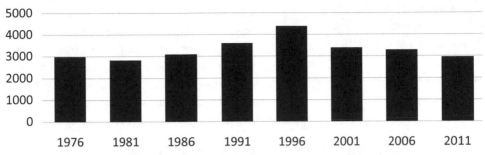

Source: Statistics Canada 2012a.

Percentage of Persons in Low-Income

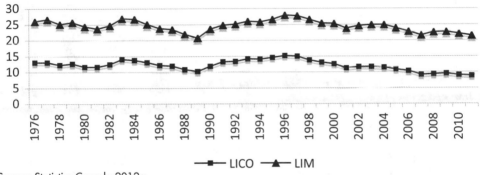

Source: Statistics Canada 2012a.

Whichever of these measures we use, poverty continues to be a major problem in Canada.

Other countries, especially the Nordic countries, have much lower poverty rates than Canada. Dennis Raphael shows that using the LIM, Canada performs "very poorly in terms of poverty, ranking 19th of 30 industrialized nations for adults, 21st for families with children, and 20th for children" (Raphael 2009: 8). Four countries — Denmark, Finland, Sweden and Norway — have child poverty rates of 5 percent or lower, while Canada's is triple that, at 15 percent (Mikkonen and Raphael 2010: 25).

People at Risk of Poverty

In Canada, particular categories of people are more likely than others to be poor. One important determination is family type: single mothers and unattached individuals are more likely than couples to be poor. In 2011, 21.2 percent of single mothers — just over one in every five — had incomes below the poverty line. As high as this is, it is less than half the level of 1996. This decline is likely attributable to the federal government's Canada Child Tax Benefit (CCTB) and the National Child Benefit Supplement (NCBS), introduced in 1997. The CCTB paid a fixed, tax-free amount per child to all parents; the NCBS was an additional amount based upon income. Together with the GST credit, these benefits have moved large numbers

> That some family types are more likely to be poor than others is largely a function of their differing relationships to the paid labour force.

of Canadians with children above the poverty line. It is likely that the federal Liberal government's proposed Canada Child Benefit will move even more children out of poverty. Unattached individuals experienced poverty rates ranging from just over 12 percent to 36 percent, depending upon the sex and age of the individuals. Rates for elderly married couples, by contrast, were just under 2 percent, while the average for two-parent families with children was just over 5 percent. The fact

PERCENTAGE OF FAMILY TYPES, LOW-INCOME AFTER-TAX LICO, 2011

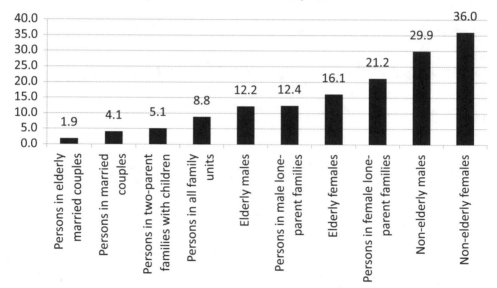

Source: Statistics Canada. 2011.

PERCENTAGE OF WOMEN AND MEN IN LOW-INCOME, LICO AFTER-TAX

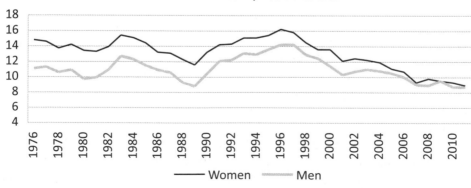

Source: Statistics Canada 2012a.

that some family types are more likely to be poor than others is Llargely a function of their differing relationships to the paid labour force.

Women are more likely than men to be poor. Since 1976, poverty rates for women have consistently been higher than for men, although in recent years the gap has been narrowing.

The higher rates of poverty experienced by women are due in part because women are paid lower wages than men. Monica Townson (2009: 16) found that 10 percent of men, but 20 percent of women, are in low-wage occupations. In Canada, the gender gap is "among the highest in the world." Women earn, on average, 71 percent of what men earn (Ontario Common Front 2012: 19). Approximately 60 percent of minimum wage earners in Canada are women; more than 70 percent of part-time workers are women (Cornish 2013: 7-8; Cornish 2012: 6).

Poverty among young people, both women and men, is relatively high. For all family types, those under the age of 25 years have a much higher incidence of poverty than do those 25 years and over (NCW 2004: 44). Low wages are a particularly important factor, and they are a function of the fact that young people comprise a large and growing proportion of workers employed in precarious jobs — jobs that are part-time, low-wage, non-union and without benefits or job security. For those young workers without post-secondary education, it is worse: as of 2013, "only one in two women and two in three men between 15 and 29 without a high school education are working" (Betcherman 2016). Economist Benjamin Tal (2013: 3) reports that a record high number of youth have *never* held a job, and without policy changes they are likely to remain chronically unemployed.

As shown below, from 1981 to 2011, younger men experienced a reduction in real wages — for men aged 17–24 years, between 13 and 14 percent, and for men 25–34 years, from 3 percent to a small gain of 1 percent. Older men experienced a net gain in real wages, ranging from 13 to about 20 percent. For women the trend is similar, although not as pronounced: younger women aged 17–24 years experienced reduced real income; women 25 years and older experienced real wage gains.

REAL HOURLY WAGE CHANGE (2010 $), MEN EMPLOYED FULL-TIME, 1981–2011

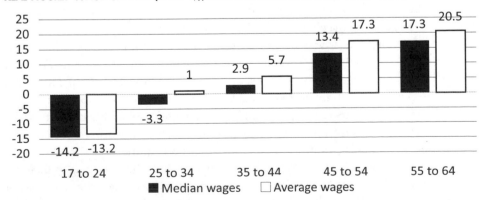

Source: Morissette, Picot, and Lu 2012.

For younger Canadians, this relative loss of purchasing power is made worse when related to changes in housing prices. While real incomes have remained relatively constant between 1976 and 2011, residential housing prices have risen more than six-fold. The growing gap between real incomes and housing prices is striking.

HOUSING PRICES COMPARED TO HOUSEHOLD INCOME

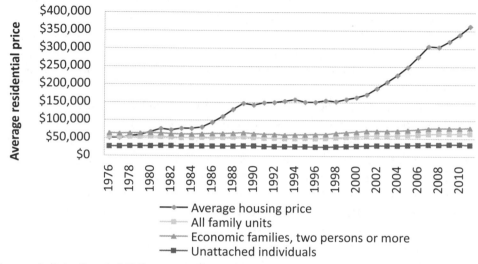

Sources: Statistics Canada 2012b; CREA 2013.

Rising housing prices are more likely to accrue to the benefit of older Canadians, who are more likely to be homeowners. The value of their homes has appreciated dramatically. For younger Canadians who may want to start a family and own a home, however, the rise in housing prices is a major disadvantage. Royal Bank of Canada data show that "to qualify to buy the average-priced two-storey home in Toronto and Vancouver ... a couple would need a gross annual household income of $132,100 and $156,200, respectively" (Carrick 2013). However, the average Canadian worker earned $47,358 in 2013 (Mackenzie 2016: 2). The result is that "houses are being priced out of reach for first-time buyers and households with income levels at or even a little above average" (Carrick 2013).

University tuition has also risen faster than real wages. Governments are reducing the share of universities' costs that they cover, meaning that students' tuition and other fees pay an ever-growing proportion of university costs — an increase from 12 to 35 percent from 1979 to 2009 (OCF 2012: 33), and to 37 percent by 2012 (Shaker and Macdonald 2015: 7).

Housing and education are two important means of establishing future security. Both are much more expensive today than in the past. Younger Canadians are particularly disadvantaged: their real wages are declining while the cost of housing and education is rising. As Angela MacEwen, economist with the Canadian Labour Congress, said when referring to their difficult job prospects: "It's a pretty bleak picture for young people, especially when you factor in rising house prices and the high cost of tuition" (quoted in *Winnipeg Free Press* 2013). This squeeze between reduced incomes and rising costs will likely lead to more poverty in the future.

Members of racialized groups — people (other than Indigenous people) who are non-Caucasian or non-white (Galabuzi 2001: 7) — are more likely than members of non-racialized groups to be poor. In 1996, the incidence of poverty for members of racialized groups was double, and by 2006 it was triple that for the Canadian population overall (Galabuzi 2006: 183; 186l; Block and Galabuzi 2011: 5). This is in large part because racialized Canadians are

> In 1996 the incidence of poverty for members of racialized groups was double, and by 2006 was triple, that for the Canadian population overall; by 2031 it's estimated racialized Canadians will make up 32 percent of the population.

over-represented in low-paid service sector jobs — janitors and security guards, for example. This is the "colour coded nature of work" (Block and Galabuzi 2011: 7). Racialized men are 24 percent more likely, and racialized women 48 percent more likely, to be unemployed than non-racialized men; racialized women earn, on average, 55.6 percent of what non-racialized men earn. These numbers are particularly significant because while in 2006 just over 16 percent of Canadians were part of a racialized group, by 2031 "it's estimated racialized Canadians will make up 32 percent of the population" (Block and Galabuzi 2011: 4).

For Indigenous people, rates of poverty are even higher. For example, in Winnipeg, home to Canada's largest urban Aboriginal population, 33 percent of Aboriginal households had incomes below the LIM in 2006, compared to 13.7 percent of non-Aboriginal households (Lezubski 2014: 120–121). In Canada in 2006 the median income for Aboriginal people was 30 percent lower than for the rest of Canadians. That gap had narrowed since 1996, but the rate at which Indigenous people were catching up was such that "it would take 63 years for the gap to be erased" (Wilson and Macdonald 2010: 8).

The problem is especially severe for Indigenous children. While 17 percent of all children in Canada in 2006 lived in families with incomes less than the LIM, the corresponding rate for all Indigenous children was 40 percent, and for First Nations children it was 50 percent. In Manitoba and Saskatchewan — each of which has large Indigenous populations — the rate of poverty for First Nations children was 62 and 64 percent, respectively. These are appalling rates of poverty.

A similar pattern prevails with children in racialized families. For example, one in three children in Ontario living in a racialized family is in poverty. In the Greater Toronto Area, while 10 percent of children of European ancestry live in poverty, the incidence of poverty increases to 20 percent for children in East Asian families, 33 percent for children in Arab and West Asian families and 50 percent for children of African families (OCF 2012: 24, 6).

If we consider these three categories of people together — young Canadians, racialized Canadians and Indigenous people, and especially children living in racialized and Indigenous families — and extrapolate into the future, there are reasons for concern. Indigenous Canadians constitute the youngest and the fastest growing demographic group in the country (Macdonald and Wilson 2013: 5); racialized Canadians comprised about 16 percent of Canada's population in 2006, but by 2031 they are predicted to be 32 percent of the population. So if current trends continue unabated, the number of people in poverty and the incidence of poverty will grow. And when we consider the circumstances of young

Canadians generally, we see that their real wages are stagnant while the costs of establishing some security in life via housing and education are rising rapidly. This too causes concern for future levels of poverty.

Food bank usage also reflects the continued need to be concerned about poverty. In March, 2015, 852,137 Canadians used food banks — more than the population of relatively large cities such as Hamilton and Winnipeg. The numbers of people using food banks have grown by 26 percent since 2008, following the severe economic crisis of 2007–08 (Food Banks Canada 2015). At the beginning of the 1980s there was no such thing as a food bank in Canada. It speaks volumes about the problem of poverty that in a country as rich as Canada we now take the existence of food banks for granted. And as Food Banks Canada (2012: 2) explains, "The key factor at the root of the need for food banks is low income," including people "working in low-paying jobs."

Poverty and the Labour Market

A person's relationship to the paid labour force — that is, whether they have a paid job at all, and if they do, how much it pays — is the most important determinant of poverty. Those who are unemployed are at high risk of poverty because of a shortage of income. Typically, the higher the rate of unemployment, the higher is the level of poverty. When unemployment declines, so does poverty.

Similarly, two-parent families and couples without children have the lowest incidence of poverty because they are most likely to have a second wage earner in the family — an option not available, by definition, to unattached individuals. Single-parent families have relatively high rates of poverty, largely because of the much greater likelihood that they will have no wage earners. A single parent with children under 5 years of age is more likely to be poor because of the difficulty of working when the children are not yet in school. Racialized Canadians and Indigenous people are more likely to be poor because they are more likely either to be unemployed or employed in a poorly paid job. In 2008, approximately two-thirds of poor families in Canada had at least one family member in the paid labour force (Canada 2012: 28). These are families of the working poor.

UNEMPLOYMENT AND POVERTY RATES

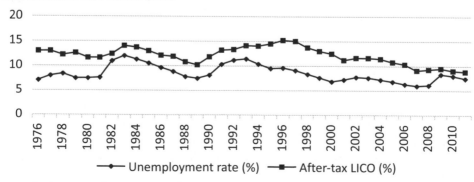

Sources: Statistics Canada 2012c, 2012d.

Families are especially vulnerable to being among the working poor when the sole income earner is working part-time, has a temporary job or is self-employed. Part-time jobs grew steadily from under 5 percent of all jobs in the 1950s to 19 percent by the early-mid 1990s. Since then the rate has stayed at about 19 percent — almost one in five. Part-time workers, on average, earn lower wages than full-time workers and are less likely to be unionized and to have a benefits package, such as pensions, medical/dental and paid sick leave, for example. In clerical, sales and service occupations, six of every ten workers — 60 percent — are part-time, so a relatively high proportion of people in those occupations are among the working poor (Statistics Canada 2009). In 2012 a record number of youth between 15 and 24 years of age were working part-time, and about 70 percent of them were "doing so involuntarily — meaning that they want to work full-time" (Tal 2013: 4).

PART-TIME WORK AS % OF TOTAL EMPLOYMENT

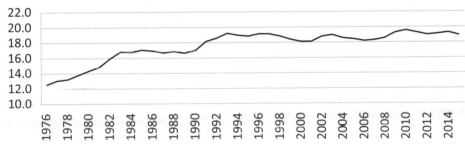

Source: Statistics Canada 2015a.

The same is the case for temporary workers, whose numbers are growing. In 2012, there were just over two million temporary workers in Canada, with the growth occurring primarily in the service sector. A growing proportion of temporary workers are young people, especially in the 15–24 age category.

Self-employment also contributes to low incomes. The downsizing of corporations and layoffs of government employees have made self-employment not only an option but also a necessity for many people. From 1976 to 2015, the number of self-employed Canadians more

SELF-EMPLOYMENT AS % OF TOTAL EMPLOYMENT

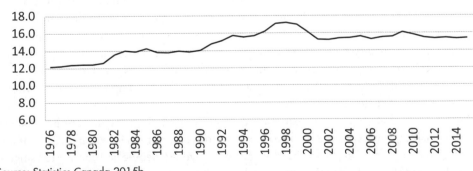

Source: Statistics Canada 2015b.

than doubled, from 1.2 million to 2.7 million; their share of the total numbers of employed grew from 12.2 percent to 15.4 percent. Self-employed workers earn less than paid employees, with the result that in 2001 "the incidence of poverty was four times higher among the self-employed than among salaried workers" (Fleury and Fortin 2006: ii).

Child Poverty

The Conference Board of Canada (2013) ranks Canada an abysmal fifteenth out of seventeen industrialized countries in the incidence of child poverty, and observes that this "is not only socially reprehensible, but it will also weigh heavily on countries' capacity to sustain economic growth in years to come." Worse, particular categories of children — those living in racialized and Indigenous families, for example — experience much higher rates of poverty, and these families are growing especially rapidly in Canada. The notion of "child poverty" is misleading. The National Council of Welfare (1996: 13) observed two decades ago that, "Children are poor because their parents are poor." The issue is poor families.

PERCENTAGE OF PERSONS 18 AND UNDER IN LOW-INCOME, LICO AFTER-TAX

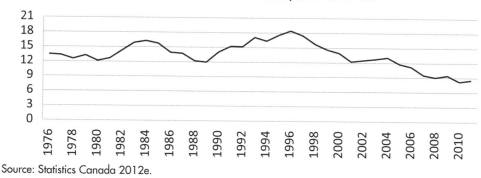

Source: Statistics Canada 2012e.

Growing up in a poor family can severely harm a child's life chances. David P. Ross and Paul Roberts examined the correlation between family income and twenty-seven indicators and found that children living in low-income families were "at a greater risk of experiencing negative outcomes and poor living conditions than those in higher-income families" (Ross and Roberts 1999: 3). For example, delayed vocabulary development occurs four times more frequently among children from low-income than high-income families; and "about one in six teens from low-income families is neither employed nor in school, compared to only one teen in twenty-five from middle- and high-income families." The result is what Ross and Roberts call "poverty of opportunity." Children who grow up in poor families are, on average, less likely to do well in life than are children who grow up in non-poor families (Ross and Roberts 1999: 8, 25, 34, 36).

This truth — that poverty, and especially complex poverty, harms children's life chances — is especially apparent in certain northern Indigenous communities. In March, 2016, it was reported that in Cross Lake, in northern Manitoba, six young people had committed suicide in the three months and more than one hundred children in that community of 6,000 were on suicide watch. As columnist Gary Mason (2016) reported: "Young people in remote towns such as Cross Lake are being overwhelmed by feelings of hopelessness and despair," with little to do "and even less to aspire to, especially a decent job … [since] unemployment is estimated at 80 percent."

The effects of poverty on educational attainment, to take another related example, are clear. Jane Gaskell and Ben Levin (2012: 12) have observed that "socio-economic status (SES) is the single most powerful factor associated with educational and other life outcomes, as has been found in virtually every important study of these issues, over time, in every country where such studies have been conducted." This is exemplified by studies done by Marni Brownell and her colleagues (2015: 43-45): in Winnipeg's highest-income quintile, more than 98 percent of young people graduated high school within six years of entering grade nine; in the lowest-income quintile, this proportion drops to 55 percent; and in some neighbourhoods where complex, racialized and spatially concentrated poverty prevails, only 25 percent of young people graduate high school within six years of entering grade nine (Brownell et al. 2006: 11; 2004: 6).

Poverty also adversely affects health. If we ask, "Why are some groups of people healthier than others?" the answer has far less to do with bio-medical and/or lifestyle factors (whether one smokes or is overweight or fails to exercise, for example), than with the social determinants of health (Wilkinson and Pickett 2009; Fernandez, MacKinnon, and Silver 2015; Raphael 2008). It is our living conditions — quality of housing, employment status and poverty — that are particularly important in shaping health outcomes. Those who are poor are much more likely to suffer poor health.

> Children raised in poverty, and especially complex poverty, are likely to experience more difficulties and are more likely to be poor themselves than children who do not grow up in poverty. Child poverty matters.

Children raised in poverty, and especially complex poverty, are likely to experience more difficulties and are more likely to be poor themselves than children who do not grow up in poverty. Child poverty matters.

The Problem of Inequality

Inequality "has become another inconvenient truth of our era, as challenging to our economy, our health, and our future as climate change" (Yalnizyan 2013: 1). In the past forty years, the gap between the richest Canadians and the rest of us has widened dramatically. For example, the 100 most highly paid Canadian Chief Executive Officers (CEOs) earned 106 times what the average Canadian worker earned in 1998; by 2005 they earned a remarkable 240 times the income of the average Canadian worker (Yalnizyan 2007: 28). In 2010 there were 61 billionaires in Canada. They owned twice as much wealth as the approximately 17 million Canadians in the bottom half of the income distribution (Stanford 2011: 2). By 2015 there were 89 billionaires in Canada (*Business Week* 2015). Economist Hugh Mackenzie (2016: 7) has calculated that by 12:18 PM on January 4, 2016, the second working day of the year, the average member of Canada's 100 highest-paid CEOs earned as much as the average Canadian

By 12:18 PM on January 4, 2016, the second working day of the year, the average member of Canada's 100 highest-paid CEOs earned as much as the average Canadian worker earned in the entire year.

worker earned in the *entire year*. The total compensation received by these one hundred highest-paid CEOs in 2014 ($896 million) "exceeds the reported budgetary deficits for 2014–15 of every province in Canada with the exception of Ontario, Quebec and Newfoundland and Labrador." This astonishing gap between the rich and the rest of us is important not only for reasons related to fairness, but also because the social determinants of health literature has shown definitively that a wide range of social ills — poor educational outcomes, poor health, a higher incidence of crime, for example — are a product not just of poverty, but also of inequality.

Adding up the Numbers

A quantitative analysis of poverty reveals many serious problems. The gap between the rich and the rest of us grows ever wider, with negative consequences for the rest of us. Poverty persists, and complex poverty in particular produces great damage. Women continue to experience a greater likelihood of being poor than men, in large part because of their relatively disadvantaged relationship to the labour market. Young people and children in both racialized and Indigenous families experience a much higher incidence of poverty than the population at large. In some cases — Indigenous children, for example — the shockingly high incidence of poverty is shameful and completely unacceptable in a country as wealthy as Canada. This is especially important given that it is young people generally, and the children of the fastest growing populations in Canada — racialized and Indigenous people — who are experiencing the highest rates of poverty. Therefore, we can anticipate a growth well into the future in the incidence of poverty and poverty-related problems.

Changes in the Economy over the Past Three Decades

These problems are in large part a function of the kind of economy we have in Canada and of the changes in the economy in recent decades. The Canadian economy — like virtually all economies in the industrialized world — was much weaker in the 1980s and first half of the 1990s than during the long, post-Second World War economic boom. The average annual rate of growth in gross domestic product (GDP) from 1950 to 1980 was about 1.5 times the rate from 1981 to 1989 and about 2.5 times the rate from 1990 to 1997. The average annual rate of employment growth from 1950 to 1980 was about four times the rate for 1990 to 1997. From 1998 to 2007, the rate of growth in GDP returned to levels about the same as 1981 to 1989, but it was still well below the 1950 to 1980 level, and it dropped further in the 2008–14 period to its lowest level, which is largely attributable to the financial crisis of 2007–08. Unemployment rates from 1981 to 1997 were almost double the rates from 1950 to 1980, and they remained almost half again as high from 1998 to 2014. It is no surprise, therefore, that the incidence of poverty as measured by the A/T LICO peaked at 16.2 percent in 1996 and that the numbers of those who were poor in 2011 were roughly the same as in 1976.

ECONOMIC PERFORMANCE INDICATORS, VARIOUS PERIODS

	Golden age (%)	Recessionary period (%)		Resumption of growth (%)	Period reflecting economic crisis and recovery (%)
	1950–1980	1981–1989	1990–1997	1998–2007	2008–2014
Average annual growth, real GDP	4.7	3.0	1.8	3.2	1.6
Average annual growth, real GDP per capita	2.8	1.7	0.7	2.2	0.5
Average annual growth, total employment	2.6	1.9	0.7	2.0	0.9
Average unemployment	5.4	9.6	10.0	7.2	7.3
Change in government spending (% of GDP) [A][B]	18.5	4.3	-3.5	-5.9	5.9
	1950–1980	1981–1996	1997–2007	2008–2015	
Annual federal deficit (% of GDP) [C]	0.3	-5.4	0.8	-1.0	
Closing federal debt (% of GDP) [D]	23	49.8	47.2	31.6	

A - General government spending (all levels).
B - Change in spending, as % of GDP, last year of period compared to first.
C - Annual federal deficit averaged over era.
D - Annual closing federal debt, averaged over era.
Sources: Government of Canada 2015; Stanford 1995, 1999; Statistics Canada 2016a, 2016b, 2015a, 2012f, 2007.

Why did the Canadian economy experience such a decline in the twenty-five years or so leading up to the late 1990s? The character of the capitalist global economy is a partial explanation. Capitalism has certain intrinsic features, chief among which is the constant competitive drive of individual business firms to earn the highest possible profits. This never-ending drive for ever more profits produces inevitable results. One is a constant revolutionizing of the means of production, leading to rapid technological change, as firms relentlessly innovate to find ways to gain an advantage over their competitors. Another is the constant drive to expand, which results in both ever-larger firms and geographic expansion, as transnational corporations scour the globe in search of lower wages, bigger markets and cheaper raw materials in order to maximize their profits. One of the results these trends is that many manufacturing firms have left Canada in search of greater profits elsewhere, creating a loss of very large numbers of well-paid jobs.

Job loss has been accentuated by the microelectronics revolution. By the mid-1970s, computers were beginning to be widely employed in factories and offices, resulting in massive job losses and an acceleration of the ease and rapidity by which investments can be moved around the globe, leading to still more job losses.

This trend has been accelerated by international trade agreements, such as the Canada-U.S. Free Trade Agreement, the North American Free Trade Agreement and potentially the Comprehensive Economic and Trade Agreement (CETA) and the Transpacific Partnership (TPP), both of which are in negotiation when this chapter was written. Trade agreements reduce the capacity of elected governments to place limits on the profit-seeking activities of transnational corporations (TNCs). They free TNCs from many of the "obstacles" — what most of us would look upon as benefits, such as environmental regulations and labour stand-ards — formerly imposed on corporations by governments, thus increasing the freedom not of individual citizens, but of TNCs. This is where the term "free trade" comes from — TNCs are freed from government restrictions. This makes it easier for them to scour the globe in search of the most profitable production sites, making it more likely that the corporations will set up shop wherever they can maximize their profits. This is especially the case for heavily unionized, relatively high-wage, mass-production industries that have left North America in large numbers over the past forty years.

For example, whereas one in three Americans worked in manufacturing in the 1960s, today only one in ten holds a manufacturing job (Hartmann and Sacks 2012). In Canada, manufacturing has declined from just under 20 percent of the economy in 1970, to about 10 percent in 2010 (I.M.F. 2013: 42). These jobs have relocated elsewhere, been eliminated by technology, been replaced by low-wage and often part-time and/or temporary work in the service sector or been replaced with various forms of self-employment. The labour market has increasingly become bifurcated, with a gap between very well-paid jobs, and contingent or precarious jobs that are poorly paid and insecure. Companies have sought not only to reduce wage levels, but also to create what the corporate sector calls more "flexible" workforces. Corporations have sought to move away from the relatively fixed and permanent high-wage regime characteristic of the mass-production industries of the 1950s and 1960s — sometimes called "Fordism," after the mass-production, relatively high-wage system introduced early in the century by Henry Ford — to a more flexible labour force, increasingly characterized by employment that is part-time, low-waged, non-union and without benefits or job security — what is referred to above as "precarious labour." Examples of this are the growth in part-time and temporary employment and in self-employment.

Another example of "flexibility" is the Canadian government's policies in recent years promoting the use of temporary foreign workers. Don Drummond, former Chief Economist at the Toronto-Dominion Bank, has said: "For sure it's depressed wage growth — with over 300,000 [foreign temporary] work-ers, I would use the word significantly" (quoted in Grant 2013; see also Yalnizyan 2013: 6). Just how significantly is revealed by Unifor economist Jim

> In Canada, manufacturing has declined from just under 20 percent of the economy in 1970, to about 10 percent in 2010. These jobs have relocated elsewhere or been eliminated by technology, replaced by low-wage and often part-time and/or temporary work in the service sector, or various forms of self-employment.

Stanford (2013), who found "over one in five net new jobs created in the entire economy from 2007 through 2012 went to one of these temporary foreign workers."

The increase in these kinds of precarious jobs and the related decrease in wages at the lower end of the income scale have been significant factors in the widening gap between the rich and the rest of us and in the persistence of poverty in Canada.

The Role of Unions

These trends have been worsened by the decline in the proportion of Canadian, private-sector workers who are unionized. Unions produce significant benefits for their members such as higher wages, improved benefits and job security (Ross et al. 2015: 138–140). Unions also bring the rule of law to the workplace. Rather than being subject to the arbitrary decisions of an owner or supervisor, unionized workers have the protection of rules and procedures embodied in a collective agreement negotiated and agreed to by management and workers. In this respect, one can see unions, however imperfect some specific unions may be, as important factors in contributing to both a vibrant economy — they add to the total purchasing power available — and a more democratic society. However, the proportion of Canadian workers in the private sector who enjoy the benefits of a union has been in decline in recent years.

UNION COVERAGE RATE

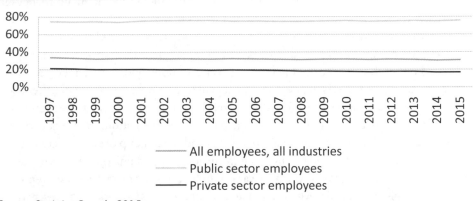

Source: Statistics Canada 2015c.

In the U.S.A., the decline has been dramatic, with the proportion of private sector workers who are unionized dropping below 7 percent in 2013. The weakening of unions is a key factor in the rise of income inequality and the related decline of the middle class. Jordan Brennan (2012: 17), an economist with the Canadian union Unifor, argues that the postwar growth in union density was a major cause of the creation of a robust middle class in Canada, while the more recent trend of de-unionization has contributed to the rich getting richer and the middle class eroding. American economist and former secretary of labor Robert Reich (2013) argues that "the decline of labour unions in America tracks exactly the decline in the bottom 90 percent share of total earnings, a shrinkage of the middle class." In Europe and

> Jordan Brennan, an economist with the Canadian union Unifor, argues that the post-war growth in union density was a major cause of the creation of a robust middle class in Canada.

North America the same is the case: "the really big story is the slow, inexorable decline of the middle class" (Freeland 2013). Increased unionization contributed dramatically to the rise of a relatively well-off middle class in the postwar years; the relative decline of unions is a major factor in the erosion of the middle class and the growing inequality of the neoliberal era.

Social Policy

The high poverty levels of the 1980s and 1990s were made worse by the dismantling during that period of the many social policy mechanisms put in place during the post-Second World War boom as a means of protecting individuals from the hazards of the inevitable ups and downs of the capitalist economy. Overall government spending — particularly on social programs — was dramatically reduced during the 1980s and 1990s. For expenditures on social programs, Canada ranks a low twenty-fourth out of thirty OECD nations (Mikkonen and Raphael 2010: 35). In addition, during the 1980s and 1990s, unemployment insurance was restructured to the disadvantage of unemployed workers, and the social safety net was significantly weakened.

These and other changes in social policy were directly related to the dramatic changes in the economy. The social policy initiatives from the 1950s to the early 1970s — Medicare, the Canada Assistance Plan, the Canada Pension Plan, the addition of the Guaranteed Income Supplement to Old Age Security and reforms to Unemployment Insurance, for example — were funded out of the proceeds of the long postwar economic boom. Sustained economic growth and relatively low levels of unemployment generated government revenue, the "fiscal dividend," to pay for new social programs. With the end of the postwar boom in the early 1970s and its replacement with a long period of relative economic stagnation, the fiscal dividend disappeared and was replaced by government deficits and the buildup of accumulated debt.

Most governments responded by choosing to cut social spending. The various elements of the welfare state erected during the postwar boom had, at least to some extent, removed the fear of unemployment and poverty that made people anxious to work at whatever wages and under whatever conditions were on offer. As early as 1975, advocates of unfettered, free enterprise were expressing concerns about the perceived consequences of the redistributive character of the welfare state at that time in advanced capitalist economies. As the Trilateral Commission (a non-governmental body founded by U.S. billionaire David Rockefeller in 1973, and comprised of corporate and other leaders from the U.S., Europe and Japan) put it, Western states had too much democracy — an "excess" of democracy — and the solution was to attack "big government" (Crozier et al. 1975). If profitability was to be fully restored, the relative security created by the welfare state had to be eroded.

In Canada, federal program spending as a share of GDP began to decline after 1974–75, when it was 20 percent of GDP. In the 1996–97 fiscal year it was about 13 percent of GDP, the lowest level as a share of the Canadian economy since 1950–51 (Yalnizyan 1998: 64).

It continued to decline, to 12 percent of GDP for fiscal years 1999–2000 and 2000–01, and in 2014–15 was at 13 percent (Canada 2012).

FEDERAL PROGRAM EXPENSES AS % OF GDP

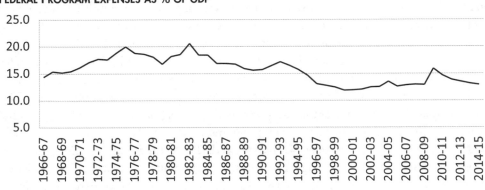

Source: Government of Canada 2015.

Cuts to public spending and thus to public sector jobs disproportionately affect women and disproportionately affect the social services that assist in the "reproduction" of families — childcare, social housing, for example — producing a deeply gendered impact. The purpose of such cuts is "to individualize and re-privatize the responsibility for caring, socially reproductive labour," and when such supports to families are cut, the burden falls most heavily on women (Naylor 2012). But also, the public sector jobs by which such services are delivered are disproportionately held by women, and because public sector jobs tend to be unionized, they are relatively well-paid. Austerity measures that cut social services hurt women in this way as well. And now seniors may be at risk: "After decades in decline, the incidence of poverty among seniors (aged 65 and older) rose 25 percent from 2007 to 2008," a shift that has disproportionately affected women and racialized seniors (OCF 2012: 22). Economist Andrew Jackson (2016: B2) reports that for Canadians over 65 years, the incidence of low income (as measured by the LIM) has grown from 7.6 percent in 2000, to 11.1 percent in 2013, while in that same year "senior singles (who are disproportionately women) had a very disturbing low-income rate of 27.1 percent."

Large cuts have been made, especially in the mid-1990s, to federal programs that transfer funds to the provinces. The amount transferred to the provinces for health, post-secondary education and social assistance by the federal Liberal government in 1996–97 and 1997–98 was $7 billion *less* than what would have been the case under the previous arrangements (Pulkingham and Ternowetsky 1999: 93; Yalnizyan 1998: 56), and the federal government got out of social housing at about the same time, contributing greatly to today's low-income housing crisis that is such a central part of complex poverty (Brandon and Silver 2015).

The standards that had existed under the postwar Canada Assistance Plan (CAP) — the cost-shared, federal-provincial program under which welfare and social assistance services were financed — were eliminated. Certain forms of assistance were "no longer mandated by legislation or directly supported by cost-shared transfers" (Pulkingham and Ternowetsky

1999: 94). Previously, under CAP, in order to receive federal funds for social assistance provinces were required to ensure that all people judged to be in need received funding, that benefit levels met basic needs, that an appeal procedure existed, enabling people to challenge welfare decisions, and that no work requirement was imposed as a condition of receiving social assistance. The removal of these standards, critics warned, would open the door "for jurisdictions to provide little or no assistance to those in need" (CCSD 1996).

That is precisely what happened after 1995. Most provinces cut back their benefit rates and/or shelter allowances and altered the rules of eligibility to programs of assistance (Yalnizyan 1998: 57). The Ontario government cut welfare rates by 21.6 percent in 1995; rates today are 55 percent lower than they were in the 1990s (Gaetz et al. 2013: 15). Several provinces introduced provincial workfare programs.

The social safety net has been badly damaged. The United Nations' Committee on Economic, Social and Cultural Rights, in a 2006 report on human rights in Canada, "notes with concern that in most Provinces and Territories, social assistance benefits are lower than a decade ago, that they do not provide adequate income to meet basic needs for food, clothing and shelter, and that welfare levels are often set at less than half the Low Income Cut-Off" (quoted in Osberg 2008: 31–32).

The trend in the U.S. has been the same. In 1996 President Bill Clinton committed to "end welfare as we know it" (Edelman 2012). He replaced the Aid to Families with Dependent Children program with a new program, Temporary Assistance for Needy Families, which tightened eligibility, cut the length of time one could be on welfare and reduced benefits. The numbers of low-income Americans receiving welfare benefits has been reduced dramatically — the Urban Institute "found that one in four low-income single mothers nationwide — about 1.5 million — are jobless and without cash aid" (DeParle 2012).

Changes to Canada's Unemployment Insurance (UI) had the same effect. In 1989–90 the federal government effectively privatized UI. With Bill C-21 the government withdrew from its role as financial contributor to this crucial program, leaving its financing completely in the hands of employees and employers. There followed a series of changes to UI in the early to mid-1990s, including stricter qualifying requirements and reductions in the level and duration of benefits, for example (Pulkingham and Ternowetsky 1999: 86). These trends were intensified with the introduction in 1996 of Bill C-12, which saw the creation of the new, re-named Employment Insurance (EI) system. The more restrictive provisions applying to EI served to accelerate the downward trend in the proportion of unemployed Canadians receiving benefits. While 74 percent of unemployed Canadians received UI benefits in 1990, only 39 percent received EI benefits in 2001 (CLC 2003), and the proportion remains roughly the same today. "Jobless benefits are at levels last seen in the early 1940s," more than seventy years ago (Yalnizyan 2010: 20). The erosion of EI continues. Changes in 2012 have produced "lower benefits and more stringent requirements that force [people] to commute long distances and accept lower pay and inferior working conditions," producing what has been described as "a bad-jobs policy that rewards low-road employers by forcing job-seekers to accept low pay and bad working conditions and that will, in short order, drive down community standards" (Guard 2012: 16–17).

All of this has taken place, not coincidentally, while the gap between the rich and the rest of us has grown ever wider, and poverty has persisted.

The cuts in social spending and the erosion of social programs were the result not only of dramatic economic changes, but also of conscious government policy. Governments have *chosen* to make certain economic and social policy changes, and not to make different kinds of policy changes. The Ontario Common Front (2012: 5), for example, has said: "It is not the inexorable march of global economics alone, but rather choices — choices in public budgets, and in economic and social policy" — that are driving growing levels of inequality and poverty.

> The cuts in social spending and erosion of social programs were the result not only of dramatic economic changes, but also of conscious government policy.

Today's dominant neoliberal ideology and related government policies — that is, choices that governments have made — have dramatically reduced the role of governments in providing support to those most in need. The result has been, among other things, a widening gap between the rich and the rest of us and the persistence in Canada of unacceptably large numbers of people living in poverty.

Blaming the Poor for Poverty

Why are Canadians not outraged by levels of poverty that are persistently much higher than the Nordic countries, for example, and much higher than they need to be? Why do we not demand that policies that benefit the richest Canadians be replaced by policies that produce greater equality and dramatically reduce the numbers in poverty?

A part of the reason is the dominance in this country of a "blame the victim" philosophy (Swanson 2001). Rather than explaining poverty as a function of dramatic changes in the economy and in the role of governments — as this chapter has attempted to do — high levels of poverty are attributed to the personal failings of those who are poor. In many cases the poor are demonized. When a large enough proportion of the population can be led to believe that high levels of poverty are caused by the personal failings of the poor themselves — because they are lazy or don't take enough initiative, or they drink too much or have too many children, for example — then it becomes difficult to mount an effective opposition to the policies that make people poor. In the U.S., this trend is, if anything, even worse (Greenbaum 2015). T-shirts worn by members of the National Rifle Association say: "I hate welfare," and "If any would not work neither should he eat" (Giroux 2013: 46). It is attitudes such as these that have led Frances Fox Piven (2011), long-time scholar of American poverty, to say that the U.S. has "been at war for decades now ... [and] it's been a war against the poor." Similar attitudes exist in Canada. In December, 2013, for example, then minister of industry James Moore said, in response to a journalist's question about child poverty: "Is it my job to feed my neighbour's child? I don't think so." Moore's statement reflects the pervasive view that the poor should be left to their own devices.

In other cases the political right attempts to define poverty out of existence. The Fraser Institute, via the work of Professor Christopher Sarlo, has sought to redefine poverty in a

narrow, purely monetary fashion to include only those unable to afford basic physical necessities, the absence of which would jeopardize one's "long term physical well being" (Sarlo
1996: 196). Using this narrow and "mean-spirited" (NCW 1998/99: 27) definition, Sarlo
(1996: 2) is driven to say, in defiance of the evidence, that "poverty, as it has been traditionally understood, has been virtually eliminated. It is simply not a major problem in Canada."

As long as the belief is maintained that the problems of the poor are their own fault, rather
than the product of economic structures and government policy choices, or that there really
are no genuinely poor people in Canada at all, we are more likely to continue to vilify or ignore
the poor than to mobilize to demand the changes that could dramatically reduce poverty.

Solutions to Poverty

Persistently high levels of poverty are not inevitable. Nations are fully capable of achieving
greater degrees of equality and dramatically lower levels of poverty. We know with certainty
that this is the case because, as shown above, other advanced industrialized nations have
poverty rates lower, and in some cases much lower, than Canada's. What can be done to
reduce Canada's persistently high levels of poverty?

Poverty exists when people do not have good jobs, and it is particular categories of
people — Indigenous people, single mothers and racialized minorities for example — who
are least likely to hold good jobs. Because a good job is a way out of poverty, a job creation
strategy would need to be a central part of a poverty reduction plan. At the heart of a good
job creation strategy is building things that Canada needs, hiring people to do the building
and related work and, in particular, hiring from those groups of people most detached from
the labour market.

Canada needs infrastructure — flood prevention in the face of climate change; repair,
maintenance and replacement of sewage and water systems; rapid transit in major Canadian
cities, for example. Canada would also benefit enormously from a green jobs strategy
— retrofitting public buildings and older residential homes would not only benefit the
environment, but also create very large numbers of jobs, and the cost of creating those
jobs and doing that work would be paid back in a relatively short period out of the resulting energy savings. Everyone would benefit. Hiring and training Indigenous people in
green jobs in Winnipeg's inner city, for example, has produced a significant ripple effect:
"successful trainees are often proud to become positive figures in their children's lives ...
[and] this can help break the cycle of family poverty" (Bernas and Hamilton 2013: 8). An
effective poverty reduction plan would include a national housing and a national childcare
strategy; the building and related work associated with these initiatives would also create
large numbers of jobs (Silver 2014).

Almost every aspect of a good poverty reduction plan would benefit from the application
of a community economic development (CED) approach. Good CED requires the active participation of, and takes its direction from, members of the low-income communities in which
it is being practiced on the grounds that poor people have crucial experiential knowledge of
their community's needs and strengths that outsiders are not likely to have. The best CED is
asset-based, which means that it identifies strengths in a low-income community — even

the most challenged communities have many strengths — and builds on those strengths. And the best CED uses a "convergence approach" (Loxley 2010), which is characterized by training and employing local people, purchasing locally, investing locally and producing to meet local peoples' needs. An example of a convergence approach is a housing strategy that builds rental housing for low-income people because that is the kind of housing that is most needed, trains and hires local, low-income people to do the building because they need the jobs, purchases building supplies from local suppliers who also hire and train low-income people and invests any surplus that may be earned back into the low-income community to continue to meet people's needs.

A CED approach applied to a national childcare strategy would build childcare centres across the country, targeting low-income communities in particular, hire from communities most marginalized from the paid labour force to construct the new childcare centres, train people from marginalized communities to become childcare workers, develop strategies to train and hire culturally appropriate childcare workers and purchase supplies for childcare centres — food for snacks for example — from local food providers that themselves employ people from marginalized communities.

The combination of these measures — building things that Canadians need, such as infrastructure, housing and childcare, and ensuring that among those hired to do the building and all the related work are large numbers of Canadians now detached from the labour market — would be a major step toward the elimination of poverty. And all Canadians would benefit, not only from the cost savings that would arise when the numbers in poverty are reduced, but also from their use of the things that would be built in this process.

Additional measures would include moving minimum wages toward a living wage, together with legislation to make it easier for those who choose to do so to form unions. An expansion of the benefits of trade unionism to the retail and service sectors, for example, would help to push up wage levels at the lower end of the income scale and thus address the problems of the working poor (Black and Silver 2008). Mikkonen and Raphael (2010: 54) observe that "there is strong evidence that an essential aspect of improving the quality of the social determinants of health is making it easier for Canadians to unionize their workplace."

To make such changes will require concerted political action that *demands* government policies that benefit the majority of Canadians, including those who are poor. At the moment there are few signs that we will soon see the emergence of this kind of socially and economically progressive political action. However, there are reasons to believe that such a campaign, if properly constructed, could find resonance among the broad Canadian population.

Canadians' Attitudes about Poverty

At the moment, most Canadians believe that poverty simply cannot be solved, that the problem is too overwhelming. Most Canadians see themselves as "middle class," and they are worried about their own economic circumstances, and quite rightly, given the growing gap described above. Canadians are concerned about their growing levels of personal indebtedness and fear that the "intergenerational bargain" — the deeply held assumption, and hope, that their children and grandchildren will do as well as they did, or better — is slipping away.

They see the poor as the "Other," and are inclined to place the blame for poverty on poor people themselves. All of this makes the development of an effective anti-poverty strategy particularly difficult.

Yet at the same time Canadians see themselves as being, and have aspirations to be, a caring society. They want leadership from political leaders in the development of specific plans to create opportunities for people who are poor:

> In an Environics poll taken in the fall of 2008, 90 percent of Canadians said they wanted the federal government to take leadership in reducing poverty. In virtually equal numbers (89%), they called for the Prime Minister and the Premiers to set targets and timelines to achieve this objective. (Broadbent 2010: 8)

This widely felt desire could be the basis upon which to build an effective anti-poverty strategy.

At the moment, what prevents this happening is the absence of organized political pressure — from trade unions and social movements and citizens in general — that *demands* such a rational, ethical and economically beneficial approach to public policy. Those currently exercising political power will continue to promote the neoliberal strategies of disinvestment at the lower end of the income scale until they are forced to do otherwise. It is in the interests of the vast majority of Canadians, including but not only the large numbers who are poor, to force them to do otherwise.

Glossary of Key Terms

Commodification: Turning something into a commodity, to be bought and sold for profit. Housing is a good example. Housing is a basic human need, and as a matter of human rights, decent quality housing ought to be available to all Canadians at a price they can afford. This is not the case because in our system housing is commodified — it is bought and sold for profit, like any other commodity — and there are no profits to be made in producing low-income rental housing, however great the need. The profits are made in producing housing that is so expensive that increasingly it is beyond the means of younger people and others with low incomes.

Complex poverty: Exists when people experience not only a shortage of income, but also some or all of the additional and interrelated problems of poor housing, poor health, low educational outcomes, exposure to street gang activity and related violence, social exclusion, racism and the stigmatization and stereotyping of entire communities and their residents. The effects of complex poverty are often internalized by the poor, resulting in a loss of self-confidence, an erosion of self-esteem and in some cases even a sense of hopelessness. Often this poverty is racialized and spatially concentrated. Its complexity and deep-rootedness is such that although we could solve it, there are no quick or easy solutions.

Free trade agreements (FTAS): Reduce the capacity of elected governments to place limits on the profit-seeking activities of transnational corporations (TNCS). FTAS free TNCS from many of the "obstacles" — (which most of us would look upon as benefits) such as environmental regulations and labour standards formerly imposed on corporations by governments, thus increasing the freedom not of individual citizens, but of TNCs. This is where the term "free trade" comes from — TNCs are freed from government restrictions. This makes it easier for them to scour the globe in search of the most profitable production sites, making it more likely that corporations will set up shop wherever they can maximize their profits.

Neoliberalism: The form of governance that seeks to reduce the role of the state and increase the role of the market. The means of this reduction include de-regulation, privatization, cuts in taxes, which are done in order to reduce the resources available to the state for public purposes and to leave more money in the hands of individuals for private purposes, and cuts in public spending.

Precarious jobs: The increasingly large numbers of jobs that are part-time and low-wage, and have no benefits, no security and no union protections. Such jobs are sometimes called "contingent" jobs.

Racialized poverty: Members of racialized groups — people (other than Indigenous people) who are non-Caucasian or non-white — are more likely than members of non-racialized groups to be poor. In 2006, the incidence of poverty for members of racialized groups was triple that for the Canadian population overall. Racialized Canadians are over-represented in low-paid service sector jobs such as janitors and security guards, for example. Racialized men are 24 percent more likely, and racialized women 48 percent more likely, to be unemployed than non-racialized men. Racialized women earn, on average, 55.6 percent of what non-racialized men earn.

Social determinants of health: Our health is shaped much more by our living conditions — quality of housing, employment status, access to food, for example — than by bio-medical determinants such as medicines and hospitals and forms of surgery, or our lifestyles, such as the extent to which we exercise or smoke. Poverty, in particular, makes people sick.

Workfare: A program in which government forces people on social assistance to work in order to qualify for social assistance benefits. It is rooted in the assumption — many believe a false assumption — that people are not working because they do not have the incentive to work and therefore must be forced.

Working poor: People who are employed, but whose employment earnings generate incomes that are below the "poverty line."

Questions for Discussion

1. Discuss the relationship between poverty and family type. How are changes in the structure of the family over the past thirty-five years related to poverty? What kinds of solutions to poverty could be designed in response to changes in family type?

2. Why are women more likely to experience low incomes than men?

3. What relationship does poverty have to jobs? How are changes in the structure of the labour market over the past thirty-five years related to poverty? What kinds of solutions to poverty could be designed in response to changes in the labour market?

4. Who, or what, is "freed" by free trade agreements, and what are the consequences for corporations and for working people?

5. How are changes to Canada's social welfare system over the past thirty-five years related to poverty? What kinds of solutions to poverty could be designed in response to changes in the social welfare system?

6. What is CED? How and why could it be useful in combating poverty?

7. What do we mean when we say that all quantitative measures of poverty are, at least in part, arbitrary?

8. Why are poverty levels so high in Canada compared to many European countries? Why have governments failed to institute policies that are known to reduce poverty levels? What might be done to encourage governments to introduce such policies?

Resources for Activists

Caledon Institute of Social Policy: www.caledoninst.org
Campaign 2000: www.campaign2000.ca
Canada Without Poverty: www.cwp-csp.ca
Canadian Association of Food Banks: www.foodbankscanada.ca
Canadian Centre for Policy Alternatives: www.policyalternatives.ca
Make Poverty History: www.makepovertyhistory.ca
PovNet: www.povnet.org
Wellesley Institute: www.wellesleyinstitute.com

Acknowledgements

I am pleased to acknowledge the generous financial support of the Social Sciences and Humanities Research Council of Canada through the Manitoba Research Alliance grant titled "Partnering for Change — Community-Based Solutions for Aboriginal and Inner-City Poverty." A particular thanks to Matthew Rogers for his work in preparing the figures in this chapter.

References

Bernas, K., and B. Hamilton. 2013. *Creating Opportunities with Green Jobs: The Story of* BUILD *and* BEEP. Winnipeg: Canadian Centre for Policy Alternatives–Manitoba.
Betcherman, G. 2016. "No Work, out of school — they need opportunities too." *Globe and Mail, Report on Business,* January 5.
Black, E., and J. Silver. 2008. *Building a Better World: An Introduction to Trade Unionism in Canada, 2nd edition.* Halifax and Winnipeg: Fernwood Publishing.
Block, S., and G. E. Galabuzi. 2011. *Canada's Colour Coded Labour Market.* Ottawa and Toronto:

Canadian Centre for Policy Alternatives and the Wellesley Institute.

Brandon, J., and J. Silver (eds.). 2015. *Poor Housing: A Silent Crisis.* Halifax and Winnipeg: Fernwood Publishing.

Brennan, J. 2012. *A Shrinking Universe: How Concentrated Corporate Power Is Shaping Income Inequality in Canada.* Ottawa: Canadian Centre for Policy Alternatives.

Broadbent, E. 2010. *The Rise and Fall of Economic and Social Rights: What Next?* Ottawa: Canadian Centre for Policy Alternatives.

Brownell, M., R. Fransoo, and P. Martens. 2015. "Social Determinants of Health and the Distribution of Health Outcomes in Manitoba." In L. Fernandez, S. MacKinnon, and J. Silver (eds.), *The Social Determinants of Health in Manitoba, 2nd edition.* Winnipeg: Canadian Centre for Policy Alternatives--Manitoba.

Brownell, M., N. Roos, and R. Fransoo. 2006. "Is the Glass Half Empty? A Population-Based Perspective on Socio-Economic Status and Educational Outcomes." *Choices.* Montreal: Institute for Research on Public Policy.

Business Week. 2015. "Canada's Richest People." January 15.

Canada. 2012. *The National Child Benefit Progress Report 2008.* Ottawa: Public Works and Government Services.

Carrick, R. 2013. "The Scary Decline of Housing Affordability." *Globe and Mail,* June 18.

CCPA–Mb (Canadian Centre for Policy Alternatives–Manitoba). 2005. *The Promise of Investment in Community-Led Renewal: State of the Inner City Report 2005. Part II. A View for the Neighbourhoods.* Winnipeg.

CCSD (Canadian Council on Social Development). 1996. *Maintaining a National Social Safety Net: Recommendations on the Canada Health and Social Transfer.* Ottawa.

CLC (Canadian Labour Congress). 2003. *Falling Unemployment Insurance Protection for Canada's Unemployed.* Ottawa: Canadian Labour Congress.

Conference Board of Canada. 2013. *How Canada Performs: A Report Card on Canada.* Ottawa: Conference Board of Canada. <conferenceboard.ca/hcp/details/society/child-poverty.aspx>.

Cornish, M. 2012. *A Living Wage as a Human Right.* Toronto: Canadian Centre for Policy Alternatives–Ontario.

____. 2013. *Ten Ways to Close Ontario's Gender Pay Gap.* Toronto: Canadian Centre for Policy Alternatives–Ontario.

CREA (Canadian Real Estate Agency). 2013. "Canada, average house price." Internal data, available upon request from CREA.

Crozier, M., S.P. Huntington, and J. Watanuki. 1975. *The Crisis of Democracy: Report on the Governability of Democracies to the Trilateral Commission.* New York: New York University Press.

DeParle, J. 2012. "Welfare Limits Left Poor Adrift as Recession Hit." *New York Times,* April 7.

Edelman, P. 2012. *So Rich, So Poor: Why It's So Hard to End Poverty in America.* New York: New Press.

Fernandez, L., S. MacKinnon, and J. Silver (eds.). 2015. *The Social Determinants of Health in Manitoba, 2nd edition.* Winnipeg: Canadian Centre for Policy Alternatives–Manitoba.

Fleury, D., and M. Fortin. 2006. *When Working Is Not Enough to Escape Poverty: An Analysis of Canada's Working Poor.* Ottawa: Human Resources and Social Development Canada.

Food Banks Canada. 2012. *Hunger Count: A Comprehensive Report on Hunger and Food Bank Use in Canada, and Recommendations for Change.* Toronto: Food Banks Canada.

____. 2015. *Hunger Count: A Comprehensive Report on Hunger and Food Bank Use in Canada, and Recommendations for Change.* Toronto: Food Banks Canada.

Freeland, C. 2013. "Fear of Falling Out of Middle Class Stalks U.S." *Globe and Mail, Report on Business,*

April 26.

Gaetz, S., J. Donaldson, T. Richter, and T. Gulliver. 2013. *The State of Homelessness in Canada 2013.* Toronto: Canadian Homelessness Research Network Press.

Galabuzi, G-E. 2001. *Canada's Creeping Economic Apartheid: The Economic Segregation and Social Marginalization of Racialized Groups.* Toronto: Centre for Social Justice.

____. 2006. *Canada's Economic Apartheid: The Social Exclusion of Racialized Groups in the New Century.* Toronto: Canadian Scholars' Press.

Gaskell, J., and B. Levin. 2012. *Making a Difference in Urban Schools: Ideas, Politics and Pedagogy.* Toronto: University of Toronto Press.

Giroux, H. 2013. "Violence, USA: The Warfare State and the Hardening of Everyday Life." *Monthly Review* 65, 1 (May).

Government of Canada 2015. *Fiscal Reference Tables.* Ottawa: Department of Finance.

Grant, Tavia. 2013. "Employers' boon, Canada's not so much." *Globe and Mail Report on Business,* April 20: B4.

Greenbaum, S.D. 2015. *Blaming the Poor: The Long Shadow of the Moynihan Report on Cruel Images about Poverty.* New Brunswick, New Jersey and London: Rutgers University Press.

Guard, J. 2012. "Conservatives' EI Reform is a Bad-Jobs Policy." *Canadian Dimension* 46, 4 (July–August).

Hartmann, T., and S. Sacks. 2012. "America the Third-World Nation in Just 4 Easy Steps." *The Daily Take, Op-Ed,* November 10.

Hennessey, T. 2010. "The Great Communications Challenge: The Growing Gap." Presentation to an ad-hoc anti-poverty group in Winnipeg, July 20.

IMF (International Monetary Fund). 2013. *Canada: 2012 Article IV Consultation.* Washington, D.C.: International Monetary.

Jackson, A. 2016. "Ottawa Should Reconsider Seniors' Policy." *Globe and Mail Report on Business,* January 7.

Katz, M.B. 1989. *The Undeserving Poor: From the War on Poverty to the War on Welfare.* New York: Pantheon Books.

Lezubski, D. 2014. *Demographic Review and Update of Selected Manitoba Urban Aboriginal Populations.* Winnipeg: Intergovernmental Strategic Aboriginal Alignment Working Group.

Loxley, J. 2010. *Aboriginal, Northern and Community Economic Development: Papers and Retrospectives.* Winnipeg: Arbeiter Ring.

Macdonald, D., and D. Wilson. 2013. *Poverty or Prosperity: Indigenous Children in Canada.* Ottawa: Canadian Centre for Policy Alternatives.

Mackenzie, H. 2016. *Staying Power: CEO Pay in Canada.* Ottawa: Canadian Centre for Policy Alternatives.

Mason, G. 2016. "Behind the Tragedy of Cross Lake." *Globe and Mail,* March 18.

Mikkonen, J., and D. Raphael. 2010. *Social Determinants of Health: The Canadian Facts.* Toronto: York University School of Health Policy and Management. <thecanadianfacts.org/>.

Morissette, R., G. Picot, and Y. Lu. 2012. *The Evolution of Canadian Wages Over the Last Three Decades.* Ottawa: Statistics Canada.

NCW (National Council of Welfare). 1996. *Poverty Profile 1995.* Ottawa: National Council of Welfare.

____. 1998/99. *A New Poverty Line: Yes, No or Maybe?* Ottawa: National Council of Welfare.

____. 2004. *Poverty Profile 2001.* Ottawa: National Council of Welfare.

Naylor, A. 2012. "Economic Crisis and Austerity: The Stranglehold on Canada's Families." *Socialist Project, E-Bulletin* 614, April 9.

OCF (Ontario Common Front). 2012. *Falling Behind: Ontario's Backslide into Widening Inequality, Growing Poverty and Cuts to Social Programs.* Toronto: Ontario Common Front.

Osberg, L. 2008. *A Quarter Century of Economic Inequality in Canada: 1981–2006.* Ottawa: Canadian Centre for Policy Alternatives.

Piven, F.F. 2011. "The War Against the Poor." *TomDispatch,* November 11 <tomdispatch.com/post/175463/tomgram%3A_frances_fox_piven%2C_the_war_on_the_home_front/>.

Pulkingham, J., and G. Ternowetsky. 1999. "Neoliberalism and Retrenchment: Employment, Universality, Safety Net Provisions and a Collapsing Canadian Welfare State." In Dave Broad and Wayne Antony (eds.), *Citizens or Consumers? Social Policy in a Market Society.* Halifax: Fernwood Publishing.

Raphael, D. 2008. *Social Determinants of Health: Canadian Perspectives, 2nd edition.* Toronto: Canadian Scholars' Press.

_____. 2009. "Poverty, Human Development, and Health in Canada: Research, Practice and Advocacy." *Canadian Journal of Nursing Research* 41, 2.

Reich, R. 2013. "The Non Zero-Sum Society." *Huffington Post,* August 18.

Ross, D., and P. Roberts. 1999. *Income and Child Well-Being: A New Perspective on the Poverty Debate.* Ottawa: Canadian Council on Social Development.

Ross, S., L. Savage, E. Black, and J. Silver. 2015. *Building a Better World: An Introduction to the Labour Movement in Canada, 3rd edition.* Halifax and Winnipeg: Fernwood Publishing.

Sarlo, C. 1996. *Poverty in Canada, 2nd edition.* Vancouver: Fraser Institute.

Shaker, E., and D. Macdonald. 2015. *What's the Difference? Taking Stock of Provincial Tuition Fee Policies.* Ottawa: Canadian Centre for Policy Alternatives.

Silver, J. 2006. *In Their Own Voices: Building Urban Aboriginal Communities.* Halifax: Fernwood Publishing.

_____. 2014. *About Canada: Poverty.* Halifax and Winnipeg: Fernwood Publishing.

Stanford, J. 1995. "The Economics of Debt and the Remaking of Canada." *Studies in Political Economy* 48: 113–135.

_____. 1999. *Paper Boom.* Ottawa: Canadian Center for Policy Alternatives.

_____. 2011. "Canada's Billionaires." *The Monitor.* Ottawa: Canadian Centre for Policy Alternatives, November.

_____. 2013. "It'll Take More Than Window-Dressing to Fix This Problem." *CCPA Monitor,* June.

Statistics Canada. 2007. "Gross domestic product at 2007." Table 380-0106. <www5.statcan.gc.ca/cansim/pick-choisir?lang=eng&p2=33&id=3800106>.

_____. 2009. "Labour Force Historical Review 2009." Table 002. Catalogue No. 71F0004XVB.

_____. 2011. "Persons in low income, by economic family type." Table 202-0804. <www5.statcan.gc.ca/cansim/a05?lang=eng&id=2020804>.

_____. 2012a. "Persons in Low Income." <statcan.gc.ca/tables-tableaux/sum-som/l01/cst01/famil19e-eng.htm>.

_____. 2012b. "Average after-tax income, by economic family type." Table 202-0603. <statcan.gc.ca/tables-tableaux/sum- som/l01/cst01/famil21a-eng.htm>.

_____. 2012c. "Unemployment rate, Canada." Table 109-5324, CANSIM. <statcan.gc.ca/cansim/a03?lang=eng&pattern=109-5324..109-5326&p2=31>.

_____. 2012d. "Persons in low income families, annual." Table 202-0802, CANSIM. <statcan.gc.ca/tables-tableaux/sum-som/l01/cst01/famil19e-eng.htm>.

_____. 2012e. "Persons in low income families." Table 202-0802. <statcan.gc.ca/tables-tableaux/sum-som/l01/cst01/famil19e-eng.htm>.

____. 2012f. *National Income and Expenditure Accounts: Data Tables.* Catalogue number 13-019-X. <statcan.gc.ca/olc-cel/olc.action?objId=13-019-X&objType=2&lang=en&limit=0>.

____. 2015a. "Labour force survey estimates (LFS), by sex and age group." Table 282-0002. <www5. statcan.gc.ca/cansim/pick-choisir?lang=eng&p2=33&id=2820002>.

____. 2015b. "Labour force survey estimates (LFS), employment by class of worker." Table 282-0012. <www5.statcan.gc.ca/cansim/pick-choisir?lang=eng&p2=33&id=2820012>.

____. 2015c. "Labour force survey estimates (LFS)." Table 282-0078. <www5.statcan.gc.ca/cansim/ pick-choisir?lang=eng&p2=33&id=2820078>.

____. 2016a. "Gross domestic product (GDP) and Gross National Product (GNP)." Table 380-0030, CANSIM. <www5.statcan.gc.ca/cansim/pick-choisir?lang=eng&p2=33&id=3800080>.

____. 2016b. "Revenue, expenditure and budgetary balance." Table 380-0080. <statcan.gc.ca/ cansim/a26?lang=eng&id=3800080>.

Swanson, J. 2001. *Poor-Bashing: The Politics of Exclusion.* Toronto: Between the Lines.

Tal, B. 2013. *Dimensions of Youth Unemployment in Canada.* Toronto: CIBC World Markets Inc.

Townson, M. 2009. *Women's Poverty and the Recession.* Ottawa: Canadian Centre for Policy Alternatives.

Wilkinson, R., and K. Pickett. 2009. *The Spirit Level: Why More Equal Societies Almost Always Do Better.* London: Allen Lane.

Wilson, D., and D. Macdonald. 2010. *The Income Gap Between Aboriginal Peoples and the Rest of Canada.* Ottawa: Canadian Centre for Policy Alternatives.

Winnipeg Free Press. 2013. "Youth Still Face Gloom; Issue Gets Political." May 11.

Yalnizyan, A. 1998. *The Growing Gap: A Report on Growing Inequality Between Rich and Poor in Canada.* Toronto: Centre for Social Justice.

____. 2007. *The Rich and the Rest of Us: The Changing Face of Canada's Growing Gap.* Ottawa: Canadian Centre for Policy Alternatives.

____. 2010. *The Rise of Canada's Richest 1 Percent.* Ottawa: Canadian Centre for Policy Alternatives.

____. 2013. "Study of Income Inequality in Canada—What Can Be Done?" Presentation to the House of Commons Standing Committee on Finance, April 30.

7

Embodied Oppression

The Social Determinants of Health

Elizabeth McGibbon

YOU SHOULD KNOW THIS

- The richest 20 percent of Canadians own nearly 70 percent of the wealth. The bottom 20 percent own almost nothing (less than 1 percent). The richest eighty-six families own more than the bottom 11 million people combined. If we consider financial assets such as stocks and bonds, the top 10 percent own 60 percent of financial assets — more than the bottom 90 percent combined. Canada's CEOs make 206 times the salary of their average worker, one of the worst wage gaps of any advanced country.
- The erosion of the social safety net has taken place during a time when uncollected corporate taxes amount to $88 billion dollars a year, which corporations and wealthy individuals are estimated to divert to overseas tax havens every year.
- From 2000 to 2010, studies comparing lung, breast, prostate and colorectal cancer mortality rates and mortality trends for Blacks and whites in the U.S. showed that survival rates are consistently lower in Black people that in white people. The breast cancer mortality disparity ratio between Black and white women increased from 30.3 to 41.8 perecnt.
- Among patients fifty years or older in Canada, women are less likely than men to be admitted to an ICU and to receive selected life-supporting treatments, and they are more likely than men to die after a critical illness. Older lesbians often experience triple discrimination because of their status as women, older adults and lesbians, while ethnic minority LGBT older adults face a "quadruple whammy."
- Excess hospitalization rates associated with low socio-economic status account for an estimated 33 to 40 percent of hospitalizations in Canada. The economic burden is substantial. In fifteen metropolitan areas in Canada, the total yearly estimated excess costs were $123 million for males and $125 million for females. National costs are therefore likely in the multibillion dollar range
- At least 200,000 Canadians experience homelessness in any given year. At least 30,000 Canadians are homeless on any given night. At least 50,000 Canadians are part of the "hidden homeless" on any given night, staying with friends or relatives on a temporary basis because they have nowhere else to go.
- Each year, 19,000 day-surgery operations are performed to treat cavities among children younger than age six. Surgery rates are significantly higher for children from Indigenous populations (8.6 times higher), least affluent neighborhoods (3.9 times higher) and rural areas (3.1 times higher). In more than one in five day-surgery visits (22.3 percent), families travelled two or more hours for care.
- In 2010 Canada dropped from sixth to twenty-fourth on international infant mortality indicators, just above Hungary and Poland. The main causes cited by researchers are poverty, isolation and premature births.

Sources: O'keefe, Meltzer and Bethea 2015; Fowler, Sabur, Li et al. 2007; Clay 2014; CIHI 2010, 2012; Priest 2010.

When one individual inflicts bodily injury upon another such that death results, we call the deed manslaughter; when the assailant knew in advance that the injury would be fatal, we call this deed murder. But when society places hundreds of pro-letarians in such a position that they inevitably meet a too early and an unnatural death, one which is quite as much a death by violence as a sword or bullet; when it deprives thousands of the necessities of life, places them under conditions which they cannot live — forces them through the strong arm of the law, to remain in such conditions until that death ensues, which is the inevitable consequence — knows that these thousands of victims must perish, yet permits these conditions to remain, its deed is murder just as surely as the deed of the single individual; disguised malicious murder, murder against which none can defend himself, which does not seem what it is, because no man sees the murderer, because the death of the victim seems a natural one, since the offense is more one of omission than commission, but murder it remains. (Engels 2009 [1845]: 152)

HUMAN HEALTH IS INTIMATELY TETHERED to its social, political, economic and cultural contexts. In all countries, whether low, middle or high income, there are wide disparities in the health status of different social groups. The lower an individual's socio-economic position, the higher their risk of poor health (WHO 2011). We live and die according to our food and housing security, the neighbourhoods we live in, our access to health and social care and education and the wider set of forces and systems shaping the conditions of daily life. These forces and systems include economic policies and systems, development agendas, social norms, social policies and political systems (WHO 2011). Oppression is a process that involves all of these institutionalized procedures and practices of domination and control that create and sustain injustice. The specifics of people's health, and how disease and ill-ness are inscribed on the body, are all central aspects of understanding how oppression is embodied, on the ground, in people's everyday struggles across the lifecourse. Oppression is also embodied in our planet — it is the living, breathing ecological context for all our lives.

According to Juha Mikkonen and Dennis Raphael (2010), the primary factors that shape the health of Canadians are not medical treatments or lifestyle choices, but rather the living conditions they experience. These conditions have come to be known as the social determinants of health (SDH). They include early childhood development, employment and working conditions, income and its equitable distribution, food and housing security, health care access, education, social exclusion, social safety nets and self determination. Despite substantial evidence that these social determinants are the strongest determinants of health, an individualistic, largely apolitical stance about health persists. Notable exceptions include inno-vations in community health, Indigenous health and public health. Over the past few decades, the emergence of critical health studies is providing a counter-narrative to this acontextual approach to analyzing and tackling human and ecological health

> Critical health studies provide a counter-narrative to an acontextual approach to analyzing and tackling human and ecological health inequities.

inequities. Health inequities, the systematic differences in the health status across different population groups, have significant social and economic costs to individuals and societies. We are in dire need of a critical counter-narrative to continue to create an intellectual and ethical space where we care about each other and the planet and where we understand that human suffering and ecological degradation have political origins that we can challenge and change.

Health and Wellness: Contrasting Dominant and Critical Perspectives

Critical perspectives about health and wellness help us understand the root causes of health inequities and identify some of their unjust structural, public policy–created origins. A central aspect of our counter-narrative is a deliberative and detailed critique of current health paradigms, particularly biomedical influences that remain so dominant and so intransigent. Skipping this analytic step makes it difficult to sustain action to destabilize the dominance of biomedical thinking and its influence on the ways that health is framed.

Persistent Dominance of the Biomedical Model

The most accurate predictor of health outcomes is socio-economic status (ses). Yet, we are inundated with the rhetoric of improving our lifestyles, losing weight, quitting smoking and getting more exercise, despite the fact that obesity and smoking rates are most strongly related to social class — poverty is not a lifestyle. Biomedical "neutrality" has played, and continues to play, a central role in social control. If we can keep citizens and public policy–makers boxed into an apolitical body-part-focused framing of human health, then there is little room for questioning the politics and economics of health and well-being. Although the dominance of biomedicine has been critiqued extensively (see Breggin 2008, 1991; Breggin and Ginger 1998; Caplan 1996; Illich 1976; Zola 1978), it is centrally important to continually underscore and make visible its profound and persistent influence on the ways that we understand health.

Even when we think about health from a Eurocentric perspective, most of us are already thinking from a biomedical perspective. We are all familiar with this framing of health because health knowledge continues to be grounded in biomedicine and its philosophical underpinnings in positivism. We grew up with it. Judy Lorber (1994) famously stated that asking people to notice gender is like asking fish to notice water. In the health world, asking people to notice the everyday, societally embedded dominance of biomedicine is also akin to asking fish to notice water. Despite the language of "holism" in policy and practice, the biomedical model continues to be largely based on the belief that the whole can be reduced to the sum of its parts, as if families, communities or nations exist in these discrete, apolitical forms. If we have any doubt that this is still the case, we need only think about our health system encounters. If we have a problem with one of our bones, we go to, or are referred to, the bone specialist (orthopod); if we have a problem with our skin we go to the skin specialist (dermatologist); if we have a problem with our ovaries we go to the ovary specialist (the gynecologist); if we have a problem with depression we go to the depression specialist (psychiatrist) and so on. Eurocentric thinking about health is so grounded in a focus on body parts that it is very difficult for many of us to even envision a reconfigured Canadian perspective on health.

Another cornerstone of the biomedical model is empiricism — the claim that *a priori* facts and truths exist and that knowledge of these facts or truths may be developed from that which is directly observable (Cruickshank 2012). The unobservable thus becomes suspect. Important examples include mental health struggles such as post-traumatic stress. Combat soldiers have been met with many decades of denial of the impact of war on front-line military personnel. Directly observable medical measures of traumatic stress are not possible in the same way that, say, medical problems such as diabetes and infection can be detected through laboratory tests. In the context of the biomedical model, soldiers were therefore simply not believed, a practice that continues to this day as veterans lobby for their rights to be provided with funding for crucial counselling supports.

The biomedical version of empiricism is especially problematic because choices about where and how to even look for "facts and truths" are filtered through the lens of isms such as ableism, ageism, classism, colonialism, ethnocentrism, heterosexism, racism, sexism and genderism. This is one reason it has taken health field knowledge so long to integrate ideas from the social sciences and humanities. The relatively recent rhetoric of evidence-based practice, grounded in empiricism, also becomes open for scrutiny. Evidence according to which worldview? Evidence according to whose voice, whose ways of knowing? Empiricism, the dominant mode of thinking in the health fields, supports the invisibility of practices such as colonialism and post-colonialism, where truth and reconciliation have taken centuries for settlers to begin to acknowledge. A central pathway for the biomedical reinforcing of oppressions such as colonialism is through assessments and interventions that are focused almost exclusively on the individual. This micro focus locates the problem within the individual, while at the same time reinforcing the powerful message that micro-analyses are sufficient and desirable.

The biomedical model continues to provide a well-established and significant barrier to opening up our minds and hearts to "other" ways of knowing and public policy–making due to the global dominance of biomedicine. Biomedically infused thinking permeates our own worldviews and the worldviews of system decision-makers in the socio-political institutions of health, justice and education, to name a few. The key idea to grasp here is that the power and influence of these societal structures are largely invisible to most of us. Although they shape and control our ways of thinking, societal processes and structures operate mostly without our direct observation or any sort of explicit critique.

As feminist sociologist Dorothy Smith (1987) pointed out, in order to make sense of how we are part of these larger processes, and here I would add the dominance of biomedicine, it is important to identify how they impact our everyday lives. Smith calls these processes "ruling relations" and describes them as a complex of organized practices, including government, law, business and financial management, professional organizations and education institutions as well as the discourses and texts that interpenetrate these sites of power. Ruling relations socially organize and regulate our lives in contemporary society. When we enter into discussions of oppression and health, one of the most enlightening places to start is with an interrogation of the persistent dominance of biomedicine. The biomedical model, centred around positivism, empiricism and supposed neutrality, continues to be a significant barrier to tackling inequities in the SDH.

The Counter-Narrative: Emergence of Critical Health Studies

The social contexts of health have been publically emphasized for decades. However, the adage that "health is not only about disease and illness and acute care" is becoming outdated in favour of explicit critical examination of the root or structural causes of disease and illness — the causes-of-the-causes. Critical health studies is a relatively new field of knowledge that synthesizes critical perspectives in the social sciences and humanities with deliberative examination of the structural mechanisms that impact human and ecological health. The focus is on synthesizing critical social scientific knowledge (i.e., the isms, social justice and social change, human rights violations, emancipation from oppressive social circumstances, the politics of climate change) with health field knowledge (that is spiritual, mental and biophysical health, oppression stress and allopathic load related to chronic stress, oppressive origins of population health outcomes, primary health care, millennium development goals, synergies between ecosystem and human health).

The result is a rich and social change–oriented body of knowledge. For example, from a critical perspective, we can discuss cardiac health outcomes in the context of colonialism and imperialism. Indigenous and African Canadians have higher rates of heart disease, by far, than the general public. We know that oppression impacts the body's physiological stress handling systems — the immune system is compromised in specific ways, blood pressure increases, diabetes increases and depression very often increases as a result of the chronic, intergenerational stress of racism. Each of us has built-in processes that help us handle stress. Our body's adrenal system adjusts itself to give us the energy and concentration to handle the everyday ups and downs of stress, such as navigating urban traffic, meeting deadlines and mentoring our children through their school exams. Our adrenal system also adjusts to help us cope with crises, such as job loss, serious illness and loss of a loved one.

However, when individuals and families live in a chronic state of stress due to the relentlessness of racism, or a chronic state of crisis about where money for the rent cheque or the next family meal is coming from, then the adrenal system becomes fatigued. It is literally too tired to keep up. Results include immunosuppression, diabetes, heart disease, obesity and depression. In other words, the body's stress handling system becomes chronically over-burdened by the experiences of grinding poverty, discrimination and oppression. Yet when people seek treatment for these health problems, they are told that the cause is their individual lifestyles, such as faulty diets and not enough exercise. Although obesity and high-fat diets can and do contribute to high blood pressure, a core problem with the biomedical model is that it reinforces oppression by failing to identify and address the root causes of heart disease. A core difference between biomedical perspectives and critical health perspectives is that critical perspectives expose and problematize the root or structural causes of ill health, rather than focusing on individual faults or deficits. The root causes of markedly increased rates of heart disease in Indigenous peoples and peoples in the African diaspora are the persistent intergenerational stresses of colonialism, neo-colonialism, environmental racism and the grinding health impacts of everyday racism.

Critical health studies integrate a lifecourse perspective, rather than the commonly used lifespan perspective, where ages and stages are largely discrete periods of analysis in human life: infancy, childhood, young adulthood, adulthood, middle age and old age. In contrast, a lifecourse perspective reflects evidence that health status at any given age reflects not only current conditions but prior living circumstances *in utero* onwards (Kuh and Ben-Shalmo 1997). The lifecourse perspective underscores intergenerational impacts of poverty, or near poverty, for the working poor. The cumulative embodiment of colonialism for Indigenous peoples becomes more clearly visible, particularly the intergenerational traumatic impacts of colonial oppression and genocide. A lifecourse perspective also helps us deliberatively identify the cumulative bodily impacts of commonly used environmental toxins such as pesticides and herbicides. We know that along the lifecourse, chronic exposure to farming pesticides eventually produces higher rates of breast and prostate cancer (Engel et al. 2005). Lifelong exposure to vehicular exhausts and industrial air pollutants produces higher rates of asthma among children who live near factories or highways (Barret 2012). It turns out that many of these increased risks also fall along income, social class and geographic lines. For example, low-income housing is most prominent near factories or major motorways, and rural people are more likely to be exposed to industrial farming toxins. In this way, the lifecourse perspective also underscores the synergies among ecological health and human health, increasingly referred to as ecohealth. Ecohealth is a field that builds international expertise by linking a range of knowledge traditions to improve the health of humans, animals and ecosystems (International Association for Ecology and Health 2016). In the field of critical health studies, human and ecological health are viewed as inseparable, hence the increasing use of the term ecohealth.

Seeing the Pointy Edges of Injustice: Walking on a Different Moral Terrain

Ideas and definitions of the SDH range from conventional, biomedically oriented perspectives to critical perspectives. Conventional perspectives go something like this: societal contexts such as how much education and income we have, whether or not we have adequate food and housing, and so on, have been shown to determine our health outcomes (Raphael 2016). When individuals, families and communities have more formal education, they are more likely to secure full-time, meaningful employment with employer-provided health and social benefits and are thus more likely to have the financial capacity to have safe, adequate housing, fresh, nutritious food and access to health care. Our health is a result of these SDH as well as our lifestyles and our motivation to exercise and eat healthy diets. If we have more of these health-enhancing determinants, we and our families will be healthier. We, as a society, need to make sure that people have an equal share of these determinants. Health and social care practitioners need to help individuals and families in their quest to attain these determinants through healthy lifestyles. You will note that these conventional perspectives keep the conversation squarely focused on the individual, and sometimes the family. Responsibility for the solution therefore rests carefully and deliberatively in the microcosm of the individual-family realm. Conventional perspectives identify individual behaviours as key influences on health, yet fail to identify how SDH come to be unequally distributed (Raphael 2012). These perspectives imply some sort of nebulous force that can be held accountable to "make sure" that people do not fall through the cracks, or suffer, or die due to inequities in the SDH.

For example, let's say you receive $900 per month from social assistance. Your $700 rent is automatically redirected to your landlord. Your home is essentially a 12x12 room with a bathroom available in a common hallway. You are caring for your adult son who has a chronic psychotic illness. He would be homeless if he was not living with you. The social assistance rules in your province dictate that your son cannot apply for assistance because he is living with you, his mother. He has little to no coverage for his medications and you are in a chronic state of outright crisis or semi-crisis because you are a loving, competent mother who wants to provide the very best of a decent life for your children, regardless of their age. Conventional approaches to the SDH are of little relevance for you and your son. Who, actually, is "making sure" that you have an "equal share"? Or, more importantly, who is failing to make sure? No amount of lifestyle coaching, anti-smoking conversations and comprehensive tips about thrifty shopping will be of any value whatsoever to you in your day-to-day struggle to stay alive. In fact, suggesting that these are solutions is morally reprehensible.

In contrast, critical perspectives on the SDH go something like this: societal structures most potently determine our health outcomes. These structures and processes are dominated by a very few people in society, and economic and political power rests with these few people. According to Raphael (2012), the SDH and their distribution are the results of the power and influence of those who create and benefit from social and health inequities. Vast wealth accumulation for the very few means proportional deprivation at the bottom, where this family is located. The richest 20 percent of Canadians own nearly 70 percent of the wealth. The bottom 20 percent own almost nothing (less than 1 percent). The richest eighty-six families own more than the bottom 11 million people combined. If we consider financial assets such as stocks and bonds, the top 10 percent own 60 percent of financial assets — more than the bottom 90 percent combined. Canada's CEOs make 206 times the salary of their average worker, one of the worst wage gaps of any advanced country (Broadbent Institute 2014).

> Societal structures most potently determine our health outcomes across the lifecourse.

So, from a critical perspective, tackling root causes of inequities in the SDH, such as the growing income gap, will have a far more long-term impact on this family's chances of escaping poverty. Yes, they need help in their day-to-day struggles, a burden that is increasingly being borne by food banks, shelters and soup kitchens in Canada. But what longer-term root structures and process are at play here? Although the answer is complex, a critical perspective sheds light on the root causes of wealth inequality. Support for the social safety net, an ethical imperative in social democratic countries, has traditionally come from the taxation base — our taxes are used to support these social expenditures. However, social support expenditure in Canada (that is, financial support of education, health and social care, child care, transportation, housing) has steadily decreased since the 1980s (Broadbent Institute 2014). The erosion of the social safety net has taken place during a time when uncollected corporate taxes amount to $88 billion dollars a year, which corporations and wealthy individuals are estimated to divert to overseas tax havens every year (Finn 2012).

The creation and maintenance of a strong social safety net in Canada is a matter of choice and preference, not a matter of available money. Most of the countries in Europe, many with less income than we potentially have at our disposal, have been able to establish a wide range of social programs that far surpass ours in quality and accessibility. (Finn 2012: 1)

Here, we see that critical perspectives on the SDH extend critical social science to integrate the root causes of ill health: economic oppression and unequal distribution of wealth that lead to disenfranchisement, human rights violations and social exclusion. Another important aspect of a critical perspective on the SDH is the insistence on spotlighting the beneficiaries of persistent inequity. When societal deprivations increase for some people, there is a corresponding increase in the wealth and power of another group of people: those who successfully lobby for tax structures that favour the corporate sector and the wealthy, reduction in public expenditures, controlling wages and worker benefits and decreasing worker rights and protection (Raphael 2012). Furthermore, Raphael emphasizes that this situation is morally indictable. Specifically:

> When societal deprivations increase for some people, there is a corresponding increase in the wealth and power of another group of people.

- Individuals experiencing adverse-quality SDH do so because others experience excessively favourable SDH;
- Individuals experiencing adverse quality SDH —low income; insecure employment, food and housing; lack of health and social services; and social exclusion— have no means of having policy-makers address their situations; and
- These processes are clearly unjust and unfair. (46)

Raphael thus calls on us to reject acontextual, individualistic perspectives on the SDH in favour of a view that takes aim at the causes-of-the-causes of health inequity. Here, there is an intentional use of "equity" rather than "equality." Equality is when everyone is treated equally, or in the same way. Equity is when we address unfairness and policy-created unequal distribution of the material goods necessary to sustain a decent and productive quality of life for Canadians. These moral dimensions of unfairness are consistently interrogated within a critical perspective on the SDH.

Intersections of the Social Determinants of Health

The concept of intersectionality highlights important insights about the pointy edges of injustice — the places and spaces where unfair distribution of wealth plays itself out on the ground in the social determinants of people's everyday lives. One of the most interesting aspects of the SDH is that they do not happen in isolation of each other. Let's consider Shafik, a 12-year-old boy who lives in Montreal. If Shafik has no access to open play spaces, it is likely that his parents do not have adequate income for safe, affordable housing. Since the best predictor of income is formal education level, it is also likely that his parents have not had the opportunity to achieve adequate education to ensure employment security in a meaningful well-paying job with employer-provided health and social care benefits. All these SDH (geographic access to play space, adequate income, affordable housing, formal education) combine or intersect to deepen disadvantage, and the result is not four times the disadvantage for Shafik and his family. Rather, there is a health-damaging, intergenerational synergy among these SDH as they interact and intersect to persistently and negatively impact mental, spiritual and physical health outcomes across the lifecourse.

Intersectionality provides important insights about the complexities of the SDH and the significant barriers in developing public policy that will tackle health inequities. Intersectionality theory has its origins in critical feminist perspectives, most notably introduced by Black feminist scholars such as Kimberle Crenshaw (1989), bell hooks (1990), Patricia Hill Collins (1990, 2002, 2005) and Agnes Calliste (2000). Collins (1990) describes how oppressions in society do not operate independently. Rather, they intersect in complex patterns — persepctives that view each oppression as additive rather than interlocking, fail to stress the centrality of power and privilege. The oppressions of sexism, racism, heterosexism and ageism, to name a few, can and do happen together to create a synergy of social and material disadvantage, the parts of which interact to form a complex whole that cannot be disentangled into any single phenomenon (McGibbon and McPherson 2012).

The mental and physical health impacts of the intersections of race, class, gender and ethnicity have been known for decades. However, SDH-specific intersectionality applications are relatively new. Hankivsky and Christofferson (2008) argues that intersectionality helps us to better understand and respond to the foundational causes of illness

> The oppressions of sexism, racism, heterosexism and ageism, to name a few, can and do happen together to produce a complex synergy of material and social disadvantage.

and disease. Wilkinson (2003) adds that public programs and policies do not often reflect the lived experience of Canadians and that individuals with many different intersecting identities should be considered when legislation is proposed and programs are designed. Hankivsky and Cormier describe how intersectionality can inform women's health research and policy:

> Intersectionality is increasingly being adopted as a new paradigm which seeks to counteract one-and two-dimensional approaches by bringing to the forefront the complexity of social locations and experiences for understanding differences in health needs and outcomes. (2010: 1)

An intersectionality lens has also informed policy to improve the social determinants of child mental health, where factors such as early childhood education often intersect with housing security, racism and ghettoization (McPherson and McGibbon 2014). Health-related intersections of the SDH, the isms as SDH and geographies as SDH were first introduced in 2007 (McGibbon 2007). Specifically, health inequities were described

INTERSECTIONS OF THE SOCIAL DETERMINANTS OF HEALTH

Intersections of
**SOCIAL DETERMINANTS
OF HEALTH (SDH)**
Early Childhood Development
Employment and Working Conditions
Income and Its Equitable Distribution
Food and Housing Security
Health Care Access
Education, Social Exclusion
Social Safety Nets
Self Determination

Intersections of
GEOGRAPHIES as SDH

Urban, Rural, Remote Location
Segregation, Ghettoization
Geographic Access to Goods,
Services
The Built Environment
EcoHealth Impacts: pollution
dispersion, toxin location, worker
health . . .
And so on...

Intersections of
the ISMS as SDH

Abelism
Ageism
Classism
Colonialism, Ethnocentrism
Heterosexism, Homophobia
Religious oppression
Racism
Sexism, Genderism
And so on...

as intersections of three spaces of inequities: the SDH as laid out in the Toronto Charter (Raphael 2004), the isms as SDH and the geographic or spatial contexts of oppression as SDH.

On the Ground: Intersectionality, Health Care Access and the SDH

Access to health care involves complex pathways of discrimination. For example, in the point-of-care context, the personal experience of racially discriminatory practices, such as clinician stereotyping and expressing prejudice in the health care setting, can reduce patients' use of health care services and have a negative impact on patients' capacity to follow-up on medical recommendations as well as their satisfaction with medical treatments (Mody, Gupta, Bikdeli et al. 2012). These practices may be overt or covert and they can happen whether or not clinicians are aware of their discriminatory actions or inactions. It has also been shown that members of racialized groups continue to experience inequities in effective acute cardiac care therapies and life-saving heart health interventions (Brewer and Cooper 2014). Among American patients who arrive in the emergency department with a heart attack, Black people are less likely to be admitted to medical facilities with cardiac treatment capabilities and high-quality cardiac outcomes (Mody, Gupta, Bikdeli et al. 2012). Studies in the Unites States have also found evidence of racism in areas such as clinicians failing to prescribe correct or sufficient medications, provide increased necessary treatment and provide needed surgical intervention, even after controlling for clinical and socioeconomic factors.

Moreover, women of colour are under threat of double jeopardy as sexism intersects with racism to prevent timely access to health care (McGibbon, Waldron and Jackson 2013). Breast cancer patients have reported experiencing different forms of medical discrimination related to social class, race and language. These discriminations included study participant's descriptions of inadequate or insufficient care based on their income levels, as well as clinicians making race, ethnicity and education assumptions that compromised quality of care (Quach et al. 2012). A 2000–2010 review compared lung, breast, prostate and colorectal cancer mortality rates and mortality trends for Blacks and whites in the U.S. (O'keefe, Meltzer and Bethea 2015). The purpose of the review was to statistically track cancer deaths according to race, ethnicity and socio-economic status. Across all four cancers, survival rates were consistently lower in Black people than in white people. The causes of these premature deaths are far-reaching; however, there is a growing body of literature that links cancer and other health disparities with institutional racism (see Krieger 2003, 2014). Breast cancer statistics in the review were particularly troubling. The authors found that the gap in breast cancer mortality between Black and white women is increasing, and, between 2000 and 2010, the breast cancer mortality disparity ratio increased from 30.3 percent to 41.8 percent. In Canada, there is, as yet, little evidence about inequities in breast cancer detection and treatment, although there are some important targeted efforts (Yavari, Barroetavena, Hislop et al. 2010).

Sexism has also been found to be a significant barrier in access to care. A Canadian study of almost half a million critical care patients' charts found that women were less likely than men to receive care in an intensive care unit (icu), and the difference was most pronounced when women were older than fifty years of age (Fowler, Sabur, Li et al. 2007). These outcomes persisted, even when women and men had the same severity of cardiac problems and therefore required comparable treatment. After adjusting for illness severity, older women were also less likely to receive life-saving interventions such as mechanical ventilation (assisted breathing) or pulmonary artery catheterization (a common procedure that aids in the diagnosis and management of numerous cardiovascular illnesses). The authors concluded that among patients fifty years or older, women are less likely than men to be admitted to an icu and to receive selected life-supporting treatments, and they are more likely than men to die after a critical illness (Fowler et al. 2007). These statistics point to the spectre of ageism in women's access to acute care. Although there are few studies about how ageism intersects with heterosexism and racism in health care access, Clay discusses how older lesbians experience multiple discriminations: "Older lesbians often experience triple discrimination because of their status as women, older adults and lesbians, while ethnic minority LGBT older adults face a quadruple whammy" (2014: 46).

On the Ground: Intersectionality and Rural People's Health

An intersectionality perspective also underscores the multiple inequities associated with rural health outcomes. Marya is seven years old. She has recently been diagnosed with juvenile rheumatoid arthritis (JRA), an autoimmune condition that causes, among other problems, painful and possibly deforming swelling in her joints, particularly her ankles, her wrists and her knees. Her family lives in a rural area where there are no health care providers with expertise in rheumatology, or its sub-specialty, JRA. The nearest pediatric rheumatologist is a two-and-a-half hour drive away. Appointments are routinely booked without consultation regarding family availability, and cancelling an appointment results in delays of up to six months for another appointment, even if Marya's condition worsens. Mom works as a cashier at a large supermarket ($10.60/hr.), and dad works as a carpenter ($23/hr.). His work is seasonal. Since the family must travel two-and-a-half hours to the city for an appointment, one of the parents must negotiate a full day off work, thus losing a day's pay ($79–$172 net lost wages). Marya also has other autoimmune conditions, and her long-term prognosis remains precarious and thus very worrisome for her parents. The family has a car, but it is only used for local travel due to its condition. They borrow a neighbour's car (gas and mileage equaling $175 return). Even though the neighbours will not charge mileage, the material cost is still incurred.

The appointment with the rheumatologist happens in tandem with other specialist appointments with an occupational therapist and a physiotherapist. At the occupational therapy appointment, the therapist fits Marya with special support braces for her wrists. After the fitting and moulding of the braces is complete, the parents are told that they must pay for the braces. They receive the bill two weeks later ($210). The occupational therapist recommends over-the-counter ankle supports for both ankles. Marya finds these very helpful in decreasing her ankle pain ($90). Marya's wrist movements are also increasingly painful, and the physiotherapist recommends regular warm wax treatments at home. The device for warm wax treatments costs $425. The family opts for a double boiler ($60) and buys the first batch of wax at the grocery store ($35); however, mom and dad worry about the safety of implementing the wax treatments at home.

The physician recommends Methotrexate, an immune system suppressant. Neither of the parents has a drug plan through their employment. The drug costs $55 per month, and Marya requires three refills before her next appointment ($165). Between appointments, the family has access to the clinic's nurse practitioner, who provides expertise via phone consultation as needed. Due to complications with medication, it has been necessary to consult the nurse clinician five times since Marya's last appointment ($120 long distance charges). Marya develops movement-restricting deformities in some of her fingers. Her parents try to negotiate some adjustment with her school, and they are told that they will have to go through a process of having Marya declared disabled in order to obtain the laptop computer she needs to be able to write in class ($1,500). Dad works with his extended family to navigate the application process, but Marya must go without the computer and is unable to take notes without a high level of pain, for at least her first term in grade two. Marya's parents strongly desire the expertise of a naturopathic doctor who will work with their rheumatologist ($125 initial consultation). They have friends who have had very encouraging results with such as arrangement, and there is a respected naturopath with a rural practice near their home. The family cannot afford the naturopath. Rurality tax and excess burden of uninsured health care needs total $3,109:

Rurality Tax per Year: $2,549
- Long distance phone calls = $120/year
- Return trip gas and mileage: $175 per visit; Lost wages due to full day travel: $172; both multiplied by seven visits per year = $2,429/year
Excess Burden of Uninsured Health Care Needs: $560
- Bill for braces, wrist and ankle supports, wax treatments, drug costs: $534

Marya's situation is not dissimilar to the expenses and constraints experienced by thousands of Canadian families with children who have chronic conditions. Her story illustrates the myth of universality in Canadian health care access. Marya's long-term prognosis is heavily influenced by her family's socio-economic circumstances. Parental unemployment at any time in the course of Marya's illness will have a devastating impact on their ability to maintain contact with health services and thus on Marya's health. Her family's rural location sets in motion an ongoing rurality tax that is inconsistent with her legal right to health care. Rurality tax is defined as the extra amount of money that rural and remote individuals and families must pay if they are to have the same possibilities of access to health care as urban people. If Marya's family is from a racialized group, she will experience additional and powerful barriers related to well-documented racism in the health care system.

Embodied Oppression and Its Root Causes

Embodied oppression occurs when the structural, systemic, institutionalized root causes of ill health produce illness and suffering across the lifecourse. The interplay of politics, economics and policy, referred to as the political economy of health, is an important aspect of this process. Oppression becomes inscribed on the body, inside and outside, from the cellular level, as in immunosuppression caused by chronic experiences of heterosexist hatred, to the outside body that we can see, as in obesity caused by colonial disruption of Indigenous nutritional lifeways and the chronic stress of racism. The body becomes the terrain where oppression plays itself out, from the

> Embodied oppression occurs when the structural, systemic, institutionalized root causes of ill health produce illness and suffering across the lifecourse.

suffering of toddlers due to preventable dental cavities, to the myriad diagnoses of poorer people who fill hospital beds at a disproportionate rate. This collective, oppression-caused suffering is a wake-up call for all of us and an indictment to a public system that is failing millions of Canadians.

Social Epidemiology, Political Economy and Oppression

Epidemiology is the study of patterns, causes and effects of disease and illness across defined populations or groups of people. Some branches of epidemiological science have evolved over time to encompass the social, political and economic root causes of illness and suffering. An example is the germinal work of Shaw, Dorling, Gordon and Smith (1999) in the United Kingdom. In their book *The Widening Gap: Health Inequalities and Policy in Britain*, the authors combined mortality and morbidity statistics across the lifecourse and analyzed these statistics in the context of poverty, housing insecurity and public policy. This integration of social science and epidemiology is an increasing global trend with its genesis in concern and even alarm about the growing poverty rates in Western countries around the world, including so-called rich countries such as Canada, England and the United States. The term social epidemiology was first used in an article in the *American Sociological Review* in 1950: "The relationship of fetal and infant mortality to residential segregation: An inquiry into social epidemiology" (Krieger 2001). According to Krieger, this topic is as timely now as it was in 1950, and the need to fully integrate social and biological origins of disease continues to be centrally relevant:

> Grappling with notions of causation, in turn, raises not only complex philosophi-
> cal issues but also, in the case of social epidemiology, issues of accountability and
> agency: simply invoking abstract notions of "society" and disembodied "genes" will
> not suffice. Instead, the central question becomes: Who and what is responsible
> for population patterns of disease and wellbeing, as manifested in present, past and
> changing social inequalities in health. (2001: 688)

Social epidemiology provides the theoretical context for us to understand why patterns of good and bad health mirror inequitable distributions of deprivation and privilege across the SDH. As described earlier in this chapter, these inequities are the result of political decision-making and public policies that favour wealth concentration among relatively few individuals, and this trend is growing.

The recognition that politics and health are intertwined is surprisingly old. Almost 200 years ago, Rudolf Virchow (1821–1902), a Polish anthropologist and physician, noted that all diseases have two causes: one pathological, the other political. More recently, Vincente Navarro, stressing the importance of the relationship between social class and health, called for a materialist epidemiology, one that integrates the ways that the societal hierarchy of class relations "conditions most potently how other variables affect the population's health" (2002: 21). Navarro (2002, 2004) and Esping-Anderson (2002), for example, outline a political economy approach about how we can tackle health inequities and their genesis in material and social deprivation. A political economy approach interrogates economic doctrines to disclose their sociological and political premises "In sum, [it] regards economic ideas and behavior not as frameworks for analysis, but as beliefs and actions that must themselves be explained" (Mayer 1987: 3). The political economy of health refers to a close examination of how economic doctrines most powerfully determine the health of citizens over time.

Marx (1977 [1845]) was the first to describe a methodological approach to understanding the linkages among society, economics and history. Rather than viewing the field of economics as consisting of objective and quantifiable sets of measurements and models, he explored a new way to think about economics, where the politics of a nation very much influenced the direction and outcomes of its economic policy. Marx explained that in order to survive and continue existence from generation to generation, it is necessary for human beings to produce and reproduce the material requirements of life. Materialist approaches are based in his assertion that economic factors — the way people produce these necessities of life — determine the kind of politics and ideology a society can have. A political economy lens is central to modern efforts to understand and tackle the root causes of social problems, including growing inequities in health outcomes.

These structural determinants of health, although rarely listed in most national health plans, are the most important policies in determining a population's health outcomes (Navarro 2007). However, political will, and hence capacity to address inequities in the SDH, varies from state to state according to prevailing political ideologies. Inequities in the SDH are particularly evident in neoliberal political economies, where the prevailing ideology is that individuals have the right and responsibility to look after themselves and that the state should only intervene when people are already destitute. Economic policies are market driven and corporate profit is viewed as an essential aspect of a robust economy. In contrast, social democratic political economies are grounded on the ideological inspiration of reduction in poverty, inequality and unemployment. The organizing principles are universalism (for example universal access to education and health and social care) and the socialist ideals of equality, the social rights of all citizens, justice, freedom and solidarity (Bryant 2009; Esping-Anderson 2002). Social democratic policies lead to better health outcomes across all social classes, races, ethnicities and ages (Raphael 2016).

THE CYCLE OF OPPRESSION

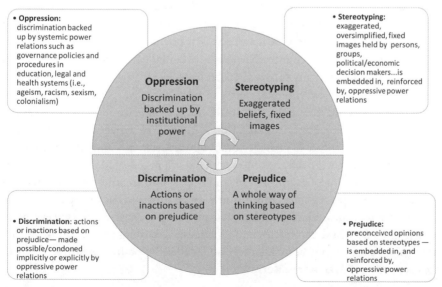

• **Oppression:** discrimination backed up by systemic power relations such as governance policies and procedures in education, legal and health systems (i.e., ageism, racism, sexism, colonialism)

• **Stereotyping:** exaggerated, oversimplified, fixed images held by persons, groups, political/economic decision makers...is embedded in, reinforced by, oppressive power relations

Oppression
Discrimination backed up by institutional power

Stereotyping
Exaggerated beliefs, fixed images

Discrimination
Actions or inactions based on prejudice

Prejudice
A whole way of thinking based on stereotypes

• **Discrimination:** actions or inactions based on prejudice— made possible/condoned implicitly or explicitly by oppressive power relations

• **Prejudice:** preconceived opinions based on stereotypes — is embedded in, and reinforced by, oppressive power relations

Social epidemiology and political economy perspectives provide tools to understand how a nation's politics and economics become central drivers of health outcomes. The cycle of oppression underscores the social, political and economic chain of causation that creates and sustains the systemic causes of ill health. Oppression is deeply embedded in systemic ruling relations resulting in persistent and toxic consequences for the mental, physical and spiritual health of oppressed peoples. Health outcomes of oppressed peoples and groups are significantly worse when compared to Canadian averages. The following on-the-ground examples illustrate how the cycle of oppression operates to reinforce systemic causes of health and social inequities.

On the Ground Oppression: Homelessness and Ill Health

Consider homelessness in Canada. Starting with biased information and lack of accurate information about homeless people, we develop commonly held stereotypes about homeless people. For example, they are all "lazy" and "crazy." Stereotypes are exaggerated, oversimplified, fixed images that are held by persons, groups, politicians, policy-makers and so on. Stereotyping leads to prejudice, a preconceived opinion about particular groups of people, such as the homeless, that is based on stereotypes: homeless people are a drain on the system; they don't deserve to be taken seriously, don't want employment, like to sit around and do nothing, and don't care about their families. After all, aren't social outcasts a common or even necessary feature in modern societies? In the case of homeless young people, why don't they just "buck up" and work for a change instead of mooching off the system? Why should I have to put up with these lazy, good-for-nothing kids who run at my car in the traffic and expect me to give them some of my hard-earned money just to clean my windshield? Why stand around on the street begging for my money when they're there just because they don't like the rules at home? Why don't more municipalities have laws to keep these vermin away? These prejudices about homeless people are common and they persist in the face of actual facts about the complex circumstances and public policies that promote increasing homelessness in Canada.

Discrimination involves actions or inactions based on prejudicial thinking. Here, we enter into the world of unethical individual and collective behaviour that sets aside homeless people as pariahs in their own country. There is substantial evidence of discrimination against homeless people across many spheres of their lives. Health and social care are often exceedingly difficult to access and when homeless or near-homeless people do manage to navigate the maze of access and then arrive for care, there is persistent and sometimes deadly discrimination at point-of-care. Here, lack of action is often a key aspect of discrimination — lack of timely treatment, failure to provide competent assessments and failure to ensure access to comprehensive follow-up referrals, all of which result in repeated worsening of their illnesses and suffering over time. Discrimination and oppression are intertwined aspects of these experiences for homeless people. Oppression is discrimination backed up by systemic or structural power, sometimes referred to as institutionalized power, including government, education, legal and health system policies and practices. According to the authors of the first comprehensive report about homelessness in Canada, the pathways into and out of homelessness are neither linear, nor uniform:

Individuals and families who wind up homeless may not share much in common with each other, aside from the fact that they are extremely vulnerable and lack adequate housing, income, and the necessary supports to ensure they stay housed. The causes of homelessness reflect an intricate interplay among structural factors (poverty, lack of affordable housing), systems failures (people being discharged from mental health facilities, corrections or child protection services into homelessness) and individual circumstances (family conflict and violence, mental health and addictions). (Gaetz et al. 2013: 4)

The perpetuation of stereotypes about homeless people is made possible through a complex of well-organized practices that produce a system of oppression that becomes inscribed on the bodies, minds and spirits of homeless people. The current problem of homelessness is not limited to individual crises. Rather, the homelessness crisis in Canada was created through neoliberal government decisions to drastically reduce investments in affordable and social housing in the 1990s, decreases in income supports and the declining spending power of almost half of the Canadian population since that time (Gaetz et al. 2013). At least 200,000 Canadians experience homelessness in any given year. At least 30,000 Canadians are homeless on any given night. At least 50,000 Canadians are part of the "hidden homeless" on any given night, staying with friends or relatives on a temporary basis because they have nowhere else to go. Currently, many Canadians are at risk of homelessness due to the high cost and unavailability of housing, inadequate incomes and family violence (Gaetz, Donaldson, Richter and Gulliver). Moreover, personal crises related to family violence and violence against women are, at their root, caused by patriarchal societal systems that condone and promote misogyny.

On the Ground: Hospitalization by Socio-economic Status

There are numerous stereotypes about people, families and communities who have low, or no, income. Prejudicial thinking reflects that poverty is the result of lack of moral fortitude and laziness. Discrimination involves countless micro and macro aggressions against people who live in poverty, from the undignifying bureaucratic hurdles that families must overcome to prove that they are worthy of social assistance, to the legislative organization of the remarkable income gap in Canada. Illness rates mirror socio-economic status — the lower the SES, the higher the rate of hospitalization (CIHI 2010). Excess rates refers to rates that are above the average Canadian hospitalization rates. The rapidly increasing income gap is writ large in the hospitals of the country. For males and females, excess rates associated with socio-economic status account for an estimated 33 to 40 percent of hospitalizations (CIHI 2010). In other words, if you are poor, you are 33 to 40 percent more likely to be hospitalized than the average Canadian. For mental illness, excess hospitalization rates are higher for males than for females. In the U.S., findings from a country-wide statistical analysis indicated that the rate of hospital stays among patients between the ages of 45 and 64 was nearly 50 percent higher for people in the lowest-income communities (Wier, Merrill and Elixhauser 2009).

Excess hospitalization rates reflect SDH outcomes related to food and housing insecurity, racism and inequities in early childhood education, to name a few. The economic burden is substantial. In a CIHI study of only fifteen metropolitan areas in Canada, the total yearly estimated excess costs of hospitalization were $123 million for males and $125 million for females. National costs are therefore likely in the multi-billion dollar range. Since up to 40 percent of hospitalizations are related to having a lower SES, it is no leap of logic that health care cost increases are heavily bound to social injustice in Canada. When examined through a political economy lens, the same neoliberal public policy-making that causes homelessness also causes increasing numbers of hospitalizations for low-income people.

Social Pathogens: The Causes of the Causes

Inequities in the SDH are caused by social pathogens. For example, asthma rates are higher in children whose families live in poverty. This is because they are more likely to live in damp, mouldy housing, or near a major road or factory. The physical cause of increased asthma is damp housing, but it is poverty that causes people to live in damp housing. These root causes of ill health, such as poverty and racism, are often called the causes of the causes, also referred to as social pathogens — the political, economic and social root causes of compromised health and well-being. These pathogens do not have the same visibility of well-known physiological pathogens such as cancer, bacteria and so on. In the area of human and ecological health, the origins of social pathogens remain largely hidden. One of the main ways that this invisibility is created and perpetuated is through the discourses of "vulnerability" and "at-risk" people, populations and species.

> Social pathogens are the political, economic, and social root causes of compromised health and wellbeing.

The vulnerability discourse implies that a person, ecosystem, plant or animal, for example, is somehow more prone to experiencing health inequities in much the same way as one might be more prone to catching a cold. These discourses imply an unknown force that is somehow causing the same people, over and over, to have chronic diseases and serious health difficulties. Similarly, in the ecological context, plant and animal species are said to be at risk due to the degradation of their environments. This cause is most often taken for granted, rather than linked to capitalism and weak or non-existent environmental protection legislation. The at-risk discourse effectively hides the structural, root causes of ill health and suffering by limiting the analysis to the micro context. Yes, there are risk factors, such as watershed pollution in the case of endangered waterfowl and poverty in the case of human families, but what is causing these risks in the first place? What and who are creating these risks for at-risk people, species and biospheres? Some of the social pathogens that cause health inequities are structural violence, slow violence and social murder.

On the Ground: Structural Violence and Childhood Suffering

Structural violence refers to the violent impacts of systemically produced, sustained and avoidable damage to human and ecological health. The word "structural" is used because its origins are explicitly traceable to societal structures or ruling relations such as government, law, business and financial management, professional organizations and education institutions. In other words, suffering and death related to homelessness are directly traceable to housing policy in the 1990s. Prolonged suffering related to lack of timely medical care in rural communities is directly traceable to persistent government refusal to divert financial support to life-saving community health centres. Structural action or lack of action is violent because it results in suffering and death.

An example of unnecessary suffering caused by structural violence involves childhood dental cavities. Early dental carries (EDC) is an infectious disease resulting in decay of a child's primary teeth. It is the leading cause of day surgery for children in Canada (CIHI 2013). The public cost associated with one aspect of day surgery for EDC — hospital care — is significant: $21.2 million nationally per year for children aged one to younger than five. This is a fraction of the total cost of care for EDC because it excludes costs associated with care providers, such as dental surgeons and anesthesiologists, as well as costs associated with travel to care (CIHI 2013). Not surprisingly, disproportionate suffering is along cultural, racial and social-class lines. The information in the box on the next page illustrates how childhood suffering is sustained through structural violence.

On the Ground: Slow Violence and Environmental Racism
Slow violence is a form of structural violence. It refers to long-term assaults on planetary life and ecosystems and a broad range of environmental and structural damage, such as toxic dumping, greenhouse gas production, desertification and climate change. These casualties produce cataclysmic changes that are felt over time, for generations, hence the term slow violence. In all forms of structural violence, the perpetrators are very difficult to hold accountable, but death and destruction persist on a grand scale nonetheless.

> To confront what I am calling slow violence requires that we attempt to give symbolic shape and plot to formless threats whose fatal repercussions are dispersed across space and time. Politically and emotionally, different kinds of disaster possess unequal heft. Falling bodies, burning towers, exploding heads have a visceral, page-turning potency that tales of slow violence cannot match. Stories of toxic buildup, massing greenhouse gases, or desertification may be cataclysmic, but they're scientifically convoluted cataclysms in which casualties are deferred, often for generations. In the gap between acts of slow violence and their delayed effects, both memory and causation readily fade from view and the casualties thus incurred pass untallied. (Nixon 2007: 14)

Impacts of the transnational petroleum industry are an important Canadian example of slow violence. Oil sands are found in about seventy countries. Alberta is home to the largest oil sands deposits. When oil is processed, the remaining water and solids are discharged into vast tailings ponds at the rate of 1.8 billion litres of waste per day, covering more than 130 square kilometres in northern Alberta (Dyer and Woynillowicz 2008; Tenenbaum 2009). The oil company Syncrude's tailings ponds, at 540 million cubic metres in volume, form one of the world's largest dams, second only to China's Three Gorges Dam. Statistically

STRUCTURAL VIOLENCE CAUSES CHILDHOOD SUFFERING ALONG SOCIAL-CLASS, GEOGRAPHIC AND RACIAL LINES IN CANADA.

"Suffer the little children": Evidence about Early Dental Carries (EDC)

- Each year, 19,000 day-surgery operations are performed to treat cavities (due to caries) among children younger than age six. This occurs despite the fact that EDC is generally preventable and, when caught early, is treatable in community-based settings (CIHI 2013).
- EDC surgery rates are significantly higher for children from Indigenous populations (8.6 times higher), least-affluent neighbourhoods (3.9 times higher) and rural areas (3.1 times higher). In more than one in five EDC day-surgery visits (22.3 percent), families travelled two or more hours for care (CIHI 2013).
- The consequences of EDC can be dire. Pain, difficulty eating and sleeping, speech difficulties and poor self-esteem may occur, affecting growth and the ability to concentrate and function. Quality of life can be seriously impaired (CIHI 2013).

Structural Causes of Childhood Suffering Related to EDC

- Federal funding of dental care has gradually eroded in favour of allowing the market (private funding) to determine dental care access. From 2000–2010, average annual growth in spending on dental services was 6.7 percent for the private sector in contrast with 3.5 percent in the public sector (CIHI 2010).
- The scope, design and financing of public programs in place to improve access to dental services among children from low-income families vary greatly by jurisdiction, since there is no federal mandate to ensure universal access to care (CIHI 2013).
- Dental care is almost wholly privately financed, with approximately 51 percent of the population paying for care through employment-based insurance and 44 percent through out-of-pocket expenditures (CIHI 2010).
- High-income Canadians are 80 percent more likely to have visited a dentist in the past twelve months compared to low-income families (Devaux and de Looper 2012).
- There is only 5 percent of public financing for dental care. Almost all is targeted to socially marginalized groups and delivered in the private sector through public forms of third-party financing (Quinonez et al. 2005). In other words, millions of families are left scrambling for dental care, even if they do manage to navigate complex means-testing procedures.
- According to the Canadian Centre for Policy Alternatives (2011), it's time we put the mouth back in the body and create public dentistry. Currently, each province varies widely regarding what ages can access public health care and which services are covered. In 2011, publicly funded dental care ranged from a low of 1.5 percent in Ontario to 77 percent in Nunavut.

significant increases in cancers of the blood and lymphatic system, biliary tract and soft tissue were found in individuals, including many Indigenous families living in Fort Chipewyan, which lies in a depositional basin of tar ponds byproducts. The incidence of a rare form of biliary duct cancer has steadily increased over the past thirty years in Alberta, and rates are two to three times higher in First Nations communities, when compared with non-First Nations populations (Tenenbaum 2009). This form of environmental racism shows that the social determinants of human health are intimately tied to social determinants of ecosystem health. Environmental byproducts of corporate profit interact to damage both human and ecosystem health over time.

In Alberta, "the feverish expansion of oil sands development is based on the untested assumption that mined landscapes can be recovered to something close to the pre-development ecosystem after mining is complete. Reclamation is the final step that mining companies are required to complete before mine closure" (Dyer and Woynillowicz 2008: 1). The Government of Alberta has certified as reclaimed less than 1 percent of the total land base disturbed by mines. This percentage does not include tailings that companies propose to incorporate into the reclaimed landscape — a fantastically erroneous proposition, given that the toxic tailing lakes are the largest human-made structure in the world and can be seen from space (Hatch and Price 2008). A development with significant human, environmental, social and economic costs, the tar sands provides a disturbing modern instance of the ways that the pursuit of profit can trigger direct and indirect ecosystem impacts and human health impacts that are wide-ranging and distributed unequally across the population.

On the Ground: Social Murder and Deaths due to Poverty and Racism

Social murder is a form of structural violence that results in early death (Chernomas and Hudson 2009). Engel's 2009 [1845] treatise on social murder over a century and a half ago remains urgently relevant today. Engels explained that when society deprives thousands of the necessities of life so that they die an early death, this is social murder — death that is caused by societal conditions rather than a gun or a knife, but murder nonetheless. The perpetrators are therefore not easily identifiable. Engels' words of 1845 are eerily prophetic: the measure of a society is its willingness to provide for the collective well-being of all citizens, especially those who are most under threat of social and material deprivation. Countries such as Sweden have demonstrated that social democratic public policy supports health for all, along with a strong, fiscally responsible economy. These facts demonstrate that ill health is tied to a nation's political will to make (or not to make) socially just public policy decisions over time. One of the most documented examples of social murder involves the death of infants and newborns. Infant mortality is a well-known global benchmark for measuring equity across the lifecourse. A 2010 Organization for Economic Cooperation and Development (OECD) report stated that Canada had dropped significantly on infant mortality indicators. "Once able to boast about its high world ranking for low infant mortality, Canada has now dropped from sixth to twenty-fourth place, just above Hungary and Poland … the main causes cited by researchers are poverty, isolation, and premature births" (Priest 2010: 1). The response from the Society of Obstetricians and Gynecologists of Canada was to propose a national birthing plan that would focus on accurate data gathering, maternity patient safety and the creation of a model of sustainable maternity and newborn care. These are no doubt reasonable suggestions, but they fail to reflect evidence about the social distribution of infant mortality: racism-related stress and socio-economic hardship (Giscombe and Lobel 2005); high prevalence of low income among women who experience serious hardships during pregnancy (Braveman et al. 2010); high poverty rates and lack of access to a socialized health care system, as is the case on the United States (Tillett 2010); significant correlation of high poverty rates with infant mortality rates among minority and white mothers in the U.S. (Sims, Sims and Bruce 2007); significant correlation among poverty level, racial composition of geographic areas and infant mortality rates (Eudy 2009) and a high correlation of inequality and child relative poverty with infant mortality rates in rich societies (Pickett and Wilkinson 2007).

Current data does not allow for nationwide statistical analyses of newborn death rates in industrialized countries along socio-economic or racial lines; however, it is known that one of the main causes of newborn death is prematurity (Save the Children 2013). The U.S. has one of the highest preterm birth rates (one in eight) in the industrialized world and a correspondingly high newborn death rate. Most preterm births occur when the mother is an adolescent, and the U.S. also has the highest adolescent pregnancy rate in the industrialized world. Evidence also shows that newborn and infant mortality are often higher among poor and racial and ethnic minority mothers. Poor and minority groups also suffer higher burdens of prematurity and low birth weights (Save the Children 2013). Root causes are persistent racism and the long-term erosion of social safety nets in Canada and other rich countries in the industrialized world.

Another Canadian example of social murder is the death of Brian Sinclair. Sinclair was a vulnerable Indigenous man who was also a double-amputee. He went to the Health Sciences Centre in Winnipeg in 2008 complaining of abdominal pain and a catheter problem. "He was told to go and wait in the waiting room. He was never called back. Ever. He was ignored to death. He had a bladder infection. He just needed antibiotics and a catheter change. [At the inquest] the chief medical examiner said: 'If the treatment had been given ... he would not have died on that day'" (Zbogar 2014: A9). Hospital staff walked past Sinclair many times and did not intervene. He vomited as he went into shock, and someone gave him a basin. This was the sum total of medical intervention. The inquest revealed that some of the staff assumed that he was drunk. Sinclair was left in distress and without the emergency care he needed for thirty-four hours. He died in the emergency department and was then ignored for several more hours until rigor mortis set in. At the inquest, the Sinclair family, and their lawyer, Victor Zbogar, rejected the euphemisms that were used to identify causation of the death: "access block" and "patient flow" problems. Rather, we see the cycle of oppression operating here: stereotyping about Sinclair as a drunk and homeless Indigenous man led clinicians to assume that he did not need emergency care; stereotyping led to discrimination, in this case lack of action until he died; this discrimination was backed up by institutional power, in this case a health care system with embedded allowances for clinical incompetence related to the SDH, as well as a legal system that hid this racist act under the guise of patient flow problems.

Personal and Collective Action for Change

Social pathogens, such as structural violence, slow violence and social murder, are very difficult to expose. When we hear or see these pathogens, our first task is to mourn. Then it is important to continually move to a different moral terrain where our own humanity is implicated in each and every transgression. Lila Watson, an Australian Aboriginal woman, responded to mission workers by saying,, "If you have come to help me, you are wasting your time. But if you have come because your liberation is bound up with mine, then let us walk together." Acting for change is about realizing that our own liberation is connected to the liberation of all people. Depending on the social or ethical issue at hand, we may find ourselves in various stages in our commitment to taking action and our ability to see how our own social justice actions are part of a larger justice movement that impacts all of us and the planet. Perhaps we see tackling health inequities as someone else's responsibility. Or perhaps we are not particularly interested in acting against climate change at this time in our lives. We may have significant barriers to action because we are experiencing oppression in our own lives. Social action is difficult because it challenges oppressive structures that are deeply embedded in social, cultural, political and economic processes and decision-making over time.

Personal action for social change is perhaps the most difficult place to start because it is often easier to think about what other people, politicians and the government can do. Personal action can also be an integral part of collective or social action. Personal action for social change happens on a continuum from supporting oppression to confronting oppression. Wijeyesinghe, Griffin and Love (1997) provided a detailed description of the stages that we can consider in our own action for change. On one end of the continuum we actively participate in oppression. When we support oppression our actions maintain oppressive social structures and ruling relations. It is crucial to note that we can support oppression *without actually noticing* that we are doing so. For example, this process is frequently a conundrum for white people, since the prevailing thinking is that we must actually be able to identify our white privilege before it can be said to exist.

Peggy MacIntosh's (1998) work, "White Privilege: Unpacking the Invisible Knapsack," uncovers how white skin affords unearned and unacknowledged daily privileges for white people. The same holds true for unearned privileges associated with higher social class, heterosexual orientation and being male. These privileges exist regardless of whether or not the bearers are aware of their privilege. One of the most important starting points in working for social change is to embrace the fact that oppressions often flourish without the oppressors

SOCIAL CHANGE CONTINUUM

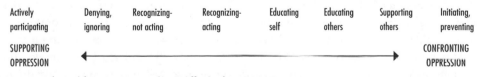

| Actively participating | Denying, ignoring | Recognizing- not acting | Recognizing- acting | Educating self | Educating others | Supporting others | Initiating, preventing |

SUPPORTING OPPRESSION ⟵————————————————————⟶ CONFRONTING OPPRESSION

Source: Adapted from Wijeyesinghe, Griffin and Love 1997.

being willing or able to name their participation. We support oppression when we actively participate in oppression, deny or ignore oppression or recognize oppression but take no action. For example, it is known that toxic waste dumps and landfills are consistently located near communities of colour the world over, including many of our own communities. When we know this fact, yet take no notice of where our own garbage is going when it leaves our curb, then we are participating in the problem.

Noticing or witnessing oppression, and taking the moral stance that it is none of our business, or that it is someone else's responsibility to speak up, is the same as not doing anything in the face of need. Silence is assent. Reverend Martin Niemöller's famous story reminds us that claiming neutrality, or standing by, has ethical consequences that are directly measureable:

> In Germany they first came for the Communists, and I didn't speak up because I wasn't a Communist. Then they came for the Jews, and I didn't speak up because I wasn't a Jew. Then they came for the trade unionists, and I didn't speak up because I wasn't a trade unionist. Then they came for the Catholics, and I didn't speak up because I was a Protestant. Then they came for me and by that time no one was left to speak up.

It is very difficult to understand how silence is assent because it is an absence of action. Silence is often disguised as neutrality. We may decline to join conversations about pressing social justice concerns, such as the missing and murdered Indigenous girls and women in Canada. Our silence is likely to be interpreted as neutrality, implying that we do not have an opinion about, say, the connections between colonialism, residential schools and the disproportionately high rate of murders of Indigenous girls and women in Canada. However, there is no neutral seat on a moving train. Let's say we are in a train that is moving dangerously fast. We are asked to help slow down the train but we say that we would rather remain neutral and let someone else take action. Our inaction thus becomes a powerful action that contributes to the possible crashing of the train.

As we move along the continuum we consciously become more aware of the injustices around us. At this location on the continuum, we often feel guilt once we see the enormity of the problems and instances of our own complicit behaviour. Everything from buying fruit out of season and using plastic grocery bags to not participating in local anti-poverty work may weigh on our minds. These are the turning points where we can consciously turn guilt into actions. As the social change continuum illustrates, we can continue to educate ourselves and/or educate others about the issues where we feel the most passion. We can support others who are taking a public stance or we join them.

Personal action for change often leads to collective action and both rest on the idea that "the personal is political." Collective action most often happens in the structural realm, where social, political and economic root causes operate. Here, social change often supports democracy and human rights related to health, such as lobbying municipal (for example, non-racist landfill locations), provincial or territorial governments (such as community-driven food collectives and community gardens) and federal governments (for example, halting the privatization of health care) for just public policy. In many cases of collective action for social justice and health there is no streamlined separation among the levels of governmental and regional policy-making bodies. When lobbying for community-driven health and social care, discussions and action will need to happen within the local or district health and social services jurisdictions as well as the provincial and federal jurisdictions. Ideas for change often emanate from anger or outrage about erosion of existing justice-based policies or services, such as provincial withdrawal of funding for women's shelters or the federal withdrawal of funding for the Sisters in Spirit Campaign (a database of missing and murdered Indigenous women) under the Harper government in 2010. Action for social justice and health tackles these root causes of embodied oppression, and even in a democracies such as Canada, there are significant barriers to action. The challenge is to continually find our own entry points in a global movement that is increasingly being framed in the context of an ethical commitment to act for change.

Glossary of Key Terms

Critical health studies: A relatively new field of knowledge that synthesizes critical perspectives in the social sciences and humanities with deliberative examination of the mechanisms that impact human and ecological health across the lifecourse.

Ecohealth: An emerging field of knowledge and action that links human health with ecological health across the planet.

Embodied oppression: Occurs when the structural, systemic, institutionalized root causes of ill health produce illness and suffering across the lifecourse — oppression is inscribed on the bodies, minds and spirits of oppressed groups and peoples.

Health inequities: Systematic differences in the health status of different population groups. Social factors, including education, employment status, income level, gender and ethnicity have a marked influence on health and illness. The lower an individual's socio-economic position, for example, the higher their risk of poor health across the lifecourse.

Intersectionality: The ways oppressions intersect. Sexism, racism, heterosexism and ageism, to name a few, can and do happen together to produce a complex synergy of material and social disadvantage. These oppressions work together, fusing into a complex whole that cannot be disentangled into any single phenomenon.

Oppression: A cyclical process involving institutionalized procedures and practices of domination and control that create and sustain injustice. Stereotyping leads to prejudicial thinking, which leads to discriminatory action or inaction. Discrimination is backed up by institutional power, the organizational structures in society (law, health care, education).

Oppression stress: Our body's adrenal system adjusts itself to give us the energy and concentration to handle everyday ups and downs of stress and even crises. However, when individuals and families live in a chronic state of stress due to oppressions such as racism, sexism or heterosexism, or a chronic day-to-day money crisis related to their rent cheque or meals, then the adrenal system becomes fatigued. Results include immunosuppression, diabetes, heart disease and depression.

Political economy of health: Interrogates economic doctrines to disclose their sociological and political premises. The political economy of health refers to a close examination of how economic doctrines most powerfully determine the health of citizens.

Slow violence: A form of structural violence referring to long-term assaults on planetary life and ecosystems and a broad range of environmental and structural damage to the planet. Some examples are toxic buildup, massing greenhouse gases, desertification and climate change. These casualties produce cataclysmic changes that are felt over time, for generations.

Social murder: A form of structural violence. When public policy decision-making and social structures deprive thousands of the necessities of life and force them to remain in such conditions so that they die an early death, this is social murder — death that is caused by societal conditions rather than a gun or a knife, but is murder nonetheless.

Structural violence: The violent impacts of systemically produced, sustained and avoidable damage to human and ecological health. The origins are explicitly traceable to societal structures or ruling relations. Slow violence and social murder are examples of structural violence.

Questions for Discussion

1. What are some of the differences between a "lifestyle" approach to understanding health problems and a structural perspective? Why and how does the lifestyle approach persist? Who benefits and who is disadvantaged by the persistence of a lifestyle approach?

2. What are some of the ways that the biomedical model continues to block progress on tackling inequities in the social determinants of health?

3. What are some case study examples of how inequities in the three areas of the SDH (SDH as laid out in the Toronto Charter, the isms as SDH and geographies as SDH) operate on the ground in people's everyday lives? Use the SDH intersectionality figure to guide your discussion.

4. Debate the following statements: People can choose to be healthy if they really want to. Women can leave an abusive relationship if they really want to. In countries such as Canada, people can achieve pretty much anything they want to if they try hard enough.

5. Talk about the idea of ecohealth. Think about some of the ecological issues that you are most concerned about. List and then discuss some of the specific ways that this slow violence impacts human health across the lifecourse.

6.   Think about and list some of the social justice and health issues that you are most passionate about. Using the social action continuum, locate yourselves (individually and/or in groups) on the social change continuum. Then talk about what actions you can take to move to the next stage on the continuum.

Resources for Activists

Canadian Health Coalition: healthcoalition.ca

Idle No More: idlenomore.ca

LeftStreamed: youtube.com/user/LeftStreamed/featured

Stop Racism and Hate Canada: stopracism.ca

Upstream: thinkupstream.net

Voices-Voix: voices-voix.ca/en

References

Barret, J.R. 2012. "Proximity Plus Pollution: Understanding Factors in Asthma Among Children Living Near Major Roadways." *Environmental Health Perspectives* 120, 11: A436.

Braveman, P., K. Marchi, S. Egerter, S. Kim, M. Meltzer, T. Stancil, and M. Libet. 2010. "Poverty, Near Poverty, and Hardship Around the Time of Pregnancy." *Maternal and Child Health Journal* 14, 1: 20–35.

Breggin, P.R. 2008. *Brain-Disabling Treatments in Psychiatry: Drugs, Electroshock and the Psychopharmaceutical Complex, 2nd edition.* New York: Springer Publishing Company.

____. 1991. *Toxic Psychiatry: Why Therapy, Empathy and Love Must Replace the Drugs, Electroshock, and Biochemical Theories of the "New Psychiatry."* New York: St. Martin's Press.

Breggin, P.R., and G.R. Ginger. 1998. *The War Against Children of Color. Psychiatry Targets Inner City Youth.* Monroe, ME: Common Courage Press.

Brewer, L.C., and L.A. Cooper. 2014. "Race, Discrimination, and Cardiovascular Disease." *American Medical Association Journal of Ethics* 16, 6: 455460.

Broadbent Institute. 2014. *The Wealth Gap: Perceptions and Misconceptions in Canada.* Ottawa: Broadbent Institute.

Bryant, T. 2009. *An Introduction to Health Policy.* Toronto: Canadian Scholars Press.

Calliste, A. 2000. *Anti-Racist Feminism: Critical Race and Gender Studies.* Halifax, NS: Fernwood Publishing.

Caplan, P. 1996. *They Say You're Crazy: How the World's Most Powerful Psychiatrists Decide Who's Normal.* New York: Perseus Books.

CCPA (Canadian Center for Policy Alternatives). 2011. *Putting Our Money Where Our Mouth Is: The Future of Dental Care in Canada.* Ottawa.

Chernomas, R., and I. Hudson. 2009. "Social Murder: The Long Term Effects of Conservative Economic Policy." *International Journal of Health Services* 39, 1: 107–121.

CIHI (Canadian Institute for Health Information). 2010. *National Health Expenditure Trends, 1975–2010.* Toronto.

____. 2013. *Treatment of Preventable Dental Cavities in Preschoolers: A Focus on Day Surgery Under General Anesthesia.* Toronto.

Clay, R.A. 2014. "Double-Whammy Discrimination: Health Care Providers' Biases and Misunderstandings Are Keeping Some Older LGBT Patients from Getting the Care They Need." *Monitor on Psychology* 45, 10: 46--49.

Collins, P.H. 1990. *Black Feminist Thought: Knowledge, Consciousness and the Politics of Empowerment.* Boston: Unwin Hyman.

____. 2002. "The Politics of Black Feminist Thought." In C.R. McCann and S. Kim (eds.), *Feminist Theory Reader: Local & Global Perspectives.* London: Routledge.

____. 2005. *Black Sexual Politics: African Americans, Gender, and the New Racism.* New York: Routledge.

Crenshaw, K. 1989. "Demarginalizing the Intersection of Race and Sex: A Black Feminist Critique of Antidiscrimination Doctrine, Feminist Theory, and Anti-Racist Politics." *University of Chicago Legal Forum,* 14: 538–554.

Cruickshank J. 2012. "Positioning Positivism, Critical Realism and Social Constructionism in the Health Sciences: A Philosophical Orientation." *Nursing Inquiry* 19: 78–82.

Devaux, M., and M. de Looper. 2012. "Income-related inequalities in health service utilisation in 19 OECD countries." OECD *Health Working Papers,* No. 58, OECD Publishing.

Dyer, S., and D. Woynillowicz. 2008. *Oil Sands Reclamation: Fact or Fiction?* Drayton Valley, AB: Pembina Institute.

Engel, L.S., D.A. Hill, J.A. Hoppin, J.H. Lubin, C.F. Lynch, and J. Pierce. 2005. "Pesticide Use and Breast Cancer Risk Among Farmers' Wives in the Agricultural Health Study." *American Journal of Epidemiology* 161, 2: 121–135.

Engels, F. 2009 [1845]. *The Condition of the Working Class in England.* New York: Penguin Classics.

Esping-Anderson, G. 2002. *Why We Need a New Welfare State.* Oxford: Oxford University Press.

Eudy, R.L. 2009. "Infant Mortality in the Lower Mississippi Delta: Geography, Poverty and Race." *Maternal Child Health Journal* 13, 6: 806–813.

Finn, E. 2012. "Government's Forgone Income: Huge Tax Cuts, Uncollected Taxes Starve Our Social Programs." *The Monitor,* July 12. Ottawa: Canadian Center for Policy Alternatives.

Fowler, R.A., N.S. Sabur, P. Li, D.N. Jurrlink, R. Pinto, M.A. Hladunew, N. Adhikari, et al. 2007. "Sex- and Age-Based Differences in the Delivery and Outcomes of Critical Care." *Canadian Medical Association Journal* 177, 12: 1513–1519.

Gaetz, S., J. Donaldson, T. Richter, and T. Gulliver. 2013. *The State of Homelessness in Canada, 2013.* Toronto: Canadian Homeless Research Network Press.

Giscombe, C.L., and M. Lobel. 2005. "Explaining Disproportionately High Rates of Adverse Birth Outcomes among African Americans: The Impact of Stress, Racism, and Related Factors in Pregnancy." *Psychological Bulletin* 131, 5: 662–683.

Hankivsky, O., and A. Christoffersen. 2008. "Intersectionality and the Determinants of Health: A Canadian Perspective." *Critical Public Health* 18, 3: 271–283.

Hankivsky, O., and R. Cormier. 2010. "Intersectionality and Public Policy: Some Lessons from Existing Models." *Political Research Quarterly* 63, 2.

Hankivsky, O., R. Cormier, and D. de Merich. 2009. "Intersectionality: Moving Women's Health Research and Policy Forward." Vancouver: Women's Health Research Network. <bccewh.bc.ca/wp-content/uploads/2012/05/2009_IntersectionaliyMovingwomenshealthresearchandpolicyforward.pdf>.

Hatch, C., and M. Price. 2008. *Canada's Toxic Tar Sands: The Most Destructive Project on Earth.* Toronto: Environmental Defense.

hooks, b. 1990. *Yearning: Race, Gender & Cultural Politics.* Toronto: Between the Lines.

IAEH (International Association for Ecology and Health). 201). *Welcome.* Victoria, BC. <ecohealth-live.net/>.

Illich, I. 1976. *Limits to Medicine: Medical Nemesis. The Expropriation of Health.* Middlesex, UK: Penguin.

Krieger N. 2001. "Theories for Social Epidemiology: An Ecosocial Perspective." *International Journal of Epidemiology* 30.

____. 2003. "Does Racism Harm Health? Did Child Abuse Exist Before 1962? On Explicit Questions, Critical Science, and Current Controversies: An Ecosocial Perspective." *American Journal of Public Health* 93, 2: 194–199.

____. 2014. "Discrimination and Health Inequities." *International Journal of Health Services* 44: 643–710.

Kuh, D., and Y. Ben-Shalmo. 1997. *A Lifecourse Approach to Chronic Disease Epidemiology.* Oxford: Oxford University Press.

Lorber, J. 1994. *Paradoxes of Gender.* New Haven, CT: Yale University Press,

Marx, K. 1977 [1845]. *A Contribution to the Critique of Political Economy.* Moscow: Progress Publishers.

Mayer. C.S. 1987. *In Search of Stability: Explorations in Historical Political Economy.* Cambridge: Cambridge University Press.

McGibbon, E. 2007. "Health inequities and the social determinants of health: The spatial contexts of oppression." Invited keynote speaker, Health Geomatics Conference, Nova Scotia Health Research Foundation, Halifax, NS, October.

McGibbon, E., and C. McPherson. 2012. "Applying Intersectionality and Complexity Theory to Address the Social Determinants of Women's Health." *Women's Health and Urban Life: An International Journal* 10, 1: 59–86.

McGibbon, E., I. Waldron, and J. Jackson. 2013. "The Social Determinants of Cardiovascular Health: Time for a Focus on Racism. Guest Editorial." *Diversity and Equality in Health and Care: An International Journal* 10: 139–142.

McPherson, C., and E. McGibbon. 2014. "Intersecting Contexts of Oppression Within Complex Public Systems." In A. Pycroft and C. Bartollas (eds.), *Applying Complexity Theory: A Whole Systems Approaches to Criminal Justice and Social Work.* Bristol: Policy Press.

Mikkonen, J., and D. Raphael. 2010. *Social Determinants of Health: The Canadian Facts.* Toronto: York University.

Mody, P., A. Gupta, B. Bikdeli, J.F. Lampropulos, and K. Dharmarajan. 2012. "Most Important Articles on Cardiovascular Disease Among Racial and Ethnic Minorities." *Circulation: Cardiovascular Quality and Outcomes* 5, 4: e33–41.

Navarro, V. 2002. "A historical review (1965–1997) of studies on class, health & quality of life: A personal account." In V. Navarro (ed.), *The Political Economy of Social Inequalities: Consequences for Health and Quality of Life.* New York: Baywood Publishing.

____. 2004. *The Political and Social Contexts of Health.* New York: Baywood Publishing.

____. 2007. "What Is National Health Policy?" *International Journal of Health Services* 37, 1: 1–14.

Nixon, R. 2007. "Slow Violence, Gender, and the Environmentalism of the Poor." *Journal of Commonwealth and Postcolonial Studies* 13.2–14.1.

O'Keefe, E.B., J.T. Meltzer, and B.N. Bethea. 2015. "Health Disparities and Cancer: Racial Disparities in Cancer Mortality in the United States, 2000–2010." *Frontiers in Public Health* 3, 51: 1–15.

OECD (Organization for Economic Cooperation and Development). 2010. *Health at a Glance: OECD Indicators.* Paris: OECD Publishing.

Pickett, K.E., and R.G. Wilkinson. 2007. "Child Wellbeing and Income Inequality in Rich Societies: Ecological Cross Sectional Study." *British Medical Journal Online* 24; 335(7629): 1080.

Priest, L. 2010. "Why are our babies dying?" *Globe and Mail,* May 22: 1.

Quach, T., A. Nuru-Jeter, P. Morris, L. Allen, S. Shea, and J.K. Winters. 2012. "Experiences and Perceptions of Medical Discrimination Among a Multiethnic Sample of Breast Cancer Patients in the Greater San Francisco Bay Area, California." *American Journal of Public Health* 102, 5: 1027–1034.

Quinonez, C., D. Locker, L. Sherret, P. Grootendorst, A. Azarpazhooh, and R. Figueiredo. 2005. *An*

Environmental Scan of Publicly Financed Dental Care in Canada. Ottawa: Community Dental Health Services Research Unit and Office of the Chief Dental Officer, Health Canada.

Raphael, D. 2004. "Strengthening the Social Determinants of Health: The Toronto Charter for a Healthy Canada." In Dennis Raphael (ed.). *The Social Determinants of Health: Canadian Perspectives.* Toronto: Canadian Scholars Press.

____. 2012. "Critical Perspectives on the Social Determinants of Health." In E. McGibbon (ed.), *Oppression: A Social Determinant of Health.* Halifax: Fernwood Publishing.

____. 2016. *Critical Perspectives on the Social Determinants of Health.* Toronto: Canadian Scholars Press.

Save the Children. 2013. *Surviving the First Day: State of the World's Mothers, 2013.* London.

Shaw, M., D. Dorling, D. Gordon, and G.D. Smith. 1999. *The Widening Gap: Health* Inequalities and Policy in Britain. Bristol: Policy Press.

Sims M., T.L. Sims, and M.A. Bruce. 2007. "Urban Poverty and Infant Mortality Rate Disparities." *Journal of the National Medical Association* 88, 4: 349–356.

Smith, D. 1987. *The Everyday World as Problematic: A Feminist Sociology.* Toronto: University of Toronto Press.

Tenenbaum, D.J. 2009. "Oil Sands Development: A Risk Worth Taking?" *Environmental Health Perspectives* 117, 4.

Tillett, J. 2010. "Global Health and Infant Mortality: Can We Learn from Other Systems?" *Journal of Perinatal and Neonatal Nursing* 24, 2: 95–97.

Virchow, R. 1842. Report to Her Majesty's Principal Secretary of State for the Home Department, from the Poor Law Commissioners on an Inquiry into the Sanitary Condition of the Labouring Population of Great Britain. London: W. Clowes and Sons, for H.M.S.O.

WHO (World Health Organization). 2011. "Ten Facts on Health Inequities and Their Causes." *Fact Files*, October.

Wier, L.M., C.T. Merrill, and A. Elixhauser. 2009. "Hospital stays among people living in the poorest communities, 2006." Health Care Cost and Utilization Project, May.

Wijeyesinghe, CL., P. Griffin, and B. Love. 1997. "Racism: Curriculum Design." In M. Adams, L. Bell and P. Griffin (eds.), *Teaching for Diversity and Social Justice: A Sourcebook.* New York: Routledge.

Wilkinson, L. 2003. "Advancing a Perspective on the Intersections of Diversity: Challenges for Research and Social Policy." *Canadian Ethnic Studies* 35, 3: 26–34.

Yavari, P., M.C. Barroetavena, T.G. Hislop, and C.D. Bajdik. 2010. "Breast Cancer Treatment and Ethnicity in British Columbia, Canada." *BioMedCentral Cancer* 10: 154.

Zbogar, V. 2014. "Brian Sinclair's death was a homicide: But call it whatever you want, just address the discrimination." *Winnipeg Free Press* Print Edition, June 16: A9.

Zola, I.K. 1978. "Medicine as an Institution of Social Control." In J. Ehrenreich (ed.), *The Cultural Crisis of Modern Medicine.* New York: Monthly Review Press.

8

Occupy Democracy

Exploring Democracy as a Relationship

Dennis Pilon

IN THE FALL OF 2011, A GLOBAL PROTEST MOVEMENT emerged seemingly overnight: Occupy. Inspired by the public activism that fueled the "Arab Spring" earlier that year, as well as a call by Vancouver-based counter-culture magazine *Adbusters* for activists to challenge the forces behind the world financial crisis, the first occupation was established on September 17 as Occupy Wall Street. What began as a tent city occupation of Zuccotti Park in the financial district of New York City soon spread to cities around the world. Occupy denounced the very top wealth and income earners and the power they wielded over the rest of society, despite the existence of formal democratic institutions and processes. In their view, it was the 1 percent versus the 99 percent. This simple rendering of the power dynamics of wealth inequality proved incredibly popular with political activists and the general

> Occupy denounced the very top wealth and income earners and the power they wielded over the rest of society, despite the existence of formal democratic institutions and processes. In their view, it was the 1% versus the 99%.

public alike (Byrne 2012). By October 15, over 900 cities in more than eighty countries around the world participated in an Occupy-orchestrated Global Day of Action (Addley 2011). In Canada, impromptu Occupy settlements emerged in public spaces in more than twenty cities (Elash 2011; Habib 2011). While media commentators focused attention on the broad Occupy theme of inequality, participants went much further, speaking of their experiences in the camps as anticipating a whole new and better way of doing democracy. No political parties, no elections, no media, no formal leaders or organized factions — just people, present in the same space, making decisions for their own collective self-governance (Syrek 2012; Roberts 2012).

Occupy was a spectacular and highly visible example of a deep dissatisfaction with Canadian democracy, but it was just one manifestation of these feelings. Survey researchers had long noted a decisive and strongly negative shift in public attitudes about politics and politicians starting as far back as the 1970s, a trend that had only intensified over time (Clarke and Kornberg 1993). While Canada's electoral processes are lauded around the world for their transparency, fairness and legitimacy, our politics appear to have fallen short of inspiring very many people recently. Voter turnout has been in fairly steady decline, public engagement on political issues appears low and poorly informed, and politicians as a group are viewed with contempt by a considerable amount of the public (Pammett and Leduc 2003). There is much debate and disagreement about just who or what is to blame for this state of affairs (see, for instance, Lenard and Simeon 2012). Some target political parties and party discipline, complaining that parties dominate our politics and force individual politicians to ignore local constituents to toe the party line. Others point to institutions — be it Parliament, the voting system or the courts — as the source of political dysfunction. Another line of criticism highlights the negative role of money in politics, underlining how campaign finance laws allow the wealthy to unduly influence political parties and elections. And these are just a few of the complaints.

Canada's present democratic deficit has inspired different responses, though nearly all seem to want to empower local communities. From the progressive side of politics, the Occupy experience would call for replacing Canada's delegated and hierarchical form of electoral representation with local and direct citizen participation: pure self-governance — no delegation. But Canada's political right also talk up local power when they argue to increase the influence of local MPs or through the

> But what if democracy is not a place or institution or set of rules? A very different take sees democracy as a relationship among people for their own self-government.

greater use of referenda or recall (Laycock 2002). Yet both sides of this critique of Canada's conventional institutionalized democracy focus on the locale or processes or institutions as the stuff that democracy is made from, the inference being that if we get them right more democratic results will emerge. But what if democracy is not a place or institution or set of rules? A very different take on democracy will be explored here, one that sees democracy as a *relationship* amongst people for their own self-government. As such, it must be judged in terms of the depth of that relationship. This requires a *relational* theory of democracy, one that can assess how the broader social relations that exist in any given society influence attempts to deepen or diminish the democratic experience.

Elections = Democracy?

The first issue we need to take up is the relationship of elections to democracy. For most media commentators, politicians and social scientists, this is a no brainer: elections equal democracy, full stop. For instance, Canada is generally referred to as an electoral democracy, a representative democracy and/or a liberal democracy because we have regular elections, fairly open rules about who can participate in them and alternation in the ranks of government (that is, different parties come to power at fairly regular intervals). This understanding of democracy is premised on the twin themes of representation and majority rule, meaning, respectively, that elections produce representatives who will speak for the populace, and decisions about governing and policy are made on the basis of gaining majority support, typically by winning a majority of votes from those representatives. Thus, as long as the public can choose from different candidates running for office, we are told, we have democracy (Courtney 2004).

The main problem with the elections = democracy formula is that Canadian elections generally fail to meet the representation/majority rule standard. Canada's voting system misrepresents what voters say with their votes in a host of ways (the following problems are dealt with in detail in Pilon 2007). It regularly overrepresents more popular parties and under-represents less popular ones; it overrepresents geographically concentrated voters while under-representing voters that are more spread out across the country. It creates incentives for voters to vote strategically for perceived winners and avoid wasting their vote on perceived losers. It makes the entry of new parties

> The main problem with the elections = democracy formula is that Canada's voting system misrepresents what voters say with their votes in a host of ways.

and new ideas more difficult while inflating the support of more established political forces. Even the dominant parties are negatively affected as the system tends to unduly regionalize their success, creating a distorted picture of their national support. And it wastes a lot votes — typically more than 50 percent of the votes cast in a Canadian election do not contribute to the election of anyone. Nor do Canadian elections meet the standard for majority rule, as governments with a majority of seats almost never reflect an actual majority of voters. Since 1921, only two federal elections out of twenty-nine have seen one party clearly secure more than 50 percent of the popular vote. Even the much vaunted choice that is the supposedly the hallmark of competitive elections is mostly illusory in Canada, given the very narrow set of options voters typically face. For instance, voters unhappy with a left-wing government have the option of choosing a right-wing one as an alternative, which is not really much of a choice for those voters.

The gap between public expectations and the skewed electoral results that are typical in our representative system fuels public complaints about politicians losing touch with their constituents and political parties breaking with their campaign promises. Some blame politicians or political parties and/or institutions, and some call for the abolition of parties, the reform of institutions and/or the rejection of elite brokered politics altogether in favour of direct democracy, participatory democracy or even an end to democracy. But a key part of the problem is with the equation elections = democracy itself. People respond as if elections were invented as means of doing democracy and have somehow been subverted since then. Yet it doesn't take much historical digging to find out that elections are not necessarily synonymous with democracy. In fact, they precede the democratic era by many centuries. Most of Europe held elections stretching far back into the Middle Ages (Myers 1975). Initially, and until recently, elections were about providing representation to electors, who were typically a privileged group, be they aristocrats, religious leaders or wealthy merchants. The first battles over representation in Western Europe were about gaining governing influence for the wealthy, not democracy for the many (von Beyme 2000). The American choice to govern by elections was widely recognized in the eighteenth century as a rejection of democracy in favour of "representative government," a system its founders thought would allow the better class of people, the economically privileged, to guide public affairs (Manin 1997). In British colonial jurisdictions like Canada, New Zealand and Australia, elections were designed to maintain order and bind local people to governing elites and their economic projects (Brady 1952).

Just holding elections does not prove anyone is democratic. Throughout its existence, the Soviet Union held elections every four years like clockwork, but only members of the ruling Communist Party could run (Pravda 1978). The Vatican selects its pope by election, but only church leaders (who are not themselves elected) can vote. Board members of joint stock companies and corporations vote on a host of issues and leaders — they are not democracies. And, by contrast, a lack of elections does not prove an absence of democracy either. The ancient Greeks eschewed elections as undemocratic and preferred to select those who would govern randomly by lot (Ober 1996). New England still has locales ruled by a town hall meeting of citizens — there is no elected council (Bryan 2004). And there are a host of examples of small scale decision-making in groups that operate on principles of broad inclusion and building consensus as a way of doing democracy, rather than taking votes or holding elections (Gastil 1993).

> Just holding elections does not prove anyone is democratic.

Canada has had a long experience with elections, stretching back decades before Confederation. But these elections were not exemplars of democracy (for examples, see Abella 1966; Cadigan 1991). In fact, Canada was arguably founded in 1867 as the world's first anti-democracy, so clear were the founders in their distaste for and rejection of democratic values (Pilon 2016). Even twenty years later neither the Conservatives nor Liberals were prepared to introduce universal male suffrage. And this disdain for democracy remained a defining characteristic of Canadian elite politics well into the twentieth century, shifting only during World War I as the political class attempted to mobilize a country for war and the privations and sacrifices that would accompany it (Dupuis-Deri 2010). Still, while the discourse changed — suddenly Canadian political aims were cloaked in a democratic rhetoric — little else did. The point

> This disdain for democracy remained a defining characteristic of Canadian elite politics well into the twentieth century.

being, the existence of elections does not prove democracy is going on. Indeed, the attempt to reduce democracy to elections is itself a political strategy with an undemocratic pedigree (Maloy 2008). On the other hand, elections might be democratic, depending on a great many other factors. But there is nothing intrinsically democratic about elections.

Democracy: What's in a Name?

So what is democracy then if not elections, or representation, or any group of people involved in making a decision? Not surprisingly, there is little consensus about a definitive answer. People have quite literally fought over what democracy means, and the path of political development across Western countries in the twentieth century has been described as a long struggle to define, control and contain that meaning (Pilon 2013). Academics have declared democracy an "essentially contested concept," basically admitting that they have given up seeking a consensus definition (Green 1993). Some suggest that democracy's meaning depends on how it is "adjectified": populist democracy, capitalist democracy, liberal democracy, socialist democracy and so on (Held 2006). Others argue that democracy as a term has no fixed meaning; it is primarily a site of struggle for those seeking to associate themselves and their processes and/or actions with its positive connotations (Whitehead 1997). But these observations seem either incomplete or unsatisfying. As a term denoting something specific, democracy can't just mean anything, or it is meaningless. Here some historical context is most useful to understand where the term "democracy" came from and what its various proponents and detractors thought it would amount to.

The common lineage of democracy traces its origins back to antiquity, specifically ancient Greece and the city of Athens in particular. Indeed, the term democracy combines the Greek words for people (*demos*) and power (*kratos*). Traditional Greek society was ruled by a small aristocracy, but in the fifth century A.D. a new, more open governing system was established that dramatically increased the number Greek citizens able to participate in governing. By shifting from a system where a handful of governors made all the decisions to one where tens of thousands could participate dramatically altered the balance of social power in Athens, creating a relationship amongst its people for self-government that proved difficult for traditional elites to overthrow. Of course, by today's standards Greek democracy hardly looks that inclusive: women, slaves and non-property-owners were all excluded from participating. But such criticisms miss the larger point. If the Greek experience could survive as a positive example for centuries, despite fragmentary records and elite opposition, it was because it captured something important about power, not institutions (Ober 1996). The "*demos-kratos*" or "people-power" in Athens, despite its limitations in modern terms, decisively altered the balance of power in favour of the masses and against traditional ruling elites.

> Greek democracy was less about majority rule and more about the "capacity to do things": the power to do, to have impact, to influence what was going on.

Greek democracy accomplished this through a focus on doing and getting results, rather than by simply defining process and institutional forms. Josiah Ober argues that Greek democracy was less about majority rule and more about the "capacity to do things": the power to do, to have impact, to influence what was going on (Ober 2008). And this is why democracy was, until recently, strenuously opposed by traditional leaders and ruling elites everywhere because the last thing they wanted was for their subjects to decide for themselves how to contribute to society (Macpherson 1965). Of course, we needn't necessarily go back to the Greeks to discover this democratic ethos — there have been many examples of societies operating on just these sorts of egalitarian governing ideas (for example, Indigenous peoples in Canada and around the world) (Paley 2002). If we boil down these many experiences, summing the basic gist of the democratic concept is fairly simple: democracy denotes an ability to influence the decisions that affect one's own life. Thus the check on whether democracy exists is not *where* it happens or *what* institutions it uses, but whether average people really have an ability to influence things.

It should be underlined that establishing and maintaining a democratic relationship amongst people generally does not go unopposed, particularly by those used to enjoying superior social and economic power. Thus the relational aspect of democracy involves an ongoing social struggle against those who do not want such a relationship to exist or would seek to weaken it precisely to limit its "capacity to do" anything on behalf of the masses. These insights give us a very different starting point in examining Canadian democracy, its

> The check on whether democracy exists is not where it happens or what institutions it uses, but whether average people really have an ability to influence things.

origins and development. If we want to understand how and why Canadian democracy works as it does, we have to explain how this struggle to establish a democratic relationship has occurred and assess what factors have been strengthening or weakening it, an approach that requires historical analysis rather than "ideal type" institutional comparison (for example, comparing how different kinds of legislatures, say American and Canadian, enact laws) or a blind nationalist championing of a romantic past (celebrating the "founding fathers" and their role in creating Canada at Confederation, for example).

Canadian Democracy: From Liberal Order to Liberal Democracy

The founders of Canada were not democrats. What they sought was a "liberal order" — a system of rule that would protect property rights through the rule of law, the point being to create legal barriers to state interference with, or seizure of, private property (McKay 2000). The "order" (or governing system) was considered liberal because the founders believed that the economy should be organized to allow individual property owners maximum freedom to influence the broader economic market and that such "free markets" were the best way to provide what society needed. They were reacting against the particular mercantilist, government-directed form of capitalism that had been established in the British colonies in North America, one where an artificial ruling elite had been created to dispense patronage and influence so as to create a British-style three-class system (aristocracy, middle class, working class). Reformers railed against the arbitrary way that the British-installed governors wielded free grants of land, patronage and corruption to rule. They complained that the colonies were effectively controlled by a "family compact" that was immune to electoral pressure or influence (Patterson 1977). But they did not call for democracy to replace it. What they wanted was a system where control over patronage and influence was decided through a competitive electoral process controlled by those with property (Curtis 1989). The Canadian struggle was not out of line with developments in Europe, where traditional ruling elites — notables, the aristocracy, the church, royalty — were also being challenged by an emerging wealthy merchant and industrial class that also demanded influence over government for themselves, not the masses (Birch 1964; von Beyme 2000).

A host of international and colonial changes weakened the family compact and ultimately led to the creation of Canada in 1867. Mercantile capitalism had relied on an imperial trading system where Britain agreed to support its colonies economically in the hopes of profit in the long term. But by the mid-nineteenth century the world's most advanced capitalist country began dismantling this system in favour of one based on free trade. The colonies of the British Empire needed to develop a new model of economic governance (Semmel 1970). The Canadian colonies had already begun this process when they achieved responsible government in the 1840s, basically by forcing their various governors to secure legislative approval for any government spending. Confederation would see Canadian politicians have to take even more responsibility for the design and maintenance of the whole economic order (Buckner 2008). The plan, as Canada's first Prime Minister John A. Macdonald described it, was to establish a system of "constitutional liberty," as opposed to democracy, a liberal order or system of rule that would set the ground rules for governing competitive capitalism so as to respect property rights and grant those with superior resources superior political influence. But how exactly to

> The plan, as Canada's first Prime Minister John A. Macdonald described it, was to establish a system of "constitutional liberty," as opposed to democracy.

carry this out was a matter of dispute and eventually led to the division of the polity into factions that would become our Conservative and Liberal political parties. Both groups were essentially small 'l' liberals (that is, they were influenced by liberal ideas about property rights and markets) but disagreed about how to organize and manage a liberal economy (McKay 2000). The Conservatives supported tariffs to give preference to Canadian business within Canada while the Liberals advocated free trade to further the expansion of Canadian business worldwide. Both sides fought pitched electoral battles to gain control of the state and put their views into practice (Underhill 1935).

A side effect of establishing this liberal order was a dramatic reorganization of society. As a competitive economic system, capitalism ruthlessly tore down existing economic structures and relationships in the search for greater profits, aided by state support for crucial infrastructure like transportation (such as railways). Over time, employment in traditional rural farming gave way to resource exploitation, manufacturing and service work, much of it centred in urban locales (Wallace 1950; Katz 1972). Such social upheaval required ongoing political management through a combination of incentives (patronage, for example) and coercion (such as open non-secret voting). Amidst this social change, various reforms — the secret ballot, re-districting and changes to the franchise — were introduced to advance the competitive position of these parties. These were not characterized as democratic accomplishments but as pragmatic accommodations meant to gain advantage over competitors while recognizing that old methods of social control would not work in a rapidly changing environment (MacDermot 1933). For instance, the 1885 *Franchise Act* altered how voters' lists were put together, accommodating the fact that a significant number of potential voters were regularly moving to and from the United States in search of work (Forster 1986).

Ironically, the same capitalism that disrupted traditional economic relationships also broke down traditional forms of social surveillance and order, creating space for genuinely democratic demands to emerge. Traditional forms of rule saw elites directly supervise the lower orders (for example, the lord and his peasants), but the scope and complexity of the new urban capitalist society made that much more difficult, allowing the poor and working classes to meet and organize outside the scrutiny of employers and politicians (Hobsbawm 2011). For instance, organized labour arose in the nineteenth century across Western countries to contest the workings of the emerging liberal order (understood as the method of governing economic development), particularly the way in which it created extreme poverty, exploited workers and resulted in steep inequality in terms of who benefited from capitalist productivity. Attempts by workers to resist their exploitation on the shop floor were met with the violent force of the state, operating at the behest of capitalists. This forced organized labour to direct some of their reforming energies to the state level, calling for democracy to politically temper the economic and social inequalities created by the liberal order (Sassoon 1996). To accomplish this, a number of strategies were adopted, including the use direct action, the creation of mass political parties and involvement in electoral campaigns (Eley 2002).

Across Western Europe and the Anglo-American countries what we can see historically is that occupy-like events and electoral movements were a direct response to the liberal order, utilizing the organizing space created by it to contest its workings and demand something better: democracy. The most striking example was undoubtedly the Paris Commune, a spontaneous take-over of that city by workers following the French defeat in the Franco-Prussian war in 1871, an occupation that lasted months and involved tens of thousands of people. Though the Commune was brutally suppressed, it remained a forceful example of working-class self-organization and democracy well into the twentieth century. In the late nineteenth century, a variety of strategies were deployed by organized labour and social-ist parties across Western countries to force concessions from the state (Tombs 2013). In Belgium workers staged general strikes to gain the franchise; in Germany socialists formed a mass political party that organized many aspects of worker's lives and became the country's largest political party by 1912. In the U.K., organized labour launched a political party that quickly became an electoral threat (Sassoon 1996; Eley 2002).

These efforts gained concessions, but it would take more cataclysmic circumstances to shift from a liberal order to liberal democracy, circumstances that would expand the scope of influence on government to include workers, particularly those without property. Nineteenth-century elites were not convinced that democracy could be embraced without sacrificing liberal property rights: you could have one or the other, they thought, but not both. Across Western countries, the circumstances that finally forced democracy onto the agenda were primarily the product of the dramatic social upheaval created in fighting in and recovering from World War I. The war altered the balance of class power, strengthen-ing the working classes and exposing the unequal class burden of prosecuting the war. While workers went to war and their families suffered sacrifices at home, war-profiteering businesses made massive profits from corrupt government contracts for a host of products and services related to the war. At the war's end, returning soldiers and workers made common cause in demanding something better from the countries they had fought for (Eley 2002). In Russia, a revolution had swept away the old regime, suggesting change could happen with dire consequences for traditional elites. In various countries across Europe, demonstrations and occupations centred around democ-ratizing the political system. In Sweden, street demonstrations forced the Crown to accept parliamentary supremacy and democracy, while in Italy demands for greater workplace democracy led to massive factory occupations (Pilon 2013).

In Canada, these tensions manifested in a host of ways. During the war the One Big Union had formed and managed to sign up tens of thousands of members in a very short period of time by promoting a radical agenda of economic democracy. After the war, the Winnipeg General Strike broke out on May 15, 1919, and for six weeks the workers replaced the civic administration in running the city. Sympathy strikes quickly emerged in more than twenty locales across the country (Heron 1998). The response to these efforts was a mixture of force and concessions. The RCMP brought the Winnipeg General Strike to a close by kill-ing two unarmed strikers, but at the same time the traditional political class began using a discourse of democracy to justify the inclusion of workers' political representatives, if that is what voters wanted (Pilon 2012). For a time, it appeared that political parties organized to represent unions and farmers might make a breakthrough in Canada — they did become the provincial government in Ontario in 1919 and the second largest party in Ottawa in

1921 — but on the whole such efforts quickly faded as traditional political forces reasserted control by various means (Naylor 1991).

While a discourse of democracy emerged in Canada after WWI, its substance was distinctly lacking. Throughout the 1920s, workers and farmers would suffer from the instability of the capitalist economy and politically the state did little to offset its effects for them. As things worsened with the onset of the Great Depression in the 1930s, progressive forces regrouped, embarking on a series of direct actions and creating new political organizations. Again, a host of occupy-like events were staged in western Canada. In 1935, the failed "On to Ottawa" trek saw unemployed men from western Canada attempt to travel on railway boxcars to Ottawa to demand the government do something about the terrible economic situation in the country, but they were dispersed and many were arrested in Regina amidst a hail of bullets. Later, in 1938, unemployed men again protested the poor pay and conditions in the work camps set up for men without work by occupying the Vancouver Post Office, Art Gallery and Hotel Georgia for a number of weeks (Howard 1985). A new left party, the Co-operative Commonwealth Federation (CCF), attempted to bring together organized labour, progressive farmers, socialists and liberal reformers and quickly became a competitive force in a number of western provinces and at the federal level (Naylor 2016). But despite the obvious dysfunction of the economic system and the organization of considerable opposition, what is striking is the resilience of those supporting a liberal order over democracy. In Canada, both Conservative and Liberal governments did little to counter or respond to the economic crisis (Horn 1984). In Europe, even a liberal democracy proved too much in a number of places, giving way to authoritarian regimes in Italy, Germany, Spain and France.

As with the previous world war, World War II altered the balance of class power in Western societies, empowering working-class movements and political parties. In Europe, socialist and labour parties came to power in the immediate postwar period and began introducing significant social and economic reforms (Eley 2002). In North America, however, a number of occupations and strikes were required in the late 1940s to move political elites to grant concessions around labour organizing, working conditions and various social entitlements. For instance, 1946 strikes of Stelco, Westinghouse and Firestone workers are widely credited with solidifying wartime gains in union recognition, seniority and grievance procedures (Palmer 1992). The emergence of a superpower brinkmanship between the Soviet Union and the United States in the form of the Cold War, one with possibly atomic destructive force, also influenced events, contributing to a negotiated political consensus around full employment and the welfare state. Basically, Western countries faced a legitimacy problem if they did not accede to longstanding public demands for full employment and a modicum of social services.

But these developments also eventually contributed to restricting the space for dissent (Maloy 2008). Democracy was increasingly defined as choice-making through elections, preferably cast in terms of two parties that were roughly similar.

> Democracy was increasingly defined as choice-making through elections. Public aspirations to participate in the decisions that affected their own lives were channelled into consumption, i.e., choice-making through the market.

Public aspirations to participate in the decisions that affected their own lives were chan-
nelled into consumption, that is, choice-making through the market. This deal, often dubbed
the "postwar economic comprise," saw many workers get decent jobs and social services in
return for reduced democratic aspirations. Union recognition and bargaining rights led to
better wages and a greater ability of working people to purchase goods and services from
the market. Additionally, the welfare state expanded considerably with the creation of
unemployment insurance, family allowances and Medicare. The compromise eventually fell
apart in the 1970s when the wage demands of working people and corporate profits came
into conflict. Right-wing critics of even this limited democracy quickly blamed the postwar
compromise for the economic failure and the increasing social upheaval in the 1960s and
1970s, seeking a return to a more pure liberal order, what would become neoliberalism
(Crozier, Huntington and Watanuki 1975). Since then, neoliberalism's supporters have been
chipping away at previous democratic accomplishments, seeking to weaken the democratic
relationship amongst Canadians, while traditional democratic supporters on the left have
increasingly lost their bearings.

Strengthening the Democratic Relationship

In response to the shallowness of Canadian electoral democracy, some seek alternatives:
direct democracy, anti-politician and anti-party movements, electoral reforms or something outside electoral politics altogether. But on their own, these proposals won't work.
Despite their various diagnoses of the problem and the different details for their projects,
all these critics share a fundamental misreading of Canadian democratic practice. They
start from what we might call an "idealist" understanding, that democracy was the product
of ideas and values that were then embodied in our institutions like political parties and
elections. From there it follows that our present democratic dysfunction can be understood
as a product of a betrayal of those values by those with power or a malfunctioning of the
institutions. In other words, they apply a *normative* judgment to Canadian elections/
party politics and find it wanting. But what they should be doing is applying an *analytical*
approach — why does Canadian politics operate as it does? Only by understanding this,
can we strengthen the democratic relationship amongst Canadians. Contra the idealist view,
Canada's electoral and governing institutions (who could vote, the workings of parliament,
the emergence of political parties, etc.) were not designed or intended to be democratic,
and their transition to being considered democratic was mostly a matter of discourse rather
than the result of any substantive process of change, a concessionary response of political
elites to political struggle from those really interested in democracy. Such challenges did
establish a democratic relationship amongst Canadians, though it should be considered
rather weak when compared to more equalitarian countries in Western Europe where left-
wing parties were stronger, and, as a result, undemocratic elites had to concede more in
the way of social entitlements (for example, welfare states) and citizenship rights (that is,
influence over governing decisions). Improving this relationship will not be accomplished
simply through critique, institutional reforms or dropping out of conventional political
spaces for self-made alternatives. It requires connecting a substantive democratic vision

> Those opposed to democracy benefit disproportionately from capitalism's high productivity, and they use their resources to maintain and reform the state regulation of the economy and society in their interest.

with a mobilization of the people who need it most: the 99 percent.

At this point, the challenges are mostly material rather than ideal. The quality or substance of our democratic relationship is affected by the material resources that different groups in society can bring to bear on the struggle. Those opposed to democracy benefit disproportionately from capitalism's high productivity, and they use their resources to maintain and reform the state regulation of the economy and society in their interest. Specifically, they fund the key governing parties, own the media that shape the agenda of public debate and actively organize to discredit political forces that would damage their interests. We can see examples of this in the active media opposition to the introduction of most aspects of the Canadian welfare state (pensions, unemployment insurance, hospital and medical insurance, for example) or in the well-funded campaigns targeting the electoral left and various social movements. Another example is the collusion between state security services and dominant political elites to spy on left-wing politicians and civil society activists to discredit them and/or disrupt their efforts (Whitaker, Kealey and Parnaby 2012). Blatant media bias is clearly revealed in the media's support for different political parties. In federal elections in 2006, 2008, 2011, and 2015, every significant daily newspaper but one supported the Conservative Party, even though only a distinct minority of Canadian voters did (O'Keefe 2015). This is not a recent trend.

By contrast, democratic forces rely on the mobilization of masses of people rather than money, the creation of permanent organizational bodies (like parties and unions) and using pre-existing social organizations and experiences (churches, community organizations, working-class culture). In different eras, the material constraints and opportunities are different.

We can break down the Canadian experience of such struggle into three broad eras: local, mediated and neoliberal. The period from 1867 to roughly 1930 witnessed Canada's transition from a rural and small town capitalist farming society to a more urban and industrial one, but people brought with them the experience of collective action from their former lives to help them organize against the powerful in their new circumstances. Working-class and co-operative farming cultures aided in political organizing. It was no-brainer to tell former farmers that workers were the ones with the know-how and didn't need bosses — they were accustomed to making their own clothes, fixing their own machinery and working with their neighbours to deal with crises and seasonal deadlines. It helped that political struggle in this period remained profoundly local and social. Prior to the advent of mass radio broadcasting in the 1930s, public meetings were the main forum for political encounters. Politics happened in the streets or in meeting halls. Left parties attempted to organize workers into a political force, while divisions amongst economic and political elites become opportunities to extract concessions. But, on the whole, Canada's anti-democratic forces maintained control, either ignoring calls for democracy or effectively shunting off significant challenges (like the post-WWI social upheaval) with delays and distractions.

The period from the 1940s through to the 1970s shifted the terrain of politics from a strictly local encounter to a mediated one. Initially, post-WWII social and union organizing forced concessions from the state around union recognition and social welfare as the kind of capital (business)-labour compromise discussed earlier as the postwar economic compromise. Political organizing was still fought at the local level, which required politicians to secure local patronage and investments to maintain full employment even while mostly serving the interests of capitalists. All this helped strengthen the democratic relationship. But contradictory elements emerged too. The rise of radio and then television broadcasting created a very different relationship between the public and political elites, ultimately weakening the ability of people to self-identify who they were and what they wanted. Instead of confirming their own sense of identity through direct interactions with political events, people increasingly observed politics indirectly through TV and radio news programs, while a decidedly skewed version of public opinion was given shape by these new profit-oriented media enterprises. The rise of postwar consumerism and the atomizing effects of the welfare state (people feeling "like a number") eroded the collective action mentality shaped in the pre-WWII era through the experience of the Great Depression and mobilizing for war. The 1970s witnessed a return to significant job action as a result of serious economic crisis, but the organizing seemed more narrowly economic (increasing wages and benefits) than political. This left traditional democratic forces like unions and left parties vulnerable when a serious anti-democratic mobilization was launched around what would become known as neoliberalism.

Neoliberalism was a project that emerged across Western countries to roll back the welfare state, privatize public services and use market-based incentives to motivate human behaviour. From the 1980s on, Canada's democratic forces have focused their attention and organizing on containing the neoliberal assault. Ongoing and significant cuts to social programs have been accompanied through serious reductions in tax rates for the wealthy and corporations. While the 1 percent have disproportionately benefited, the 99 percent have seen their standard of living decline. Though the left and unions have tried to resist these initiatives, their efforts have been largely defensive: to hold on to previous gains, rather than open up space for a more searching critique of the limits of the postwar economic compromise (Panitch and Swartz 2008). This lack of leadership and vision has contributed to a significant decline in working-class and poor participation in politics, be it through membership in political parties or just voting in elections. At the same time, divisions amongst ruling elites, particularly the capitalist class, have narrowed considerably, with a broad consensus on their part for small government, reduced welfare states and worldwide free trade (Panitch and Gindin 2012). The dilemma of the current moment is to figure out how to combine effectively against such anti-democratic opponents.

While the challenges are many, there are many positive signs that today's society expects and will demand more from our limited democracy. The transformation in social attitudes around issues

> The transformation in social attitudes around issues like gay marriage, traditional gender roles and the recognition of past wrongs all suggest that contemporary Canadian society is more willing to challenge dominant ideas and act on questions of social justice.

> Social media is a weak form of politics because simply liking a Facebook page doesn't necessarily mean anything concrete will happen.

like gay marriage, traditional gender roles and the recognition of past wrongs like the Chinese Head Tax and the internment of Japanese Canadians during WWII, and the terrible impact of residential schools and other manifestations of colonialism on Indigenous peoples all suggest that contemporary Canadian society is more willing to challenge dominant ideas and act on questions of social justice. Much has been made of the opportunities afforded by new technology and social media, with significant attention paid to the role it played in recent democratization efforts around the world (as in Egypt and Tunisia, for example). Certainly efforts like Occupy demonstrated how social media could be brought to bear in organizing and communicating a different kind of politics (DeLuca, Lawson, and Sun 2012; also see Chapter 16 in this book). However, on its own, social media is a weak form of politics because simply liking a Facebook page doesn't necessarily mean anything concrete will happen — people can take up social causes on social media like consumers purchase products. And unlike traditional organizing, social media can be decidedly unsocial, experienced in an individual and isolated way (Conover et al. 2013; James 2014). In a world where an individual's identity appears to be increasingly defined online, dropping out of material encounters becomes much easier.

Fighting for democracy against those that seek to limit or eliminate it requires collective action to push back. This is the difficulty with many of the more creative alternative forms of dissent today: they have failed to connect their democratic challenge with the masses of people who could give it heft. Thus challenges like Occupy succeed at the spectacular level — as a spectacle of opposition, Occupy signalled that dissent is possible and potentially popular. Occupy's messages — the 1 percent versus the 99 percent, the immorality of Wall Street, the wastefulness of contemporary capitalism and the shallowness of conventional electoral democracy — struck a chord with the great mass of people. Even their intransigence in refusing to decamp was inspiring for its doggedness to keep the focus on the unacceptability of the present state of economic affairs (Stechyson 2012). But Occupy, on its own, could not act as a template to remake democracy for the simple reason that their involved, maximally participative, non-delegated form of participation assured that only a very privileged group of people would have the time, material resources and social capital required to be present (Roberts 2012). Occupy meetings would go on for hours, and the level of discourse often assumed some post-secondary education.

> Occupy's involved, maximally participative, non-delegated form of participation assured that only a very privileged group of people would have the time, material resources and social capital required to be present.

As countless studies show, the poor and working class do not have the time or confidence to actively participate in such settings (discussed in Pilon 2015). Indeed, research shows that the further one moves from conventional electoral politics, the more socially unequal participation becomes, particularly in class terms (Dalton, Scarrow and Cain 2003).

By contrast, with a relational view of democratic struggle, our efforts must take place on multiple fronts: Occupy-like confrontations at a spectacular level to open up the discourse and let people see that others are unhappy too, organizational bodies that take account of how class and other forms of inequality and oppression limit how or whether marginalized groups can participate and a state-level strategy (for example, a party with a program to democratize the economy) that can threaten the interests of capital and leverage such threats into a strengthened democratic relationship among the many for their collective self-governance. These three strategies actually work together, mutually influencing and reinforcing each other. For instance, Occupy-like events do not stand apart from other social mobilizing efforts; indeed, they often rely on economic and organizing support from more conventional organizations like unions (Rowe and Carroll 2014). Or we can see how the work done by Occupy in raising the profile of inequality and expanding the scope of what could be discussed also was manifest in the unexpected popularity of the Bernie Sanders' bid for the presidential nomination of the Democratic Party (Gabbatt 2015; Kreig 2016).

The point being, these are not separate, alternative political strategies but complementary and necessarily interactive aspects of the same critical and democratic politics that affect the broader democratic relationship. This view is not simply a matter of choice, reflecting our values and preferences, but a decision informed by our analysis of how power works and how it can be challenged in the present moment. Thus we do what we must, not necessarily what we prefer.

The Project of Self-Rule

The seemingly overnight success of the Occupy movement caught most pundits and long-time political activists by surprise. For a moment it captured the attention of the media, who didn't seem to know how to respond to its unconventional organization and unclear objectives. Of course, others found the spontaneous and egalitarian milieu of Occupy exciting and inspirational, especially when compared to more staid and less radical political spaces like political parties and elections. But Occupy should not be seen as an alternative to other forms of political activism and engagement. Rather, it is a necessary and constitutive part of any effort to further democracy in capitalist societies. This is because democracy is not a place or particular form of organization or specific set of rules — it is a relationship amongst people for their own self-governance, one that we must struggle to establish and enhance against considerable and myriad forms of inequality. Occupy alone won't do this. What we must do is take the inspiration of Occupy and combine it with other strategies to occupy democracy.

To occupy democracy is to be present in the power constellations that affect it, to mobilize people-power to counter the material privileges produced by capitalism for anti-democratic forces. That means being present in the streets, in the organizations that further collective action by the many and, yes, in elections that crucially affect the governing of

> To occupy democracy is to be present in the power constellations that affect it, to mobilize people-power to counter the material privileges produced by capitalism for anti-democratic forces.

the state. It must be necessary to act in all these spaces because only by bringing together all three can we strengthen and further our democratic relationship. Capitalists have their own problems, not least of which is their need to compete against each other for profit, a factor that prevents a unified political ruling class from emerging. Despite the apparent solidity and stability of our present liberal order, an enormous effort involving considerable resources must be mobilized on an ongoing basis to maintain and reproduce a less-than-democratic capitalist form of rule. Countering this mobilizing effort must be a collective force that challenges the key pillars sustaining and strengthening it, via spectacular challenges to the democratic imaginary, through a solid and substantial organization of the masses of people to participate by permanent bodies and with a clear political project aimed at the state to limit and reshape its defence of capitalists. Of course people can and should choose where they want to put their energy, but our many efforts are in aid in one project: to strengthen the democratic relationship amongst us and make more real the project of self-rule.

Glossary of Key Terms

Democracy: A contested concept, defined by some as a process where the public can partici-pate in competitive elections to choose representatives and influence government formation and policy. In more robust accounts, democracy exists where people, regardless of social differentiation, can participate in meaningful ways in the decisions that affect their own lives. That is, democracy should be understood as a relationship amongst people for their collective self-governance, one that is affected by the broader social relations and inequality existent in any given society.

Democratic deficit: A generic term invoked to highlight the lack of depth in democratic proc-esses in Western countries. While countries have extensive procedural norms of "democracy," their substantive quality is called into question with such terms, particularly as regards public engagement and unequal participation.

Elections: Used as a synonym for democracy in most Western countries, elections actually precede the democratic era by many centuries. These ritualized and highly staged events involve outlays of millions of dollars, usually in an attempt to control and shape the outcome. Nevertheless, they are moments of great potential instability for the powerful and opportunity for the masses, and they have led to reforms that have benefited many.

Liberal: Generally denotes a set of ideas emerging in the nineteenth century that defended individual property rights and market-based economic regulation, with an accompany-ing governing order to support this (for example, the rule of law). Liberalism was initially contrasted with conservatism, which supported a hierarchical social order (monarchy, aristocracy) governed by a hereditary social class, though later it would be contrasted with any political ideas that attempted to balance collective well-being with individual freedom.

Liberal democracy: A post-hoc characterization of the grafting of popular consultation mecha-nisms (like elections) onto an essentially liberal order of governing. Liberals and their critics both admit that the "liberal" element essentially limits the democratic one, though liberals think it is an essential protection for property holders, while their critics see it as weakening of the democratic promise of equality.

Liberal order: The ongoing political struggle to shape government and state actions to support and enhance liberal property relations and the capitalist economy that results from them. In Canada, both Conservative and Liberal parties have been involved in this project, though with different ideas about just how to carry it out. A number of political movements have arisen contesting aspects of the liberal order (Canada's farmers in the 1920s, for example) or calling for its replacement with something else (for example, the socialist Co-operative Commonwealth Confederation in the 1930s through 1950s), but more recently, Canada's party system appears to have moved to consensus on the desirability of the liberal order approach.

Mercantilism: An early form of capitalist development involving considerable state investment in, and guarantees for, colonial enterprises, with some simply focused on resource exploitation overseas while others combined emigration and colonization of subject lands with resource extraction. By the mid-1850s, mercantilism had been abandoned by the U.K. in favour of a free-trade regime of capitalism.

Occupy: The name taken by the protest movements around the world in 2011 contesting the undue influence of financial elites on government policy and economic regulation. With their catchy slogans (the 1 perecnt versus the 99 percent) and distinctive forms of organization (fully participative governance, no hierarchy), they gave voice to a widespread frustration with government accommodation of the business class at the expense of social needs.

Postwar compromise: The broad political accommodation achieved after WWII across Western countries that saw the introduction of full employment and various social services in return for a labour peace that would assure maximum productivity. Existing roughly from 1945 to 1975, it was the most dynamic period of capitalist development in history. However, it broke down in the 1970s for various reasons but mostly because of the clash between demands for increased wages and declining profits for capitalists.

Representative government: A system of governing where electors choose representatives who govern, rather than governing directly themselves. This system can be democratic, if the franchise rules for electors are broad enough to include most adults.

Responsible government: In the Canadian context, the term refers to a governing order where the government of the day must be drawn from and maintain majority support in the legislature. Prior to the 1840s, the pre-Canadian colonies had elected legislatures but the representatives did not control what the government did. The achievement of responsible government is a necessary but insufficient condition of electoral democracy, especially if the franchise is restricted or electors are subject to coercion at the polls.

Self-rule: The idea that people can govern themselves rather than needing to be governed by someone else, typically a ruler, monarch or social superior. Though the concept is of ancient origin, it is only in relatively recent times that it has become widely accepted as both possible and desirable, though mainstream notions of self-rule are usually limited to representative democracy. More radical versions envision everyone in society playing a larger role in governing.

Questions for Discussion

1. What are the strengths and limits of the Occupy approach to democratic participation?

2. How democratic are Canadian elections? What government policies or institutional reforms might deepen their democratic substance?

3. Is a "liberal order" the same as capitalism? Can you think of an example of a country with a non-liberal capitalist system?

4. Canadian history is replete with examples of social groups and political parties that supported or opposed democracy in Canada. Who are the social groups that are for and against furthering democracy in Canada today?

5. How do the broader social relations of inequality that exist in Canadian society (class, gender, race, sexuality, ability, Indigeneity) impact our democratic relationship?

6. What steps should we take to deepen our democratic relationship right now?

Resources for Activists

The Broadbent Institute: broadbentinstitute.ca
Council of Canadians: canadians.org
Democracy Watch: democracywatch.ca
Fair Vote Canada: fairvote.ca
The Media Democracy Project: mediademocracyproject.ca
Project Democracy Canada: facebook.com/Project.Democracy.Canada/
Unlock Democracy: unlockdemocracy.ca

References

Abella, I.M. 1966. "The 'Sydenham Election' of 1841." *Canadian Historical Review* 47, 4 (December): 326–343.
Addley, E. 2011. "Occupy movement: from local action to a global howl of protest." *The Guardian*, October 18.
Birch, A.H. 1964. *Representative and Responsible Government*. Toronto: University of Toronto Press.
Brady, A. 1952. *Democracy in the Dominions*. Toronto: University of Toronto Press.
Bryan, F.M. 2004. *Real Democracy: The New England Town Hall Meeting and How It Works*. Chicago: University of Chicago Press.

Buckner, P.A. 2008. *Canada and the British Empire*. Oxford: Oxford University Press.

Byrne, J. (ed.). 2012. *The Occupy Handbook*. New York: Little, Brown.

Cadigan, S. 1991. "Paternalism and Politics: Sir Francis Bond Head, the Orange Order, and the Election of 1836." *Canadian Historical Review* 72, 3: 319–347.

Clarke, H.D., and A. Kornberg. 1993. "Evaluations and Evolution: Public Attitudes toward Canada's Federal Political Parties, 1965–1991." *Canadian Journal of Political Science* 26, 2: 287–311.

Conover, M.D., E. Ferrara, F. Menczer, and A. Flammini. 2013. "The Digital Evolution of Occupy Wall Street." *PLOS/One* 8, 5 (May 29): 1–5.

Courtney, J. 2004. *Elections*. Vancouver: UBC Press.

Crozier, M., S. Huntington, and J. Watanuki. 1975. *The Crisis of Democracy: Report on the Governability of Democracies to the Trilateral Commission*. New York: New York University Press.

Curtis, B. 1989. "Representation and State Formation in the Canadas, 1790–1850." *Studies in Political Economy* 28 (Spring): 59–87.

Dalton, R., S. Scarrow, and B. Cain. 2003. "Democracy Transformed? Expanding Political Opportunities in Advanced Industrial Democracies." Center for Study of Democracy Working Papers. University of California Irvine.

DeLuca, K.M., S. Lawson, and Y. Sun. 2012. "Occupy Wall Street on the Public Screens of Social Media: The Many Framings of the Birth of a Protest Movement." *Communication, Culture & Critique* 5, 4 (December): 483–509.

Dupuis-Deri, F. 2010. "History of the Word 'Democracy' in Canada and Quebec: A Political Analysis of Rhetorical Strategies." *World Political Science Review* 6, 1: 1–23.

Elash, A. 2011. "The Canadian response: Many cities, one unifying cause." *Globe and Mail,* Oct. 14.

Eley, G. 2002. *Forging Democracy: The History of the Left in Europe*. Oxford: Oxford University Press.

Forster, B., M. Davidson, and R.C. Brown. 1986. "The Franchise, Personators, and Dead Men: An Inquiry into the Voters' Lists and the Election of 1891." *Canadian Historical Review* 67, 1: 17–41.

Gabbatt, A. 2015. "Former Occupy Wall Street Protesters Rally Around Bernie Sanders Campaign." *The Guardian*, September 17.

Gastil, J. 1993. *Democracy in Small Groups: Participation, Decision-Making, and Communication*. Philadelphia: New Society Publishers.

Green, P. 1993. "'Democracy' as a Contested Idea." In P. Green (ed.), *Democracy*, New Jersey: Humanities.

Gustein, Donald. 2009. *Not a Conspiracy Theory: How Business Propaganda Hijacks Democracy*. Toronto: Key Porter Books.

Habib, M. 2011. "Occupy Canada rallies spread economic 'awakening.'" *CBC.ca*, October 13.

Held, D. 2006. *Models of Democracy, 3rd edition*. Cambridge: Polity.

Heron, C., ed. 1998. *The Workers' Revolt in Canada, 1917–1925*. Toronto: University of Toronto Press.

Hobsbawm, E. 2011. *Uncommon People*. London: Orion.

Horn, M. 1984. "The Great Depression in the 1930s in Canada." Ottawa: Historical Booklet #39, Canadian Historical Association.

Howard, V. 1985. " 'We Were the Salt of the Earth!': The On-To-Ottawa Trek and the Regina Riot*. Regina: University of Regina Canadian Plains Research Centre.

James, M. 2014. "Occupy: History, Physicality, Virtuality." In M. Smith (ed.), *Group Politics and Social Movements in Canada, 2nd edition*. Toronto: University of Toronto Press.

Katz, M. 1972. "The People of a Canadian City." *Canadian Historical Review* 53, 4 (December): 402–426.

Kreig, G. 2016 "Occupy Wall Street Rises up for Bernie Sanders." *CNNPolitics.com*, April 13.

Laycock, D. 2002. *The New Right and Democracy in Canada: Understanding Reform and the Canadian Alliance*. Toronto: Oxford University Press.

Lenard, P., and R. Simeon. 2012. *Imperfect Democracies: The Democratic Deficit in Canada and the United States*. Vancouver: UBC Press.

MacDermot, T.W.L. 1933. "The Political Ideas of John A. Macdonald." *Canadian Historical Review* 14, 3 (September): 247–264.

Macpherson, C.B. 1965. *The Real World of Democracy*. Toronto: Anasi Press.

Maloy, J.S. 2008. "A Genealogy of Rational Choice: Rationalism, Elitism, and Democracy." *Canadian Journal of Political Science* 41, 3 (September).

Manin, B. 1997. *The Principles of Representative Government*. Cambridge: Cambridge University Press.

McKay, I. 2000. "The Liberal Order Framework: A Prospectus for a Reconnaissance of Canadian History." *Canadian Historical Review* 81: 617–645.

Myers, A.R. 1975. *Parliaments and Estates in Europe to 1789*. London: Thames and Hudson.

Naylor, J. 1991. *The New Democracy: Challenging the Social Order in Industrial Ontario*. Toronto: University of Toronto Press.

____. 2016. *The Fate of Labour Socialism: The Co-operative Commonwealth Federation and the Dream of a Working Class Future*. Toronto: University of Toronto Press.

O'Keefe, D. 2015. "Did the Owners of Canada's National Newspapers Order Them to Endorse Harper?" *Ricochet*, October 16.

Ober, J. 1996. *The Athenian Revolution: Essays on Ancient Greek Democracy and Political Theory*. New Jersey: Princeton University Press.

____. 2008. "The Original Meaning of 'Democracy': Capacity to Do Things, not Majority Rule." *Constellations* 15, 1: 3–9.

Paley, J. 2002. "Toward an Anthropology of Democracy." *Annual Review of Anthropology* 31, 1.

Palmer, B. 1992. *Working-Class Experience: Rethinking the History of Canadian Labour, 1800–1991*. Toronto: McClelland & Stewart.

Pammett, J., and L. Leduc. 2003. "Explaining the Turnout Decline in Canadian Federal Elections: A New Survey of Non-Voters." Elections Canada, March.

Panitch, L., and S. Gindin. 2012. *The Making of Global Capitalism: The Political Economy of American Empire*. London: Verso.

Panitch, L. and D. Swartz. 2008. *From Consent to Coercion: The Assault on Trade Union Freedoms, 3rd edition*. Toronto: University of Toronto Press.

Patterson, G. 1977. "An Enduring Canadian Myth: Responsible Government and the Family Compact." *Journal of Canadian Studies* 12, 2 (April): 3–16.

Pilon, D. 2007. *The Politics of Voting: Reforming Canada's Electoral System*. Toronto: Emond Montgomery.

____. 2012. "Labour and the Politics of Voting System Reform in Canada." In S. Ross and L. Savage (eds.), *Rethinking the Politics of Labour in Canada*. Halifax: Fernwood Publishing.

____. 2013. *Wrestling with Democracy: Voting Systems as Politics in the Twentieth Century West*. Toronto: University of Toronto Press.

____. 2015. "Researching the Electoral Subaltern and Voter Turnout: Utilizing 'Class' as Identity." *Studies in Political Economy* 96 (Autumn): 69–91.

____. 2016. "Canadian Confederation and Democracy." *Canada Watch* Spring: 18–20.

Pravda, A. 1978. "Elections in Communist Party States." In G. Hermet, R. Rose, and A. Rouquie (eds.), *Elections Without Choice*. New York: John Wiley and Sons.

Roberts, A. 2012. "Why the Occupy Movement Failed." *Public Administration Review* 72, 5: 754–762.

Rowe, J.K., and M. Carroll. 2014. "Reform or Radicalism: Left Social Movements from the Battle of Seattle to Occupy Wall Street." *New Political Science*.

Sassoon, D. 1996. *One Hundred Years of Socialism*. New York: New Press.

See, S.W. 1991. "Polling Crowds and Patronage: New Brunswick's 'Fighting Elections' of 1842–3." *Canadian Historical Review* 72, 2: 127–156.

Semmel, B. 1970. *The Rise of Free Trade Imperialism: Classical Political Economy the Empire of Free Trade and Imperialism 1750–1850*. Cambridge: Cambridge University Press.

Stechyson, N. 2012. "Half of Canadians sympathized with Occupy movement: poll." *National Post*, January 20.

Syrek, S. 2012. "'Why Am I Talking?' Reflecting on Language and Privilege at Occupy Wall Street." *Critical Quarterly* 54, 2: 72–75.

Tombs, R. 2013. *The Paris Commune, 1871*. New York: Routledge.

Underhill, F.H. 1935. "The Development of National Political Parties in Canada." *Canadian Historical Review* 16, 4 (December): 367–387.

von Beyme, K. 2000. *Parliamentary Democracy: Democratization, Destabilization, Reconsolidation, 1789–1999*. Houndsmill: Palgrave Macmillan.

Wallace, E. 1950. "The Origin of the Social Welfare State in Canada, 1867–1900." *Canadian Journal of Economics and Political Science* 16, 3 (August): 383–393.

Whitaker, R., G. Kealey, and A. Parnaby. 2012. *Secret State: Political Policing in Canada from the Fenians to Fortress America*. Toronto: University of Toronto Press.

Whitehead, L. 1997. "The Vexed Issue of the Meaning of Democracy." *Journal of Political Ideologies* 2, 2.

9

Corporatizing Public Universities

The Transformation of Higher Education in Canada

Jamie Brownlee

YOU SHOULD KNOW THIS

- Between 1991 and 2011, the proportion of employed persons aged 25 to 34 with a university degree rose from 17 to 27 percent among men, and from 19 to 40 percent among women.
- At the national level, public funding made up 84 percent of university operating revenues in 1979; by 2009 this figure was reduced to 58 percent.
- The cost of undergraduate tuition has grown from an average of $1,706 in 1991–92 to $5,772 in 2013–14, an increase of 238 percent. Students requiring a Canada student loan now graduate with average debts of more than $28,000.
- In 2010, 20 cents was spent on central university administration costs for every dollar spent on teaching and non-sponsored research, up from just 12 cents in 1988.
- Between 1998 and 2009, the Canadian Foundation for Innovation disbursed over $4.2 billion to fund university infrastructure projects. Ninety percent of this funding went to the physical sciences, health sciences and engineering, while the arts, literature, humanities and social sciences received just 5 percent.
- One study found that 94 percent of articles that had authors who were affiliated with the tobacco industry concluded that secondhand smoke was not harmful. In contrast, only 13 percent of articles where the authors had no ties to tobacco reached the same conclusion.
- An investigation of cancer drug studies found that those funded by drug companies were nearly eight times less likely to reach unfavourable conclusions compared with similar studies funded by non-profit organizations.
- An analysis of the world's leading medical journals suggests that the majority of articles on lucrative pharmaceutical drugs are wholly or partially ghost-written by corporate medical writers and pharmaceutical company personnel.

Sources: Barnes and Bero 1998; Burley and Awad 2015; CAUT 2010, 2012, 2014; Friedberg et al. 1999; Healy and Cattell 2003; Guppy, Grabb and Mollica 2013; Smith 2010; Uppal and LaRochelle-Côté 2014.

UNIVERSITIES ARE CRITICALLY IMPORTANT INSTITUTIONS in the lives of Canadians and in Canadian society as a whole. When parents think about their children's future, a growing number see a university education as important to their success. According to a national poll, 93 percent of Canadians report that saving for their children's education is a top financial priority (CBC News 2011). Canadians are also strong believers in generous public education funding and the principle of universal access. Opinion surveys have found that a majority of Canadians (in all regions of the country) believe that governments should invest more in higher education, and 93 percent of Canadians agree that cost should not prevent qualified students from attending university (CAUT 2011; CCL 2009; CFS 2012; Ipsos Reid 2004).

Recent trends in enrolment and employment also underscore the importance of university education in today's society. Between 2000 and 2011, the number of full-time undergraduate students rose by 44 percent, while those enrolled in graduate degree programs grew by 82 percent (AUCC 2012). In 2011, the number of those enrolled in Canadian undergraduate programs surpassed one million students, setting a new enrolment record. University education is also increasingly important for securing stable and meaningful employment. Statistics Canada reports that between 1991 and 2011, the proportion of employed persons aged 25 to 34 with a university degree rose from 17 to 27 percent among men, and from 19 to 40 percent among women (Uppal and LaRochelle-Côté 2014). According to Universities Canada (2015), between 2008 and 2015, twice as many new jobs were created for university graduates than for college and trades graduates combined. While obtaining a university education is no guarantee of stable employment (young people in Canada are increasingly vulnerable to the current environment of precarious and insecure work), many predict continued growth in employment opportunities for occupations requiring a university education (Miner 2010).

Of course, universities play critical roles in other areas of Canadian society as well. They are widely understood to have an immeasurable impact on our individual and collective identities, our communities, our culture and our ability to understand and resist other powerful institutions. They have also been implicated as sites of social change. In this sense, universities occupy a complicated and, in many ways, contradictory role in society. On the one hand, universities are institutions that function to preserve class privilege and protect and legitimate the social order. As Pierre Bourdieu (1988) and other critical education scholars have argued, universities legitimate structural inequalities by "normalizing" the capitalist production process, socializing students to accept existing distributions of power and wealth and preparing them for work in occupational hierarchies. In other words, universities are agencies of social control, promoting a strong identification with the values, attitudes and beliefs necessary for the maintenance of the capitalist system.

On the other hand, it would be a mistake to view universities as simply the instruments of dominant social groups or defenders of the status quo. Throughout history, universities have been expected to teach the "truth," to liberate the mind from conventional thought and to advance democratic and egalitarian concerns. Universities are generally equated with a public service/social justice mission to prepare people to be active citizens, to produce and disseminate public knowledge and to inform public life and civic participation. As leading education scholar Henry Giroux (2008: 148–149) explains: "While the university should equip people to enter the workplace, it should also educate them to contest workplace inequalities, imagine democratically organized forms of work, and identify and challenge those injustices that contradict and undercut the most fundamental principles of freedom, justice, and respect for all people." Given these functions, the university has often been cast as the social critic or conscience of society. It also has a key role to play in transforming society,

> The public service mission of the university is being reduced in favour of private and commercial interests.

including through dedicated curricular programs such as labour, urban, environmental, women's and Indigenous studies. The university remains one of the only institutions in modern society that explicitly claims, as part of its mission, to raise questions about the social order and offer challenges to society's most fundamental beliefs.

As numerous analysts have observed, however, the nature of Canada's university system has been changing in recent years. A new, market-based vision for higher education has taken shape, and the direction and priorities of Canadian universities have shifted alongside it. As part of this shift, the public service mission of the university — which has often emphasized democratic goals, service to the broader community and a commitment to progressive social change — is being reduced in favour of private and commercial interests. I liken these changes to a process of "corporatization," which refers to the process and resulting outcomes of the ascendance of business interests, values and models in the university system. The remainder of this chapter focuses on some of the key outcomes and implications of the corporatization

> The term corporatization refers to the process and resulting outcomes of the ascendance of business interests, values and models in the university system.

process. I argue that although corporatization may provide some benefits to the private sector and particular individuals, it does not serve the interests of the Canadian population as a whole. Rather, corporatization poses significant threats to many who learn and work within universities, as well as the public and future generations.

Corporatizing Higher Education: A Process of Institutional Transformation

For university students and faculty, corporatization is often most visible in their everyday environments. Corporate advertising on university campuses is growing every year. University facilities and lecture halls are increasingly branded with corporate logos and the names of wealthy elites. Linda McQuaig and Neil Brooks (2010: 192) note that in contrast to past years, when buildings were often named in honour of distinguished academics, today "campus buildings and auditoriums have been named almost exclusively after people whose distinctive characteristic is the possession of lots of money." One of the most noticeable commercial shifts has been the practice of contracting-out campus services to private companies, especially in the area of food services. In return for cash, universities grant exclusive licenses to food providers — often fast-food giants and soft drink chains — allowing them effective monopolies over campus cuisine. These kinds of practices have become so pervasive that, according to one study, the "commercial and corporate presence" in Canadian universities has become "normalized as part of campus culture" (CCPA 2008: 2). These direct manifestations of business influence are obvious indicators of corporatization. However, corporatization actually reflects a deeper process involving a transformation of university teaching, learning, research and governance.

Universities have always functioned, to some extent, to serve the practical interests of businesses and their other stakeholders. What has changed over the past few decades is the nature and extent to which corporate values, decision-making criteria and modes of governance are permeating public universities. The corporatization process is associated with a number of key indicators and outcomes. One indicator is the enhanced institutional integration between universities and corporate institutions through, for example, the expansion of public-private research partnerships and donor agreements, and the acceptance of corporate control over university curriculum and infrastructure development. Other indicators include the increasing use of "business-like" practices and objectives by universities themselves. These practices can be seen in new policies and incentives that direct research missions toward commercialization and private gain, the increasing reliance on contract faculty in university teaching, new restrictions on academic freedom in both teaching and research and the adoption of corporate management models.

> University presidents have been recast as "CEOs," students as "customers," graduates as "products" and professors as "service providers."

The outcomes or consequences of corporatization are numerous. University presidents have been recast as "CEOs," students as "customers," graduates as "products" and professors as "service providers." Contractual business relationships and measures of financial viability have been elevated in relation to public and social commitments. Profit has become a leading goal of academic inquiry and a guiding principal for deciding what products and services to offer. Decisions about course offerings, research funding, and hiring and enrolment practices are assessed less in terms of academic criteria and more on whether they represent good business decisions. At a more general level, corporatization is associated with the conversion of higher education from a public to a private good. Higher education as a private good is reflected in the growing reliance on student tuition fees and the redefinition of students as educational consumers and a shift in the university's mission away from the provision of liberal arts education. Corporatization involves providing businesses with the means to socialize the risks and costs of university research while privatizing the benefits and to accrue advantages through the transfer of technology to the private sector. Corporatization subsidizes the retraining of the corporate workforce through an increasingly vocational curriculum. And it provides the corporate sector with greater control over an institution that has, at times, challenged its power. Rather than being "sold off" to the private sector, the uses and benefits of university resources and knowledge production are being handed over to private interests at the public's expense.

Taken together, these changes have resulted in a process of institutional transformation. As Claire Polster (2004: 95) has argued, the corporatization process is not "additive," it is "transformative." That is, the increasing ties between corporations and universities "are not an 'add-on' to the university, such that after their establishment we have the old university plus these links." On the contrary, these relationships are changing the nature and function of the public university through qualitative changes to its culture and its system of governance as well as its approach to teaching and research.

The fact that Canadian universities are being transformed is not really in question. But there remains considerable debate around the sources of this transformation. Who or what is responsible? There are some who argue that corporatization is a positive (even a "natural") development, one that reflects the inevitable progression of market forces. These analysts contend that the nature of a nation's higher educational institutions has become a marker of its competitive position in the global economy and of its capacity to attract and retain a skilled workforce. Seen in this light, educational restructuring is a rational response to the inevitabilities of a changing market because it strengthens Canada's economic position, and the process of corporatization is presented in technocratic rather than political or ideological terms. For its proponents, a more corporatized educational system makes universities more efficient, "relevant" and effective, which serves the interests of Canadian business and improves the lives of Canadian citizens.

From a more critical perspective, corporatization is generally understood within a wider political or neoliberal context. Here, neoliberalism is not a natural or inevitable development but a carefully crafted political project involving broad economic and political transformations. And a key part of this project has involved changing the way that universities function, from institutions that serve the public good to those that provide a more profitable ground for capitalist expansion. Neoliberal ideology rests on a familiar set of principles and policies, including the downsizing of the public sector and reductions in social spending. One of the most pivotal factors in facilitating the corporatization of higher education has been the sharp and prolonged reduction in government funding that has taken place over the past four decades. At the national level, public funding made up 84 percent of university operating revenues in 1979; by 2009 this figure was reduced to just 58 percent (CAUT 2012). While these austerity programs may have reflected resource scarcity on the part of governments to some extent, it is important to understand that they were also part of a deliberate plan to link universities more closely to the needs of the market and lay the foundation for corporatization.[1]

Public funding cuts, in concert with other changes to Canada's education system and broader political economy, have weakened the university's public service mission and its ability to disseminate knowledge in the public interest. Further, this process has resulted in a wide range of negative consequences for teachers, students, researchers and the public at large. In the remainder of the chapter, I focus on four key aspects of the corporatization process in order to highlight some of these consequences and to illustrate why this transformation should be resisted.

University Teaching and the Casualization of Academia Labour

Many aspects of university teaching have been affected by corporatization. In today's academy, teaching is seen as having less "value" relative to university research. The result is that an institution's status is now generally defined more by the name recognition of its researchers than by quality teaching or student learning. Moreover, universities are devoting a larger and larger proportion of their resources to research. Sponsored research in Canada's twenty-five largest universities accounted for 15 percent of university expenditures in 1988; by 2008, this figure had grown to 25 percent (Smith 2010). This increase in research-related expenditures has coincided with parallel declines in teaching.

With less and less money reaching the classroom, universities are relying on limited-term contract faculty to perform a greater share of their teaching responsibilities. This shift runs alongside developments in the larger corporate economy, where workplace restructuring has resulted in more "labour flexibility" and a situation where the number of part-time and temporary workers continues to grow in relation to secure, full-time positions. Whereas tenured and tenure-track professors are expected to perform the full range of academic activities — including teaching, research and service — contract instructors are hired solely to teach. Their salaries are usually a fraction of those earned per course by tenured professors, and their benefits — including sick leave, parental leave, health and disability insurance, vision and dental care — are often limited or non-existent. Although some contract faculty have full-time careers outside of the university, most are not well-paid professionals. Rather, the majority of contract faculty are individuals whose livelihoods are dependent on part-time teaching and who desire a full-time academic career.

Documenting the increase in contract faculty hiring — or the casualization of academic labour — has been difficult for Canadian researchers. There is currently no reliable national data on the number of contract faculty working in Canadian universities. The primary reason for this data scarcity is that universities have been reluctant to release the information. However, I was able to gather some Canadian data using Ontario's *Freedom of Information and Protection of Privacy Act* (FIPPA). The employment data I received from my freedom of information requests (which mainly included faculties and departments within the humanities and social sciences) confirmed there has been a growing reliance on contract faculty in Ontario universities.

At several Ontario institutions, the increase in contract hiring has been dramatic. For example, in those departments that are now part of the Faculty of Liberal Arts and Professional Studies at York, the number of part-time contract appointments increased from 531 to 1,253 (136 percent) between 2000–01 and 2009–10, while the number of tenure-stream faculty grew from 493 to 593 (18 percent). The growth in part-time positions was especially prominent in certain departments, such as English (564 percent); Languages, Literatures and Linguistics (180 percent); Administrative Studies (174 percent); and Philosophy (169 percent). In the sixteen departments I reviewed at Trent, the number of part-time positions increased from 66 to 200 (203 percent). At the same time, the number of tenured/tenure-track positions increased from 138 to 156 (13 percent). For Carleton, I was able to obtain data for the university as a whole. Across all departments, the number of part-time appointments increased from 475 to 821 (73 percent) between 2001–02 and 2011–12, while those in the tenure stream rose from 608 to 745 (23 percent) over roughly the same period. In 2003–04, contract faculty were responsible for teaching one out of every five undergraduate courses at Carleton; eight years later, they were teaching one in three. Across all fifteen institutions I surveyed for which comparative data were available, the number of part-time appointments increased by 69 percent between 2001–02 and 2009–10. Over the same period, the number of tenure-stream positions increased by 30 percent. Put another way, in 2001–02 tenure-stream appointments outnumbered part-time appointments by 637 (3,113 versus 2,476); by 2009–10, there were fewer tenure-stream appointments than part-time appointments

(4,060 versus 4,173) in the faculties and departments under review (see Brownlee 2015).

One reason why more data is needed to fully document the casualization of academic labour is that the conditions of contract faculty work are often precarious. As noted above, limited-term contracts rarely recognize the research and service components of academic work, or provide employees with appropriate resources and protections to participate in a full academic career. As a result, contract workers often do not have the time or the financial security to engage in sustained research and other collegial responsibilities, which diminishes their future ability to obtain permanent positions. Contract faculty are also generally not required, and usually not encouraged, to participate in university governance. In fact, they are often excluded from even the most basic collegial decision-making bodies, such as departmental committees.

Given their level of education, contract faculty in Canada are paid very poorly. In some

PART-TIME CONTRACT FACULTY APPOINTMENTS (FIFTEEN INSTITUTIONS)

University	Year										
	2000	2001	2002	2003	2004	2005	2006	2007	2008	2009	2010
Ottawa	304	295	327	382	378	395	408	410	418	396	425
Windsor	118	116	123	136	136	146	144	158	169	160	160
Trent	66	69	94	123	141	170	183	153	197	189	200
UOIT *	-	-	-	19	33	47	83	105	120	117	153
Waterloo	141	133	153	146	150	169	168	164	153	152	181
Queen's	56	67	59	74	63	65	98	103	84	70	n/a
Brock	51	50	62	37	38	59	78	71	75	69	n/a
Ryerson	39	45	40	33	49	52	71	73	79	53	47
	Academic Year										
	2000 /01	2001 /02	2002 /03	2003 /04	2004 /05	2005 /06	2006 /07	2007 /08	2008 /09	2009 /10	2010 /11
York	531	681	758	675	882	746	883	1047	1027	1253	n/a
Carleton*	n/a	475	520	521	519	628	671	700	761	794	815
Western	n/a	263	320	351	334	340	353	363	347	315	n/a
Nipissing	42	37	56	56	44	70	88	82	83	89	72
Guelph	104	123	109	92	125	145	174	177	219	204	n/a
Laurentian	40	37	42	50	45	61	75	76	66	68	n/a
Toronto	n/a	85	149	153	187	265	261	285	256	244	n/a
Total Contract Faculty	n/a	2476	2812	2848	3124	3358	3738	3967	4054	4173	n/a
Total Tenure Stream Faculty	n/a	3113	3189	3337	3513	3522	3696	3943	4019	4060	n/a

* Includes totals for entire university.

instances, contract salary levels are shocking. At the University of Winnipeg, for example, a contract instructor teaching five single-term courses (a full course load) would make approximately $20,000, which is right around the city's low-income cut-off (Canada's version of the poverty line). Substandard pay is often compounded by a lack of pensions and other benefits. In fact, some contract instructors are not even provided with basic services that permanent faculty take for granted (for example, photocopying, computers, clerical support and office space). Contract faculty typically lack job security as well, having to re-apply for their jobs as often as every few months, with no guarantees of reappointment. In the absence of job security, contract workers are easily at risk of a contract not being renewed. This means, in effect, that the protections of academic freedom do not apply to this segment of the academic workforce, as controversial positions or viewpoints can result in a lost contract.

Research has found that the casualization of academic labour can also negatively impact students. Although many contract faculty are outstanding teachers, the precarious nature of their employment can result in barriers and disincentives to quality teaching. For example, the "just-in-time" approach to contract hiring means that instructors often receive their course assignments just days or weeks before courses begin. This translates into insufficient time to prepare, to incorporate and update materials for students and to explore innovative pedagogical methods and materials (Street et al. 2012). Poor pay also forces many casual employees to teach multiple courses at a time, sometimes at different institutions. As a result, many are overburdened by heavy teaching loads, and have little time to do the writing and research necessary to keep up with their disciplines. Perhaps most importantly, the demanding schedules of contract faculty often mean that they interact with students less frequently. This lack of interaction is especially significant given the positive outcomes associated with contact between professors and students, such as improved academic performance, increased cognitive development and a greater degree of satisfaction with the educational experience (Jaeger 2008).

Supporters of corporatization maintain that a greater utilization of contract faculty produces educational efficiencies because it contains costs in tough economic times and offers managerial flexibility. However, these claims are largely unjustified. The displacement of secure, full-time professors with contract academics may be "efficient" from a strict economic point of view, but it does not take into account the human, social and educational costs. For the instructors, this practice is consistent with job insecurity and a more precarious working environment. For students, it often means reduced faculty-student interaction time and other impediments to learning. For tenured faculty, there are costs associated with increased demand for administrative service and, for the faculty as a whole, a weakening of collegial governance. As permanent faculty positions are systematically eliminated in the corporate university, university teaching — and the lives and livelihoods of university teachers — have suffered.

Tuition, Debt and the Rise of the Student-Consumer

There is a longstanding debate about whether the goals of a university education should focus on providing a broad liberal education or specific job training skills. The terms of this debate have shifted under corporatization. Today, the ideals of a liberal education are no longer considered sufficient to prepare graduates for the workforce or for life, and practical, applied or vocational pursuits are seen as the most "relevant" options. This perspective ignores the fact that liberal arts graduates generally perform well in the Canadian labour market (discussed in the next section). Moreover, shifting to a narrow, vocational set of criteria to define the public university's role has been associated with a number of negative implications for students and for society. Most notably, it has helped to transform students into educational consumers — or as customers purchasing a service or private good — who are encouraged to extract maximum "value" for their tuition dollars. The new "student-consumer" model of higher education is impacting students' values and educational choices, learning experiences, finances, career prospects and relationship with the university. It is also associated with a shifting political economy of student life that includes rising tuition fees and student debt.

Canadian universities have come to embrace many elements of a corporate "service culture." Reduced public funding and a greater reliance on tuition revenues have led many institutions to focus on customer service, consumer satisfaction and "product quality." As universities employ customer and marketing narratives to guide their relationship with students, it is only natural that students would incorporate a consumerist model in their relationship with the university. In part, this shift has contributed to a more narrow, consumerist orientation on the part of university students. Recent surveys suggest that today's students are far more likely to say that "getting a good job" and making more money are the most important reasons for attending university (Maritime Provinces Higher Education Commission 2008; Prairie Research Associates 2010; Singleton-Jackson, Jackson and Reinhardt 2010). There is also evidence that more students today view higher learning as a "service encounter" (or a passive commercial transaction), rather than an active process of discovery and mutual engagement between student and professor (Côté and Allahar 2011). Although not indifferent to the economic value of higher learning, students in earlier generations were more willing to endorse values such as social engagement, the acquisition of knowledge and intellectual self-development in education. The growing importance students attach to career and monetary advancement has coincided with changes in student enrolments, which have moved away from basic arts and sciences and toward applied fields such as commerce, business and management (Statistics Canada 2005, 2009, 2010).

The student-consumer identity has been further entrenched by a "customers pay" orientation to university financing on the part of successive federal administrations and most provincial governments in Canada. This orientation rests on the assumption that the benefits of higher education accrue primarily to individuals rather than to society (that is, education is a private rather than a public good) and, therefore, student-consumers should pay most of the costs. As a result, Canada has some of the highest tuition fees in the world. While tuition varies considerably across provinces, the cost of undergraduate tuition grew from an average

AVERAGE UNDERGRADUATE TUITION

Year	Province										
	NL	PE	NS	NB	QC	ON	MB	SK	AB	BC	CA
1991–92	$1,544	$2,141	$2,232	$2,046	$1,311	$1,818	$1,848	$1,859	$1,544	$1,970	$1,706
2013–14	$2,644	$5,696	$6,185	$6,133	$2,653	$7,259	$3,779	$6,394	$5,670	$5,029	$5,772
% Increase	71.2	166.0	177.1	199.8	102.4	299.3	104.5	243.9	267.2	155.3	238.3

Source: *Canadian Association of University Teachers Almanac of Post-Secondary Education in Canada, 2014–2015.*

of $1,706 in 1991–92 to $5,772 in 2013–14, an increase of 238 percent (CAUT 2014). Of course, escalating costs have not had an equal impact on all Canadians.[2]

Not surprisingly, escalating fees has also meant escalating student debt. Federal government student loan debt in Canada has risen to approximately $15 billion. When provincial and commercial bank loans are included, the total is closer to $20 billion. A study by the Canadian Federation of Students shows that students requiring a Canada student loan now graduate with average debts of over $28,000 (Burley and Awad 2015). Of course, tuition is not the only culprit. According to the Organization for Economic Co-operation and Development's (OECD) *Education at a Glance 2014*, student aid in the form of grants (as opposed to loans which need to be paid back) now covers a much smaller proportion of the direct costs of post-secondary education in Canada than it does in most other OECD countries.

Growing tuition and student debt do not merely reflect an economic strategy or the inevitable impact of public funding cuts. On the contrary, downloading the costs of higher education to stu-

> Rising tuition and debt levels are blocking access to higher education for underprivileged families.

dents and their families is a political choice based on particular assumptions about public education and what constitutes a just society. For example, Canadian federal governments chose to forgo approximately $48 billion in revenue through tax cuts during the 2000s, with much of it going into the pockets of Canada's largest corporations. Just 10 percent of that money could have funded the elimination of tuition fees for all students currently enrolled in Canadian universities. The impacts have been felt most acutely by low-income groups. Research has shown that rising tuition and debt levels are blocking access to higher education for underprivileged families (Coelli 2005, 2009; Neill 2009). Students with high debt levels are also more likely to take on paid employment with adverse academic effects (Callender 2008; Côté and Allahar 2007; Motte and Schwartz 2009), more likely to complete their studies at a slower pace (Ekos 2006), less likely to graduate or pursue further education (Maritime Provinces Higher Education Commission 2007; Prairie Research Associates 2007; Williams 2012) and less likely to consider employment or training in public service occupations (Chernomas and Black 2004; Field 2009; Tannock 2006). Debt dependence also permeates our broader political culture. As more and more students are forced to confront the debt "time bombs" that await them after graduation, they are less and less likely to participate in social activism. In this way, debt dependence is contributing to the creation of a fragmented society where individuals are focused on individual concerns and less likely to engage in collective struggles.

Managing Universities like a Business

Over the past few decades, the management of Canadian universities has shifted to a more corporate model of organization. This shift has led to changes in the role of university administrations and in the makeup of individuals who occupy their leading positions. As universities have increasingly turned to private sources of financial support, they have also devoted a greater share of institutional resources to external relations, such as fundraising and the expansion of corporate-university partnerships. In addition, growing financial concerns and a rise in secretive corporate agreements within universities have allegedly required management that is free from faculty influence. The result has been that there are more and more career administrators who are hired from outside of the university to govern with a corporate, managerialist approach.

Under corporatization, university administrations have expanded considerably.[3] So too have the salaries of senior administrators. In Ontario, executive pay across all universities increased by 40 percent in real terms between 1996 and 2006, this at a time when these institutions were ostensibly under severe financial stress (Essaji and Horton 2010). This trend is especially evident in the case of university presidents, whose salaries are now more than double the level that would have been considered generous in the 1990s. In 2010, twenty cents was spent on central administration for every dollar spent on teaching and non-sponsored research in Canadian universities, up from twelve cents in 1987–88 (Smith 2010). Just as escalating corporate salaries are justified by the "pressures" associated with cost cutting and labour market restructuring, university administrators are getting paid more to pursue a similar mandate.

> Preoccupation with brand image means that "controversial" research by professors, criticism of universities by faculty and students, and public displays of dissent or resistance on campuses are increasingly viewed as a threat to the university's brand name.

Administrations have also assumed greater command over institutional objectives and policies, leading to a significant shift in the power of administrations relative to professors. Administrators have appropriated power from faculty and academic bodies in a number of ways. At some institutions, administrators have replaced collegial processes — where decisions affecting faculty and students are made collectively by academics — with "consultation" exercises that limit faculty participation in governance. At others, educational issues have been redefined as purely administrative and therefore not subject to faculty input, especially those that involve finance. A corporate management style also means that faculty members are increasingly treated as subordinate workers, rather than autonomous professionals, through intensified workloads, closer monitoring and enhanced performance evaluations.

Like their counterparts in the private sector, today's university administrators are increasingly concerned about the marketing, ranking and "brand image" of their institutions. This new marketing focus has led to a significant growth in the share of institutional resources devoted to advertising and promotional campaigns. It has also been associated with the suppression of academic freedom. Preoccupation with brand image means that "controversial" research by professors, criticism of universities by faculty and students and public displays of dissent or resistance on campuses are increasingly viewed as a threat to the university's brand name. On some campuses, new student conduct and use-of-space policies are denying students the opportunity to assemble and speak freely.[4] It has also been suggested that concerns about brand reputation have led some universities to ignore allegations of sexual assaults on their campuses (Mayor 2015). In addition to policing teachers and students to protect their own brands, administrators also prioritize shielding corporate sponsors from criticism. It was this concern that motivated the University of Ottawa to prevent a prominent Burmese human rights activist from speaking on campus in 2007. The subject of the activist's talk was the unethical Burmese business activities of Total S.A., a French oil company whose board members included the wealthy Desmarais family, one of the university's largest benefactors.[5]

> In the corporate university, where introspective questions about morality, society and the common good are considered less important, no area of study is more under threat than the humanities

Another aspect of these administrative changes is that curriculum, program and infrastructure development are much more closely tied to corporate interests. Academic departments that are more removed from labour and commercial markets have been deemed less relevant to the university's mission, which has led to an inequitable distribution of funding. Universities are devoting more resources to vocational and applied fields, while arts and basic science programs are downgraded. In the corporate university, where introspective questions about morality, society and the common good are considered less important, no area of study is more under threat than the humanities. Books and articles discussing the supposed incompatibility of the humanities with neoliberal restructuring now saturate academic and popular presses (see, for example, Burgan 2008; Cohen 2009; Donoghue 2008; Mignolo 2003). The neglect of humanities, liberal arts and basic science programs has been accompanied by the growth and construction of new management schools, engineering facilities and other "relevant" curricula and infrastructure on campuses across the country. These changes are occurring in spite of the fact that liberal arts graduates have performed well in the Canadian labour market, even when compared to university graduates from applied disciplines (Council of Ontario Universities 2011, 2012; Finnie et al. 2014; Liu, McCloy and DeClou 2012).[6]

It is not only university administrators that are working to corporatize university governance. Government funding mechanisms have also had a big impact, including in infrastructure development. Capital funding for universities accelerated during the 2000s, largely through Ontario's SuperBuild program, funding for research infrastructure provided by the Canadian Foundation for Innovation (CFI) and the federal government's Knowledge Infrastructure Program. All of these programs were designed to secure matching funds from the private

CANADIAN FOUNDATION FOR INNOVATION (CFI) FUNDING BY DISCIPLINE, 1998–2009

Area	No. of Projects	Total Funds ($)	% of Funds
Arts and Literature	73	39,709,673	0.9
Health Sciences	1,177	1,394,523,033	32.5
Humanities and Social Sciences	561	176,315,717	4.1
Multidisciplinary	86	200,634,279	4.7
Natural Sciences and Engineering	4,413	2,473,718,765	57.7
Total	6,310	4,284,901,467	100

Source: Guppy, Grabb and Mollica 2013.

sector, which means they have a structural preference for infrastructure projects in certain disciplines. Between 1998 and 2009, for example, the CFI disbursed over $4.2 billion to various projects, with about 90 percent of this funding going to the physical sciences, health sciences and engineering. In contrast, arts, literature, humanities and social sciences received just 5 percent of funds (Guppy, Grabb and Mollica 2013). Governments have also provided tens of millions in taxpayer dollars to support contentious "donor agreements" — such as the Munk School of Global Affairs at the University of Toronto and the Clayton H. Riddell Graduate Program of Political Management at Carleton — which have provided private sector donors with more direct control over academic decision-making.[7] These measures mean that universities are not only being run more like businesses, they are increasingly being run *by* members of the private sector.

Commercializing and Corrupting Academic Research

In the 1960s and 1970s, there was relatively little collaboration between academic researchers and members of the business community. In the 1980s and 1990s, however, research alliances between universities and the private sector began to expand and have continued to increase ever since. Supporters of corporatization contend that university-industry research ties are beneficial for many reasons, including because that they provide financial support for universities, commercially valuable product development, faculty access to research and development opportunities and enhanced technological innovation. While there may be some truth to these claims, I argue that the corporatization of academic research has not been beneficial for universities or for society and that the negative impacts far outweigh any benefits. Corporatization has corrupted the basic values that have historically defined scientific and other academic research and compromised the ability of the university to act as a site of independent inquiry and thought.

> Corporatization has corrupted the basic values that have historically defined scientific and other academic research, and compromised the ability of the university to act as a site of independent inquiry and thought.

Corporate influence crosses all aspects of the academic research process, including at the outset with the selection of research topics and projects. Rather than setting their own research agendas in response to social needs, academics are increasingly joining with partners from the private sector to define their research priorities. As a result, the basis for deciding what knowledge is worth pursuing is defined more and more by the criteria of profitability and corporate demand. Many areas of university research have been affected by this shift, including health research. For example, corporate influence has diverted academic attention away from vaccine research and diseases that affect the world's poor (such as malaria, schistosomiasis, tuberculosis and dengue fever). A recent study of the top fifty-four Canadian and U.S. research universities found that less than 3 percent of research funding is now devoted to diseases that affect the world's poorest people (Universities Allied for Essential Medicines 2013). The report also notes that more than a billion people currently suffer from "neglected diseases," or diseases that are "rarely researched by the private sector because most of those affected are too poor to provide a market for new drugs." For commercial reasons, the majority of research funding and investments by the pharmaceutical industry (and increasingly universities who partner with it) focus on what are called "lifestyle drugs" — high-profit treatments for things like obesity, baldness, wrinkles and sexual dysfunction.

Another consequence of corporatization has been growing research secrecy. One of the ways that corporatization has fostered research secrecy is through the creation of a more competitive and performance-based research culture (Chan and Fisher 2008; Polster 2007). But secrecy is produced in other ways too, including through non-disclosure and intellectual property agreements. In some cases, contractual arrangements can force academics to transfer the results of their research to the companies who paid for it. In others, the publication of findings may be delayed until a corporate sponsor obtains a patent on its intellectual property. Selective disclosure and withholding of data may also occur if the research results are potentially damaging to the corporation and/or its bottom line. The implications of these practices are numerous. Within the academy, secrecy reduces knowledge sharing and promotes waste as researchers needlessly duplicate work that was not made freely available. Secrecy also restricts the course of knowledge production because scientific progress depends on researchers building on the findings of others. Most importantly, research secrecy inhibits the amount of knowledge that is available in the public domain, including in areas central to human health and well-being.

Corporatization has also compromised university research by introducing a fundamental bias brought on by conflicts of interest. In this context, conflict of interest situations are those in which financial or other personal considerations may compromise a researcher's professional judgement in conducting research or reporting research results. One of the consequences is research bias. In some cases, research bias results from direct corporate censorship or academic corruption. However, a much more common cause of research bias is the unconscious or internalized effect of financial benefit or career advancement. A substantial body of empirical evidence suggests that researchers with a vested interest in reaching a particular conclusion will tend to weigh arguments and evidence in a biased fashion. This is sometimes known as the "funding effect," where projects financed by big business are far more likely to reach conclusions that support the interests of their sponsor (Krimsky 2013).

Many areas of academic research have been affected by research bias. In the area of food and nutrition, researcher Marion Nestle (2007) reports that sponsorship almost invariably predicts research results. Tobacco research is another example. One study found that 94 percent of articles that had authors who were affiliated with the tobacco industry concluded that secondhand smoke was not harmful. In contrast, only 13 percent of articles where the authors had no tobacco ties reached the same conclusion (Barnes and Bero 1998). Conflicts of interest and research bias are perhaps most common in the area of drug research.[8] One investigation found that studies of cancer drugs funded by drug companies were nearly eight times less likely to reach unfavourable conclusions about the drug compared with similar studies funded by non-profit organizations (Friedberg et al. 1999). Similarly, medical researchers in Toronto reported a strong association between purported drug safety and financial conflicts of interest (Stelfox et al. 1998). More specifically, they found that 96 percent of authors whose findings supported the safety of a particular class of drug had a financial relationship with the drug manufacturers, compared with 60 percent of "neutral" authors and 37 percent of authors who were critical of the drug's safety.[9]

Another disturbing aspect of corporatized research is that corporate employees (for example, medical writing and communications firms) are now writing many of the "academic" papers that emerge from corporate-sponsored research. This practice is often referred to as "ghost-writing." Frequently, the academic who assumes authorship will not have had access to the data on which the study is based and, in some cases, is simply paid to have his or her name appear on the publication. Given the inherent secrecy of the process, not much information is available about ghost-writing. Existing evidence suggests, however, that the practice is common and even extends to medical textbook publishing (Basken 2009; Lacasse and Leo 2010; Wilson 2010). In fact, one study estimates that the majority of articles on lucrative pharmaceutical drugs in leading medical journals are wholly or partially ghost-written (Healy and Cattell 2003).[10] As troubling as these practices are, ghost-writing is only one part of an increasingly sophisticated system of "ghost-management" in medical research (Sismondo 2007, 2009). Ghost-management refers to the broader phenomenon whereby drug companies and their agents direct and shape the entire research process, from funding and design to publication and promotion. According to Sergio Sismondo (2009: 172), up to 40 percent of "important journal reports of clinical trials of new drugs (and, more anecdotally, perhaps a higher percentage of meeting presentations on clinical trials) are ghost-managed through to publication."

It is important not to overlook the role that federal government policy has played in corporatizing academic research. For example, the federal Conservatives under Prime Minister Stephen Harper oversaw a strategic reorientation of the federal research granting councils. In 2009, it was announced that scholarships granted by the Social Sciences and Humanities Research Council (SSHRC) would focus on "business-related degrees." The Canadian Institutes of Health Research (CIHR) also was given a new commercial mandate. And the National Science and Engineering Research Council (NSERC) got a complete overhaul. As part of NSERC's new focus on "innovation," the government redirected public funds to programs to help solve company-specific problems, which is tantamount to providing free labour for the corporate sector. Between 2009 and 2013, company-specific research funding grew by more than 1,000 percent (Seidman 2013). In 2012, NSERC was even offering to organize "speed dating" events to bring interested researchers and corporations together. At the same time, NSERC's Discovery Grants program — the main funding source for basic research in the natural sciences and engineering — has declined significantly, from two-thirds of the Council's budget in 1978 to one-third in 2010 (CAUT 2010).

> Corporatizing academic research has gone hand in hand with the decline of basic research funding, even though it is basic research that has yielded many of the world's most important scientific and technological advancements.

The corporatization of academic research has had a profound impact on universities, researchers and the public. For universities and the medical profession, it has produced an unprecedented crisis of credibility in the published literature and tarnished the academy as a source of unbiased research. For researchers, it has reduced their ability to pursue independent lines of scholarship and increased restrictions on academic freedom. The public impact, however, goes much deeper. In addition to the life-threatening risks associated with research bias in academic medicine and other health research, corporatizing academic research has gone hand in hand with the decline of basic research funding, even though it is basic research that has yielded many of the world's most important scientific and technological advancements. In fact, the majority of scientific breakthroughs in virtually every field have resulted from basic research conducted in academic settings built and supported largely by public funds. The strategy of defunding basic research and throwing resources at the narrow fields of commercial application has been highly damaging from a public interest perspective.

Resisting the Corporatization of the University

Higher education has undergone a series of dramatic changes under corporatization. More and more, teaching is focused on vocational training and is carried out by casualized labour, governance models reflect business objectives and modes of operation, and research is conducted to serve corporate interests. Taken together, these changes are threatening many of the defining characteristics of the public university, and they reveal a fundamental conflict between university and corporate priorities. They also reveal how the corporate university's approach to teaching, research and governance has resulted in a range of negative consequences for instructors, for researchers, for students and for the public. Canadian universities are approaching a critical juncture. If they do not reverse the current move toward corporatization, they risk being permanently transformed into institutions whose primary purposes are job training and enhancing corporate profits.

In the face of this growing crisis, many people are fighting back. Corporate management models are being challenged by faculty members and faculty associations across the country. New rules and guidelines for reducing conflicts of interest in corporate-university research partnerships have been produced, and some progress has been made in improving the lives and working conditions of contract faculty through union activism and other means. There has even been some movement in the direction of prohibiting corporate funding and other institutional ties. Several medical schools, for example, have restricted ties between drug companies and physicians and eliminated industry support for continuing medical education. Moreover, academic associations like the American Association of University Professors (2014) are now calling for a prohibition on academics and administrators participating in certain industry-financed events and for barring pharmaceutical and biotechnology companies from operating freely on campuses.

While all of these reforms have the potential to improve our higher education system, I believe there remains a deep incompatibility or mismatch between university and corporate institutions. This means that strategies that merely aim to "regulate" corporatization — or accommodate the broader process through piecemeal reforms — will be largely ineffective in the long term. Furthermore, to meaningfully challenge corporatization and its impacts, we also need to recognize that universities are simply one target of corporate/political forces that are attempting to weaken the public sphere. In this way, the problems confronting universities are akin to the problems facing other public institutions and Canadian society more broadly. As public intellectual and activist Ursula Franklin (2000: 21) explains, corporatization is "not so much a university problem, but the university manifestation of a general, technologically-facilitated shift of power and accountability. The impact of this new misdistribution of power is felt in many other public institutions in Canada; solidarity with them should be part of our response."

It follows that efforts to transform universities are inextricably linked to struggles to democratize social, political and economic life and that there will be inherent challenges in trying to develop free and democratic universities within a society replete with power imbalances and social inequality. This point was recognized by Canadian student activists back in the 1960s, who argued that the problems of education were rooted in socio-economic structures and that solutions needed to alter these structures in the direction of a more equitable society. One of the necessary conditions to oppose corporatization, then, is to connect these resistance efforts to broader social movements operating outside of the university and to locate education-based struggles within a wider critique of neoliberalism and the capitalist system.

> Today's student movements are locating educational concerns within the larger context of government austerity agendas, attacks on worker's rights, declining social programs, environmental destruction and climate change, and the expansion of corporate power.

Many of today's student movements exemplify this orientation and strategy. Around the world, there has been a substantial increase in the level of student activism, the use of more militant activist tactics (such as occupations) and the creation of linkages with broader movements for change. In the past decade alone, students in California engaged in a mass walk-out and a series of occupations across the entire University of California system (Wollan and Lewin 2009); massive student demonstrations in England were followed by a wave of occupations that spread to dozens of universities (Coughlan 2010); students and educators in

Italy organized against public disinvestment by occupying campuses, train stations, highways and airports; students in Austria occupied classrooms and offices for an entire semester in defiance of financing reforms; in Greece hundreds of schools and university departments came under student occupation as the government faced mounting opposition to its higher education agenda (Marseilles 2011); student groups in Puerto Rico engaged in a series of mass strikes and occupied university buildings for several months in opposition to tuition increases; and thousands of students, teachers and activists in Columbia organized actions against their government's plan to introduce for-profit universities.

What is particularly striking about these contemporary student movements is that they are locating educational concerns within the larger context of government austerity agendas, attacks on worker's rights, declining social programs, environmental destruction, climate change and the expansion of corporate power. These developments are indicative of new inter-sectoral alliances that are beginning to form among university-based and other social movements. In Chile, for example, hundreds of thousands of students began a series of mass demonstrations in 2011 against tuition increases. Over the next few years, this initial upheaval progressed into a broad-based movement composed of students, teachers, academics, unions, civil servants and human rights organizations. As the diversity of its participants grew, the movement began to challenge class inequality, health care privatization, ecological devastation, the activities of foreign mining companies and even the basic structure of the capitalist economy (Bernasconi 2012; Larrabure and Torchia 2011).

Of course, there is also evidence of these kinds of alliances in the Canadian context. The 2012 Québec student strikes began as a series of actions opposing planned tuition increases and evolved into action about issues much broader than tuition. One major branch of the movement — represented by the Coalition large de l'Association pour une solidarité syndicale étudiante (CLASSE) — consisted largely of students who located the tuition hikes as part of a broader neoliberal program and as a symptom of a failing and unjust social order. Consequently, the students held general assemblies, organized alternative education events and built alliances with outside organizations. According to Ingar Solty (2012), the success of the student strikes rested upon the solidarity and support the movement received from the "Red Hand Coalition" — an alliance of 125 organizations including anti-poverty groups, environmental groups and public sector unions that formed in 2009 to resist privatization and neoliberal restructuring. The students also received widespread support from teachers, parents, university professors and other civil society organizations in part because of the broad social and political mandate the movement had come to represent.

It is also vital to recognize that students, faculty and others who are resisting corporatization in Canada have a firm ally in the public. On virtually every measure, the Canadian public opposes a corporatization agenda. A majority of Canadians strongly disagree with a "customers pay" model of university financing, with most agreeing that tuition fees should be eliminated altogether (CAUT 2009). They are vehemently opposed to public funding cuts (CCL 2009; CFS 2012; Ipsos Reid 2004). They believe that teaching — not research — is the most important factor in considering university quality (Ekos 2003). A majority also believe that the best strategy to compensate for funding shortfalls would be to reduce central university administration costs (CAUT 2011). And, although the opinions of university scientists have been largely ignored by Canadian political leaders, the public believes they should be taken seriously. According to a nation-wide poll, 44 percent of Canadians said they find the opinions of university scientists to be the most trustworthy in debates over university research funding. In sharp contrast, 10 percent said corporations were the most trustworthy source, 9 percent said university administrators, and just 9 percent said the federal government (CAUT 2009).

In spite of what those in power tell us, the greatest challenges facing public universities today are not related to economic growth, "innovation" or national competitiveness. They centre on the willingness and capacity of these institutions to confront the myriad of global problems that are producing needless human suffering, increasing social exclusion, inequality, chronic poverty and unemployment, and contributing to a rapidly deteriorating natural environment and climate change. The causes of these complex and related challenges are rooted in society's major institutions and structures of power. Therefore, it is vital that these institutions and their supporting ideologies be subject to critical analysis and, ultimately, to direct challenge. Universities should be subject to such analysis, and, just as importantly, they should provide a venue — an institutional position of authority and influence — within and through which this analysis and activism takes place. In order for this to happen, Canadians must do everything in their power to resist the corporatization of our universities.

Glossary of Key Terms

Academic freedom: The idea that the freedom of inquiry by university faculty is essential to the mission of universities and the principles of academia. In practice, it refers to the freedom of a university teacher or researcher to investigate, discuss and communicate any issue without interference or penalty from university administrators or external university funders/stakeholders.

Casualization of academic labour: The process through which full-time tenure-stream academic appointments are converted into part-time, contractually limited appointments. It is associated with the increased use of contract faculty in university teaching.

Collegial governance: A form of university governance where the decisions affecting faculty and students are made collectively by academics. Examples of collegial structures within universities are senates and faculty councils. As universities have shifted to a more corporate governance model, administrations have assumed greater command over university decision-making, including defining institutional objectives and policies.

Corporatization: The process and resulting outcomes of the ascendance of business interests, values and models within public institutions. In the context of universities, the corporatization process has been characterized by the enhanced institutional integration of universities and corporate institutions, the increasing use of "business-like" practices by universities themselves and the conversion of higher education from a public to a private good.

Public service mission: In discussions about universities, public service mission refers to there being an emphasis on democratic goals, service to the broader community and a commitment to social change in the public interest. It centres on the ability (and responsibility) of the university to produce and disseminate public knowledge and to inform public life and civic participation. Corporatization has weakened the university's public service mission and its ability to disseminate knowledge in the public interest.

Research bias: Refers to, among other things, research being biased as a result of inherent conflicts of interest in the research process. Conflict of interest situations are those in which financial or other personal considerations may compromise a researcher's professional judgement in conducting research or reporting research results. Research bias can also be produced by attaching monetary incentives to discovery, where a commercial orientation creates a preoccupation with particular kinds of outcomes. It can also be related to the "funding effect," where projects financed by big business are more likely to reach conclusions that support the interests of their sponsor.

Student-consumer: A transformation in student identity whereby students are redefined as educational consumers or as customers purchasing a service or private good. This transformation is associated with a "customers pay" orientation to university financing, which has resulted in increased tuition fees and student debt.

Questions for Discussion

1. Have you noticed any visible indicators of corporatization on your campus? If so, what kinds? What are their impacts on the university environment?

2. As a student, are you aware of whether your classes are taught by tenure-track professors or contract instructors? How do you think the casualization of academic labour affects teaching and learning?

3. What has been the impact of rising tuition and student debt on your own experience at university, and the experience of your peers?

4. Do you agree that, as a student, you are a "consumer" of education? If tuition were free, do you think this would change your university experience, including in the selection of areas of study and your engagement in the work?

5. Can you think of examples of potential conflicts of interest or research bias in research you are aware of or have cited in your work?

6. Are you aware of any actions that have been taken by students and faculty on your campus to challenge the impacts of corporatization? What strategies might be useful in not only bringing this issue to people's attention, but also resisting the changes that are taking place?

Resources for Activists

Canadian Association of University Teachers: www.caut.ca

Canadian Centre for Policy Alternatives – Education Project: www.policyalternatives.ca/projects/

Canadian Federation of Students: www.cfs-fcee.ca

Coalition of Contingent Academic Labour: www.cocalinternational.org

New Faculty Majority: www.newfacultymajority.info

Ontario Confederation of University Faculty Associations: www.ocufa.on.ca

Notes

1. This desire to shift to a more corporate university model has been clearly articulated by political, business and even university leaders. In the 1980s and 1990s, for example, the Business Council on National Issues launched a sustained attack to undermine public confidence in public education and repeatedly called for government cutbacks to universities. At the same time, the Corporate Higher Education Forum (CHEF) — an alliance of twenty-five corporate CEOs and twenty-five university presidents — explicitly advocated government underfunding to make universities more responsive to private interests. As part of these campaigns, the university was portrayed as unresponsive to market demands and the home of a lot of useless learning. These campaigns placed universities alongside other supposedly "outdated" public programs and entitlements, such as health care and social security.

2. Between 1980 and 2007, undergraduate tuition as a proportion of average net income grew from 8 to 18 percent for those in the lowest income quintile. For those in the highest income group, it grew from just 2 to 3 percent (Motte, Berger and Parkin 2009). In 1990 in Ontario, a middle-income family could earn the equivalent of four years of tuition in 87 days; by 2012, the average time required had increased to 195 days (CCPA 2013).

3. The growth in university administrations has been disproportional to other dimensions of educational expansion (for example, student enrolment and faculty hiring). While there is no reliable information on administrative growth at the national level, many provincial examples illustrate this shift. At the Université de Montreal, for instance, the relative weight of administrative personnel increased from 10 to 15 percent of total university staff between 2000 and 2008 (or from 817 to 1,712 employees). Over the same period, the proportion of professors fell from 26 to 22 percent (Martin and Tremblay-Pepin 2011). At the University of Saskatchewan, the number of full-time equivalent academic staff increased from 984 in 2003–04 to 1,119 in 2009–10 (13.7 percent increase), whereas the number of full-time equivalent positions increased by 33.2 percent for administrative, technical, clerical and other support staff, or from 2,993 to 3,986 employees (Gingrich 2011).

4. One infamous case was the administrative crackdown that took place at York University several years ago. In response to student unrest in 2004, the York administration overhauled the university's Temporary Use of Space Policy by outlawing any unauthorized use of university buildings and restricting freedom of assembly. The administration also stipulated that students and faculty needed permission to bring guest speakers to York. As David Noble (2005: 24), writing at the time as a professor at York, explains: "In the manner of all private-sector owners and managers, [the administration] deemed the ... university campus ... to be 'private property' and formulated official policy on its use." The following year, police were invited onto campus by the administration and subsequently violently dispersed students who were protesting, among other things, the corporate representation on York's Board of Governors.

5. According to documents obtained by the Canadian Friends of Burma through freedom of information requests, members of the senior administration used a number of strategies to block the event. In internal correspondence, university officials appeared to be aware that they were violating elementary codes of academic freedom in the service of their corporate sponsor; in an email to then university president Gilles Patry, one vice president noted that preventing the talk "flies in the face of many principles we hold dear in the University world, but I think we have other interests at stake" (Morgan 2010).

6. A paper commissioned by the Social Sciences and Humanities Research Council (SSHRC) found that "social sciences and humanities-based industries" account for more than three-quarters of all employment in Canada and that these disciplines influence more than $388 billion in economic activity, which is roughly equivalent to the amount influenced by science, technology, engineering and medicine (Impact Group 2008). While the importance of the liberal arts cannot and should not be measured primarily by economic or employment criteria, these trends run counter to the widely held assumption that a liberal arts education has little value in today's economy.

7. Supported by a multi-million dollar donation by Peter Munk (chair and founder of the mining company Barrick Gold), the Munk School of Global Affairs was established in 2010 at the University of Toronto. A major portion of Munk's money is released only after the Munk board of directors is satisfied that the school has achieved certain donor-defined objectives, and Munk has the authority to withdraw funds over any aspect of the school with which he disapproves. This means that Munk is effectively buying influence over academic decisions. Given his connections to mining giant Barrick Gold, it is unlikely, for example, that the school will conduct any research that is critical of the crimes of Canadian mining companies, let alone Barrick's own human rights and environmental record.

8. The most typical conflicts are financial in nature; these range from the provision of "hands-off" corporate sponsorships to situations where researchers hold a personal financial stake in their research outcomes. The latter cases are especially troublesome, yet surprisingly common. In his seminal study, Sheldon Krimsky and his colleagues (1996) studied the industry connections of the authors of 789 scientific papers published by 1,105 researchers in fourteen major life science and biomedical journals. They found that 34 percent of the articles (267) had at least one lead author with a financial interest in the outcome of the research (not one article disclosed this interest).

9. More recently, several meta-analyses of the biomedical literature have provided even stronger evidence of these linkages, pointing to strong and consistent correlations between industry sponsorship and pro-industry conclusions (Bekelman, Li and Gross 2003; Lexchin et al. 2003; Sismondo 2008).

10. Healy (2008, 2012) has even suggested that in some areas — such as on-patent drugs and the safety/effectiveness of antidepressants for children — virtually all of the published literature includes material that is authored by medical writers or pharmaceutical company personnel. It follows that studies of antidepressants in children "offer the greatest known divide in medicine between what published reports in the scientific literature say on the one side and what the raw data in fact show" (Healy 2012: 149). What published reports say is that these drugs are remarkably safe and effective. What the data show is that children are committing suicide at a much higher rate while they are on some of these drugs.

References

American Association of University Professors. 2014. "Summary of Recommendations: 56 Principles to Guide Academy-Industry Engagement." <aaup.org/sites/default/files/files/Principles-summary.pdf>.

Association of Universities and Colleges of Canada. 2012. "Back to School Quick Facts." Ottawa.

Barnes, D., and L. Bero. 1998. "Why Review Articles on the Health Effects of Passive Smoking Reach Different Conclusions." *Journal of the American Medical Association* 279, 19.

Basken, P. 2009. "'Ghostwriting' Is Still a Common Practice, Study Shows." *Chronicle of Higher Education*, September 10.

Bekelman, J., Y. Li, and C. Gross. 2003. "Scope and Impact of Financial Conflicts of Interest in Biomedical Research: A Systematic Review." *Journal of the American Medical Association* 289, 4.

Bernasconi, A. 2012. "Not Another Brick in the Wall: Capitalism and Student Protests in Chile." *Academic Matters* November.

Bourdieu, P. 1988. *Homo Academicus*. Cambridge: Polity Press.

Brownlee, J. 2015. *Academia, Inc.: How Corporatization Is Transforming Canadian Universities*. Halifax: Fernwood Publishing.

Burgan, M. 2008. "Production in the Humanities." In J. Turk (ed.), *Universities at Risk: How Politics, Special Interests and Corporatization Threaten Academic Integrity*. Toronto: James Lorimer.

Burley, G., and A. Awad. 2015. "The Impact of Student Debt." Ottawa: Canadian Federation of Students.

Callender, C. 2008. "The Impact of Term-Time Employment on Higher Education Students' Academic Attainment and Achievement." *Journal of Education Policy* 23, 4.

Canadian Association of University Teachers. 2009. "Public Opinion of Post-Secondary Education Issues." <caut.ca/uploads/Summary_Spring_2009.pdf>.

____. 2010. "NSERC Discovery Grants Spiral Downward." *CAUT Bulletin* 57, 8. Ottawa.

____. 2011. "Decima Summary: Public Opinion and Post-Secondary Education." <caut.ca/uploads/DecimaSummary_Fall2011.pdf>.

____. 2012. *CAUT Almanac of Post-Secondary Education in Canada 2012–2013*. Ottawa.

____. 2014. *CAUT Almanac of Post-Secondary Education in Canada 2014–2015*. Ottawa.

CBC News. 2011. "Canadians Save Too Little for Children's Schooling, TD Says." July 19. <cbc.ca/news/business/story/2011/07/19/td-survey-education-finances.html>.

CCL (Canadian Council on Learning). 2009. "2008 Survey of Canadian Attitudes Toward Learning: Results for Learning Throughout the Lifespan." Ottawa.

CCPA (Canadian Centre for Policy Alternatives). 2008. "Corporate Initiatives on Campus: A 2008 Snapshot." Ottawa.

____. 2013. "Not Your Parents Education: Ontario Tuition Fact Sheet." Ottawa.

CFS (Canadian Federation of Students). 2012. "Public Education for the Public Good: A National Vision for Canada's Post-Secondary Education System." Ottawa.

Chan, A., and D. Fisher. 2008. "Academic Culture and the Research-Intensive University: The Impact of Commercialism and Scientism." In A. Chan and D. Fisher (eds.), *The Exchange University: Corporatization of Academic Culture*. Vancouver: UBC Press.

Chernomas, R., and E. Black. 2004. "Fast Facts: Should University Students Pay More?" Winnipeg: Canadian Centre for Policy Alternatives.

Coelli, M. 2005. "Tuition, Rationing and Inequality in Post-Secondary Education Attendance." University of British Columbia Working Paper.

____. 2009. "Tuition Fees and Equality of University Enrolment." *Canadian Journal of Economics* 42, 3.

Cohen, P. 2009. "In Tough Times, the Humanities Must Justify Their Worth." *New York Times*, February 24.

Côté, J., and A. Allahar. 2007. *Ivory Tower Blues: A University System in Crisis*. Toronto: University of Toronto Press.

____. 2011. *Lowering Higher Education: The Rise of Corporate Universities and the Fall of Liberal Education*. Toronto: University of Toronto Press.

Coughlan, S. 2010. "Students Stage Day of Protests over Tuition Fee Rises." BBC *News*, November 24.

Council of Ontario Universities. 2011. "Employment Outcomes of 2008 Graduates of Ontario University Undergraduate Programs: 2010 Survey Highlights." Toronto.

____. 2012. "Employment Outcomes of 2009 Graduates of Ontario University Undergraduate Programs: 2011 Survey Highlights." Toronto.

Donoghue, F. 2008. *The Last Professors: The Corporate University and the Fate of the Humanities*. New York: Fordham University Press.

Ekos Research Associates. 2003. "Public Perceptions on Quality: Final Report." Ottawa: Council of Ontario Universities.

____. 2006. "Investing in Their Future: A Survey of Student and Parental Support for Learning." Montreal: Canada Millennium Scholarship Foundation.

Essaji, A., and S. Horton. 2010. "Silent Escalation: Salaries of Senior University Administrators in Ontario, 1996–2006." *Higher Education* 59, 3.

Field, E. 2009. "Educational Debt Burden and Career Choice: Evidence from a Financial Aid Experiment at NYU Law School." *American Economic Journal: Applied Economics* 1, 1.

Finnie, R., S. Childs, D. Pavlic, and N. Jevtovic. 2014. "How Much Do University Graduates Earn?" Ottawa: Education Policy Research Initiative.

Franklin, U. 2000. "What Is at Stake? Universities in Context." In J. Turk (ed.), *The Corporate Campus: Commercialization and the Dangers to Canada's Colleges and Universities*. Toronto: James Lorimer.

Friedberg, M., B. Saffran, T. Stinson, W. Nelson, and C. Bennett. 1999. "Evaluation of Conflict of Interest in Economic Analysis of New Drugs Used in Oncology." *Journal of the American Medical Association* 282, 15.

Gingrich, P. 2011. "After the Freeze: Restoring University Affordability in Saskatchewan." Saskatchewan: Canadian Centre for Policy Alternatives.

Giroux, H. 2008. "Marketing the University: Corporate Power and the Academic Factory." *Our Schools, Our Selves* 17, 3.

Guppy, N., E. Grabb, and C. Mollica. 2013. "The Canada Foundation for Innovation, Sociology of Knowledge, and the Re-engineering of the University." *Canadian Public Policy* 39, 1.

Healy, D. 2008. "Academic Stalking and Brand Fascism." In J. Turk (ed.), *Universities at Risk: How Politics, Special Interests and Corporatization Threaten Academic Integrity*. Toronto: James Lorimer.

____. 2012. *Pharmageddon*. Los Angeles: University of California Press.

Healy, D., and D. Cattell. 2003. "The Interface between Authorship, Industry and Science in the Domain of Therapeutics." *British Journal of Psychiatry* 182.

Impact Group. 2008. "The Economic Role and Influence of the Social Sciences and Humanities: A Conjecture." Toronto.

Ipsos Reid. 2004. "Canadians Attitudes Towards Financing Post-Secondary Education: Who Should Pay and How?" Montreal: Canada Millennium Scholarship Foundation.

Jaeger, A. 2008. "Contingent Faculty and Student Outcomes." *Academe* 94, 6.

Krimsky, S. 2013. "Do Financial Conflicts of Interest Bias Research? An Inquiry into the 'Funding Effect' Hypothesis." *Science, Technology and Human Values* 38, 4.

Krimsky S., L.S. Rothenberg, P. Stott, and G. Kyle. 1996. "Financial Interests of Authors in Scientific Journals: A Pilot Study of 14 Publications." *Science and Engineering Ethics* 2, 3.

Lacasse, J., and J. Leo. 2010. "Ghostwriting at Elite Academic Medical Centers in the United States." *PLoS Medicine* 7, 2.

Larrabure, M., and C. Torchia. 2011. "'Our Future Is Not for Sale': The Chilean Student Movement Against Neoliberalism." *The Bullet*, Socialist Project E-Bulletin 542 (September 6).

Lexchin, J., L. Bero, B. Djulbegovic, and O. Clark. 2003. "Pharmaceutical Industry Sponsorship and Research Outcome and Quality: Systematic Review." *British Medical Journal* 326.

Liu, S., U. McCloy, and L. DeClou. 2012. "Early Labour Market Outcomes of Ontario College and University Graduates, 1982–2005." Toronto: Higher Education Quality Council of Ontario.

Maritime Provinces Higher Education Commission. 2007. "Two Years On: A Survey of Class 2003 Maritime University Graduates." Fredericton, NB: Maritime Provinces Higher Education Commission.

____. 2008. "Intentions of Maritime University Students Following Graduation." Fredericton, NB: Maritime Provinces Higher Education Commission.

Marseilles, M. 2011. "Protests Erupt Over Higher Education Reforms." *University World News* 187 (September 4).

Martin, E., and S. Tremblay-Pepin. 2011. "Do We Really Need to Raise Tuition Fees? Eight Misleading Arguments for the Hikes." Montreal: IRIS. <iris-recherche.s3.amazonaws.com/uploads/publication/file_secondary/Brochure-English-web.pdf>.

Mayor, L. 2015. "UBC 'Abandoned' Women Who Reported Sexual Assaults." CBC News, November 20.

Miner, R. 2010. *People Without Jobs, Jobs Without People: Ontario's Labour Market Future*. Toronto: Miner Management Consultants.

McQuaig, L., and N. Brooks. 2010. *The Trouble with Billionaires*. Toronto: Viking Canada.

Mignolo, W. 2003. "Globalization and the Geopolitics of Knowledge: The Role of the Humanities in the Corporate University." *Views from South* 4, 1.

Morgan, M. 2010. "University of Ottawa Spied on Leading Burmese Activist." *Rabble.ca*, May 14. <rabble.ca/news/2010/05/university-ottawa-spied-leading-burmese-activist>.

Motte, A., J. Berger, and A. Parkin. 2009. "Paying for Post-Secondary Education." In J. Berger, A. Motte and A. Parkin (eds.), *The Price of Knowledge: Access and Student Finance in Canada*. Montreal: Canada Millennium Scholarship Foundation.

Motte, A., and S. Schwartz. 2009. "Are Student Employment and Academic Success Linked?" Montreal: Canada Millennium Scholarship Foundation.

Neill, C. 2009. "Tuition Fees and the Demand for University Places." *Economics of Education Review* 28, 5.

Nestle, M. 2007. *Food Politics: How the Food Industry Influences Nutrition and Health*. Los Angeles: University of California Press.

Noble, D. 2005. "Private Pretensions: The Battle for Canada's Universities." *Canadian Dimension* September/October.

OECD (Organization for Economic Cooperation and Development). 2014. *Education at a Glance 2014: OECD Indicators*. Paris.

Polster, C. 2004. "Rethinking and Remaking Academic Freedom." In D. Doherty-Delorme and E. Shaker (eds.), *Missing Pieces V: An Alternative Guide to Canadian Post-Secondary Education*. Ottawa: Canadian Centre for Policy Alternatives.

____. 2007. "The Nature and Implications of the Growing Importance of Research Grants to Canadian Universities and Academics." *Higher Education* 53, 5.

Prairie Research Associates. 2007. "Report on Student Debt: Canadian College Student Survey and Canadian Undergraduate Survey Consortium." Montreal: Canada Millennium Scholarship Foundation.

———. 2010. "2010 First-Year University Student Survey: Master Report." Ottawa: Canadian University Survey Consortium.

Seidman, K. 2013. "Universities Urged to Put Focus Back on Basic Research." *Montreal Gazette*, April 25.

Singleton-Jackson, J., D. Jackson, and J. Reinhardt. 2010. "Students as Consumers of Knowledge: Are They Buying What We're Selling?" *Innovative Higher Education* 35, 5.

Sismondo, S. 2007. "Ghost Management: How Much of the Medical Literature is Shaped Behind the Scenes by the Pharmaceutical Industry?" *PLoS Medicine* 4, 9.

———. 2008. "Pharmaceutical Company Funding and its Consequences: A Qualitative Systematic Review." *Contemporary Clinical Trials* 29.

———. 2009. "Ghosts in the Machine: Publication Planning in the Medical Sciences." *Social Studies of Science* 39, 2.

Smith, W.D. 2010. "Where all that Money Is Going." *Maclean's*, January 14.

Solty, I. 2012. "Canada's 'Maple Spring:' From the Quebec Student Strike to the Movement Against Neoliberalism." *The Bullet*, Socialist Project E-Bulletin 752, December 31.

Statistics Canada. 2005. "University Enrolment." *The Daily*, October 11. <statcan.gc.ca/daily-quotidien/051011/dq051011b-eng.htm>.

———. 2009. "Postsecondary Enrolment and Graduation, October 2009." Ottawa. Catalogue No. 81-599-X. <statcan.gc.ca/pub/81-599-x/81-599-x2009003-eng.htm>.

———. 2010. "University Enrolment." *The Daily*, July 14. <statcan.gc.ca/daily-quotidien/100714/dq100714a-eng.htm>.

Stelfox, H., G. Chua, K. O'Rourke, and A. Detsky. 1998. "Conflict of Interest in the Debate Over Calcium-Channel Antagonists." *New England Journal of Medicine* 338, 2.

Street, S., M. Maisto, E. Merves, and G. Rhoades. 2012. "Who Is Professor 'Staff'?" *Center for the Future of Higher Education*, Policy Report #2.

Tannock, S. 2006. "Higher Education, Inequality, and the Public Good." *Dissent* 53, 2.

Universities Allied for Essential Medicines. 2013. "University Global Health Impact Report Card." <globalhealthgrades.org/>.

Universities Canada. 2015. "Back to School 2015 Quick Facts." Ottawa.

Uppal, S., and S. LaRochelle-Côté. 2014. "Changes in the Occupational Profile of Young Men and Women in Canada." Statistics Canada, Catalogue No. 75-006-X.

Williams, J. 2012. "Academic Freedom and Indentured Students." *Academe* 98, 1.

Wilson, D. 2010. "Drug Maker Hired Writing Company for Doctor's Book, Documents Say." *New York Times*, November 29.

Wollan, M., and T. Lewin. 2009. "Students Protest Tuition Increases." *New York Times*, November 20.

10

Power, Participation and State Legitimacy in the Alberta Tar Sands

The Rise and Fall of a Democratic Mirage

Mark Hudson

YOU SHOULD KNOW THIS

- In order to have a two-thirds chance at staying below the 2 degree "safe level" of global warming, human societies can pump about 800 gigatonnes of carbon dioxide (or its equivalent in other greenhouse gases) into the atmosphere.
- 2 degrees of warming used to be considered the "safe level," but many scientists now believe that 1.5 is a more accurate figure and governments have pledged to strive for this lower target.
- Canada's proven oil reserves hold about 91 gigatonnes — the vast majority in the oil sands — and adding "probable reserves" brings it up to 174 gigatonnes. That's more than one-fifth of the entire global carbon budget.
- In September 2016, First Nations from across North America asserted their sovereignty and expressed their opposition to further expansion of the oil sands by signing the Treaty Alliance Against Tar Sands Expansion, in which they agree to "officially prohibit and to agree to collectively challenge and resist the use of our respective territories and coasts in connection with the expansion of the production of the Alberta Tar Sands, including for the transport of such expanded production, whether by pipeline, rail or tanker."

Sources: United Nations 2015; Lee 2013; Treaty Alliance n.d.

IN NORTHERN AND CENTRAL ALBERTA, beneath the boreal forest, a mixture of sand, clay, water and bitumen has attracted large volumes of both capital and controversy. When heated sufficiently, the bitumen can be separated from the rest of the material — a process that was initially developed in the 1920s, but only implemented on an industrial scale in the late 1960s — and then refined into oil. From 1973 to 2015, tar sands production, as it was initially known,[1] rose from being a tiny drop in Canada's flow of crude oil (2.6 percent) to making up almost two-thirds (62 percent) of the total (CAPP 2016). Today, at an estimated 166 billion barrels, tar sands deposits make up 97 percent of Canada's oil reserves, which are the third largest in the world. This substance, the geological product of tiny, long-dead marine organisms, has become an economic pillar of Alberta, as well as a political flashpoint due to the environmental issues stemming from its extraction, transportation and combustion.

This chapter provides an introduction to the economic and the ecological stakes of bitumen extraction in Alberta and makes the case that these stakes are high enough to warrant a broad and open process of democratic decision-making. Unfortunately, what we see instead is a systematic closure of public participation in energy resource management in Alberta.

This in turn suggests that the state may no longer see democratic participation as an integral part of its legitimacy — a major issue in relations of power and resistance.

At Stake in the Sands

Profit, Taxes and Jobs: The Tar Sands and the Alberta Economy

The tar sands are a pretty small piece of the Canadian economy. Unconventional oil extraction — which includes the tar sands — made up about 2 percent of the Canadian economy in 2013, prior to the precipitous decline in world oil prices beginning in the latter half of 2014. For comparison, forestry made up about 1.25 percent of GDP in the same year. Manufacturing accounts for 11 percent or so. In Alberta, however, oil sands extraction is a substantial piece of the pie. In 2012, the oil and gas sector made up 18 percent of the Alberta economy (second only to its share in Newfoundland and Labrador, at 25 percent) (Osberg et al. 2016). This doesn't include any indirect effects, so the figure underestimates the economic impact of the oil and gas sector overall, and as suggested above, tar sands makes up a large and growing share of the sector. Anything that puts a serious brake on the development of oil sands in the province presents a serious drag on economic growth and on government revenues.

This became painfully clear for many Alberta oil patch workers and for the provincial government after the collapse of oil prices in 2014–15, as the economy shrank by 1.5 percent in 2015 and as government revenue tumbled by just more than 16 percent — a loss of $8.1 billion — from 2014–15 to the forecast for 2016–17 (Government of Alberta 2016a: 15). Bitumen royalties directly accounted for about one-tenth of provincial government revenue in 2014–15. This fell to 2.5 percent in 2015–16. Corporate income tax also falls considerably for the province when oil and gas development is in the doldrums (Government of Alberta 2016a: 15). Corporations also feel the impact of low oil prices. Profitability for a barrel of oil from the tar sands requires a price of between US$44–$50. New steam-assisted gravity drainage (SAGD) projects are reported to need a price of US$80 to generate long-term profit (Dawson 2015). As a result, at current prices, major corporate investors in the oil sands have been "bleeding cash on every barrel of bitumen," according to TD Securities (Dawson 2015). While the Fort MacMurray wildfires in May of 2016 exacerbated corporate losses, the underlying issue of low oil prices drove them. Despite these losses, the Canadian Association of Petroleum Producers anticipate a 30 percent increase in output from the oil sands between 2015 and 2020, based on large projects already under construction (Dawson 2015).

The oil sands also matter for employment. The Canadian Energy Research Institute (2015) estimated that about 150,000 jobs directly result from oil sands production, though the drop in oil prices resulted in 36,000 oil sector layoffs, with 24,400 more predicted for 2016 (Government of Alberta 2016b: 6). Thus, for Alberta, the economic stakes of the tar sands are high. Corporations, the state and workers all have an immediate interest in keeping development humming (or, from the perspective of the current doldrums, revving it up). This dependency, it must be noted, does not follow necessarily from the fact

> Corporations, the state and workers all have an immediate interest in keeping development humming.

that there is oil in the ground but is rather the product of a long history of policy choices. The Alberta government's reliance on energy-sector royalties, for example, arises from its decision to forego revenue from other potential sources, such as income, sales or corporate taxes. Similarly, Alberta could have focused its early oil revenue on supporting economic diversification, seriously reducing working families' vulnerability to oil price swings. As it stands, however, the pressures of the "treadmill of production," first theorized by Allan Schnaiberg in the 1980s, are brought to bear in the oil sands. Schnaiberg (1980) made the case that within capitalism, as technological development raised the productivity of labour by using more energy and more capital, there was a requirement to constantly accelerate growth in order to keep people employed, keep profits up and keep government tax revenues growing. Corporations, government and labour, each for their own reasons, share a powerful interest in ramping up production. All the while, the increase and acceleration of production takes a growing toll on the environment, as, in Schnaiberg's terms, companies withdraw more resources from nature and put back more waste and pollution.

The Environmental Effects of Bitumen Extraction: Oil at What Cost?

There's no doubt that Schnaiberg's treadmill of production is occurring on a grand scale in the tar sands. As significant as the economic stakes are, they are both temporally and spatially exceeded by the ecological issues, which stretch well beyond Alberta and well into the future. Unsurprisingly, extracting, refining, transporting and burning tar sands oil are each environmentally destructive and destructive of livelihoods that are closely connected to the land — most especially those of First Nations and Métis people. Bitumen is extracted either through surface mining, in which the material is dug up and carted off in massive trucks, or "in situ," in which steam is injected into the ground to make the bitumen flow, at which point it is pumped out of the ground. Each method has its own land, soil, water and climate impacts.

Surface mining projects have a larger footprint, since they involve clearing the boreal forest, finding somewhere to dump this "overburden" and the creation of tailings ponds. Tailings are a mixture of the sand, clay and water left over after processing. This sounds fairly harmless, but the slurry is laced with dissolved metals and high levels of toxic residue, including polycyclic aromatic hydrocarbons (PAHs). PAHs are listed by the U.S. as priority pollutants because they are carcinogenic, mutagenic and can affect the development of fetuses and embryos (Schindler 2013). The growing problem of tailings was launched into the international spotlight in 2008, when a flock of ducks seeking shelter from a snowstorm alighted on a Syncrude tailings pond and 1,600 of them promptly died (Steward 2015). Tailings volumes have been growing steadily, and government efforts to regulate this growth have been ineffective so far. The previous regulatory body, the Energy Resources Conservation Board (ERCB) attempted in 2009 to set targets for the reduction of so-called "fine tailings," but the directive was revoked in 2015 because of enforcement problems (Snyder 2015). Mine operators were not complying, either due to unwillingness or inability. The Alberta Energy Regulator (AER) has only recently released a new directive, whose effectiveness remains to be seen. As of 2015, the liquid in tailings ponds would fill about 390,000 Olympic swimming pools, and they cover 176 square kilometres — not including the earthen walls and infrastructure. Tailings volumes have grown ten times over the past two decades (Steward 2015). Storage of these tailings is imperfect, and PAHs can find their way into rivers, lakes, soils and animals via a variety of pathways, despite a "zero discharge" policy touted by mining companies (Parajulee and Wania 2014: 3344).

The environmental hazards of oil sands mining carry on even when the mines are tapped out. Once operations cease, mining companies are charged with reclaiming the area, which is proving problematic as well. The cheapest option, and one being planned for thirty mine pits, is to fill the bottom of the pit with tailings, and then cap it with a mixture of fresh and mine-processed water, creating what is known as an end pit lake. It is hoped that these will eventually become fully-functioning, healthy ecosystems and recreation spaces in a decade or two. However, while companies have built small test-ponds with promising results, end pit lakes are unproven on any large scale. The *Globe and Mail* summarized the nature of the gamble nicely, reporting that "it could one day be Alberta's very own Lake District, a recreational haven complete with campgrounds, boating, fishing — even swimming. Or it could turn into a landscape of ponds sullied by toxins and oil, a malingering presence left by an industrial experiment gone wrong" (Vanderklippe 2012).

Oil sands operations have also been found to be a significant producer of airborne pollutants, including PAHs, nitrogen and sulfur oxides, metals and particulates (Hodson 2013: 1569). Kurek et al. (2013), using dated lake sediment cores, linked the rise of PAHs in the Athabasca river and its tributaries to the rise of oil sands activity. Additionally, volatile organic compounds from mined material interact with sunlight and air to produce secondary organic aerosols linked with lung disease and heart problems. These compounds travel in windborne plumes from the source. Research using fly-overs of the oil sands area — in which other sources of secondary organic aerosol formation are largely absent — shows that the sands produce at least 45–84 tonnes per day of these pollutants. These levels, from a single industry, and in a relatively small geographical area, are comparable to the totals produced in megacities like Paris and Mexico City (Liggio et al. 2016).

For in situ processes, the environmental impacts are largely related to the required infrastructure — central processing facilities, seismic lines, roads, pipelines and well pads. While this involves a smaller footprint, it also involves fragmentation of forest habitat, as things like seismic lines, roads and pipelines, which cover large linear distances, carve the boreal forest into discontinuous chunks. The fragmented landscape that develops around in situ extraction can disrupt species migration patterns, reducing diversity and species viability for birds, caribou and carnivores (Jordaan 2012: 3612). Some research has found that because of this infrastructure, in situ extraction actually has a larger land-use intensity (LUI) than surface mining. That is, for every cubic metre of bitumen produced, in situ extraction disturbs more land than surface mining (Yeh et al. 2015: 13). This becomes more pronounced if the land disturbance from natural gas extraction is included. Both in situ and mining processes use natural gas, but in situ uses about four times as much (Jordaan 2012: 3612).

Both modes of extraction also require significant volumes of water — about 4.4 percent of the mean flow of the Athabasca River. Again, this sounds minor, but recent research suggests that over the long term, the Athabasca river basin exhibits huge variation in flows, including decades-long periods of low flow and a declining long-term trend (Sauchyn et al. 2015). That is, for long periods of time, the river's volume has been much lower than it is now. Currently, the allocations of water for tar sands use do not account for this. The amounts of water that have been committed to use in the oil sands are thus based on the "untenable assumption" (Sauchyn et al. 2015: 12621) that short-term instrumental measurements are representative of the long history of the Athabasca river basin. The implications of oil sands expansion on the availability of water in the Athabasca basin are thus likely more severe than planners and policy-makers imagine.

Finally, both in situ and mining operations also contribute significantly to Canada's greenhouse gas (GHG) emissions, thwarting our pledges made under the United Nations Framework Convention on Climate Change (UNFCCC) at the Paris meeting of the Convention in 2015, in the interests of doing our part in keeping the world below an average of 2 degrees of warming, While 2 degrees is a somewhat arbitrary target chosen through diplomacy, the International Panel on Climate Change (IPCC) does suggest that 2 degrees is the level of warming beyond which climate change will produce very serious risks to ecosystems and societies (which should not be understood as materially distinct from one another). For example, coral reef degradation or Arctic sea ice loss are likely to be severe above this temperature. We are likely to see increased frequency and severity of extreme weather like heat waves, heavy precipitation and coastal flooding. Species extinction rates would likely increase beyond their already intolerable levels (IPCC 2014: 72). Canada pledged to reduce its GHGs by 30 percent relative to 2005 levels by 2030. This means chopping 208 million tonnes of GHG emissions relative to their currently projected levels for 2030. Two things about this pledge must be noted. The first is that current, international GHG reduction pledges are not enough to get us to the "safe level" of 2 degrees average warming — a level that itself only carries a probability of being non-catastrophic. Many nations, scientists and activists are calling for a target of 1.5 degrees. If every government with an existing pledge actually honours it (and Canada, along with many others, failed to honour its previous pledges), we are still looking at a likely average warming of 2.7 degrees (see the Climate Action Tracker at www.climateactiontracker.org). The second point is that without getting some control over our emissions from the oil and gas sector, and from the oil sands in particular, we have no hope of reaching our national target. The oil and gas sector as a whole is currently the largest contributor to our total GHG emissions in Canada (25 percent), and oil and gas emissions are projected by Environment Canada to grow by 45 percent between 2005 and 2020, while all other significant sectors are projected to grow only slightly or decline. Within the oil and gas sector, bitumen from the oil sands is the dominant driver by far, with a projected emissions growth of 67 percent between 2005 and 2020. These emissions only account for the production, transmission, processing, refining and distribution of oil and gas, not the eventual combustion of the product. While Alberta has legislated a cap of 100 megatonnes (MT) of carbon emissions annually from the oil sands, research suggests that if this cap is hit, together with other

> The oil and gas sector as a whole is currently the largest contributor to our total GHG emissions in Canada.

planned liquid natural gas production in British Columbia, achieving our Paris targets becomes "near impossible without severe economic consequences" (Hughes 2016: 6).

The fate of the oil sands, then, has considerable economic significance for Albertans and carries massive environmental consequences locally, regionally, nationally and even globally. Given the high stakes, then, one might expect — or at least hope — that decisions about whether, how and how quickly bitumen is extracted would be reflective of an expressed democratic will. Of course, this raises the sticky question of which *demos* is relevant. Whose "collective will" should determine things? Given the implications of global climate change — for example, the prospect of inundation for small island states and coastal regions, the increased frequency and intensity of severe weather, like floods, hurricanes and droughts, and the reduced productivity of agriculture in many parts of the world — one might argue that the relevant public is not limited even to Canada. However, the Canadian Constitution assigns responsibility for natural resources to the provinces. While the federal government is the signatory to the Paris Agreement, and while it can claim some jurisdiction over specific aspects of oil and gas development, the province of Alberta has constitutional authority over the disposition of the oil and gas deposits within its territory. So, do Albertans have a say in the fate of the tar sands? To what extent do ordinary citizens of the province get a chance to intervene and affect the process of oil sands development?

In order to get a handle on whether resource development in the Alberta sands is driven by and for the people of Alberta, it is helpful to take a small detour northwest to the Yukon Territories to look at a recent, illustrative court case. This will help us develop a better understanding of what "participation" in natural resource decision-making means in practice and to begin asking what it ought to mean going forward.

Yukon Justice?

In 2011, after seven years of consultation and public planning, three First Nations and the Yukon territorial government arrived at a land-use plan for the Peel River region. The plan as it was initially agreed upon protected about 80 percent of the watershed from mining and oil staking, which was viewed as a compromise by the First Nations involved from their initial position of 100 percent protection. However, in the final stage of the process, the territorial government made a set of unilateral changes to the plan that left about 71 percent of the area open to staking. Unsurprisingly, the First Nations, along with environmental groups from the area, took exception and dragged the Yukon government to court.

On November 4, 2015, the Yukon Court of Appeal released its Peel River decision, which was seen to have some potential implications for public participation in resource projects not just in the Yukon but across Canada (Olynyk et al. 2015). The decision was that the Yukon government had not followed proper procedure — especially with regard to consultation — in making extensive changes to an existing land-use plan.

In making the initial decision that was, in many parts, upheld by the Court of Appeal, the trial judge declared that the Yukon government's procedure in changing the plan represented "an ungenerous interpretation not consistent with the honour and integrity of the Crown." Odd and quaint though it may seem, in Canada, the "honour and integrity of the Crown" carries some importance. At its most basic, it is a judge's way of opining on whether the state is behaving "sincerely" in its dealing with Indigenous peoples. The honour of the Crown requires that governments must interpret their obligations generously, work to carry out their promises and ensure their obligations are fulfilled.

So, the Peel River decision by the Yukon Court of Appeal seemed partially like good news. It maintains that governments must attempt to reconcile Indigenous rights with broader societal interests (which are almost always understood exclusively in terms of economic development). It also told the Yukon government it could not go ahead with its plan to leave 71 percent of the Peel River region open to resource development. However, the First Nation (Na-Cho Nyak Dun, Tr'ondëk Hwëch'in) and the two environmental groups (the Yukon chapter of the Canadian Parks and Wilderness Society and the Yukon Conservation Society) that initially took the Yukon government to court, along with the Vuntut Gwitchin First Nation, are challenging this ruling at the Supreme Court of Canada, attempting to get the Yukon government to implement the land-use plan agreed upon at the end of the consultations. They are doing so because the Court of Appeal also ruled that while the Yukon government failed to uphold the honour of the Crown, the government nonetheless holds ultimate authority over public land and resource management. In making this ruling, the honour of the Crown was understood to hinge not on the breadth and depth of participation, not the meaningful extension of public power over resource management, but on "transparency in government communication with First Nations" (Olynyk et al. 2015). governments must, in this ruling, simply communicate clearly enough that those being consulted can comment effectively.

This case is significant because it is representative of a shift in the basis of state legitimacy — one that also pertains to the case this chapter deals with in more detail: the regulatory overhaul currently occurring in the tar sands of Alberta, as the new Alberta Energy Regulator (AER) solidifies its place as the sole regulator of Alberta energy development. The cases are very different, as in Canada the state has certain specific obligations toward Indigenous peoples that the Alberta government does not with regard to other Albertans or settler-Canadians, generally. Nonetheless, just as in the Yukon case, it appears that the Alberta regulator perceives that broad and meaningful participation in resource management is no longer a necessary condition for legitimacy.

> Broad and meaningful participation in resource management is no longer a necessary condition for legitimacy.

Drawing on an analysis of public participation mechanisms, the rest of this chapter examines the shift in regime that occurred in 2014 as regulatory power passed to the new AER. It highlights the limits of public participation in both the old and the new regimes, exploring the extent to which legitimation processes remain important to state and private-sector actors in resource-intensive economies and whether the bases for legitimacy have shifted. Specifically, while states observed a period in which public participation was understood to be crucial to legitimacy, recent developments in Alberta raise the question of whether this remains the case. In the case of the AER, the state's self-presentation suggests that it understands legitimacy to rest on perceptions of its transparency alone, while participation has drifted from the spotlight.

Participation's Day in the Sun

There was, following the late 1960s in North America, a period in which states opened up a number of channels for more citizen participation, in response to demands from the public. These demands took the form of protest and legal challenges, and they were widely understood as a "withdrawal of consent" — a collective expression of the fact that the state was not acting as a legitimate defender of the public good.

This marked one of several historical and contemporary moments in which the state and/or business have been compelled by their need for legitimacy to open up avenues of political struggle over access to and control over what we now commonly think of as "the environment." While Brown (2003) argues that neoliberal states have side-stepped the danger of legitimation crisis — a term used to describe a mass withdrawal of consent by the governed — by tying their legitimacy directly to their ability to serve the market and maintain economic growth above all else, some states, at some times, have found it necessary to appear responsive to citizens' environmental concerns. One manifestation of this is the range of legal provisions for public participation in decision-making over resource extrac-tion and development. Indeed, the increasing presence of citizens and their organizations in day-to-day functioning of state agencies was seen, in the 1970s, as a major shift in the administrative landscape — and not an exclusively positive one. Writing in 1977, Stephen Cupps (478) claimed:

> Over the last decade and a half … citizen groups have besieged administrative agencies and courts at every level of government with demands that they be able to participate fully in administrative proceedings, that they be given greater access to agency information, and that they be permitted to present any and all evidence in behalf of their interests before appropriate administrative and judicial tribunals.…
> Furthermore, both the participants themselves and knowledgeable observers have predicted that the torrent of citizen suits and public interest activity seen thus far is only a small fraction of the deluge yet to come.

Cupps warned of the dangers for effective state management contained within this com-ing flood of citizen demands concerning the conduct of their government. Here we see the expression of one of the most significant barriers to meaningful public participation in decisions about resource extraction (or almost anything else). Politics — particularly deliberative politics that aim to include a broad array of voices — take time. Participatory processes are nowhere near as quick and efficient as autocratic and exclusionary ones. The slower process of meaningful public participation — that is, the practice of democracy — runs up against one of the primary pillars of capitalism: the acceleration of the circuit that connects investment of capital to the realization of profit on that investment. State regulation, including the process of granting private corporations access to nature such that they might

> Governments felt compelled for a time to display openness to citizen input.

profitably extract its innards, stands in the middle of this circuit, and it becomes ever more sclerotic as it becomes more inclusive and participatory (Dörre et al 2015: 84–85). Nonetheless, despite Cupps's warnings and his belief that public participation would completely gum up the efficient functioning of the bureaucracy — and thus the circuit of investment and profit — governments felt *compelled* for a time to display an openness to citizen input.

With regard to natural resources specifically, Marshall and Goldstein argue, also in the context of the United States, that the shift from a "scientific expertise era" (2006: 224) of natural resource management (from the start of the twentieth century to the passage of the United States' NEPA in 1969) to a "NEPA participation era," and finally to a "collaborative decision-making" era beginning in the 1990s, has been driven by the need to manage environmental legitimacy crises. The state's perception of a withdrawal of mass loyalty in the 1960s and again in the 1980s based on its failure to protect the environment spurred it to progressively open the previously exclusive realm of management to the public, democratizing the process and moving toward increasingly more "authentic" forms of participation over time.

Canadian federal and provincial governments also launched a flurry of participation-enhancing legislation and regulation during this period. Alberta got into the game late, following a public relations disaster experienced by the government in 1988, when it approved a couple of highly controversial projects — the Alberta-Pacific pulp and paper mill and the Oldman River Dam — against the recommendations of federal environmental review panels. Alberta's subsequent review of environmental legislation wrapped up in 1993 with the implementation of the *Environmental Protection and Enhancement Act* (EPEA), which was hailed by the provincial government and the press as a model of participatory legislation — both in terms of its process and its effect.

When the EPEA was implemented, it was beneath a snowstorm of government rhetoric suggesting that the Act was both developed through participatory processes and would open new doors for citizen participation. To take just one sample flake from this storm, Brian Evans (who shortly after became environment minister), at the Bill's second reading, claimed that "this government recognizes that Albertans today demand the opportunity to participate in democracy and to participate in a meaningful way. That is exactly what is provided for in the (Environmental Protection and Enhancement) Act" (Alberta *Hansard*, April 4, 1991). Following on the heels of the approval of the Alberta-Pacific pulp and paper project in 1988, until the eventual implementation of the EPEA, Alberta's record of legislative proceedings is full of very similar comments highlighting the government's unswerving commitment to participatory democracy, particularly with regard to energy and natural resources. It is fairly clear from this history that governments across North America viewed public participation as one axis upon which they would be judged in terms of their legitimacy.

Participation as Legitimation in the Old Regime

Amidst the heat of the government's rhetoric touting the rise of public participation, there arose a mirage of democracy — an apparition that vanished when viewers got close enough. Participation's "day in the sun" was not a period characterized by real democratization of resource management. For all of the cracks that it may have opened, public participation was, from the state's perspective, largely about controlling dissent, managing citizen demands in a way that did not put at risk a policy agenda established well in advance and making the state *appear* as legitimate. Simon Kiss (2014: 26) describes the rise of this regime of "managed participation" in Alberta in the early 1990s in response to increasingly loud calls for public participation. In Kiss's terms, it was designed to use strategic communications to "manage processes without jeopardizing the government's re-election or policy agenda." Under such a managed strategy, citizens are included as window dressing, since all of the important decisions have already been made. Control over the agenda (and thus control over what will be discussed, and what will not) as well as over the terms on which citizens might intervene within that agenda are extraordinarily powerful tools (Lukes 2005), which the Alberta government kept tightly to itself.

> Under such a managed strategy, citizens are included as window-dressing, since all of the important decisions have already been made.

The effect was a great deal of lip service to democracy and participation, while in practice, through a variety of legal mechanisms, the thrust of Alberta resource management has been to exclude any possibility that citizens might be able to effectively slow down the rate of (let alone halt) energy development. With regard to bitumen extraction in the province, this continues to be true today (Bowness and Hudson 2014). Before the AER took over, under the joint rule of the Energy and Resource Conservation Board and Alberta Environment, there were two primary means of citizen involvement in the provincial licensing and approval of tar sands projects: hearings and appeals. If a citizen or group of citizens managed to jump through a set of hoops on deadline, they could force a public hearing by the ERCB on an application for a bitumen development. It was also possible to appeal decisions made by the regulator. Try as you might to find evidence that public participation in hearings and appeals had some influence on bitumen development, next to none can be found. To give just one indicator of the lack of effective citizen influence, there were 175 applications to operate an oil sands project (extraction, upgrading or pipeline) between 2004 and 2011. Only twenty-four of these sparked public hearings pitting a real person (not a corporation) against a project developer. Of these, twenty-three of the projects were approved, and one application was withdrawn (Bowness and Hudson 2014: 8–9). An update up to 2014 found thirty-three new licence application hearings, resulting in thirty-one approvals and two applications withdrawn. The appeals process has an equally bleak record. Essentially, once an application was in, the likelihood of a concerned citizen or group of citizens stopping it was

> Try as you might to find evidence that public participation had some influence on bitumen development, next to none can be found.

miniscule. Nonetheless, the regulator and the government *presented* the process as though Albertans could effectively intervene, that it was a meaningfully participatory process. They felt as though there would be consequences to a widespread perception that the process was not open to public participation.

The New Regime: From Participation to Transparency

In 2014, however, the Alberta government ushered in what it claimed would be a new era in energy regulation in the province with the implementation of the *Responsibly Energy Development Act* and the transfer of regulatory power from the old ERCB and Alberta Environment to the new AER.

From all early evidence and appearances under the new regime, "participation" has faded from view almost entirely as the key concept for legitimation, having been replaced by an emphasis on "transparency." These two concepts are often discursively linked and sometimes erroneously treated as a single concept. While they are indeed linked, we need to be attentive to each concept's relevance for the extent of public control over those packets of nature that come to be socially recognized as resources.

Participation is, in and of itself, a slippery term that is mobilized to describe anything from informing the public, consulting the public, learning from the public or actually enabling democratic control over whether and how resource extraction occurs (see, for example, Arnstein 1969).

A variety of terms are also used to stand in for "participation" in different literature. "Public engagement" is a popular one, and indeed, it serves to obscure the actual gap between participation and transparency. Effective participation is defined here as taking an active role in the determination of an outcome — a weaker criterion than actually determining an outcome, but one that doesn't presume that we will be able to see influence in every case. However, influence should be evident over a sufficiently large number of cases (through a connection between expressed interests and outcomes, through changes in the structure of participation itself and through changes in the agenda of regulators).

"Transparency," on the other hand, is a simple prerequisite for participation (and it presumes — not unrealistically but also uncritically — from the get-go, a radical separation between the regulator and the affected public). Transparency is a one-way process of revelation. It makes no promises or even suggestions about the distribution of effective power or influence. Any redistribution or effective action flowing from "transparency" is only possible if legitimacy requires more than the simple act of revelation. Participation, in contrast, if it is meaningful, is a necessarily interactive process in which citizen influence over an outcome is a possibility.

The *Responsible Energy Development Act* (REDA) and the Rules of Practice laid down by the AER do indeed require the AER to increase its transparency. The AER has made the *process* of participation more transparent by explaining on its website how a member of the public can get involved and by posting an "EnerFAQ" to spell out the hearings process. It has made its own activities more transparent by posting incidents (such as spills, or enforcement actions) promptly on its own website. It has a duty to publish its decisions on applications, which it seems to be complying with. It has also recently decided to post all of its participation decisions (what used to be called "standings decisions") online, as well as the substantive procedural decisions made by AER hearings panels. If you want to watch a hearing, they plan on allowing people to do so online.

Having posted very few of these things up to 2015, this is a substantial commitment to transparency. There are still problems — internet access for Indigenous communities is far from universal, for example — but transparency has been improved relative to the previous regime.

However, while it shines up the window between itself and the public, the AER continues to use a very restrictive definition to determine who can and cannot actually participate, mostly through the language of "directly and adversely affected." If you can back up a claim to be "directly and adversely affected" by a proposed project, and your concerns have not been dealt with elsewhere, then the regulator will hold a hearing. Unfortunately, the phrase "directly and adversely affected" has been interpreted by Alberta resource agencies in an unnecessarily narrow and restrictive way since the 1990s — and that interpretation has been largely upheld by courts (Fluker 2014).

Albertans and the rest of Canada wondered whether the AER would drift from past practice on this narrow interpretation of "directly and adversely affected." The Rules of Practice that guide the AER's operationalization of legislation didn't give much room for optimism. The AER makes participation decisions based on section 9(3) of the AER's Rules of Practice, which read as follows:

> The Regulator may refuse to allow a person to participate in the hearing on an application if the Regulator is of the opinion that any of the following circumstances apply:
> (a) the person's request to participate is frivolous, vexatious, an abuse of process or without merit;
> (b) the person has not demonstrated that the decision of the Regulator on the application may directly and adversely affect the person;
> (c) in the case of a group or association, the request to participate does not demonstrate to the satisfaction of the Regulator that a majority of the persons in the group or association may be directly and adversely affected by the decision of the Regulator on the application;
> (d) the person has not demonstrated that
>   (i) the person's participation will materially assist the Regulator in deciding the matter that is the subject of the hearing,
>   (ii) the person has a tangible interest in the subject-matter of the hearing,
>   (iii) the person's participation will not unnecessarily delay the hearing, and
>   (iv) the person will not repeat or duplicate evidence presented by other parties;
> (e) the Regulator considers it appropriate to do so for any other reason. (AER 2014)

The Kirby Expansion

The first glimpse of how the AER would actually put these rules into practice came in a 2014 ruling on a project application by Canadian Natural Resource Limited (CNRL) — the Kirby Expansion Project. The Kirby Expansion is an in situ project that, at the time of application, would have more than doubled the production of an existing project, taking it to about 140,000 barrels per day, establishing seventy-two new surface well pads and expanding already approved processing facilities, utilities and other infrastructure.[2] The expansion plans were eventually dialled back significantly from about $6.5 billion of new investment to just over $2 billion when the price of oil collapsed, but at the time of the application, it looked to be very substantial.

The AER initially decided to hold a hearing. They put out a notice asking interested parties to submit the nature of their interest in the project. Five First Nations (Beaver Lake Cree Nation, Whitefish Lake First Nation, Cold Lake First Nation, Fort McMurray First Nation and Kehewin Cree First Nation) and an environmental group called the Oil Sands Environmental Coalition (OSEC) filed submissions. Upon review of those submissions, the AER ruled that none of them adequately demonstrated that they were "directly and adversely affected," despite the fact that at least one of the First Nations claimed that its members exercised treaty rights and conducted traditional land uses in and adjacent to the project area. In its rejection of OSEC's rights to participation, the AER claimed that OSEC's membership had no "tangible interest in the subject matter of the application," and that its concerns were "general … and not related to the project." As a result of AER's rejection of each of these groups' applications to be heard, there were no applicants with standing, and the hearing was cancelled (Bankes 2014).

> The AER will likely continue to choke out the possibility of effective citizen participation.

With this early decision, the AER signalled that those motivated to participate because of concerns that are not immediately financial, those whose concerns are public and those who cannot demonstrate a threat to personal, individual interests will be filtered out of the process. The end result is that the AER will likely continue to choke out the possibility of effective citizen participation, while unabashedly and transparently demonstrating that fact to the public over its website. It is difficult not to draw the conclusion that the state has no fear of the participation bogeyman. As long as the state reports and communicates clearly to the public that it is busy denying groups and individuals the right to participate in resource management, then its legitimacy is not, in its view, up for grabs.

It seems that this is not an isolated case but is representative of a broad drift among public regulators. By way of illustration, we can refer to AER's commissioned study into how it might achieve "regulatory excellence." AER turned to the Penn Program on Regulation (PPR), housed at the University of Pennsylvania Law School, to guide it toward this goal. As part of their research, the PPR surveyed twenty recent summations on the attributes that are alleged to define regulatory excellence, from a variety of public regulators around the world, and distilled them into a set of principles. Transparency appears as one such attribute in ten of them. Participation features in just two of the twenty (Coglianese 2015: 23–24).

There is some speculation on whether this restrictive approach to participation might be expected to change given the election of an allegedly less oil-dominated NDP government. As was mentioned earlier, the NDP has passed legislation establishing an annual allowable cap on carbon emissions of 100 megatonnes. However, the province remains financially dependent on bitumen development. The 2015 NDP budget presumes a 21 percent increase in bitumen production between 2014–15 and 2017–18, resulting in an overall 26 percent rise in bitumen-derived revenues (Government of Alberta 2015: 28). Bitumen revenues are down by several billion dollars from the period prior to 2014, but not as a result of declining production — only as a result of lower global oil prices. So, if anything, the political and economic stakes of increasing bitumen development for the state have grown, rather than diminished. That makes it unlikely that we are going to see any state-directed opening of public participation or control over the rate and terms of oil sands extraction. The government is only likely to re-emphasize public participation in energy development if it feels as though its withdrawal will have some political consequence. So far, it clearly feels as though it is on safe ground by increasing their transparency alone.

Resistance Remains

This is not to say that some people and communities are not still insisting on expanded public participation, despite the state's apparent sense that participation is not a relevant aspect of legitimation. Indigenous peoples both in and outside of the extractive zone itself, as well as other Canadians concerned about the effects of pipelines and tankers, have called the legitimacy of the regulatory regime into question specifically on the basis of its exclusionary rules on participation.

Pipeline resistance outside of Alberta has proven particularly effective. In part, this is because the economic and political forces that drive fossil fuel extraction are weaker outside of the immediate zone of extraction. There are fewer interests vested in the construction of a pipeline that passes through Manitoba, Ontario or Quebec — less tax revenue on the line, fewer profits to be made, fewer jobs on offer or at risk — and plenty of people who understand that pipelines carry significant risks such as leaks, spills or explosions. There is also a widespread understanding that pipelines, by enabling more up- and down-stream fossil fuel combustion, erode our ability to honour our climate commitments. The geography of petro-economies, which involve sprawling transportation infrastructures, dis-aligns Schnaiberg's "treadmill of production." The fact that profitability for oil companies in Alberta means asking people who are outside of their sphere of influence to take on serious risks for little reward shifts the political economic vectors and the calculations of political risk. So, while public participation remains moribund in the actual site of extraction, it seems to be rising as a demand elsewhere.

> The economic and political forces that drive fossil fuel extraction are weaker outside of the immediate zone of extraction.

The joined forces of resistance to pipeline projects like the Enbridge Northern Gateway, the Kinder-Morgan Trans Mountain and TransCanada's Energy East have, for example, forced the Canadian federal government to promise an overhaul of how the National Energy Board (NEB) reviews and approves pipeline applications. A major plank in the 2015 federal electoral victory of the Liberal Party was a promise to reform the NEB review process, which the Liberals characterized as a rubber-stamp: untrustworthy, exclusionary and lacking the confidence of Canadians. The deeply problematic approval process was thrust into the national spotlight when a former Kinder Morgan consultant was appointed to the NEB, which occurred amidst widespread cries from municipal governments, mayors and citizens that the review provided no means for meaningful public participation (McSheffrey and Uechi 2016). Interim reforms to the NEB following the election of the Liberal government included increased consultations with Indigenous groups, but criticism of the process as an "insider's game" persists. Whether the federal government actually does make significant reforms aimed at increasing public participation in pipeline development, they clearly believe that making a show of doing so (much like Alberta in the 1990s) is important to get "buy-in" for pipeline construction and to maintain consent. Participation — albeit likely a managed form of it — may indeed still be an active factor in the calculation of legitimacy at the federal level, thanks largely to the efforts of those protestors and activists who have raised the political costs of exclusion.

Glossary of Key Terms

Alberta Energy Regulator (AER): The regulatory agency established in 2014 to oversee the development of energy resources in Alberta. The AER took over regulatory functions formerly handled by the Energy Resources Conservation Board and Alberta Environment.

Directly and adversely affected: The term by which the Alberta Energy Regulator determines whether an individual or group is eligible to participate in decision-making about energy resource development. The narrow interpretation given to this term by regulators and supported by courts has excluded those who cannot demonstrate an individual, financial threat, or whose concerns are motivated by non-monetary notions of the public good.

Honour of the Crown: Originally a term grounded in the responsibility of anybody acting on behalf of a sovereign to act honourably, in Canadian Indigenous law it acts as a standard for the comportment of Canadian government agencies in relation to First Nations. The honour of the Crown requires that governments must interpret their obligations to Indigenous peoples generously, work to carry out their promises and ensure their obligations are fulfilled.

Oil sands/Tar sands: Officially known as "bituminous sands," the terms "oil sands" and "tar sands" have become politically charged, with opponents of their further development preferring "tar sands," and proponents (including the provincial government of Alberta) sticking with "oil sands." They were once used interchangeably by both industry and government. Bituminous sands are a mix of sand, clay, water and bitumen, the latter of which can be refined for use as an energy source.

Public participation: According to Arnstein (1969: 216), "the means by which [members of the public] can induce significant social reform." More specifically in the case of government, it can mean any form of engagement with the public in the process of decision-making for planning, legislative or regulatory purposes. It can take any number of forms with varying levels of inclusivity and public power.

Tailings: Byproducts of resource extraction, especially mining. In the case of oil sands, tailings consist of water, clay, sand, silt and residual bitumen and are stored in tailings ponds.

Transparency: A one-way process of revelation, involving the provision of information about process and/or outcomes; a basic enabling requirement of public participation. It involves no necessary intention of redistributing power within processes or influence over outcomes.

United Nations Framework Convention on Climate Change: The framework governing climate change negotiations, as initiated at the 1992 Rio Earth Summit. The latest agreement of the parties to the Convention — the Paris Agreement — commits national governments to achieving a target of no more than 2 degrees average global warming and to "striving" toward the lower target of 1.5 degrees.

Questions for Discussion

1. What do you think the public's role in energy resource development ought to be?

2. Are the limits on who can and can't participate in decisions about oil sands development appropriate, in your view? Why?

3. Why do you think that the Alberta Energy Regulator enforces such a strict definition of "directly and adversely affected"?

4). One possible principle of justice that government could act on suggests that those most affected by a particular decision should have the greatest influence in the outcome. How might that principle be enacted? What would this mean for different peoples' "voices" in the oil sands? Do you think it a wise principle to follow?

Resources for Activists

DeSmog Canada: www.desmog.ca
Dogwood Initiative: www.dogwoodinitiative.org
EcoJustice: www.ecojustice.ca/blog
FossilFree Canada: www.gofossilfree.ca
Keepers of the Athabasca: www.keepersofthewater.ca/athabasca

Notes

1. Industry and the Alberta government led a push to re-brand from "tar sands" to "oil sands." Throughout the chapter, I use the two terms interchangeably.
2. The Kirby Project Description is available at <aer.ca/applications-and-notices/notices/hrg-1712215#sthash.zBPuc1UJ.dpuf>.

References

AER (Alberta Energy Regulator). 2014. Alberta Energy Regulator Rules of Practice. Alberta Regulation 99/2013. Edmonton. <qp.alberta.ca/documents/Regs/2013_099.pdf>.

Arnstein, S. 1969. "A Ladder of Citizen Participation." *Journal of the American Institute of Planners* 35, 4: 216–224.

Bankes, N. 2014. "Directly and Adversely Affected: The Actual Practice of the Alberta Energy Regulator." <ABlawg.ca>.

Bowness, E., and M. Hudson. 2014. "Sand in the Cogs? Power and Participation in the Alberta Tar Sands." *Environmental Politics* 23, 1: 59–76.

Brown, W. 2003. "Neo-liberalism and the End of Liberal Democracy." *Theory and Event* 7, 1: 1–21.

Canadian Energy Research Institute. 2015. "Canadian Oil Sands Supply Costs and Development Projects (2015-2035)." Calgary: CERI. <resources.ceri.ca/PDF/Pubs/Studies/Study_152_Full_Report.pdf>.

CAPP (Canadian Association of Petroleum Producers). 2016. *Statistical Handbook for Canada's Upstream Petroleum Industry*. Calgary.

Climate Action Tracker. n.d. "Major challenges ahead for Paris Agreement to meet its 1.5deg warming limit." <climateactiontracker.org/news/265/Major-challenges-ahead-for-Paris-Agreement-to-meet-its-1.5deg-warming-limit-.html>.

Coglianese, C. 2015. "Listening, Learning, Leading: A Framework for Regulatory Excellence." Philadelphia: UPenn Law School. <law.upenn.edu/live/files/4946-pprfinalconvenersreport.pdf>.

Cupps, D.S. 1977. "Emerging Problems of Citizen Participation." *Public Administration Review* 37: 478–487.

Dawson, C. 2015. "Canadian Oil-Sands Producers Struggle." *Wall Street Journal,* August 19. <wsj.com/articles/oil-sands-producers-struggle-1440017716>.

Fluker, S. 2014. "The Right to Public Participation in Resources and Environmental Decision-Making in Alberta." *Alberta Law Review* 52, 3 (April 30). <ssrn.com/abstract=2438979>.

Government of Alberta. 2015. "Budget 2015: Revenue." <finance.alberta.ca/publications/budget/budget2015-october/fiscal-plan-revenue.pdf>.

____. 2016a. "Budget 2016: Fiscal Plan." <finance.alberta.ca/publications/budget/budget2016/fiscal-plan-complete.pdf>.

____. 2016b. "Alberta Oil Sands Industry Quarterly Update, Summer 2016." <albertacanada.com/business/statistics/oil-sands-quarterly.aspx>.

Hodson, P.V. 2013. "History of Environmental Contamination by Oil Sands Extraction." *Proceedings of the National Academy of Sciences* 110, 5: 1569–1570.

Hughes, J.D. 2016. *Can Canada Expand Oil and Gas Production, Build Pipelines, and Keep Its Climate Change Commitments?* Edmonton: Parkland Institute.

IPCC. 2014. *Climate Change 2014: Synthesis Report. Contribution of Working Groups I, II and III to the Fifth Assessment Report of the Intergovernmental Panel on Climate Change* [Core Writing Team, R.K. Pachauri and L.A. Meyer (eds.)]. Geneva, Switzerland.

Jordaan, S.M. 2012. "Land and Water Impacts of Oil Sands Production in Alberta." *Environmental Science and Technology* 46: 3611–3617.

Kiss, S.J. 2014. "Responding to the 'New Public': The Arrival of Strategic Communications and Managed Participation in Alberta." *Canadian Public Administration* 57, 1: 1–182.

Kurek J., J.L. Kirk, D.C.G. Muir, X. Wang, M.S. Evans, and J.P. Smol. 2013. "Legacy of a Half Century of Athabasca Oil Sands Development Recorded by Lake Ecosystems." *Proceedings of the National Academy of Sciences* 110, 5: 1761–1766.

Lee, Marc. 2013. "Global carbon budget is a harsh reality check for Canadian investors." Globe and Mail October 30. <theglobeandmail.com/report-on-business/economy/economy-lab/global-carbon-budget-is-a-harsh-reality-check-for-canadian-investors/article15158549/>.

Liggio, J., S.M. Li, K. Hayden, et al. 2016. "Oil Sands Operations as a Large Source of Secondary Organic Aerosols. " *Nature* 354 (June): 91–106.

Lukes, S. 2005. *Power: A Radical View, 2nd edition.* New York: Palgrave Macmillan.

Marshall, B.K., and W.S. Goldstein. 2006. "Managing the Environmental Legitimation Crisis." *Organization & Environment* 19, 2: 214–232.

McSheffrey, E., and J. Uechi. 2016. "NEB Sides with Texas-based Pipeline Company Against B.C. Citizens, First Nations." *National Observer*, May 19. <nationalobserver.com/2016/05/19/news/neb-expected-approve-kinder-morgan trans-mountain-expansion-today>.

Olynyk, J., K. Bergner, and T. Kruger. 2015. "Losing the Battle but Winning the War?" *Project Law Blog*, Nov. 6. <projectlawblog.com/2015/11/06/losing-the-battle-but-winning-the-war/>.

Osberg, L., A. Sharpe, and J. Thomas. 2016. "How Much Do Changing Terms of Trade Matter for Economic Well-Being in Canada?" Working paper. <csls.ca/events/cea2016/osberg.pdf>.

Parajulee, A., and F. Wania. 2014. "Evaluating Officially Reported Polycyclic Aromatic Hydrocarbon Emissions in the Athabasca Oil Sands Region with a Multimedia Fate Model." *Proceedings of the National Academy of Sciences* 111, 9: 3344–3349.

Sauchyn, D., J-M. St-Jacques, and B. Luckman. 2015. *Proceedings of the National Academy of Siences* 112, 41 <pnas.org/content/112/41/12621.full.pdf>.

Schindler, D. 2013. "Water Quality Issues in the Oil Sands Region of the Lower Athabasca River, Alberta." *Geoscience Canada* 40: 202–214.

Schnaiberg, A. 1980. *The Environment: From Surplus to Scarcity.* New York: Oxford University Press.

Snyder, J. 2015. "A Fine Mess: The AER's Directive 074." *Alberta Oil* July 28. <albertaoilmagazine.com/2015/07/alberta-energy-regulator-directive-074/>.

Steward, G. 2015. "Tailings ponds a toxic legacy of Alberta's oil sands." *Toronto Star*, September 4. <thestar.com/news/atkinsonseries/2015/09/04/tailings-ponds-a-toxic-legacy-of-albertas-oilsands.html>.

Treaty Alliance Against Tar Sands Expansion. n.d. The Treaty (English). <treatyalliance.org/wp-content/uploads/2016/12/TreatyandAdditionalInformation-20161216-OL.pdf>.

United Nations (Framework Convention on Climate Change). 2015. Report on the structured expert dialogue on the 2013–2015 review. UNFCCC: Bonn.

Vanderklippe, N. 2012. "Ambitious plans for oil sands would create lakes from waste." *Globe and Mail*, October 3 <theglobeandmail.com/news/national/ambitious-plans-for-oil-sands-would-create-lakes-from-waste/article4583817/>.

Yeh, S., A. Zhao, S.D. Hogan, et al. 2015. "Past and Future Land Use Impacts of Canadian Oil Sands and Greenhouse Gas Emissions." Research report – UCD-ITS-RR-15-01. Davis: UCDavis Institute of Transportation Studies.

11

Making Universities Safe for Women

Sexual Assault on Campus

Elizabeth Sheehy

YOU SHOULD KNOW THIS

- Annually, 460,000 Canadian women report that men have sexually assaulted them. This is a conservative estimate since it is based on self-reports by women to interviewers from Statistics Canada whom they do not know and in circumstances where the legal definition of sexual assault is not presented to them.
- Among perpetrators of sexual assault, 0.3 percent are held accountable under Canadian law; 99.7 percent are not held accountable.
- Only one in three Canadians understands the criminal law of consent to sexual activity; two in three Canadians mistakenly believe that affirmative consent is not required (saying "yes," initiating or enjoying the activity) or that ongoing consent to the sexual activity is not required. One in ten does not know that consent is required between spouses, and 21 percent of those aged 18–34 believe that when a woman sends a sexually explicit photo she is "consenting."
- The rate at which women students are sexually assaulted by men during their college years in the U.S. sits between 15 and 34 percent.
- By June 2016, U.S. federal authorities had opened 246 investigations of 195 colleges and universities for Title IX violations regarding their responses to campus sexual violence.
- Seventy-eight percent of University of Ottawa students have experienced face-to-face harassment, including 44 percent who experienced unwanted physical contact, and 67 percent had experienced online harassment.
- Women students reported 179 sexual assaults to their campus authorities in Canada in 2013, a rate that is 21 percent higher than assaults reported in 2012 and 66 percent higher than 2009.
- Only twenty-four of one hundred post-secondary institutions in Canada had, by 2016, adopted a stand-alone policy for sexual violence on campus.

Sources: Johnson 2012; Hill 2015; Cantor et al. 2015; Krebs et al. 2007; Kingkade 2016; Johnson 2015b; Sawa and Ward 2015a; Kane 2016b.

SEXUAL ASSAULT PERPETRATED BY MEN IN CANADA constitutes a major barrier to women's freedom, security of their person and their right to equality before and under the law. Women students in post-secondary institutions suffer additional consequences beyond the trauma and chaos of rape: they may be unable to avoid the perpetrator if he shares a residence, classes, activities or even campus routes; their academic success will be imperiled such that they may fail their courses or be forced to withdraw from their programs; and they face financial penalties of wasted tuition, loss of teaching and research assistantships and the costs of counselling. Men's sexual violence thus has material consequences for women's access to educational equity.

> Men's sexual violence has material consequences for women's access to educational equity.

Perpetrators often target young women aged 15–24 (Perreault and Brennan 2010), placing university and college students among those women most at risk. The legal system remains a hostile place for women who report sexual assault to the police, despite substantive reforms to the law intended to change both the outcomes and experiences of women who initiate criminal legal intervention. When men assault women while they are pursuing post-secondary degrees, additional issues arise that are not taken up by the criminal law, for example the need for a safety plan for her on campus, the need to remove the perpetrator from the university community to alleviate the risk he poses to her and to other students, the need to denounce the behaviour as fundamentally inconsistent with the university's mission and the need to accommodate and support the student herself in recovery and in academic success. Women students are therefore demanding that their universities and colleges respond to the destructive behaviour of campus perpetrators.

This chapter will first situate campus sexual assault on the current political agenda in Canada and the United States, including the agenda of frontline women's groups who support and advocate for women who have been raped. In order to articulate the dimensions of the issue, it will second review the data on men's commission of sexual assault both off and on campus. Third, it will describe the criminal law of sexual assault, and fourth, it will outline the many obstacles women face in the legal processing of sexual assault reports when they turn to the criminal justice system.

Finally, this chapter will examine the processes available to women on campus in Canada, including sexual harassment policies and student codes of conduct, pointing out the perils of both, before turning to consider new legislation in Ontario, British Columbia and Manitoba requiring universities and colleges to develop sexual violence policies and provide resources to support students who experience sexual violence. Finally, the chapter will conclude by identifying three challenges that universities and colleges face in developing and defending campus sexual violence policies: the dearth of input from frontline anti-violence feminist advocates, the lack of uniformity among campus policies and the agenda of the campus anti-feminist men's rights movement.

Women Students Put Campus Sexual Assault on the Agenda

Women students are turning to their universities and colleges in increasing numbers for alternate processes and interim measures to allow them to continue their educational programs after men have sexually assaulted them. While women students' demands appear to be a relatively new phenomenon in Canada, the lack of data collection by post-secondary institutions and the effort by some administrators to silence women who report sexual assault on campus precludes firm conclusions on just how "new" women students' demands are (Laychuk 2016).

And in fact, frontline women's rape crisis centres have been dealing with the aftermath of campus sexual assault for the decades during which they have operated across North

> Women students are turning to their universities and colleges in increasing numbers for alternate processes and interim measures to allow them to continue their educational programs after men have sexually assaulted them.

America. By supporting these students, women's centres have contributed to the educational mission of universities, and some have also advocated on behalf of students to their universities. Women's frontline organizations thus have critical expertise when it comes to developing responses to campus sexual assault.

The evidence from the most impressive study to date, which examined seventy countries over forty years, shows that the autonomous women's movement worldwide is the single most important factor in producing positive policy change on male violence against women (Htun and Weldon 2012). Thus it is also important to consider campus sexual assault in the wider context of the women's movement's analysis and strategy around men's violence against women and to recall that this form of sexual violence is not uniquely or differently experienced by students than by other women.

Despite the fact that men's sexual violence has long been on the feminist agenda in Canada, a series of highly publicized events at Canadian universities starting in 2013 has catapulted men's sexual violence on campus into a national conversation for the first time ever. Rape chants by frosh students, men and women alike (CBC News Online 2013b), racist songs that insulted Indigenous women (Justice 2013) and a series of rapes on campus by a serial predator, all in the fall of 2013, put the University of British Columbia under intense scrutiny (Bailey 2013). A rape chant scandal also rocked Saint Mary's University (Taber 2013), while Lakehead University's failure to respond to a student's sexual assault report was exposed when she described what it was like to attend classes with her alleged perpetrator in a letter to the editor of a local paper (CBC News Online 2013a).

Months later, a report of sexual assault by several hockey players on the University of Ottawa team was exposed at almost the same time as Facebook pages were made public in which five male student leaders at the same university denigrated sexually and threatened their female student president (CBC News Online 2014b; CBC News Online 2014a). Dalhousie University experienced its moment in the media glare when the Facebook posts of male dentistry students commenting sexually on their female colleagues and discussing using chloroform to drug and then rape women patients were shared (Hampson 2015). A Mount St. Vincent professor who engaged in inappropriate sexual and academic conduct with respect to a female student was fired by his university (Zaccagna 2015). A student at Brandon University was required to sign a contract, as part of the investigation of her complaint, agreeing not to discuss another student's sexual assault against her with anyone other than a counsellor, upon pain of suspension or expulsion (Laychuk 2016).

It is difficult to determine why this category of sexual assault and bureaucratic misfeasance attracted such a media profile at this particular moment: was it the privilege — and presumed whiteness — of university students that made this category of victims newsworthy? Were these events galvanizing because parents expect their daughters to be safe on campus, or that university administrators will take sexual violence seriously and respond in a timely and compassionate manner? Possibly the overlap of the unfolding Jian Ghomeshi allegations that emerged in October 2014, and his subsequent trial helped keep the campus sexual assault story alive in the media. Or was it Canadian journalists chasing the U.S. news who saw the opportunity for breaking similar stories in Canada?

Canadian students and activists have looked to the U.S. as a frontrunner in developing responses to men's assaults on campus. There, a student-led movement successfully campaigned for federal intervention to ensure that post-secondary institutions either implement sexual assault policies that support women students or risk losing federal funding. President Obama responded with the White House Task Force to Protect Students from Sexual Assault in early 2014 to enforce federal laws aimed at the institutional response to men's sexual violence on campus. Although sex discrimination in education has long been prohibited under Title IX of the *Education Amendments of 1972* for institutions that receive federal financial support, historically the litigation that forced compliance had been focused on discrimination in athletic programs rather than other forms of discrimination.

Title IX can now be invoked by students against universities and colleges that fail to respond appropriately to sexual harassment and sexual violence as conduct that has a discriminatory impact on them as women students. In fact, Title IX has been interpreted by the U.S. government as precluding mediation for sexual assault reports and as requiring a "preponderance of the evidence" standard in adjudication of such allegations (Sheehy and Gilbert 2015). Other federal laws require institutions to make public their data on sexual assault reported by students (*The Jeanne Clery Disclosure of Campus Security Policy and Campus Crime Statistics Act (Clery Act)* 2012) and to engage in educational and preventative programing regarding sexual assault.

By March 2016, 208 federal investigations of 167 colleges and universities for Title IX infractions regarding their failure to develop and enforce appropriate sexual assault policies and practices had been initiated (Cohen and St Clair 2016). As of June 2016, the numbers of U.S. federal investigations for Title IX violations regarding responses to campus sexual violence had climbed further to 246 ongoing investigations of 195 colleges and universities (Kingkade 2016).

Unlike their U.S. counterparts, women students in Canada have exerted pressure at the university and provincial levels because our federal government has mostly withdrawn from funding post-secondary institutions. The exposés of Canadian universities' institutional failures to respond to sexual assault on campus, as well as journalists' investigations revealing that as of 2014 only nine of eighty-seven Canadian universities even had a "sexual assault" policy (Mathieu and Poisson 2014), generated enormous political pressure for social and legal change. A few universities have been proactive: for example, the University of Manitoba began consulting students about developing a new sexual violence policy without waiting for a crisis to explode or the province to force them to act (Kroeker 2016).

> The exposés of Canadian universities' institutional failures to respond to sexual assault on campus as well as journalists' investigations generated enormous political pressure for social and legal change.

In order to understand why students are turning to their post-secondary institutions for responses to sexual assault and what those institutions might offer, it is necessary to situate the issue in relation to the social and legal realities of sexual assault both off and on campus in Canada. Whose and which knowledge informs our understanding of this crime? What do we know about men's sexual assaults upon women students? To whom do women students turn in these circumstances?

The Social Reality of Sexual Assault in Canada

Sexual assault is a deeply gendered crime: 92 percent of those victimized are female (Vaillancourt 2010) and 94 percent of the perpetrators are male (Perreault 2015). Men are also the vast majority of perpetrators — 79 percent — of violent victimization against other men (Vaillancourt 2010). Sexual assault is also a persistent crime. Despite the drop in all other forms of violent crime in Canada over the past decade, men's commission of sexual assault remains constant such that for the first time ever women have surpassed men at the rate at which they are victimized violently (Statistics Canada 2015).

We do not know how many men engage in sexually assaultive behaviour. In fact we also do not know with certainty how many women they assault each year, although we do know that it appears to be one of the most under-reported of crimes. The widely cited statistic is that one in ten women who experience sexual assault report it to police. However, Statistics Canada recently reported that the numbers are such that only one in twenty women report their experience of sexual assault to police (Statistics Canada 2015).

But even still, we cannot be certain that the reporting rates are not far lower than this. This lacuna in our knowledge is due to the reality that rape is a crime that silences women: it is a terrifying crime during which the victim may not know if she will be killed, producing long-term trauma responses; it is a crime that denies the personhood of the victim, rendering her an object to be used by another person and shattering her sense of safety in the world; it is a crime that produces shock and disbelief, such that many women try to rationalize or normalize the perpetrator's behaviour or to lock away the memory rather than confront him or others with his acts; it is a crime that commonly produces a freeze response, making women ashamed that they did not somehow "fight"; it is a crime for which many in our society blame women themselves — for their manner of dress, their consumption of alcohol, their "flirtatious" behaviour, their decisions that others perceive as "risk-taking" — leading victims to engage in self-blame and self-censorship; it is a crime overwhelmingly committed by men known to the woman, making it very complicated for a victim to report; and it is a crime that we as a society deny, minimize and rationalize, convincing victims that they are unlikely to be believed. No wonder so few women "break the silence."

Men who rape count on the silencing effect of this crime. The social construction of knowledge about men's violence against women abets this silencing. Police data has been recognized as incomplete both because so few women choose to report to police but also because police recording practices for this category of crime are deeply problematic given the documented biases that infect them, as discussed below. Crime victimization surveys are inadequate because they are not specifically tailored to identify for women the range of behaviours that constitute "sexual assault" in legal terms, nor are the interviewers trained to spend time gaining the confidence of interviewees and responding with empathy. As Holly Johnson argues, the low incidence rates produced by these forms of "knowledge" allowed criminologists and others to claim that women's fear of sexual violence was groundless and disproportionate to their documented risk (Johnson 2015c). However, the best study available of the actual incidence of men's sexual offending against women produced startling new knowledge: men assault 39 percent of Canadian women, who experience this crime at least once over their lifetimes (Statistics Canada 1994). This study was undertaken by Statistics Canada in 1993 under the direction of Dr. Holly Johnson. The Violence Against Women Survey (vaws), as it was called, avoided many of the known problems with other efforts to survey women about sexual assault. The vaws introduced a woman-centred survey that asked women about their experiences from the age of 16 forward (as opposed to the past year) and specified the acts considered criminal, including sexual assaults where the woman did not resist or where she was incapable of consent — categories of criminal offending that many, including women, erroneously believe do not amount to sexual assault in law. The interviewers were trained to ensure the woman's safety needs were met and to respond to the emotional turmoil that their questions might provoke.

When we turn to sexual assault on the campus, our knowledge is even more limited, and most of it is based on the U.S. experience. Two recent studies place the rate at which college women are raped by men during their college years at between 15 and 34 percent, illustrating substantial variance in offending rates across institutions (Cantor et al. 2015; Krebs et al. 2007). Some of the research on U.S. campuses suggests that approximately 6 percent of male students are perpetrators, but that many of them are serial predators, accounting for an average of six rapes each (Lisak and Miller 2002).

Further, older research by Malamuth and Dean (1991) found that 16–20 percent of male students claim that they would commit rape if they thought they could get away with it; when they changed the wording from "rape" to "force a woman to have sex," the numbers soared to 36–44 percent (Malamuth and Dean 1991: 234). There is also evidence that fraternities and sports teams, especially football and hockey, both contribute to rape culture — a culture in which rape is encouraged, tolerated or minimized — and provide the social context in which men who commit sexual assault are hidden and protected (Martin 2016).

In Canada, some of the earlier work by DeKeseredy and Kelly (1993) surveyed students in forty-four Canadian post-secondary institutions for their experience of either perpetrating sexual assault or being perpetrated against. They found that 11 percent of males reported abusing their dating partners sexually, while 27.7 percent of females reported experiencing this behaviour. When the researchers included all forms of abuse — physical and psychological as well as sexual — their numbers rose to 19.5 percent males self-reporting such behaviour and 45.1 percent female students responding that they had been targeted by this behaviour (DeKeseredy and Kelly 1993). DeKeseredy, Schwartz and Tait (1993) examined sexual aggression by non-strangers and strangers against women at one Canadian university in an exploratory study and found that men had sexually assaulted 32.8 percent of the 259 women in the past twelve months.

Both studies used broad definitions of sexual assault, specific questions that allowed women to measure their experience against legal understandings of sexual assault, and provided follow-up support for women surveyed. The authors concluded, however, that even these numbers are undercounts because they did not involve interviews during which women are known to make belated disclosures (DeKeseredy, Schwartz and Tait 1993: 274). Only three of the approximately 120 students who experienced sexual assault in this study said that they had reported their victimization to police — a reporting rate that sits significantly below even the rate of one in twenty women reporting to police.

Recently in Canada, journalists collected the data from Canadian universities about reporting rates among students who experience sexual violence both to police and to their post-secondary institutions (Sawa and Ward 2015a). Several things are striking about the data. First, women students are putting pressure on their colleges and universities by reporting in increasing numbers: "In 2013, 179 assaults were reported, a 21 per cent rise over 2012 and a 66 per cent rise over the number of sexual assaults reported in 2009" (Sawa and Ward 2015a: n.p.).

Second, for many universities there is a mismatch — in fact a reversal — of women's reporting rates to their institutions as opposed to police. For example, while UBC's data shows that sixteen sexual assaults were reported to campus security for the period 2009–13, the RCMP data shows seventy sexual assaults for the same period (Sawa and Ward 2015b). Thus many more women reported to police than to their campus authorities, which suggests that many students were either unaware of the university's policy or had more confidence in police than in their university.

> Many more women reported to police than to their campus authorities, which suggests that many students were either unaware of university policies or had more confidence in police than in their universities.

Third, those numbers of students reporting sexual violence, whether to police or their schools, are only the tip of the iceberg in terms of the disconnect between what happens to women on Canadian campuses and what campus officials are asked to respond to. Dr. Holly Johnson designed and administered Canada's first campus survey for sexual violence in 2015 at the University of Ottawa (Johnson 2015b). She found that 44 percent of students surveyed online reported that they had experienced some form of sexual violence while at the university. In contrast, the University of Ottawa received only ten reports of sexual violence from its students in the period 2009–13 (Sawa and Ward 2015a).

Beyond the silencing effect of sexual assault, why do so few women students report to police or to their university? Does the criminal law fairly define the wrong of sexual assault and provide appropriate legal rules for the prosecution and defence of this crime?

Sexual Assault Law

Canada's sexual assault law is recognized as one of the most progressive in the world for women. In 1983, in response to feminist demands made by the women's movement in Canada, it shed many of the most sex discriminatory rules that plagued the prosecution of rape for centuries (Boyle 1984). *Criminal Code* reforms made wife rape a crime for the first time, eliminated the requirement that penetration be proven and reformed the previous evidentiary rules that had invited judges and juries to acquit on the basis of the doctrine of "recent complaint," a lack of corroborating evidence or a woman's prior sexual experience being used to make her an incredible victim. More reforms to the criminal law of sexual assault, including the definition of legally valid "consent" and limits on the "mistaken belief in consent" defence followed in 1992, led by the proposals and energy of the violence against women's movement in Canada.

Between statutory definitions and judicial rulings, Canadian law supports the following propositions: sexual contact without the "voluntary agreement" of the other person is criminal (*Criminal Code of Canada* s 273.1); voluntary agreement is a subjective state of mind of the other person — it cannot be "implied" or presumed from the circumstances (*R v Ewanchuk* 1999); those who are asleep, severely intoxicated (by drugs or alcohol) or passed out are legally incapable of consent (*Criminal Code of Canada* s 273.1); voluntary agreement must be expressed by words or actions of that person, and failure to resist or passivity does not amount to consent in law (*R v M(.M.L.)* 1994) and voluntary agreement must be obtained for "the sexual activity in question" (meaning our law does not recognize global consent); and consent can be withdrawn by words or conduct and must be contemporaneous with the sexual activity (there is no "advance consent") (*R v J.A.* 2011).

Further, a man cannot defend himself by arguing "mistaken belief in consent" if his error arose from his intoxication or recklessness as to the woman's consent or if he failed "to take reasonable steps, in the circumstances known to him at the time, to ascertain consent" (*Criminal Code of Canada* s 273.2(b)). Our law places limits on accused men's access to women's sexual history and their private counselling and other records, based on women's competing equality rights and the recognized need to eliminate discriminatory rape myths from the criminal law (*Criminal Code of Canada* ss 276, 278). However, resort to either women's past sexual experience or their private records is not absolutely prohibited, such that no woman considering reporting sexual assault can be guaranteed that the lawyer defending the accused will not be able to cross-examine her about her sexual experience or her private counselling records (Craig 2016b). But our criminal law does protect complainants from being identified in the media by name or descriptions that effectively disclose their identities (*Criminal Code of Canada* s 486).

The Legal Processing of Sexual Assault in Canada

In spite of the strong and clear jurisprudence governing sexual assault, the criminal law is not applied consistently by police, prosecutors and judges. At the level of police, their failures include refusal to investigate women's reports or to send their rape evidence kits for forensic testing, treating women with disbelief and hostility and charging or threatening to charge women with "mischief" or "obstruction" for allegedly false reports of rape, among other responses. These failures are so pervasive and persistent that U.S. scholar Corey Rayburn Yung argues that police are effectively "hostile gatekeepers who prevent rape complaints from progressing through the criminal justice system by fervently policing the culturally disputed concept of 'rape'" (2016: 1).

The "unfounding" rate — the rate at which police disbelieve women and decide that no crime has been committed — is higher for sexual assault than any other crime in Canada. The rate of "unfounding" on average among police departments studied is 25–43 percent, meaning that in many cities, police turn away at least one in four women who report rape, devastating the women who turned to police for aid and emboldening perpetrators (DuBois 2012:194-95). In Ottawa between 2009 and 2013, police unfounded 38 percent of women's sexual assault complaints; by 2014, the rate had dropped to 21 percent, but at the same time the category of founded, unsolved cases had risen from 32 to 47 percent (Johnson 2015a).

Men who rape their fellow students are particularly likely to benefit from unfounding because of police adherence to rape myths that view "stranger" rape as more serious and credible than "acquaintance" rape. For example, in 2013 fifty sexual assaults were reported by UBC students to the RCMP. Of these, forty-one were unfounded — a shockingly high rate of police disregard (UBC Campus Security 2016).

Often, as Yung demonstrates with terrifying examples, police are impervious to legal reform of the definitions used to criminalize sexual violence, continuing to focus on women's behaviour, not men's, when deciding whether to investigate and lay charges. Consider, for example, the Ottawa police decision not to investigate the rape of a first-year University of Ottawa student (CBC News Online 2015). This student reported on September 26, 2015, to police after she had gone to hospital and undergone medical examination. She told them that another student had punched, strangled, raped and then spat upon her at his home the night before.

Over a month later the investigator contacted her to tell her that police had decided not to lay charges after interviewing the alleged perpetrator. Since he claimed that he thought the interaction was consensual, the officer concluded that it was a "misunderstanding" (CBC News Online 2015). Such an interpretation of the facts and law would see virtually all per-petrators left untouched by criminal law, if all they need do is allege "mistake." But further, in the case of this degree of violence, "mistaken belief in consent" is practically unavailable as a legal defence.

Only after this student abandoned her right to anonymity and went public with her name and face did police reverse and claim that the investigation was "ongoing." Another two months went by before police announced that they had "laid charges," but only after the man had left Canada, and no arrest was made (Sibley 2016). Only in August 2016 was this man arrested when he audaciously re-entered Canada (Gillis 2016). To date, the student has been unable to return to complete her academic year.

If police do in fact lay charges, they are overwhelmingly likely to charge at the level of simple sexual assault, even in those cases where the facts support more serious charges of sexual assault causing bodily harm or using a weapon, or aggravated sexual assault, whereby the man either maims or endangers the life of the complainant (Du Mont 2003). This lower level of charge means that the degree of men's violence in many sexual assaults is rendered invisible, and we are left with a misleading statistical portrait about this crime in Canada.

The immediate consequence of this practice of under-charging is that the maximum sen-tence an accused is liable to is ten years imprisonment, with the average length of incarceration in Canada of adult men for sexual assault standing at 1,406 days (Boe et al. 2004). Further, the lower level of charging also makes it possible for some men to receive non-jail sentences such as suspended sentences and conditional imprisonment, also known as "house arrest" (Balfour and Du Mont 2012).

Prosecutors provide another barrier for women who report sexual assault, even if police arrest a suspect and/or recommend charges. Prosecutors may drop charges laid by police: they use a charge screening test that looks at the likelihood of conviction and the public interest in proceeding with a case, both of which may lead them to abandon prosecution. Holly Johnson shows that about 50 percent of sexual assault charges are dropped at this stage of the legal process (Johnson 2012). For example, at the University of Victoria the police arrested a male student in relation to sexual assaults he allegedly committed against four women (Zinn 2016). However, the Crown's office refused to lay charges on the basis that the evidence did not meet their charge assessment standard, meaning that prosecutors doubted whether there was a substantial likelihood of conviction (*Globe and Mail* 2016).

Crown attorneys (or Crowns) may accept a guilty plea in exchange for lesser charges of assault or a minor sentence in order to save resources and shield the complainant from the trial process. Or they may proceed to trial, but without a deep understanding or commitment to the reformed law of sexual assault (Vandervort 2012). Some Crowns hold erroneous or unchallenged beliefs about women and sexual assault, such that they may not object to defence cross-examination of the complainant that exceeds legal limits by, for example, touching on women's past sexual relationships (Lazar 2010; Vandervort 2012).

Further, the Crown represents the state, not the individual woman — meaning the Crown is not *her* lawyer — and should maintain some degree of neutrality. This is because Crown attorneys have different ethical obligations than do defence lawyers. Defence lawyers are charged with the responsibility of doing their utmost, within the limits of the law, to secure acquittal for their clients (Law Society of Upper Canada 2016: Chapter 5.1-1). In contrast, Crowns must act dispassionately and must not seek conviction, but rather to ensure that justice is done through a fair trial on the merits (Law Society of Upper Canada 2016: Chapter 5.1-3).

Unlike defence lawyers, therefore, Crowns do not "prepare" their witnesses for testifying, so as to avoid any suggestion that the witness's evidence has been "tainted." Crowns may also not have the budget allocation to call expert evidence to challenge erroneous beliefs about how women who experience sexual assault behave, allowing defence lawyers to impugn women's credibility by suggesting, for example, that maintaining contact with the perpetrator post-offence is inconsistent with a "real rape" having occurred.

Finally, legal aid is unavailable in most of the country for women who are sexual assault complainants, meaning that the overwhelming majority of women will testify without any legal advice or assistance. Ontario is currently running a pilot project in Toronto, Ottawa and Thunder Bay for sexual assault complainants to receive four hours of legal advice paid for by Legal Aid Ontario. Even so, or even if women have the resources to hire their own lawyer, that lawyer does not have "standing" to intervene in the trial to supply expert evidence or to protest cross-examination by defence counsel. This design of criminal trials is premised on the idea that an accused facing the prosecutorial arm of the state, where they might be out-resourced and liable to loss of liberty, should not be rendered vulnerable to additional adversaries. The more fortunate women who have sought support from frontline women's groups will at least have accompaniment and emotional support for the trial.

The trial, if it proceeds, will usually take place before a judge sitting alone without a jury. Women who testify can expect to undergo lengthy, repetitive, aggressive and sometimes sex discriminatory cross-examination by defence counsel in the public space of the courtroom and under the gaze of the alleged perpetrator (Craig 2016a). Women's credibility will be attacked on the basis that they made bad decisions to consume alcohol, to enter a private space alone with the accused, to continue to associate with him after the assault or to wait days, months or years to report the offence to authorities.

Women's reliability as witnesses will be undermined if they did not tell the exact same account each time they relayed the details of the assault or if they were impaired by alcohol or drugs at the time of the assault. Their private counselling records and their previous sexual experiences may be used as part of cross-examination. Certainly women's social media accounts and texts will be used to embarrass and discredit them if a defence lawyer can get their hands on these records.

A judge may put limits on abusive or discriminatory cross-examination, but judges also exercise caution in appearing to favour one side or disrupting the adversarial process at the risk of their decisions being appealed and overturned (*R v Schmaltz* 2015). However, not all judges succeed at "neutrality," and some share the same discriminatory beliefs as police and lawyers, as was vividly illustrated by the remarks made by Justice John McClung for the Alberta Court of Appeal in *R v Ewanchuk* (1998) and more recently by Justice Robin Camp in *R v Wagar* (2015; Crawford and Tasker 2016).

Justice Robin Camp told the complainant that if she didn't want "it" all she had to do was keep her knees together. He also refused to apply the law limiting access to the complainant's prior sexual history because he did not agree with the law, and he asserted that sex and pain "sometimes go together" and that "young women want to have sex, particularly if they're drunk," among numerous other problematic comments. His fitness for judicial office is under review by the Canadian Judicial Council as a result of a complaint made against him (In the Matter of an Inquiry 2016), but since 1971 the Council has recommended judicial removal in only two cases (Ireland 2015).

Except for attempted murder, sexual assault has the lowest conviction rate of any crime in Canada (Nicol 2013). Johnson (2012) reports that of the 2,824 sexual assaults that were prosecuted in 2006, 1,519 resulted in conviction. Her overall data, using women's self-reported sexual assaults and these outcomes, indicates that only 0.3 percent of men's sexual assaults ultimately result in conviction (Johnson 2012).

Our criminal law has been particularly ineffective in grappling with men's perpetration against unconscious women, whether the women are medicated, sleeping or passed out from alcohol or drug intoxication. In many such cases, judges have acquitted based on men's claims that they mistakenly believed the women were awake and indicating consent by their bodily movements (Sheehy 2012). In one particularly egregious case where the complainant fell asleep at a party fully clothed only to wake up to a complete stranger penetrating her, the Ontario Court of Appeal ruled that "it would be too onerous a test of willful blindness to require an accused to stop the activity and, in effect, say, 'Wait a minute; do you know who I am?'" (*R v Osvath* 1996).

> Our criminal law has been particularly ineffective in grappling with men's perpetration against unconscious women, whether the women are medicated, sleeping or passed out from alcohol or drug intoxication.

The problem areas identified above — cases where women consumed alcohol, where they were unconscious when the men initiated sexual contact, where women remained in social contact after the assault or where they failed to report immediately — are all common situations that men can exploit on a university or college campus. For example, one study (Du Mont et al. 2009) reports that "suspected drug-facilitated sexual assault is a common problem," affecting one in five women who report to hospital-based sexual assault units in Ontario, and that one-third of them were students. The inability of the law to respond effectively to these types of cases makes it all the more important that post-secondary institutions provide alternative processes for women students.

University and College Sexual Assault Policies

Campus sexual assault policies hold the potential to provide different kinds of support to women students. First and foremost, universities can and should engage in prevention and education about sexual assault by training students, faculty and staff around the legal parameters of sexual assault, offering self-defence and resistance strategies geared to women, and instigating bystander intervention, among other programs. Second, they must provide emergency aid and easy access to clear information for those students who have been assaulted. It is critical that students who report be told about the option of reporting to police, not discouraged from doing so, and supported, if at all possible, by members of the university should the student need their help with going to police. Students must also be told about campus protocols and processes that they may wish to invoke. Third, post-secondary institutions need to provide on-campus resources: counselling services and academic accommodation for students at the receiving end of sexual violence, regardless of whether or not they pursue a formal complaint against the perpetrator.

Fourth, universities can craft policies and procedures to deal with students, staff and faculty who sexually assault others in the university community. Because the mandate of a university is not to punish "crime" but rather to provide a safe environment and educate its students equitably, a university is free to develop alternate definitions, processes and consequences that avoid some of the problems of the criminal justice system. Therefore, universities can use broad definitions of sexual violence that might capture behaviour that is not a criminal offence — for example, cyber-sexual violence and online sexual assault (University of Ottawa 2016). Universities can place limits on what is "relevant" for the purpose of responding to a report of sexual violence, as St. Thomas University has done in its code of conduct wherein it prohibits reliance on the manner of dress or sexual history of the complainant in determining consent (St. Thomas University 2012).

> Because the mandate of a university is not to punish "crime" but rather to provide a safe environment and educate its students equitably, it is free to develop alternate definitions, processes and consequences that avoid some of the problems of the criminal justice system.

Universities can also devise less adversarial adjudicative processes and impose different consequences, all within far shorter timelines than the criminal law response. Thus, instead of the criminal law standard of "proof beyond a reasonable doubt," university policies can use a "preponderance of the evidence" standard. University processes can bar lawyers from participating and can preclude cross-examination of the parties. Universities can also administer consequences that range beyond the criminal law's sanctions of imprisonment, fine and supervision in the community. They can impose apologies, educational measures and limits on the perpetrator's movements on campus, as well as removal from residence, suspension and expulsion, among other possible responses.

But overwhelmingly, post-secondary institutions in Canada have not seized this opportunity to respond to sexual violence on campus. Instead, the vast majority of post-secondary institutions — 75 percent — have failed to adopt stand-alone sexual assault policies: as of 2016 only twenty-four of one hundred Canadian institutions had a stand-alone policy for sexual violence (Kane 2016b). Most universities therefore continue to rely on their student codes of conduct and their anti-harassment and discrimination polices to resolve allegations of sexual assault. But because sexual assault is not like other campus misbehaviour, and sits on the outer edge of the continuum of sexual harassment, neither process is ideal for responding to allegations of sexual assault.

Student conduct codes are usually focused on non-academic behaviours far less serious than sexual assault, such as drinking on campus, academic fraud or damaging university property. They may use academic sanctions like suspension or expulsion for academic offences, but use small fines for enforcement for non-academic violations. Student codes of conduct may require face-to-face confrontation between complainant and defendant or allow the two parties to directly question each other. Both of these practices are particularly difficult for those who have experienced sexual violence. Some codes also provide for adjudication of the alleged infraction by faculty and students from the same department as the complainant, putting the woman's privacy and dignity at serious risk.

Human rights–based processes are designed primarily for discrimination and harassment and tend to involve lengthy periods for resolution. When instigated in the university context, harassment complaints may be resolved by senior administrators, such as deans, who may be or be perceived to be in a conflict of interest. These persons may also be untrained for such a role, which requires awareness of the rape myths that permeate our culture, understanding of the traumatic effects of sexual harassment and assault and knowledge of knowledge of the legal definitions and methods of proof (University of Ottawa Task Force on Respect and Equality 2015: 19–21).

Processes for sexual harassment complaints are predominantly focused on mediation as a method of resolution, even if a formal complaints process is available. For example, a recent *Globe and Mail* study found that at the high end, only two universities saw 26.67 and 22.94 percent, respectively, resolved formally. The rest were informally resolved, whether by support to the complainant, mediation or education for the perpetrator (Chiose 2016). Data from the University of Toronto's Sexual Harassment Office shows that of the 137 complaints made over the course of 2015, not one resulted in suspension or expulsion (Negrin 2016). Students criticize informal processes on the bases that they may be administered in a discretionary fashion, no record may be kept (Chiose 2016), penalties are either small or non-existent and results of an investigation may be kept from the student who reported the misconduct (Negrin 2016).

> Students criticize informal processes on the basis that they may be administered in a discretionary fashion, no record may be kept, penalties are either small or non-existent, and results of an investigation may be kept from the student who reported the misconduct.

It seems clear that human rights–based processes are not often perceived by students as viable options to respond to harassment. For example, Holly Johnson's campus climate survey at the University of Ottawa found that 78 percent of women students have experienced face-to-face harassment, including 44 percent who experienced unwanted physical contact that would arguably qualify as sexual assault, and 67 percent had experienced online harassment (Johnson 2015b). However, only 6 percent of those harassed and 9 percent of those who said they had been sexually assaulted had sought aid from the university and student resources, including the human rights office.

Some of the universities that have been exposed in the media for their failure to respond to sexual violence have launched task forces and committed to revised policies aimed at education, prevention and punishment of sexual violence on campus (UBC Point Grey Campus Safety Working Group 2015; St. Mary's President's Council 2013; University of Ottawa Task Force on Respect and Equality 2015; UBC's President's Task Force on Gender-based Violence and Aboriginal Stereotypes 2014). But even among those universities that have created a sexual violence policy, most have placed it within a complex web of potential avenues of redress including student codes of conduct and sexual harassment and discrimination policies. Thus, students looking for answers are faced with university websites that provide conflicting information about to whom the complainant should first report and about how investigations will proceed.

For example, graduate student Mandi Gray is challenging York University's claims to have remedied its sexual violence policy. She has initiated a human rights complaint that paints York's policy as "smoke and mirrors": unclear in its application, un-resourced and contradictory (Hoffman 2015; Negrin 2016). These vague policies have the potential to re-victimize students who report by, for example, requiring that they consult with the alleged perpetrator's class schedule and figure out how to avoid accidental contact on campus, requiring students to recount their traumatic experiences to several different individuals, or forcing them to participate in adjudicative processes regardless of their wishes.

Ontario women's groups and the provincial government have provided guidance and encouragement to post-secondary institutions in developing policies and protocols for sexual violence (Ontario Women's Directorate 2013; METRAC Action on Violence 2014). Ontario enacted legislation (Bill 132 2016) and regulations that require universities and colleges to develop policies and protocols, in co-operation and consultation with students, that address raising awareness about sexual violence, preventing and reporting sexual assault, training of students, staff and faculty, developing complaint mechanisms and response protocols and making public their activities and data. Ontario regulations further specify that universities provide detailed information to students regarding the processes for investigation and adjudication, including the "due process" measures the institution provides, the rights to legal or other representation and the available appeal processes (Ontario Regulation 131/16 2016).

Apart, however, from dictating that support and accommodation be made available to students regardless of whether they engage a formal disciplinary process to condemn sexual violence committed against them, and prohibiting universities from requiring that victims participate in adjudicative processes, the Ontario government has not provided guidance to post-secondary institutions as to what ought to be the detailed content of their policies. B.C. has followed Ontario's lead, although it has not required its post-secondary institutions to report their data, instead reserving the power to the minister to require an institution to develop a survey to assess the effectiveness of its policy (Bill 23 2016). B.C. has also required consultation with students in the development and review of the adopted policy but has left open the possibility that the regulations to come may require that other persons or classes of persons be consulted. The law will come into effect in 2017, giving institutions a year to come into compliance.

Manitoba has also proposed a bill quite similar to Ontario's that is still in the legislative process (Private Member's Bill 204 2016). Like that of Ontario's, the bill requires consultation with students. Both B.C. and Manitoba have followed Ontario's approach of legislating generalized requirements for universities and colleges to develop sexual violence policies, but, again, without specific direction as to the details.

Future Challenges

Responses to campus sexual assault are evolving rapidly in Canada, as legislation, litigation and student activism emerge and converge. In this changing context, we can expect to see the other provinces follow suit, under pressure from women students and media exposure, and pass laws that require post-secondary institutions to develop policies and practices and meet certain minimal standards for supporting students and preventing sexual violence. However, given that two of the three provincial laws require universities to consult only students, not other designated groups such as women's anti-violence advocates, in their development of sexual violence policies, given the lack of uniformity among the detailed policies being adopted by these institutions, as well as their lack of experience in adjudicating sexual violence, and combined with the agitation of men's rights and anti-feminist groups on campuses, we can expect turmoil and uncertainty in the years to come as sexual violence policies are tested on campus, in the courts and in the media.

While it is laudable that provincial governments are stepping into the gap by requiring

post-secondary institutions to grapple with campus sexual violence and legislating that student
voices be included in devising responses, there
are serious problems with this direction. The laws
give no indication as to which students or groups
must have a voice or whose input should be valued. Universities seem to be free to consult with

> We can expect turmoil and
> uncertainty in the years to come as
> sexual violence policies are tested
> on campus, in the courts and in
> media.

the individual students or groups of their choosing. Many student groups have taken a
position opposing rape culture, but not all articulate a feminist commitment; some have
voiced opposition to policies that implicate any form of discipline for offending students
(University of Ottawa Task Force on Respect and Equality Task Force 2015: 22); and
others, as discussed below, are downright hostile to measures supporting women against
male violence on campus.

Even those students and groups who are politically aligned with supporting sexual violence policies may have neither the expertise nor the long-term commitment to developing,
maintaining and refining campus responses. Of course individual women students who have
been assaulted by men are experts in their own experience; they may not, however, have
the broader or systemic understanding of men's sexual violence needed to inform policy
development. Turnover is the norm in student groups as they graduate, and a sense of history of the women's anti-violence movement — what has been theorized from decades of
experience, what has been tried and failed and where current resources and struggles are
focused — may also be lacking. It is simply not possible to develop optimal responses to
sexual assault on campus without the expertise of women's frontline anti-violence activists.
This gap — or legislative preference — to require universities to negotiate with individual
students or student groups rather than women's organizations may temper the sexual violence
policies that are adopted and jeopardize their longevity.

The provincial governments' decision to leave the development of the details of sexual
violence policies to individual institutions adds to the volatility of this political and legal
situation. As has already been mentioned, most institutions — with the exception of a few
leaders like the University of Ottawa and the University of Manitoba — seem to be simply
tacking on a sexual violence policy to pre-existing student codes of conduct or harassment
and discrimination policies, neither of which have any track record of successfully responding
to sexual assault. Between reliance on these other — sometimes confusing and conflicting
— mechanisms and the fact that each university will have divergent procedures, practices
and expertise, we can expect that both women students who report and those men asked
to respond to complaints will have unmet expectations about how their rights and interests
should be respected in this context. As mentioned earlier, women students are already
instigating complaints to provincial human rights bodies about university policy failures
(Kane 2016b).

Furthermore, the issue of campus sexual assault sits within a much larger political and
legal context in which men accused of sexual violence on campus are aggressively contesting
campus adjudications of responsibility by seeking judicial review and arguing that their "due

process" rights have been violated. The pattern has emerged powerfully in the U.S., whereby universities are being sued by lawyers representing aggrieved male students who have been found responsible for sexual assault and disciplined by academic sanctions, such as suspension or expulsion (Gutierrez 2016). These lawsuits challenge the university findings on the basis of violation of fundamental fairness because, for example, they have denied the respondent student access to legal representation or to an appeal process, among other issues. Many of these claims have failed, but others have resulted in settlements by universities wishing to avoid the glare of litigation, and a few have been successful in court (Watanabe 2014).

This context, as well as the litigation efforts of some male students in Canada (Seymour 2015) ought to caution universities and student groups to tread carefully in devising campus policies. The generalized standards of fairness that our courts require of university disciplinary processes are "justification, transparency, and intelligibility" (*AlGhaithy v University of Ottawa* 2012). This means, at a minimum, setting up mechanisms for the investigation of the allegation, ensuring that the investigator is not also the adjudicator, allowing both parties to provide written submissions and to see both the investigator's report and each other's submissions, providing reasons for any decision and providing avenues for appeal of the decision to both parties.

Canadian judges have often taken a deferential approach to how universities regulate and discipline their students, recognizing both the independence and the educational mission of universities that justify departures from criminal law due process protections. However, the Canadian and U.S. case law suggests that the more campus policy, procedure and penalty resembles quasi-judicial models, the higher the level of due process measures judges will require. Further, in cases where consequences for students have been considered "serious," such as loss of an academic year, some judges have ruled that the student is entitled to legal representation and the right to cross-examine witnesses (*Telfer v University of Western Ontario* 2012; *Hajee v York University* 1985).

Although the provincial laws adopted in Ontario, B.C. and (likely) Manitoba require that sexual violence policies articulate what due process measures will be provided, the fact that universities are free to pick and choose these measures means that there is potential for considerable variance among universities, making them even more vulnerable to legal challenge, which will weaken the integrity and finality of university processes and decisions. The lack of uniformity also means that it will be difficult to build expertise across universities and among those charged with administering these policies, increasing the potential for litigation.

These risks — that policies will be developed without the input of those with the most expertise in women's experience of sexual violence and that universities will have their various and disparate policies undermined by judicial intervention — are only increased by the presence of campus-based men's rights groups dedicated to "pro-redressing what they see as a gender imbalance in the current debate about equality, namely the obvious: That women are more often the victims of sexism and abuse" (McLaren 2015). Men's rights activists have launched campus campaigns at the University of Alberta, by removing and replacing the anti-rape slogans on posters with "rape-apologist" messages (Sands 2013). They have also targeted a well-known feminist professor whose research and leadership focuses on sexual assault with posters that read "Just because you are paid to demonize men doesn't mean rape is gendered. Don't be that bigot" (*Huffington Post* 2013).

One men's rights group, the Canadian Association for Equality (CAFE), claims to have set up student groups on sixteen campuses across Canada (Anderson 2016). CAFE has the benefit and status of a charitable organization under the taxation laws of Canada, even though there is some suggestion that their filing as a charity was less than forthcoming (McLaren 2015). Their activities have focused on hosting public speaking events for anti-feminists, whose talks are focused on re-positioning men as the victims of women's violence and minimizing women students' sexual violence reports. These events are not uncontested by other student groups, but it seems likely that CAFE, among others, will seek to oppose and upend university sexual assault policies.

In conclusion, several provincial governments and numerous post-secondary institutions in Canada have been forced, by the combined power of individual women students, women's anti-violence advocates and dogged journalism to set upon the path of generating campus polices for sexual assault. Even as U.S. legal developments suggest that court challenges from male students are a predictable risk of this endeavour, provincial governments are forging ahead with boilerplate legislation that leaves each university to its own designs and hence open to litigation. The lack of policy response grounded in either feminist expertise, with a broader political base to back it, or a collective commitment across and among universities to produce uniform policies and practices, means that the defence of campus sexual assault policies will be fraught. The emergence of men's rights groups on Canadian campuses creates the potential for further instability with regard to the enforceability of sexual violence policies. In the long term, therefore, the enterprise of responding to men's violence against women in this context rests where it always has: in the hands of the autonomous women's movement in Canada.

> The lack of policy response grounded in either feminist expertise, with a broader political base to back it, or a collective commitment across and among universities to produce uniform policies and practices, means that the defence of campus sexual assault policies will be fraught.

Glossary of Key Terms

Advance consent: Consent cannot be obtained when the other person is unconscious, and so in *R v J.A.* (2011), the defence tried to argue that the complainant had given consent "in advance" of being rendered unconscious through strangulation. The Supreme Court rejected this argument and the concept of advance consent. To be valid in law, consent must be contemporaneous with the sexual activity in question so that participants remain free to change their minds and withdraw consent at any time.

Autonomous women's movement: A feminist movement dedicated to women's liberation from oppression. It is led by women and is independent of institutional support or affiliation. It prioritizes the rights and needs of women and believes in collective functioning.

Bystander intervention: Bystander training, aimed at involving men in preventing and calling out sexual violence, is in place across many campuses in Canada and the U.S. Bystander programs teach participants to be aware of possible risks before they occur, to challenge the normalization of sexual violence against women, to evaluate the costs and benefits of stepping in and to attempt intervention when possible.

Doctrine of Recent Complaint: This historical legal doctrine, also called the "hue and cry" doctrine, was premised on the (false) idea that if a woman or girl had truly been raped she would have reported the violation at the first opportunity presented to her. It has been repealed from Canadian law, but defence lawyers continue to argue that delayed disclosure of sexual violence ought to reflect poorly on the woman's credibility.

Due process rights: These are the constitutional legal rights that government must respect when invoking a legal proceeding that may result in loss of life, liberty or property. Due process rights involve certain standards of procedure, such as the individual's right to know the case against them and the right to be heard in one's own defence, which are aimed at ensuring fair treatment through the justice system.

Incapable of consent: In sexual assault law, a person is unable to consent to sexual activity, for example, when they are under the age of 14, between the ages of 14 and 16 (depending on the age of the other person), and when they are incapable of consent due to mental disability, unconsciousness or incapacitation caused by alcohol or drug intoxication.

Preponderance of the evidence: A legal standard of proof (also called proof on a balance of probabilities) used in civil (as opposed to criminal) proceedings. Rather than "proof beyond a reasonable doubt," which is required for the Crown to prove that the accused committed a criminal offence, this standard requires only that the pursuer prove that it is more likely than not that the prohibited act occurred.

Sexual history evidence: Evidence of the complainant's prior sexual activity, whether with the alleged perpetrator or any other person. Because lawyers can use sexual history evidence to intimidate and humiliate the woman, and because its introduction has an unreasonable and prejudicial impact upon fact-finding, it is generally prohibited under Canadian law in the absence of a compelling case for its relevance.

Standing: Only lawyers with standing can participate and advocate before a judge or a jury. In the criminal trial, only the Crown and the defence have standing, unless the defence attempts to secure access to the complainant's private records (in which case her counsel has standing to oppose the motion), or a successful motion is made by a lawyer to the judge for standing for a particular aspect of a trial.

Questions for Discussion

1. This chapter discusses the growing pressures on Canadian post-secondary institutions to develop and enforce policies offering preventative, remedial and disciplinary responses to sexual assaults perpetrated by men against women students. What are the risks that this focus on universities will effectively decriminalize sexual assault and take pressure off police and the criminal justice system to respond effectively to sexual assault? Are there dangers associated with this effort to hold universities and colleges to account?

2. You may have noticed that this chapter has frequently foregrounded the agents of sexual assault — overwhelmingly men — in discussing the data and the issues. What implicit critique and messaging does the chapter convey by avoiding the passive tense, eschewing nominalization and naming the perpetrators of sexual violence? Is language power? What are the costs of so overtly naming this form of violence in law and policy?

3. This chapter discusses the roles of the autonomous women's movement, student organizations, the media and government in generating social and legal change in response to sexual violence in post-secondary institutions. What are the structural limits and the potentialities of these sites to contribute to positive change in this regard?

4. In both government policy-making and media, "gender neutral" linguistic choices have become the norm, even when discussing social problems like men's violence against women. What are the benefits of laws and policies that focus on "gender-based violence"? What do we lose when we discuss "people" or "folks" who commit sexual assault or those who experience it?

Resources for Activists

METRAC: www.metrac.org.
Ontario Women's Directorate: www.women.gov.on.ca/english/.
Ottawa Rape Crisis Centre: www.orcc.net.
U.S. Department of Justice, Not Alone: www.justice.gov/ovw/protecting-students-sexual-assault.
Vancouver Rape Relief and Women's Shelter: www.rapereliefshelter.bc.ca.

References

AlGhaithy v University of Ottawa, 2012 ONSC 142.
Anderson, J. 2016. "Men's issues on campus: examining men's groups on Canadian campuses and the controversy surrounding them." *The Charlatan*, March 22. <charlatan.ca/2016/03/mens-issues-on-campus-examining-mens-groups-on-canadian-campuses-and-the-controversy-surrounding-them/>.
Bailey, I. 2013. "RCMP hunting serial predator in UBC sexual assaults." *Globe and Mail*, October 29. <theglobeandmail.com/news/british-columbia/one-suspect-now-believed-responsible-for-

six-ubc-campus-sex-assaults/article15141220/>.

Balfour, G., and J. Du Mont. 2012. "Confronting Restorative Justice in Neo-Liberal Times: Legal and Rape Narratives in Conditional Sentencing." In Elizabeth Sheehy (ed.), *Sexual Assault in Canada: Law, Legal Practice and   Women's Activism.* Ottawa: University of Ottawa Press.

Bill 23, *Sexual Violence and Misconduct Policy Act,* 5th Sess, 40th Parliament, British Columbia, 2016.

Bill 132, *An Act to amend various statutes with respect to sexual violence, sexual harassment, domestic violence and related matters,* 1st Sess, 41st Leg, Ontario, 2016.

Boe, R., L. Motiuk, and M. Nafekh. 2004. "An Examination of the Average Length of Prison Sentence for Adult Men In Canada: 1994 to 2002." *Correctional Service Canada* March <csc-scc.gc.ca/research/r136-eng.shtml>.

Boyle, C. 1984. *Sexual Assault.* Toronto: Carswell.

Cantor, et al. 2015. *Report on the AAU Campus Climate Survey on Sexual Assault and Sexual Misconduct.* September 21. <aau.edu/uploadedFiles/AAU _Publications/AAU_Reports/Sexual_Assault_ Campus_Survey/AAU_Campus_Climate_Survey_12_14_15.pdf>.

CBC News Online. 2013a. "Lakehead student's rape allegation prompts taskforce." October 22. <cbc.ca/m/news/canada/thunder-bay/lakehead-student-s-rape-allegation-prompts-task-force-1.2159004>.

____. 2013b. "UBC frosh students sing pro-rape chant." September 7. <cbc.ca/news/canada/british-columbia/ubc-investigates-frosh-students-pro-rape-chant-1. 1699589>.

____. 2014a. "Allan Rock calls University of Ottawa incident 'repugnant.'" March 5. <cbc.ca/news/canada/ottawa/allan-rock-calls-university-of-   ottawa-incidents-repugnant-1.2561604>.

____. 2014b. "Anne-Marie Roy, uOttawa student leader, subject of explicit online chat." March 2. <cbc.ca/news/canada/ottawa/anne-marie-roy-uottawa-student-leader-subject-of-explicit-online-chat-1.2556948>.

____. 2015. "Ottawa woman says police told her assault was 'misunderstanding.'" November 5. <cbc.ca/news/canada/ottawa/ottawa-woman-says-police-told-her-sexual-assault-was-misunderstanding-1.3307830>.

Chiose, S. 2016. "Harassment on campus: 90 per cent of cases kept quiet." *Globe and Mail,* April 2. <theglobeandmail.com/news/national/education/canadian-universities-under-pressure-to-formalize-harassment-assaultpolicies/article29499302/>.

Cohen, J., and S. St Clair. 2016. "Federal authorities investigating sexual violence complaints at several area colleges." *Chicago Tribune,* March 1. <chicagotribune.com/news/local/breaking/ct-universities-sexual-violence-investigations-20160301-story.html>.

Craig, E. 2016a. "The Inhospitable Court." *University of Toronto Law Journal* 66, 2.

____. 2016b. "Section 276 Misconstrued: The Failure to Properly Interpret and Apply Canada's Rape Shield Provisions." *The Canadian Bar Review* 94, 1.

Crawford, A., and J.P. Tasker. 2016. "Robin Camp, Federal Court Judge, faces inquiry after berating sexual assault complainant." *CBC News,* January 7. <cbc.ca/news/politics/federal-court-judge-robin-camp-inquiry-1.3393539>.

Criminal Code of Canada, RSC 1985, c C-46.

DeKeseredy, W., and K. Kelly. 1993. "Woman Abuse in University and College Dating Relationships: The Contribution of the Ideology of Familial Patriarchy." *Journal of Human Justice* 4, 2 (Spring).

DeKeseredy, W., M. Schwartz, and K. Tait. 1993. "Sexual Assault and Stranger Aggression on a Canadian University Campus." *Sex Roles* 28, 5.

Du Mont, J. 2003. "Charging and Sentencing in Sexual Assault Cases: An Exploratory Examination." *Canadian Journal of Women and the Law* 15, 2.

Du Mont, J., et al. 2009. "Factors Associated with Suspected Drug-Facilitated Sexual Assault." *Canadian Medical Association Journal* 180, 5.

DuBois, Teresa. 2012. "Police Investigation of Sexual Assault Complaints: How Far Have We Come Since Jane Doe?" In Elizabeth Sheehy (ed.), *Sexual Assault in Canada: Law, Legal Practice and Women's Activism*. Ottawa: University of Ottawa Press.

Gillis, M. 2016. "Suspect arrested at airport in relation to 2016 sex-assault allegations." *Ottawa Citizen*, August 12. <ottawacitizen.com/news/local-news/suspect-arrested-at-airport-in-2015-sex-assault-allegations>.

Globe and Mail. 2016. "No charges for man accused of sexually assaulting women at UVic." *Globe and Mail*, April 8. <theglobeandmail.com/news/british-columbia/no-charges-for-man-accused-of-sexually-assaulting-four-women-at-uvic/article29575761/>.

Gutierrez, T. 2016. "Colleges slammed with lawsuits from men accused of sex crimes." *CBS News*, March 23. <cbsnews.com/news/colleges-slammed-with-lawsuits-from-men-accused-of-sex-crimes/>.

Hajee v York University, (1985) 11 OAC 72.

Hampson, S. 2015. "How the Dentistry-school scandal has let loose a torrent of anger at Dalhousie." *Globe and Mail*, March 6. <theglobeandmail.com /news/national/education/how-the-dentistry-school-scandal-has-let-loose-a-torrent-of-anger-at-dalhousie/article23344495/>.

Hill, D. 2015. "Two Reasons Canadians Are Confused About Sexual Consent." *Huffington Post*, May 28. <huffingtonpost.ca/diane-hill/sexual-consent-confusion_b_7453718.html>.

Hoffman, K. 2015. "York University's sexual assault policy sparks human-rights complaint." *Globe and Mail*, June 30. <theglobeandmail.com/news/national/education/york-universitys-sexual-assault-policy-sparks-human-rights-complaint/article25194134/>.

Htun, M., and S.L. Weldon. 2012. "The Civic Origins of Progressive Policy Change: Combatting Violence Against Women in a Global Perspective, 1975–2005." *American Political Science Review* 106, 3.

Huffington Post. 2013. "Men's Rights Edmonton Rape Posters Target List Gotell." *Huffington Post*, September 16. <huffingtonpost.ca/2013/09/16/mens-rights-edmonton-rape-posters_n_3938004.html>.

"In the Matter of an Inquiry Pursuant to s. 63(1) of the *Judges Act* Regarding the Honourable Justice Robin Camp." 2016. *Canadian Judicial Council*, May 2. <cjc-ccm.gc.ca/cmslib/general/Camp_Docs/2016-05-02%20Notice%20Allegations.pdf>.

Ireland, J. 2015. "Robin Camp case: What does it take to remove a judge from the bench?" *CBC*, November 12. <cbc.ca/news/canada/judge-removal-canadian-judicial-council-1.3314962>.

Jeanne Clery Disclosure of Campus Security Policy and Campus Crime Statistics Act (Clery Act), 20 USC S. 1092(f)(1)-(15) (2012).

Johnson, H. 2012. "Limits of a Criminal Justice Response: Trends in Police and Court Processing of Sexual Assault." In Elizabeth Sheehy (ed.), *Sexual Assault in Canada: Law, Legal Practice and Women's Activism*. Ottawa: University of Ottawa Press.

____. 2015a. "Improving the Police Response to Crimes of Violence Against Women: Ottawa Women have their Say." *Faculty of Social Sciences University of Ottawa*. <socialsciences.uottawa.ca/criminology/sites/socialsciences.uottawa.ca.criminology/files/h.johnson_research_summary.pdf>.

____. 2015b. "Campus Climate Survey." *Report of the Task Force on Respect and Equality: Ending Sexual Violence at the University of Ottawa*. <uottawa.ca/president/sites/www.uottawa.ca.president/files/report-of-the-task-force-on-respect-and-equality.pdf>.

____. 2015c. "Degendering Violence." *Social Politics* 22, 3.

Justice, D. 2013. "What's wrong with the CUS FROSH Pocahontas chant?" *Artswire* UBC, September 20. <wire.arts.ubc.ca/featured/whats-wrong-with-the-cus-frosh-pocahontas-chant/>.

Kane, L. 2016a. "B.C. introduces law to require universities to have sexual misconduct policies." *Vancouver Observer,* April 28. <vancouverobserver.com/news/bc-introduces-law-require-universities-have-sexual-misconduct-policies>.

____. 2016b. "Sexual assault policies lacking at most Canadian universities, say students." CBC, March 7. <cbc.ca/news/canada/british-columbia/canadian-universities-sex-assault-policies-1.3479314>.

Kingkade, T. 2016. "There Are Far More Title IX Investigations of Colleges than Most People Know." *Huffington Post,* June 16. <huffingtonpost.com/entry/title-ix-investigations-sexual-harassment_us_575f4b0ee4b053d433061b3d>.

Krebs, C.P. et al. 2007. "The Campus Sexual Assault (CSA) Study." *National Institute of Justice.* <ncjrs.gov/pdffiles1/nij/grants/221153.pdf>.

Kroeker, C. 2016. "U of M Consulting Students on Sexual Assault Policy." *The Manitoban,* January 30. <themanitoban.com/2016/01/u-of-m-consulting-students-on-sexual-assault-policy/26899/>.

Law Society of Upper Canada. 2016. *Rules of Professional Conduct.* <lsuc.on.ca/lawyer-conduct-rules/>.

Laychuk, R. 2016. "Brandon University sexual assault victims forced to sign contract that keeps them silent." CBC, April 5. <cbc.ca/news/canada/manitoba/brandon-university-behavioural-contract-1.3520568>.

Lazar, R. 2010. "Negotiating Sex: The Legal Construct of Consent in Cases of Wife Rape in Ontario, Canada." *The Canadian Journal of Women and the Law* 22, 2.

Lisak, D., and P.M. Miller. 2002. "Repeat Rape and Multiple Offending Among Undetected Rapists." *Violence and Victims* 17, 1.

Malamuth, N., and K. Dean. 1991. "Attraction to Sexual Aggression." In A. Parrot and L. Bechofer (eds.), *Acquaintance Rape: The Hidden Crime.* New York: Wiley.

Martin, P.Y. 2016. "The Rape Prone Culture of Academic Contexts: Fraternities and Athletics." *Gender & Society* 30, 1.

Mathieu, E., and J. Poisson. 2014. "Canadian post-secondary institutions failing sex assault victims." *Toronto Star,* November 20. <thestar.com/news/canada/2014/11/20/canadian_postsecondary_schools_failing_sex_assault_victims.html>.

McLaren, L. 2015. "Leah McLaren: How men's rights groups are distorting the debate about equality." *Globe and Mail,* March 13. <theglobeandmail.com/life/relationships/leah-mclaren-are-men-really-the-victims/article23426535/>.

METRAC Action on Violence. 2014. "Sexual Assault Policies on Campus: A Discussion Paper." <metrac.org/resources/sexual-assault-policies-on-campus-a-discussion-paper-2014/>.

Negrin, S. 2016. "Negrin: Sexual assault looks different than we think and university policy must reflect that." *Ottawa Citizen,* May 11. <ottawacitizen.com/opinion/columnists/negrin-sexual-assault-looks-different-than-we-think-and-university-policy-must-reflect-that>.

Nicol, J. 2013. "Under-Reporting and Low Conviction Rates for Sexual Assault." Library of Parliament Research Publications, April 17, HillNote 2013-16-E.

Ontario Regulation 131/16. 2016. *Sexual Violence at Colleges and Universities.*

Ontario Women's Directorate. 2013. *Developing a Response to Sexual Violence: A Resource Guide for Ontario's Colleges and Universities.* <citizenship.gov.on.ca/owd/english/ending-violence/campus_guide.shtml>.

Perreault, S. 2015. "Criminal Victimization in Canada, 2014." *Statistics Canada.* <statcan.gc.ca/pub/85 002-x/2015001/article/14241-eng.htm>.

Perreault, S., and S. Brennan. 2010. "Criminal Victimization in Canada, 2009." *Statistics Canada* 30, 2. <statcan.gc.ca/pub/85-002-x/2010002/ article/11340-eng.htm>.

Pietch, N. 2010. "'I'm Not That Kind of Girl': White Femininity, the Other and the Legal/Social Sanctioning of Sexualized Violence Against Racialized Women." *Canadian Woman Studies* 28, 3 (Fall/Winter).

Private Member's Bill 204. 2016. *The Post-Secondary Sexual Violence and Sexual Harassment Policies Act,* 1st Sess, 41st Leg, Manitoba.

R v Ewanchuk (1999), 57 Alta. L.R. (3d) 235 (CA).

R v J.A., 2011 SCC 28.

R v M.(M.L.), [1994] 2 SCR 3.

R v Osvath (1996), 46 CR (4th) 124 (Ont CA).

R v Schmaltz, 2015 ABCA 4.

R v Wagar, 2015 ABCA 327.

Sands, A. July 10, 2013. "'Troubling' posters that parody successful 'Don't Be That Guy' anti-rape campaign appear in Edmonton." *National Post.* <nationalpost.com/m/wp/blog.html?b=news. nationalpost.com/2013/07/10/troubling-posters-that-parody-successful-dont-be-that-guy-anti-rape-campaign-appear-in-edmonton>.

Sawa, T., and L. Ward. 2015a. "Sex assault reporting on Canadian campuses worryingly low, say experts." CBC, February 6. <cbc.ca/news/canada/canadian-campuses-lack u s-style-transparency-on-sex-assault-reports-1.2953078>.

____. 2015b. "UBC sex assault reports out of sync with police statistics." CBC, February 9. <cbc.ca/news/canada/ubc-sex-assault-reports-out-of-sync-with-police-statistics-1.2950264>.

Seymour, A. 2015. "Hockey players can sue U of O, judge rules." *Ottawa Citizen,* July 10. <ottawacitizen.com/news/local-news/hockey-players-can-sue-u-of-o-judge-rules>.

Sheehy, E. 2012. "Judges and the Reasonable Steps Requirement: The Judicial Stance on Perpetration Against Unconscious Women." In Elizabeth Sheehy (ed.), *Sexual Assault in Canada: Law, Legal Practice and Women's Activism.* Ottawa: University of Ottawa Press.

Sheehy, E., and D. Gilbert. 2015. "Responding to Sexual Assault on Campus: What Can Canadian Universities Learn From US Law and Policy?" Forthcoming in E. Quinlan, A. Quinlan, C. Fogel, and Gail Taylor (eds.), *Sexual Assault on Canadian University and College Campuses.* Waterloo: Wilfrid Laurier University Press.

Sibley, R. 2016. "Police lay sexual assault charges in three-month-old case." *Ottawa Citizen,* January 4. <ottawacitizen.com/news/local-news/police-lay-sexual-assault-charges-in-three-month-old-case>.

St Mary's President's Council. Report of the President's Council. 2013. *Promoting a Culture of Safety, Respect and Consent at St Mary's University and Beyond.* December 15. <smu.ca/webfiles/PresidentsCouncilReport-2013.pdf>.

St Thomas University. 2012. "Disciplinary Processes for Cases of Social Misconduct, Appendix B, *Procedures with respect to Sexual Assault Complaints by Students."* December. <w3.stu.ca/stu/currentstudents/policies/documents/CodeofConductDecember2012.pdf>.

Statistics Canada. 1994. *Violence Against Women, 1993.* Ottawa: Housing, Family, and Social Statistics Division. <www23.statcan.gc. ca/imdb/p2SV.pl?Function=getSurvey&SDDS=3896>.

____. 2015. *Self-Reported Victimization, 2014.* <statcan.gc.ca/daily-quotidien/151123/dq151123a-eng.pdf>.

Taber, J. 2013. "Saint Mary's student president says rape chant was 'biggest mistake... probably in my life'." *Globe and Mail,* September 5. <theglobeandmail.com/news/

national/saint-marys-student-president-says-rape-chant-was-biggest-mistake-of-my-life/article14142351>.

Telfer v University of Western Ontario, 2012 ONSC 1287, [2012] O.J. No. 1500.

UBC Campus Security. 2016. "Sexual Assault Statistics." <security.ubc.ca/ubc-sexual-assault-statistics/>.

UBC Point Grey Campus Safety Working Group. 2015. "Interim Report of the UBC Point Grey Campus Safety Working Group." February. <vpstudents.ubc.ca/files/2014/02/Interim-Report-from-the-UBC-Point-Grey-Campus-Safety-Working-Group.pdf>.

UBC's President's Task Force on Gender-based Violence and Aboriginal Stereotypes. 2014. "Transforming UBC and Developing a Culture of Equality and Accountability: Confronting Rape Culture and Colonialist Violence." February 18. <equity2.sites.olt.ubc.ca/files/2014/05/Task-Force-on-IGBVAS-Final-Report-March-28-2014.pdf>.

University of Ottawa. 2016. "Sexual Violence: Support and Prevention." June. <uottawa.ca/sexual-violence-support-and-prevention/definitions>.

University of Ottawa Task Force on Respect and Equality. 2015. "Report of the Task Force on Respect and Equality: Ending Sexual Violence at the University of Ottawa [report]." January 29. <uottawa.ca/president/sites/www.uottawa.ca.president/files/report-of-the-task-force-on-respect-and-equality.pdf>.

Vaillancourt, R. 2010. *Gender Differences in Police-Reported Violent Crime in Canada, 2008*. Ottawa: Canadian Centre for Justice Statistics.

Vandervort, L. 2012. "Legal Subversion of the Criminal Justice Process? Judicial, Prosecutorial and Police Discretion in Edmondson, Kindrat and Brown." In Elizabeth Sheehy (ed.), *Sexual Assault in Canada: Law, Legal Practice and Women's Activism*. Ottawa: University of Ottawa Press.

Watanabe, T. 2014. "More college men are fighting back against sexual misconduct cases." *Los Angeles Times*, June 7. <latimes.com/local/la-me-sexual-assault-legal-20140608-story.html>.

Yung, C. 2016. "Rape Law Gatekeeping." 12 August. Forthcoming: *Boston College Law Review*. SSRN <https://ssrn.com/abstract=2742855>.

Zaccagna, R. 2015. "MSVU dismisses instructor who had sexual relationship with student." [Halifax] *Chronicle Herald*, 15 January. <http://thechronicleherald.ca/metro/1263504-msvu-dismisses-instructor-who-had-sexual-relationship-with-student>.

Zinn, J. 2016. "Charges recommended against UVic student for alleged sexual assaults." *Saanich News*, March 1. <saanichnews.com/news/370676511.html? mobile=true>.

12

Resisting Conformity

Women Talk about Their Tattoos

Jessica Antony

YOU SHOULD KNOW THIS

- Tattooing, as defined by Health Canada, is the art of depositing pigment 1-2mm into the skin, creating a design. A tattoo gun, which is used for this practice, involves a cluster of small needles that vibrate hundreds of times per minute, puncturing the skin to deposit the ink.
- In the mid to late 1990s, tattooing was listed as one of the top growing businesses in the U.S.
- In a 2000 study of teens aged 12 to 19, 29 percent had a tattoo or were planning on getting a tattoo.
- According to the CBC's survey of Canadian prisons in 2004, 47 percent of males and 53 percent of females were tattooed.
- A 2013 study found that 21 percent of all Canadians had at least one tattoo.

Sources: CBC 2004; Kosut 2006: 1036; Health Canada 2001; Faille and Edminston 2013.

HISTORICALLY, TATTOOS HAVE HAD A NEGATIVE IMAGE. Tattooed bodies were thought to be monstrous — as examples of bodily excess, as sex objects or hypersexual beings, or as primitive, threatening or circus-like spectacles. Tattoos were associated with dangerous under classes and sexual behaviour — a "destructive decoration that flouts the possibility of untainted flesh" (Braunberger 2000: 1; see also Hawkes et al. 2004: 593). Situated within a racist ideology, tattooing and body art were interpreted not as "the rational choice of an enlightened individual, but constitute[d] instead a primitive response more usually associated with the uncivilized behaviour of savages" (Widdicombe and Wooffitt 1995: 139). Lower-class, marginalized people embodied the notion of tattooing —sailor, military man, biker, gang member or prisoner — and were seen as deviant or at least counter cultural.

Today, however, what was once a practice reserved for the so-called "seedy underbelly" of society has become, in the eyes of some, just an appropriated marketing tool. Over the last decade, convenience store chains have seen a rise in energy drinks — like Inked, Rockstar or Wicked — that use tattoo culture as a marketing tool. Inked, in particular, is aimed at tattooed customers or "those who want to think of themselves as the tattoo type" (Associated Press/CBS News 2007). The drink's can features tribal-style designs, while the promotional posters include the outstretched, tattooed arm of a white male. This new marketing strategy, said 7-Eleven's manager of non-carbonated beverages, was created to sell a drink "that appealed to men and women, and the tattoo culture has really become popular with both genders." Tattooing can be used to sell products to the young or those who, according to 7-Eleven, "think and act young" (Associated Press 2007). Other corporations are jumping on this marketing bandwagon as well, with Hard Rock Energy drink supporting tattoo artists and shops by showcasing them on their website and social media platforms, for example. It would seem that tattooing's dubious past has all but disappeared.

The Western history of tattooing, however, has posed a conundrum for contemporary North American capitalist culture: in order to create a tattoo market by commodifying tattoos in the pursuit of profit, a distance from this history had to be established. While tattoos were once a form of deviance, they are now much more embedded in mainstream culture — they are made normal through reality television shows, such as *Miami Ink, Ink Master* and *Tattoo Nightmares*; through increasingly tattooed professional athletes and musicians, such as David Beckham, Rihanna and Lady Gaga; or even simply through the proliferation of tattoo shops and parlours throughout North America. In order to enable their capitalist commodification, tattoos and body art required a social acceptability — especially for the middle-class consumer.

One way in which social acceptability has been accomplished is through appropriating Eastern culture (DeMello 1995, 2000, 2014) — a culture in which tattoos have had considerable significance and mark a rite of passage in the achievement of personal growth. This new generation of tattooing is one that has been defined both by rejecting the traditional association to working-class and under-class meanings and history associated with the practice and by appropriating and creating new meanings, a new history and a new discourse surrounding tattooing practices. The focus of this new generation is on the tattoo as a means of personal and spiritual growth and the creation of individuality (DeMello 2000, 2014), a set of meanings that differ significantly from the working-class meanings traditionally associated with tattooing, such as masculinity and patriotism. Furthermore, the creation of an entirely new history focuses on the roots of tattooing in Japanese and Polynesian cultures, rejecting the association of tattooing with the low-class and marginalized individuals that originally introduced the practice to Western society. As well, this new discourse surrounding tattooing borrows from the self-help discourse of the 1970s and 1980s, as tattoo enthusiasts now locate tattooing as an identity-altering practice.

Nevertheless, the remnants of Western history have not been completely erased. There is still the association of tattoos as a sign of difference and resistance. In this regard, the mainstream acceptability and popularity of tattoos have proved problematic for women who want to use tattooing as a means of expressing particular identities. The tattoo is, in this context, strange as it represents at once permanence and change. While in the physical it is permanent (tattoos are very difficult, almost impossible to remove from the skin), the meanings surrounding tattoos change over time. The problem for women, then, becomes two-fold: within our capitalist and patriarchal society, how do tattooed women negotiate the tension between tattoos as a sign of conformity (to mainstream consumer culture) and one of resistance or reinvention (as a challenge to patriarchal gender roles)? Given the increasingly commodified nature of tattooing in mainstream Western culture, are women's tattoos merely a reflection of that consumerist culture? Or, are women's tattoos a flouting of gender roles and resistance to a patriarchal culture that pushes women to act and carry themselves in certain, oppressive ways? Are so called "feminine" tattoos — butterflies and flowers, for example — considered not subversive enough to be seen as a resistance of patriarchy?

I am interested in addressing these questions not only as a fan of tattoos, but also as a tattooed woman myself. I acquired my first tattoo at the age of eighteen while on a trip to Australia, shortly after I graduated from high school. Since then I have become a collector, adding many more tattoos to my body — including a full sleeve on my right arm and a number of other large pieces on my legs, ribs and left arm. I became interested in the

> The problem for women, then, becomes two-fold: within our capitalist and patriarchal society, how do tattooed women negotiate the tension between tattoos as a sign of conformity (to mainstream consumer culture) and one of resistance or reinvention (as a challenge to patriarchal gender roles)?

problem of tattoos for women as I experienced some of them myself — feeling unfeminine with such large, prominent tattoos, or thinking about my own tattoos as a commodity in comparison to those whose skin has not been inked.

In order to explore the social and individual meaning of women's tattoos, I spoke with eighteen tattooed women. These women told me the stories of their tattoos: why they got them, how they decided on them and how they feel about them. These "tattoo narratives" (cf. DeMello 2000) serve as a means of making connections between each tattoo project and a broader historical context, ultimately reconciling for these women the tension between conformity and resistance.

Authenticity, a key theme in my analysis and the women's stories, has a number of meanings. It is used to refer to the desire, expressed by the women I spoke with, to create a legitimate, original self-identity through their tattoo projects; a sincere, long-term commitment to a tattoo; and the sense of uniqueness that comes from being marked as different. The women acknowledged the nuances of authenticity not overtly, but through the ways in which they explained and understood tattooing. DeMello argues that, in appropriating the Eastern history of tattooing, contemporary North American tattoo enthusiasts have created a new tattoo "text." This new tattoo text, in presenting tattoos as a symbol of individuality, allows for tattoos to become a part of the mainstream — it allows for them to be culturally commodified.

Cultural commodification, or the repackaging of once "low-class" cultural symbols into products for the consumption of the mainstream, is what bell hooks describes as "eating the Other" (hooks 1992). She argues that, through cultural commodification, the media inundate us with "messages of difference" in which your sense of self-identity can be found in the Other or, in the case of tattoos, in a practice that was once reserved for the marginalized. The Other then becomes a product, commodified for the mainstream, as the media tell us that "the 'real fun' is to be had by bringing to the surface all those 'nasty' unconscious fantasies and longings about contact with the Other" (hooks 1992: 21) that are entrenched in Western culture.

Commodification is an integral process in capitalism. As Karl Marx and Friedrich Engels (1998) argued long ago, in capitalism there is an incessant, relentless search by capitalists for new markets, for constantly pushing the market into areas of human life that have not been turned into products to buy, sell and consume. As they put it in *The Communist Manifesto,* over 160 years ago:

> The bourgeoisie, wherever it has got the upper hand ... has left no other nexus between man and man [sic] than naked self-interest, than callous "cash payment." It has drowned out the most heavenly ecstasies of religious fervour, of chivalrous enthusiasm, of philistine sentimentalism, in the icy water of egotistical calculation. It has resolved personal worth into exchange value, and in place of the numberless indefeasible chartered freedoms, has set up that single, unconscionable freedom — Free Trade. (Marx and Engels 1998: 3)

There are no bounds to the desire to turn everything into products for sale. We see this in the attempts in Canada to make education and knowledge not a right of human beings but a privilege of those able to pay for it (see Jamie Brownlee in this book on the corporatization of the university; also see Sally Miller on the commodification of the right to eat). This desire to turn everything into a product takes many forms, ranging from the socialization of labour, to privatization and corporatization (see Marxists.org n.d.). As we will see, even self-identity is fair game in the push for commodification.

Commodification can indeed be found all around us, whether we're conscious of it or not. One example is evident in the drive to turn drinkable water into a product to be bought and sold. Maude Barlow, in her book *Blue Gold: The Global Water Crisis and the Commodification of the World's Water Supply* (2001), argues that as the global demand for drinkable water increases beyond sustainable levels, governments around the world are pushing to privatize water as a means of controlling its distribution. This will turn what is a basic human need — water to drink, grow crops and feed livestock — into a product that only those with the money to buy it can afford. Adrienne Roberts (2008: n.p.) similarly argues that "water production and distribution has come to be regulated by an economic logic that implicitly assumes that water shares the characteristics of other commodities produced for sale on the capitalist market." Turning water into a commodity to be bought and sold is a fundamental problem: "Instead of allowing this vital resource to become a commodity sold to the highest bidder, we believe that access to clean water for basic needs is a fundamental human right" (Barlow 2001: 4).

Another example of commodification can be found all over Canada and the Western world. Che Guevera, an Argentinean revolutionary who is most famous for leading the Cuban Revolution with Fidel Castro in the late 1950s, was a Marxist who fought against the economic injustices in Latin America and the capitalist dictators that did nothing to alleviate their people's poverty. He fought specifically against the capitalist system of commodification — that is, the fruits of impoverished people's labour being exploited by those from wealthy countries. Now, we find T-shirts, mugs, hats, posters and calendars emblazoned with Che's image, mass-produced — often by the labour of marginalized or impoverished people who are not paid a fair wage — and sold to the mainstream as an image of so-called rebellion, rebellion devoid of Che's original meaning. Elizabeth Hurley, a British movie star, was photographed a few years ago holding a Louis Vuitton handbag embroidered with an image of Che. Alexander Boldizar summed up this example of commodification quite succinctly:

> Fans would point out that he was a Marxist fundamentally opposed to the fetishization of commodities. Detractors would mention that at La Cabana he executed several thousand of exactly the sort of people who'd be most likely to shell out several thousand for a handbag. Lawyers would point out that Korda [the photographer of the famous Che image] was never paid for the intellectual property rights of the photograph. And even those who are neither fans, nor detractors, nor lawyers, who simply admire his picture as a countercultural symbol, must get a bit of cognitive dissonance when that symbol is on the most bourgeois of bags. (2008)

In short, the image of a man who spent his life fighting the commodification of labour has now been commodified. This example points to the deep underlying dynamic of the commodification imperative: empty the meaning from anything and everything human and humane; reduce all to the essence of capitalism — things, people, emotions and rights are only meaningful as products to be bought and sold as the basis for profit-making. Yet, is this process complete and all encompassing? Does everyone go along with the commodification imperative?

This new text, then, that is created when the practice of tattooing is appropriated from Eastern cultures is important in making sense of the ways in which the women I spoke with understand their tattoos. But to see this tattoo process as only commodification falls short because it does not recognize the constant shifting in the specific meanings of and narratives surrounding tattoos,

> The commodification imperative: empty the meaning from anything and everything human and humane; reduce all to the essence of capitalism — things, people, emotions and rights are only meaningful as products to be bought and sold as the basis for profit-making.

political or otherwise. The ways in which we talk about tattoos has changed (as analysts like DeMello argue). I agree it has and must in order for tattoos to reach the place in mainstream culture where we see them today. However, I suggest that, though tattoo discourse has changed as tattoos have become commodified, tattoo wearers — particularly women — are not merely marking themselves with a product devoid of any meaning except that of a popular commodity. That is, tattoos are not simply a commodification meant to represent a sense of false individuality — they are more complex than that, and they can represent genuine cultural connections made by women as they undertake their tattoo projects. More generally speaking, the sense of individuality and authenticity that tattoos represent for some women constitute one of the ways in which women negotiate conformity and resistance in a patriarchal, capitalist culture. In this sense, then, cultural commodification is nuanced and, in the case of tattoos as a form of self-identification, the struggle for self-identity is indeed one of the ways in which women confront and resist the on-going capitalist effort to turn everything into a commodity, including permanent body modifications. The ways in which women negotiate and interpret seemingly traditionally feminine tattoo images also represents women's abilities to be agents in the resistance of patriarchy. While tattoo culture often relegates women to consumers of acceptably feminine tattoo designs and placements, women often create and negotiate their own fluid meanings for their tattoos, thus rejecting the need to conform to socially acceptable forms of expression. Tattoos and tattooing are, then, a window to this process of commodification and the resistance to it in patriarchal capitalism.

Historical Context

Tattooing reaches back thousands of years and can be found in nearly all parts of the world at some time (Caplan 2000: xi). Going back to colonial times, Westerners have had contact with cultures that revered tattooing. These practices eventually found their way into Canadian and U.S. culture.

North American (colonial) tattooing is rooted in the sea voyages of early European travellers of the late eighteenth and early nineteenth centuries. Explorers to the South Pacific came into contact with the tattooed Other in Polynesia, Micronesia and Melanesia. While Europeans had experienced tattooing as early as the 1600s, it was James Cook who first documented the "pervasiveness of 'tattooing' (a derivation of the Tahitian term *ta-tu* or *tatau*) among South Pacific cultures" (Atkinson 2003: 31).

European explorers' exposure to tattooed tribal natives had a profound effect — the explorers considered the tattooed natives to be savage and weird and saw tattooing as a frightening foreign ritual. Native peoples were captured and transported back to Europe with the explorers as "living evidence of primitivism in the New World" (Atkinson 2003: 31). Sold and paraded through European museums and sideshows, these individuals — women especially — were seen by Europeans as the "radical self-expression, physical vanity, and exuberant sexuality they had denied themselves ... in the service of their restrictive deity" (Atkinson 2003: 31). Many Natives were baptized and given new, Christian names in an attempt to liberate them "from their 'spiritual and physical slavery'" (Oettermann 2000: 195). Many European sailors returned home decorated with tattoos, exposing the upper and middle classes of European society to the practice and arguably "reaffirming [their] understanding of their own cultural advancement and progress, as the outwardly uncontrolled libidinal bodies of 'backward' tribal cultures of the world articulated a brutality long overcome in Western cultures" (Atkinson 2003: 31).

The practice among South Pacific Islanders changed too as a result of colonizers' visits. Tattoo designs soon came to include images such as ships, flags, guns, cannons and even portraits of European royalty. Their meanings shifted, as well. For example, Hawaiian tattoos were once thought to protect the person from harm, but after the introduction of guns and other weapons the significance of protective tattooing dwindled away. The Maori of New Zealand have traditionally tattooed their faces as a sign of status and lineage; however, after European explorers and colonizers began trading goods for the tattooed heads they found so fascinating, the Maori stopped tattooing their faces in fear of being decapitated (Govenar 2000: 213; Atkinson 2003: 32).

During this period, Europeans saw tattooing as both fascinating and deplorable — a paradox of sorts — and interpreted the tattooed body as a source of exotic entertainment. Sailors tattooed their bodies as both a keepsake of their overseas adventures and as a form of excitement, setting themselves apart from the majority in European society. With more and more sailors coming home with cultural inscriptions permanently marked on their bodies, tattooing started to creep into mainstream European culture and eventually (colonial) North American culture (Atkinson 2003: 33). In 1876 at the Centennial Exposition in Philadelphia, some of the first tattooed native people were put on display for the enjoyment and wonder of the audience. Even as members of the Navy were coming home adorned with tattoos, the majority of European and North American society had little to no knowledge of the practice.

Taking their cue from the success of tattooed sideshow performers, tattooed Navy servicemen coming back from

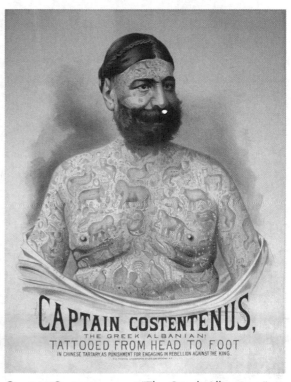

Captain Costentenus, or "The Greek Albanian," was first put on display at the 1876 Centennial Exposition and later toured with P.T. Barnum's New and Greatest Show on Earth
Source: Wikimedia Commons <https://commons.wikimedia.org/wiki/File:Captain_Costentenus.jpg>.

overseas started to exhibit themselves in travelling circuses and sideshows. Part of the attraction, however, was the notion of a savage native from a foreign land covered in frightening markings. As the Navy men were obviously of European heritage, they concocted elaborate back-stories to accompany their exhibitions. Many would claim to have been captured by savages and tattooed against their will, thus perpetuating the notion of tattooing as the frightening ritual of an "uncivilized Other" (Atkinson 2003).

The designs that were popular largely consisted of patriotic symbols, religious imagery and erotic illustrations of women. These designs, Alan Govenar (2000: 217) argues, constituted a "folk art form" generated by word of mouth and imitation. This folk art provides, to some extent, insight into the cultural context of the time, as tattoo artists were necessarily aware of the demands of their audience. The social coercion that the designs adhered to promoted not only conformity but also tradition, thus serving as a visual representation of important symbols of the day. Primarily patriotic and religious, these designs communicated loyalty, devotion and (oddly enough) conservative morals (Govenar 2000).

By the end of the 1930s, tattoo exhibits were becoming less exciting and exotic as more

Maud Stevens Wagner, wife of tattooer Gus Wagner, was a circus performer and one of the first known female tattoo artists in the U.S.
Source: Wikimedia Commons <https://commons.wikimedia.org/wiki/File:Maud_Stevens_Wagner.jpeg>.

and more people were becoming tattooed and exposed to tattoos. Tattooed performers then had to develop more elaborate back-stories to entice their audiences — such as the "abducted farmer's daughter," who was tattooed against her will — and women, in particular, found it necessary to dress more provocatively in order to maintain the interest of the audience (Govenar 2000: 225). As tattoos became more common, sideshow audiences turned to the circus for entertainment. To attract audiences, women took centre stage as tattooed attractions — women who were often the wives and girlfriends of tattooists or were simply lured into the profession with the promise of fame and fortune (Atkinson 2003: 35). The show then became somewhat pornographic, as women would take the stage and strip before the crowd, displaying their tattooed bodies. These shows became some of the most popular midway attractions through to the 1940s.

The introduction of tattoos into the carnival and sideshow exhibitions ultimately served as a means of exploring desires and emotions that were socially repressed at the time in a controlled way. Tattoos were seen as a form of deviance and tattooed bodies were considered savage and frightening. The sideshows provided the means for "North Americans to experience subversive pleasures with and tortures of the flesh without sacrificing commonly held cultural understandings of corporeal respectability" (Atkinson 2003: 36); that is, North Americans were able to enjoy these pleasures from a distance, without subjecting their own bodies to the taboo of marking the skin, which was seen as lacking respectability. This era firmly established the association between tattooing and social deviance, a particularly important connection to note as this association has carried through to the present. Returning home after the Second World War, servicemen found that their symbolically patriotic tattoos now held a great deal of negative social value. The significance and patriotism once associated with tattooing started to diminish, and by 1946 new recruits were no longer interested in becoming tattooed. Tattoos were even restricted in the military in the 1950s — if they limited the effectiveness of a man's ability to work (due to infection, for example), he would be prosecuted. In the context of the increasingly urban, family-centred nature of North American culture in the 1950s, tattoos were once again associated with disrepute and deviance. Societal values shifted toward material comfort and middle-class conformity, and tattoos were strongly identified with lower-class, criminal individuals and groups. Once a symbol of group expression and national pride, tattoos were now interpreted as a widespread sign of criminality (Govenar 2000).

Radical Shifts: Contemporary Commodification

The political upheaval of the 1960s and 1970s brought with it a great many cultural shifts, including the popular conception of tattooing. Women, in particular, began to question and fight normative notions of femininity and gender roles, resurrecting tattoos as a means of redefining themselves as women. Margot Mifflin explains:

> [Women] began casting off their bras as they had their corsets a half-century earlier, tattoos were rescued from ignominy and resurrected in the counterculture by women who were rethinking womanhood. The arrival of the Pill in 1961 had given women a new sexual freedom; a little over a decade later legalized abortion secured their reproductive rights. Not surprisingly, the breast became a popular spot for tattoos—it was here that many women inscribed symbols of their newfound sexual independence. (1997: 56)

With the swell of popularity — especially among women — in tattooing, the middle classes began to become involved in the historically marginalized practice. Cultural icons such as musicians and actors started to embrace the practice, thus enticing young, middle-class individuals to follow suit. While the popularity of the practice was already entrenched among the marginalized classes, the 1960s and 1970s saw an increase in its popularity among more privileged classes, thus introducing tattooing to the mainstream and drawing widespread attention to the practice. The designs that had held up since the early 1900s, however, were no longer of interest to young people. Not able to identify with the extremely patriotic imagery, they demanded more customized, personal images, which opened up the art to the appropriation of designs from other cultures. Tattoo artists as a whole also became a more educated, artistic group in keeping with the demand for more complicated, personalized designs. Young tattoo artists began to see tattooing as a representation of identity, "treating the body as less and less of a canvas to be filled with tattoos and more as an integral part of the self, the young middle-class insurgence into the tattoo artist profession redefined many of the old ideologies held strongly in the trade" (Atkinson 2003: 45). Artists experimented with different styles. and shops moved from the urban ghetto to the youth centres of the city.

The 1970s and 1980s saw more people than ever before embrace tattooing as a form of self-expression. Michael Atkinson explains this process:

> Influenced by political movements that shook conservative understandings of the body to the ground, interpretations of tattoos were more varied and subject to contextual

construction. As women and more "respectable" social classes participated in tattooing it transformed into a practice of political identity construction. (2003: 46)

By the 1990s tattoos had become mainstream phenomena, with scores of tattoo shops cropping up in many major North American cities. In the present context, therefore, artists must now be able to adapt to new styles, designs and needs of their customer base. New methods of communication, and thus, marketing, have brought a whole new dimension to the tattoo industry, with tattoo magazines, websites, message boards and online communities developing and flourishing, bringing artists and enthusiasts alike together "into an information-rich community of social actors" (Atkinson 2003: 48). As people are now able to learn more about the process of tattooing via online resources, as well as communicate with tattoo enthusiasts around the world, more and more people are being drawn into the practice as both tattoo artists and tattooees. According to the *National Post*, 21 percent of Canadians in 2013 had at least one tattoo (Faille and Edmiston 2013). The Pew Research Centre, based in Washington, noted in their 2010 report that "tattoos have become something of a trademark" for Americans entering adulthood (Kwong 2012).

As tattooing becomes more and more a mainstream phenomenon, the ability to decipher a tattooed body's authentic membership in a particular counter culture, while once quite apparent, now becomes not so easily done. Tattoos have become commodified — a trend, an immediate mark of individuality that can be bought and sold. Nevertheless, tattoos still serve as a means of communication. *What* they communicate, however, is indeed more difficult to determine.

Appropriation or Connection?

A typical non-critical commodification analysis argues that tattoos have become a false representation of self-identity — one that has been appropriated from the so-called dangerous classes and is lacking any real political meaning. Margo DeMello (2000, 2014), for example, makes just such an argument by examining the role of class hierarchy in the tattoo community, coupled with the re-inscription of the culture with the influx of middle-class wearers and artists in the so-called new generation of tattooing.

DeMello begins her investigation by outlining the history of Western tattooing and examines the state of the practice after World War Two, as technological, artistic and social changes were affecting tattooing. The introduction of academically trained tattoo artists, the use of tattooing as a counter-cultural symbol and the appropriation of exotic designs and images (as opposed to traditional, old-school Americana designs) created a shift in the culture, which DeMello refers to as the "Tattoo Renaissance." As a result of this cultural transformation, tattooing began to appeal to a more middle-class clientele. Within the new tattoo generation, there is the distinction between "high" and "low" tattooing practices, which have been perpetuated and maintained within the tattoo culture through media interpretations, academic approaches and publications produced from within the community. Media accounts in particular — both those produced within and outside the tattoo community — have had a significant effect on the polarization of the tattoo culture. Mainstream media have focused on the increased popularity of tattooing among more conventional individuals, ultimately softening the public image of the practice and making it easier to digest. Tattoo publications produced within the community have focused on fine art tattooing (or "high" tattooing), moving away from the biker and sailor image traditionally associated with tattooing (or "low" tattooing). These two main sources of information dissemination have redefined the tattoo community.

The reappropriation of what was considered a low-class art form is similar to the appropriation of 1940s Hollywood glamour in gay camp: camp being the "re-creation of surplus value from forgotten forms of labour ... by liberating the objects and discourses of the past from disdain and neglect" (DeMello 1995: 11). In this sense, camp involves the resurrection of objects and discourses of the past that are generally seen as negative and are forgotten — they are discourses that are taboo and lack respectability and are generally ignored by mainstream society. They are resurrected and reimagined for the dominant class's purposes. The problem being, however, that these forms are not forgotten but are actually still used by those so-called low-class people. DeMello argues that while the middle-class appropriation of tattooing may seem liberatory, it is in fact an illustration of how "characteristics of social difference are appropriated within our culture to provide the trappings of individual difference" (Williamson, cited in DeMello 1995: 11). The cultural appropriation of many traditions, then, is based on a pre-existing text through which new cultural symbols can be created; however, the middle-class appropriation of tattooing is different in that middle-class tattoo wearers do not possess the lower-class text (such as a similar socio-economic status) — thus that previous text is ignored and the new, middle-class text is created. Put another way, the appropriation of tattoos results in tattoos' origins and history in the practices of the "deviant" and marginalized (bikers, sailors, punks) being erased as middle-class tattoo wearers have no connection to or use for that history.

Perpetuating this new tattoo cultural text is the separation of low-class from middle-class (or biker versus fine art) tattoos. The separation of the two allows middle-class tattoo wearers to reject and separate themselves from a tradition historically seen as negative but still maintain the symbolic individuality. The distinction, DeMello argues, is upheld not for aesthetic reasons, but for political and social ones. Since the prior text has been rejected, and with it the prior history of tattoos (including their association with bikers, prisoners, sailors and prostitutes), a new history must be developed — one based on a "mythical, primitive past" (DeMello 1995: 13). This new, fictionalized past legitimizes a tradition historically seen as negative. It is through middle-class tattoo magazines (like *TattooTime* or *Inked Magazine*) that this past is perpetuated and introduced into the public discourse. *TattooTime's* first edition (*The New Tribalism*), as well as RE/Search's *Modern Primitives,* represents this desire to return to a primitive past and to naturalize the practice of tattooing.

So has tattooing's negative past been effectively eliminated? DeMello argues that it has not, the evidence being tattoo culture's increasing presence in the mainstream, especially given tattooing's shady roots, through both mainstream and alternative media publications. She argues that, if anything, this presence illustrates "the power of the media to effect, if not real social change ... at least symbolic transformations" (DeMello 1995: 14).

While the cultural appropriation of Eastern tattooing history is important in understanding the context in which the contemporary tattoo industry resides, I found that the women I spoke with used the stories or narratives about their tattoos as a means not of appropriating something, but rather of connecting them *with* something: a history, a cultural belonging or a sense of identity. Tattoos have necessarily become commodified and bereft of meaning, partly in using the narratives from Eastern culture, in order for them to be made acceptable to the mainstream and middle-class. The women I spoke with, however, recognized their tattoos' commodified nature and were able to find meaning through connecting their tattoos with their sense of identity. Thus, these links are not understood as cultural appropriation, but rather cultural *connection*. In these terms, we can see the nuances of appropriation and the complexity of the ways in which it permeates contemporary tattooing practices. Moreover, the ways in which the women used tattoo narratives to make connections and to give meaning is representative of the struggle and tension that they face as tattooed women and the ways they reconcile these challenges. It is in hearing these narratives that we can see how, like cultural narratives generally, they are changing and shifting over time, from one historical era to another. That is, tattoos can be seen and interpreted as a fad or a commodity by some, but their meanings to tattoo wearers are nuanced and shifting. For the wearers, tattoos have meaning beyond their appropriation by mainstream culture as a meaningless product to be bought and sold.

The Fluidity of Tattoo Discourse

As the meanings of tattoos change so too does the language we use to discuss them. How do we understand them? How do we think about them? Analyses not critical of the commodification process often say that the mainstream media, academic publications and tattoo artist/enthusiast publications are responsible for shaping the way that the tattoo community is presented and understood and thus the way people, both tattooed and not, talk about tattoos.

The mainstream media have portrayed tattooing and the tattoo culture in the past as something to fear (tattoos are for deviants, tattoos are dangerous, and so forth). Media coverage now focuses on the increasing popularity of tattoos. Explaining what tattooing *used* to be and who *used* to get tattooed illustrates the practice's "seedy" roots and association with nefarious characters and then focusing on the new generation of tattooed people — the middle-class, educated people — effectively silences those groups of people (such as bikers and prisoners) who were traditionally associated with the practice. By selecting those who are interviewed, the mainstream media choose who is allowed to talk and who is given a voice. Academic representations of the practice are similar in that they highlight the distinctions between middle- and low-class tattoo users and fail to recognize the possibility of the media's role in creating this distinction in the first place. Also in line with mainstream media's presentation of the practice is academia's failure to elaborate on low-class tattooing, such as the distinctions between the tattoo use of bikers, sailors and prisoners, for example. This is dismissed in favour of a focus on the popular use of artistic tattooing.

Those who are given a voice all seem to say the same thing and use the same discourse to talk about their tattoos. Borrowing from the self-help discourse of the 1970s and 1980s, these new-generation tattooed individuals discuss how tattoos have given them a sense of individuality, aided in their personal growth or heightened their spirituality. These motivations for becoming tattooed can be easily contrasted with the reasons people (such as bikers) *used* to give for getting tattoos: they were drunk, they wanted to prove their masculinity, they were rejecting middle-class life and all of its meanings or they had no real reason at all. Mainstream media representations are made to be easily accessible and understandable to even non-tattooed readers:

> By first focusing their articles around a select group of middle-class individuals, most of whom have relatively small, inoffensive tattoos; by second, denying all of those who do not fit into this category the right to be represented, except as the absent unit of comparison; and third, by centering the discussion around ideas which are very popular outside of the tattoo community, the journalists are able to make the world of tattooing a safe and understandable place. (DeMello 1995: 6)

While tattoos may be seen as counter-cultural, the contemporary discourse around them is not: combining popular self-help and personal growth discourse with middle-class, educated tattooers and tattooed people, contemporary representations of tattooing feature it as a safe and accessible phenomenon.

The new discourse surrounding tattooing borrows from the self-help discourse of the 1970s and 1980s, as tattoo enthusiasts see tattooing as an identity-altering practice. The self-help movement is a combination of pop-psychology and self-awareness that began in the 1970s and still continues today:

> Self-help describes a movement whose adherents use psychotherapy, twelve-step programs, and other psychological techniques to become happier and to eliminate negative behaviours or attitudes such as codependency, depression, and eating disorders, or to achieve loving relationships with others. (DeMello 2000: 144)

This movement appealed to "therapeutic sensibilities" (Lasch, cited in DeMello 2000: 144) and an increasing interest in mental and emotional health and the power that is "ascribed to the individual will in achieving this" (ibid.). Additionally, the new age movement, which began around the same time, saw middle-class individuals experimenting with Eastern religions and "consciousness-transforming techniques" (ibid.), borrowing practices like Buddhism, tarot, Wicca and meditation. Within this social climate, tattoos came to be interpreted as a transformative practice, a way of getting in touch with one's spiritual essence. Many popular tattoo images and designs are derived from this new age philosophy, such as zodiac signs, yin yang or Sanskrit and Japanese writing. With modern Western society seen as repressive, alienating and lacking ritual, non-Western symbols and practices were adopted as they were thought to be more meaningful than those found in Western culture. It is through narratives derived from the self-help and new age movements that people developed meaning for their tattoos. DeMello argues that these meanings are especially important "within a middle class context that traditionally has not viewed tattoos in a positive light," and that they "form the basis of the individual's personal understanding of his/her tattoo" (2000: 149).

Judy, thirty-two, has one tattoo and explained that while she is proud of it, and sees it as a symbol of her strength and independence as a woman, most people are shocked to find out that she has one:

> I think sometimes it surprises people when they find out that I have a tattoo. Like, I have a fairly recent new group of friends that I've been hanging out with. I happened to mention that I had a tattoo and all of the girls were very shocked. I know this group of friends happens to be middle class to upper middle class. I think they don't really see a white, middle-class girl getting a tattoo. Those are the people that are a little more shocked and don't see it blending with my personality.

Judy's friends seem to understand tattooing as a practice that derives its meaning from the marginalized classes.

Thus, three main narratives have shaped the new generation of tattooing — its redefinition and reinscription — and are used to describe tattoos by this new generation of tattooed individuals: individuality, spirituality and personal growth. These themes, DeMello argues, have shaped both the nature of the tattoo community and the meaning of the tattoo. The increasing middle-class participation in tattooing has resulted in a transformation of the tattoo culture itself.

DeMello found that while both men and women favour narratives of individuality, spirituality and personal growth, women alone also explain their tattoos in terms of control, healing and empowerment. Women were more apt to interpret their tattoos as a means of reclaiming their bodies — women's bodies are, as many scholars (see Butler 1999 and Grosz 1994, for example) have argued, the site "for the inscription of power and the primary site of resistance to that power" (2000: 173); thus women may interpret their tattoos as a means of marking their bodies in an effort to negate the marks of oppression and patriarchy they feel on their bodies. While the most common narratives have been popularized and are thus more popular among the middle class, the themes of empowerment common among tattooed women do not fall within such definitive class boundaries. Lower-class women, DeMello notes, have had much more experience using their bodies as a site of resistance (through, for example, clothing and hairstyles) and, similarly, have been getting tattooed for much longer than middle-class women have. Despite this, however, DeMello argues that heavily tattooed women of both classes "can be said to control and subvert the ever-present 'male gaze' by forcing men (and women) to look at their bodies in a manner that exerts control" (2000: 173). DeMello even connects this sense of control and empowerment to the tattooed ladies of the 1920s and 1930s circuses and sideshows — in important ways, these women were independent and decided to make a living for themselves. While women today do not get tattooed to earn a living, it can be argued that tattoos on women serve as a sign of independence.

These anti-patriarchal discourses have, indeed, been influenced by dominant middle-class liberatory discourses, and the women (myself included) who see their tattoos as a means of securing an empowering identity connect with and infuse their own tattoo narratives with references to opposing the male gaze. Nevertheless, tattoo narratives, like any discourse, are constantly changing. They are used to "re-create," both for the teller and the listener, the complex justifications for the tattoos — justifications that are constantly changing. As tattooing becomes mainstream, however, many tattooed people's claims that their tattoos are deeply meaningful and spiritual come into question, which, according to DeMello, suggests a class backlash: "The very same middle-class tattooists who were at the forefront of the renaissance now look nostalgically back to the old days of blue-collar values" (2000: 191). While Judy may not necessarily subscribe to the "blue-collar values" of earlier tattoo wearers, she recognizes and notes the ways in which the mainstreaming of tattoos has left many, as some would argue, devoid of meaning:

> When I see women with flowers and Chinese characters, they don't know what they're saying. They're white like me and they have Chinese chicken-guy-cue on the back of their neck or on their foot. That really irritates me. They're trying to be cool. They're trying to be something and that's not the way to do it. I don't feel tattooing is the way to make you free and strong and independent. It might be a symbol of that for some people but, just looking at other women, it really depends on the individual tattoo.

Judy interprets the preponderance of tattooing as having a negative effect on the practice as a whole, with symbols and designs permeating the industry and effectively lessening the power of some individual tattoos. The increasing popularity of tattoos creates a whitewashing effect: in order to stand out, one will have to wear increasingly more visible and subversive tattoos. Sara echoed this sentiment:

> It's become such an everyday thing that it really takes something quite extraordinary for me to be like, "Wow, that's cool." Like, if I see a woman who has a whole back piece or something insane, that's rad. … Women who aren't tattooed, I look at them and I'm like, "Wow, you're pure."

Sara's comment illustrates the changing discourse around tattooing. While at one time a tattoo can be seen as shocking — to Judy's friends, for example — in another context, tattoos become an "everyday thing" and it is instead those *without* tattoos that become shocking.

While the research on tattoo discourse is indeed helpful in understanding the ways in which the women I spoke with tell their tattoos, much of it falls short in that there is the argument, or often just the assumption, that contemporary tattooing has lost its message or become meaningless outside of the capitalist culture of commodification and consumerism. It is here that we need to turn again to the fluidity of tattoo discourse (as with all discourse) rather than to glorify the easy-to-read tattoos of the days of sailors and bikers. While it has been argued that the traditional, working-class tattoo was characterized as "lacking in sophistication and significance and is worn by people who put very little thought into their tattoos" (DeMello 2000: 193), a number of tattoo artists today are arguing that classic Western tattooing did, in fact, have a simple, recognizable message that has been lost in contemporary fine art tattoo imagery, tattoo trends and tattoo magazines. DeMello notes:

> The traditional American tattoo — with its easy-to-read imagery that reflected the old-fashioned values of God, mother, and country — is being displaced in favor of the contemporary tattoo, with its often unrecognizable imagery and exotic content. The contemporary tattoo is high fashion, but at the same time alienates those whose tattoos are no longer favored. (2000: 193)

These traditional tattoos are able to tell a story all by themselves while contemporary tattoos often require the wearer to construct a narrative in order to explain them. Given the discussions I had with the tattooed women, I maintain that contemporary tattoos hold just as much meaning as did the traditional designs. It is through adapting their tattoo narrative to the historical, social and cultural context of the moment that contemporary tattoos remain meaningful to tattoo wearers through the wearer's lifespan. While traditional designs may have seemed simplistic in their message, I believe that the overarching association with deviance was perhaps the most overt message they delivered. The story they are able to tell all by themselves is one that we have come to understand through a changing discourse. Just as an eagle meant something in the early part of the century, a Chinese character or a flower means something today. After all, not all tattoo wearers construct elaborate stories to connect their tattoos to a larger history. As with Sara, for example, some women find meaning not in the specific tattoo but in its resultant marking, that is, in the experience of being marked as tattooed.

> It is through adapting their tattoo narrative to the historical, social and cultural context of the moment that contemporary tattoos remain meaningful.

Five Tattooed Women

Karen is a 38-year-old Mohawk mother of two. She teaches Aboriginal History of Canada and works as a student advisor. She got her first tattoo, a unicorn on her arm, when she was sixteen, and since then has collected five more tattoos, the majority of which hold personal family and cultural significance for her. At nineteen, she had a dragon tattooed on her hip, "Just for fun … because dragons are cool," and a small frog and mushroom on her shoulder that she told me she would likely get covered up in the future. Years later she had the unicorn covered with a large tribal piece on her left arm and shoulder that is based on tribal designs from around the world, which is "intended to represent the concept of all [her] relations." On her right arm she has a wolf that was done in honour of her grandfather, who is a member of the Wolf Clan. On her right leg is a turtle surrounded by Celtic knot work, which she explained is in honour of her parents: "Because my father's Turtle Clan, because my grandmother's Turtle Clan, it's matrilineal, and my mom's British so I have the Celtic knot work." Most recently, she's had the confederacy wampum belt tattooed across her back. She had been intending to get this particular tattoo for the past ten years, but the time wasn't right until recently, when she completed her master's degree. "And then when I start my Ph.D., I'm going to get my status card tattooed on my ass," she said.

When Karen started getting tattooed as a young girl, however, tattooing wasn't the mainstream practice that it is today. "I'm old enough to remember when it was an act of rebellion, not conformity, and that's exactly what it was. I left home at a very young age, so I was a street kid, and it was part of that culture," she said. When I asked her what made her choose her first design, a unicorn, Karen told me about her experience getting that tattoo:

> I was at a big house party at a flop house, because I mean we were all street kids, and there was some guy who had just gotten out of Stoney [Mountain Penitentiary] with his little homemade jail gun and was like, "Hey anybody want a tattoo?" And that was pretty much what he knew how to draw, one of the things he knew how to do. So [I said] "Okay." So that's kind of how I got that one. But, I mean, it's covered up now.

Karen describes her tattoos as an expression of her identity, of her self. For her, tattoos represent both her "ethnic and cultural identity as well as [her] spiritual beliefs." "Your body's a temple," Karen continued. "You've only got it once, you might as well paint the walls, right?" In addition to representing her cultural and spiritual identity, her tattoo projects have all been thought out and planned in consultation with her artist to balance both her body and the art. "All of my tattoos have been thought out," Karen said, "I mean, there's a reason behind them all. They either mark a point in my life or they have some sort of meaning. It's never just sort of 'Oh that looks cool, put it here,' which so many tattoos today are."

Sara is 26 years old and a recent graduate from a community college communications program. She has three tattoos, the first of which, a line drawing of a woman that would eventually become a part of Salvador Dali's painting "The Burning Giraffe," was a gift from her parents for her twenty-first birthday. Six months after her first tattoo, she had a piece done on her calf — a collection of images from one of her favourite books, Clive Barker's *The Thief of Always*, that represent key ideas that the book portrays. "It's a tree with a tree house in it and its got a kite and the tree house has a ladder doing down and then there's a fish coming up on the bottom; it's all just different parts from the book," said Sara. A short while later, Sara had three large peonies, her favorite flower, tattooed on her right arm.

Unlike many women that I talked to, Sara doesn't associate any deep, personal significance with her tattoos: "I didn't get them because I had gone through some horrible trauma, and I didn't get them because I wanted to make a particular statement." Sara explained to me that she got her tattoos for aesthetic reasons — "Because I like them" — rather than to cover a particular body part or relay a particular message to others through her choice of design. Sara explained that she does not immediately identify as a "tattooed person" and chooses not to show them off. What is important to her, however, is that her tattoos are unique, not easily defined and not something you would see on either the wall of a tattoo shop or the arm of another tattoo enthusiast. She takes pride in her tattoos, even though, as she explained, some think of them as "weird."

Kendra e-mailed her responses to my questions, as she is currently living and teaching

English in Thailand. A 23-year-old, Kendra had the Chinese characters for "true love" tattooed on her left calf seven years ago, at 17. She chose this design because, as she explained, true love is something she believes in and aspires to. After spending some time in Paris, France, the "city of romance," ideas of love were floating around in her head: "True love represented the hope I had (and still have) for the future. I decided on Chinese because my best friend is Chinese Canadian and I always thought the language looked beautiful." Kendra's tattoo makes her feel special and hopeful, and it serves as a reminder for her never to "settle." She sees her tattoo as a legacy, a means of self-expression, "like holding the answers to a secret."

Kendra told me that once she was tattooed, she felt older, if at times a bit "cliché" given the popularity of Chinese characters as a tattoo design. At one time shy about her body, Kendra started wearing clothing in an attempt to show off her tattoo and is now really happy with her choice of location, as it is a place on her body that won't change as she ages: "At least it won't get saggy and gross like if it was on my boob or my tummy."

Kendra was initially worried about the pain and the ability to cover the tattoo, as once she is finished with her time in Thailand she will be working as a teacher in Manitoba, where there are strict guidelines concerning the visibility of body modifications. She explains, "When I was in university and student teaching I heard a principal say he would 'never hire anyone with a visible tattoo.' Funny thing was the grade 1, 2, 5, and 6 teachers all had tattoos. Guess they never told him. I stuck to wearing pants."

Katie is a 28-year-old graduate student of theology. She has two tattoos, both of which were completed within a year and a half of each other: one is a simple, open concept line drawing of a dove on her left shoulder; the other is a large "vine with Greek text as the trunk" starting at her foot and ending about five inches above her knee. The text is "Koine Greek, which is what the New Testament was written in, and it's a Bible passage, and it translates into 'Lord I believe help my unbelief.'" Raised Mennonite and having worked as a youth pastor for four years, Katie's faith has been and still is a large part of her identity. As well, the image of peace that she has tattooed on her left shoulder is something she feels constitutes her self. While Katie is proud of her faith, she told me that people react to her differently once they find out that her leg piece holds religious connotations:

> That's probably one thing that makes me uncomfortable with my leg piece, is when people ask what the text means, all of a sudden they find out that I'm a person of faith, and they react to me differently. I don't want people to feel like I'm trying to evangelize to them because I've got this, it's my faith and it's my faith struggle and my faith journey. That's why I got it. It had nothing to do about wanting the world to know.

Despite some of the negative reactions to her tattoos that she gets from people, Katie finds the fun in it as well: "In the back of my mind I have a couple of joking translations that I would give people because who the hell's going to understand Greek? Like, if I'm out at a bar and some person is like, 'Hey what's that mean?' [I'll say] 'Look but don't touch' or 'It's all Greek to you.'"

Once she had the piece on her leg done, Katie realized she was "that girl with the huge-ass tattoo on her leg." But she doesn't mind the attention. Alternative culture has always appealed to her, so she felt that it made sense for her to have such a visible tattoo. While being so visibly tattooed noticeably changes the interactions she has with people, Katie isn't ashamed of her artwork, but rather sees her body now as more of a potential canvas for future projects.

Lynda is 54 years old and has two sons, aged 13 and 29. She got her first tattoo for her fiftieth birthday, and her eldest son went along and got one too. The tattoo, a small purple lily on her chest just under her collarbone, symbolizes a number of things for Lynda: lilies are a symbol of rebirth, which correlates to her entering a new stage in her life and celebrating moving forward; she chose purple as it is one of the highest energy centres for chakras; and purple is also a colour associated with royalty, as she explained that "anyone who knows me knows that I kind of like to be the Queen of Everything." Lynda had also given considerable thought to the placement of her tattoo. It was located on a part of her body that wouldn't change much over time and could be easily covered, and because the location was easily visible to her, the tattoo acts as a reminder that this is a good stage in her life. She researched tattoo studios in Winnipeg with her eldest son, who had already been tattooed and was quite encouraging of her decision to be tattooed, for about two to three years before she had it done. Lynda first spoke with an artist at one studio with whom she did not feel comfortable before finally finding a place that felt right.

Lynda explained to me that fifteen years ago she thought of tattooing as a strange practice, but now she finds happiness in having this pretty piece of art permanently on her skin. While she told me that she has always had issues with her body image, Lynda said that her tattoo has changed how she sees herself. "Finally having something that is quite pretty that I chose leaves me more open to accepting [my body] because it's the part of me that's always going to be beautiful," she said. Being tattooed later in life has made an impact on her self-identity as well:

> I think it did make a difference because reaching your 50s is a difficult age, I think as women we all have those goddess archetypes in us and I know my Aphrodite had been submerged for many years and it was like a coming out, and I mean, it's very simple, it's just a little tattoo, but it really is quite powerful.

Additionally, because her generation has not subscribed to tattooing in the same way that younger generations have embraced it, she enjoys the "shock impact" when people see that she is tattooed. Working with a number of people who are younger than her, she said, "I'm the age of their mothers and their mothers aren't getting tattooed, so that obviously sort of switches things around for them, and somehow this tattoo takes a few years off, makes me more contemporary maybe?" In this regard, she has fun with her tattoo — keeping it covered most of the time at work, as it is still something that is personal for her, but showing it off in particular settings or when the topic comes up in conversation. "People don't know what to do with it sometimes, so I just have fun with it; it's just fun!"

These women use tattoo narratives to make connections to a number of things: for

Karen, her tattoos connect her to her cultural heritage and to a past in which tattooing was considered an overt form of rebellion; for Sara, tattoos serve as a means of marking her as different; Kendra's tattoo connects her to culturally important notions like friendship and love; for Katie, her tattoo is a connection and reminder to her struggles with her faith; and for Lynda, her tattoo connects her with a sense of identity. However, the connections made are done so in the context of a capitalist and patriarchal culture.

Tattoos Commodified

While these five women all have different reasons for being tattooed, and approach tattooing in different ways, they share the fact that they have become a part of a culture that is growing like wildfire. Tattooing has moved from the sphere of the rebellious and into the mainstream over the past few decades, helped in part by its use in advertising campaigns (7-Eleven's Inked energy drink, for example) or television programming, such as *Miami Ink* and *LA Ink*. Tattoos have saturated our culture to the point where they no longer garner the immediate shock and attention that they did many years ago. In some important ways, tattoos have become normalized.

This normalization of tattooing was not lost on the women I interviewed. During our conversations many of the women said they regard tattoos in much the same way they do any other element of fashion. As Breccan, 27, told me: "It's like permanently wearing a very flashy skirt or something." Katie said that she doesn't particularly feel a bond with other tattooed women, as it has become such a popular form of body modification: "It would be the same as walking down the street and seeing someone dressed in the same style that you dress." Karen associates her tattoos with fashion as well, in the sense that they are an extension of her personality, "like wearing fancy shoes or a really nice dress or something like that, except it's permanent."

Some of the women I spoke with commented that today there are so many people with tattoos, piercings and other body modifications that it is those who are "pure" — those who are without any modifications — that may be the true rebels. That is, they see tattoos as having become "trendy." Sara noted that as tattoos have become so much a part of our culture now, when you see someone who doesn't have a tattoo, "they're almost prevailing more, and they're almost like the anti- or counter-culture now."

So, knowing and given this (commodified) context in which the practice of tattooing is presently situated, is that all there is to the story? Do women simply see tattoos as fashion or do they see them more as a struggle to incorporate resistance, to invest their tattoos with some political context and meaning? The women I spoke with understand that tattoos have become commodified, rendered "normal" and fashionable, but how do they negotiate this? Given the context in which tattooing has become normalized, what, in spite of this process, makes them different? Despite the inarguably powerful effects of patriarchy and its ability to shape and influence the lives of women and how they consume popular culture (including tattoos), women remain active participants in this process. Women are, as Brenda Austin-Smith (2007: 83) argues, "capable of constructing alternative and often resistant meanings from the most conventional and conservative texts." There are a number of ways in which the women I interviewed negotiate this tension between the conformity associated with tattooing, given its mainstream popularity in Western culture, and their efforts to resist that commodification in the endeavour to construct an authentic sense of self.

Reconciling Trendiness/Maintaining Authenticity

> I don't think I would relate to somebody who had a massive tribal tattoo on their arm just for the sake of getting one. I think that's, I think that's part of the big issue is just, like, getting one just to say you have one. (Amber, 21, five tattoos)

As I mentioned at the outset, authenticity is a theme and term that is used in a variety of ways. For the women, authenticity can be an expression of long-term commitment, uniqueness and individuality, as well as a partial reaction to trendiness and fashionability, as Amber alludes to. Each woman I spoke with understood and talked about authenticity — overtly or otherwise — and desired to make connections that are shifting or to locate herself in a larger historical context. The nuances of what it means to be authentic and how one can connect in a legitimate way through her tattoos ultimately highlighted for me that appropriation is complex and certainly not a linear process. The nuances represented by the women's understandings of their tattoos also put DeMello's argument in a new and more complicated light.

The women I spoke with have agency — they aren't, and none of us are, empty vessels into which mainstream (and shifting) culture is simply poured. While they are aware that tattooing has become a trend, they are constantly both reconstructing and relocating themselves within this process of mainstreaming, of trendiness. Reconciling the desire to express themselves on their own terms and the desire to be regarded as authentic is not an easy task. Karlie, a 22-year-old insurance claims adjuster with three tattoos, reflected this point:

> Well, I think there's a lot of people who, you know, critique tattoos, think that every tattoo has to be very personal, have huge deep meanings, and it can't be like, funny or whatever. But as much as I do agree with them in some sense, that your tattoos should mean something, they don't always have to be serious. That's just me. I plan on getting some ridiculous tattoos, but other people would look at those and be like "Well why the hell did you get that? That's absolutely ridiculous." But, I don't know, I think some people take it a little bit too seriously, and sometimes I'm completely guilty of that. Even though I'm getting them, I'm judging people for them. But a lot of people just take it really seriously and they don't always need to. But on the flip side, some people don't take it seriously enough and get little fluffy unicorns on their lower back.

Karlie's comments illustrate the complexity of issues that tattooed women are faced with in their decision to get tattooed. Rejecting the need for a personal story to contextualize a tattoo design, which in its mainstream popularity has become a sign of *in*authenticity to some tattooed women, can lead to the opposite: choosing a tattoo design that is devoid of meaning, which Karlie suggests is similarly inauthentic. The women I spoke with have recognized this difficult binary; yet, they have found ways in which to work around it and justify for themselves the legitimacy of their tattoo projects.

Karen has tattoos that are all strongly connected to her family and spiritual identity. Although, when she started getting tattooed in the late 1980s and early 1990s, tattooing was a means of rebellion for her:

> Well, I guess there was always a push [for me] to be unique and different. I was never mainstream. You know, I was never one with the crowd and it was just one way of making myself distinct and making myself unique, right? I don't fit in and that's totally cool. So it's just another way of expressing that, really.

Karen has also witnessed the change in the industry itself, along with the public perception of tattooing:

> Back in the day it was illegal, right? We just did it out the kitchen, right? I mean, like, I'm old enough to remember when getting tattoos were an act of rebellion as opposed to conformity. Which is really what all mine are, um, and, I mean, back in my day people would cross the street to avoid you if you had piercings and tattoos and looked like a punk rocker, with purple hair, right? And they did, people would look at me like "Holy shit, you're a freak." Now people don't even blink twice, it's become mainstream. So yeah, some of my earliest tattoos were work done in the kitchen, with home made guns and things like that, the jail house style, because, I mean, you really didn't have much of a choice back in the 80s.

Despite the development of the industry into a mainstream practice, Karen locates herself as someone who remains committed to tattooing's rebellious roots. She doesn't see herself as subscribing to trends. Rather, given her own lengthy history with the practice, tattooing constitutes for her an act of rebellion *and* a means of adornment — no matter how much more difficult it may be to define tattooing as rebellious in today's culture.

For Sara, the uniqueness of her tattoos serves as means of separating herself from the mainstream. She explained, "I never felt the need to be like, 'Oh I think I'm so boring-looking that I need to go do this or that,' because I think everybody fits in their own niche. But I think my tattoos just sort of set me apart a little bit more." When she made the decision to get tattooed, Sara knew she wanted to get something that was a little different: "I didn't want to just go down and pick out from all the artist flash …. I didn't want to get something that everybody else would have." In this way, Sara locates herself outside of the trendiness and the mainstream because her tattoo projects are not easily defined and not something typically found on the walls of a tattoo studio. She explains her "unusual" tattoos:

> I guess you have to kind of really look at it and sort of figure out and discern what everything is. … So, I think that they make a statement that I've chosen to do something

to myself to sort of differentiate myself from the masses. But in the same breath, I don't want it to seem like I felt that I was some ordinary plain Jane to begin with.

Despite her tattoos setting her apart from the mainstream, Sara recognizes that tattooing is still very much "an everyday thing," but she doesn't get wrapped up in the popularity and hype of the practice: "People make a much bigger deal out of it than I ever made out of getting them, and, like, honestly sometimes I forget I have them." This suggests that, while her tattoos serve as a connection to a counter-cultural practice that is seen as somewhat deviant, Sara has chosen to reject the claims to celebrated, definitive individuality that has propelled the practice into the mainstream to begin with. It is clear that, in these terms, authenticity is a complex phenomenon.

Additionally, the women find their own meaning and context within the practice by connecting it with events in their lives, honouring their family members or honouring their faith. For Lynda, the decision to become tattooed wasn't one that was tied up in her subscription to a new trend. In fact, she admitted that in the past she found the practice strange. Instead, she sees tattooing as a permanent way to celebrate herself — as a rite of passage in turning fifty. She explained, "Well a lily is a symbol of rebirth, and I was very excited about getting it to symbolize entering a new stage in my life, becoming a crone, that whole moving forward celebration." She also expressed her understanding of tattooing as a new art form for women to explore:

> I think mostly men had owned the art, or the realm, and I think it's our new art form. Maybe we've pushed the limits more, because I don't think anyone's really encouraged us, women, to get tattooed. But I think it could have to do with it being a safe way for women to express themselves, because you can do it but not be in somebody's face about it. You don't have to talk about it. It's just a statement.

Katie sees her tattoos as a part of her identity. Her faith is a large part of her identity, and her tattoos reflect that. For her, tattooing is not about participating in a trend, but rather is about her struggle with her own faith: her leg piece reads, "Lord I believe help my unbelief." In her words:

> That's the story of my faith. I've spent a lot of years not believing and a lot of years believing but still being uncomfortable with believing. I've been a minister; I was a youth pastor for four years, full time. It was really hard. I mean this, it comes from the book of Mark, and I'm not really one of those people to sit around and quote Bible passages, but this one just stuck with me because it takes faith to say "Lord I believe help my unbelief." It really leaves room for questions and doubts and insecurities about it and all that kind of stuff.

It is also evident that the women are not all getting tattooed for the same reason; they have very different, and often very personal, reasons for getting a tattoo. What is similar among the women, however, is the personal narrative that each constructs by way of explaining her tattoos. These narratives, like other cultural discourses, are expressed in similar, learned terms. Kendra, for example, attaches a great deal of personal meaning to her calf tattoo — the notion of "true love" is something that holds a lot of significance for her in her life. She explains:

> True love is something that I believe in. True love meaning the ultimate love — something that is real, romantic, unique, extraordinary, beautiful, passionate and life long. I got the tattoo when I was quite young and I saw true love in everything. I was really hopeful about love despite never having been in a relationship at that point. I saw relationships in movies, on television, in magazines and in school. The concept of true love was always floating around in my head. What sealed the deal was when Pacey on Dawson's Creek named his boat "True Love" in an episode. I could see true love everywhere and knew that it had a strong meaning for me. I wanted something as special as that in my life, I believed in it.

This idea of love is one that is learned through dominant discourse — television shows, for example — and Kendra's tattoo, as it connects her to the idea of true love, suggests an expression of emotional value. Tattoos, in this regard, can connect us with learned cultural values. For Kendra, being tattooed was a way of expressing her desire for true love and having a tattoo feels like "a legacy." Her tattoo provides her with a message of hope:

> Sometimes women settle, and I wanted my tattoo to remind me to never settle. I have seen love fall apart and I have seen people fool themselves into thinking they are in love. True love is the ultimate experience in love and something that I hope to experience in my life. I think I am on my way. In fact, I know I am.

While Kendra acknowledges the "cliché" of having Chinese characters tattooed on her, she maintains her claim to authenticity — her justification for the originality of her tattoo — as she was the first of her friends, and the first of many of her classmates, to be tattooed:

> It made me feel special to have something with so much personal meaning in it. I also felt a little cliché at times. Chinese characters aren't exactly unique. I got a lot of attention for being the first kid in my class to have a tattoo. Soon after, two of my friends got one. They both got lower back tattoos and both regretted their decisions afterwards. They didn't spend a lot of time thinking about their designs. One decided in two weeks, the other in one week. But as for me, I was really proud of my tattoo and thought it was special. It made me feel special and hopeful to have the message on me.

In this way, authenticity can take on several meanings — in Kendra's case, being the first of her classmates and friends to be tattooed lent her tattoo (which she acknowledged as "cliché") a sense of legitimacy in its originality. The meaning of her tattoo has shifted, as she implied, as the design she chose has become quite popular — at once new and original, the symbol of the Chinese character is familiar. For Kendra, the meaning of her tattoo remains a permanent reminder of her hope for true love being a part of her life. In this regard, tattoos are somewhat paradoxical, as they are about permanence, but at the same time their meanings shift and change.

In the same way that the reasons for getting tattooed vary from woman to woman, the importance placed on tattoo projects by the women shifts over time, suggesting that significance is a fluid concept. Jenn, a 28-year-old legal assistant, who sports a large tribal back piece in addition to a group tattoo that she had done with her sisters, explained to me that tattooing has become less of a priority as she's grown older:

> Yes, the years I was getting my back done, it seemed like the most important thing to do. But now with a mortgage and trying to start a family it's not really something I think about. I mean, it's there and it's part of me but it's not something I think about every day — it doesn't define me anymore.

Interestingly, some of the women reject the need to attach personal significance to their tattoos, thereby resisting the self-help discourse that locates tattooing as a means of personal growth. For instance, Sara was aware that some women were motivated to get tattooed as a way of coping with difficult life experiences: "I think it's great, you know, if somebody who's had some horrible trauma done to them and then they need, this is something that they need to do to heal themselves, then right on." But this was not Sara's motivation. April, 27, who has a chrysanthemum tattooed on the side of her torso made this point more directly:

"Well I'll just find a meaning for tattoos after I get them. Meanings of tattoos will always change too."

> I don't personally think that everyone does it to make a statement, because, like mine, a lot of people ask me if there's any meaning behind it, and I'm like "No not really."… It shouldn't have to mean anything. If you want there to be a meaning behind it, look up the actual meaning of it, like the phoenix rising out of the fire, or the particular type of flower. Like, there's always going to be a meaning behind something. If it's personal, for personal taste, then that's your meaning. Like, the meaning is who you are and why you have it on you.

Similarly, Ryse, a 21-year-old woman with five tattoos, told me that her notion of meaning is not static, but rather always changing: "Well I'll just find a meaning for tattoos after I get them. Meanings of tattoos will always change too."

Commodification or Resistance?

With the new generation of tattoo enthusiasts comes a new text through which tattooing is understood — a new history, focusing on the Japanese or Polynesian roots of tattooing, effectively distances middle-class tattoo wearers from Western tattooing's low-class, marginalized roots. In order to market tattooing as a safe, acceptable commodity by which to mark your individuality or identity, capitalist culture has framed the practice in terms

> Their construction of tattoo narratives to tell the story of their tattoos were ways that these women could make connections with, rather than appropriate, a larger history.

of its ability to aid in personal growth, as a rite of passage or a marker of strength similar to the uses of tattooing among tribal cultures.

DeMello's theory helps to make sense of the ways in which tattoo discourse has changed over the years and the nuanced and often complex ways in which tattooing is interpreted and perceived by contemporary enthusiasts. Indeed, the women I spoke with echoed the complexity of issues that arise with the decision to become tattooed and the motivations for becoming tattooed. The ways in which these women understand and talk about the meanings of their tattoos, necessarily shaped and informed by the discourse of tattooing that permeates the current social climate, reflect DeMello's argument. Personal significance and authenticity play large roles in the ways in which these women construct their tattoo projects, and the fluidity of meaning and authenticity then necessarily affects the ways in which tattoos are perceived and discussed. Their construction of tattoo narratives to tell the story of their tattoos were ways that these women could make connections with, rather than, as DeMello argues, appropriate, a larger history.

Additionally, the messages relayed by the women show that the commodification argument may be too simple. Rather than see contemporary fine art tattoos as unrecognizable and exotic, the women find meaning in their tattoos through their adaptation to the changing nature of tattoo discourse. It is through their tattoo narratives that their tattoos resist conformity and remain authentic — be that original, legitimate or sincere long-term commitments to the culture of tattooing — *despite* its commodification. This would suggest, more broadly speaking, that the commodification of cultural artifacts does not necessarily strip them of their political content. While cultural commodification, or "eating the Other," is a mechanism in consumerist capitalism by which the culture of marginalized people can be and is appropriated and repackaged to be sold to the mainstream — what would appear to be the process of stripping those aspects of their meaningful, non-consumption, non-market content — the political content does not, it seems, disappear entirely. While capitalist culture often neglects human rights and human-ness in the interests of marketing goods that are seen as having no meaning other than profit, rendering them devoid of real human meaning, it would appear the commodification of tattoos is not complete. It is true that tattoos have now become a means of selling products: blockbuster films often use tattoos as a way to distinguish rebellious or edgy characters; more and more popular musicians of all genres are tattooed, and ad campaigns use tattoos to sell anything from energy drinks to credit cards (see Kosut 2006). They have gone from being a sign of deviance to a form of body modification that is acceptable by the mainstream. The difference, however, is that the tattoo is one product that cannot be bought without being intimately linked to its actual production. As Mary Kosut notes:

> While capitalist culture often neglects human rights and human-ness in the interests of marketing goods that are seen as having no meaning other than profit, the commodification of tattoos is not complete.

As a tattooed person, you are the witness, participant, and life-long bearer of a unique production process; a process in which the producer and consumer unite in complicated exchange that is simultaneously ritualistic, economic/consumeristic, and individualistic. (2006: 1041)

Along with the actual process of getting a tattoo, the women I spoke with were able to find meaning, meaning that often shifted over time and adapted to their lives and identities, while recognizing the commodified and gendered nature of their tattoos. People want and need meaning in their lives, meaning deeper than fashion and consumerism — that is what underlies the narratives the women attached to their tattoos. Oppressive institutions like capitalism and patriarchy can be and are resisted on a number of levels. In the case of tattooing, the women I spoke with were able to access aspects of tattooing's past — despite its commodification — to find meaning and value.

Glossary of Key Terms

Appropriation: The ways in which cultural practices, often those of marginalized classes or peoples, are claimed by dominant society and re-purposed for their own use. An example would be the ways in which Eastern tattooing practices were claimed and re-purposed by Western society in an attempt to legitimate tattooing for mainstream society.

Authenticity: The desire to create a legitimate, original self-identity through tattoo projects in the face of the commodified and gendered nature of tattoos; a sincere, long-term commitment to a tattoo; and the sense of uniqueness that comes from being marked as different.

Commodification: The inherent process in capitalism to extend the market into ever more areas of human life, rendering all things, including humans themselves, meaningful only as products to buy, sell, and consume as a means to making profit.

Cultural commodification: bell hooks, for example, refers to cultural commodification as "eating the Other." Cultural commodification is the practice in capitalism within which a particular cultural aspect, often of a marginalized group, is appropriated, stripped it of its original meaning and repackaged for the consumption of mainstream society.

Identity: A person's sense of self, those aspects that distinguish a person from those around him or her.

Old school tattoos/tattoo designs: Images made popular with the introduction of tattooing to Western culture by sailors are referred to as old school tattoos/tattoo designs. These images — such as flags, ships, knives, snakes, panthers, roses and erotic images of women and mermaids — invoked patriotism and masculinity.

Other: Othering refers to the way in which those not a part of the dominant class, race or gender are (mis)represented and (mis)treated by mainstream society. Marginalized classes are seen as different and inferior and treated as such. Othering is an expression of power by the dominant over the marginalized.

Questions for Discussion

1. What are some cultural artifacts, other than tattooing, that have been appropriated by Western society?

2. What kinds of problems can arise when subcultures are commodified? What benefits are there?

3. What are your own impressions of the practice of tattooing? What do you think of someone when you see that they are tattooed?

4. Were you surprised at all by the ways in which the women talked about their own tattoos?

5. How does the way in which the women in this chapter interpret their own tattoos and resist conformity reflect on the ways in which everyday people can resist capitalism and patriarchy?

Resources for Activism

Body Modification Ezine: www.bme.com
Inked Magazine: www.inkedmag.com/tattoos
Margot Mifflin: www.margotmifflin.com
Sailor Jerry Tattoos: www.sailorjerry.com/tattoos/
Tattoo Artist Magazine: www.tattooartistmagazine.com

References

Associated Press/CBS News. 2007. "Tattoos Lose Their Cool: Want a Blasting Berry Tattoo with That Fruit Roll-Up?" December 4. <cbsnews.com/stories/2007/12/04/entertainment/main3573970.shtml>.

Atkinson, M. 2002. "Pretty in Ink: Conformity, Resistance, and Negotiation in Women's Tattooing." *Sex Roles* 47.

Austin-Smith, B. 2007. "Feeling Framed: Emotion and the Hollywood Woman's Film." In L. Samuelson and W. Antony (eds.), *Power and Resistance: Critical Thinking About Canadian Social Issues, 4th edition*. Halifax: Fernwood Publishing.

Barlow, M. 2001. *Blue Gold: The Global Water Crisis and the Commodification of the World's Water Supply, revised edition*. Ottawa: Council of Canadians. <canadians.org/water/publications/Blue_Gold.html>.

Boldizar, A. 2008. "Handbags of the Apocalypse." *Asian Contemporary Arts and Culture*. <cartsmag.com/articles/detail.php?Title=Handbags%20of%20the%20Apocalypse&ID_Comment=29>.

Braunberger, C. 2000. "Revolting Bodies: The Monster Beauty of Tattooed Women." *NWSA Journal* 12, 2.

Butler, J. 1999. *Gender Trouble: Feminism and the Subversion of Identity*. New York: Routledge.

Caplan, J. 2000. "Introduction." In J. Caplan (ed.), *Written on the Body: The Tattoo in European and American History*. London, UK: Reaktion Books.

CBC. 2004. "Body Art: The Story Behind Tattooing and Piercing in Canada." *CBC News Indepth* <cbc.ca/news/background/tattoo/>.

DeMello, M. 1995. "Not Just For Bikers Anymore: Popular Representations of American Tattooing." *Journal of Popular Culture* 29, 3.

____. 2000. *Bodies of Inscription: A Cultural History of the Modern,* Durham & London: Duke University Press.

____. 2014. *Body Studies: An Introduction,* New York: Routledge.

Faille, M., and J. Edminston. 2013. "Graphic: The Tattoo Industry." *National Post online*, August 16. <news.nationalpost.com/news/graphics/graphic-the-tattoo-industry>.

Govenar, A. 2000. "The Changing Image of Tattooing in American Culture, 1846–1966." In J. Caplan (ed.), *Written on the Body: The Tattoo in European and American History*. London, UK: Reaktion Books.

Grosz, E. 1994. *Volatile Bodies: Toward a Corporeal Feminism*. Indiana: Indiana University Press.

Hawkes, D., C.Y. Senn, and C. Thorn. 2004. "Factors That Influence Attitudes Toward Women with Tattoos." *Sex Roles* 50.

Health Canada. 2001. "Special Report on Youth, Piercing, Tattooing and Hepatitis C: Trendscan Findings." <phac-aspc.gc.ca/hepc/pubs/youthpt-jeunessept/>.

hooks, b. 1992. *Black Looks: Race and Representation*. Cambridge, MA: South End Press.

Kosut, M. 2006. "An Ironic Fad: The Commodification and Consumption of Tattoos." *Journal of Popular Culture* 39, 6.

Kwong, M. 2012. "Tattoo culture making its mark on millenials." *CBC News Canada*, September 19. <cbc.ca/news/canada/tattoo-culture-making-its-mark-on-millennials-1.1149528>.

Marx, K., and F. Engels. *The Communist Manifesto*. Halifax: Fernwood Publishing.

Marxists.org. n.d. "Encyclopedia of Marxism: Commodification." <marxists.org/glossary/terms/c/o.htm#commodification>.

Mifflin, M. 2001. *Bodies of Subversion: A Secret History of Women and Tattoo*. New York: Juno Books.

MSNBC. 2007. "Tattoo Ads Turn People into 'Walking Billboards.'" November 26. <msnbc.msn.com/id/21979076/ns/business-us_business/t/tattoo-ads-turn-people-walking-billboards/#.Tr7WmPFZQZc>.

Oetterman, S. 2000. "On Display: Tattooed Entertainers in America and Germany." In J. Caplan (ed.), *Written on the Body: The Tattoo in European and American History*. London, UK: Reaktion Books.

Roberts, A. 2008. "Privatizing Social Reproduction: The Primitive Accumulation of Water in an Era of Neoliberalism." *Antipode* 40, 4. <onlinelibrary.wiley.com/doi/10.1111/j.1467-8330.2008.00623.x/full>.

Torgovnick, M. 1991. *Gone Primitive: Savage Intellects, Modern Lives*. Chicago: University of Chicago Press.

Widdicombe, S., and R. Wooffitt. 1995. *The Language of Youth Subcultures: Social Identity in Action*. New York: Prentice Hall.

13

Hidden Rainbows in Plain Sight

Human Rights Discourse and Gender and Sexual Minority Youth

Tracey Peter and Catherine Taylor

You Should Know This

LGBTQ Rights in Canada Timeline

- 1967 - Justice Minister Pierre Elliott Trudeau declares, "There's no place for the state in the bedrooms of the nation."
- 1969 - Consensual sex between two adults of the same sex over the age of twenty-one is decriminalized.
- 1977 - Quebec prohibits discrimination on basis of sexual orientation.
- 1992 - Justice Minister Kim Campbell ends ban on gay and lesbian people in the armed forces.
- 1995 - Supreme Court rules that "sexual orientation" should be read into the list of prohibited grounds of discrimination in the *Charter of Rights and Freedoms*.
- 1996 - Sexual orientation is added to the *Canadian Human Rights Act*.
- 1999 - Supreme Court rules in favour of same sex couples' adoption rights.
- 2005 - Canada legalizes same-sex marriage.
- 2009 - Ontario Ministry of Education requires school districts to implement policies and programming to support LGBTQ -inclusive education.
- 2013 - As a way to promote safe and inclusive educational practices, the Manitoba Legislature passes into law Bill 18, which, among other things, amends the *Public Schools Act* that requires educators to accommodate students who want to start LGBTQ clubs, such as gay-straight alliances. Similar legislation is being passed or considered in other provinces/territories.
- 2016 - The federal Liberal government introduces Bill C-16, which will update the *Criminal Code* and the *Canadian Human Rights Act* to include "gender identity and gender expression" as protected grounds from discrimination and hate. The Bill is the first to be put forth by the governing party in the House of Commons.

IN THE YEARS SINCE IT WAS PROCLAIMED IN 1982, the *Charter of Rights and Freedoms* has come to function as Canada's chief nation-building document in the crucial sense of providing a mechanism to protect disenfranchised citizens from forms of racism, sexism and other systems of oppression "in and before the law." Because of the Charter, lesbian, gay and bisexual (LGB) people have been able to use the court system to overturn provincial and federal laws that discriminated against them in areas such as property, hospital visitation, marriage and adoption rights. Because of this progress on the juridical front, it is often said that discrimination against "gay" people is a thing of the past. Legislation that would also protect transgender people from discrimination on the grounds of gender identity or gender expression was introduced by federal Liberal Minister of Justice Jody Wilson-Raybould on May 17, 2016. Even though several private member's bills have been introduced in the past, this is the first bill that has been put forth by the governing party in the House of Commons. The Charter has been opposed all along by socially conservative groups, who regard it as Left-wing social engineering: those same groups still denounce the inclusion of sexual and gender minority people in Charter protections, since they see this as caving in to the "homosexualist agenda" (see, for example, Canada Family Action Coalition). Nevertheless, while activists and social theorists alike are well aware that discrimination persists in the Charter era, and that legal equality does not necessarily translate into social justice or social equality, the Charter has tremendous symbolic value in legitimizing marginalized people, a value that goes beyond its admittedly limited spheres of legal application. Indeed, the symbolic value of the Charter has been so broadly endorsed in Canada that it is now a cornerstone of social studies curricula in which school children and youth across the land learn that Canada has a proud tradition of upholding minority rights and celebrating diversity.

Yet there is a disconnect between official Canadian human rights discourse and the experiences of sexual- and gender-minority people, who continue to suffer from discrimination in various spheres of everyday life, both public and private. For example, even the innocuous everyday practice (for cisgender heterosexual [CH] couples) of holding hands with one's partner is still unsafe for sexual minority couples in the vast majority of public places in Canada, and identifiably transgender people remain at high risk of harassment and assault in the simple act of entering a public washroom. Sexual- and gender-minority Canadians encounter discrimination and disrespect in their families (being evicted, not being allowed to be alone with family children, partners not being welcome at family gatherings); in their religion (being shunned, expelled, required to be celibate); in employment (being denied an interview or advancement within an organization for reasons ostensibly unrelated to sexual or gender identity) and in housing (being denied rental accommodation, being ostracized or harassed by hostile neighbours). They may encounter hostility from homophobic and transphobic restaurant staff, sales clerks and health care providers who express their disapproval of LGBTQ people in ways ranging from the subtle (being less respectful than with other clients) to the blatant (flat refusal of service).

Admittedly, this grim picture is not universally true of life for all LGBTQ Canadians, nor in all places in Canada. Although most LGBTQ Canadians are resigned to enduring the daily indignity involved in not demonstrating public affection for their partners, many live relatively openly, in stark contrast to the almost unbroken practice of self-concealment, known as being in the "closet," of a few decades ago. This is especially true of middle- or professional-class Canadians living in major urban centres who seem conventionally gendered (masculine male or feminine female), are not members of socially conservative groups or faith traditions, are not Indigenous or members of racialized groups and are not under the age of eighteen.

In fact, most Canadian youth spend much of their lives in a world seemingly untouched by the legal and social advances of recent decades: the world of school culture. The disconnect between human rights discourse (legal equality) and lived experience (social equality) is demonstrated acutely in the high levels of both symbolic violence and direct harassment of all kinds that sexual- and gender-minority youth reported in the "First National Climate Survey on Homophobia in Canadian High Schools" (Taylor et al. 2011). The findings of this study are referred to throughout this chapter. Findings from several additional projects – namely, the "Every Teacher Project" (Taylor, Peter, Short et al. 2016, 2015), the first national survey of trans youth (Veale et al., 2015) and a national survey of school superintendents (Taylor, Peter, Edkins et al. 2016) — are highlighted here as well.[1] While distinct in ways suggested here, the experiences of high school students illustrate, at least in part, the contours of experience for all LBGTQ people in Canada.

What Does LGBTQ Stand For?

LGBTQ is an acronym for "Lesbian, Gay, Bisexual, Trans, Two Spirit, Queer and Questioning" people and is an umbrella term for all sexual-minority (lesbian, gay, bisexual) and gender-minority (transgender and transsexual) people. Gender minority ("trans people") includes transgender people, whose gender expression and sense of self do not match mainstream gender conventions for their birth sex, and transsexual people, who seek sex reassignment surgery in order to bring their bodies into alignment with their sense of gender. "T" also stands for "Two Spirit," which is an identity term used by many Indigenous LGBTQ people. Some LGBTQ people identify as "Queer," often to signify their opposition to what can be seen as an apartheid-like system of sexual and gender categories that oppresses anyone outside the mainstream. "Q" also stands for "Questioning" since high school-aged youth in particular are often just figuring out their own sexual and gender identities. They may feel same-sex attractions, for example, but wonder if they can be heterosexual, or they may think they are gay but realize eventually that they are transgender.

What Is Homophobia?

Homophobia denotes a broad spectrum of social-climate indicators of hostility to LGBTQ people, ranging from casual use of pejorative language to violent personal attacks. Although a problematic term in some ways, "homophonbia" is a much clearer term than alternatives, such as "heterosexism" and "heteronormativity," since it keeps the focus on active hostility to LGBTQ people rather than broadening the focus to include subtler forms of discrimination (an issue that is also worthy of study and critique). The term is used here not to invoke an individualistic concept denoting an irrational fear of homosexuals, but instead to refer to a sociological concept with an established history of denoting hostility to LGBTQ people. This hostility is the logical and often intended product of social institutions (such as families, places of worship and school systems) that are implicated in creating and re-creating relations of inequality (see, for example, Pharr 1988; Murray 2009).

What Is Transphobia?

Transphobia refers to discrimination against individuals based on their expressions of gender or gender identity. Many trans people also experience homophobia, when their gender identity is incorrectly equated with homosexuality. The experiences of LGB people (who experience attractions to people of their own sex, and who may or may not be conventional in their gender identity and gender expression) should not be confused with those of trans people (whose gender identity or gender expression does not match societal conventions of their birth sex, and who may or may not experience same-sex attractions). Transgenderism is in contrast to cisgenderism (or simply cis), which denotes someone whose gender

> Cisgenderism (or simply cis), denotes someone whose gender identity and expression match social conventions for the sex they were assigned at birth based on their body parts: the feminine female or masculine male.

identity and expression match social conventions for the sex they were assigned at birth based on their body parts: the feminine female or masculine male. To this end, CH-normativity represents a cultural and societal bias, often unconscious, that privileges CH identities and conventional forms of gender expression.

Why the Fuss?

Initiated by the 'It gets better' campaign, which was in response to several high profile suicides by LGBTQ youth, there has been a greater appreciation of hostile school climates and the negative impact they have on the wellbeing of Canadian youth. For example, in 2011 Jamie Hubley of Ottawa, Ontario, died by suicide. He was only 15 years old. After Jamie's death, his father, Allan Hubley, spoke out about how his son was repeatedly victimized at school. In one account, Hubley's father described how schoolmates tried to stuff batteries down his throat on the school bus. Jamie's "offense?" He was gay. Media attention to his and other young LGBTQ people's deaths brought the issue of homophobic bullying into the living rooms of the nation and the committee rooms of school systems.

In order to understand the more specific contexts that put LGBTQ youth at risk for suicide and other negative health and educational outcomes, we draw on theoretical perspectives that offer a more in-depth analysis of school climate. In this regard, school culture can be examined from a poststructuralist perspective, which enables us to appreciate how school climate is characterized by CH-normative discourse practices that are hostile to LGBTQ wellbeing.

Post-Structuralism

It is crucial to social change movements to examine discourse and language practices because they powerfully structure our sense of self and our social relations. This is the subject of post-structural analysis. Post-structuralists question the status of "common sense" and challenge mainstream assumptions (for example, that all teenagers are CH). To do this, they critically examine how social patterns become constituted, reproduced and contested — which are important analytical tools for resistance to oppression and working for change (Ristock 2002; Weedon 1997).

Within the context of homophobia and transphobia in Canada, post-structuralism is especially useful because it offers an approach whereby dominant discourses of CH-normativity can be critically analyzed in order to understand how life experiences are influenced by various social constructions. For example, heteronormativity is short for "normative sexuality," which refers to the way in which social institutions (especially familial, educational, religious and legal) overtly or covertly work to reinforce CH standards (Weiss 2001). Included within these dominant standards is the belief that all individuals fall into one of two, and only two, distinct cisgender categories: male or female; that sexual attraction is only "normal" when it occurs between two people of opposite genders and that each gender has certain natural or essential roles and behaviours to which all individuals should conform, depending on which sex they are assigned at birth based on their body parts. Those who critique CH-normative discourse argue that it stigmatizes alternative sexualities and ways of "doing gender" that do not conform to mainstream notions of heterosexuality or masculinity/femininity. Thus, critically investigating CH-normativity enables an exploration of the ways in which homophobia and transphobia become constituted through the power of discourse and how that power can be resisted.

Discourse

The study of discourse primarily stems from Michel Foucault's (1979, 1980, 1981) work. Foucault argued that, as humans, we are in a constant state of incarceration — we are imprisoned by the practices (including language practices) of modern social systems and institutions, which he calls "discourses." Foucault promoted the study of discourses (instead of focusing strictly on structural inequalities like capitalism and patriarchy) in order to analyze how "regimes of truth" are socially constructed or produced and attain the status of common sense that structures our lives. Drawing on Foucault's work, Janice Ristock (2002) maintains that critically analyzing discourses is useful because assumptions of what is normative are maintained through categories that include some (that is, those who are CH) and exclude others (such as LGBTQ people). Discourse analysis, then, can describe how who we think we are and how we act are created through an interplay of power and knowledge. As such, we can explore how the social constructions of cisgender heterosexuality (masculinity and femininity) form dominant discourses, which create truth claims and normalize the way all people should act and behave. Dominant discourses provide a working language to which all should conform (what Foucault called "docile bodies"). Similar to the position taken by symbolic interactionists, individuals become themselves the "bearers of discourse" by thinking and acting as though they really are what discourse requires them to be; however, a Foucauldian approach differs from symbolic interactionism in that the former draws on the "microphysics of power" to explain how power is imbedded within social structures and relations, while the latter is primarily focused on the micro-level aspects of daily social interactions without a specific theory of power (Dennis and Martin 2005).

   In Foucault's (1979) analysis, the social regulation of human behaviour through dominant discourses is labelled as "normalized judgement." Normalized judgement refers to a desire to produce conformity through the creation of a homogenous group whereby everyone is encouraged to adopt the same behaviour and enforce it in others. There is, however, an individualizing effect because each person is measured against the dominant discursive norm. This is achieved by measuring an individual against an essential criterion (or ideal type) of appropriate behaviour and then assessing how much of a gap exists between this individual and the desired norm. For LGBTQ people, the outcome of such discourse calculations is the effective stigmatization of their sexuality and gender expression/identity through CH-normativity.

The significance of normative discourses can be seen if we examine how social rules are often followed because of the threat of stigma on those who disregard or violate them. For instance, in order to secure normative ideals of cisgender heterosexuality, there need to be individuals who "fall" outside these socially constructed expectations. Creation of sexual and gender outliers or "others" is one of the ways that cisgender identity and heterosexuality are normalized.

Normalizing Gender

Feminist writers, such as Judith Butler (1987, 1990, 1993, 1996) and Denise Riley (1988), question approaches that dichotomize man and woman. They argue that the binaries of man/woman, or heterosexual/homosexual reflect universal, static and ahistorical assumptions where some individuals, women and homosexuals are oppressively relegated to the subordinate end of the dichotomy. Such dualisms deal strictly with difference and opposition. The problem with the rigid dichotomy within gender is that it depends on an obviously false binary split of femininity and masculinity as opposites that are strictly attached to female and male bodies, respectively. Only through deconstructing such social constructions can the regulative and normative formations of gender identity be exposed.

Especially in the case of gender identity, feminist theory has contested the presumed fundamental assumptions of masculinity and femininity because, like heterosexism, they prohibit the possibility of alternative accounts and experiences. Linda Alcoff (1988), for instance, acknowledges that gender is not a pre-discursive entity. In other words, gender does not exist prior to the ways we think and talk about it. Rather, it is a construction that is logically formalized through a matrix of practices and customs that most people consent to perform. Likewise, for Butler (1990), identity does not precede the performance of one's gender ("doing gender"), which is instead constituted through the convergence of multiple discourses (those of family, religion, media and so on) in our lives that supply the social and language practices appropriate to our assigned sex. Over the course of countless repetitions of these performances in childhood and adolescence, assigned gender comes to feel natural to many people, as though it arises directly from one's birth sex. "Doing gender," then, encompasses how males and females "perform" different roles in society, as though it is natural that they do so. But if gender is performative rather than a natural function of birth sex, why should all young people be expected to "perform" the feminine female or the masculine male and be stigmatized when they do not?

Within a performative framework, the ideals inherent in dominant discourses of masculinity and femininity are not suitable to all males and females. Although it could be argued that most people are more or less comfortable with playing their parts as laid out in CH-normative discourse, many are not, and it is nevertheless possible to resist discursively dictated norms of masculinity and femininity and to create alternative or resistant identities that perform subcultural variations of gender roles or identities.

Normalizing Heterosexuality

In *The History of Sexuality,* Foucault (1981) explores the "truth effects" of sex rather than its "origins." This is a crucial distinction, as the study of truth effects is much more interested in the consequences of beliefs being accepted as true than in whether they do in fact correspond to some objective reality. Because sexuality, as we experience it, is so powerfully structured by discourse, it cannot be specifically located or contained within an individual's body, nor is it a natural phenomenon. Rather, sexuality is formed within and informed by social forces. Sexuality, then, is something that is culturally constructed, sustained and reproduced through a collection of socially prescribed norms. That does not mean that without discourse there would be no sexual desire (or death, or sunrises); it means, rather, that our experience of sexuality is inseparable from the discourses about sexuality in which our lives are lived and that the feeling of "naturalness" is itself a product of discourse.

Foucault explains the inseparability of sexuality from discourse by arguing that the Victorian era (mid to late nineteenth century) saw a "proliferation of discourse" around sex in which sexual relations needed to be strictly regulated in order to produce and reproduce docile bodies that served the interests of the new industrial economy and social order. Sexuality was no longer seen as the property of just a body. Instead, it became the quintessential representation of self, which influenced the way people talked about sex. This "deployment of sexuality" operated through normalizing techniques, and created — via social discourse — "compulsory heterosexuality" (Rich 1980), which continues to be socially enforced.

As mentioned earlier, even today, years after the repeal of most discriminatory laws against lesbian, gay and bisexual people, heteronormative categories resonate in various communities. Implicit in CH assumptions are normalcy and naturalness, which thereby construct all other sexualities as abnormal and unnatural. Same-sex attractions and/or transgenderism continue to be stigmatized as deviant, and cisgender heterosexuality continues to be maintained in part through the social penalties for failing to conform, which range from fairly minor to brutal (an example of such brutality is Scott Jones of Nova Scotia, who was left a paraplegic in 2013 from being stabbed in the neck and the back because he is gay — see CBC News 2013). Cisgender heterosexuality, then, becomes regulated and is regarded as not just the normalized, but the *normal,* form of sexuality and gender identity.

> Same-sex attractions and/or transgenderism continue to be stigmatized as deviant, and cisgender heterosexuality continues to be maintained in part through the social penalties for failing to conform, which range from fairly minor to brutal.

Power/Knowledge/Resistance

Also central to a post-structuralist framework are the interrelated concepts of power, knowledge and resistance. Specifically, Foucault (1979, 1980) maintains that a conventional model of power focuses on the repressive state apparatus of law enforcement, overlooking the complex and multi-faceted existence of domination via the knowledge-producing institutions of society — institutions such as religion, psychiatry and education — which produce knowledge that comes to be accepted as the truth in our society. Foucault (1980) contends that power and knowledge are so implicated in each other that the two are inseparable; hence his use of the term "*pouvoir/savoir*" or "power/knowledge." Producing knowledge is seen as having powerful effects on people — a very different idea from the truism that (acquiring) knowledge results in one having power. However, Foucault was not interested in the exercise of juridical power through incarceration or corporal punishment, where there is little or no possibility of resistance, but rather in the kinds of power that are exercised throughout our social relations and that exist without use of brute force. For him, therefore, "where there is power, there is resistance" (1979: 95). Resistance is like power in that it has no life outside the relationship in which it is occurring; as a result, power and resistance can be examined only in particular contexts, and thus not by using generalities. Finally, resistance manifests itself in multiple ways because it is not a homogeneous, fixed phenomenon.

Such theorizing enables the examination of situations where someone, for example, may feel powerless in one instance (for example, students among teachers and school administrators) but powerful in another (for example, the same students participating in homophobic and transphobic bullying). The interrelatedness of power and powerlessness also allows us to conceptualize how people can be in a privileged and an oppressed situation at the same time.

LGBTQ and CHpeople alike are bound to dominant sexual discourses that locate them in very different positions in the social-sexual hierarchy — a hierarchy hat subordinates LGBTQ individuals. Nevertheless, it is possible to disrupt this control of sexuality by engaging in counter-discourses, such as LGBTQ rights, that challenge what is accepted as "real" or "natural." This allows space for "agency," or living out alternatives, where individuals do not behave like docile bodies; they thereby jeopardize the "naturalness" of everyday sexual knowledge and custom, exposing it as a set of oppressive fictions, and thus open up spaces for others to act in ways that dominant discourses otherwise foreclose.

Language

Knowledge is embedded in language, which does not always reflect "reality." Instead, language reproduces a world that is constantly in transition and is never definitive. Language, then, organizes experience and is not an expression of unique individuality; put another way, we are "born into language" and its representations of ourselves and our world. Its social influence in the construction of an individual's subjectivity is enormous. However, that process is neither fixed nor stable. We can conceive of language as a system of "signs." Embedded in each sign is a "signifier" (a sound, text or image) and a "signified" (the meaning of the signifier). For instance, there is nothing inherent to the term "faggot" — rather the meaning of faggot is produced in relation to other signifiers of sexuality, such as "straight," to which meaning is attached, and vice versa (Weedon 1997: 23). Language, then, is a powerful tool of oppressive discourses; in the spheres of gender and sexuality, language classifies and orders experiences by signifying cisgender heterosexuality as normal and any other ways of doing gender and sexuality as abnormal.

The best way to understand the effects of language is to analyze the discourse systems in which it is used. For example, language like "that's so gay" is pretty much an everyday occurrence that both draws on and reinforces homophobic and transphobic discourses. When such language is used, normalized discourses of femininity and masculinity as well as compulsory heterosexuality are reinforced because statements like "that's so gay" are usually used as analogous to "that's so stupid" and in so doing reinforce heterosexuality as "not stupid."

These processes of discourse and language play out in everyday life, not only enforcing CH-normativity, but also producing the counter-discourses of diverse sexuality and gender identities. Examining the discourses around gender and sexuality show that the "promise" of the *Charter of Rights and Freedoms* has been far from achieved when it comes to gender and sexuality.

Experiences of LGBTQ Youth

The case of homophobia and transphobia in high schools illustrates these general processes of CH-normativity, and resistance to it, in Canadian society. To give empirical substance to the general and theoretical discussions above, the results of a major study of homophobia and transphobia among students and young people in Canada are discussed below

A Questionnaire and Its Participants

The student climate survey questionnaire,[2] which was hosted on its own website in 2008–09, asked participants a series of questions on their school climate in the past year, with a particular focus on experiences of hostile climate, targeted harassment, impacts and interventions.[3] In total, 3,607 individuals answered the questionnaire. Their social characteristics are broad, representing much of Canada:

- Nearly three-quarters (71 percent) identified as straight/CH. One-quarter (26 percent) identified as LGB or Q, and 3 percent as trans.
- Participants were distributed among the regions of Canada (except Quebec): 25 percent were from British Columbia, 24 percent from the Prairie provinces (Alberta, Saskatchewan and Manitoba), 30 percent from Ontario, 15 percent from the Atlantic provinces (New Brunswick, Nova Scotia, Prince Edward Island and Newfoundland), and 6 percent from the North (Northwest Territories, Yukon, Nunavut and Labrador).
- Participants approximately represented the ethnic diversity of Canada, with 66 percent identifying as white/Caucasian, 19 percent as Asian, 6 percent as Indigenous, 6 percent as mixed ethnicity and 3 percent as "other."
- Almost half (46 percent) indicated that they lived in a small city or suburban setting, followed by 43 percent from urban areas and 11 percent from rural environments, First Nation Reserves or Armed Forces bases.
- The average age of respondents was 17.4 years, with a median age of 17 years.

The Hostile Discourse within Canadian Schools

It would appear that, despite any popular conceptions to the contrary, Canadian schools, like Canadian society generally, are an extremely hostile place for LGBTQ students. There is a good deal of symbolic violence in schools and elsewhere — LGBTQ people hear lots of homophobic comments, either directed at them or just voiced generally, all the time. Seventy percent of the surveyed students, for example, reported hearing expressions like "that's so gay" every day in school, and only 2 percent commented that they never heard such remarks in school. In addition, almost half (47 percent) of the students reported hearing remarks such as "faggot," "queer," "lezbo" or "dyke" daily in school, while only 6 percent commented that they never heard such remarks in school. The Every Teacher project (Taylor et al. 2015), conducted in 2013, confirms the widespread use of homonegative language in Canadian schools. Of the 3,319 educators surveyed across Canada, nearly half (49 percent) reported hearing comments like "that's so gay" at least weekly in their school, and only 12 percent indicated that they had never heard such comments. Over one-quarter (27 percent) of educators reported hearing homophobic comments such as "faggot" or "dyke" at least weekly at their school. The lower numbers from the Every Teacher project are to be expected given that such language is often used when teachers are not present (in hallways, washrooms and change rooms, for example). The societal persuasiveness of homonegative language ("that's so gay"), however, is so widespread that even teachers reported hearing it from their peers (22 percent), with 20 percent indicating that it was only in the staff room (and other non-student places) and 4 percent reporting that such language was used in the presence of students.

> Seventy percent of students, for example, reported hearing expressions like "that's so gay" every day in school, and only 2 percent commented that they never heard such remarks in school.

Not surprisingly, those who belong to LGBTQ groups are more likely to recall the use of hostile language. For instance, 81 percent of transgender identified students and 76 percent of LGBQ students recalled hearing the expression, "that's so gay," daily in school, compared to 68 percent of non-LGBTQ students. In terms of expressions like "faggot," "queer," "lezbo" or "dyke," over half of transgender (54 percent) and LGBQ (53 percent) participants reported hearing such remarks daily, compared to 45 percent of non-LGBTQ students. Similar differences were found in the Every Teacher project where 56 percent of LGBTQ educators (versus 47 percent of CH educators) reported hearing homonegative comments at least weekly in their school.

Even though the signifier "that's so gay" does not directly mean "homosexual," its signified message is that something is stupid or worthless. As one student wrote:

> The expression "that's so gay" is extremely commonly used but I've found that, more often than not, people don't use it as a way to verbally bash gay people, just simply as a synonym for "stupid" or "weird" and don't actually have the anti-gay beliefs behind the phrase.

For LGBTQ students, that means hearing a word that goes to the core of their identity used as a synonym for stupid or loser:

> Sometimes, people don't even realize what they're saying (that's so gay!). A lot of people don't care, even if they do offend others. Sometimes it is done on purpose to offend. Sometimes people "joke" about it ("Shut up faggot"). Then they laugh and say they were just joking, even though it could have been offensive anyway. Overall, people are becoming more and more negative towards people's sexual nature. Sometimes it is referred to as a joke, but anyone who is LGBTQ could be deeply offended by "joking."
>
> Fun Fact: I've counted myself hearing "that's so gay" and other homophobic terms up to around fifteen times per class. That's up to sixty times a day and usually (depending on the teacher and other students around of course) the language never gets dealt with unless I say something to try and stop it. I have never been a victim of homophobia, but I hear comments like "that's so gay" every single day at my school. Who wants to come out to that negativity?

As in all contexts, language is relational and is a powerful tool of oppression because it structures experience by signifying what is normal and what is not. Since the majority of students in the majority of schools across Canada regularly are subjected to hearing "that's so gay" in their school, the implicit message is that homosexuality is stupid and worthless and that heterosexuality, conversely, is cool and valuable. Such homophobic language practices draw on and reinforce heteronormative discourse in which LGBTQ identities are not recognized as acceptable or natural.

Negative gender-related or transphobic comments are very common in our society, as common as homophobic comments. For instance, men and boys who display feminine qualities are often chastised for acting like a woman/girl. Schools clearly illustrate this kind of discursive oppression. "Don't be a girl" is a common phrase directed at boys in high schools. Sexual- and gender-minority students were somewhat more likely to notice the use of transphobic language. More specifically, 79 percent of transgender and 69 percent of LGBQ students indicated that they frequently (daily) or sometimes (weekly) heard comments about boys not acting "masculine" enough, compared to 59 percent of non-LGBTQ participants. Further, 62 percent of transgender and 53 percent of LGBQ students reported hearing comments about girls not acting "feminine" enough on a daily or weekly basis, compared to 42 percent of non-LGBTQ students. Similarly, the U.S. Gay, Lesbian, Straight Education Network (GLSEN) survey found that 82 percent of transgender students heard remarks about boys not acting "masculine" enough sometimes, often or frequently, while 77 percent of their transgender participants indicated hearing comments about girls not acting "feminine" enough (Greytak, Kosciw and Diaz 2009). It is not surprising that trans students reported hearing transphobic comments more frequently than CH students, given that they would be the most aware about the rules of CH-normative discourse and the penalties for departing from them. In addition to trans students being more acutely aware of these remarks, it is also likely that such remarks are deliberately made in their presence.

Consequences of Violating Dominant Discourse

There are significant consequences for individuals, whether LGBTQ or CH, who violate the CH-normative rules of dominant sexuality and gender discourse. The contours and variations of these negative consequences are well illustrated by life in high schools. For students, this process occurred in three contexts: unsafe spaces, more directed forms of violence (that is, verbal and physical harassment as well as other forms of victimization) and the impact of such CH-normative violations.

Unsafe Spaces

There are a variety of spaces in everyday life that are not safe for LGBTQ people; spaces that CH people take for granted as non-threatening — some highly visible and public, some more hidden from view — ranging from restaurants to workplace hallways to elevators and stairwells. We gave students a list of places involved in everyday life at school (hallways, the cafeteria, classrooms, the library, stairwells/under stairs, the gymnasium, physical education change rooms, the school grounds, washrooms, school buses and spaces occupied while travelling to and from school) and asked them to identify any that they thought would be unsafe for LGBTQ students. Overall, 53 percent of all students identified at least one area at school that was unsafe for LGBTQ individuals. Not surprisingly, there was a positive relationship between sexual orientation/gender identity and how unsafe high school seems for LGBTQ students, with the students most stigmatized in CH-normative discourse being most likely to see school as unsafe for LGBTQ students. For example, 79 percent of transgender and 70 percent of LGBQ participants acknowledged at least one area of their school as being unsafe for LGBTQ students, compared to 47 percent of non-LGBTQ respondents. Moreover, compared to non-LGBTQ students, LGBTQ youth were significantly more likely to see the physical education change room (49 versus 30 percent), washrooms (43 versus 28 percent), and hallways (43 versus 25 percent) as unsafe, which is consistent with the GLSEN study (Kosciw et al. 2014) and the Canadian trans youth survey, where 44 percent of trans students reported feeling unsafe in school change rooms and 40 percent in school washrooms (Veale et al., 2015). It is interesting to note that two of these spaces are private areas (physical education change rooms and washrooms), while the third (hallways) is a public place. However, these three spaces are largely unsupervised, which makes them easy sites for student-to-student harassment.

The prevalence of homophobic harassment was highlighted by several students:

> During phys. ed. in grade 9, we could hear the guys in the boys' change rooms making fun of the other boys who weren't as "manly" as they would say, or as muscular as they were. They would call them pansies, fags, butt pirates, queers, anything homophobic … you name it, they most likely called them it.

> I was forced to drop my phys-ed class when my peers decided to not let me in the change rooms. I was forced to skip my wood shop class due to peers threatening me with equipment.

> I've been spit on by students and called a faggot, and each time I was in the hallways and there were like three teachers watching and they didn't do anything.

> I was threatened by a group of eight girls who cornered me in the washroom and demanded that I "shut my mouth, or they will shut it for me."

As is evident in these narratives, prejudice is more likely to occur in some places than others, depending on factors such as opportunity, exposure, presence of potential witnesses and the type of activity associated with the place (for example, showering and contact sports).

Directed Violence

The safety of a space is largely determined by the likelihood, or the perception of the likelihood, of encountering some kind of violence. LGBTQ people find many "normally" safe places to be ones in which they often encounter violent behaviour — verbal and physical — directed at them by others. This represents another more direct way that CH-normativity is enforced. Three out of five (60 percent) transgender students, 46 percent of LGBQ and 8 percent of CH students reported having had rumours or lies spread about their sexual orientation or their perceived sexual orientation at school during the last twelve months. Almost two-thirds of transgender (64 percent), 50 percent of LGBQ and 8 percent of CH youth were verbally harassed about their sexual orientation or perceived sexual orientation at school. In addition, 74 percent of transgender, 55 percent of LGBQ, and 26 percent of CH identified respondents reported being the targets of verbal harassment because of their gender expression. Tragically, 37 percent of transgender, 21 percent of LGBQ and 10 percent of CH students indicated that they had been physically harassed or assaulted due to their gender expression, while 25 percent of LGBQ and 20 percent of transgender reported they were physically bullied due to their sexual orientation. Findings from the trans youth project reveal that more than one in three (36 percent) transgender students reported experiencing an act of physical violence, and 9 percent indicated being threatened or injured with a weapon in the past year (Veale et al 2015). Similar results were found in the Every Teacher project (Taylor et al. 2015). For example, 67 percent of teachers were aware of verbal harassment of at least one LGBTQ student in the past year, 55 percent knew of incidents where rumours or lies were spread about a student's sexual orientation (or perceived sexual orientation) or his/her gender identity and one-third (33 percent) were aware of physical harassment.

These are not just statistics. They are real people suffering the real humiliation of a high level of directed violence:

> I got beat up in grade 10 for dating a girl. The people who jumped us got suspended, but we did also. It wasn't fair, I never asked to get beat up and I surely didn't deserve getting suspended because I got beat up.

> My friend and I both got sent to the hospital — and he's straight, but was just trying to help me. I feel bad that he got hurt, and we don't talk anymore 'cuz afterwards he had to leave the school as well for being labelled a fag for being known as my friend.

[I don't tell people I'm transgender] because I am worried what most people will think or say to me — I already get teased enough and I don't want to lose friends for being trans.

It isn't safe. I learned that the hard way at other schools. I had to transfer out of the public school system and my parents now pay tons of cash per year to keep me in a secluded school — and at this new place I don't risk my parents' investment by outing myself.

I can see why other people wouldn't want to come out here. It's because, quite simply, it's not a safe move. People here are VERY homophobic; to the point of violence/hate mail.

Clearly, there is a high level of victimization (as well as the depression, anxiety and fear associated with it) endured by LGBTQ students in Canadian schools. It is also important to point out that anywhere between 8 percent and 25 percent of CH-identified students reported experiencing directed violence due to their gender expression or perceived sexual orientation. In a school of 1,000 students, where up to, say, 90 percent are CH, translates to approximately ninety straight youth who are physically harassed or assaulted because they don't live up to the dominant discourses of gender within a school culture (that is, girls who are not feminine enough or boys who are not masculine enough).

> In a school of 1000 students, where up to, say, 90 percent are CH, translates to approximately ninety straight youth who are physically harassed or assaulted.

LGBTQ people experience many forms of physical violence up to, and including, murder. Certainly the tragic killing of forty-nine individuals at a gay nightclub in Orlando, Florida, by a lone gunman in June 2016 provides a frightful reminder of the horrifying consequence of some people's hate (see *New York Times* 2016). While such brute force is an extreme state and unlikely to occur in a school setting (we hope), educational institutions are not immune to horrible forms of violence. In schools, such brute force most often takes the form of bullying because of one's sexual orientation and shows clearly that gender makes a significant difference to the quality of the lives of sexual-minority students. Interestingly, female LGBQ students were more likely to be verbally and physically harassed than male LGBQ students (59 versus 43 percent, respectively, for verbal harassment and 25 versus 17 percent for physical assault). Female LGBQ levels of harrassment were similar to those of transgender students for most of the directed violence indicators (for example, 59 versus 63 percent for verbal harassment). It is sometimes perceived that the school climate (and the climate elsewhere in society) is less targeted at lesbians than at gay males because society in general is more tolerant of lesbians — being a lesbian or a bisexual female can even be trendy. The lives of sexual-minority girls and women refute these popular conceptions (see also Peter et al. 2015).

Impacts

Not surprisingly, these levels of violence and abuse have dire consequences for LGBTQ people. Harassment, violence and verbal abuse can only add to the stress levels in their lives. They feel emotionally distressed as well as alienated from the communities they live in. These stresses can lead to serious health consequences and are repeatedly regarded as factors leading individuals toward suicidal feelings that are often still acute in adulthood (Peter, Taylor, and Campbell 2016; Peter and Taylor 2014; Veale et al. 2015). Several students talked about the link between homophobia and suicidal behaviour:

> I was bullied so bad in grade 10 that I attempted suicide. I dropped out of school after that, after being pressured by my counsellor and principal to stay in the school, because they were afraid of increasing the drop-out rate.

> Bullies, I already get bullied enough and I self-harm and always think about suicide. I don't need any more things to deal with at school. If I came out about being bisexual, the bullying [would] increase!

Fortunately (as far as we know) these students did not commit suicide. Unfortunately, however, Jamie Hubley did, and the premature death by suicide of LGBTQ youth occurs far too often. For Jamie, being gay was certainly a factor in his suicide. In Jamie's situation, his family was supportive of him being gay; however, his school climate was full of mistreatment and misery.

The connections between homophobia/transphobia and acute mental distress are stark. For instance, over half (55 percent) of educators in our Every Teacher project were aware of LGBTQ students who had self-harmed due to experiencing homophobic or transphobic harassment, and 47 percent knew of a LGBTQ student who considered suicide. In terms of emotional distress, in our student climate survey we found that 78 percent of transgender and 63 percent of LGBQ students felt unsafe at school, compared to 15 percent of CH-identified participants. Moreover, 58 percent of transgender and 56 percent of LGBQ respondents indicated that sometimes they felt depressed about school, compared to 28 percent of straight students. Two students indicate just how hard it is to be a sexual minority (or to be perceived as one) in Canadian schools:

> Public school is probably one of the worst places to be different. I can't speak from experience, but homosexuals must have it so incredibly hard. To go into school each day knowing that people in those hallways would tear you apart....

> The vice-principal of my school used to be my guidance counsellor. I went to her because I was extremely depressed and wanted to commit suicide. She then found it necessary to point out that she goes to church every Sunday, and that all these things had nothing to do with me wanting to commit suicide.

Skipping school is one way to deal with feeling unsafe either at school or on the way to school. Thirty percent of sexual and gender minority students, compared to 11 percent of non-LGBTQ respondents, reported skipping because they felt unsafe at school or on the way to school. Transgender students were even more likely to miss school because they felt unsafe (44 versus 29 percent for LGBQ respondents). They

> Transgender students were even more likely to miss school because they felt unsafe.

were also more likely to have skipped more than ten days because they felt unsafe at school (15 percent, compared to 5 percent of LGBQ and 1 percent of non-LGBTQ). GLSEN reports similarly: 46 percent of transgender students skipped school due to feeling unsafe, and 13 percent indicated that they skipped more than five days (Greytak, Kosciw, and Diaz 2009).

Homophobic and transphobic bullying also leads students to feel less attached to their school communities. For instance, almost half of the LGBTQ participants (44 percent) strongly agreed (16 percent) or somewhat agreed (another 29 percent) with the statement "It is hard for me to feel accepted at my school," compared to fewer than one in six non-LGBTQ students (4 percent strongly and 12 percent somewhat). Transgender students were also more likely (55 percent) to disagree with the statement, "I feel like a real part of my school," compared to 41 percent of LGBQ and 25 percent of non-LGBTQ students.

These statistics are important, not only because of what they reveal about the degree of fear sexual- and gender-minority students experience on a regular basis, but also because of the potential impact missing classes can have on the academic achievement for these students. In short, the experiences of these students do seem to suggest that being on the outside of CH-normative discourse in a school setting where sexuality and gender norms are strictly regulated makes it much harder for LGBTQ students to engage with school life, either socially or academically.

Conflicting Discourses: Human Rights Versus Hallway Pedagogy

> Most of the gay community in my school are bullied. We all stick together, but that doesn't always help. Many gays are depressed because of this, and teachers and adults need to help and stand up for our community. We are not aliens, we're people, and we have rights.

Time spent in high school is very tumultuous for most students. However, as this student suggests, for sexual- and gender-minority students, high school represents not only a hostile experience, but also one that occurs in a deeply contradictory discourse context. On the one hand, schools promise safety and respect for all students. For example, students learn in social studies that Canada defends everyone's human rights and celebrates diversity/ multiculturalism. On the other hand, however, students witness the disrespect of LGBTQ students every day, and they often see their teachers look the other way. The combined pedagogical effect of these conflicting discourses is the message that the *Charter of Rights and Freedoms* applies to everyone but gay people — if it applied to them, more teachers would be saying something about all the abuse they take. It is no different for LGBTQ people in general — we live in a society that constantly proclaims the great freedoms we all enjoy.

Canada's twelve-year participation (ending in March 2014) in the war in Afghanistan, and the more recent bombing campaign of the Islamic State of Iraq and the Levant (ISIL), was defended everywhere as bringing freedoms, such as those expressed in the Charter, to people on the other side of the world. Yet, the promises of "life, liberty, and security of person" (as outlined in Section 7 of the Charter) conflict with the lived experiences of LGBTQ people.

> The combined pedagogical effect of these conflicting discourses is the message that the Charter of Rights and Freedoms applies to everyone but gay people.

Many school systems have begun to implement interventions that are designed to send the message that LGBTQ people are indeed entitled to the same rights as everyone else and that LGBTQ students are fully welcome in the school community. These interventions, such as gay straight alliance/gender and sexuality alliance clubs (GSAs), LGBTQ-inclusive curriculum and anti-homophobia and anti-transphobia harassment policies, can be thought of as counter-discourse and resistance strategies. Recently, superintendents across Canada reported on the forms and extent of school system interventions made in support of the wellbeing of LGBTQ students and staff in school districts (Taylor, Peter, Edkins et al. 2016). In total 141 school districts (36 percent of all districts in Canada) participated in the 2014 survey. Over one-third (38 percent) reported that their district has a policy that specifically addresses LGBTQ-inclusive education, which most often covered issues pertaining to harassment. But, what is the student knowledge of, and experiences with, anti-homophobia policies as well as GSAs?

GSAs

GSAs are official student clubs with LGBTQ and CH student membership and typically one or two teachers who serve as faculty advisors. In our Every Teacher project, over half of high school teachers indicated that their school had a GSA (Taylor et al., 2015). Superintendents report that 51 percent of their districts had at least one GSA or some other LGBTQ-specific club (Taylor, Peter, Edkins et al. 2016).

The purpose of GSAs is to provide a much-needed safe space in which LGBTQ students and allies can work together on making their schools more welcoming for sexual and gender minority students. As one questioning student commented:

> At this point I'm not really comfortable talking to other people about it, when I don't even know what's going on myself. I think if I did come out eventually it would be okay, because I'm a fairly private person and probably only my friends would know about it. I'm also a member of our school's GSA so I know I would have somewhere safe to be if it came to that.

GSA's have been shown to have many benefits (Saewyc et al., 2014), one of which is greater awareness to the school community as a whole. One teacher from our Every Teacher project commented:

Individual teachers are improving with regards to addressing homophobic and transphobic harassment issues. We have an active GSA in the school and they work on educating both staff and students through school activities. (Taylor et al. 2015: 36)

This educator's experience has occurred elsewhere. Our study found a positive correlation between the presence of a GSA and participation in LGBTQ-awareness days (for example, LGBTQ Pride events, LGBT History Month and so on). Educators from schools with a GSA are more likely to acknowledge the helpfulness of such clubs in creating safer schools for LGBTQ students (79 precent versus 58 percent for those from high schools without a GSA). Students from schools with GSAs are much more likely to agree that their school communities were supportive of LGBTQ people, compared to participants from schools without GSAs (53 versus 26 percent). LGBTQ students in schools with GSAs were much more likely to be open with some or all of their peers about their sexual orientation or gender identity (82 versus 68 percent) and were somewhat more likely to see their school climate as becoming less homophobic (75 versus 65 percent).

As a staple of recent Canadian legislation (as seen in Ontario, Manitoba and Alberta), and one of the simplest interventions to implement, GSAs function as effective protective factors for LGBTQ youth. It is important to note, however, that not all GSAs are the same. For instance, Fetner and colleagues (2012) contend that even though generally GSAs serve a positive function, each club creates its own character based on its school and community context, the openness around membership and the group's commitment to activity or activism within their school or wider community (see also Poteat et al. 2015). Unfortunately, however, there is too much of a "one and done" mentality whereby school administers permit (or are forced to through provincial legislation) a GSA, but fail to encourage capacity-building or provide resources and/or funding for on-going programming (Russell 2011; Taylor, Peter, Edkins et al. 2016).

Institutional Responses

Sexual- and gender-minority students in schools with comprehensive safe-school policies that clearly address homophobia report lower levels of harassment, fewer homophobic comments, more staff intervention when such comments are made and more willingness to report harassment and assault to staff members (Kosciw et al. 2014). Moreover, in the U.S., generic safe-school policies that do not include specific measures on homophobia are ineffective in improving the school climate for LGBTQ students. We asked Canadian students whether their schools had anti-homophobia policies or procedures as a context for their reporting about their lives at school. Asking students about policy, of course, does not indicate whether or not schools actually have policies, only whether or not students think that they do. It is likely that some students were wrong about their schools or school divisions not having policies. However, students reporting either that anti-homophobia policies do not exist when in fact they do, or that they do not even know whether or not their schools or school boards have such policies, suggests that schools need to make further efforts to publically implement their policies among their student bodies: a procedure for reporting homophobic incidents that youth do not know about is not effective.

Several students who did go to schools without anti-homophobia policies indicated that overall the climate was not supportive of sexual and gender minority issues:

> If my school had breached the topic of homosexuality in the classroom and had teachers who were not afraid to discuss it, my school would have been a much better place. I feel that the students in my school had the ability to accept gay people but were never given a reason to question their stance that gay people were bad and immoral.

> My school has absolutely no support (no awareness) of the LGBTQ community within and around it. The biggest fear for myself is the unknown, not knowing how people will accept someone who is LGBTQ.

> Nobody is stepping up to the plate (especially adults/teachers) to stop it. It's really pretty depressing that this piece of society is not being respected.

> I've never seen the issue discussed in any class or assembly (despite our school having at least two anti-racism assemblies a year) nor does the school apparently have any policies on queer issues. If they do have policies, they obviously don't enforce them, as students make anti-queer slurs all the time, in front of teachers, and nothing is said to the students.

Sexual- and gender-minority students who reported that their schools had anti-homophobia policies were significantly more likely to feel that their school community was supportive of LGBTQ individuals (58 versus 25 percent); to report homophobic incidents to teachers or other staff (58 versus 34 percent); to comment that teachers or other staff intervened more effectively (71 versus 31 percent) and to feel more attached to their school (for instance, 77 percent of students who went to schools with anti-homophobia policies agreed with the comment, "I feel like a real part of my school," compared to 62 percent of participants who did not go to such schools).

What about educators and institutional/school policies? In the Every Teacher project, the presence of a policy aids in administrators' commitment to provide resources for LGBTQ issues. For instance, two-thirds (67 percent) of educators from schools with an anti-homophobic harassment policy and almost three-quarters (74 percent) of those from schools with an anti-transphobic harassment policy reported having a resource person specializing in LGBTQ issues, versus 32 percent of those from schools without an anti-homophobic policy and 34 percent without an anti-transphobic harassment policy. For teachers who indicated that their school had progressive policies, those educators who responded that they had not received sufficient training or had not been trained at all were significantly more likely to report being aware of verbal harassment (80 percent) than those who felt that they were very well or adequately prepared (60 percent). As one teacher comments:

> I feel sometimes teachers choose to ignore a comment so they don't have to deal with it. There is no direction on who to give the problem to or what the follow up

would be. We have an equity binder but were told to read it on our own with no direction. So basically it will be shelved and not looked at.

Thus, while anti-homophobic and/or anti-transphobic harassment policies on their own are not enough to lower the incidence of harassment, a policy effectively implemented by incorporating staff training can.

Little is known about the outcomes of LGBTQ-inclusive curriculum (because there has been very little of it in existence). It is an established principle of inclusive education that it is important for marginalized students to see their identity group represented in the curriculum to counter the impacts of stigmatization they experience elsewhere (much like seeing racialized individuals in mainstream television commercials). We found, for example, that students who learned about LGBTQ issues in school felt more attached to their school. Elsewhere, LGBTQ-inclusive curriculum is correlated with students feeling safer at school, experiencing less harassment and achieving better academic outcomes (Kosciw et al. 2014). Even though widespread inclusion of LGBTQ curriculum is rare, the majority of Canadian educators (78 percent) report having included LGBTQ content in some way in their classroom, ranging from one-off references to repeated occasions and multiple methods (Taylor et al. 2015). However, while these attempts at LGBTQ inclusion are increasingly common, the need for greater resources and professional development is still needed, as one in five educators reported not knowing of any LGBTQ education resources, including inclusive curriculum guides.

The Bad News and the Good News

As the experiences of students and educators show, the bad news is that both homophobia and transphobia are widespread in Canadian schools, thereby casting doubts that LGBTQ people have achieved social equality within the Canadian landscape. The good news, however, is that in schools where even small efforts have been made, students and teachers report better climates, thereby providing support for the importance of legal rights for LGBTQ people. The substantial improvements in school culture associated with even modest interventions such as minor curricular inclusion suggest that even though the problem of homophobia and transphobia may be widespread in Canadian schools, it is perhaps not very deeply rooted. In this regard, much like the "legal equality" guaranteed through official legislation as well as the Charter, institutional legislation within schools does provide students with some safety.

And yet, there is even better news. Fifty-eight percent of CH-identified students, or roughly 1,400 of the 2,400 straight students, found it upsetting to hear homophobic remarks. There are many reasons why so many CH students would be upset by homophobic (and transphobic) bigotry. For some of these students, they are perceived to be LGBTQ themselves and targeted accordingly. Statistically, if there are upwards of ten times as many CH students as LGBTQ students (assuming that roughly one in ten students identify as LGBTQ), and some of them are homophobically or transphobically harassed because they are seen as queer. In raw numbers this translates to a larger number of CH students than LGBTQ students who are bullied in this manner. Other students are upset by homophobia/transphobia because they have an LGBTQ parent or sibling, or they are friends with an LGBTQ peer. Still other students are simply kind and feel empathy for their peers who are being grossly mistreated. And then there are those who are ashamed of themselves for participating in it or for remaining silent when it was going on. Finally, some simply find the presence of homophobia/transphobia depressing to the human spirit and are disheartened to be a part of a school community that continually abuses people who have done nothing to deserve it. This 58 percent suggests that there is a great deal of untapped solidarity for

> Fifty-eight percent of CH-identified students, or roughly 1400 of the 2400 straight students, found it upsetting to hear homophobic remarks.

their LGBTQ peers among CH students and that the majority of students, LGBTQ and CH, would welcome some help from the adult world in shifting their school culture towards a social justice approach. The Every Teacher project suggests that help could be on its way. In fact, the vast majority of educators surveyed (85 percent) reported that they approve of LGBTQ-inclusive education, and almost all (96 percent) see LGBTQ rights as human rights.

If so many students are upset by such degradation and so many teachers are supportive of LGBTQ rights, why do so few intervene when homophobic/transphobic comments are made or they witness homophobic/transphobic harassment and abuse? Many students are afraid to act because they are well aware that challenging CH-normative discourse puts them in danger of being perceived as LGBTQ and becoming the targets of name-calling and violence. For them, the costs of speaking up outweigh the benefits. We must never forget that high school is a time in the human life course when fitting in is one of the most important elements of well-being and survival. Teenagers fall into line with using language like "that's so gay" or "you faggot" without fully understanding the painful bite of these words for LGBTQ people, who are well aware of their lowly positions in CH-normative discourse. Students using such language may not like these phrases, but the thought of leaving the "group" and finding themselves in the uninhabitable zone of schoolyard discourse is also inconceivable. This is not to suggest that students are blind followers with no agency or ability to engage in transformative social change on issues pertaining to social justice or human rights; indeed, in some schools, students have led the way on this and other social justice issues, lobbying the school administration to implement GSAs, organizing LGBTQ-inclusive events, participating in LGBTQ Pride marches and speaking up in class to critique homophobia or to address the absence of LGBTQ content. It is simply to remind us that young people learn life lessons not only when adults demonstrate apparent hypocrisy, but also when they demonstrate the courage of their convictions as well.

It is unrealistic to always expect students to carry the heavy intervention load when incidents of homophobia/transphobia take place in school culture, which then leaves teachers and other educational personnel to step up to the plate. The Every Teacher project asked educators who reported hearing homonegative ("that's so gay") and homophobic comments (faggot or dyke) from students whether they had intervened. Nearly two-thirds (64 percent) indicated that they always intervened when they heard homonegative comments, and 70 percent always intervened when they heard homophobic comments. Intervention in incidents involving gender-negative remarks was less common. For example, 54 percent of educators reported that they always intervene when they hear negative remarks about boys acting "too much like a girl," and 53 percent when they hear negative comments about girls acting "too much like a boy." Moreover, only 30 percent of teachers felt that their schools responded effectively to incidents of LGBTQ harassment (Taylor et al. 2015). As one teacher comments,

> I believe that my school is poorly equipped/prepared to deal with such incidents. They would rather pretend that these students do not exist. Nobody wants to talk about it. I know LGBT students who are getting bullied and I don't think anything is done.

Educators from schools with either anti-homophobia or anti-transphobia harassment policies were far more likely to report that their school responded effectively to incidents of LGBTQ-based harassment. For instance, in schools with an anti-transphobia policy, 44 percent of participants felt their school responded effectively, compared to only 14 percent in schools without a policy. The effective intervention gap widens when comparisons are made between staff who were very well or adequately trained on this policy (61 percent), staff who were adequately trained but would have liked more (28 percent) and staff who had no training or inadequate training (11 percent).

The Every Teacher project illustrates that while some educators are stepping up and intervening when they witness incidents of LGBTQ bullying, far too many still do not. The silence from these teachers helps to not only validate homophobia and transphobia, but also ensure the recirculation of fear by teaching young people that they are on their own on this issue and that adults will not help them. Sadly, some school authorities and some parents tacitly approve of homophobia as an efficient strategy for enforcing compulsory heterosexuality. Unfortunately, some parents are so terrified of their children turning out gay that they would rather see them unhappy than see them un-heterosexual. Yet, if all teachers, administrators and school boards started to speak respectfully of LGBTQ people (literally and through specific interventions both at the school and district levels), the silent majority of students — the 58 percent of CH students and the approximately 10 percent of students who are LGBTQ — would have more reason for courage. Young people may learn new ways to say "that's stupid," without insulting categories of people, and they may come to understand that most of their peers are not committed to homophobic behaviours either. LGBTQ youth and the 58 percent of young CH people who quietly wish

> Sadly, some school authorities and some parents tacitly approve of homophobia as an efficient strategy for enforcing compulsory heterosexuality.

for something better would have a solid group of allies, backed by numerous human rights legislations, that could alter the discourse systems of students across Canada.

Social Change

If sexual and gender minority students are experiencing disproportionate amounts of bullying, yet the majority of CH students are distressed by this and most teachers are supportive of LGBTQ-inclusive education, where do we go from here to change the homophobic and transphobic landscape across Canadian schools and in Canada generally? There is a clear disconnect between Canada's official human rights discourse, endorsed broadly in society and specifically in classrooms, and the homophobic/transphobic discourse of Canadian high schools. On one hand, public opinion polls consistently show that the majority of Canadians believe that homophobia is wrong, support gay marriage and believe that being gay, lesbian or bisexual is simply what one is — like being Jewish, Indigenous, or female — and is not a moral issue or lifestyle choice that can be turned on and off. Even the federal Conservative Party in May 2016 voted 1,036 to 462 to change its political stance on same-sex marriage from one of opposition to one of being neutral, which is in stark contrast to their vocal disapproval when the law was passed in 2005 (CBC News 2016). Yet, on the other hand, Canadian school systems, and other social institutions, remain frozen in time, often fearful of backlash from extreme right-wing religious organizations that tirelessly work to deride LGBTQ people as sinful and dangerous to society (see, for example, Canada Family Action Coalition). The end result is that schools are too often failing the children and youth they are sworn to protect and respect, and as a result too many LGBTQ students are going through school being abused and disrespected.

> The majority of Canadians believe that homophobia is wrong; they support gay marriage; and they believe that being gay, lesbian, or bisexual is simply what one is.

What needs to change? School system officials at all levels of the education system, from ministries of education to school principals, need to mandate the development of LGBTQ-inclusive interventions in the form of thoroughly implemented policy and resource development. Parents/guardians, students and communities need to put pressure on these school systems and make it known that they will not settle for anything less. As mentioned, some provinces are embracing such change, most notably through GSA legislation, but there is still much more work to do especially from a "whole-system approach." Such an intervention mandates the inclusion of gender and sexual minority content throughout the education system including appropriate policy, programs, professional development and curriculum.

School system policies cannot in themselves produce respectful school climates for LGBTQ students any more than declaring that the *Charter of Rights and Freedoms* has suddenly produced a discrimination-free society across Canada. However, what human rights policies and laws can do, apart from their general symbolic value of conferring institutional legitimacy on marginalized groups, is support the efforts of people working at the forefront of change. Classroom teachers are expected to do the heavy lifting where changing school culture is concerned: if they are to fulfill their professional obligations to practise truly inclusive education (which our research shows they really want to do), they need policies that require their principals to support them if complaints are made. Similarly, principals need to know that school district directors will support them, and directors need to know that education ministers will support them. A positive start would be a strong mandate from ministries of education to integrate sexual and gender diversity into classroom teaching, complete with curriculum resources and professional development opportunities, just as ethnic diversity is now integrated into the curriculum. Without such a high level of government commitment, both the fear of repercussions and the lack of training and resources will continue to prevent school districts as well as teachers and administrators from finding the courage to implement the interventions required to disrupt the homophobic and transphobic discourses that dominate Canadian school cultures.

A number of factors converge to make high schools a particularly hostile environment for LGBTQ people: the concurrence of adolescents' fascination with sexuality, the existence of a generalized culture of bullying and exclusion, the fear of the repercussions for opposing homophobia and transphobia among students, teachers and administrators and the disconnect between a heartily endorsed official discourse promising respect for all and a widespread, unofficial (but institutionally rooted) discourse that disrespects LGBTQ people. All of these combine to create the heightened levels of abuse and degradation experiences by many LGBTQ individuals within school climates.

At the beginning of the chapter we mentioned the tragic suicide of Jamie Hubley, and the 'It gets better' campaign that resulted from his death (and others). To date there are over 50,000 YouTube videos made mainly by adults (such as U.S. President Obama, CBC celebrity Rick Mercer and a group video by the Royal Canadian Mounted Police) telling LGBTQ youth to: "hang on; endure high school; don't kill yourself; life gets better once you get out of that environment." The international campaign www.itgetsbetter.org has done a remarkable job bringing awareness to LGBTQ issues and has over 600,000 members and over 50 million views on YouTube. Despite being well intentioned, we believe that telling kids that life gets better after high school is insufficient and misguided. For many LGBTQ adults, life does indeed get better. For many others, however, the pervasiveness of homophobic and transphobic discourse practices are so entrenched in social institutions that life does not get better in adulthood. Telling youth "it gets better" is not an acceptable reply to a situation in which students are in a state of emergency. It was simply not enough for youth like Jamie, who could not wait three more years to escape school bullies — coupled with the knowledge that a high school diploma will not eradicate bigotry, intolerance, and pure hate that exists even in the adult world.

Instead of telling youth that "it gets better," we need to work together to "make it better." In coming years, we will see continued arguments against human rights for LGBTQ people by members of radically conservative communities who claim religious authority for their positions. On the legal front, the clash of LGBTQ Charter rights and Charter rights to freedom of religious "conscience" will be seen in areas including the right of Justices of the Peace to refuse to marry a same-sex couple, the right of psychologists to refuse to provide treatment that supports LGBTQ identity and the right of religious schools and other organizations to refuse to employ LGBTQ people. On the social front, we can expect continued harassment of LGBTQ couples and indeed of any person who falls outside the binary system of conventionally cisgendered heterosexuality that remains dominant in our society. To this end, official policies denouncing homophobia and transphobia will not eliminate such discrimination in Canadian schools — much like the Charter does not necessarily translate into social (as compared to legal) equality for LGBTQ individuals — but it is a good place to start; after all, a waterfall begins with a single drop, and look what becomes of that.

Glossary of Key Terms

Bisexual: A person who is attracted physically and emotionally to both males and females.

Cisgender: often abbreviated to "cis," represents a person whose gender identity aligns with conventional social expectations for the sex assigned to them at birth (e.g., a cisgender female is someone who identifies as a woman and who was assigned female sex at birth).

Gay: A person who is physically and emotionally attracted to someone of the same sex. Gay can include both males and females, or refer to males only.

Gender expression: The way a person publicly shows their gender identity through clothing, speech, body language, wearing of make-up and/or accessories,and other forms of displaying masculinity or femininity.

Gender identity: A person's internal sense or feeling of being male or female. Gender expression relates to how a person presents their sense of gender to the larger society. Gender identity and gender expression are often closely linked with the term transgender.

Gender minority: A transgender or transsexual person.

Homosexual: In contrast to heterosexual, the word homosexual is deeply connected with pathologizing and oppressive meanings from legal, religious and medical institutions and thus is not commonly used in the LGBTQ community.

Lesbian: A female who is attracted physically and emotionally to other females.

Perceived sexual orientation: When someone wrongly assumes that you are lesbian, gay or bisexual without knowing what your true sexual orientation really is (heterosexual).

Queer: Historically, a negative term for homosexuality, but more recently reclaimed by the LGBT movement to refer to itself. Increasingly, the word "queer" is popularly used by LGBT youth as a positive way to refer to themselves.

Questioning: A person who is in the process of figuring out their sexual orientation or gender identity.

Sexual minority: Persons who think of themselves as other than completely heterosexual.

Sexual identity/orientation: A person's deep-seated feelings of emotional and sexual attraction to another person. This may be with people of the same gender (lesbian or gay), the other gender (heterosexual/straight) or either gender (bisexual).

Straight/heterosexual: A person who is sexually and emotionally attracted to someone of the "opposite" sex.

Transgender: A person whose gender identity, outward appearance, expression and/or anatomy does not fit into conventional expectations of male or female. Often used as an umbrella term to represent a wide range of nonconforming gender identities and behaviours.

Transsexual: A person who experiences intense personal and emotional discomfort with their assigned birth gender. Some transsexuals may undergo treatments (sex reassignment surgery and/or hormone therapy) to physically alter their body and gender expression to correspond with what they feel their true gender is.

Two Spirit: Some Indigenous people identify themselves as two spirit rather than as lesbian, gay, bisexual or transgender. Historically, in many Indigenous cultures, Two-Spirited persons were respected leaders and medicine people. Two-Spirited persons were often accorded special status based upon their unique abilities to understand both male and female perspectives.

Questions for Discussion

1. Thinking back to when you were in high school, would you agree that there was a disconnect (that is, a contradictory experience) between human rights discourse and the discourse of your school environment (high levels of homophobia and transphobia)? How widespread were homophobic and transphobic language and harassment in your school?

2. Why do you think narratives like "that's so gay" are used so frequently in high school and among young people?

3. In your high school, was there a GSA club? Were there specific anti-homophobic policies and procedures for reporting incidents of abuse and harassment? If yes, do you think it made your school community a more welcoming environment? If no, do you think your school community would have benefited from being a more accepting place for LGBTQ youth?

4. Discuss the aggressive gender policing that youth participate in with reference to Foucault's concept of docile bodies and the constitutive effects of dominant discourse. What practices are involved in gender policing? What might happen if students stopped acting as agents of CH-normative discourse in school culture?

5. Some people prefer "queer" to "LGBT" because it signifies a rejection of the CH-normative system of sexuality and gender categories. If that system has always oppressed sexual and gender minority people, why would some still prefer the

identity terms "lesbian," "gay," "bisexual," "trans," and "Two-Spirit" over the term "queer"? Account for this using some of the discourse concepts discussed in this chapter. What difference might it make if LGBTQ people and their allies stopped referring to themselves as LGBTQ or "straight," and instead started using "queer" this way?

6. It is often said that homophobia is a "natural" response to "unnatural" sexual practices and gender expression. However, now that dominant discourses such as those emanating from health care, law and the media have become more LGBTQ-inclusive, polls show that far fewer Canadians are homophobic. This suggests that homophobia is not natural, but discursively constructed. If homophobia is not natural, and seems to be on the decline, why might some discourse communities be so adamantly opposed to LGBTQ-inclusive education? In other words, who benefits from the maintenance of homophobia and transphobia? What is all this discrimination for? In your answer, think about how homophobia and transphobia might function to serve the interests of dominant culture by maintaining socially conservative family and economic arrangements.

Resources for Activists

Egale (Equality for Gays and Lesbians Everywhere) Canada: egale.ca

Gay, Lesbian, Straight Education Network (GLSEN): glsen.org

Institute for Sexual Minority Studies and Services (ISMSS): ismss.ualberta.ca

McCreary Centre Society: mcs.bc.ca

MyGSA.ca: egale.ca/portfolio/mygsa/

Stonewall: stonewall.org/uk

Notes

1. The First National Climate Survey on Homophobia, Biphobia and Transphobia in Canadian Schools was based on a large-scale study of over 3700 youth. The study was conducted in partnership with Egale Canada Human Rights Trust (ECHRT), which provided a major grant, with additional funding from the University of Winnipeg and the Canadian Institutes of Health Research (CIHR)-funded research team, SVR (see Peter, Taylor, and Campbell 2016; Peter, Taylor, and Edkins 2016; Peter, Taylor Ristock, and Edkins 2015; Peter, Taylor, and Chamberland 2015; Taylor and Peter 2012; Taylor and Peter 2011; Taylor, Peter, et al. 2011). The Every Teacher Project on LGBTQ-inclusive Education in Canadian Schools was conducted in partnership with the Manitoba Teachers' Society (MTS) and funded by the Social Sciences and Humanities Research Council of Canada, MTS, the University of Winnipeg, and the Legal Institute of the University of Manitoba (see Meyer, Taylor & Peter 2015; Taylor et al., 2015; Taylor, Peter, Short et al. 2016) The National Inventory of School District Interventions in support of LGBTQ youth wellbeing was funded by CIHR as part of a larger project led by Dr. Elizabeth Saewyc at University of British Columbia (see Taylor, Peter, Edkins et al. 2016).

2. Two methods were used to reach participants in the student survey. First we compiled a list of every organization in the country known to have LGBTQ youth group components or clients and provided them with information about the survey. In addition, a link to the survey was posted on

the Egale Canada website and Facebook site in order to encourage participation from individuals who may not be associated with any LGBTQ youth groups. Some participants learned of the survey through mainstream and LGBTQ media coverage. Others were informed of the survey by educators, whose boards had approved the survey, but had not implemented it in their schools. Finally, although not specifically asked of respondents, a number of participants certainly heard about the survey through a friend or acquaintance. The second method was based on formal research applications to a random selection of forty school districts proportionally distributed across the regions and population densities of Canada to conduct the survey during class time. In the end, twenty school districts representing all regions of Canada except Quebec approved the study (A parallel study was conducted at the same time by Line Chamberland, Université du Quebec à Montréal of which we provided an aggregate analysis of the two studies – see Peter, Taylor, and Chamberland 2015).

3. The questionnaire was drafted in consultation with members of the Education Committee of Egale Canada. The questionnaire was finalized after pre-testing for age-appropriate vocabulary, clarity/unambiguity, neutrality, relevance, and completeness by administering it to members of an LGBTQ youth group. Finally, an Ethics Protocol was approved by the Senate Committee on Ethics in Human Research and Scholarship at the University of Winnipeg.

References

Alcoff, L. 1988. "Cultural Feminism versus Post-Structuralism: The Identity Crisis in Feminist Theory." SIGNS: *Journal of Women in Culture and Society* 13, 3.

Butler, J. 1987. "Variations on Sex and Gender: Beauvoir, Wittig, and Foucault." In S. Benhabib and D. Cornell (eds.), *Feminism as Critique*. Minneapolis: University of Minnesota Press.

____. 1990. *Gender Trouble: Feminism and the Subversion of Identity*. New York: Routledge.

____. 1993. *Bodies that Matter: On the Discursive Limits of "Sex."* New York: Routledge.

____. 1996. "Sexual Inversions." In S. Hekman (ed.), *Feminist Interpretations of Michel Foucault*. University Park: Pennsylvania State University Press.

Canada Family Action Coalition. <familyaction.org>.

CBC News. 2013. "Scott Jones says he was attacked for being gay." December 11. <cbc.ca/news/canada/nova-scotia/scott-jones-says-he-was-attacked-for-being-gay-1.2459289>.

____. 2016. "Freedom and respect: Conservative strike marriage definition from party policy." May 28. <cbc.ca/news/politics/conservative-convention-saturday-votes-1.3604990>.

Dennis, A., and P.J. Martin. 2005. "Symbolic Interactionism and the Concept of Power." *The British Journal of Sociology* 56, 2: 191–213.

Fetner, T., A. Elafros, S. Bortolin, and C. Drechsler. 2012. "Safe Spaces: Gay-Straight Alliances in High Schools." *Canadian Review of Sociology* 49, 2, 188–207.

Foucault, M. 1979. *Discipline and Punish: The Birth of the Prison*. Translated by A. Sheridan. New York: Vintage Books.

____. 1980. *Power/Knowledge: Selected Interviews and Other Writings*. Translated by C. Gordon. New York: Pantheon Books.

____. 1981. *The History of Sexuality: An Introduction*. Translated by R. Hurley. Harmondsworth: Penguin.

Greytak, E.A., J.G. Kosciw, and E.M. Diaz. 2009. *Harsh Realities: The Experiences of Transgender Youth in Our Nation's Schools*. New York: GLSEN. <glsen.org>.

Kosciw, J.G., E.A. Greytak, N.A. Palmer, and M.J. Boesen. 2014. *The 2013 National School Climate*

Survey: The Experiences of Lesbian, Gay, Bisexual and Transgender Youth in Our Nation's Schools. New York: GLSEN. <glsen.org>.

Meyer, E.J., C. Taylor, C., and T. Peter. 2015. "Perspectives on Gender and Sexual Diversity (GSD) Inclusive Education: Comparisons Between Gay/Lesbian/Bisexual and Straight Educators." *Journal of Sex Education* 15, 3: 221–234.

Murray, D. (ed.). 2009. *Homophobias: Lust and Loathing Across Time and Space.* Durham: Duke University Press.

New York Times. 2016. "Orlando Gunman Attacks Gay Nightclub, Leaving 50 Dead." June 12. <nytimes. com/2016/06/13/us/orlando-nightclub-shooting.html?_r=0>.

Peter, T., and C. Taylor. 2014. "Buried Above Ground: A University-Based Study of Risk/Protective Factors for Suicidality among Sexual Minority Youth." *Journal of LGBT Youth* 11, 2: 125–149.

Peter, T., C. Taylor, and C. Campbell. 2016 (online). "'You can't break … when you're already broken': The importance of school climate when examining LGBTQ youths' experiences with suicide and suicide behaviour." *Journal of Gay and Lesbian Mental Health.*

Peter, T., C. Taylor, and L. Chamberland. 2015. "A Queer Day in Canada: Examining Canadian High School Students' Experiences with School-Based Homophobia in Two Large-Scale Studies." *Journal of Homosexuality* 62, 2: 186–206.

Peter, T., C. Taylor, and T. Edkins. 2016. "Are the Kids All Right? The Impact of School Climate Among Students with LGBT Parents." *Canadian Journal of Education* 39, 1: 1–25.

Peter, T., C. Taylor, J. Ristock, and T. Edkins. 2015. "Pride and Prejudice: Factors Affecting School Attachment Among Lesbian, Bisexual, and Heterosexual Girls." *Journal of Lesbian Studies* 19, 2: 249–273.

Pharr, S. 1988. *Homophobia: A Weapon of Sexism.* Inverness: Chardon Press.

Poteat, V.P., H. Yoshikawa, J.P. Calzo, et al. 2015. "Contextualizing Gay-Straight Alliances: Student, Advisor, and Structural Factors Related to Positive Youth Development among Members." *Child Development* 86, 1: 176–193.

Rich, A. 1980. "Compulsory Heterosexuality and Lesbian Existence." *SIGNS: Journal of Women in Culture and Society* 5, 4.

Riley, D. 1988. *"Am I That Name?" Feminism and the Category of 'Women' in History.* Minneapolis: University of Minnesota Press.

Ristock, J.L. 2002. *No More Secrets: Violence in Lesbian Relationships.* New York: Routledge.

Russell, S.T. 2011. "Challenging Homophobia in Schools: Policies and Programs for Safe School Climate." *Educa em Revista, Curitiba, Brasil* 39: 123–138.

Saewyc, E., C. Konishi, H.A. Rose, and Y. Homma. 2014 "School Based Strategies to Reduce Suicidal Ideation, Suicide Attempts, and Discrimination among Sexual Minority and Heterosexual Adolescents in Western Canada." *International Journal of Child, Youth and Family Studies* 5, 1: 89–112.

Taylor, C., and T. Peter. 2011. "'We Are Not Aliens, We're People, and We Have Rights': Canadian Human Rights Discourse and High School Climate for LGBTQ Students." *Canadian Review of Sociology* 48, 3: 631–668.

____. 2012. "Left Behind: Sexual and Gender Minority Students in Canadian High Schools in the New Millennium." In T. Morrison, M. Morrison, D.T. McDermott, and A. Carrigan (eds.), *Sexual Minority Research in the New Millennium.* Hauppauge: Nova Science.

Taylor, C., T. Peter, C. Campbell, E. Meyer, J. Ristock, and D. Short. 2015. *The Every Teacher Project on LGBTQ-Inclusive Education in Canada's K-12 Schools: Final Report.* Winnipeg, MB: Manitoba Teacher's Society.

Taylor, C., T. Peter, T. Edkins, C. Campbell, and E. Saewyc. 2016. "Final report of the national inventory of school district interventions in support of LGBTQ student wellbeing." Vancouver, BC: Stigma and Resilience Among Vulnerable Youth Centre, School of Nursing, University of British Columbia.

Taylor, C., T. Peter, D. Short, J. Ristock, E. Meyer, and C. Campbell. 2016. "Gaps between Beliefs, Perceptions, and Practices: Findings from The Every Teacher Project on LGBTQ-Inclusive Education in Canadian Schools." *Journal of LGBT Youth* 13, 1--2: 112–140.

Taylor, C., and T. Peter, with T.L. McMinn, K. Schachter, S. Beldom, A. Ferry, Z. Gross, and S. Paquin. 2011. "Every Class in Every School: Final Report on the First National Climate Survey on Homophobia, Biophobia, and Transphobia in Canadian Schools." Toronto: Egale Canada.

Veale, J., E. Saewyc, H. Frohard-Dourlent, S. Dobson, B. Clark, and the Canadian Trans Youth Health Survey Research Group. 2015. "Being Safe, Being Me: Results of the Canadian Trans Youth Health Survey." Vancouver, BC: Stigma and Resilience Among Vulnerable Youth Centre, School of Nursing, University of British Columbia.

Weedon, C. 1997. *Feminist Practice and Poststructuralist Theory, 2nd edition*. Cambridge: Blackwell.

Weiss, J.T. 2001. "The Gender Caste System: Identity, Privacy, and Heteronormativity." *Law and Sexuality* 10.

14

Making Drug Use into a Problem

The Politics of Drug Policy in Canada

Susan Boyd, Connie Carter and Donald MacPherson

YOU SHOULD KNOW THIS

- In 2015, two-thirds (61 percent) of all drug offences involved cannabis.
- Cannabis possession charges accounted for 51 percent of all drug charges.
- Criminal justice statistics in 2015 highlight that the rate of persons accused of drug offences is highest for the 18- to 24-year-old age group (1,108 per 100,000 population), followed by youth (ages 12 to 17) (657 per 100,000).
- In addition, 75 percent of police-reported drug offences in 2015 involved possession, not drug trafficking, importing or production (see Allen 2016: 42).

IN THIS CHAPTER, WE ARGUE THAT SOCIAL PROBLEMS, such as the "drug problem," are socially constructed. Social constructionist analyses also draw our attention to the institutionally based claims-makers who shape our understanding of drugs as a social problem, such as the Royal Canadian Mounted Police, municipal police forces, politicians, physicians, researchers and others. On a daily basis, spokespeople in Canada use a variety of forums, including radio, newspapers, television, films and numerous websites and social media forums to make claims about drugs as a social problem. These claims-makers help to define the nature of the "drug problem," and they also offer solutions to this problem that correspond with their institutional priorities and concerns (Best 1995). Social constructionist analyses also draw our attention to the contradictory nature of claims about "social problems" (Reinarman and Levine 2000). This is no less the case with drugs. Even a cursory examination of websites devoted to this topic will reveal competing and contradictory ideas about drugs. These same sites will also offer contradictory analyses of why drugs are a problem and how we should respond to this problem. The voices behind these claims and counter-claims often compete with each other to define the drug problem, but they are also challenged by others' voices, including spokespeople from groups supporting drug policy reform, academics and groups of people who use drugs.

This chapter draws on sociological perspectives to explore how our ideas about drugs have deeply rooted cultural and historical origins. This same sociological approach suggests that ideas about drugs are produced by humans in daily interactions in political, social and cultural contexts. The notion that some drugs are good and some are bad, for example, is not necessarily based on the supposed health or social harms of a drug but is instead related to the history of claims made about that substance. Indeed, as is the case in Canada, many of these socially constructed ideas about drugs have been codified into laws that govern how we may access and use these same drugs.

> Social problems, such as the "drug problem," are socially constructed.

Criminalized drugs are most often those substances that a variety of institutionally based groups condemned in a specific historical era. As we will discuss more fully below, specific substances like opium, heroin and cocaine were criminalized in the early 1900s in Canada. Prior to and following the legal prohibition of these substances, ideas about drugs were under considerable public debate, debates that shaped how we understand these drugs and their effects to this day.

In the early part of the twentieth century, drugs such as opium were associated with a variety of supposed social ills, including interracial relationships, white slavery, degradation and loose sexual morals. The historical literature on Canadian drug policy suggests that periods of heightened concern about drugs were often driven by a combination of newspaper campaigns and interest and advocacy group activities, resulting in changes to Canada's drug policy laws (Boyd 2015; Carstairs 2006; Grayson 2008; Martel 2006; Valverde 1998). Drug prohibition in Canada did not begin until the passage of the *Opium Act* in 1908 (however, alcohol prohibition for those labelled "Status Indian" began in 1868). Prior to this point, nineteenth-century opiate use, alcohol consumption and tobacco smoking were "widely embedded in social custom" and practised by white citizens in Western nations (Berridge 2013: 12). At that time, anyone could buy, without a prescription, a wide array of opiate-, cocaine- and cannabis-based products, such as tinctures, creams, pills, patient medicines and powders (15).

Following a notorious race riot in Vancouver's Chinatown in 1907, an event that was fuelled by the race and class concerns of white workers against Chinese labourers at that time, the Canadian federal government sent politician (and later prime minister) William Lyon Mackenzie King to Vancouver to investigate the causes of this riot. King's report on this riot borrowed from racist newspaper accounts that claimed that smoking opium led ordinarily moral and upstanding white Canadians to ruin in opium dens thought to be run exclusively by Chinese Canadians. His report also included the testimony of prominent anti-opium reformers who made similar claims about the effects of opium. Following this event, King is quoted as declaring, "We will get some good out of this riot yet" (N. Boyd 1984: 115; Comack 1986). King's report to the federal government recommended that opium prepared for smoking and powered and crude opium be criminalized. In response, Parliament passed the *Opium Act* in 1908. The Act regulated crude and powdered opium and opium prepared for smoking and made it an offence to import, manufacture, offer to sell, sell or possess to sell opium for non-medical reasons. Thus, early on, law enforcement focused on closing opium dens and policing those associated with the smoking of opium — almost exclusively

> Nineteenth-century opiate use, alcohol consumption and tobacco smoking were "widely embedded in social custom" and practised by white citizens in Western nations.

Chinese residents living in Canada (N. Boyd 1984), while many other Canadians still consumed opiates in patent medicines such as cough syrups and laudanum. In 1923, the Canadian Parliament criminalized marijuana, but without debate. Over the following decades, more drugs were criminalized and Canada adopted a primarily criminal justice approach rather than a health or human rights approach to drug policy.

> In Canada today, the use of particular drugs is regulated and controlled by the federal *Controlled Drugs and Substances Act* (CDSA), which includes possession, trafficking, importing and exporting, and production-related offences.

In Canada today, the use of particular drugs is regulated and controlled by the federal *Controlled Drugs and Substances Act* (CDSA), which includes possession, trafficking, importing and exporting and production-related offences. The seriousness of penalties included in the CDSA is related to the *perceived* levels of harm caused by each drug. The CDSA does not recognize that drugs such as alcohol and tobacco are at least as harmful as some illegal drugs. Historically, concerns about public safety have been linked to illegal drug use or drug dealing. Until recently, in Canada, as in many nations around the world, the response to these concerns has been to increase the scope of laws, the severity of punishments and the scale of policing. Canada is also a signatory of the prohibitionist United Nations global drug control treaties: the 1961 Single Convention on Narcotic Drugs, the 1971 Convention on Psychotropic Substances and the 1988 Convention against Illicit Traffic in Narcotic Drugs and Psychotropic Substances.

Crime Rates and Drug Crime

In Canada, although law agents and government officials claim that drug policy and associated government funding are directed at stopping high-level production and selling of criminalized substances, drug statistics over time demonstrate that it is young, poor and marginalized users who are most vulnerable to arrest, not high-level traffickers. In addition, rather than trafficking and production, the majority of arrests in Canada are for drug possession. In 2013, 71 percent of all drug offences were for possession, and cannabis possession made up the majority of these arrests (54 percent) (Cotter, Greenland and Karam 2015: 3, 5). Cannabis possession charges numbered 59,965 in 2013, a rate of 168 per 100,000 people in Canada. The rate of police-reported incidents of cannabis possession are far higher than for any other illegal drug (at 22 per 100,000 for cocaine possession and a rate of 32 per 100,000 for all other illegal drugs combined) (Boyce, Cotter and Perreault 2014: Table 5). The rate of cannabis possession offences has more than doubled since 1991 (Cotter, Greenland and Karam 2015: 7).

Carol Bacchi's framework for policy analysis provides an "opportunity to question taken-for-granted assumptions that lodge in government," such as medical and other policies related to the problem of illegal drugs. She claims that law-and-order discourse makes "drug use a matter of illegal behaviour" and people who use illegal drugs are "marked as addicts" (2009: 92). Compared to the U.S., where drug crime has been a main driver of incarceration, Canada can seem like a more compassionate place when it comes to the regulation of drugs.

But, people who use illegal drugs are also marked as criminals and subject to discrimination and punishment, and Canada has a record of increasing numbers of drug crimes and high levels of incarceration due to drug convictions. Although there has been a steady decrease in the crime rate in Canada — for example, in 2013, the crime rate was at its lowest since 1969 — the number of drug offences has been increasing since the early 1990s with a slight decrease of 2 percent in 2013 and 9 percent in 2015 from the years before then (Allen 2016: 23; Boyce, Cotter and Perreault 2014; Brennan 2012). In fact, from 1998 to 2011, the drug offence rate increased 39.5 percent (Public Safety Canada 2012: 1).

Similar to previous years, in 2013, B.C. reported the highest overall rate of drug offences among the provinces. While B.C. also had the highest rate for cannabis offences, Saskatchewan reported the highest rate of cocaine offences (Boyce Cotter and Perreault 2014: Table 6). However, in 2015, Yukon, Northwest Territories and Nunavut had the highest cannabis offences rates in Canada, 337, 785, and 729 respectively (Allen 2016: 46).

Keep in mind that "rates" measure police-reported offences per 100,000 population. Thus, due to its larger population, more people in B.C. are arrested for drug offences than in Saskatchewan.

Increases or decreases in police-reported drug crime do not necessarily represent real changes in actual occurrences of crime. Police-reported crime statistics in Canada are compiled using the Uniform Crime Reporting (UCR) survey, which collects information on all criminal incidents reported to, and substantiated by, Canadian police services. These data are based on a nationally approved set of common crime categories and definitions that have been developed in cooperation with the Canadian Association of Chiefs of Police. Data provided by the UCR reflects crime that comes to the attention of police and does not include crime that does not come to their attention.

In addition, official crime statistics (and many crime surveys) disproportionately capture street crime and low-level crime rather than white collar or corporate crime. The focus on property crime and street crime (including drug offences) is directly related to legislation, the criminal code, selective police enforcement and priorities and profiling. Thus, crime statistics and data can be influenced by policing priorities that allocate time and resources to the detection of certain categories of crime (Brennan 2012: 11). The increase in police-reported drug offences may also be related to policy practices, resources, enforcement priorities and targeting of particular offenders or offences (Boyce, Cotter and Perreault 2014).

Crime rates are also shaped by the size of youth populations (historically, crime rates are higher for youth and crime rates increase when baby boom generations become young adults) in specific eras, police profiling, new laws and shifting police-enforcement practices, technological developments, political pressures and societal "intolerance for specific forms of behaviour" (Balfour and Comack 2006: 63). The increase in drug offences over the last thirty years does not reflect a rise in drug-use rates in Canada; thus, we can assume that the rise in drug arrests in Canada is largely due to other factors.

Youth (aged 12 to 17) crime also fell in 2014, continuing a downward trend that has been apparent for a number of years (Boyce, Cotter and Perreault 2014). These declines are explained by the enactment of the *Youth Criminal Justice Act* in 2003, which provided clear guidelines for the use of extrajudicial measures (that is, informal sanctions) (Brennan 2012: 21). Regardless, in 2014, roughly 15,300 youth were arrested for a drug violation, and 81 percent of these arrests were for possession of cannabis (Allen and Superle 2015: 5, 31). Youth are charged with drug offences under the CDSA at a rate of 657 per 100,000 youth compared to a rate of 215 per 100,000 adults (aged 25 and older). However, the arrest rates for drug offences for young adults aged 18 to 24 are the highest at 1,108 per 100,000. Thus, our drug laws disproportionately impact youth and young adults in Canada (Allen and Superle 2016: 5).

Given the steady increase in the percentage of Canadians who favour decriminalization or drug reform in relation to cannabis possession — in 2012, 66 percent of Canadians and 75 percent of British Columbians surveyed favoured the decriminalization of cannabis (Angus Reid 2012, 2011) — societal intolerance may not be at play in relation to rising drug arrests (the largest category of arrests is for possession of cannabis). Rather, the steady increase in drug offences is more likely linked to increased law-enforcement focus on this particular criminal activity, increases in resources for police enforcement, police targeting of drug offenders and specific urban and rural areas, all of which are shaped by the claims made about drugs by key representatives of policing and by politicians seeking to make drugs an electoral issue.

Renewed focus by the past Conservative-led government of Prime Minister Stephen Harper, for example, helped to shape drug arrest rates in Canada. It would, however, be a mistake to assume that all federal Conservative politicians are in favour of tough drug laws or that all federal Liberal and New Democratic Party politicians favour drug reform. But over the last thirty years, the Conservative Party of Canada has taken on a law-and-order and tough-on-crime stance that includes drug offences and, with the enactment of the *Safe Streets and Communities Act* in 2012, harsher drug laws. Critics have long argued that, since the 1980s, the renewed "war on drugs" in many Western nations is fuelled by the Conservative response to both the perceived increasingly liberal social morals and their loss of power in the 1960s and 1970s (Willis 1992). While Canada has long had harsh drug laws, this country has lagged behind the U.S., which, beginning in the 1980s, enacted very harsh drug laws and sentencing practices that resulted in mass incarceration of its citizens. By the early 2000s in Canada, the Conservative Party had successfully reinforced and capitalized on fears about illegal drug use, and beginning in 2007, after its election, the Harper government renewed and extended a Canadian version of the "war on drugs." For example, the *Safe Streets and Communities Act* introduced mandatory minimum penalties for some drug offences. However, signalling a shift in policy, in 2015 the Liberal-led federal government pledged to end cannabis prohibition. The Government of Canada is moving ahead on this promise and plans to introduce a framework for the legal regulation of cannabis by 2017.

Prisons in Canada

When a person is convicted of a crime in Canada, the judge imposes a sentence or punishment for breaking the law. A judge could impose a fine, probation, community service or imprisonment. Imprisonment is most often reserved for society's most heinous crimes. Even though Canada's crime rate has been falling, prison populations are rising. Between 2003 and 2013, the total prison population in Canada increased by 16.5 percent (an increase of almost 2,100 prisoners) and visible minority prisoners increased by 75 percent in that ten-year period (Sapers 2013).

About 55 percent of people incarcerated in federal prisons have problems with substance use (ibid.). Despite this clear need for in-prison treatment, prison-based substance-use programming is also in decline; the Correctional Service of Canada budget for these programs fell from $11 million in 2008–09 to $9 million in 2010–11 (CIC 2012: 16). In addition, health care is the most common area of complaint received by the Office of the Correctional Investigator in Canada by people incarcerated in federal prisons (Public Safety Canada 2012: 31). Though Canada's rate of incarceration in 2013–14 was 118 per 100,000 people, a middle rate compared to many other nations in the world (for example, the U.S. at 707 and Iceland at 45), mandatory minimum sentences for some drug crimes have the potential to push rates of incarceration higher in Canada (Correctional Services Program 2015). In fact, in 2013–14, although provincial/territorial incarceration rates fell by 3 percent from the previous year, the federal incarceration rate increased by 3 percent during the same period (Correctional Services Program 2015).

Programs and other services inside prison that help inmates transition to life after prison are also either in decline or plagued by lack of available resources. For instance, the safer tattooing initiative in prisons was cancelled in 2006 despite the effectiveness of such programs in curbing the spread of HIV and HCV (Harris 2009). This program recognized that tattooing takes place inside prison walls and that the sharing of used equipment could potentially result in HIV and HCV infections. The Correctional Service of Canada (CSC) evaluated the program and found positive results, including an enhanced level of knowledge and awareness amongst staff and inmates regarding blood-borne infectious disease prevention practices. The evaluation also found that the initiative had the potential to reduce exposure to health risks and enhance the safety of staff members, inmates and the general public. The initiative also provided additional employment opportunities for inmates in the institution and work skills that are transferable to the community (Correctional Service of Canada 2009). The passage of the *Safe Streets and Communities Act* in 2012 follows on these and other moves by the former Conservative-led federal government that make prisons less safe and reduce the discretion of the judicial system in developing appropriate sentences for individuals convicted of drug crimes.

Canada's federal prison system is severely overcrowded, leading to increasing volatility behind bars. In the two-year period between March 2010 and March 2012, the federal in-custody population increased by almost a thousand inmates, or 6.8 percent, which is the equivalent of two large male medium-security institutions. As of 2013, more than 20 percent of people in Canada's prisons are double-bunked (meaning that two people are incarcerated in a cell that was built for only one occupant) (Sapers 2013). This increase occurred even before the imposition of mandatory minimum sentences, which will stress Canada's incarceration system even further. It is important to remember that in 2012, the year mandatory minimum drug sentences were enacted, already 26.7 percent of female federal offenders and 15.7 percent of male offenders were serving a sentence for a drug crime (Public Safety Canada 2012: 61).

To accommodate increases in Canada's prison population, the federal government planned to add 2,700 cells to thirty existing facilities at a cost of $630 million. By 2013, the government closed three federal facilities as part of budget-reduction plan (Kingston Penitentiary and the Regional Treatment Centre in Ontario, and Leclerc Institution in Quebec). These closures affected a thousand people, who were relocated, including 140 people residing at the Ontario Regional Treatment Centre, a stand-alone facility at Kingston Penitentiary. The government argued that the closure of the three federal institutions and the transfer of prisoners to other facilities would save over a million dollars a year, yet there is little evidence of these savings. Rather, critics of the government's prison closures and transfers point to the social and personal cost of overcrowding, double-bunking and elimination of effective prison programs in Canada (Sapers 2013, 2014).

Prisons, Race and Gender in Canada

The racial composition of prison populations in Canada is a stark reminder that prison sentencing is racially motivated. In addition, the increasing numbers of women in prison suggest the increased meting out of harsh sentences for low-level drug crimes. The number of Black prisoners increased by almost 90 percent between 2002 and 2013 (Sapers 2013). Over the last thirty years, the number of women charged with a criminal offence has also risen in Canada and the increase is also reflected in the women's prison population (Mahony 2011). Although Indigenous people (including Métis and Inuit) make up 4.3 percent of the total Canadian population, Indigenous women make up over 35 percent of all federally incarcerated women in Canada, compared to 21.5 percent of Indigenous men, an increase of 85.7 percent over the last ten years (Statistics Canada 2013: 4, 9; Office of the Correctional Investigator 2012: 4; Public Safety Canada 2012: 51; Public Safety Canada 2012: 53; Sapers 2016: 43).

In 2012, the Office of the Correctional Investigator noted that the overrepresentation of Indigenous people in prison is worse in many provincial prisons, especially in the Prairie provinces (CIC 2012: 11). In B.C., 47 percent of the women in provincial prisons in 2013 were racialized women (non-white women); of these, 38 percent were Indigenous women (B.C. Corrections 2014). In addition, 50 percent of the total number of women serving time in a B.C. provincial prison in 2013 were sentenced for a drug offence compared to 31 percent of men (ibid.). In addition, almost 27 percent of women compared to 16 percent of men were serving time in federal prison for a Schedule II drug offence in 2012 (Public Safety Canada 2012: 61).

The overrepresentation of Indigenous and racialized peoples in Canadian prisons, and the higher percentage of women serving prison time for drug offences than men, are disproportionate to their drug-arrest rates, their drug-use rates and their involvement in the illegal drug trade. In fact, only 18 percent of all people accused of a drug offence in 2013 were women and drug-use rates for women are much lower than men, and most often women are not major players in the drug trade (Cotter, Greenland and Karam 2015: 16). Indigenous drug-use rates are not higher than rates for Caucasian people. However, women's involvement in the drug trade mirrors their social status in Canada; they are often at the lowest echelons of the drug trade, engaged in importing or exporting drugs, selling small amounts of illegal drugs on the street to support themselves and their families, or to support their own drug use (Boyd 2006). In 2013, drug offences for importing and exporting drugs had the highest proportion of women accused (29 percent) (Cotter, Greenland and Karam 2015: 16).

Most criminalized drugs enter Canada hidden in planes, boats, trucks and other transport vehicles that hold much larger quantities than what can be found on (or in) an individual body or a suitcase. There is a growing body of research about women's involvement as drug couriers (or drug mules) in the drug trade (importing or exporting drugs). The research demonstrates that women drug couriers are most often poor, first-time offenders and that their decision to carry drugs is economic. They are most often paid a flat fee and they do not share in any drug trade profits (Boyd 2006; Office of the Sentencing Council 2011). Women drug couriers are also poorly paid (given the risk) and are the most "disposable of workers" (Boyd 2006; Sudbury 2005: 175).

In Canada (and the U.S. and U.K.) the majority of women sentenced to prison for drug importation and exportation are foreign nationals; poor, racialized women whose choices are framed by global and national political and economic concerns and Western demand for specific substances (Boyd 2006: 145). In 2011–12, 53 percent of Black women in federal prison were incarcerated for a Schedule II drug offence (Sapers 2014). Some of these same conditions shape the experience of poor, racialized men. Police profiling and harsher sentencing of both Black and Indigenous peoples are systemic practices in Canada (Wortley 2004; CIC 2012; Sapers 2014). The Office of the Correctional Investigator also claims that the disproportionate rates of incarceration for Indigenous and Black peoples reflect gaps in Canada's "social fabric and raise concerns about social inclusion, participation and equality of opportunity" (Sapers 2013). The Office of the Correctional Investigator also argues that Indigenous overrepresentation in prison is "systemic and race-related" and exacerbated by the Canadian criminal justice system and colonial history (Sapers 2013).

> The Office of the Correctional Investigator also claims that the disproportionate rates of incarceration for Indigenous and Black peoples reflect gaps in Canada's "social fabric and raise concerns about social inclusion, participation and equality of opportunity."

Safe Streets and Communities Act and the Social Construction of Safety

With the introduction of the National Anti-Drug Strategy (NADS) in 2007, the Conservative-led government at that time signalled its intention to "get tough" on drugs. This approach meant more public spending on law enforcement and more severe penalties. In 2012, Canada's federal government passed and enacted the *Safe Streets and Communities Act* (SSCA). The SSCA is an omnibus law that introduces a wide variety of changes, including amendments to currently existing laws and the enactment of new laws. The law ends house arrest for property and other serious crimes, focuses on detaining supposedly violent young offenders, requires the Crown to consider seeking adult sentences for youth convicted of violent crimes, eliminates pardons for serious crimes, adds additional criteria for the transfer of Canadian offenders back to Canada, allows Canadians to sue organizations that supposedly support terrorism and protects foreign nationals from exploitation by making it more difficult for them to enter the country (Department of Justice 2012).

Among the vast array of changes is the introduction of mandatory minimum sentences for some drug crimes, including production, trafficking, importing and exporting. Mandatory minimum sentences reduce the discretion used by justice officials through the application of predefined minimum sentences for some crimes. These changes apply to drugs listed in both Schedule I (heroin, cocaine, methamphetamine) and Schedule II (marijuana) of the *Controlled Drugs and Substances Act*. These changes also increase the maximum penalty for the production of marijuana from seven to fourteen years and add more drugs to Schedule I, including amphetamine-type drugs, which will result in higher maximum penalties for activities involving these drugs (Department of Justice 2012). The SSCA was touted as an effort to extend greater protection to the most vulnerable members of society, enhance the ability of the justice system to hold offenders accountable and "improve the safety and security of all Canadians" (Department of Justice 2012).

Throughout the federal government materials on the SSCA, notions of safety and security are wielded in support of increased criminalization and decreased judicial and criminal justice discretion. "Tough on crime" approaches, such as mandatory minimum sentences, are often touted as efforts to attack the "big players" in underground drug markets rather than focusing on individuals who possess drugs for personal use. When the Conservative-led government announced the NADS in 2007, Stephen Harper's speech sharply delineated between drug users and drug sellers and producers. As he said:

> Our government recognizes that we also have to find new ways to prevent people from becoming enslaved by drugs. And we need to find new ways to free them from drugs when they get hooked. That's what the new National Anti-Drug Strategy I'm unveiling today is all about. Our message is clear: drugs are dangerous and destructive. If drugs do get a hold of you — there's help to get you off them. And if you sell or produce drugs — you'll pay with jail time. (Government of Canada 2016)

This approach by the past federal government ignores research noted above that found that dealers who are often drug users are more likely to be caught up in police efforts against drug crime.

The passage of the SSCA followed a protracted media campaign by law enforcement in Canada to depict Canada's court system as too lenient on offenders despite the harshness of its treatment of drug offenders (Boyd and Carter 2014: 68). The imposition of mandatory minimum sentences for some instances of cultivating marijuana is the also the logical extension of a protracted media-based drug scare about the impacts of marijuana-growing operations, which extended from the late 1990s to the present day. During this period newspaper reports carried extensive coverage of the threats to public safety and other dangers of these operations by drawing on police-based spokespeople. These stories continually reiterated the notion that marijuana-growing operations bring other crime, undesirable people and dangers such as house fires to otherwise supposedly innocent residential homeowners and neighbourhoods (Boyd and Carter 2014: 186).

The SSCA was passed into law despite extensive opposition from numerous parties, organizations and experts in Canada. In particular, criticism of this legislation focused on the approach to crime highlighted by these changes — a reactive approach that focuses on punishment after the fact, instead of a proactive approach that focuses on key issues like early learning and development, overall health promotion and community and economic development as a means to lower crime.[1] The Canadian Bar Association, for example, warned that mandatory minimum sentences subvert important aspects of Canada's sentencing regime, including principles of proportionality and individualization and judges' discretion to impose a just sentence after hearing all the facts in the individual case. Before the SSCA, judges could weigh each case and assess aggravating factors, such as violence, presence of weapons and the proximity of a crime to children, to determine a sentence. Judges could also determine the likelihood of an offender committing further crimes and mete out a sentence appropriate to these issues (Canadian Bar Association 2009). As we pointed out previously, without mandatory minimum sentences, sentencing practices in Canada were already discriminatory. Critics of the new law have pointed out that these new sentencing provisions are unlikely to be meted out fairly. Two cases below are illustrative of how some women come into conflict with the law for transporting drugs.[2] The lenient sentence that they both received was heralded as a breakthrough at the time. If the women had been arrested and sentenced today, the judge would have had to abide by the mandatory minimum sentences implemented in 2012. Thus, both women would have been sentenced to prison.

In Canada, even before the enactment of mandatory minimum sentences for some drug offences, drug couriers are typically sentenced harshly. But two different Canadian cases in 2004 had a different outcome (*R. v. Hamilton* 2004; see Boyd 2006).[3] In both cases, women were arrested at Toronto's Pearson International Airport after returning from visits to Jamaica. Marsha Hamilton was arrested in 2000, and Donna Mason in 2001. The trial judge sought to place the participation of both of these women as drug couriers against a backdrop of race, gender, poverty and inequality. His analysis of the cases speaks to the social conditions that shape women's conflict with the law.

Marsha Hamilton is a Black woman with a grade 9 education. At the time of her arrest she was unemployed and living in Canada, with family in Jamaica. She was 28 years old and a single parent with three children under the age of eight. She had made a trip home to Jamaica and, in preparation for returning to Canada, had swallowed ninety-three pellets of cocaine with an estimated $69,000 street value. She almost died on the trip because the pellets leaked cocaine into her body. Marsha had no prior arrests or police record, and she stated that she had committed the crime for financial reasons.

Donna Mason is a Black woman with a grade 12 education. At the time of her arrest she was 33 years old and living in Canada. She had three children whom she solely supported on a limited income. Prior to the birth of her third child, she had worked full-time at a Wendy's restaurant for $8 an hour, supplemented by welfare assistance. She was also the choir leader at her church. Before returning to Canada from Jamaica she had swallowed just under one kilogram of cocaine pellets. She had no prior arrest or police record, and she also said that financial hardship was the main reason she committed the crime.

Both women pleaded guilty to importing cocaine, in an amount of under one kilogram, from Jamaica. Both were Black women of limited economic means. Both had dependent children. Both were first-time offenders. Their profile is similar to that of other women in prison for drug importation in Canada, Britain and the U.S. In 2003, both women were sentenced by Justice Hill of Ontario's Superior Court of Justice. Their cases are ground-breaking because both women were given conditional sentences and not sent to prison. Hamilton was given a conditional sentence of twenty months; Mason of twenty-four months less a day.

The defence in each of these cases highlighted the role of the judiciary, and specifically the sentencing judge, in addressing injustices against Indigenous peoples in Canada — injustices recognized in *R. v. Gladue* (1999). The defence argued that Black women should be granted similar consideration when the evidence presented at the trial suggests a history similar to that of Indigenous women: poverty, discrimination and overrepresentation in the criminal justice system (*R. v. Hamilton* 2003). Judge Hill's decision was significant for its recognition of systemic factors in the imposition of conditional sentences. Nevertheless, it did little to challenge Canada's drug laws, nor did it recognize the criminal justice system as a site of conflict and oppression. In addition, it did not entirely dispel well-worn myths about Black women and crime. Yet, even with the limitations of the case, today the outcome and the issues addressed in court would not have prevailed because mandatory minimum sentencing allows no room for recognition of systemic factors in the imposition of sentencing. Thus, under the *Safe Streets and Communities Act*, Marsha Hamilton and Donna Mason would have been sentenced to a mandatory minimum prison sentence leaving their children at risk of entering the foster care system.

Mandatory minimum sentences and three-strike laws were implemented extensively in the U.S. between the mid-1970s and 2006. As the U.S. experience shows, the brunt of mandatory minimum sentences was borne by people who are drug dependent and by those facing economic challenges, and not those involved in the higher levels of drug selling and production. Moreover, although rates of drug use and selling are comparable across racial and ethnic lines, Blacks and Latinos are far more likely to be criminalized for drug law violations than whites (U.S. Department of Health and Human Services, Substance Abuse and Mental Health Services Administration 2012; Human Rights Watch 2008). In addition, individuals who sell drugs at the street level are more often than not involved in tasks such as carrying drugs and steering buyers towards dealers; real profiteers in the drug market distance themselves from visible drug-trafficking activities and are rarely captured by law-enforcement efforts (Chu 2012). One of the effects of mandatory minimum sentencing laws in the U.S. is to give the country the distinction of having by far the highest rates of incarceration in the world, the largest proportion of which is attributable to drug offences. Despite high rates of incarceration, data supplied by the U.S. government shows that it has one of the highest levels of drug use and a vast and increasing supply of illegal drugs (SAMHSA Office of Applied Studies 2012).

The imposition of mandatory minimum sentences for drug crimes in Canada also flies in the face of evidence of their ineffectiveness. The potential deterrent effects of these laws are often touted as the key reason for their implementation. Studies

> Putting people in prison does not reduce levels of harmful drug use or the supply of drugs.

of mandatory sentencing laws in the U.S. and Australia, however, have found no convincing evidence that the imposition of these laws deters crime (Tonry 2009). Most of the reviews of the effects of these penalties were conducted well before the imposition of the SSCA. In fact, the 1987 Canadian Sentencing Commission report, a 1993 report of the Committee on Justice of the Canadian Parliament and the 2002 Department of Justice review all concluded that the effects of these laws on deterrence was negligible. The 2002 Department of Justice report concluded that mandatory minimum sentences are "least effective in relation to drug offences" and that "drug consumption and drug related crime seem to be unaffected, in any measurable way, by severe mandatory minimum sentences" (Gabor and Crutcher 2002: 31). Putting people in prison does not reduce levels of harmful drug use or the supply of drugs. Instead, the effects of mandatory minimum sentences include increases in the prison population in already overcrowded prisons, increases in the costs to the criminal justice system and a number of well-documented consequences on already marginalized populations (Canadian Bar Association 2009; Mallea 2010). In Canada, as was the case in the U.S., mandatory minimum sentences have the potential to increase the numbers of people in prison, thus exposing more people for longer periods of time to increased potential for violence and an environment characterized by mental, emotional and physical degradation (Iftene and Manson 2012).

> In Canada, as was the case in the U.S., mandatory minimum sentences have the potential to increase the numbers of people in prison, thus exposing more people for longer periods of time to increased potential for violence and an environment characterized by mental, emotional and physical degradation.

Incarceration is costly and the introduction of mandatory minimum sentences only serves to increase these costs. Even very cautious estimates suggest that changes associated with the *Safe Streets and Communities Act*, including the imposition of mandatory minimum sentences, will cost the Canadian federal government about $8 million and the provinces another $137 million annually. In fact, as noted above, in 2012 the federal government budgeted $67.7 million above the NADS' budget for mandatory minimum penalties (Department of Justice 2012). These facts fly in the face of the federal government's claim that these changes would not cost anything (Yalkin and Kirk 2012). A study by the Quebec Institute for Socio-economic Research and Information suggests that the costs for the provinces will be much higher due to increases in the prison population, as much as $1,676 million (Institute de recherché et d'informations socio-economiques 2011). Already annual expenditures on federal corrections have increased to $2.375 billion in 2010–11, a 43.9 percent increase since 2005–06. The annual average cost of keeping a federal inmate behind bars has increased from $88,000 in 2005–06 to over $114,364 in 2010–11. The annual cost of incarcerating women in federal prison is much higher, costing $214,614 (Public Safety Canada 2012: 25). This is due to the fact that there are fewer women's prisons and a much smaller female prison population. The daily cost of federal imprisonment increased to $313 from $255 in 2006–07 (Public Safety Canada 2012: 25). In contrast, the daily average cost to keep an offender in the community is $80.82, or $29,499 per year (CIC 2012). Given these soaring costs, Canada's Correctional Investigator, Howard Sapers, has suggested that "at a time of wide-spread budgetary restraint, it seems prudent to use prison sparingly, and as the last resort it was intended to be" (ibid.).

A 2013 report by the B.C. Provincial Health Officer also warned that changes to sentencing and other justice practices brought about by the enactment of the *Safe Streets and Communities Act* would be extremely impactful on Indigenous peoples. These changes put Indigenous people at greater risk for incarceration and the resulting consequences of incarceration, including lack of access to culturally safe services that support healing and reintegration (Office of the Provincial Health Officer (B.C.) 2013). This report also noted that the SSCA appears to conflict with other federal programs aimed at reducing prison time, specifically section 718.2(e) of the *Criminal Code*, which requires sentencing judges to consider all options other than incarceration (ibid.: 43).

An October 2012 report by the Correctional Investigator of Canada entitled *Spirit Matters: Aboriginal People and the Corrections and Conditional Release Act* echoed these concerns (CIC 2012). This report speaks to the lack of resolve on the part of the Correctional Service of Canada (CSC) to meet the commitments set out in the *Corrections and Conditional Release Act*. Sections 81 and 84 of this Act were meant to help mitigate the overrepresentation of Indigenous peoples in federal prison and to provide a healing path based on cultural and spiritual practices. Healing lodges were originally conceptualized by the Native Women's Association as a way to "connect Aboriginal women to their communities and traditions as *the* method of providing correctional services for Aboriginal women." (ibid.: 52). "Section 81 of the CCRA was intended to give CSC the capacity to enter into agreements with Aboriginal communities for the care and custody of offenders who would otherwise be held in a CSC facility. ... Section 84 was to enhance the information provided to the Parole Board of Canada and to enable Aboriginal communities to propose conditions for offenders wanting to be released into their communities" (Office of the Provincial Health Officer (B.C.) 2013: 4). Included among these requirements was the establishment of healing lodges that emphasize Indigenous beliefs and traditions and focus on preparation for release (Office of the Provincial Health Officer (B.C.) 2013). Although the original intent of the healing lodge has never been fully realized, eight healing lodges are now operating, four operated by CSC and their staff, and four operated by CSC and community partner organizations.

The report found that in B.C., Ontario, Atlantic Canada and the North there were no section 81 healing lodge spaces for Indigenous Women (Office of the Provincial Health Officer (B.C.) 2013). In addition, because healing lodges limit intake to minimum-security offenders, 90 percent of Indigenous offenders were excluded from being considered for a transfer to a healing lodge. The report concludes with a critique of the lack of action by the Correctional Service of Canada.

Consistent with expressions of Indigenous self-determination, sections 81 and 84 capture the promise to redefine the relationship between Indigenous people and the federal government. Control over more aspects of release planning for Indigenous offenders and greater access to more culturally-appropriate services and programming were original hopes when the CCRA was proclaimed in November 1992. (2012: 33)

The report concludes by calling on the CSC to ensure that the provisions of the Act are implemented in good faith.

The implications for Canadian drug policy are clear: rising rates of incarceration of Indigenous peoples, higher rates of substance-use problems combined with a lack of commitment to social structural change and alternative healing paths means more federally and provincially sentenced Indigenous people will not receive the services they need. In fact, recognizing the high financial and social costs of mandatory minimum sentences, as well as their widespread failure, by 2013, the states of New York, Michigan, Massachusetts and Connecticut have repealed these sentences for non-violent drug crimes, with other U.S. jurisdictions set to follow. New York in particular repealed all of what were called the Rockefeller Drug Laws (Wood et al. 2012: 37; Tonry 2009: 69). In August 2013, U.S. Attorney General Eric Holder announced the softening of the application of minimum sentencing laws on federal offenders. Most recently a task force appointed by the U.S. Congress to investigate and report on possible reforms to the U.S. federal corrections system recommended reserving mandatory minimum sentences for only the most serious federal drug crimes (CCTF 2016). In Canada, the implementation of the SSCA was accompanied almost immediately by court challenges. In 2014, a B.C. provincial court judge found mandatory minimum sentences for drug trafficking to be a violation of the Canadian Constitution (*R v. Lloyd* 2014). The Crown pursued this case to the Canadian Supreme Court, which ruled in a 6–3 decision that mandatory minimums violate provisions against cruel and unusual punishment by forcing judges to hand out long prison sentences without consideration of the mitigating details of the case (*R. v. Lloyd* 2016). The Liberal federal government has responded by to noting that it is reviewing mandatory minimum sentencing for some crimes.

Does the "War on Drugs" Work?

When it comes to drug use, the major institutional claims-makers in Canada, such as the RCMP, claim that the problem of drug use is primarily one of drug supply, making only small concessions to the need for drug prevention programs. For this reason, extensive public monies and effort is put into curbing the drug supply without regard for how these efforts, in fact, produce the very problems they seek to alleviate. Perhaps the most stunning display of unimaginative thinking when it comes to solving current drug problems is

> Far from eliminating drug use and the illicit trade, prohibition (making some drugs illegal) has inadvertently fuelled the development of the world's largest illegal commodities market, estimated by the U.N. in 2005 at approximately $350 billion a year.

the refusal by governments to consider the failure of the overarching policy framework that not only creates much of the drug crime in Canada but also constrains our ability to address many drug-related health harms. Far from eliminating drug use and the illicit trade, prohibition (making some drugs illegal) has inadvertently fuelled the development of the world's largest illegal commodities market, estimated by the U.N. in 2005 at approximately $350 billion a year. Just as with alcohol prohibition in the early twentieth century, the profits flow untaxed into the hands of unregulated, sometimes violent, criminal profiteers (Count the Costs 2012a). Banning drugs and relying on enforcement-based supply-side approaches to discourage their use has not stemmed the increase in drug use or the increase in drug supply. Despite Canada's significant investment in drug control efforts, drugs are cheaper and more available than ever (Werb et al. 2010). There is a growing consensus among international experts that drug prohibition has failed to deliver its intended outcomes and has been counter-productive (London

> There is a growing consensus among international experts that drug prohibition has failed to deliver its intended outcomes and has been counter-productive.

School of Economics 2014; Global Commission on Drug Policy 2011, 2014).

A growing body of evidence has a suggested that rather than protecting public health and safety, the current overarching policy framework of prohibition not only constrains our ability to address many drug-related health harms, but also produces other harms, listed below.

Increases in Violence

Because of the lack of formal regulation used in the legitimate economy, violence can be the default regulatory mechanism in the illicit drug trade. It occurs through enforcing payment of debts, through rival criminals and organizations fighting to protect or expand their market share and profits and through conflict with drug law enforcers. In Canada, gang violence sometimes results from turf wars over control of illegal drug markets. A "get tough" approach to crime assumes that more enforcement will eliminate the problem of gang violence. But as a comprehensive review by the International Center for Science in Drug Policy states: "Contrary to the conventional wisdom that increasing drug law enforcement will reduce violence, the existing evidence strongly suggests that drug prohibition likely contributes to drug market violence and higher homicide rates" (Werb et al. 2010: 91). Indeed, the demand for drugs means that as soon as one dealer is removed others are there to take their place. The Global Commission on Drug Policy supports these findings:

> Vast expenditures on criminalization and repressive measures directed at producers, traffickers and consumers of illegal drugs have clearly failed to effectively curtail supply or consumption. Apparent victories in eliminating one source or trafficking organization are negated almost instantly by the emergence of other sources and traffickers. Repressive efforts directed at consumers impede public health measures to reduce HIV/AIDS, overdose fatalities and other harmful consequences of drug use. Government expenditures on futile supply reduction strategies and incarceration

displace more cost-effective and evidence-based investments in demand and harm reduction. (Global Commission on Drug Policy 2011: 2)

The Creation of Unregulated Drug Markets

Drug policies that prohibit some substances actually eliminate age restrictions by abandoning controls to an unregulated market. In addition, when we prohibit rather than regulate substances, it becomes impossible to control the purity and strength of drugs. Illegally produced and supplied drugs are of unknown strength and purity, increasing the risk of overdose, poisoning and infection (Health Officers' Council of B.C. 2011). When people buy from the illegal market, they have no way to determine the quality of the drugs they purchase (all legal drugs are regulated for quality). For example, heroin bought on the street varies in strength. Hypothetically, heroin could be 100 percent unadulterated; however, this is unlikely and most often heroin bought on the illegal market ranges in purity and strength. Because the drug trade is

> When people buy from the illegal market, they have no way to determine the quality of the drugs they purchase (all legal drugs are regulated for quality).

unregulated, buyers have no way to ascertain the purity or strength of the heroin they purchase. One day's purchase could be 10 percent pure, another day's purchase could be 30 percent pure. Thus, users are vulnerable to drug overdose. Also, on the illegal market, other substances are added to increase weight and volume, hence more profit. Sometimes these substances are benign, other times not.

In 2015, B.C. saw a rise in drug overdoses from fentanyl, a strong synthetic opiate being sold on the street as heroin (CBC 2015c). Because this drug is a much stronger opiate than heroin, its use led to an alarming spike in drug overdoses (ibid.). In 2016, the B.C. provincial health officer declared a public health emergency due to the increase in overdose deaths in the province. The case of fentanyl illustrates the point that drugs bought on the illegal market can vary drastically in terms of potency and purity because there are no controls on quality. Thus, rather than reducing the supply of drugs, prohibition abdicates the responsibility for regulating drug markets to organized crime groups and increases the risk of harm to people who use criminalized drugs.

Substance Displacement

As the United Nations Office on Drugs and Crime reports, if the use of one drug is controlled by reducing supply, suppliers and users may move on to another drug with similar psychoactive effects, but less stringent controls (Count the Costs 2012b). For example, studies of the effects of banning mephedrone (a cathinone analogue) in the U.K. suggest that people who used this drug before the ban either continued their use, or switched back to prohibited substances like ecstasy and cocaine, both of which are unregulated and thus of unknown purity and strength (Van Hout and Brennan 2012; Winstock, Mitcheson and Marsden 2010).

Market Displacement

Studies suggest that geographically specific enforcement practices tend to displace drug markets to other locations rather than eliminate them (Kerr, Small,and Wood 2005). This is due to the fact that "drug supply networks are generally not limited to a few central 'kingpins,' but rather include numerous diverse enterprises, and therefore removing the entire supply network is beyond the resources and scope of even the most well-supplied enforcement agency" (215). In addition, the supply network is made up of small, diverse and fluid groups of people rather than cartels or kingpins (Tickner and Cepeda 2012). Many people who sell drugs, especially street-level sellers, are unorganized and have no established ties to organized crime (Dorn and South 1993). Yet, they are most vulnerable to arrest and quickly replaced by other sellers (Dorn and South 1993; Kerr, Small and Wood 2005). These findings raise serious concerns about the capacity of law-enforcement strategies to eliminate drug supply.

The Neglect of Medical Applications

The complete prohibition of some substances curtails their potential medical uses and benefits, as well as research into potential beneficial applications of controlled substances. An example is the use of pharmaceutical-grade heroin to treat individuals for whom other treatments have not worked. For example, the findings of a Canadian trial of heroin-assisted treatment — the North American Opiate Medication Initiative (NAOMI) study conducted in Vancouver and in Montreal in the 2000s — were positive and noted benefits such as improved physical and psychological health for participants in this study. Yet the continued prohibition of prescribed heroin hinders the use of this drug in treatment settings. Indeed, the implementation of medical cannabis programs in Canada has been repeatedly thwarted by the prohibited status of this drug despite evidence that shows it has beneficial effects for many patients (Grindspoon 1998). Canada has a federal medical marijuana program, yet the past Conservative-led government changed the policies regulating medical marijuana use and production, eliminating both personal and designated growers, although a recent Charter challenge at the Supreme Court (*Allard et al. v. Canada* 2016) successfully challenged the new policy. In August 2016, Health Canada responded to the Allard decision by enacting new policy; the Access to Cannabis for Medical Purposes Regulations (ACMPR) replaced the Marihuana for Medical Purposes Regulations (MMPR).

An Inability to Limit Use

Comparisons between states or regions show no clear correlation between levels of drug use and the toughness of laws and penalties (Count the Costs 2012a; Degenhardt, Chiu et al. 2008). Similarly, studies tracking the effects of relaxation in policy do not show drug use increases(Hughes and Stevens 2010). For instance, when Portugal decriminalized possession of all drugs for personal use, drug use and addiction rates did not rise (Moreira et al. 2011; Murkin 2014). In short, any deterrence is at best marginal compared to the wider social, cultural and economic factors that drive up levels of drug use. A study at the B.C.-based International Centre for Science in Drug Policy culled from two decades (1990 to 2010) of government databases on illegal drug supply and found the supply of major illegal drugs has (with a few exceptions) increased. Regardless of harsh federal and state drug laws, with the exception of powder cocaine, the purity and/or potency of illegal drugs in the U.S. has generally increased. Their findings also confirm that the price of illegal drugs has generally decreased (Werb et al. 2013). These findings once again throw into question the effectiveness of current government-level drug policies that emphasize supply reduction at the expense of other goals. These deficiencies are aptly illustrated by the World Drug Report, an annual publication of the United Nations Office on Drugs and Crime that relies on reports of police drug seizures (that is, the size and estimates of drugs found in raids) along with police-based estimates of crop size (for cannabis and coca) to evaluate the effectiveness of drug policies. The larger the seizure, the more enforcement officials assert the effectiveness of their approaches. But the findings described above suggest that no matter how hard we try to apply supply-side drug enforcement, drugs are still widely available, cheap and increasingly potent.

An Increase in the Negative Effects of Drug Use

The reality is that making some drugs illegal does not stop people from using substances. This is evident from the United Nations data demonstrating increasing levels of drug use over the past three decades (United Nations Office on Drugs and Crime 2013). Criminalization of substance use further stigmatizes people who use drugs, making it more difficult to engage people in health care and other services. Criminalization also increases marginalization and encourages high-risk behaviours among people who use drugs, such as injecting in unhygienic environments, poly-drug use and binging. Evidence from other countries suggests the stigma and fear of arrest deter people from seeking treatment and it is more effective to divert users into treatment without harming their future prospects with a criminal record for drug use (Room and Reuter 2012).

Trying to manage drug use through incarceration diverts law enforcement away from efforts to improve community safety with crime prevention programs. Funding prisons and police also takes away precious resources from services like adequate housing and family income, and robust educational programs, all of which have the potential to address the root causes of crime (Canadian Council on Social Development 2014). None of these strategies were at the forefront of the approach taken by Canada's Conservative federal government from 2007 to 2015. Yet, readers should keep in mind that in Canada, the U.S. and the U.K. drug possession charges (the majority being for cannabis) make up the bulk of drug arrests (Boyd 2015). Even though federal governments have chosen to criminalize this activity, critical drug researchers argue that marijuana users are not "criminals" and past theories about the causes of criminality are not relevant due to the fact that marijuana use is prevalent in Western countries and is a normalized youth practice (Boyd and Carter 2014; Manning 2007).

Despite the well-documented failures of prohibition, Canada pursued a strictly prohibitionist approach to many drugs and in fact, scaled-up this approach from 2007 to 2015.

Cannabis as a Case in Point

In the lead up to the 2015 federal election, Liberal Party leader, Justin Trudeau, promised to legalize, regulate and tax cannabis. The Liberals won a majority government in the election and in his throne speech in December 2015, Prime Minister Trudeau reaffirmed that he would create a legal regulatory framework for cannabis following consultation with all levels of government and experts in public health and substance use and policing (Bronskill 2015). However, as this chapter goes to press, Canada's cannabis laws remain unchanged even though the government announced that a new legal framework will be introduced by 2017.

In Canada, next to alcohol and tobacco, cannabis is the most often-used drug. Young people in Canada use cannabis extensively (depending upon the province, 30 percent to 53 percent of grade 12 students reported using cannabis during their lifetime) (Canadian Centre on Substance Abuse 2011). In fact, a report from UNICEF suggests that Canada has the highest rate of youth cannabis use among developed countries, but one of the lowest rates of tobacco use (UNICEF 2013). Heavy use, including using more than once daily, can have negative impacts on lung health, cognition and mental health. Yet, the overall public health impacts of cannabis use are low compared with other illicit drugs, such as opioids, or with alcohol. The risk of overdose is very low, as is the risk of cannabis-related accidents (Fischer, Rehm and Hall 2009; Room, Fischer et al. 2008). In addition, death due to cannabis overdose is "difficult, if not impossible" (Deganhart and Hall 2012: 62). A review of the harms of various substances published in the medical journal the *Lancet* was based on a study that called on drug specialists to meet and score each of twenty drugs on "16 criteria, nine related to the harms that a drug produces in the individual and seven to the harms to others" (Nutt, King and Phillips 2010: 1558). The criteria included measuring drug-specific mortality (such as risk of overdose), drug-specific damage to physical health, crime, impact on family and community and economic costs (1560). This review found that alcohol was the most potentially harmful drug over even heroin and cocaine. Of the twenty drugs assessed by this study cannabis was ranked at eight in terms of harmfulness behind most major illegal substances.

Cannabis-control policies, whether harsh or liberal, appear to have little or no impact on the prevalence of its consumption and production (Potter et al. 2015; Room, Fischer et al. 2008). Police reports tell us that Canada has a robust (underground) cannabis industry. The RCMP and police agencies regularly report the amount of marijuana seized in drug busts, including kilograms of marijuana and marijuana plants (Boyd and Carter 2014). However, police drug seizures only tell us part of the story. Although researchers provide estimates, due to the fact it is a hidden economy, no one can accurately state how prevalent marijuana growing is in Canada. However, one study suggests that retail expenditures in Canada on cannabis are as high as $4.6 billion annually (Kilmer and Pacula 2009: 94). The most recent estimates of the size of the underground cannabis economy in Quebec peg it at three hundred tonnes in 2002; in B.C. estimates of the size of the economy suggest it could reach as high as $7 billion annually (Easton 2004). However, a 2012 study estimated that annual retail expenditures on cannabis by British Columbians was $407 million and daily users accounted for the bulk of the cannabis revenue, with a median estimated expenditure of approximately $357 million (Werb et al. 2012: 1). The authors of this study conclude that given the size of the cannabis industry in B.C., it would be worthwhile to legally regulate the activity and the province would benefit from taxing its sale. Clearly, cannabis is a popular drug, but the potential financial benefits of a regulated and taxable product like cannabis (for recreational use) were completely lost to past federal and provincial treasuries (Werb et al. 2012). In 2013, Uruguay became the first nation to repeal cannabis prohibition. In addition, eight U.S. states and the District of Columbia have also repealed cannabis prohibition. In Uruguay, these states and the District of Columbia, cannabis is now legally regulated (both production and sale) by the state and taxed.

One of the arguments put forward for legally regulating cannabis relates to the sizeable costs of criminalizing cannabis, including policing, courts and corrections, which are borne by governments and Canadian taxpayers. In 2013, for example, there were 58,965 incidents reported to police involving possession of cannabis for the whole of Canada. Police-reported incidents of cannabis possession are far higher than any other illegal drug. The rate of 168 per 100,000 population far exceeds the rate of 22 for cocaine possession and a rate of 32 for all other illegal drugs combined. Indeed, the rate of cannabis possession arrests in Canada have more than doubled since 1991 (Cotter, Greenland and Karam 2015: 7). Between 2012 and 2013, drug offences decreased by 2 percent; however, cannabis possession offences increased by 1 percent (Boyce, Cotter and Perreault 2014: 20, 33). From 2013 to 2015 there has been a slight decrease in the total number of drug offences, including cannabis possession offences (Allen 2016: 23). Even with these decreases, drug arrests remain higher than ten years ago.

A study in B.C. suggests that charges for possession of cannabis in the province doubled between 2005 and 2011 despite low public support for the imposition of a criminal conviction for this conduct. This study also found that charges for cannabis possession vary considerably between police departments and between municipal police and RCMP detachments (N. Boyd 2013). The RCMP are responsible for an overwhelming majority of the charges in B.C. Due to the RCMP's "investment" in drug crime, in 2013 (for the fourth consecutive year), Kelowna, B.C., reported the highest rates of possession charges in Canada — 80 percent of all drug offences were for possession. Seventy percent of the total possession charges in Kelowna were for cannabis. Kelowna has a rate of 707 possession offences per 100,000 population, almost double the rate of Vancouver (Cotter, Greenland and Karam 2015: 12). It is conservatively estimated that it costs about $10 million annually in B.C. alone to enforce criminal prohibition against cannabis possession (N. Boyd 2013). Given the relatively low impact cannabis has on public health compared to other drugs, and the significant limitations placed on people with criminal convictions (employment and travel restrictions), research suggests that our current policies likely do more to undermine collective respect for the law and law enforcement than they do to protect public health (N. Boyd 2013).

If the goals of our current laws are to reduce cannabis production and consumption, clearly these laws are not effective. Even though, as shown earlier, there is high use among young people, there are no regulatory controls, such as age restrictions, on cannabis as there are on tobacco. Nor can purchasers reliably determine the dose (that is, the level of THC) or the origin of the substance. When it comes to tobacco use, a regulatory system that includes age restrictions on purchase, prohibiting lifestyle marketing and focusing on clean air initiatives has been effective in making Canada safer and healthier. Recognizing the unique challenges presented by cannabis policies, and the potential of a public health regulatory framework to control the use and availability of this drug, in 2012 the Union of British Columbia municipalities endorsed a motion to encourage the B.C. provincial government to support the decriminalization and regulation of cannabis.

Polls also suggest that a majority of Canadians (57 percent) support the legalization and regulation marijuana. In B.C., 77 percent of respondents to a poll indicated support for cannabis law reform (Angus Reid 2012). They are not alone. In an effort to stem the damage that underground drug markets create, leaders in Central and South America have called for changes to the way cannabis is regulated. In 2011, the Global Commission on Drug Policy encouraged governments to experiment with the regulation of cannabis with goals of safeguarding health and safety of all citizens (Global Commission on Drug Policy 2011).

The Curious Case of Canada's Marijuana for Medical Purposes

Although marijuana for recreational use is illegal in Canada, the federal government has operated the Medical Marihuana [sic] Access Program since 2001, prompted by court rulings that upheld the right to access cannabis for serious and chronic medical conditions (Belle-Isle and Hathaway 2007). That program underwent a major overhaul and the federal government established new regulations for the program, passing them in 2013 (Government of Canada 2012). Thus, the old program, the Medical Marihuana Access Program (MMAP) was replaced by the Marihuana for Medical Purposes Regulations (MMPR) on April 1, 2013. The MMPR program requires patients to obtain a prescription-like document from a physician or nurse practitioner, rather than applying for an "Authorization to Possess" through Health Canada. The elimination of the very cumbersome application process and the addition of nurse practitioners as authorized health care prescribers are welcome moves. But in Canada too few physicians currently know enough about the benefits and risks of cannabis for medical purposes to make sound medical judgments and recommend it to their patients, nor are enough physicians sufficiently aware of the appropriate use of cannabis for medical purposes (Canadian Medical Association 2013). More education of physicians is needed to ensure that patients will have adequate access to the program.

The MMPR eliminated the Personal Use Production Licences (PUPL) and Designated Licences, which allowed people or a designated person to grow their own cannabis. This was a concern for several reasons. Many people choose to produce their own supply because current prices of available cannabis are prohibitive (Lucas 2012). Producing their own cannabis also enables patients to select the strain(s) that work best for them and to grow them without an undue financial burden (Health Canada 2013). The elimination of the PUPL responds to concerns expressed by law enforcement and vocal claims-makers about the cultivation of medical cannabis in residential homes (Boyd and Carter 2014). Rather than eliminating this option, the MMPR could have addressed these concerns through routine inspections and certification of home gardens. Health Canada's decision to centralize the cultivation of cannabis for medical purposes in the hands of licensed corporate producers has increased the costs substantially because patients have to turn to a limited number of commercial producers (Government of Canada 2012). The MMPR requires that cannabis production be located in indoor sites away from residential homes, that access to these operations be restricted with the use of visual monitoring systems and intrusion-detection equipment and that personnel hold a valid security clearance issued by the federal minister of health. These requirements mean that producers will need to heavily capitalize just to start an operation. As of 2016, there are thirty-four corporate producers approved although Health Canada has received more than a thousand applications (Health Canada 2015; Lupick 2015: 14). In addition, the security requirements alone are so extensive that small growers find that they cannot afford them, thus eliminating them from participating legally in the market (Lupick 2015). However, a recent Charter challenge at the Supreme Court (*Allard et al. v. Canada* 2016) successfully challenged the MMPR policy. In August 2016, Health Canada responded to the Allard decision by enacting new policy, and the Access to Cannabis for Medical Purposes Regulations (ACMPR) replaced the Marihuana for Medical Purposes Regulations (MMPR). Under the ACMPR patients are able to apply for Personal Use Production Licences (PUPL) and Designated Licences.

The new regulations also exclude currently existing medical cannabis dispensaries in the supply and distribution system. These dispensaries are not legal; however, they have long played a key role in disseminating information about cannabis and they offer a range of cannabis strains, products and services, such as peer counselling and referrals to other services. As we write, Health Canada–licensed medical marijuana producers can only sell dried cannabis and cannabis oil via mail order. No other cannabis products, such as tinctures, creams and edibles, can be produced or sold. Medical marijuana patients are not allowed to buy on the premises. Including medical cannabis dispensaries in the distribution system would have addressed some of the barriers to access to cannabis for medical purposes that Canadians currently experience. In response to the high cost of marijuana from licensed producers and the lack of cannabis edibles and other services, medical marijuana users continue to turn to illegal medical marijuana dispensaries in cities throughout Canada.

Since the new medical marijuana policies came into effect, the number of illegal cannabis dispensaries has increased in many cities in Canada, particularly in B.C. In Vancouver alone, it is estimated that there were about twenty illegal dispensaries before 2012 (Woo 2015). That number increased to one hundred in 2015 (CBC 2015b; Lepard 2015). In April 2015, the City of Vancouver responded to the rapid growth of unregulated illegal medical marijuana dispensaries with proposed new regulations to control these outlets. The proposed regulations prohibit dispensaries from operating near schools or community centres, require a licensing fee of $30,000 and a development permit, among other requirements (CBC 2015a; Woo 2015).

Vancouver's proposal to use municipal bylaws to regulate the operations of cannabis dispensaries revealed the deep differences in approach to drugs that exists between some municipal, provincial and federal authorities in Canada. Just one day after the City's proposals were released, then federal health minister Rona Ambrose warned the mayor of Vancouver not to regulate the dispensaries because they are illegal and it would "encourage drug use and addiction" (Woo 2015). She also claimed that regulating the dispensaries would send a "dangerous message to youth." In response to the health minister's warning, City Councillor Kerry Lang reported that the City drafted the regulations to "keep marijuana away from children" and to regulate the growing number of dispensaries. He also reported that Vancouver has been examining the findings from Colorado and other jurisdictions that have legalized and regulated recreational cannabis use (CBC 2015a). Following these events, Health Minister Terry Lake announced that the B.C. provincial Liberal-led government supports the City of Vancouver's proposed marijuana dispensary regulations. On April 24, 2015, federal Health Minister Ambrose commented to the media that "marijuana is not medicine" (CBC News 2015a), thus reiterating the former Conservative government's position on medical marijuana. Despite Ambrose's objections, on June 24, 2015, Vancouver city councillors voted in favour of the new regulations to license medical marijuana dispensaries, becoming the first city in Canada to take this step. Even policing in Canada is not always supportive of federal approaches to drug laws. In response to a complaint, the Vancouver Police Department (VPD) released a report on marijuana dispensaries in September 2015, in which they argue the following:

> Using the criminal law to close marihuana dispensaries is generally ineffective, raises concerns about proportionality, and is a significant drain on valuable police resources that is difficult to justify in the absence of overt public safety concerns. …. Bylaw enforcement, however, is an effective tool to shut down a business that isn't compliant with municipal bylaws. (VPD 2015)

This statement reveals the high level of discord between various levels of government in Canada when in comes to addressing cannabis laws.

In fact, Health Canada's website for the past MMPR, includes a disclaimer in a bolded box that states:

> Dried marijuana is not an approved drug or medicine in Canada. The Government of Canada does not endorse the use of marijuana, but the courts have required reasonable access to a legal source of marijuana when authorized by a physician. (Health Canada 2015)

In 2016, the website was updated, and it now states: "Cannabis is not an approved therapeutic product and the provision of this information should not be interpreted as an endorsement of the use of cannabis for therapeutic purposes, or of marijuana generally, by Health Canada." However, by blaming the courts for the continuance of, though greatly reorganized, federal medical marijuana program, the Conservative-led government at that time condoned it publicly. However, the government's policy changes have not gone unnoticed. Prior to the policy changes, medical marijuana scholars and advocates presented research and evidence to the government about the benefits of the plant for medicinal purposes and the need to keep intact personal and designated grower options. The Conservative-led federal government at that time failed to listen and eliminated personal and designated growers. Following these events, as noted above, a challenge was initiated by four plaintiffs (*Allaird et al. v. Canada*). The issue before the Supreme Court was whether the new medical marijuana policy (MMPR) put into place in 2014 by the federal government violated section 7 of the *Canadian Charter of Rights and Freedoms*. It was argued successfully that the elimination of personal and designated growers infringe on the plaintiffs' liberty and security of the person. This case and others related to cannabis will impact the Liberal-led federal government's legal regulatory framework for cannabis.

Alternatives to Prohibition

In this chapter we argue that drug use is a health and social, not criminal, matter and should be treated as such. We also note that not all drug use is problematic and that cultural and social factors shape drug use. Prohibition does not deliver on its intended goals, but it does result in the marginalization of whole groups of people and in some cases their deaths. It is time to consider an approach that helps to contain the negative effects of drug use, provides a variety of treatment modalities and harm reduction services and avoids criminalizing those who choose to use drugs.

New models for addressing drug-related problems are also emerging across the globe. In fact, since 2012 the international consensus on prohibition seems to be coming apart. Countries are beginning to experiment with approaches that show more promise for achieving the health and safety goals for their communities. At least twenty-five jurisdictions around the world are currently deploying some form decriminalization of drugs (Rosmarin and Eastwood 2012). Portugal, Uruguay, Guatemala, Colombia and the Czech Republic, as well as some U.S. states, are among the jurisdictions experimenting with either decriminalization or legal regulation of some drugs. Portugal decriminalized all illegal drugs in 2001 and adopted a more health-oriented approach by increasing social supports, harm reduction and diverse drug treatment services (Moreira et al. 2011; Murkin 2014). In Portugal, decriminalization has had the effect of decreasing the number of people injecting drugs, decreasing the number of people using drugs problematically and decreasing trends of drug use among 15- to 24-year-olds. The Czech Republic also decriminalized all drugs in 2010 after undertaking a cost-benefit analysis of their policies that found that the penalization of drug use had not affected the availability of illegal drugs, increases in the levels of drug use had occurred and the social costs of illicit drugs had increased considerably. After decriminalization, and similar to the case of Portugal, drug use has not increased significantly, but the social harms of drug use have declined. The lesson from these two jurisdictions appears to be to that decreases in drug use can achieved by rejecting law-and-order approaches and ramping up other social supports.

In 2014, Uruguay became the first nation to end cannabis prohibition at the federal level when legislators voted to create a legally regulated and state-controlled regime for cannabis. In November 2012, the U.S. states of Washington and Colorado also voted to create regulated markets for cannabis for adults. In 2014, Alaska, Oregon and the District of Columbia followed suit. In 2016, California, Maine, Massachusetts and Nevada also voted to legalize and regulate cannabis. These events follow on a long history of decriminalization of cannabis, including the Dutch coffee shop model (which allows for the legal sale of small amounts of cannabis in select coffee shops in the Netherlands) and the decriminalization of cannabis in several Australian and U.S. states.

Canada has contributed some of the best thinking in the world when it comes to offering alternatives to prohibition. Since 1998, the Health Officers Council of British Columbia has created a series of discussion papers that recommend an end to prohibition and its replacement with a regulated market for all substances based on the principles of public health (Health Officers Council of British Columbia 2011). The latest of these papers, published in 2011, describes how the public health–oriented regulation of alcohol, tobacco, prescription and illegal substances can better reduce the harms that result both from substance use and substance regulation, compared to current approaches.

A model for legalizing and regulating cannabis draws on a public health approach that includes price controls through taxation, restriction of advertising and promotion, controls on the age of the purchaser, driving restrictions, limited hours of sale, labelling that contains information on potency and health effects, plain packaging and licensing guidelines for producers of cannabis. Similar approaches could be taken to cannabis to balance the need to limit use but avoid re-creating an illegal market for contraband (Emont, Choi, Novotny and Giovino 1993; Levy, Chaloupka and Gitchell 2004; Lewit et al. 1997; Room, Babor and Rehm 2005).

Taxation has been shown to decrease levels of alcohol and tobacco use, and similar strategies could be applied to cannabis. For example, Stockwell et al. (2007: 6) outline three approaches for using alcohol taxation strategies to reduce harm: 1) taxing the alcohol content of drinks, 2) linking tax rates to the cost of living and 3) raising small additional taxes to fund treatment and prevention programs. The researchers also explain that there is "strong evidence from other countries for the effectiveness of such tax changes." A relevant example is Australia, where the sale of low-alcohol beverages (rather than high-alcohol beverages) increased due to their taxation changes:

DECRIMINALIZATION VERSUS LEGALIZATION

Decriminalization refers to the removal of criminal penalties for possession of small amounts of currently criminalized drugs. Possession would remain a criminal offence "subject to civil or administration sanctions" such as fines (Transform 2014: 83). Critics argue that prohibition-related harms would remain in tact, such as illegal drug markets and organized crime. Further, they argue that drug users would remain at risk because the quality of the drugs bought would remain unknown. Portugal decriminalized all drugs for personal use in 2001.

Legalization refers to removing all criminal penalties for the possession of currently criminalized drugs. These drugs would be legally regulated by the state (just as alcohol and prescription drugs are). Furthermore, policies for the production, sale and taxation of some drugs such as cannabis would be enacted. In 2014 Uruguay became the first nation to end cannabis prohibition. Four U.S. states and the District of Columbia have also enacted legislation to legally regulate the use, production, sale and taxation of cannabis.

With the major success of low to mid-strength beers (2.5% to 3.8% alcohol by volume), after tax incentives to encourage the production of these products were introduced in the late 1980s.... The market share of these beverages in terms of value reached 40% of the total Australian beer market by the late 1990s. These products are also widely used at large-scale sporting venues as a way of reducing problems with alcohol-related violence. (ibid.)

The graph illustrates the relationship between drug control and its supply and demand. When a drug is fully prohibited it ends up being controlled by underground organizations. When a drug is legalized and promoted without regard for public health impacts, there are similar consequences for supply and demand. From the perspective of public health, the ideal mode of regulation sits in the middle, where a substance is available in a regulated market with appropriate age and other controls and appropriate programs that address the harms and benefits of its use.

This model draws on the kinds of evidence presented in this chapter and focuses on the prevention of illness, injury and mortality. We do not suggest that a completely free drug market be established; instead careful thought must be put into all aspects of a regulatory model for drugs that draws on the mistakes and successes of regulation of other legally available psychoactive substances such as tobacco and alcohol. We also recognize that given the propensity for social conditions to shape the harms of drug use, changing how we control substances requires a robust governmental response that includes adequate health care and other social supports that address issues of poverty, isolation and oppression.

Drug prohibitionist approaches have been shown to be ineffective at reducing drug use and promoting pubic safety in other places around the world. In fact, drug prohibition and increasingly punitive policies have been demonstrated to create harms that undermine public safety and human rights (Count the Costs 2012a; Global Commission on Drug Policy 2011; Room and Reuter 2012). Internationally, drug reform efforts are moving forward despite the reality that Canada and other nations are signatories on a number of United Nations drug control treaties that espouse punitive prohibitionist policies.

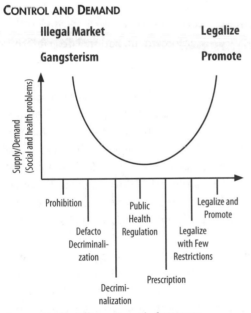

CONTROL AND DEMAND

Illegal Market   **Legalize**

Gangsterism   **Promote**

Supply/Demand (Social and health problems)

Prohibition — Public Health — Legalize and Promote

Defacto Decriminalization — Regulation — Legalize with Few Restrictions

Decriminalization — Prescription

Source: Health Officers Council of BC 2011.

Drug Policy in the Future

A new direction in drug policy is required. We can continue to work within the paradigm of drug prohibition, or we can begin to explore alternative approaches and chart a new course that can help save lives, respect human rights and foster social inclusion while being more cost effective at the same time.

Fortunately, as the discussion above about emerging legal regulatory frameworks for cannabis illustrates, drug policies and law are not unchanging. Sometimes, drug reform is incremental. At other times, small policy shifts slowly evolve over time to form a larger change. With the election of a Liberal-led federal government in the fall of 2015, Canada's drug policies are about to change as the Liberal promise to end cannabis prohibition is enacted into law.

As we write, Canada still relies on the criminal law to curb illegal drug use and stem the growth of illegal drug markets. Canada also spends enormous amounts of money annually to prevent the illegal purchase, use and distribution of illegal drugs both inside Canada and beyond its borders. The Conservative-led federal government allocated $527.8 million for the NADS for 2012–17, much of it on enforcement related activities. It is too soon to know how the allocation of funds will be prioritized in the next federal budget, especially when cannabis prohibition ends and a legal regulatory framework is created in its place. However, the NADS strategy only accounts for a portion of government spending on drug control. Activities such as provincial, municipal and RCMP drug enforcement, national drug interdiction efforts and the use of military personnel in international drug control efforts, drive up policing, military and border security budgets.

Cannabis remains a key target of policing, and cannabis remains a lucrative market — the annual retail expenditures on this substance are estimated to be about $357 million per year in B.C. alone. Cannabis is a popular drug, and its effects are certainly less harmful than alcohol and tobacco. But the Liberal promise to legalize and regulate the recreational use of cannabis has many unknowns. What will this legal framework look like? Will small and local cannabis dispensaries become part of the framework? Will adults be allowed to grow a few cannabis plants for personal use? Will cannabis arrests cease now rather than waiting until after the new framework is implemented? Will people with past cannabis convictions be pardoned?

One of the most urgent issues affecting Canadians is discrimination against people who use illegal drugs. Poor and racialized women and men, especially Indigenous peoples, are discriminated against in the criminal justice system and in social welfare and health services. In fact, poor and marginalized people bear the brunt of our prohibitionist drug policies. This discrimination and the hostility towards people who use drugs can be seen in the derogatory statements that appear routinely in media reports of public debates about services. Even with cannabis reform, legal discrimination against people who use other criminalized drugs may continue. In addition, people who sell small amounts of criminalized drugs may be further demonized. Thus, a reconsideration of all drug policies would be beneficial.

Therefore, there is also a need for urgent change in three key areas: drug law reform, discrimination, services and supports. In order to move forward, we recommend the reform of Canada's legislative, policy and regulatory frameworks that address psychoactive substances. We call for the replacement of the NADS with a strategy focused on health and human rights, social inclusion and the legal regulation of all drugs for personal use (and any step forward, such as decriminalization and the elimination of criminal penalties for personal possession) and the immediate creation of a regulatory system for adult cannabis use as the Liberals propose to do. In addition, we remind readers that most drug use is not problematic; rather, drug use is a social and cultural practice. Thus, not all drug use needs to be treated (or criminalized). However, we advocate the scaling-up of comprehensive health and social services, including housing and treatment services that engage people with drug problems. In addition, we advocate increased support for efforts to reduce the harms of substance use, which includes robust educational programs about safer drug use, programs for distributing new supplies for injection and crack cocaine use, safer consumption services, opioid substitution therapies and heroin-assisted treatment. We argue that these services are part of a larger social and public health approach to substance use that respects the human rights of people who use drugs. In addition, we also advocate that social and economic supports accompany drug reform. We also support expanded efforts to implement research-based and social approaches to eliminate stigma, discrimination and social and health inequities that affect people who use drugs.

Canada has many good people working at every level from frontline services and organizations to provincial and federal ministries, whose efforts are severely hampered by fear, lack of leadership and poorly informed policies based on outdated ideas and beliefs about drugs, addiction and the people who use, produce and sell substances. At the same time, critics in Canada assert that drug prohibition causes more harm than the drugs and the people it attempts to regulate. Eugene Oscapella (2012: 12), in his report with the Canadian Drug Policy Coalition Policy Working group, *Changing the Frame: A New Approach to Drug Policy in Canada*, stresses that there is "no substantial evidence that the criminal law significantly deters drug use." In addition, a global movement of sitting and former political leaders is emerging that acknowledges that the over-reliance on the criminal law in addressing drug problems is causing more harm than good. In 2011, the Global Commission on Drug Policy stated:

> The global war on drugs has failed, with devastating consequences for individuals and societies around the world. Fifty years after the initiation of the U.N. Single Convention on Narcotic Drugs ... fundamental reforms in national and global drug control policies are urgently needed. (Global Commission on Drug Policy 2011: 2)

The Commission recommends an end to the discrimination and marginalization of people who use currently criminalized drugs. They also recommend that governments implement models of legal regulation.

As drug users themselves and service and health providers continue to operate innovative harm reduction and drug services in Canada, and press for municipal, provincial and national reform, others, such as the Canadian Drug Policy Coalition, the Global Commission on Drug Policy, Transform Drug Policy Foundation and Drug Policy Alliance (to name a few), are also pressing for change at the international level, including organizing national and international discussions and meetings prior to the United Nations General Assembly Special Session (UNGASS) in 2016 that took place in New York. UNGASS was a special deliberation by the General Assembly to discuss a pressing issue of the day relating to health, gender or, in this case, the world's drug control priorities. The previous special session on drugs, held in 1998, adopted a plan to make the world "drug free" by 2008. This plan has not been realized. UNGASS 2016 was seen as an opportunity to craft a more realistic and constructive plan.

UNGASS 2016 was precipitated by an aligned and resolute group of reform-minded Latin American countries. But calls for reform are also emanating from Europe, and even the U.S. — traditionally one of the world's staunchest proponents and architects of the war on drugs — recognizes the need for more flexible interpretations of U.N. drug treaties. Although UNGASS did not radically change the course of drug policy, important issues were raised, and the Canadian minister of health addressed the Session and made clear that Canada is moving towards a health approach to drug policy, including the legalization of cannabis by 2017.

Canada is at a crossroads; cannabis prohibition will end in 2017. Yet, it is unclear what type of legal framework will be adopted and whether Canada's drug prohibitionist stance will shift in relation to other currently criminalized drugs and the people who use them. For example, will Canada also move towards decriminalization or legalization of the possession of other currently criminalized drugs? The number of U.N. member states advocating for new approaches to drug policy is unprecedented; globally, unparalleled drug reform is taking place. In a short span of time, cannabis prohibition ended in Uruguay, eight U.S. states and the District of Columbia; the decriminalization of personal use of all drugs took place in Portugal, and Bolivia opted to allow the chewing of coca leaves. These are only a few of the many drug reform shifts happening around the world.

Glossary of Key Terms

Controlled Drugs and Substances Act (CDSA): In Canada today, the use of particular drugs is regulated and controlled by this federal Act, which includes possession, trafficking, importing and exporting and production-related offences.

Drug prohibition: Drug prohibition is a regulatory system that has been expanded on for more than a century at the local, national and international levels. Drug prohibition is primarily a criminal justice system approach in Canada.

Legalization: Legalization refers to removing all criminal penalties for the possession of currently criminalized drugs. These drugs would be legally regulated by the state (just as alcohol and prescription drugs are). Furthermore, policies for the production, sale and taxation of some drugs such as cannabis would be enacted.

Marihuana for Medical Purposes Regulations (MMPR): Since 2001, the federal government of Canada has operated a legal medical marijuana system that was prompted by court rulings that upheld the right to access cannabis for serious and chronic medical conditions.

New policy was introduced in 2013 to regulate medical marijuana, Marihuana for Medical Purposes Regulations.

Opium Act: In 1908, the first federal drug law was enacted in Canada. The *Opium Act* regulated crude and powdered opium and opium prepared for smoking and made it an offence to import, manufacture, offer to sell, sell or possess to sell opium for non-medical reasons.

Royal Canadian Mounted Police (RCMP): A militarized federal police force, and local police, are the enforcement arm of drug prohibition in Canada.

Sate Streets and Communities Act (SSCA): In 2012, Canada's federal government passed and enacted the *Safe Streets and Communities Act* (SSCA). The Act includes mandatory minimum sentences for some drug crimes, including production, trafficking, importing and exporting. Mandatory minimum sentences reduce the discretion used by justice officials through the application of predefined minimum sentences for some crimes.

Uniform Crime Reporting (UCR): Police-reported crime statistics in Canada are compiled using the Uniform Crime Reporting (UCR) survey, which collects information on all criminal incidents reported to, and substantiated by, Canadian police services.

United Nations General Assembly Special Session (UNGASS): In 2016, UNGASS took place in New York. UNGASS was a special deliberation by the General Assembly to discuss the world's drug control priorities.

Questions for Discussion

1. Why did Canada enact a federal drug law in 1908? What social factors shaped the enactment of the *Opium Act*?

2. What do drug arrest statistics tell us about the enforcement of Canada's drug laws? Who is the most vulnerable for arrest? What drug garners the most attention by law enforcement?

3. Around the world, nations are turning away from punitive drug prohibitionist policies. Why are nations searching for alternatives to this model?

Resources for Activists

Canadian Drug Policy Coalition: www.drugpolicy.ca
Global Commission on Drug Policy: www.globalcommissionondrugs.org
NORML Canada: http://norml.ca
Transform: www.tdpf.org.uk

Notes

1. See also *Development of Needs-Based Planning Models for Substance Use Services and Supports in Canada*. <needsbasedplanningmodels.wordpress.com/>.
2. See, for example, Canadian Bar Association; Collaborating Centre for Prison Health and Education, Vancouver; Assembly of First Nations; B.C. Representative for Children and Youth; St. Leonard's Society of Canada; John Howard Society; Elizabeth Fry Society.
3. The two drug courier cases described below are an excerpt from Boyd 2006.

References

Allard et al. v. Canada. 2016. No: FC 419.

Allen, M. 2016. "Police-Reported Crime Statistics in Canada, 2015." *Juristat.* Ottawa: Canadian Centre for Justice Statistics.

Allen, M., and T. Superle. 2016. "Youth Crime in Canada, 2014." *Juristat.* Ottawa: Canadian Centre for Justice Statistics.

Angus Reid. 2011. *British Columbians Link Gang Violence to Illegal Cannabis Market.* Poll commissioned by Stop the Violence BC, September. <drugpolicy.ca/wp-content/uploads/2011/12/STVBC-How-not-to-protect-community-health-and-safety.pdf>.

____. 2012. *Most Americans and Canadians Are Ready to Legalize Marijuana.* Angus Reid Public Opinion, November 29. <angusreidglobal.com/wp-content/uploads/2012/11/2012.11.28_Marijuana.pdf>.

Bacchi, C. 2009. *Analysing Policy: What's the Problem Represented To Be?* French Forest, Australia: Pearson.

Balfour, G., and E. Comack (eds.). 2006. *Criminalizing Women: Gender and (In)justice in Neo-liberal Times.* Halifax: Fernwood Publishing.

B.C. Corrections, Ministry of Justice. 2014. "Data on Women Who Received a Jail Sentence with British Columbia Corrections." Email communication with C. Gress, Director of Research and Planning, February 17.

Belle-Isle, L., and A. Hathaway. 2007. "Barriers to Access to Medical Cannabis for Canadians Living with hiv/aids." *AIDS Care* 19, 4: 500–506.

Berridge, V. 2013. *Demons: Our Changing Attitudes to Alcohol, Tobacco, and Drugs.* New York: Oxford University Press.

Best, J. 1995. *Random Violence: How We Talk About New Crimes and New Victims.* Berkeley: University of California Press.

Boyd, N. 1984. "The Origins of Canadian Narcotics Legislation: The Process of Criminalization in Historical Context." *Dalhousie Law Journal* 8: 102–36.

____. 2013. *The Enforcement of Marijuana Possession Offences in British Columbia: A Blueprint for Change.* <neilboyd.net/articles/Blueprint%20for%20Change.pdf>.

Boyd, S. 2006. "Representations of Women in the Drug Trade." In G. Balfour and E. Comack (eds.), *Criminalizing Women.* Halifax: Fernwood Publishing.

____. 2015. *From Witches to Crack Moms: Women, Drug Law and Policy, 2nd edition.* Durham: Carolina Academic Press.

Boyd, S., and C. Carter. 2014. *Killer Weed: Marijuana Grow Ops, Media, and Justice.* Toronto: University of Toronto Press.

Boyce, J., A. Cotter, and S. Perreault. 2014. "Police-Reported Crime Statistics in Canada, 2013." *Juristat.* Ottawa: Canadian Centre for Justice Statistics.

Brennan, S. 2012. *Police Reported Crime Statistics in Canada, 2011.* Ottawa: Statistics Canada. <statcan.

gc.ca/pub/85-002-x/2012001/article/11692-eng.htm>.

Bronskill, J. 2015. "Tax Revenue from Legalized Pot Should Fund Addiction Programs, Trudeau Says." *The Brandon Sun*, December 17. <brandonsun.com/national/breaking-news/taxation-of-legalized-pot-wont-be-a-government-cash-cow-trudeau-says-362833511.html?thx=y>.

Canadian Bar Association, National Criminal Law Section. 2009. *Bill C-15 — Controlled Drugs and Substances Act Amendments.* <cba.org/CMSPages/GetFile.aspx?guid=6d4e3ff7-85e3-40cb-a4f7-bac9f2de4392>.

Canadian Centre on Substance Abuse. 2011. *Cross Canada Report on Student Alcohol and Drug Use, Technical Report.* Ottawa: CCSA. <ccsa.ca/Resource%20 Library/2011_CCSA_Student_Alcohol_and_Drug_Use_en.pdf>.

Canadian Council on Social Development. 2014. *Children and Youth: Crime Prevention Through Social Development.* <ccsd.ca/resources/CrimePrevention/index.htm>.

Canadian Medical Association. 2013. CMA Response: Health Canada's Medical Marihuana Regulatory Proposal, February 28. <https://www.cma.ca/Assets/assets-library/document/en/advocacy/Proposed-Medical-Marihuana-Regulations_en.pdf>.

Carstairs, C. 2006. *Jailed for Possession: Illegal Drug Use, Regulation, and Power in Canada, 1920–1961.* Toronto: University of Toronto Press.

CBC News. 2015a. "Canada's Health Minister Says Dispensaries Normalize Marijuana Use." April 25. <cbc.ca/news/canada/british-columbia/canada-s-health-minister-says-dispensaries-normalize-marijuana-use-1.3048543>.

____. 2015b. "Federal Medical Marijuana Raids Not Part of Vancouver Police Plans." September 11. <cbc.ca/news/canada/british-columbia/federal-medical-marijuana-raids-not-part-of-vancouver-police-plans-1.3224111>.

____. 2015c. "Fentanyl Suspected in Death of Vancouver Teen." August 3. <cbc.ca/news/canada/british-columbia/fentanyl-suspected-in-death-of-vancouver-teen-1.3177987>.

Charles Colson Task Force on Federal Corrections. 2016. "Transforming Prisons, Restoring Lives: Final Recommendations of the Charles Colson Task Force on Federal Corrections." Washington, D.C.: Urban Institute. <colsontaskforce.org/final-recommendations/Colson-Task-Force-Final-Recommendations-January-2016.pdf>.

Chu, Sandra. 2012. "Thrown Under the Omnibus: Implications of the Safe Streets and Communities Act." Presentation to OHRDP 2012, The Current Political Environment: Implications for Harm Reduction and Supervised Consumption, January 30. <ohrdp.ca/wp-content/uploads/pdf/SandraKoHonChu.pdf>.

CIC (Correctional Investigator of Canada). 2012. *Annual Report of the Office of Correctional Investigator, 2011/12.* <oci-bec.gc.ca/cnt/rpt/annrpt/annrpt20112012-eng.aspx>.

Comack, E. 1986. "We Will Get Some Good Out of This Riot Yet: The Canadian State, Drug Legislation and Class Conflict." In S. Brickey and E. Comack (eds.), *The Social Basis of Law: Critical Readings in the Sociology of Law.* Toronto: Garamond.

Correctional Service of Canada. 2009. *Evaluation Report: Correctional Service Canada's Safer Tattooing Practices Pilot Initiative.* Ottawa. <csc-scc.gc.ca/text/pa/ev-tattooing-394-2-39/index-eng.shtml>.

Correctional Services Program. 2015. *Adult Correctional Statistics in Canada, 2013/2014.* Statistics Canada. <statcan.gc.ca/pub/85-002-x/2015001/article/14163-eng.htm>.

Cotter, A., J. Greenland, and M. Karam. 2015. "Drug-Related Offences in Canada, 2013." *Juristat.* Ottawa: Canadian Centre for Justice Statistics.

Count the Costs of the War on Drugs. 2012a. *Creating Crime, Enriching Criminals.* <countthecosts.org/seven-costs/creating-crime-enriching-criminals>.

____. 2012b. *The Alternative World Drug Report: Counting the Costs of the War on Drugs.* <countthecosts. org/sites/default/files/AWDR.pdf>.

Degenhardt, L., W.T. Chiu, et al. 2008. "Toward a Global View of Alcohol, Tobacco, Cannabis, and Cocaine Use: Findings from the who World Mental Health Surveys." *PLoS Med* 5, 7: e141. <plosmedicine.org/article/info:doi/10.1371/journal.pmed.0050141>.

Department of Justice, Canada. 2012. *Backgrounder — Safe Streets and Communities Act: Targeting Serious Drug Crime.* <news.gc.ca/web/article-en.do?nid=965359>.

Dorn, N., and N. South. 1993. "After Mr. Bennett and Mr. Bush: U.S. Foreign Policy and the Prospects for Drug Control." In F. Pearce and M. Woodiwiss (eds.), *Global Crime Connections: Dynamics and Control.* Toronto: University of Toronto Press.

Easton, S.T. 2004. *Marijuana Growth in British Columbia. Public Policy Sources: A Fraser Institute Occasional Paper.* Vancouver: The Fraser Institute.

Emont, S.L., W.S. Choi, et al. 1993. "Clean Indoor Air Legislation, Taxation, and Smoking Behaviour in the United States: An Ecological Analysis." *Tobacco Control* 2, 1: 13.

Fischer, B., J. Rehm, and W. Hall. 2009. "Cannabis Use in Canada: The Need for a 'Public Health' Approach." *Canadian Journal of Public Health* 100, 2: 101–103.

Gabor, T., and N. Crutcher. 2002. *Mandatory Minimum Penalties: Their Effects on Crime, Sentencing Disparities and Justice System Expenditures.* Ottawa: Research and Statistics Branch.

Government of Canada. 2012. "Marihuana for Medical Purposes Regulations." *Canada Gazette* 146, 5 (December 15). <gazette.gc.ca/rp-pr/p1/2012/2012-12-15/html/reg4-eng.html>.

Global Commission on Drug Policy. 2011. *War on Drugs: Report of the Global Commission on Drug Policy.* <globalcommissionondrugs.org/reports/>.

____. 2014. *Taking Control: Pathways to Drug Policies That Work.* <globalcommissionondrugs.org/ reports/taking-control-pathways-to-drug-policies-that-work/>.

Government of Canada. 2016. "Prime Minister Pledges Crackdown on Drug Criminal, Compassion for Their Victims." Speech, October 4, 2007. Ottawa: Government of Canada. <news.gc.ca/web/ article-en.do?crtr.sj1D=&mthd=advSrch&crtr.mnthndVl=&nid=352609&crtr.dpt1D=&crtr. tp1D=&crtr.lc1D=&crtr.yrStrtVl=2008&crtr.kw=&crtr.dyStrtVl=26&crtr.aud1D=&crtr. mnthStrtVl=2&crtr.yrndVl=&crtr.dyndVl>.

Grayson, K. 2008. *Chasing Dragons: Security, Identity, and Illicit Drugs in Canada.* Toronto: University of Toronto Press.

Grindspoon, L. 1998. "Medical Marihuana in a Time of Prohibition." *International Journal of Drug Policy* 10, 2: 145–56.

Harris, K. 2009. "Prison Tattoo Program Cut Risk of HIV: Report." *Sudbury Star*, April 15. <thesudburystar.com/2009/04/15/prison-tattoo-program-cut-risk-of-hiv-report-7>.

Health Canada. 2013. *Transition and the Marihuana for Medical Purposes Regulations.* <hc-sc.gc.ca/ dhp-mps/marihuana/transition-eng.php>.

____. 2015. *Medical use of Marihuana.* <hc-sc.gc.ca/dhp-mps/marihuana/index-eng.php>.

____. 2016. Consumer Education. <hc-sc.gc.ca/dhp-mps/marihuana/info/cons-eng.php>

Health Officers' Council of British Columbia. 2011. *Public Health Perspectives for Regulating Psychoactive Substances: What We Can Do About Alcohol, Tobacco and Other Drugs.* <canadianharmreduction. com/sites/default/files/BC2.pdf>.

Hughes, C., and A. Stevens. 2010. "What Can We Learn From the Portuguese Decriminalization of Illicit Drugs?" *British Journal of Criminology* 50, 6: 999–1022.

Human Rights Watch. 2008. *Targeting Blacks: Drug Law Enforcement and Race in the United States.* New York: Human Rights Watch.

Iftene, A., and A. Manson. 2012. "Recent Crime Legislation and the Challenge for Prison Health Care." *CMAJ*, Nov. 5.

Kerr, T., W. Small, and E. Wood. 2005. "The Public Health and Social Impacts of Drug Market Enforcement: A Review of the Evidence." *International Journal of Drug Policy* 16, 4: 210–220.

Kilmer, B., and R.L. Pacula. 2009. *Estimating the Size of Global Drug Market: A Demand-Side Approach*. Santa Monica: RAND Europe.

Lepard, D. 2015. *Service and Policy Complaint #2015-112 Regarding Enforcement against Marihuana Dispensaries*. Vancouver Police Department, September 1. <vancouver.ca/police/policeboard/agenda/2015/0917/1509C01-2015-112-Marijuana-Dispensaries.pdf>.

Levy, D.T., F. Chaloupka, and J. Gitchell. 2004. "The Effects of Tobacco Control Policies on Smoking Rates: A Tobacco Control Scorecard." *Journal of Public Health Management and Practice* 10, 4: 338.

Lewit, E.M., A. Hyland, N. Kerrebrock, and K.M. Cummings. 1997. "Price, Public Policy and Smoking in Young People." *British Medical Journal* 6 (Suppl 2): S17.

London School of Economics. 2014. *Ending the Drug Wars*. May. Report of the LSE Expert Group on the Economics of Drug Policy. London: Author.

Lucas, P. 2012. "It Can't Hurt to Ask: A Patient-Centred Quality of Service Assessment of Health Canada's Medical Cannabis Policy and Program." *Harm Reduction Journal* 9, 2: 436–441.

Lupick, T. 2015. "Corporations Move in on Canada's Medicinal Cannabis Industry." *The Georgia Straight*, March 18. <straight.com/news/413966/corporations-move-canadas-medicinal-cannabis-industry>.

Mahony, T. 2011. *Women and the Criminal Justice System*. Statistics Canada: Ministry of Industry.

Mallea, P. 2010. *The Fear Factor: Stephen Harper's "Tough on Crime" Agenda*. Ottawa: Canadian Centre for Policy Alternatives. <policyalternatives.ca/sites/default/files/uploads/publications/National%20Office/2010/11/Tough%20on%20Crime.pdf>.

Manning, P. 2007. "Introduction." In P. Manning (ed.), *Drugs and Popular Culture: Drugs, Media and Identity in Contemporary Society*. Cullompton: Willan.

Martel, M. 2006. *Not This Time: Canadians, Public Policy, and the Marijuana Question 1961–1975*. Toronto: University of Toronto Press.

Moreira, M., B. Hughes, C. Storti, and F. Zobel. 2011. *Drug Policy Profiles — Portugal*. Luxembourg: European Monitoring Centre for Drugs and Drug Addiction. <emcdda.europa.eu/publications/drug-policy-profiles/portugal>.

Murkin, G. 2014. *Drug Decriminalisation in Portugal: Setting the Record Straight*. London: Transform Drug Policy Foundation. <tdpf.org.uk/blog/drug-decriminalisation-portugal-setting-record-straight>.

NAOMI Study Team. 2008. "Reaching the Hardest to Reach – Treating the Hardest-to-Treat: Summary of the Primary Outcomes of the North American Opiate Medication Initiative (NAOMI)." <chumontreal.qc.ca/sites/default/files//documents/Media/PDF/081017-resume-resultats-etude.pdf>.

Nutt, D., L. King, and L.Phillips. 2010. "Drug Harms in the UK: A Multicriteria Decision Analysis." *The Lancet* 376, 9752: 1558–1565.

Office of the Correctional Investigator. 2012. *Spirit Matters: Aboriginal People and the Corrections and Conditional Release Act*. <oci-bec.gc.ca/cnt/rpt/oth-aut/oth-aut20121022-eng.aspx>.

Office of the Provincial Health Officer (B.C.). 2013. *Health, Crime and Doing Time: Potential Impacts of the Safe Streets and Communities Act (Former Bill C10) on the Health and Well-being of Aboriginal People in BC*. <health.gov.bc.ca/pho/pdf/health-crime-2013.pdf>.

Office of the Sentencing Council. 2011. "Drug 'Mules': Twelve Case Studies." London: Sentencing Council of England and Wales. <sentencingcouncil.org.uk/wp-content/uploads/Drug_mules_bulletin.pdf>.

Oscapella, E., with Canadian Drug Policy Coalition Policy Working Group. 2012. *Changing the Frame: A New Approach to Drug Policy in Canada*. Vancouver, BC: Canadian Drug Policy Coalition. <drugpolicy.ca/wp-content/uploads/2015/02/CDPC_report_eng_v14_comp.pdf>.

Potter, G., et al. 2015. "Global Patterns of Domestic Cannabis Cultivation: Sample Characteristics and Patterns of Growing across Eleven Countries." *International Journal of Drug Policy* 26, 3: 226–237.

Public Safety Canada. 2012. *Corrections and Conditional Release Statistical Overview 2012*. <publicsafety.gc.ca/cnt/rsrcs/pblctns/ccrso-2012/index-en.aspx>.

R. v. Lloyd. 2014. Provincial Court of British Columbia 2014 BCPC 0011. <provincialcourt.bc.ca/judgments.php?link=http://www.canlii.org/en/bc/bcpc/>.

R. v. Lloyd. 2016. Supreme Court of Canada SCC 2016 13. <scc-csc.lexum.com/scc-csc/scc-csc/en/item/15859/index.do>.

Reinarman, C., and H. Levine. 2000. "Crack in Context: Politics and Media in the Making of a Drug Scare." In R. Cruthchfield, G. Bridges, J. Weis, and C. Kubrin (eds.), *Crime Readings, 2nd edition*. Thousand Oaks, CA: Pine Forge Press.

Room, R., B. Fischer, et al. 2008. *Cannabis Policy: Moving Beyond Stalemate*. Oxford: Oxford University Press.

Room, R., T. Babor, and J. Rehm. 2005. "Alcohol and Public Health." *Lancet* 365, 9458: 519.

Room, R., and P. Reuter. 2012. "How Well Do International Drug Conventions Protect Public Health?" *Lancet* 379, 9810: 84–91.

Rosmarin, A., and N. Eastwood. 2012. *A Quiet Revolution: Drug Decriminalization Policies in Practice Across the Globe*. London: Release Legal Emergency and Drug Services. <release.org.uk/publications/quiet-revolution-drug-decriminalisation-policies-practice-across-globe>.

R. v. Gladue. 1999. 1 S.C.R. No. 699.

R. v. Hamilton. 2003. 172, C.C.C. (3d) 114, 8 C.R. (6th) 215 (S.C.J.).

R. v. Hamilton. 2004. 186 C.C.C. (3d) 129, 241 D.L. R. (4th) 490, 22 C.R. (6th) 1, 72 O.R. (3d) 1 (C.A.).

SAMHSA (Substance Abuse and Mental Health Services Administration), Office of Applied Studies. 2012. *Results from the 2011 National Survey on Drug Use and Health: National Findings*. <samhsa.gov/data/sites/default/files/Revised2k11NSDUHSummNatFindings/Revised2k11NSDUHSummNatFindings/NSDUHresults2011.htm>.

Sapers, H. 2013. *Annual Report of the Office of the Correctional Investigator 2012–2013*. Ottawa: Office of the Correctional Investigator, Government of Canada. <oci-bec.gc.ca/cnt/rpt/annrpt/annrpt20122013-eng.aspx>.

____. 2014. *Annual Report of the Office of the Correctional Investigator 2013–2014*. Ottawa: Office of the Correctional Investigator, Government of Canada. <oci-bec.gc.ca/cnt/rpt/pdf/annrpt/annrpt20132014-eng.pdf>.

____. 2016. *Annual Report of the Office of the Correctional Investigator, 2015–2016*. Ottawa: The Correctional Investigator Canada. <oci-bec.gc.ca/cnt/rpt/pdf/annrpt/annrpt20152016-eng.pdf>.

Statistics Canada. 2013. *Aboriginal Peoples in Canada: First Nations People, Métis and Inuit. National Household Survey, 2011*. Ministry of Industry. <stratejuste.ca/uploads/3/1/8/4/31849453/aboriginal_release_nhs_briefs_sept_16.pdf>.

Stockwell, T., B. Pakula, S. Macdonald, J. Buxton, J. Zhao, A. Tu, D. Reist, G. Thomas, A. Puri, and C. Duff. 2007. "Alcohol Consumption in British Columbia and Canada: A Case for Liquor Taxes that Reduce Harm." *CARBC Statistical Bulletin* 3: 1–8. University of Victoria, British Columbia. <uvic.ca/research/centres/carbc/assets/docs/bulletin3-alcohol-consumption-in-bc.pdf>.

Sudbury, J. (ed.). 2005. *Global Lockdown: Race, Gender, and the Prison-Industrial Complex*. London: Routledge.

Tickner, A., and C. Cepeda. 2012. "The Role of Illegal Drugs in Colombian-U.S. Relations." In A. Gaviria and D. Mejia (eds.), *Anti-Drugs Policies in Colombia: Successes, Failures and Wrong Turns*. Universidad de los Andes (uncorrected Proof).

Tonry, M. 2009. "The Mostly Unintended Effects of Mandatory Penalties: Two Centuries of Consistent Findings." In M. Tonry (ed.), *Crime and Justice: A Review of Research*, Volume 38. Chicago: University of Chicago Press.

UNICEF. 2013. *Child Well-Being in Rich Countries: A Comparative Overview*. <unicef.org.uk/Images/Campaigns/FINAL_RC11-ENG-LORES-fnl2.pdf>.

United Nations Office on Drugs and Crime. 2013. *World Drug Report, 2012*. <unodc.org/documents/data-and-analysis/WDR2012/WDR_2012_web_small.pdf>.

U.S. Department of Health and Human Services, Substance Abuse and Mental Health Services Administration. 2012. *National Survey on Drug Use and Health 2011*. Washington.

Valverde, M. 1998. *Diseases of the Will: Alcohol and Dilemmas of Freedom*. Cambridge: Cambridge University Press.

Vancouver Police Department. 2015. "Service and Policy Complaint #2015-112 regarding enforcement against marihuana dispensaries." Vancouver: VPD.

Van Hout, M.C., and R. Brennan. 2012. "Curiosity Killed the M-Cat: A Post Legislative Study on Mephedrone Use in Ireland." *Drugs: Education, Prevention and Policy* 19, 2: 156–162.

Werb, D., T. Kerr, B. Nosyk, S. Strathdee, J. Montaner, and E. Wood. 2013. "The Temporal Relationship Between Drug Supply Indicators: An Audit of International Government Surveillance Systems." *BMJ* 3, 9: doi: 10.1136/bmjopen-2013-003077.

Werb, D., B. Nosyk, T. Kerr, B. Fischer, J. Montaner, and E. Wood. 2012. "Estimating the Economic Value of British Columbia's Domestic Cannabis Market: Implications for Provincial Cannabis Policy." *International Journal on Drug Policy* 23, 6: 436–441. <dx.doi.org/10.1016/j.drugpo.2012.05.003 Medline: 23085258>.

Werb, D., G. Rowell, G. Guyatt, T. Kerr, J. Montaner, and E. Wood. 2010. *Effect of Drug Law Enforcement on Drug Related Violence: Evidence From a Scientific Review*. Vancouver: International Centre for Science in Drug Policy. <ncbi.nlm.nih.gov/pubmed/23085258>.

Willis, E. 1992. *No More Nice Girls: Countercultural Essays*. Hanover, NH: University Press of New England.

Winstock, A., L. Mitcheson, and J. Marsden. 2010. "Mephedrone: Still Available and Twice the Price." *Lancet* 376: 1537.

Woo, A. 2015. "Ottawa Warns Against Plan to Regulate Vancouver Pot Dispensaries." *Globe and Mail*, April 23. <theglobeandmail.com/news/british-columbia/health-minister-warns-vancouver-not-to-regulate-illegal-marijuana-dispensaries/article24090887/>.

Wood, E., M. McKinnon, R. Strang, and P.R. Kendall. 2012. "Improving Community Health and Safety in Canada Through Evidence-Based Policies on Illegal Drugs." *Open Medicine* 6, 1: 37.

Wortley, S. 2004. "Hidden Intersections: Research on Race, Crime and Criminal Justice in Canada." *Canadian Ethnic Studies Journal* 35, 3: 99–17. <who.int/healthpromotion/conferences/previous/ottawa/en/index.html>.

Yalkin, T.R., and M. Kirk. 2012. *The Fiscal Impact of Changes to Eligibility for Conditional Sentences of Imprisonment in Canada*. <parl.gc.ca/pbo-dpb/documents/Conditional_sentencing_EN.pdf>.

15

It Begins with Food

Food as Inspiration and Imperative for Social Change

Sally Miller

YOU SHOULD KNOW THIS

- One in nine people in the world are hungry while over one in ten are obese.
- In Canada, farmers receive the same prices, not adjusted for inflation, that they received in the 1970s.
- Around 12 percent of Canadian households lived with food insecurity (not knowing if they will have enough food to eat) in 2014.
- 16.7 percent of households accessing food banks in Canada have working members; one in six children lived in households that experienced food insecurity in 2015.
- Between 1993 and 2006, around 150,000 farmers in India committed suicide by drinking the pesticides that drove them into debt.
- In 2007, the Food and Agriculture Association reported that there was enough food harvested that year to feed the world 1.5 times over.
- Between 1985 and 2010, 100 percent of Canadian farmers' net income came from farm support programs, off-farm income and loans.
- The global food system accounts for one-third of all greenhouse gas emissions.

Sources: World Food Programme 2016; WHO 2016; Food Banks Canada 2016 website; Food Banks Canada 2015; Lee et al. 2010; NFU 2010; Qualman and Tait 2004; Rideout et al. 2007; Tarasuk, Mitchell and Dachner 2016; Gilbert 2012.

IN ALL SOCIAL ACTION, FROM BUYING LUNCh to marching in a rally, we shape, explore and take moral positions that define our actions. This cultural process occurs through the narratives we tell about our experience, the understanding we create and work out together in dialogue with other cultural actors. Nowhere is this more dramatic and urgent than in our words about food. Food, along with shelter, is essential to our survival, but it is also the stage for us to discuss and work out our relations with others, from our favourite childhood meals to the choice of snack between classes.

Food is an idiom for social expression, most recently as a vivid stage for the concentration of power and wealth in the hands of a few. The food system has become the focus of intensive corporate concentration, economic power and the systematic dismantling of community and democratic ownership of food and agriculture. Like all works of culture, this has proceeded through the stories we tell about the food system, from the corporations that claim their seed will feed the world to the thousands of activists working together to save local and peasant agricultures. As cultural actors and activists, we choose which stories to highlight and act upon. How did we come to shape and consent to a world in which so many people are hungry and have lost access to land to feed themselves? How do we shape and confirm new ways for eating, distributing and growing food? This chapter explores the current state of the food system, the ways in which it is failing people everywhere, including in Canada, and the movements for resistance and change that can take us beyond the current food crisis.

The Complexities of Food

Food has been the flashpoint of resistance and the tinder for the fire of change around the world for many decades. Food and agriculture are also the site of an unprecedented concentration of power. This has spectacular conjunctions of our inhumanity towards others with the systematic dismantling of democracy and equity structures, and the development of economic mechanisms devoted to profit and the consolidation of power. This tragic conjunction of circumstances is rapidly draining the earth of resources and resilience. One billion of us go to bed hungry; one billion of us are obese (Holt-Gimenez and Patel 2009: 3) — as profits shift unevenly towards the powerful, so too do the calories.

There is enough to feed the world, and there has been for many decades; the Food and Agriculture Organization calculates that in 2007 there was one-and-a-half times the food needed to feed everyone sufficiently (Holt-Gimenez and Patel 2009: 7). The problem is not with yield, but with distribution and poverty. These are issues of power, not crop failure. More recently, rampant speculation with food commodities and the growing competition between grain for food and grain for fuel have exacerbated the situation. However, as Davis (2002) has pointed out, famine and starvation are a result of human systems responding to climate variation. As wealth becomes concentrated in the hands of a few people and transnational corporations (TNCs) like Cargill, Dupont and McDonald's, the number of have-nots increases. Those with sufficient money can buy whatever food they want, including exotic items like coffee that has been squeezed through the gut of an Indonesian civet, blowfish sushi that contains a neurotoxin that may stimulate your senses or kill you, gourmet chocolates with rare salts and organic ingredients and deep sea fish that have never before seen the light of day. Those without money starve or suffer from chronic malnutrition and food insecurity leading to death.

The Moral Economies of Food

A food system based on conventional economic principles assumes that price is determined in a negotiation between supply and demand, which will always leave some people out; for widgets this is fine — you can have too many widgets. But for food, if you are one of the unlucky ones who can't afford the price, you go hungry. In the parlance of neoclassical economics, this group is called those "not willing to pay," as if it is our own choice to go hungry or watch our children starve. This fantasy removes the need for compassion from food economics. It is key to the shift that has had to take place in the cultures of food and that must be reinforced over and over again by the way corporations and governments talk about food.

We all have a great deal to say about food; opinions, knowledge, exclamations and concerns burble out of us like fast-running water in a brook. The dynamic cultures of food, which bring us together, link us to previous generations, comfort us and cause us anxiety,

> Talking about food gives us a way to change our economies of food.

also determine the place of food in resistance and social change. Most people are diffident about discussing economic issues such as our wages or the difficulties we have making car payments. In North America, poverty is considered an individual shame. Systemic concerns are nebulous in our stories about poverty. The latter tend to focus on individual effort and failure. We are more ready to discuss food issues — even those struggling with food insecurity can talk about their favourite meals, the best places to get deals or their food memories from childhood. Talking about food gives us a way to change our economies of food.

Food and Resistance

Resistance to the global food system is greatly facilitated by the fact that food plays such an important role in our social expression. Food provides a means of expression, reflection and rumination over the supreme moment of capitalism that we have reached. The choice to use food to address a global breakdown in economic and social equity is not neutral; food and agriculture hold central and defining positions in movements for alternatives (Patel and McMichael 2009; see also Goodman and Watts 1997: 7). Since the key to understanding and changing our world can be found in the narratives we use to assert, confirm and create our version of the world and our experience in it, food and narratives about it represent an ideal starting point to think about a better world.

The reasons why food provides an ideal starting point for social change are complex: they include the relation of food and agriculture to a culture's identity as well as to the imperatives of survival. Holt-Gimenez and Patel link this, as many others do, to identity (2009: 182): "Control over one's food is essential to control over oneself." Manning writes (2004: 163), "Food tells a people's collective story in the same way that the molecules we eat assemble the body." Food can be a powerful force for change, but change in action, culture, and behaviour necessarily is ignited from and invites changes in the stories we tell about ourselves.

The Power of Narrative

Narratives, whether of food, war or fairies, are not created equal. To change the identities and lives we create through food, we must address the uneven distribution of power, status and wealth, which has ensured that some stories are more heard, believed and acted on than others. Just as we are not making objective decisions in the false plenty of a supermarket, we are also facing a panoply of narratives of unequal rhetorical and political power. The failure to persuade or to become dominant is rarely intimately connected to truthfulness; it has more to do with the culture and power embodied and embedded in the story. Statistical reports of food insecurity (over three million in Canada, 14 percent of the U.S. population, 795 million hungry people in the world) seem more apt to be taken seriously than dramatic and enraged pleas. The register of numbers and science-derived facts has a higher status than tones of anger and outrage.

How we recognize or define truth ensures that we have a cultural standard for narrative: reports told with anger and passion have less chance of persuasion, at least among the powerful, than ones told without emotion. But shouldn't we be angry about so many hungry people on our doorsteps? Perhaps we should be more concerned about people who seem unmoved by the atrocities in the food system — is it really possible to speak without emotion about the 150,000 farmers in India that have committed suicide since 1993 by drinking the pesticides that drove them into debt (Holt-Gimenez and Patel 2009: 32)? To be able to talk about these things without rage seems a little pathological. The credibility of a tale is also influenced by the teller's class and political status (often measured and reflected in precisely the scientific vocabulary and accent of one's speech): the higher the class position of the speaker, the greater the credibility of their tale.

The unequal power of narratives, rhetoric and speakers creates a sense of inevitability or naturalness about narratives that are, after all, only one more way of looking at the world. This can become very dangerous, as we abide by, and shape our decisions around a narrative that has become the commonly believed context, and therefore no longer questionable. For instance, the failure of neoclassical economic solutions has become resoundingly clear. The international organizations like the World Bank, World Trade Organization (WTO), and International Monetary Fund (IMF) have recommended and enforced patterns of structural adjustment for developing countries. These prescriptions require countries to reduce their social safety nets and introduce survival necessities like food, water and land to the commodity market in order to receive the loans they need. These requirements have led to increasing hunger, lack of social protections for people who fall ill or lose their jobs and nightmare scenarios such as the situation in Bolivia, where the privatization by Bechtel Corporation of the public water led to riots. Protesters were murdered in the streets as they demanded access to water to live. A similar result of cost-cutting requirements has resulted in long-term health problems for many people in Flint, Michigan, when the city's water source was changed to the highly polluted, but cheaper, Flint River water in 2014.

The globally powerful offer solutions that are more of the same: strengthen the global institutions that oversee agriculture (like the WTO) and create even freer markets and more reduced safety nets in developing countries. This persistence in the face of unavoidable evidence is the result, not of science that is constantly available for re-evaluation, but of a deeply held religious and cultural faith.

The Globalization of Food

The question of Canada's miserable failure as a wealthy country to address the needs of many residents cannot be understood outside the context of the globalization of food. Like many other countries, Canada has been negatively affected by the increasing profit-taking of transnational corporations (TNCs). Some TNCs now rival sovereign nations in the size of their "economies." In Canada and abroad, global policies have enforced and supported the goals and purposes of these TNCs.

> The question of Canada's miserable failure as a wealthy country to address the needs of many residents cannot be understood outside the context of the globalization of food.

Canada and TNCs

The first global announcement of the international determination to eliminate hunger was made in 1948, when the *Universal Declaration of Human Rights* was declared and signed by Canada (Rideout et al. 2007: 566–567). Since that time, hunger has continued to increase, but the pronouncements and promises about eliminating hunger have become fainter and more modest. Although international agreements have confirmed the right to food, the U.S. has consistently refused to sign them and has in fact lobbied against these treaties. Since the first promises were made, subsistence farming and social supports have been systematically dismantled around the world.

The WTO and other international organizations have been instrumental in making this dismal situation a reality. Power is distributed unevenly at these international bargaining tables, with powerful factions like the U.S. and the EU driving decisions and policies. This has enabled the U.S. and the EU to use the power of international institutions to protect their agricultural subsidies (which create artificial pricing structures). Farmers in the global north, protected by taxpayer-funded subsidies that the WTO has agreed to ignore, can undercut local food pricing in developing countries. At the same time, international trade organizations, corporations and governments have prevented developing countries from either establishing their own subsidies or from protecting their markets from export dumping from farmers in the north. In addition, the powerful elites in these institutions are not neutral, objective observers, but are often the same people who rotate positions and directorships between the agro-TNCs who benefit and the institutions that regulate. For instance, Michael Taylor, appointed to the Food and Drug Administration, was Vice President for Public Policy at Monsanto from 1998 to 2001 (Kenfield 2009). As Mattera (2004) reports in *USDA Inc.*, Ann Veneman, secretary of the USDA from 2001 to 2005, had been on the board of Calgene, which later became part of Monsanto.

While the trade organizations create food regimes sympathetic to the global north, international finance institutions offer struggling countries appealing loans to re-create the industrial agriculture that dominates in the north. The debt load has been willingly taken on in Canada and in the global south. "To earn a net income dollar today, farmers must borrow and risk seven times as much debt as they did in the 1970s, and three times as much as in the '80s" (NFU 2010: 19). The debt comes with promises of higher yields and a solution to stagnant food prices in Canada and to the need for cash in the south and north. It often comes with strings attached: in Canada, it means the loss of farmer power over agriculture; in the south, it means the loss of national social safety nets and public goods like water and food.

In Canada, the result has not been prosperity but grinding debt, loss of autonomy and, eventually, forced sales of land: "Canadian farmers' net income from the markets (with farm support payments subtracted out) has totaled less than zero. Due to a grinding farm crisis, over the past twenty-five years, 100 percent of farm families' net income has come from farm support programs, off-farm jobs, and loans" (NFU 2010: 6).

The package offered to farmers to change their way of farming and eating was marketed first in the global south under the terms of the Green Revolution; similar packages were developed for the north. Industrial farming models brought farmers designer seeds that had shown higher yields in tests back in the laboratory and chemical inputs that would increase production. What was not mentioned at first was that the inputs and new hybrid seeds would starve the land of natural nutrients; that the monocropping of these cash crops would lead to rapid soil erosion and degradation; that the new regime required expensive levels of irrigation only available to wealthy farmers and that the mountain of debt the farmers would find themselves under once they started on the treadmill of feeding their soil chemically would be one from which they might never emerge. For instance, in India many farmers moved from a mix of high-yielding indigenous seeds to a focus on wheat and rice, losing a diversity of crops for food as well as fodder for animals (Shiva 1993: 45). In Canada, diverse farm regimes have been replaced by acres of corn or soybeans for export. In addition, the higher concentration of meat in global diets means that more than two-thirds of all arable land is currently put to use for livestock (both for pasture and for animal feed crops) (Weis 2007: 40).

As hunger encroached in lands where it had previously been managed through the farming of diverse crops for local consumption rather than for export, the winners of the global trade game (the U.S. and the EU) invented a new form of compassion in the form of food aid. The need for food in the south coincided with surpluses of wheat and other commodities in the north. Farmers and governments needed to find new markets for this surplus product.

The Politics of Famine

Famine often occurs in a context of plenty. As Davis (2002) reports, famines occur despite the presence of local storehouses bulging with grain, or even a busy export market that removes grain from the country even as the country's people starve. The problem is distribution and power, not lack of food (Patel 2009). Famine is not so much a matter of an unbalanced numerical formula (the amount of grain needed for a certain number of people) as it is a complex and tragic result of political decisions, social dislocations (from war and colonization) and the systematic relocation of smallholder farmers to the urban labour pool to make way for industrial agriculture or mass irrigation projects.

> Famine often occurs in a context of plenty.

In addition, the imposition of cheap food from the north puts the final nail in the coffin of local agriculture, as local farmers are unable to compete with the cheap northern food. In 1987, as Holt-Gimenez and Patel report (2009: 38), Haiti's rice was largely supplied by local growers. The U.S.-backed regime that took power after 1986 instituted neoliberal reforms to open Haiti's markets to imports. Today, most of the rice consumed in Haiti is imported, and the FAO listed Haiti as one of the twenty-two countries at greatest risk of hunger due to rising food prices. Food aid, often a response to the hunger crisis that results from this type of regime, is not a long-term practical response to hunger, as it destroys the ability of local systems to resolve current or future crises and makes them dependent on cheap food imports. Food aid is simply a management technique for surpluses from large farms in the global north, where surpluses were produced that needed to find a market. Studies have also shown that these imports are an inefficient response to hunger. Much of the aid never reaches the hungry: it is absorbed by markets and more powerful actors before it reaches the people that need it (Holt-Gimenez and Patel 2009; Pottier 1999; Pretty 1995). Notably, Canada has recently untied food aid from Canadian production, under pressure from Oxfam Canada, the Canadian Foodgrains Bank and other organizations, thus potentially redirecting some food aid to those who actually need it (Bailey 2011: 39).

In the last decade, this flawed system of so-called food aid has reached a point of cataclysm, as exporting countries have reduced or banned exports to protect their own agriculture, just as hunger has risen in southern countries that no longer have the land, knowledge or tools to produce their own food. Meanwhile, for those who have the money to buy food (many Canadians for instance), diet-related illnesses like obesity, diabetes and heart attacks are reaching epidemic proportions. We have finally reached the peculiar and desperate situation where the percentage of the world's population that is suffering from obesity is almost the same as those suffering from hunger (Holt-Gimenez and Patel 2009: 3; World Health Organization 2016; World Food Programme 2016).

Canada and the Global System

This unhappy history is by no means confined to relations between north and south. Although Canada tends to identify itself as a global economy winner, the truth is disturbing and complicated. Uneasily included at the tables of the dominant powers, Canada has more in common with developing countries. Like southern countries, Canada has lost its agriculture, land and control over its food system to systematic dumping by subsidized foreign agri-food corporations and is subject to structural adjustment pressures and liberalization of national markets that are more familiar in our tales from the south (Qualman and Wiebe 2002). NAFTA, which was hailed by many as a historic trade agreement, also exposed our markets to greater levels of imports from the U.S., where many crops are heavily subsidized. More recently, food sovereignty supporters battle the Trans-Pacific Partnership (TPP) Agreement and the Comprehensive Economic and Trade Agreement (CETA) with the European Union, both of which threaten Canada's ability to protect Canada's agriculture and food systems. The National Farmer's Union (NFU) (2015: 4-5) described key provisions in the agreements "which allow corporations to sue governments if their ability to profit is diminished by changes in government regulation, laws and policies."

> Although Canada tends to identify itself as a global economy winner, the truth is disturbing and complicated.

Canada boasts extensive fertile farmland and food resources, yet imports a great deal of its food from the U.S. (over half) and elsewhere. According to the Nova Scotia Federation of Agriculture, in 2001, 97 percent of the fruit in Canada was imported (NSFA n.d.). The Nova Scotia Federation of Agriculture estimates that only 8.4 percent of the food on Nova Scotia tables is grown locally, down from 15 percent fifteen years ago (NSFA 2011). This import trade leaves Canadian eaters at the mercy of international food price fluctuations and Canadian farmers at the mercy of prices set by associations for subsidized commodities (wheat, corn, soy, and so on). In addition, the National Farmers Union (Holtslander 2015) reports that foreign corporations have begun to set up Canadian subsidiaries in order to purchase

Canadian farmland, which now considered a lucrative investment by financial speculators.

The bare story of the global food crisis has been recapitulated in many important popular and scholarly works. It is hard to avoid a feeling of hopelessness or mounting ineffectual anger when contemplating this history. Although it is important to recognize the depth of misery and despair the current food regimes have created, the story risks missing key points that indicate ongoing resistance and hope for a better world. For instance, where does one place agency in this history? Are the international institutions maliciously and knowingly dismantling people's livelihoods, or is there an insidious and agentless force obedient to the imperatives of power and profit? Are the peasant farmers, Canadian smallholders and single mothers who pay rent before they buy food in Toronto passive victims of inexorable forces and/or evil corporations/CEOs? Or are they at all times inventive, responsive and resistant to their loss of power, resources and solutions?

It is not even accurate to say that agri-food industries are "winners" in the sense of someone who got there first on their own merits. The agri-industrial complex depends on tax breaks, taxpayer funded subsidies, free sinks (also known as the environment) for waste, subsidized oil, systemic racism, expropriation of indigenous land and exploited imported and resident labour for its success (Holt-Gimenez and Patel 2009: 85). Canada is still one of the wealthiest nations in the world, particularly if judged by the standards of GNP and GDP. Perhaps it is more accurate to say that all these stories are true at different times and in different contexts. As Gramsci has eloquently expressed it, social change (Forgacs 2000: 244–245) is like an orchestra rehearsing, a cacophony of different tunes and voices necessary to create a powerful musical pattern in the performance. The struggle over food is a struggle over different ways of telling the tale, knowing the world, and choosing to act.

Canada's Food System

Let us review the effects of the globalization of food in Canada and tease apart the stories for change that arise in this contested landscape. In Canada, a country considered "one of the wealthiest countries in the world," a grim reality mars the quality of our communal life. In 2015, 12 percent of Canadian households experienced food insecurity, including one in six children (Tarasuk, Mitchell, and Dachner 2016). In March of 2015, the number of Canadians accessing food banks reached 852,137 (Food Banks Canada 2015: 1). Food Banks Canada predicted that almost 2 million separate individuals would access food banks in 2015, making over 14.5 million visits (2015: 3). These are the stories that do not often make the front page.

Canada's Farm Crisis

At the same time, we are losing our local food producers. The number of farmers in Canada has steadily dropped for years. In the fifteen years between 1991 and 2006, over 60,000 farmers exited the profession (Statistics Canada 2011); 25 percent of farmers stopped farming between 1991 and 2011 (NFU 2015: 4). As Desmarais (2007: 64; also Qualman and Tait 2004: 14) points out, "Realized net farm incomes in 2006 were worse than the levels that farmers had experienced in the 1930s." The National Farmers' Union cites Statistics Canada figures that show that "over the past twenty-five years, 100 percent of farm families' net income has come from farm support programs, off-farm jobs, and loans" (NFU 2010: 6).

Our farmland is also disappearing, as it is sold off to housing speculators and developers and most recently to foreign investors. As the NFU reported in *Losing Our Grip*, Canadian land is up for grabs (Holtslander 2015); transnational finance corporations now rhapsodize about Canadian land as an excellent investment opportunity. Of course, we should wonder to ourselves, if it is considered so valuable for overseas investors, why are we so ready to sell it off? Or is it not so much readiness as that Canada is in the malign grip of the same pincers that captured land in Brazil for soybeans and now agri-fuels? Farmers may not want to leave the land, but between overwhelming debt loads, food prices that haven't changed since the 1970s and the tantalizing prize of immediate cash for land, who would not be "willing to sell"? The National Farmers' Union reports that in Canada "to earn a net income dollar today, farmers must borrow and risk seven times as much debt as they did in the 1970s, and three times as much as in the '80s" (2010: 19). In 2005, the NFU (2005: 2) said "Were it not for taxpayer-funded support, off-farm income, depletion of savings, and access to debt, farming in Canada would have to cease. " By 2013, the NFU reports, farm debt had increased to 78 billion (2015: 24).

Qualman and Tait (2004) write, "On a per-farm basis, adjusted for inflation, farmers' net income over the past decade has been lower than at any time since the 1930s. To stay on the land, most families must now rely on off-farm jobs." It should be no surprise that, given an opportunity, farmers in this situation are ready to sell their land. While we continue to elect governments that facilitate this crisis,[1] it seems unfair to expect farmers to care more about feeding us than we do.

Agricultural Policy in Canada

Unfortunately, governments are not innocent or passive in this project. In fact, Canadian governments have loosened the ownership regulations to facilitate the fire sale of Canadian land (NFU 2010: 14). As far back as 1969, there were recommendations from the federal government to reduce the number of Canadian farmers by 50–65 percent (Qualman and Tait 2004: 6). This goal is rapidly being achieved in Canada, and worldwide. The strategy was based on a belief that fewer and larger farms would lead to greater efficiencies, but recent research has been able to show higher yields and more efficient use of land from small-holder farms (Pretty 1995).

Although we read about consolidation and concentration in the U.S. agri-industrial complex, it is easy to forget that Canada has also done a stellar job at consolidation and oligopoly control by a few, perhaps exceeding achievements in the U.S. Qualman and Tait write, "In Canada, each link of the agri-food chain is dominated by fewer than ten (and often as few as two) multibillion-dollar transnationals. The single exception is the farm link, where nearly a billion of the world's farmers operate in an intensely competitive sector" (2004: 19). With Metro's purchase of A&P Canada, four large companies dominated Canadian grocery retail from coast to coast, with 68 percent of the market share (Sparling, Quadri, and van Duren 2005: 2). By 2013, Costco had entered the market, and the top five companies had cornered 70 percent of the market. Since 2005, mergers have increased consolidation: Sobey's purchased Safeway Canada, Loblaw's purchased Shopper's Drug Mart and Metro bought A&P Canada. Recently the grocery market control of the large Canadian companies was threatened by the food offerings of transnationals like Wal-Mart and Costco; in response, they have increased the rate of consolidation by purchasing smaller independent chains to retain market share. (Sturgeon 2014; Kwon 2014). Large agri-food TNCs also prioritize vertical integration, which means that they own and operate not just retail stores, but processing facilities, storage warehouses and distribution infrastructure — they own every aspect of food, in fact, except the high-risk agricultural sector. This is particularly true in livestock production; large TNCs like Tyson Foods own the input, processing and distribution facilities and dictate feed and pharmaceutical regimes while leaving the risk of raising the animals to the farmers (Weis 2007: 79).

Like our sisters and brothers in the south, we may soon lose the wherewithal to grow our own food and will be completely at the mercy of the price choices and export flow determined by the U.S. Canadian farmers will be tenants on their own land, if they stay in farming at all, "a situation," reports the NFU, "that would look familiar and comforting to a thirteenth century lord" (2010: 23). As Weis points out, the Canadian situation is inextricably entwined with the global food system, international corporations and global finance. He notes that "an increasingly global lens is needed to understand the problems facing farmers in most parts of the world" (2007: 177).

As Rideout et al. write (2007: 567–568), a system that is concerned with the consolidation of profit and power into the hands of a few transnational corporations is indifferent to nutritional, social and environmental health. Consumers, who are on the receiving end of an unhealthy food system, express in their bodies the toxicity of neoliberal agricultural economics. In addition to high profile food-related illnesses (e. coli outbreaks, poisoned water sources), diet-related illnesses that stem from an unhealthy food system are all on the rise, such as obesity, diabetes and heart-related illnesses. Alongside hunger, approximately one in three Toronto children (aged 2 to 11) is either overweight or obese. Toronto Public Health's report (2010) states that "according to a 2010 report from Statistics Canada, children as a group are 'taller, heavier, fatter and weaker than in 1981,' which may lead to accelerated 'non-communicable disease development, increased health care costs, and loss of future productivity.'"

In a system that provides food to those who can pay for it (despite the so-far empty declarations of the right to food in Canada, except perhaps in Quebec) (Rideout et al. 2007: 571), hunger is a demon that will continue to infect society. For example, 1.3 million households in Canada are food insecure (Tarasuk, Mitchell, and Dachner 2016: 2). The percentages are much higher in First Nations and northern regions, reaching almost 50 percent in some areas.

Like a flint that creates sparks, food is a touchstone for society's ills; hunger is exacerbated by many other ills (Scharf, Levkoe, and Saul 2010). Many working poor rely on food banks for food, as low-income wages are insufficient for shelter and food, and people living in poverty will necessarily pay rent before buying food. Supermarkets increase stress for urban poor by locating where people are able to pay for food; food deserts (where there are no food stores), food swamps (where there are only unhealthy food options) and higher food prices have been identified in low-income neighbourhoods (Larsen and Gilliland 2008). The dismantling of local food infrastructure in Ontario has included the loss of local food processing, distribution, and storage and transportation options for small to medium scale farmers (Carter-Whitney and Miller 2010). There are fewer jobs in the food sectors, and many farmers have been forced out of business. Lee et al. point out that, incredibly enough, the one hundred-mile diet may be dependent on labour from workers traveling 3,000 miles, as farm-workers are increasingly replaced by migrant labour (2010: 7).

The agri-food system also creates long-term effects in environmental degradation as well as the social costs of poor health and job loss. Holt-Gimenez and Patel (2009: 3) summarize the global situation: "A financial cornucopia producing over $6 trillion a year in wealth, industrial agri-food is tragically one of the planet's major drivers of global poverty and environmental destruction." Monocropping, the single crop focus used throughout Canada, and now imported in industrial agriculture systems to the global south, creates a perfect scenario for soil erosion. The need for straight crop rows, accessible to large-scale mechanized planters and harvesters, creates long gullies that are ideal for draining water and soil from farmers' land. Food First reports (Holt-Gimenez and Mott 2016) that "the world is losing about 75 billion tons of crop soil every year—a loss valued at US$400 billion." The loss is attributed to current agricultural methods, including intensive tillage and net loss of soil carbon from intensive agriculture (which makes soil vulnerable to erosion).

There are also more subtle losses from the triumphal progress of the agri-industrial complex. Farmers have lost more than soil, jobs and livelihood, they have also lost the knowledge to farm sustainably (Desmarais 2007: 44). As Shiva (1993) points out, farmers have been systematically removed from the place of innovation in agriculture and have had to cede the important role of problem-solving and innovation to crop scientists, seed and technology providers and other non-farming technicians. In many sectors the farmers are in the position of serfs on their own land, following recipes (for feeding regimes) and prescriptions (for hormones and low levels of antibiotics). In these factory farms, methods are dictated by the corporations who represent the farmers' only market option. The corporations may own everything on the farm except the land itself. In a few short decades, essential information has been lost about saving seed, building soil immunity, ecosystem resilience and so on. As Shiva has pointed out (1993), the change of strategies of thought is not innocent; it serves to utterly separate the course of humanity from nature, and makes our misuse of environmental resources reasonable and inevitable. In addition, the agri-food complex transfers power from peasants and farmers to an elite pool of scientists and marketers who work for the agro-TNCs and are answerable not to communities, but to the corporate CEO and shareholders.

Resistance: Beyond Victors and Victims

As resistance to the global food system rises, we begin to hear a story beyond victors and victims. Aside from the story of immiseration in Canada's rural lands and urban high rises, there are other stories that are not told often enough. These are the stories of resistance: those who have been disenfranchised, dislocated and left behind by the triumphal sweep of neoliberal economics have never taken it lying down (Patel 2009: 107; Pottier 199:

109); they have resisted from the beginning, from the first moment that the *Agreement on Agriculture* looked like a made-for-the-U.S. solution to global agriculture, to the food riots in Egypt — the culmination of decades of inequality and social injustice — that toppled an unpopular dictator.

While we are familiar with the story that a few large corporations hold all the power in the food system, we are less familiar with the story of how the power was transferred — who colluded in that transfer, which communities stood against it, what bureaucracies, coercions and duplicitous tactics brought us to where we are (see Friedmann 1993 for important analysis of this history).

The problem with ahistorical descriptions is that, if we don't know how we got here, we don't know how to get back out. For instance, it has become natural to see food as private property and to assume food must come from land that is privately owned. Yet many traditional and indigenous land users still harvest a great deal of food and fuel from common land and share communal management of irrigation, grazing rights and firewood harvest rights. (Patel 2009). As Patel (2009: 7) points out, "Private property requires society to approve of it being taken out of common hands. Property is, in other words, social — there's nothing natural about the way some people are allowed to exclude others from land, for instance" (2009: 7). As well, the determination of what should be submitted to market exchanges is a social decision; we have agreed that food should be bought and sold as a commodity for profit, available to those who can afford it. However, as the numerous movements and commitments to the right to food indicate, we are also able to think about it differently and argue that none of our neighbours or fellow planetary denizens should be hungry (Madeley 2002: 2).

Power and Story: How Telling Makes It So

Our attitudes to food and agriculture, our beliefs that we enshrine in policies, trade agreements and law, are a matter of cultural identity (Hart, in Goodman and Watts 1997: 62). Weis writes,

> From seasonal cultivation routines to harvest to preparation to mealtime, food has long been a central part of cultural identities, and a major aspect of the escalating power of agro-TNCs lies in their extraordinary ability to sever both the material and conceptual links between farmers and consumers and replace these with opaque webs of sourcing, processing, distributing, retailing and branding while ... managing to naturalize this. (2007: 186)

This severance and substitution has not succeeded completely: a trace has been left in our culture that tells a story of compassion and care for others (everyone has a right to food), of the commons and sharing and of important alternatives that have begun to collaborate to create an international resistance and an alternative food identity for us all (Bello 2004: 27).

In the negotiation of what we believe, whom we trust, who has the last word (in other words, culture), power and status have a determining effect on which stories get told. The

> Our attitudes to food and agriculture, our beliefs that we enshrine in policies, trade agreements and law, are a matter of cultural identity.

stories told by the powerful assume an artificial inevitability; as the U.K.'s Prime Minister Margaret Thatcher was wont to say as she dismantled and privatized England's public systems, "There is no alternative." If we restore an analysis of power to the equation, we see, for instance, that there is nothing free about the "free market"; the success of transnational corporations depends very much on their power to set trade rules to suit their own profit goals and to mobilize taxpayer money to subsidize their activities through price subsidies and less visible subsidies that include public funds for environmental clean-up, waste disposal, public health investments and transportation system funding. (Holt-Gimenez and Patel 2009: 2). Corporate success would not have happened without the public goods paid for by us to keep their system running.

Stories of Resistance and Protest

The work to undo the social, economic and environmental mess of global capitalism is a narrative task: it means we must begin to hear and tell alternative stories. It includes an essential recognition that capitalism itself is not monolithic — it should not take a global financial meltdown to recognize that capitalism takes different forms and breaks down in different ways depending on the cultural context (Hart, in Goodman and Watts 1997: 56).[2] The first step to thinking about alternatives is to whisk the curtain aside to see the wizard and to realize that the stories of the powerful can be changed, just as they have changed our stories beyond recognition. Whatmore (in Goodman and Watts 1997: 289) writes that globalization is "a socially contested rather than logical process in which many spaces of resistance, alterity, and possibility become analytically discernible and politically meaningful."

> The work to undo the social, economic and environmental mess of global capitalism is a narrative task: it means we must begin to hear and tell alternative stories.

For instance, the mass protests at the global trade talks in Seattle, Quebec, Doha and Cancun featured food and agriculture as prominent issues that mobilized scores of different groups, from southern peasant organizations to youth activists in the north (Weis 2007). The stories of the protests were not conveyed to us in a disinterested fashion, however; the focus was on eruptions of violence, on costumed agitators, on broken storefront windows. These versions eliminate the stories of thousands of peaceful protestors, the peasant groups and food security organizations, the children marching with parents, the network of support and planning that ensured that the protestors had backup and legal support in case the police turned violent.

Food "riots"[3] erupted around the world in response to food price rises in 2008 and in 2010 (Lee et al. 2010: 12; Holt-Gimenez and Patel 2009). According to Hendrix et al. (2009: 2), food protests took place in over thirty countries. They were a trigger point in Egypt's democracy movement that toppled Mubarak's regime; they are significant in protests around the world. Patel (2009: 132–33) reminds us that it is inaccurate to say these actions were "fueled by nothing more than mute or inarticulate pangs of hunger"; they "were also an expression of deeper anger at the politics surrounding food that had resulted in high prices and low incomes" (also see Patel and McMichael 2009).

Resistance Is Multiple

Although the mass protests have been a powerful statement, as Nierenberger (2010: 6) of the Worldwatch Institute writes, "There is no single solution. In fact, it is the one-size-fits-all approach that has been so crippling." Mass movements to change food regimes are only one part of resistance; most actors engage in more than one form of protest, combining protest, policy advocacy and alternative practice as a way of creating new communities of food. Many local non-governmental organizations (NGOs) fight to reduce poverty, recognizing that lack of access to food is often a result of unfair wage laws and practices. In addition, actors work to change the definition of food from a commodity (to be bought, sold, afforded, or not afforded) to a human right. This move has inspired important organizations like The Stop and FoodShare in Toronto and the B.C. Food Systems Network to call for the integration of social justice, environmental justice, public health and food movements (Scharf, Levkoe, and Saul 2010; Lee at al. 2010: 33).

> Mass movements to change food regimes are only one part of resistance; most actors engage in more than one form of protest, combining protest, policy advocacy and alternative practice as a way of creating new communities of food.

Alternative Food Systems

Numerous alternative practices have appeared and captured the imaginations and loyalty of Canadians. These tend to be erected somewhere between the advocacy organizations and the market economy. Many of these initiatives derive from rethinking land use: community gardens on public lands, or sometimes vacant or contested land, as in the case of the recently bulldozed South Central Farm in Los Angeles. In another model, guerrilla gardening lays claim to unused urban spaces through the "guerrilla" planting of seeds.

In Canada, the "Carrot City" exhibition mobilized activists, architects and planners to rethink the use of urban space for food, creating designs for intensive farming, vertical farming and mixed use to revivify neighbourhoods. Urban farming is no mere pipe dream; much of Havana's food is grown within the city limits (Funes et al. 2003). Other innovations that have been launched recently include various programs to link urban gardeners with people with backyards they are willing to share, providing some of the harvest in exchange for the gardening work. One enterprising urban farmer in Toronto, Erica Lemieux, is now farming a quarter-acre across eight backyards around the city and selling her produce at the Sorauren Farmers' Market (Porter 2011). As Patricia Allen (2008: 159) has pointed out, many urban agriculture initiatives in the global north are disproportionately accessed and championed by the privileged; those living in poverty may not be able to afford the time to work in exchange for food when they more urgently need cash for rent money or fuel to get to their jobs. Several farmers' markets in Toronto have piloted market voucher programs for low-income people in order to address this problem. The African Food Basket farms a significant garden area to provide culturally familiar foods for some of Toronto's ethnic populations and supports the development of community agriculture for key food-insecure groups in Toronto.

Food Relocalization Movements

Calls to relocalize food (Bello 2004; Halweil and Nieremberger 2010), which focus on growing, distributing and eating more local food, encapsulate some of the possibilities for a reframed food system. These approaches advocate changes in scale, ownership and relationships from one end of the supply chain to the other. The local food movement has captured activist and media imaginations but must be interrogated rigorously. At this point, the results of relocalization are often only available to the privileged, who can afford to pay more for food and who have a choice in their food (those who rely on drop-in centres and food banks cannot prioritize local food, as they have little choice in what they eat). Technically, relocalization is not impossible; various studies have explored the positive effects on the local economy of shifting even a few imported foods to local sources (Xuereb 2005; Stopes et al. 2002; Swenson 2009). Lee et al. (2010: 6) write that "if B.C. could shift just 1.5 percent of its overall consumption per year to local sources, the province would supply 80 percent of its food needs by 2030." The advantages are also unquestionable, as they point out: "One U.S. study estimated that if all food was localized, the reduction in emissions would be roughly equivalent to households shifting their diet one day per week from red meat and dairy to a vegetable-based diet" (28). Relocalization also provides important benefits through new jobs and manufacturing opportunities.

New Land Use Practices

More substantial changes to land use and access to food may come from the land trust movement and programs for Greenbelt protection near urban centres, or protected land for farming such as B.C.'s Agricultural Land Reserve (ALR). These programs seek to formally register lands as protected for agricultural or conservation purposes. The ALR is managed by the province and has almost five million acres that are designated as priority areas for agricultural use, with other uses restricted and controlled.[4] The Greenbelt in southern Ontario protects almost 2 million acres. In effect, by pricing the land in terms of value by use (including environmental goods) rather than market value, such initiatives contest the submission of land to the free market. Elsewhere in the world, serious land reform movements are underway. For instance, the Brazilian MST (Landless Workers Movement) has reclaimed large tracts of unused land from absentee landowners (Wright and Wolford 2003).

Power in Alternative Food Movements

In food movements and actions, it is important to continue to raise the questions of power: who is acting for change, and who has access to the alternatives (Patel and McMichael 2009: 10). Holt-Gimenez and Patel argue that the recent global food crisis has mobilized the world's poor and marginalized as they were hardest hit by the increase in food prices (2009: 159). Likewise, Patel points out that women are disproportionately affected by the globalization of food (Patel 2009; also Pottier 1999). The collaboration between democracy movements and food actions is crucial to the achievement of a more just and equitable food system. We are told that to effect change we must vote with our food dollar, but does this mean we should abandon all our fellow humans who can't afford to pay — who can't, in short, afford the kind of food dollar democracy they are offered? Real democracy rises above the impoverished rhetoric of choice offered only to those who can pay (Bello 2004: 10), replacing mere voting with true economic democracy.

Food Policy for Change

New institutions like food charters (that declare the universal right to food), food policy councils that seek to enforce it through collaboration among diverse actors and municipalities that formalize the right to food in government programs are at the forefront of the movement to restore real democracy to the food system. Belo Horizonte in Brazil became a global leader for food change by embedding the human right to food in actual government programs (Rocha 2000). These were designed to fulfill the promise of the right to food, which has remained an empty promise in places like Canada (see also Ecuador's new Food Sovereignty Law [Holt-Gimenez and Patel 2009: 180]). Organizations like FoodShare in Toronto have looked to Belo Horizonte's municipal policies for inspiration in their own work. Manitoba was the first to have a province-wide food charter stating the right to food.[5] Toronto also passed a municipal food charter in 2001.

Initiatives that establish new principles for food systems — equity, the right to food, democracy — must also consider the structure of power they inaugurate in their innovation. This consideration can enable actors to resist co-optation as their success grows. The co-operative form, as well as the radical forms, of participatory democracy (as in the case of the MST; see Wright and Wolford 2003: 35) have been at the forefront of significant movements for change in food and agriculture. In Cuba, co-operatives have been essential alternatives to state or private ownership, providing a measure of control to actors that has some advantages over a state-run system. In Argentina and Venezuela, economic catastrophe has led to the rapid rise of worker co-ops, as labour takes charge of the means of production to create an economy that works for all people rather than just a few. In Canada, important farmers' co-ops like GayLea, OntarBio and the Canadian Wheat Board (ended in 2012) have helped dairy and grain farmers stay in business and command fair prices for their goods through co-ordinated efforts. Co-operatives change the relation of people to alternatives. While community gardens may reinforce a charity model (people grow food which they often donate to food banks or provide to poor people), a co-operatively owned project like the multi-stakeholder West End Food Co-op in Toronto restores power to the actors, including workers, consumers, producers and community food agencies. In these projects, all stakeholders may participate in decision-making, equipment purchase and long-term planning, as well as growing and eating.

A democratic culture of food provisioning is no minor change; we are unused to, and largely untrained in, participatory democracy (Rebick 2000; Miller 2008). Real democracy requires much more than stating your opinion; it means listening to others, considering the good of all, considering your interests and position carefully to reach consensus through argument, negotiation and consultation. It will take many years to learn or relearn this, just as it will take years to recover lost agricultural skills for sustainable farming.

Alternatives that Reframe the Food System

Many local food movements, as well as peasant movements around the world, view the solutions and alternatives as dependent on a reorganization of every aspect of the food system, from our relations to land, to distribution, to ownership of food infrastructure and access. As Holt-Gimenez and Patel (2009: 98) point out, "ending hunger will require restructuring the ways we produce, process, distribute and consume our food." It will also require new ways of being with each other; as Patel (2009: 22) writes: "Seeing fellow human beings as mere co-consumers blinds us to the deeper connections between us, and distorts our political choices.... There's no space to renegotiate so that everyone gets to eat, no way to become a co-producer."

> Many local food movements, as well as peasant movements around the world, view the solutions and alternatives as dependent on a reorganization of every aspect of the food system, from our relations to land, to distribution, to ownership of food infrastructure and access.

Ontario is in a crisis around local food infrastructure, which has been dismantled over the years as foreign options and labour became more financially appealing for global capitalists. The last tender fruit processing plant closed in 2006. A government program pays farmers to uproot and destroy their fruit trees and to replace them with something more economically viable (though what that would be in the current agricultural climate is unclear — condominiums, perhaps). In a recent study of policies and strategies to restore local food infrastructure in Ontario (Carter-Whitney and Miller 2010; see also Atamenenko n.d.), over forty farmers and stakeholders were interviewed. Respondents recognized a catastrophic lack of options for value-added processing in Ontario and recommended solutions that reframe the food chain from farming to processing to storage, distribution and marketing. Regional food hubs have arisen as a novel solution to the problem. Stimulated by support from the U.S. Department of Agriculture, Community Development Financial Institutions and other sources, there are hundreds of food hubs in the U.S. now that provide mid-scale aggregation, marketing and distribution for regional producers. The model is on the rise in Canada as well, with a focus that includes processing and food security as well as regional distribution.

Food Sovereignty Movements

Food sovereignty movements have taken the story of a better world to a new level. They integrate the various types of resistance into alternatives that are insistently democratic and rely on principles of social justice and well-distributed power. Holt-Gimenez and Patel (2009: 86) write, "Food sovereignty proposes that people, rather than corporate monopolies, make the decisions regarding our food." La Vía Campesina is a new and powerful international peasant organization that seeks to create food sovereignty alternatives in which, as Desmarais (2007: 33) writes, "agriculture is farmer-driven and based on peasant production. It uses local resources and is geared to domestic markets. Agriculture not only plays an important social function but is also economically viable and ecologically sustainable." Patel (2009: 119) reports that La Vía Campesina boasts 150 million members in sixty-nine countries (in 2016 the count was up to 73 countries, according to their website. La Vía Campesina's member organizations are diverse and place specific; the international organization has been created out of a careful scheme of participation and representation that builds on a grassroots democracy. In Canada, the National Farmers Union is a key participant in La Vía Campesina's work.

One key point in La Vía Campesina's work is that the membership is restricted to peasants (Desmarais 2007). Across international borders, the members are therefore in an equal place of power (or disempowerment) in relation to the world food economy. Well-meaning NGOs, which do not have their biological survival at stake, are welcome to participate as allies but do not have access to membership. Members are from north and south, and include members of the various landless movements in the south, as well as Canada's National Farmers Union, and the U.S.-based Coalition of Immokalee Workers (CIW). CIW is a coalition of agricultural workers that includes the tomato workers in Florida who have forced major chains like Taco Bell and McDonald's to increase the tomato pickers' pay by one penny per pound. They have also advocated and fought against the modern-day slavery that exists for many of these workers, which includes forced confinement, inhuman working hours and workplace practices and wages that force workers into debt to sustain their families. In case the slavery comparison seems outrageous, it is important to note that the CIW cited the same laws used during the abolition of slavery to free the Immokalee workers (Desmarais 2007; Holt-Gimenez and Patel 2009: 172).

Rewriting the Narratives of the Global Food Economy: Agroecology

The narratives in these new movements for social change carry significant new principles that profoundly challenge the global economies of food. In addition to formalizing the sharing and transfer of power in strong democratic structures, La Vía Campesina and its members are reinventing ideas of property ownership and entitlement and reinventing the philosophies of interactions with the land in agricultural systems. The latter is captured under the rubric of agroecology and, together with the reinvention of the meaning of property, creates and embeds in cultures new ways of being with the land.

Agroecology is not simply a return to traditional farming methods, although it may incorporate centuries-old techniques and varieties (Holt-Gimenez and Patel 2009: 110). As an agricultural practice, it recognizes the power and sustainability of techniques and varieties that are innovations based on immediate contexts, climates and local demands and possibilities. It is a way of thinking in tune with an agricultural ecosystem that tests and solves problems where they arise, in the context of local pests and beneficials, climatic benefits and challenges and the realities of locally financed and managed farming. As Madeley writes, "Small biodiverse farms, growing a number of crops in the same field, are proving to be the new agriculture that is more likely to grow the food that is needed by this and future generations" (Madeley 2002: 41).

For instance, in agroecology, drought would not be lifted out of the particularity of place, as it is by the agro-TNCs who create designer seeds and mass irrigation projects to combat it. In a sustainable farm, unlike industrial agriculture that addresses problems with single-seed or technology solutions, the farmer will plant a mix of crops and varieties (polycultures). The rotation in drought-prone areas will include a drought-resistant variety that may not yield as well, but in drought years that variety will ensure a crop for the farmer (see Pretty's *Regenerating Agriculture* [1995] for many more examples). The examples of place-specific solutions in sustainable agriculture are a marvel of ingenuity and innovation. For instance, Featherstone Estate Winery in Ontario uses cover crops to control weeds between the vines, sheep to reduce the grape leaves and increase the fruit's exposure to light and a Harris hawk to control the incursions of birds.

As Holt-Gimenez and Patel point out, agroecology is not just crop insurance for those who cannot afford a policy; it has actually been proven to provide yields and efficiency that are the equal of industrial agriculture results (2009: 103). They report that a University of Michigan study shows that sustainable agriculture could even produce more kilocalories per person per day than industrial agriculture (2009: 107). Agroecology also mirrors other sustainable systems in solving multiple problems through one elegant solution (such as a team of sheep that both provide fertilizer and help to trim the grapevines).

New Relations to Land Through Agroecology

The agricultural thinking of agroecology changes the relations between farmers and land. An industrial agriculturalist could farm anywhere — from Zambia to Missouri, the techniques are the same: add the necessary nutrients, arrange for consistent irrigation and use high-yield hybrid varieties in a monocrop planting. For an agroecologist, their solutions, seed varieties, techniques and innovations are based on place-specific assessments and interventions; the farmers' future becomes intimately tied to the particular land they farm, and they are more attentive to things like soil degradation, soil strength and immunity, and erosion. The soil is perceived as their wealth (Wright and Wolford 2003: 288). As Weis (2007: 92) points out, the ownership and use relations to land in alternative agricultural practices are also place- and culture-specific, ranging from "from redistribution into small private holdings, to reformist land tenure restructuring, to massive nationalization and collectivization schemes."

Agroecology also changes the relations between farmers, as well as between farmers and communities. Most agroecology movements embed farmer-to-farmer education in their initiatives. Farmer Field Schools have been ignited around the world; farmers are sharing information, exchanging knowledge and providing key networks of support in their quest to reinvent agriculture. FarmStart in Ontario is an excellent example of this peer mentoring: new farmers get access to land on shared public land and can share tips and ideas as well as access expert input. The new peasant organizations are adamant and radical in their approach to democracy, inaugurating participatory practices that move well beyond voting. In the Brazilian MST for instance, peasants occupy unused land to reclaim it from absentee landholders. They farm in the face of the imminent threat of violent eviction by private security or the military. Yet they maintain an insistence on participatory democracy, with carefully designed councils and rotating representation to manage and operate the land and community, and ongoing education in the encampment, both between farmers and within the community (Wright and Wolford 2003; Patel 2007: 207). The change in decision-making and power distribution is as important as the right to food and sustainable agriculture (Hines 2000: 31; Holt-Gimenez and Patel 2009: 98).

Agroecology movements and peasant movements have restored, revived and enriched the relations between people and land, while incidentally creating alternatives to the principle that makes land a vehicle for private ownership for profit. Weis cites land reform as the key to these new ways, both in the north and south: "Ultimately, the work of building more localized, socially just and ecologically rational food economies hinges on challenging the grossly inequitable property rights that the global enclosures have wrought and working to reconfigure uneven landscapes" (2007: 182). Of the movements for resistance reviewed here, agroecology movements may be the most powerful. They have the potential to create a new way of living on our planet that will not destroy it by our use and presence.

New Ways of Thinking, New Ways of Eating

The battle for agriculture that can feed the world and not destroy the planet is a battle between different ways of thinking. The conflict engages the cultural negotiation of meaning that defines our moral structure and our relations with each other, the planet and other species. As Weis and Patel have pointed out, once we have descended the slippery slope of indus-trial agriculture and accepted its sheen of inevitability, it is hard to go back. We are set the urgent task of learning new ways of thinking (Weis 2007: 30; Patel 2009: 173). The beliefs that accompany the move to industrial agriculture have left us adrift with few resources and tools to rebuild a sustainable world.

Yet as calcified as the agro-industrial complex seems to be, it has engendered resistance and alternatives across the world, in the peasants movements described above, and in local move-ments to reclaim land and sustainability through urban agriculture, land trusts and farmer co-ops. Desmarais (2007: 24) writes, "The brutal force of globalization contributed to the emergence of a great variety of new social actors. It also led to new structures of collective action among traditional social actors, including peasant organizations." These movements are not merely angry reactions to social injustice and disempowerment; instead they reframe the moral principles and ethics of action. They eschew the celebration of individual needs and the search for power and profit accumulation in favour of shared interests, community interdependences, economic democracy and the shared management of common resources for interlocking and integrated needs. They seek to establish what Shiva calls "living economies" (2005).

Coalitions and the Power to Change

A key strategy in sustainable agriculture and similar movements is to reunite interests that have been systematically separated (Patel 2009; Pretty 1995; Lee et al. 2010: 32). Some jurisdictions have begun to address this, particularly in the realm of public health and the social determinants of health. These actors recognize that personal health cannot be separated from a healthy food system, healthy and resilient communities and a web of strong com-munity relations and supports (see Toronto's *Cultivating Food Connections* Report (2010) for an excellent example of recommendations for integrated food and health solutions). Likewise in global movements for change, the demands and interests have begun to converge in important ways. Holt-Gimenez and Patel (2009: 164) write, "The socioeconomic realities and political strategies of these actors and organizations are diverse, and have sometimes led to tensions and work at cross-purposes. However, with the food and financial crises, their demands are converging, and point to a powerful consensus."

Polanyi argued that markets have been severed from cultural and social contexts and need to be re-embedded to work and nourish people and cultures (see Patel 2009: 189). As Patel (2009: 190) remarks, "We need the imagination to reclaim both democracy and the economy — we need to understand the basic flaw in imagining the two could be separated. This means telling ourselves different stories to replace the fantasies about the free market." Markets, whether global and profit-oriented or local and community-oriented, are productions of cultures and cultural actors that are replete with a certain moral outlook and define a cultural identity that may be savoury or unsavoury. We have been led by narratives of partial truths or outright lies to believe that an agriculture that eliminates farmers and their knowledge, consolidates power and profits and requires scarcity (hunger) to survive, is the only possible historical path ("inevitability") and certainly the only one that can "feed the world" and address climate change and other environmental crises. We have continued to believe these narratives long after their ability to convince should have expired in the face of rising global temperatures and immiseration among farmers and consumers around the world. It is time to lay aside these old stories that no longer offer us acceptable precepts for action or living and to begin to tell new ways of ownership, being and identity. As one peasant organization in India pledges, "I shall adopt the broader meaning of common ownership ... instead of thinking in terms of I should get more than others, I aspire that other[s] should not get less than me" (quoted in Shiva 2005: 69). The exercise of power can be measured not by how much one can get for oneself, but in one's ability to ensure, in concert with others, that everyone has enough.

> A key strategy in sustainable agriculture and similar movements is to reunite interests that have been systematically separated.

Glossary of Key Terms

Agri-food complex (agri-food industrial complex): Large-scale agriculture focused on commodity markets rather than food production. It is characterized by consolidation and centralization of power in very large corporations and vertical integration (in which agri-food corporations own every sector of the supply chain from production to processing and distribution to retail/consumption).

Agroecology: "The application of ecological concepts and principles to the design and management of sustainable agricultural ecosystems" (Altieri 2009). "A farming philosophy that farms *with* nature, developing and maintaining soil fertility, producing a wide range of crops, and matching the farming to the needs, climate, geography, biodiversity and aspirations of a particular place and community" (Patel 2007: 306, emphasis added).

Food security: "Food security exists when all people, at all times, have physical and economic access to sufficient, safe and nutritious food to meet their dietary needs and food preferences for an active and healthy life" (FAO 1996).

Food sovereignty: "The people's democratic control of the food system, the right of all people to healthy, culturally appropriate food produced through ecologically sound and sustainable methods, and their right to define their own food and agriculture systems" (La Vía Campesina 2010).

Neoclassical economics: Neoclassical economics (expressed politically in neoliberalism) is the theory of economics that promotes the removal of social supports and safety nets to "liberalize" or "free" markets. It theorizes that greater efficiencies are achieved when market actors are allowed free reign to consolidate market power. It emphasizes the private sector as the main actor in national economies. It is argued that this approach will result in the greatest good for all.

Relocalization: The movement to reduce the long-distance transportation of food and to have food grown, produced, processed and consumed in the same region.

Transnational corporations (TNC): Corporate entities that operate in more than one country and across borders. They are able to move operations where labour and other costs of operating (like environmental penalties for pollution, or the cost of raw materials) are low. Many of them have economies that are larger than sovereign nations.

"Willingness to Pay" theory: A key concept from neoclassical economics that hypothesizes that price is identified in a free market by exchanges between supply and demand, with a balance reached where sellers are willing to sell and buyers are willing to buy. It is applied to all commodities, including land and food, and results in scarcity of the necessities of life for those who cannot afford to pay. Willingness to Pay is countered by the "right to food," and more recently, the "right to grow food," philosophies that argue that everyone has the right to the basic necessities of life.

Questions for Discussion

1.   Why is food an important trigger for social change movements?

2.   How do the following change the way people relate to food, to land and to each other: community gardens, food co-ops, Brazil's Landless Workers Movement?

3.   What are ways to change the food system that will ensure lasting change?

4.   What are the reasons that Canada is not necessarily a winner in the global food system?

Resources for Activists

Canadian Centre for Policy Alternatives: www.policyalternatives.ca

Food and Agriculture Organization of the United Nations: www.fao.org

La Vía Campesina: www.viacampesina.org

Organic Consumers Association: www.organicconsumers.org

World Food Programme: wfp.org/hunger

World Health Organization: www.who.int/en/

Notes

1. As Lester Brown (2011) reports in *World on the Edge*, farmers have begun to sell their irrigation water, as they make more selling water to municipalities than they do raising crops.
2. For an important and groundbreaking consideration of this problem, see J.K. Gibson-Graham (1996), *The End of Capitalism (As We Knew It)*.
3. Note the choice of word in most reports — "riot" seems so much more violent than "protest." "Demonstration" is even more modest, though the term seems to eliminate much hope of change, as if protest were a display in a shop window.
4. See the Agricultural Land Reserve website at alc.gov.bc.ca/alc/content/home for more information on this important initiative.
5. See Food Matters Manitoba at foodmattersmanitoba.ca/ for more on this important initiative.

References

Allen, P. 2008. "Mining for Justice in the Food System: Perceptions, Practices and Possibilities." *Agriculture and Human Values* 25.

Altieri, M.A. 2009. "Agroecology, Small Farms, and Food Sovereignty." *Monthly Review* July–August. <monthlyreview.org/090810altieri.php>.

Atamenenko, A. n.d. *Food for Thought: Towards a Canadian Food Strategy*. Special Report. New Democratic Party of Canada.

Bailey, R. 2011. *Growing a Better Future: Food Justice in a Resource Constrained World*. Oxfam. <oxfam.org/grow>.

Bello, W. 2004. *Deglobalization: Ideas for a New World Economy*. Halifax, NS: Fernwood.

Brown, L.R. 2011. *World on the Edge: How to Prevent Economic and Environmental* Collapse. New York: W.W. Norton.

Carter-Whitney, M., and S. Miller. 2010. "Nurturing Fruit and Vegetable Processing in Ontario." Metcalf Food Solutions Papers. Toronto: Metcalf Foundation.

Davis, M. 2002. *Late Victorian Holocausts: El Nino Famines and the Making of the Third World*. New York: Verso.

Desmarais, A.A. 2007. *La Vía Campesina: Globalization and the Power of Peasants*. Halifax: Fernwood Publishing.

FAO (Food and Agriculture Organization of the United Nations). 1996. "Rome Declaration on World Food Security." World Food Summit, November 13–17. <fao.org/docrep/003/w3613e/w3613e00.HTM>.

Food Banks Canada. 2015. "HungerCount 2015." <foodbankscanada.ca/HungerCount>.

____. 2016. "HungerCount 2016." <foodbankscanada.ca/hungercount2016>.

Forgacs, D. (ed.). 2000. *An Antonio Gramsci Reader: Selected Writings 1916–1935*. New York: Schocken Books.

Friedmann, H. 1993. "The Political Economy of Food: A Global Crisis." *New Left Review* 197, January–February: 29–55.

Funes, F., L. Garcia, M. Bourque, N. Perez, and P. Rosset. 2003. *Sustainable Agriculture and Resistance: Transforming Food Production in Cuba.* Oakland: Food First Books.

Gibson-Graham, J.K. 1996. *The End of Capitalism (As We Knew It): A Feminist Critique of Political Economy.* Malden, MA: Blackwell Publishers.

Gilbert, N. 2012. "OneThird of Our Greenhouse Gas Emissions Come from Agriculture." *Nature News and Comment.* October 31. Nature Publishing Group, a division of Macmillan Publishers Limited.

Goodman, D., and M. Watts. 1997. *Globalising Food: Agrarian Questions and Global Restructuring.* New York: Routledge.

Halwcil, B., and D. Nierenberger. 2010. "Charting a New Path to Eliminating Hunger." *State of the World 2011: Innovations that Nourish the Planet.* Washington, DC: Worldwatch Institute.

Hendrix, C., S. Haggard, and B. Magaloni. 2009. "Grievance and Opportunity: Food Prices, Political Regime and Protest." Paper prepared for presentation at the International Studies Association convention, New York, February 15–18.

Hines, C. 2000. *Localization: A Global Manifesto.* London: Earthscan Publications.

Holt-Gimenez, E., and K. Mott. 2016. "Ground Shaking? Assessing the FAO's 2015 International Year of Soils." *Food First Backgrounder* 22, 1 (Spring). <foodfirst.org/publication/ground-shaking-assessing-the-faos-2015-international-year-of-soils/>.

Holt-Gimenez, E., and R. Patel, with A. Shattuck. 2009. *Food Rebellions! Crisis and the Hunger for Justice.* Cape Town, Africa: Pambazuka Press.

Holtslander, C. 2015. *Losing Our Grip 2015 Update.* National Farmers Union, March. <nfu.ca/issues/losing-our-grip-2015-update>.

Kenfield, I. 2009. "The Return of Michael Taylor: Monsanto's Man in the Obama Administration." *Counterpunch* August 14–16. <organicconsumers.org/articles/article_18866.cfm>.

Kwon, N. 2014. "Independents Want More Protection Amid Industry Consolidation." *Canadian Grocer.* <canadiangrocer.com/top-stories/independents-call-for-more-protection-as-competition-gets-stiffer-39330?print>.

La Vía Campesina. 2010. "Statement from the People's Movement Assembly on Food Sovereignty." <viacampesina.org/en/index.php/main-issues-mainmenu-27/food-sovereignty-and-trade-mainmenu-38/908-statement-from-the-peoples-movement-assembly-on-food-sovereignty>.

Larsen, K., and J. Gilliland. 2008. "Mapping the Evolution of 'Food Deserts' in a Canadian City: Supermarket Accessibility in London, Ontario, 1961–2005." *International Journal of Health Geographics* 7, 16.

Lee, M., H. Barbolet, T. Adams, and M. Thomson. 2010. *Every Bite Counts: Climate Justice and B.C.'s Food System.* November. Canadian Centre for Policy Alternatives.

Madeley, J. 2002. *Food for All: The Need for a New Agriculture.* Halifax, NS: Fernwood Publishing.

Manning, R. 2004. *Against the Grain.* New York: North Point Press.

Mattera, P. 2004. "How Agribusiness Has Hijacked Regulatory Policy at the U.S. Department of Agriculture." Corporate research project of Good Jobs First. Washington DC: USDA Inc. <scribd.com/doc/73696926/USDA-INC-By-Philip-Mattera>.

Miller, S. 2008. *Edible Action: Food Activism and Alternative Economics.* Halifax/Winnipeg: Fernwood Publishing.

NFU (National Farmers Union Canada). 2005. "The Farm Crisis and Corporate Profits." National Farmers Union Canada. November 30. <nfu.ca/sites/www.nfu.ca/files/corporate_profits.pdf>.

____. 2010. "Losing Our Grip: How a Corporate Farmland Buy-up, Rising Farm Debt, and Agribusiness

Financing of Inputs Threaten Family Farms and Food Sovereignty." A report by Canada's National Farmers Union, June 7. <nfu.ca/sites/www.nfu.ca/files/06-07-losing_grip.pdf Note>.

____. 2011. "Farms, Farmers and Agriculture in Ontario: An Overview of the Situation in 2011." National Farmers Union, May. <nfu.ca/sites/www.nfu.ca/files/farm_ontario.pdf>.

NSFA (Nova Scotia Federation of Agriculture). 2011. "Reduced Food Miles Brings Benefits." <nsfa-fane.ca/programs-projects/food-miles-project/>.

____. n.d. "Reduced Food Miles Brings Benefits." <nsfa-fane.ca/programs-projects/food-miles-project/>.

Patel, R. 2007. *Stuffed and Starved: Markets, Power and the Hidden Battle for the World Food System*. Toronto: Harper Collins.

____. 2009. *The Value of Nothing*. New York: Picador.

Patel, R., and P. McMichael. 2009. "A Political Economy of the Food Riot." *Review* xxxii, 1.

Porter, C. 2011. "Backyard Farming in the GTA." *Toronto Sta*, April 6. <thestar.com/news/article/970270--porter-backyard-farming-in-the-gta>.

Pottier, J. 1999. *Anthropology of Food: The Social Dynamics of Food Security*. Malden, MA: Blackwell Publishers.

Pretty, J.N. 1995. *Regenerating Agriculture: Policies and Practice for Sustainability and Self-Reliance*. Washington, DC: Joseph Henry Press.

Qualman, D., and F. Tait. 2004. *The Farm Crisis, Bigger Farms and the Myths of "Competition" and 'Efficiency.'* Ottawa: Canadian Council for Policy Alternatives. October.

Qualman, D., and N. Wiebe. 2002. *The Structural Adjustment of Canadian Agriculture*. November. Ottawa: Canadian Centre for Policy Alternatives.

Rebick, J. 2000. *Imagine Democracy*. Toronto: Stoddart Publishing.

Rideout, K., G. Riches, A. Ostry, D. Buckingham, and R. MacRae. 2007. "Bringing the Right to Food Home to Canada: Challenges and Possibilities for Achieving Food Security." *Public Health Nutrition*. <journals.cambridge.org/article_S1368980007246622>.

Rocha, C. 2000. "An Integrated Program for Urban Food Security: The Case of Belo Horizonte, Brazil." Unpublished paper.

Scharf, K., C. Levkoe, and N. Saul. 2010. "In Every Community a Place for Food: The Role of the Community Food Centre in Building a Local, Sustainable, and Just Food System." Metcalf Food Solutions Papers. Toronto: Metcalf Foundation.

Shiva, V. 2005. *Earth Democracy: Justice, Sustainability and Peace*. Boston: South End Press.

____. 1993. *Monocultures of the Mind*. London: Zed Books.

Sinclair, S., and J. Grieshaber-Otto. 2009. *Threatened Harvest: Protecting Canada's World-Class Grain System*. Ottawa: Canadian Centre for Policy Alternatives, March. <policyalternatives.ca/publications/reports/threatened-harvest>.

Sparling, D., T. Quadri, and E. van Duren. 2005. *Consolidation in the Canadian Agri-Food Sector and the Impact on Farm Incomes*. Draft Discussion Document. June. Ottawa: Canadian Agri-Food Policy Institute. <capi-icpa.ca/archives/pdfs/PapID11_DSparling.pdf>.

Statistics Canada. 2011. *Census of Agriculture: Section 6, Characteristics of Farm Operators, Canada and Provinces: Census Years 1991 to 2006*. <statcan.gc.ca/pub/95-632-x/2007000/t/4185586-eng.htm>.

Stopes, C., C. Couzens, M. Redman, and S. Watson. 2002. "Local Food: The Case for Re-localising Northern Ireland's Food Economy." Belfast, NI: Friends of the Earth.

Sturgeon, J. 2014. "Here's Who's Really Winning Canada's Grocery Wars." Consumer Affairs, Global News. <globalnews.ca/news/1678970/heres whos-really-winning-canadas-grocery-wars/>.

Swenson, D. 2009. *Investigating the Potential Economic Impacts of Local Foods for Southeast Iowa.* Ames, IA: Leopold Center for Sustainable Agriculture, Iowa State University.

Tarasuk, V., A. Mitchell, and N. Dachner. 2016. *Household Food Insecurity in Canada, 2014.* PROOF. <proof.utoronto.ca>.

Toronto Public Health. 2010. *Cultivating Food Connections: Toward a Healthy and Sustainable Food System for Toronto.* May. Toronto: City of Toronto.

Weimer, C. 2009. *Bridging the Gap from Poverty to Independence: What Is the Role of Canadian Food Banks?* February 26. Regina: Canadian Council for Policy Alternatives. <policyalternatives.ca/publications/reports/bridging-gap-poverty-independence>.

Weis, T. 2007. *The Global Food Economy: The Battle for the Future of Farming.* Halifax, NS: Fernwood Publishing.

WHO (World Health Organization). 2016. "Obesity and Overweight-Fact Sheet." <who.int/mediacentre/factsheets/fs311/en/>.

World Food Programme. 2016. "Hunger Statistics." <wfp.org/hunger/stats>.

Wright, A., and W. Wolford. 2003. *To Inherit the Earth: The Landless Movement and the Struggle for a New Brazil.* Oakland: Food First Books.

Xuereb, M. 2005. *Food Miles: Environmental Implications of Food Imports to Waterloo Region.* Waterloo, ON: Region of Waterloo Public Health.

16

"Twitter Revolution" or Human Revolution?

Social Media and Social Justice Activism

Leslie Regan Shade, Normand Landry and Rhon Teruelle

YOU SHOULD KNOW THIS

- Canadians spend more time on the Internet than those in other countries, with the average Canadian spending 36.3 hours per month online via their desktop computer.
- In May 2011, Twitter had 200 million registered users who posted an average of 140 million tweets per day. Four years later, Twitter had 320 million registered users and reported 2015 revenue at US$550.
- The average daily active users on Facebook in 2015 was 1.04 billion, with 83.6 percent of users outside the U.S. and Canada, and in 2015 their revenue was an extraordinary US$17.93 billion.
- According to Ron Deibert, Director of the Citizen Lab at the University of Toronto, and Rafal Rohozinski, CEO of the SecDev Group in Ottawa, a heightened cyber military-industrial complex is now estimated to be worth between US$80 billion and US$150 billion annually. Authoritarian regimes are some of the largest consumers of these technological systems, which are highly complicit in shutting down opposition voices and surveilling enemies.

Sources: Bradshaw 2011; CBC News 2015a; Deibert and Rohozinski 2011; Facebook 2016; Isaac 2016; Kopytoff 2011.

IN DECEMBER 2010, A 26-YEAR-OLD UNEMPLOYED Tunisian university graduate named Mohamed Bouazizi set himself on fire in protest after the fruit he was selling in the town of Sidi Bouzid was confiscated by government officials. The officials alleged he was operating his stand without a licence. Three weeks later he died in hospital, sparking massive street revolts by Tunisian citizens frustrated by government corruption and widespread unemployment. Tunisia's repressive government intervened, imposing curfews, closing schools and universities, arresting citizens and violently setting the police on to the thousands of citizens who had taken to the street. Tunisia was infamous for its authoritarian media and Internet system, decried by the International Federation of Journalists (IFJ) and its affiliate, the Syndicat national des journalistes tunisiens (SNJT), in their campaign for journalistic independence.

Initially Western mainstream media ignored the Tunisian protests, partly because of a lack of official information from the government, but citizens, using various social media, were able to spread timely information about the protests to the world and mobilize Tunisian citizens and the Tunisian diaspora, including a large community in Montreal. Information was disseminated via Facebook (even after the government deleted pages that were critical of the government), WikiLeaks, the Tunisian blog *Nawaat*, which posted amateur videos online, proxy servers that could bypass government monitoring and Twitter, which was also able to more easily circumvent government censorship (Al Jazeera English 2011). After twenty-three years of autocratic rule, President Ben Ali fled the country, which is now undergoing a shift in governance that Tunisians hope will usher in a reign of democratic transparency. Five years after the revolution, however, while political critique is debated in a more open fashion than before, economic and security issues remain unresolved (Chomiak 2016).

Many Western commentators dubbed the actions in Tunisia "The Twitter Revolution," celebrating the use of social media for mobilizing Tunisians and toppling the Ben Ali government. But others were more cautious, attributing the actions of Tunisians to "decades of frustration, not in reaction to a WikiLeaks cable, a denial-of-service attack, or a Facebook update" (Zuckerman 2011). Jillian York, also hesitant to ascribe power to networked technologies, remarked that "I am glad that Tunisians were able to utilize social media to bring attention to their plight. But I will not dishonor the memory of Mohamed Bouazizi — or the sixty-five others that died on the streets for their cause — by dubbing this anything but a human revolution" (York 2011).

There is considerable debate over the power and influence of social media in political discourse and for activism. Technologies can embody power, and technological design can conceal vested interests and goals, values and worldviews; policy, politics and technology are thus intrinsically and inherently linked. Vested interests can run the political gamut, from social media companies that are unabashedly corporatist and oriented towards market profitability, often to the detriment of citizen's privacy rights (Facebook), to those that are communitarian in spirit, allowing users to own their own information and control their privacy (Diaspora*). Facebook exemplifies the dramatic reconfiguration of personal privacy online, with CEO Mark Zuckerberg's evangelical belief in "radical transparency'" — the

> Technologies can embody power, and technological design can conceal vested interests and goals, values and worldviews; policy, politics and technology are thus intrinsically and inherently linked.

company's credo that creating more open and transparent identities creates a healthier society (Kirkpatrick 2010). Diaspora*, the open-source social network site with its origins in the "free culture movement," was championed as the "anti-Facebook" for its principles of user control (Dwyer 2014; Nussbaum 2010) and is now run as a community project.

The use of social media as a vehicle to spark democratic reform in the Arab region elicited much conversation at that time. Several weeks after the Tunisian uproar, Egyptians took to the streets demanding reform under Hosni Mubarak's leadership; in response, the government ordered all telecommunications providers to shut down, thus "taking the country's citizens and institutions off the digital map" (El Akkad 2011). Since then, the role of digital activism in the Middle East has been a topic of considerable debate in scholarship (for instance, see Howard and Hussain 2013) and was featured in Jehane Noujaim's evocative Academy Award–nominated documentary, *The Square*, which centred on the activist locale of Tahrir Square in Cairo. The use of social media for Canadian activism has not been as fraught. It is, however, contested terrain.

Social media for activism is contested because corporate-owned social media sites such as Facebook and Twitter dictate the terms of the users' participation in their platforms, and this is related to privacy, intellectual property and freedom of speech. These terms can be contrary and even antithetical to the public interest. Privacy is one such terrain, wherein users' personal data can be tracked, targeted, mined and sold to third-party companies, who in turn use this information to selectively target the same surveilled users with personalized ads for products. This "commodification" of users on social media is skillfully adopted from the marketing sector and is a practice that has grown in stature and stealth as companies increasingly seek to develop and deepen new and more lucrative revenue streams.

> Social media for activism is contested because corporate-owned social media sites dictate the terms of the users' participation in their platforms, which can be contrary and even antithetical to the public interest.

Social media for activism is also contested because as social justice activists increasingly use social media for human rights activities, their activities may go against the corporate-owned terms of service. For instance, many social media platforms require that users use their real names to create a profile, but human rights activists who are fearful of reprisal and punishment by authoritarian regimes and have signed up using pseudonyms have found their content removed because they violated the community norms of these sites (Preston 2011a, 2011b). Facebook's real name policy came under attack when a coalition of civil rights organizations argued that the rights of marginalized communities (abuse victims, the LGBTQ community, ethnic minorities) were impacted; while Facebook has since relaxed its policy, serious issues remain regarding the vulnerability and security for many users (Hassine and Galperin 2016). Social media companies must grapple with these tensions if their platforms are to be used as an effective tool for social justice.

In this chapter, several controversial Canadian case studies of social media activism are examined: the Idle No More movement, one of the largest Indigenous mass movements in Canadian history, the 2012 Québec Student Strike, and #BeenRapedNeverReported, an example of hashtag activism protesting and publicizing violence against women. The chapter will also reflect upon whether social media are an effective tool for social justice activism, or if they have contributed towards a culture of complacent couch potato politics, or "slacktivism."

What Are Social Media?

Social media refer to a range of Internet technologies that allow for participative communicative practices; they are tools that empower users to contribute to developing, collaborating, customizing, rating and distributing Internet content. Referred to earlier as "Web 2.0" technologies, user practices are called "user-created content" (UCC), or "user-generated content" (UGC). In their 2007 study on the participative web, the Organisation for Economic Co-operation and Development (OECD) described the characteristics of UCC as content made publicly available over the Internet, reflecting some creative component, whether original or adapted. Implicit for UCC is that content is created outside of professional, paid labour, with no industry or institutional affiliation and little to no financial remuneration.

Predicated on access to good "broadband" connections and often, but not always, comprised of younger users, the motivations for those using social media and producing UCC can be many: creative and fun expression, establishing and extending communities of interest, seeking fame and notoriety or civic participation. Models for recompense include voluntary contributions, charging viewers for services, selling goods and services to the community, establishing advertising-based models and licensing content and technologies to third parties. The social impacts of UCC are multifarious: a promise of increased democratization of media production; a valorization of amateurs; a potential for increased participation, collaboration and sharing; and the facilitation of open platforms for political debate. But alongside these many opportunities are challenges, in particular, privacy (identity theft, a disregard for the protection of personal information, third-party marketing), copyright (determining what can be considered "fair dealing" with regard to the ownership of content), informational integrity (protecting against illegal and inappropriate content, promoting and preserving freedom of expression) and security and safety.

The most popular social media include social network sites, blogs/microblogs wikis, and video-sharing sites. Increasingly the mobile phone is used as a platform for social media. Intrinsic to these technologies are their facility for users to upload their own content, reconfigure, remix and comment on content; for activist purposes, mediated mobilization, which fosters collaboration and participation, is of central importance. Such mobilization, writes Leah Lievrouw, "is not merely the collection and allocation of resources (people, time, funding, technology, space), it also creates a sense of belonging, solidarity, and collective identity among participants that is expressed through their collaborative activities" (2011: 174).

Social Network Sites

Social network sites link together individuals, associations or groups sharing common interests, shared histories, backgrounds and affiliations, kinship, similar tastes or ideas. Users can post personal or institutional status, update profiles and publish information, news, pictures, links or videos. Information provided by users can either be made publicly available or restricted to areas the user deems "private." With more than 1.04 billion daily users, Facebook, for example, claims supremacy as the world's most popular social network website. Instagram, acquired by Facebook in 2012 for US$1 billion is now the most popular photo sharing platform.

Blogs

Blogs are relatively simple websites that can be operated, modified and updated by users without the need of extensive programming or technical skills. They are typically interactive in the sense that they frequently call for comments and participation from readers. They contain text, picture, sound and video files and archive past events and activities. While previously generally associated with personal journals and websites, blogs have been professionalized and are now used by corporations, journalists, free lancers, political entrepreneurs and analysts for publicity, advertising and branding activities. WordPress and Blogger are among the biggest pre-hosted blog services currently available.

Microblogs

Microblogs are registered accounts hosted by a particular social network site linking together individuals, groups and communities. Microblog accounts allow users to publish small and concise posts made of short sentences and hypertexts (links to other websites) in real-time. These posts are accessible through the social network site, smartphones and in some countries, by short message service (SMS). With more than 320 million registered users, Twitter is the definitive goliath of the microblogosphere.

Wikis

Wikis are collaborative websites that can be updated and edited by their users. Content is provided and monitored by users: web pages are created, published, edited and revised by a community of users willingly participating and investing time in a commons knowledge project. Wikis often rely on "open-source software" and are often associated with non-profit endeavours, projects and activities. The multilingual, web-based online encyclopaedia Wikipedia might just be the most successful, widespread and well-known wiki available on the web.

Video-Sharing Sites

Video-sharing sites provide a forum for viewing videos — amateur and professional — on the Internet. By far the most popular video-sharing site is YouTube, which is owned by Google. According to YouTube, they have over a billion users, with 80 percent of views from outside of the United States. While YouTube will not reveal the size of its video library, the company estimates that twenty hours of video are uploaded to the site every minute, with the average user spending fifteen minutes a day on the site (YouTube 2016; Helft 2009).

Social Media and Activism: A Primer

Technologies are designed, produced and distributed with an understanding of who its potential users are and their imagined interactions. Some of these uses are sanctioned, desired and anticipated by the technological designers and manufacturers; others are restricted, forbidden and opposed with rigour by either the proprietor of the technology or public authorities. Users can surprise technological entrepreneurs by developing innovative, original and unforeseen ways to interact and mobilize technology, but often these unintended uses are harshly resisted and suppressed by the owners of these technologies, often in the guise of morality, national security or public order.

Social media, the latest and (for the time being) the hippest infant of communication technologies, is currently at the forefront of a global struggle to shape the many ways that citizens are appropriating and using technologies to expand their boundaries of freedom. Many of these social media, some of which were mythically developed with much passion and pluck in the San Francisco Bay area by university students, are now intrinsically enveloped within the capitalist structures of commerce and entertainment and are worth billions of dollars in revenue. And in many instances, the blurring between these powerful platform producers and distributors, users and their content can be vexing, particularly as content is increasingly monetized. Under most of these platforms, terms of service for use is cavalier towards personal privacy (favouring third-party marketing), and user content is the intellectual property of the corporate owners.

History tells us that citizens and activists are quick to discover and exploit the unexplored potential of communication technology (Curran 2002; Shaw 2005; de Jong, Shaw, and Stammers 2005; Raley 2009). The subversion of technological consumer products by activists relies on a refusal to be constrained by prescribed uses and a desire to both build on technological opportunities and bypass technological constraints. The open-source movement is the perfect example of this. Reacting against the closed proprietary nature of most commercial software, open-source activists refuse the lockdown imposed by major corporations on software and instead develop their own competitive tools and applications. The Apache HTTP server, the web browser Firefox, the GNU/Linux operating system and the content management system Drupal are commonly used open-source tools. Users also commonly "jailbreak" mobile devices such as the iPhone in order to install third-party applications that are not under the sole ownership and control of the parent company — in this case the Apple Corporation. Hackers, pirates, programmers and file-sharers are also keen to write and share software that meets their needs, goals and desires without bending to the requirements of copyright holders.

Consumer products such as the personal computer, the smart phone and the video camera have become, in the hands of activists, tools of subversion and resistance. They are instruments of political information, ideological affirmation and debate, publicity, co-ordination, knowledge sharing and political action. The stories told through these devices are ones of passion and despair, of hope and change, of anger and injustice. A global network of friends, allies and supporters now fits in one's pocket. Examples of this are numerous. The cameras in mobile phones are used by activists to hold public authorities responsible for their actions, to record abuses and human rights violations (especially those that occur during public demonstrations) and to rectify, correct or challenge information provided by the mainstream media. The case of the Tunisian revolution is illustrative of this use. Other global examples include Amnesty International UK's "Break the Silence" campaign, which distributes pocket radios to allow the Burmese to bypass state censorship and to educate and inform the population about their human rights.[1] WITNESS provided training, support and video cameras to activists and local groups in many countries so they could record abuses and exactions.[2] The social and political uses of these technological devices derive from the creativity and the tactical choices made by activists.

> Consumer products such as the personal computer, the "smart" mobile phone, and the video camera have become, in the hands of activists, tools of subversion and resistance.

Social media has come to play a central role in the spontaneous co-ordination of upscale protests and demonstrations. Since the 1999 anti-globalization protests in Seattle, which effectively shut down a World Trade Organization (WTO) meeting, protesters have increasingly relied on a decentralized, nebulous, hard-to-shutdown communication architecture used for co-ordination, intelligence and publication (Karatzogianni 2006). The explosion of social media over the first decade of the twenty-first century has played an important part in the building of movements and protest activities. These media exemplify the potential that communication technology holds for social resistance and mobilization.

Social media build communities of interest: they link together individuals who share similar interests in issues and people. They are community-driven and community-fuelled technologically mediated social spaces that expand, reassert and reinforce often weak social ties. As such, they are highly relevant tools of social mobilization. They contribute to the organization of movements, protest activities and information distribution on a contagion model. They help to get the word out in ways previously unthinkable. Like a virus, politically charged information passes around people who meet online, sometimes infecting them and spreading among networks, mutating in new strains, scattering in unsuspected hubs and locations. This has major impact for recruitment activities.

> The explosion of social media over the first decade of the twenty-first century has played an important part in the building of movements and protest activities. These media exemplify the potential that communication technology holds for social resistance and mobilization.

For one, social media contribute to the establishment of relevant distribution channels among various publics, activists and sympathizers. These channels are then able to constitute the backbone of networks constituted by dormant agents, adherents and potential supporters to be called upon when needed (Carty 2011). Secondly, social media and protest activities are linked by a process of activation. Previously established networks of friends, allies and colleagues are activated in precise, often punctual, settings: a demonstration, an online protest, a boycott. And thirdly, immediacy — another essential attribute of social media — has a major impact in the recruitment process preceding protest activities. Flash-mobs (or smart-mobs), spontaneous demonstrations and public protests can be organized in a matter of hours, making them unpredictable and harder to monitor or anticipate by public authorities (Teruelle and Shade 2014).

Communication technologies have come to be seen both as tools and modes for organizing protest and dissent. As a tool for organization, communication technology has been used for movement building, as well as for tactical interventions; as a mode of organization, communication technology refocuses contentious politics — and social mobilization — around the production and distribution of alternative cultural codes, narratives and symbols. Social media provide the platforms to ease and facilitate such processes and are thus used to deploy, construct and organize epistemic communities of shared identity and meaning.

Bennett (2003) argued years ago that new communication tools change the very conduct of contentious politics. Communication technology does not merely reduce the costs or increase the efficiencies of social mobilization, but, rather, *"the nature of social transactions, themselves, is changing* due to the capacity of distributed communication networks to ease personal engagement with others" (Bennett 2003: 149, emphasis in original). The Internet and social media have fostered the widespread adoption of the SPIN organizational model among activist communities: social mobilization now has to be seen as segmented, polycentric, integrated and networked.[3]

The mainstream attractiveness of social media relies on three interrelated elements: their flexibility (people can interact with them in various ways in order to achieve numerous and often quite personal goals), their networking power (their relevance and importance grow with the number of its users or contributors) and — perhaps foremost — their ease of use. Blogs, wikis and social networking tools and websites are made to be as simple to use as possible. Their very nature is to provide considerable publishing power to non-expert users. As such, they can become powerful tools to be used by those who have much to say but cannot have their stories told in mainstream media, by marginalized communities who face issues of enduring poverty, exclusion, and criminalization and by individuals and groups who are systemically excluded from telling their very own stories.

As such, social media could be integrated into a larger category of "citizens' media," a set of media productions bringing what Clemencia Rodríguez (2004) calls a "metamorphic transformation of alternative media participants (or community media, or participatory media, or radical media, or alternative media) into active citizens." Rodríguez argues:

> Citizens' media is a concept that accounts for the processes of empowerment, con-scientisation [a process of "consciousness raising"], and fragmentation of power that result when men, women, and youth gain access to and re-claim their own media. As they use media to re-constitute their own cultural codes to name the world in their own terms, citizens' media participants disrupt power relationships, exercise their own agency, and re-constitute their own lives, futures, and cultures. (n.p.)

The flexibility, networking power and ease of use of social media can provide marginalized communities with the tools to contest social codes and legitimized identities that often criminalize or victimize them and can empower individuals and groups to transform their very lives by providing a positive and rewarding learning and communication experience.

The tactical relevance of social media for activism has further proved to be considerable. Tactical Tech, an international NGO linking progressive social activism with digital communication technology, trains people to see and use social media in order to mobilize, witness and record testimonies and events, visualize communications and messages, amplify personal stories, add humour to (sometimes tragic or grim) communications, manage contacts, use complex data, deploy the collective intelligence of the communities, allow feedback and questions and investigate and expose abuses.[4]

> The flexibility, networking power and ease of use of social media can provide marginalized communities with the tools to contest social codes that often victimize them, and also to empower individual and groups to transform their lives.

This tactical relevance of social media, however, is not confined to online activities and community-building activities. It is also found in the increasing influence of "swarming" as a confrontational doctrine applied by activists of the information age during protests and demonstrations. Swarming, which relies on "the deployment of myriad, small, dispersed, networked manoeuvre units," is defined as "a deliberately structured, co-ordinated, strategic way to strike from all directions, by means of a sustainable pulsing of force and/or fire, close-in as well as from stand-off positions" (Arquilla and Ronfeldt 2000: vii). As a tactical doctrine, swarming is used both by the military and protesters to overflow adversaries' defenses and co-ordinate action.

Swarming is especially relevant for hackers and pirates, who build botnets — networks of thousands of personal computers infested by malicious software that form an army of "zombie computers" — literally swarming (or flooding) targeted websites, addresses or portals with hundreds of thousands of requests per second. The result is a "distributed denial-of-service attack" (DDoS).

A fascinating and unique botnet experiment took place in December 2010 when a nebulous group called Anonymous harnessed the power of social media to conduct a DDoS attack against firms that collaborated with public authorities in their attempt to cut off international whistleblower organization WikiLeaks from its financial revenue sources. Using Twitter, Facebook, online handbills and other social portals, Anonymous called for the voluntary insertion of personal computers in botnets targeting firms considered corporate accomplices of state censorship. PayPal, Visa and MasterCard were notably targeted. The venture, called Operation Payback, was meant to launch a global "cyberwar" against censorship. Operation Payback was unique because it relied on social media's power and the keen co-operation of those who are usually the unwilling accomplices of hackers and pirates (Duncan 2010; Coleman 2014). Since then, Anonymous has conducted numerous actions, including attacks against the Canadian government in response to the passing of anti-terrorism legislation, Bill C-51 (CBC News 2015b).

> Social media matter for activists at organizational, tactical and political levels. However, activists must also be cognizant of the politics of these corporately owned social media platforms and their insinuation into users' everyday activities.

Microblogging further plays an increasingly important co-ordinating and informative role on the ground during public protests. Live, unfiltered feeds seeded by activists inform public demonstrators of the dangers lying ahead, the rapid shifting of adversaries' forces, the identities of those arrested (or of human-rights abusers) and the locations where the arrests are taking place. Social media participates in the establishment of an enlarged sensory system relying on the constant communication of small, simple units able to ensure global co-ordination and efficiency without a centralized architecture. It has come to play a considerable role in producing real-time, citizen-oriented coverage of protests, social uprisings and political contestation.

Social media matter for activists at organizational, tactical and political levels. However, activists must also be cognizant of the politics of these corporately owned social media platforms and their insinuation into users' everyday activities. This is especially so when it comes to the privacy rights of users amid the surreptitious surveillance possibilities wrought by digital technologies.

Surveilling Dissent

Concerns over privacy and surveillance from networked communication technologies are real and serious. Yet the massive adoption of social media by consumers has also led, to a certain degree, to a reversal, and a turnaround, about surveillance issues. The activities of public authorities, state agents and even (to a lesser degree) powerful individuals are more and more challenged by recordings produced and distributed on social media websites by private, often anonymous citizens. These recordings frequently challenge police assertions of facts and their denial of reckless brutality; they provide recordings and testimonies of human rights abuses, violations of basic civil and social rights, wrongdoings, lies, propaganda and political flip-flops. They are meant to shame power by exposing the truth, but also to request justice — either in the face of public opinion or before a court of justice. No longer can public authorities discard witnesses or activist narratives as unreliable and erroneous: the public and authorities alike are called — or forced — to bear witness.

Idle No More

Idle No More is one of the largest Indigenous mass movements in Canadian history. Its inception in 2012 stemmed from Saskatchewan activists Jessica Gordon, Sylvia McAdam, Nina Wilson and Sheelah McLean, who were concerned with the then-Harper led government's omnibus Bill C-45 that called for drastic changes to land management on reservations and the weakening of environmental laws to protect waterways. Gordon created a Facebook page entreating citizens "to get off the couch and start working," which led to the naming of the movement, Idle No More (Caven 2013).

From a series of teach-ins in Saskatchewan to a national day of action in December that aligned with the United Nations Human Rights Day, Idle No More's mission grew to encompass a range of Indigenous sovereignty issues: "Idle No More calls on all people to join in a peaceful revolution, to honour Indigenous sovereignty, and to protect the land and water" (Idle No More 2013). After C-45 passed, a series of protest flash mobs involving round dances and drumming transpired across Canada in public spaces such as shopping malls. The events were recorded and passed on virally through the hashtag #idlenomore, Facebook and YouTube, which lead to a wider public knowledge of the movement (Kuttner 2014.) Environmental and climate justice concerns, particularly the volatile debates over the Alberta tar sands and the Keystone XL and Enbridge pipelines, also became integrated into Idle No More's concerns.

Social media was important in mobilizing citizens to the movement, educating citizens about First Nations sovereignty issues, and in publicizing events. Raynauld, Richez and Antoine analyzed Twitter activity for #idlenomore and found that identity issues were key to the postings, with First Nations history and culture an integral aspect of the content, even from non-First Nations supporters (Federation for the Humanities and Social Sciences 2015). This finding was also echoed by Callison and Hermida (2015), who found that non-elite Indigenous voices on Twitter were influential, producing what they called a "middle ground" for articulation and accountability. Wood argues that the particular nature of Indigenous social networks that included the "'weak ties' of activists with dense clusters of young people" facilitated not only the rapid spread of the protest movement but also a "sovereignty challenge to the government and a resurgence movement" (2015: 620). Friedel states that by sustaining cultural teachings, Idle No More "has now brought together allies in the form of First Nations, Métis, and Inuit activists, environmentalists, academics, civil liberties experts, artists, scientists, and journalists, all interested in defending land rights and protecting democratic principles" (2015: 887).

Digital mapping was used in 2012 and 2013 to document Idle No More's myriad activities, with tactics including teach-ins, rallies, blockades, hunger strikes and flash-mob round dances, that were happening not only in Canada but also globally. Tim Groves of the Media Co-Op set up a simple Google map by placing markers on the map about events he heard about, but he quickly realized the enormity of the job and crowdsourced the information, setting up an online form for event submissions (Groves 2013).

Recently Idle No More has mobilized to draw attention to the plight of the Attawapiskat First Nation community in Northern Ontario, where an epidemic of youth suicides has led to a state of emergency. Occupying the regional offices of Indigenous and Northern Affairs Canada (INAC) in Toronto with members of Black Lives Matter in solidarity has brought renewed attention to the concerns of First Nations youth (Da Silva 2015).

Québec Student Protests of 2012

The Québec student protests of 2012 were the college and university students' response to the proposed university tuition increase by the Jean Charest-led Liberal government. Included in the relatively short-lived social movement was what many view as the largest expression of civil disobedience in Canadian history, as hundreds of thousands of individuals participated in a rally in downtown Montreal (Dolphin 2012; Gass 2012; Kanuga 2012). For the approximately 300,000 students that were involved in the protests (*McGill Daily* 2015), the reasons for the strike quickly escalated from an initial response against the proposed 75 percent tuition fee hike directed towards Québec residents, to a struggle against neoliberalism, austerity measures, economic injustice, the corporatization of the university and the criminalization of protesting and basic human rights. As part of the protests, the students utilized a number of tactics. Key among these was their tactical use of social media.

The Québec students utilized social media in a variety of ways. Their use of social media was reflective of their structure; it was uneven at best. For instance, of the three major student leadership groups involved in the strike, the Fédération Etudiante Universitaire du Québec (FEUQ) maintained the largest presence on social media because they had the funding to hire three individuals to be in charge of their social media campaign (Teruelle 2016: 167). According to student organizer Laurent Gauthier, who was a member of FEUQ at the time of the strike, "The Facebook group was up to 300,000 people at one time. We were able to get instant feedback and advertise for free. And during the strike, we used Facebook and Twitter to send as much information as possible to the students" (ibid: 167). However, although the other groups likewise utilized Facebook and Twitter during the strike, Teruelle's research shows that their use of the two largest social media sites lagged behind in comparison to FEUQ. As an example, from May 17 to May 23, 2012, which was the height of the strike, FEUQ had 191 Facebook posts as compared to 63 for Association pour une solidarité syndicale étudiante (ASSÉ) and a mere seven from Fédération étudiante collégiale du Québec (FECQ). Additionally, the Twitter results were similar in that FEUQ dominated with almost 136 tweets, followed by FECQ with 91 tweets, and ASSÉ with a mere 5 tweets. Perhaps the uneven results of the student groups' use of social media were a direct result of the organizers' attitudes.

Without a doubt, the striking students' use of social media was heavily influenced by the democratic, leaderless and egalitarian ideals promoted by CLASSE — Coalition large de l'ASSÉ — a group that was an offshoot of ASSÉ. According to respondent and former FECQ president Léo Bureau-Blouin, "As student representatives, *we were not calling the shots of mobilization. Things were moving through social media. They were organizing their own stuff, organizing their own campaign … the truth is that we didn't even know what was going on*" (ibid: 172, emphasis in original). Indeed, whether acting as a citizen journalist and documenting the strike, sharing information about the happenings or organizing, the students certainly utilized social media on their own terms.

Twitter provided explicit examples of the students' use of social media through an analysis of the more popular hashtags. For instance, Amy Luft tweeted, "I live a block west of St. Denis – loud sound of drums and cheers suddenly. Lots of horns honking (in support, I think?) #22mai #ggi" (ibid.: 190). An analysis of the hashtag #non1625 — a direct reference to the proposed tuition hike of $1,625 — revealed the following: there were 139 tweets recorded on May 17, 179 tweets on May 18, 73 tweets on May 19, 64 tweets on May 20, 93 tweets on May 21 and 139 tweets on May 22. As an example, on May 17, Olivier Lacelle's tweet encouraged the students to partake in the one-hundredth day May 22 demonstration: "Nous devons battre un record le mardi 22 mai. Rendez-vous à la Place des Festivals à partir de midi. #manifencours #ggi #non1625 #polqc," which translates to "We need to break a record on Tuesday, May 22. Meet at à la Place des Festivals to leave at noon" (ibid: 193). Certainly, social media had a great role in allowing the students and their supporters to organize.

Moreover, student-run media, CUTV, provided a live stream broadcast throughout the entire period of the strike and even documented police assaults on the protesters. It gave the students a voice, a venue to express themselves, and in their own way. By using CUTV live streaming, the students actively participated in the demonstrations while simultaneously "covering all major aspects of the strike" (Thorburn 2014: 55). CUTV's live streaming technology and footage also allowed for "the self-representation of strikers, for the subject formation of previously unconstituted activists, and for the creation of a new assemblage — the counter-hegemonic surveillance assemblage, that began to challenge and hold accountable the power of the State" (Thorburn 2014: 55). Simply put, the use of live streaming allowed the students to surveil the police and promote their own narrative.

> Not only did the organizations and the students use social media to coordinate and mobilize individuals and promote other street-level tactics, students also used social media to create their own stories and report on the events themselves.

The students were very effective in their tactical use of social media during the 2012

Quebec student strike. Students and organizations used social media not only to coordinate and mobilize individuals and promote other street-level tactics, but also to create their own stories and report on the events themselves.

#BeenRapedNeverReported

When the Canadian Broadcasting Corporation (CBC) fired superstar radio host Jian Ghomeshi on October 26, 2014, it unwillingly sparked a national debate on sexual violence against women. The layoff took place in a tense context, as the CBC was publicly accused of having tolerated abuses and improper behaviour from their star host for years (Radio-Canada 2014).

Over the following days, several women stepped forward and publicly denounced the abuse and harassment they claimed to have suffered from the charismatic celebrity. Ghomeshi responded to his dismissal by the CBC by launching a short-lived $55 million lawsuit against the CBC, claiming defamation and breach of trust (Fraser 2016). Controversy was quick to follow. While facing criminal charges of sexual assault, Ghomeshi initially found strong public support from people denouncing what they perceived as his public hanging before trial, the invasion of his private life and the inconsideration of the presumption of innocence by the media (Doucette 2014). The women who came out publicly about their assaults were questioned about their motives, their own conduct and behaviour, and why they refrained from taking legal action themselves against the radio host.

Reacting to these events, two journalists, Antonia Zerbisias and Sue Montgomery, responded by creating the hashtag #BeenRapedNeverReported and revealed themselves as victims of sexual abuse.

> It was 1969 when, if you found you were the only girl in the rec room and no parents were home, it was your fault.#BeenRapedNeverReported —Antonia Zerbisias (@AntoniaZ) October 30, 2014

> He was my grandfather. I was 3–9 yo. Cops wanted to know why I waited so long to report it. #BeenRapedNeverReported —suemontgomery (@MontgomerySue) October 31, 2014

By doing so, they opened a public window allowing victims to express their suffering and break the silence (Muise 2014). Their actions were quickly followed by tens of thousands of people (mostly women) narrating their stories of sexual violence and abuse on Twitter. The hashtag became viral, started trending, aggregated millions of tweets and sparked conversations and debates on blogs, social media platforms and mainstream media. #AgressionNonDénoncée was quickly launched in French Canada by the Fédération des femmes du Québec. Fédération president Alexa Conradi told her story of sexual abuse as well. #BeenRapedNeverReported became a movement (Zerbisias 2014).

Public discussions escalated on the role of social media in feminist activism. Concepts such as "hashtag feminism," "feminism 2.0" and "networked feminism" (which predates these events) were applied to describe the events and critically reconsidered. In these conversations, social media was described as a space in which victims of aggression, discrimination and injustice could meet and share stories, both to themselves and to a larger public. In doing so, it was said that participants could resist loneliness, guilt and shame while raising awareness on issues that were marginalized or incorrectly depicted in the mainstream media (Dixon 2014). Violence suffered in private could be expressed publicly while providing some degree of anonymity to those who spoke out (Giese 2014). Many victims of sexual assault choose to remain anonymous.

Technology was further branded as a potential ally for activist feminism. As Antonia Zerbisias claimed:

> Social media has not only resurrected feminist activism; it has redefined it and made it more inclusive, despite the differences within the movement. Feminism is no longer the purview of privileged women with the resources to devote themselves to it. Because social media is democratic, available to anybody with a smartphone, voices long silenced or marginalized now have a platform—and a megaphone. (Zerbisias 2014)

The idea of "hashtag feminism" or "networked feminism" contradicts earlier representations of online life as merely individualist or solitary. A strong commitment to collective identity and to the global feminist community was demonstrated by such viral and vibrant activism. #BeenRapedNeverReported further challenges critics of digital activism that see it as empty gestures lacking any significant impact. The actions launched a national and international momentum to address issues of sexual violence against women and allowed victims of sexual assault to frame their stories in their own words, challenging mainstream narratives about consent, violence and responsibility.

The idea of "hashtag feminism" or "networked feminism" contradicts earlier representations of online life as merely individualist or solitary.

Yet not everybody agreed with this enthusiastic appraisal of the democratic function of social media. Critics of "hashtag feminism" argued that the use of technology could not only empower communities of marginalized voices, but also reproduce and reinforce exclusion as well. Access to digital tools, to opinion leaders and to knowledge and skills needed to express grievances on social media platforms remain unequally distributed amongst social groups (Loza 2014; Latina and Docherty 2014). Furthermore, social media remains a place in which women — and especially feminists and feminist organizations — are routinely targeted with defamation, insults and threats (Ganzer 2014).

On March 24, 2016, Ghomeshi was found not guilty on all charges of sexual assault. The ruling fuelled dismay in the legal system as a safe space in which narratives about sexual violence could be heard and processed. Protestors argued that the court's decision proved that women, not the radio host, "were put on trial" and reaffirmed the need to provide victims of abuse with spaces in which they could be heard and supported (CBC 2016).

The role that social media can play in feminism remains controversial (Kaba, Smith,

Adelman and Gay 2014). The #BeenRapedNeverReported movement provided the ground-work from which intellectuals, activists and survivors of violence could engage in a discussion about feminism, inequality, empowerment and marginalization.

Am I Talking to Myself? Critiques of Online Activism

Social activism is, at its core, a communicative phenomenon. It is built upon and organizes change through communication processes: ideas, values and information need to be shared; supporters and adherents have to be recruited; antagonistic arguments and discourses need to be discarded and replied to. The role of technology and of the regulatory framework under which it operates are consequently central to the very life and dynamics of collective mobilization. As de Jong, Shaw and Stammers argue: "It should be obvious that we cannot understand activism without seeing how it communicates politically, or contemporary media without looking at how activists are both using and transforming political communication" (2005: 2).

Yet some argue that online activism — the use of digital communication technology, in general, and of social media in particular to foster social change — is of limited potential at best, or a mere illusion at worst. Online activism, such skeptics say, might just be "slacktivism" — lazy and lousy activism that makes people feel good about themselves but does not provide any real challenge to the power-holders one aims to influence. In one example, facing an unprecedented level of unpopularity, Quebec's Prime Minister Jean Charest was confronted early in 2011 by an online petition signed by nearly 250,000 people requesting his resignation. Launched a few months before as a citizen initiative, the petition found support among provincial opposition parties and was hosted on the National Assembly website. While the numbers of signatories was impressive, Quebec's civil society and political class failed to build on the momentum and to provide any meaningful political action that would have more that a symbolic and ephemeral impact.

Malcolm Gladwell, a New Yorker columnist, is one skeptic of online activism. He argues that the use of social media by activists ought to be considered as "a small change" (2010). Quoting the work of social movement expert Doug McAdam, Gladwell argues that high-risk activism is very much a "strong-tie" thing, something social media, which relies on the reinforcements and maintenance of weak social ties, can never claim to build. "Social networks," Gladwell (2010) writes, "are effective at increasing participation — by lessening the level of motivation that participation requires." When protest activities require high levels of motivation — when there is high personal involvement, risk or danger — social media become incapable of providing the fundamental strategic and motivational requirements of efficient social action. The very architectural principle of social media — the network — is further judged incompatible with significant social activism, which requires hierarchical decision-making structures.

Gladwell's comments echo those of activist and academic Angela Davis, who rose to prominence during the American struggles for civil rights and African American freedom:

> Organizing is not synonymous with mobilizing. Now that many of us have access

to new technologies of communication like the Internet and cell phones, we need to give serious thought to how they might best be used. The Internet is an incredible tool but it may also encourage us to think that we can produce instantaneous movements, movements modeled after fast food delivery. (Davis 2005: 129–30)

Evgeny Morozov, a journalist and former fellow of the Open Society Institute, is another critic. His assessment of net activism, *The Net Delusion* (2011), was published on the eve of the Tunisian unrest, and his critique about the hype of social media in fomenting popular protest in repressive regimes generated much debate in the media and in online forums.

Morozov offers a trenchant analysis of cyber-utopianism, "the idea that the Internet favors the oppressed rather than the oppressor" (2011: xiii), and blames it on the "starry-eyed digital fervor of the 1990s" (2011: xiii) led by what he claims are former hippies now ensconced in elite universities intent on resurrecting the democratic impulses of the 1960s. Morozov also blames the "Google Doctrine," "the enthusiastic belief in the liberating power of technology accompanied by the irresistible urge to enlist Silicon Valley start-ups in the global fight for freedom" (2011: xiii). He further argues that the prevalence of "Internet-centrism" has seeped into discourses on democratic reform, thus obscuring a consideration of other contextual factors that can foster such reforms.

He warns of the dangers of repressive regimes surveilling the new spaces of social media dissent more assiduously than they do anti-government gatherings in public spaces, and he is wary of the American dominance of social media infrastructures, themselves also potentially part of a larger military-industrial-security and surveillance regime. These technologies are not inherently apolitical, Morozov comments, and are instead ensconced in regimes of power operating under an often libertarian mantra of "Internet freedom." This tension has been highlighted in more recent events, discussed earlier in this chapter, wherein human rights activists in China and the Middle East have found their effective use of social media compromised by arduous terms of service exercised by American corporate social media platform companies.

Western countries are not immune from state surveillance. In Spring 2013, American whistleblower Edward Snowden revealed to the world that global surveillance programs were conducted by American intelligence agencies. Documents leaked by Snowden revealed that these agencies, especially the National Security Agency (NSA), were collecting informations on tens of millions of U.S. citizens, while numerous high profile politicians, foreigners and international institutions were monitored and surveilled (Poitras 2014; Greenwald 2015). In February 2016, a federal judge, as requested by the FBI, ordered Apple to unlock an iPhone used by Syed Farook, who shot and murdered fourteen people. Apple refused to comply, stating that this would lead to a precedent-setting situation whereby national security agencies could request access to the private data of its customers. The request was eventually dropped — and the FBI claims that it succeeded in accessing the data without the help of Apple. This case highlights the raising tension between privacy and state security (Yadron 2016).

It Is a Contested Terrain

Will the revolution be tweeted? Of course it will — as it will be broadcasted, blogged, painted, danced and screened. Social media, as all media appropriated by activists (whether they are referred to as citizens' media, alternative media, radical media or community media; see Rodríguez 2004; Downing 2001; Couldry and Curran 2003) are fundamental tools used by activists deeply immersed in cultural struggles — struggles where the meaning, importance and articulation of a society's values and beliefs are waged. As Keane argues "a healthy democratic regime is one in which various types of public spheres are thriving, with no single one of them actually enjoying monopoly in public disputes about the distribution of power" (2004: 376).

Movement-controlled media are fundamental tools of political information, ideological affirmation and debate, publicity, co-ordination, knowledge-sharing, internal cohesion and identity reinforcement, planning and political action. They can provide challenges to what Thompson (1995) defines as the "symbolic power" of authorities, referring to the "capacity to intervene in the course of events, to influence the actions of others and indeed to create events, by means of production and diffusion of symbolic forms" (Thompson 1995: 17). They are at the centre of a "delivery system for consciousness raising, political education, and training" (Barney 2004: 126). They matter.

> Social media are comprised of software products owned by capitalistic interests and invested in the reproduction of capitalistic relationships. They are deeply inserted in the global political economy of communication that marginalizes — and often criminalizes — those who resist the social, economic, and political order that nurtured their development.

Yet mainstream social media sites are not natural allies of activists. Social media are comprised of software products owned by capitalistic interests and invested in the reproduction of capitalistic relationships. They are deeply inserted in the global political economy of communication that marginalizes — and often criminalizes — those who resist the social, economic and political order that nurtured their development.

These media are further selling a very precise product: their users' private data and information. Facebook has been continuously criticized for its infringement of its users' privacy rights. An early investigation into Facebook's privacy policies was conducted by the Privacy Commissioner of Canada in 2009, following a complaint instigated by University of Ottawa students and the Canadian Internet Policy and Public Interest Clinic. The Privacy Commissioner was, among other things, concerned with the sharing of personal information with third-party developers publishing games and quizzes on the social networking site, the confusing distinction between deactivation and deletion of accounts, the privacy of non-users invited to join the site and the management of accounts of deceased users (Office of the Privacy Commissioner of Canada 2009). Facing significant political and legal pressure, Facebook agreed in August 2009 to proceed with the establishment of new privacy safeguards. Concern about adherence to the Commission's recommendations, however, remains. Facebook CEO and founder, Mark Zuckerberg argued in 2010 that privacy is no longer "a social norm," sparking international debates about user's privacy rights (*Telegraph* 2010). Facebook has further repeatedly outraged privacy groups and civil liberties organizations over the last few years by introducing privacy settings that diminish privacy while increasing the level of personal information available online to third-party marketers.

Facebook is also a tool for surveillance and monitoring owned and used by capitalist interests. This, in itself, is a matter of concern for both activist communities and ordinary citizens. Mainstream social media derive considerable — actually monumental — revenues from the selling of users' personal information to the actual customer of the social media — marketers, advertising companies, corporations and third-party companies. How they do it, following which guidelines, and with what degree of transparency and accountability is a matter of deep democratic concern. Facebook's half a billion users' habits and activities are tracked, monitored, stored and sold. This company has never intended to promote or support progressive social movements, despite the recent announcement of the Chan Zuckerberg Initiative, a limited liability company which will allow Zuckerberg and his wife to give away an estimated US$45 billion worth of their Facebook shares to causes for "personalized learning, curing disease, connecting people and building strong communities" (Sagan 2015). This example of "philanthrocapitalism" highlights the democratic stakes when ultra-rich business leaders can influence policy priorities (Cassidy 2015). Facebook, like other social media platforms, provides a formidable and highly attractive profit-oriented entry point into the personal lives of its users throughout the world who are reconfigured as consumers rather than citizens (Sarikakis 2010).

Nevertheless, like any other technological consumer product, these very features of mainstream social media can be used in subversive ways by dedicated activists. It is a matter of creativity, imagination, and resistance — attributes that have much more to do with ingenuity than with technology. And, despite painstaking and deliberate care, technology, with the assistance of diverse social actors, often detours from its original "intentionality" track. "Technology leads a double life," wrote the late York University professor David Noble, "one which conforms to the intentions of designers and interests of power and another which contradicts them — proceeding behind the backs of their architects to reveal unintended consequences and unanticipated possibilities" (Noble 1984: 324–325). The highly creative and imaginative uses of Twitter and Facebook made by activists and concerned citizens in the uprisings in the Arab world is a striking example of this double use.

Those who refuse to be monitored and confined are called to develop their own social media tools (wikis, blogs, social networking sites). And while these won't have the same outreach appeal as the tools garnering huge financial support from initial public offerings and venture capitalists, they ought to be considered as micro-social media, aimed at reinforcing social ties between activists, and highly relevant for social organization and information-sharing. The Independent Media Center, built in 1999 from the rioting streets of Seattle, might be the most famous movement-oriented, citizen-operated network of wikis publishing news and information. (See Lievrouw 2011 and Wolfson 2014 for an overview of its origins and pioneering uses of participatory journalism through its open publishing platform.)

The spread of new, high quality and affordable communication technologies among

424 Power and Resistance

citizens and activist communities also ought to be understood as providing a greater opportunity for the ordinary citizen to produce and distribute meaning, information and values and beliefs that can be highly critical of the official discourses of economic and political power holders. Over the last few years, social media have been seized by activists as an entry point to impact the mediasphere — either by generating significant online traffic on precise content or through providing mainstream media with stories, pictures, sound bites and recordings that enrich the needs of these resource-strapped media organizations.

> Social media will not create the revolution, but have become an integral component in contemporary social and political struggles, as those who struggle harness these participatory tools to tell their stories about social justice in creative, passionate, and imaginative ways.

Furthermore, in a world where control over the production and distribution of information flows is an essential attribute of power, the confinement of individuals and groups to positions of passive receptivity is equated with subordination (Melucci 1996: 180). Escaping from a status of mere media consumer is a qualitative shift from being the mere object of communication to becoming the communicative subject itself. This transformation has deep political ramifications. Speaking out is always political; it represents a refusal of noiselessness, submission, passivity and conformity. Because social media can provide the platforms to ease and facilitate such processes, they are thus used to deploy, construct and organize epistemic communities of shared identity and meaning.

In the end, the relevance of social media for activism relies on what it provides to its users: an access gate to open publication, admission to a fully customizable and near-infinite series of networks, efficient distribution channels for content and information and a collaborative space for meeting and exchanging with others. All of these can hardly be discarded as irrelevant. Yet critics of online activism are right about this: social media is a tool, not an end in itself. There is nothing inherently emancipatory about it. Social media will not create the revolution. But as many recent events demonstrate, social media have become an integral component in contemporary social and political struggles, as those who struggle harness these participatory tools to tell their stories about social justice in creative, passionate and imaginative ways.

Glossary of Key Terms

Botnet: A network frequently made of thousands of personal computers infested by malicious software and placed under control of an individual referred to as a "bot herder." Botnets are used by bot herders to launch denial-of-service attacks.

Broadband: High-speed telecommunication connectivity. Broadband connections provide greater speed than analog connections to users accessing the Internet and telecommunication services. Broadband connectivity consumes a higher amount of bandwidth and requires a technological architecture able to deliver it.

Commodification: Taking objects, or often non-commercial products, and services and trans-forming them into entities valued for their marketable function and use in exchange processes.

Cyberwar: The strategic use of digital technology and computer communications by states or politically active groups in order to infiltrate designated targets or to disrupt communications, destroy property or cause damage to their adversaries.

Denial-of-service attack (DDOS): An operation that overflows a server with requests with the goal of interrupting, disrupting or stopping activities taking place on targeted websites. DDOS occur when botnets are activated by a "bot herder."

Fair dealing: A strategy that aims at providing space for fair critique, private study and public information on material protected by intellectual property law. Fair dealing, which requires acknowledgement of the author or creator of the protected material, is a limited exception to the exclusivity of intellectual property.

Flash-mobs: Spontaneous, short-lived public events reuniting groups of people in the same location. Flash-mobs are frequently organized through the use of digital communications devices and social media technology. Though varying in scale, purposes and shape, flash-mobs rely in essence on a disruption of ordinariness and predictability.

Free culture movement: A social movement promoting the creation and distribution of content on the Internet. It advocates for copyright reform that is least restrictive and that permits the free sharing of culture under various conditions such as under Creative Commons licences.

Hackers: Individuals who use their knowledge and computer skills to break into and infiltrate digital devices and networks. Hackers have different motivations and ethics. Fame, profit, political purposes, curiosity, and personal satisfaction are among the most common incentives to hacking.

Identity theft: Assuming someone else's identity in order to access their private and personal accounts, access valuable information or steal the financial resources of the victim.

Libertarian: An individual whose political philosophy emphasizes an individualistic conception of liberty, freedom, and responsibility. Libertarians typically show hostility towards state regulation, involvement or participation in private or public life.

Open-source software: Software that allows users to access, modify and reprogram their source code in order to improve or personalize them to their needs and interests. As with closed-source software (such as Windows), open-source software (such as Linux) is protected by license agreements providing rules and regulation of uses and distribution.

Pirates: Individuals or groups who illegally modify, share or distribute privately owned information, content or data. File-sharing and website hacking are often associated with piracy by both public authorities and representatives of intellectual property rights organizations.

Slacktivism: Public demonstrations of support in regard to a particular social issue or cause that requires little or no direct commitment, participation or involvement from supporters. Slacktivism is depicted by critics as useless or personal public relations activities.

Social media: Internet technologies that allow for participative communication practices. Social media are tools that empower users to contribute to developing, collaborating, customizing, rating and distributing Internet content. Their design aims at facilitating the constitution of networks among users.

Swarming: Offensive strategy and military doctrine aimed at overrunning the adversary's defences through co-ordinated attacks coming from numerous directions and locations simultaneously.

Third-party marketing: The use of social media, Internet technology and websites by companies and entrepreneurs to interact with, gather information from and obtain feedback from targeted customers, groups and individuals.

WikiLeaks: A non-profit organization whose primary activity rests in the online publication of classified, leaked and secret information. Officially launched in 2007 as a project of the Sunshine Press, WikiLeaks relies mostly on anonymous sources and whistleblowers for obtaining sensitive information. The organization is currently headed by controversial public figure Julian Assange.

Questions for Discussion

1. Are social media a tool of control, monitoring and surveillance, or an opportunity for progressive social mobilization?

2. Is online activism "slacktivism?"

3. What uses can be made of social media by progressive activists?

4. Which specificities of social media make it relevant for social justice activism?

5. What are other Canadian examples of the use of social media for social justice activism?

Resources for Activists

Electronic Frontier Foundation — Social Network Monitoring: eff.org/foia/social-network-monitoring>
Independent Media Center: indymedia.org
International Free and Open Source Science Foundation: ifossf.org
OpenMedia: openmedia.ca
Privacy International: privacyinternational.org
Rabble.ca: Social Justice Resources: rabble.ca/podcasts/channel/social-justice

Surveillance Studies Centre — Queen's University: sscqueens.org
Tactical Technology Collective: tacticaltech.org
WITNESS: witness.org
World Association for Christian Communication: waccglobal.org

Notes

1. See <amnesty.org.uk/news_details.asp?NewsID=18827>.
2. See <witness.org>.
3. Segmentation invokes the porous boundaries between groups and organizations sharing resources and co-ordinating action. Polycentrism refers to the multiple hubs and centres around which a movement is organized. Integration refers to ideological frameworks uniting activists, where inclusiveness has come to be fostered by new communication technologies. Finally, networks of activists are found in various settings; they are active in multiple groups and hold various commitments and identities. See Bennett 2003: 22.
4. See the Tactical Tech website <tacticaltech.org>.

References

Al Jazeera English. 2011. "Social Media's Role in the Tunisian Uprising." January 15. <youtube.com/watch?v=UoRspCp5Xn0>.

Arquilla, J., and D. Ronfeldt. 2000. *Swarming and the Future of Conflicts.* Santa Monica: RAND.

Barney, D.D. 2004. *The Network Society.* Cambridge; Malden, MA: Polity.

Bennett, W.L. 2003. "Communicating Global Activism: Strengths and Vulnerabilities of Networked Politics." *Information, Communication and Society* 6, 2.

Bradshaw, T. 2011. "Bin Laden Death Sees Twitter Traffic Soar." *Financial Times,* May 3. <ft.com/cms/s/0/44a50716-757e-11e0849200144feabdc0,dwp_uuid=f39ffd26-4bb2-11da997b0000779e2340.html#axzz1LQxUGNXr>.

Callison, C., and A. Hermida. 2015. "Dissent and Resonance: #Idlenomore as an Emergent Middle Ground." *Canadian Journal of Communication* 40, 4. <cjc-online.ca/index.php/journal/article/view/2958>.

Carty, V. 2011. *Wired and Mobilizing: Social Movements, New Technology, and Electoral Politics.* New York; London: Routledge.

Cassidy, J. 2015. "Mark Zuckerberg and the Rise of Philanthrocapitalism." *The New Yorker,* December 2. <newyorker.com/news/john-cassidy/mark-zuckerberg-and-the-rise-of-philanthrocapitalism>.

Caven, F. 2013. "Being Idle No More: The Women Behind the Movement." *Cultural Survival Quarterly*, March. <culturalsurvival.org/publications/cultural-survival-quarterly/being-idle-no-more-women-behind-movement>.

CBC News. 2015a. "Desktop Internet Use by Canadians Highest in World. comScore Says." March 27. <cbc.ca/news/business/desktop-internet-use-by-canadians-highest-in-world-comscore-says-1.3012666>.

____. 2015b. "'Anonymous' Says it Cyberattacked Federal Government to Protest Bill C-51." June 17. <cbc.ca/news/politics/anonymous-says-it-cyberattacked-federal-government-to-protest-bill-c-51-1.3117360>.

____. 2016. "Jian Ghomeshi trial's not guilty decision triggers outrage, march to police headquarters." *cbc.ca*, March 25. <cbc.ca/news/canada/toronto/jian-ghomeshi-judge-ruling-1.3504250>.

Chomiak, L. 2016. "Five Years After the Tunisian Revolution, Political Frustration Doesn't Diminish Progress." *The Washington Post.* <washingtonpost.com/news/monkey-cage/wp/2016/01/14/

five-years-after-the-tunisian-revolution/>.

Coleman, G. 2014. *Hacker, Hoaxer, Whistleblower, Spy: The Many Faces of Anonymous*. London: Verso.

Couldry, N., and J. Curran (eds.). 2003. *Contesting Media Power: Alternative Media in a Networked World*. Lanham, MD: Rowman and Littlefield.

Curran, J. 2002. *Media and Power*. London; New York: Routledge.

Da Silva, C. 2015. "Idle No More, Black Lives Matter Protesters Demand Action on Attawapiskat Suicide Crisis." *CBC News*, April 13. <cbc.ca/news/canada/toronto/protesters-occupy-indigenous-northern-affairs-office-1.3533662>.

Davis, A.Y. 2005. *Abolition Democracy: Beyond Empire, Prisons and Torture*. New York: Seven Stories.

De Jong, W., M. Shaw, and N. Stammers. 2005. *Global Activism, Global Media*. London; Ann Arbor, MI: Pluto Press.

Deibert, R., and R. Rohozinski. 2011. "The New Cyber Military-Industrial Complex." *Globe and Mail*, March 28. <theglobeandmail.com/news/opinions/opinion/the-new-cyber-military-industrial-complex/article1957159/>.

Dixon, K. 2014. "Feminist Online Identity: Analyzing the Presence of Hashtag Feminism." *Journal of Arts and Humanities* 3, 7: 34–50. <theartsjournal.org/index.php/site/article/view/509>.

Dolphin, M. 2012. "Massive Montreal Rally Marks 100 Days of Student Protests." *The Canadian Press*, May 22. <theglobeandmail.com/news/national/massive-montreal-rally-marks-100-days-of-student-protests/article4198301/>.

Doucette, C. 2014. "Jian Ghomeshi Blames Firing on 'Consensual' Rough Sex." *IFpress.com*, October 27. <lfpress.com/2014/10/26/cbc-parts-ways-with-jian-ghomeshi>.

Downing, J. 2001. *Radical Media: Rebellious Communication and Social Movements*. Thousand Oaks, CA: Sage Publications.

Duncan, G. 2010. "WikiLeaks Supporters Using Volunteer and Zombie Botnets." DigitalTrends. <digitaltrends.com/computing/wikileaks-supporters-using-volunteer-and-zombie-botnets/>.

Dwyer, J. 2014. *More Awesome Than Money: Four Boys and Their Heroic Quest to Save Your Privacy from Facebook*. NY: Viking.

El Akkad, O. 2011. "In a Span of Minutes, a Country Goes Off-line." *Globe and Mail*, January 29: A16.

Facebook Corporation. 2016. "Company Information." <newsroom.fb.com/company-info/>.

Federation for the Humanities and Social Sciences. 2015. "#idlenomore and Social Media: A First Study." Press release, May 31. <ideas-idees.ca/media/media-releases/idlenomore-and-social-media-first-study>.

Fraser, L. 2016. "Timeline: What led to Jian Ghomeshi's sex assault trial." *cbc.ca*, January 29. <cbc.ca/news/canada/toronto/timeline-jian-ghomeshi-1.3417978>.

Friedel, T.L. 2015. "Understanding the Nature of Indigenous Youth Activism in Canada: Idle No More as a Resumptive Pedagogy." *South Atlantic Quarterly* 114, 4 (October): 878–891.

Ganzer, M. 2014. "In Bed With the Trolls." *Feminist Media Studies* 14, 6: 1098–1100.

Gass, H. 2012. "Record Numbers March for 100th Day of Quebec Student Strike." *McGill Daily*, May 24. <cupwire.ca/2012/05/24/record-numbers-march-for-100th-day-of-quebec-student-strike/>.

Giese, R. 2014. "#YouCantShutMeUp: Feminism goes viral." *Chatelaine*, October 31. <chatelaine.com/living/youcantshutmeup/>.

Gladwell, M. 2010. "Small Change: Why the Revolution Will Not Be Tweeted." *New Yorker*, October 4. <newyorker.com/reporting/2010/10/04/101004fa_fact_gladwell?currentPage=all>.

Greenwald, G. 2015. *No Place to Hide: Edward Snowden, the NSA, and the U.S. Surveillance State*. NY: Picador.

Groves, T. 2013. "Making a Map of Idle No More," January 3. <timgrovesreports.wordpress.

com/2013/01/03/making-a-map-of-idle-no-more/>.

Hassine, W.B., and E. Galperin. 2016. "Changes to Facebook's 'Real Names' Policy Still Don't Fix the Problem." San Francisco: Electronic Frontier Foundation. <eff.org/deeplinks/2015/12/changes-facebooks-real-names-policy-still-dont-fix-problem>.

Helft, M. 2009. "YouTube's Quest to Suggest More, So Users Search Less." *New York Times*, December 30. <nytimes.com/2009/12/31/technology/Internet/31tube.html?ref=youtube>.

Howard, P.N., and M.M. Hussain. 2013. *Democracy's Fourth Wave? Digital Media and the Arab Spring.* Oxford: Oxford University Press.

Idle No More. 2013. "The Vision." <idlenomore.ca/vision>.

Isaac, M. 2016. "Twitter User Growth Stalls, and the Chief Pledges to Make Fixes." *New York Times*, February 10. <nytimes.com/2016/02/11/technology/twitter-earnings-user-growth.html?ref=technology&_r=0>.

Kaba, M., A. Smith, L. Adelman, and R. Gay. 2014. "Where Twitter and Feminism Meet." *The Nation*, April 17. <thenation.com/article/where-twitter-and-feminism-meet/>.

Kanuga, M. 2012. "The Quebec Student Strike Celebrates its 100th Day." *Global Research*, May 23. <globalresearch.ca/the-quebec-student-strike-celebrates-its-100th-day/31002>.

Karatzogianni, A. 2006. *The Politics of Cyberconflict.* London; New York: Routledge.

Keane, J. 2004. "The Structural Transformations of the Public Sphere." In Frank Webster et al. (eds.), *The Information Society Reader.* London; New York: Routledge.

Kirkpatrick, D. 2010. *The Facebook Effect: The Inside Story of the Company That Is Connecting the World.* New York: Simon and Schuster.

Kopytoff, V.G. 2011. "Sites Like Twitter Absent from Free Speech Pact." *New York Times*, March 6. <nytimes.com/2011/03/07/technology /07rights.html?_r=1&ref=facebookinc>.

Kuttner, P. 2014. "Idle No More and the Round Dance Flash Mob." *Beautiful Trouble.* <beautifultrouble.org/case/idle-dance-flash-mob/>.

Latina, D., and S. Docherty. 2014. "Trending Participation, Trending Exclusion?" *Feminist Media Studies* 14, 6: 1103–1105.

Lievrouw, L.A. 2011. *Alternative and Activist New Media.* Malden, MA: Polity Press.

Loza, S. 2014. "Hashtag Feminism, #SolidarityIsForWhiteWomen, and the Other #FemFuture." *Ada: A Journal of Gender, New Media and Technology* 5. <adanewmedia.org/2014/07/issue5-loza/>.

McGill Daily. 2015. "Beyond Separatism: A Short Primer on Quebec's Political Landscape." January 26. <web.archive.org/web/20150109183125/http://www.mcgilldaily.com/disorientation2014/beyondseparatism.php>.

Melucci, A. 1996. *Challenging Codes: Collective Action in the Information Age.* Cambridge; New York: Cambridge University Press.

Morozov, E. 2011. *The Net Delusion: The Dark Side of Internet Freedom.* New York: Public Affairs.

Muise, M. 2014. "'Been Raped Never Reported': Why 90% of Sex Assault Victims Stay Silent Rather Than Face Trial by Ordeal." *The National Post*, November 28. <news.nationalpost.com/news/canada/been-raped-never-reported-why-90-of-sex-assault-victims-stay-silent-rather-than-face-trial-by-ordeal>.

Noble, D.F. 1984. *Forces of Production: A Social History of Industrial Automation.* New York: Knopf.

Nussbaum, E. 2010. "Defacebook." *New York Magazine*, September 26. <nymag.com/news/features/establishments/68512/>.

OECD (Organisation for Economic Co-operation and Development). 2007. "OECD Study on the Participative Web and User-Created Content: Web 2.0, Wikis, and Social Networking." <213.253.134.43/oecd/pdfs/browseit/9307031E.PDF>.

Office of the Privacy Commissioner of Canada. 2009. "Facebook Agrees to Address Privacy Commissioner's Concerns." Press release. <priv.gc.ca/media/nr-c/2009/nr-c_090827_e.cfm, August 27>.

Poitras, L., dir. 2014. *Citizen Four.* <citizenfourfilm.com/>.

Preston, J. 2011a. "Facebook Officials Keep Quiet on Its Role in the Revolts." *New York Times*, February 14. <nytimes.com/2011/02/15/business/media/15facebook.html>.

____. 2011b. "Ethical Quandary for Social Sites." *New York Times*, March 27. <nytimes.com/2011/03/28/business/media/28social.html?ref=facebookinc>.

Radio-Canada. 2014. "Jian Ghomeshi: la version de la CBC." *radio-canada.ca*, October 31. <ici.radio-canada.ca/regions/ontario/2014/10/31/011-jian-ghomeshi-version-cbc-heather-conway.shtml>.

Raley, R. 2009. *Tactical Media.* Minneapolis: University of Minnesota Press.

Rodríguez, C. 2004. "The Renaissance of Citizens Media." *Media Development* 2. <waccglobal.org/en/20042-citizenship-identity-media/506-The-renaissance-of-citizens-media.html>.

Sagan, A. 2015. "Zuckerberg, Chan $45 Billion Pledge is Not for Charity, But a Company." *CBC News*, December 3. <cbc.ca/news/business/facebook-mark-zuckerberg-charity-share-donation-1.3346966>.

Sarikakis, K. 2010. "The Precarious Citizen: Control and Value in the Digital Age." *Nordicom Review* 31. <nordicom.gu.se/common/publ_pdf/320_11%20sarikakis.pdf>.

Shaw, M. 2005. "Peace Activism and Western Wars: Social Movements in Mass-Mediated Global Politics." In Wilma de Jong et al. (eds.), *Global Activism, Global Media.* London; Ann Arbor, MI: Pluto Press.

Telegraph. 2010. "Facebook's Mark Zuckerberg Says Privacy Is No Longer a 'Social Norm.'" January 11. <telegraph.co.uk/technology/facebook/6966628/Facebooks-Mark-Zuckerberg-says-privacy-is-no-longer-a-social-norm.html>.

Teruelle, R. 2016. *Social Media, Red Squares, and Other Tactics: The 2012 Québec Student Protests.* Doctoral dissertation, Toronto: Faculty of Information, University of Toronto.

Teruelle, R., and L.R. Shade. 2014. "Flash Mobs." In K. Harvey and G.J. Golson (eds.), *Encyclopedia of Social Media and Politics.* Thousand Oaks, CA: Sage Publications.

Thompson, J. 1995. *The Media and Modernity.* Cambridge, UK: Polity.

Thorburn, E.D. 2014. "Social Media, Subjectivity, and Surveillance: Moving on From Occupy, the Rise of Live Streaming Video." *Communication and Critical/Cultural Studies,* 11, 1: 52–63.

Wolfson, T. 2014. *Digital Rebellion: The Birth of the Cyber Left.* Urbana-Champaign: University of Illinois Press.

Wood, L. 2015. "Idle No More, Facebook and Diffusion." *Social Movement Studies* 14, 5: 615–621.

Yadron, D. 2016. "FBI Confirms It Won't Tell Apple How It Hacked San Bernardino Shooter's iPhone." *The Guardian*, April 28. <theguardian.com/technology/2016/apr/27/fbi-apple-iphone-secret-hack-san-bernardino>.

York, J.C. 2011. "Not Twitter, Not Wikileaks: A Human Revolution." January 14. <jilliancyork.com/2011/01/14/not-twitter-not-wikileaks-a-human-revolution/>.

YouTube. 2016. "Statistics." <youtube.com/yt/press/statistics.html>.

Zerbisias, A. 2014. "How #BeenRapedNeverReported became a movement." *Rabble.ca*, November 5. <rabble.ca/news/2014/11/antonia-zerbisias-how-beenrapedneverreported-became-movement>.

Zuckerman, E. 2011. "The First Twitter Revolution? Not So Fast." *Foreign Policy*, January 14. <foreignpolicy.com/articles/2011/01/14/the_first_twitter_revolution?page=0,1>.

Index